THE INTERNATIONAL
BUSINESS ENVIRONMENT

Second edition

THE INTERNATIONAL BUSINESS ENVIRONMENT

CHALLENGES AND CHANGES

Ian Brooks, Jamie Weatherston and Graham Wilkinson

Financial Times Prentice Hall is an imprint of

PEARSON

Harlow, England • London • New York • Boston • San Francisco • Toronto
Sydney • Tokyo • Singapore • Hong Kong • Seoul • Taipei • New Delhi
Cape Town • Madrid • Mexico City • Amsterdam • Munich • Paris • Milan

Pearson Education Limited
Edinburgh Gate
Harlow
Essex CM20 2JE
England

and Associated Companies throughout the world

Visit us on the World Wide Web at:
www.pearsoned.co.uk

First published 2004
Second edition published 2011

ISBN: 978-0-273-72566-4

British Library Cataloguing-in-Publication Data
A catalogue record for this book is available from the British Library

Library of Congress Cataloging-in-Publication Data
Brooks, Ian, 1956–
  The international business environment : challenges and changes /
Ian Brooks, Jamie Weatherston and Graham Wilkinson. —2nd ed.
     p. cm.
  ISBN 978-0-273-72566-4 (pbk.)
 1. International trade.   2. International finance.   3. International economic relations.
4. International business enterprises.   I. Weatherston, Jamie.   II. Wilkinson, Graham, MBA.
III. Title.
HF1379.B765 2010
658'.049—dc22   2010020300

10 9 8 7 6 5 4 3 2 1
15 14 13 12 11

Typeset in 10/12 pt and Minion by 75
Printed and bound by Graficas Estella, Navarra, Spain

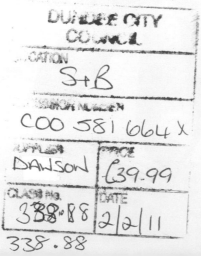

Contents

Preface

The first version of this book was published in 1997 under the title *The Business Environment: Challenges and Changes*; a second edition followed in 2000. In 2004 the increasingly interconnected, global nature of both business and the environment in which it operates was recognised by many changes in the emphasis of the text; these were encapsulated in the change of title to *The International Business Environment*. This new edition continues that approach, but has been extensively rewritten and updated to reflect the increasingly turbulent and internationalised setting in which modern businesses, of all sizes, now operate. Given the importance of the subject, a clear understanding of the theories and models outlined in the text is valuable in itself for a clearer understanding of modern business in undergraduate and professional educational programmes. It also provides a fundamental building block for the study of corporate strategy, a subject which is included at more advanced levels of the business curriculum.

The overall structure of this edition remains the same as before, including both theory and practical examples. This allows students to use theory as a framework, a tool, to better analyse and understand the nature of the international business environment. However, some changes have been made in response to requests and observations by readers. We have broadened the international aspects of the book to give more examples from around the world, rather than concentrating quite so heavily on European matters. Much attention has been given to the development of material to do with global challenges and changes, particularly areas of recent concern such as global warming, terrorism, the financial crisis and recession. The long cases at the end of the first edition were not widely liked. We have, therefore, deleted these in favour of including half a dozen minicases within each of the nine chapters. These cases have been carefully selected to illustrate an array of organisational types, operating environments and geographic locations from around the world. The structure of the book is explained and explored in Chapter 1, but we provide a brief outline here.

Chapter 1 sets the scene and delineates the scope of the book. In it we recognise that a number of interrelated international environmental forces act upon a variety of types of organisation. These forces are grouped under the acronym PESTLE C (for political, economic, social, technological, legal, ecological and competitive), but form an interrelated and complex whole. These environmental forces influence different types of organisation in different ways and act at a number of geo-political scales. Additionally, the impact of individual perception and organisational filters and the influence they have on the business environment and forecasting is explored. The chapter concludes with a brief consideration of the links between environmental analysis and business strategy.

Chapter 2 seeks to identify the nature and complexity of the competitive environment. We then try to determine how its dynamic nature and structure affects both the level of competition that organisations may face and their future profitability. The increasingly global nature of competition in many industries is one key issue that is identified and examined, as we introduce some of the tools and models that organisations can use to understand their own position and that of their competitors. As markets left to their own devices may become anti-competitive, we examine the circumstances in which government intervention may be necessary. We also examine the role that governments can play in providing support for new, fledgling industries to allow them to grow and become competitive in the international arena.

In Chapter 3 we consider the changes in government priorities within the macroeconomic environment in recent decades. The four main macroeconomic policy areas – economic growth, inflation, employment and the balance of trade – are explored in some detail. We discuss different exchange rate systems in the international macroeconomic environment, paying particular attention to the European Union and the impact of the single currency on organisations both within and outside the Eurozone.

Chapter 4 takes a broad view of the technological environment. We begin by defining technology and its importance, drawing distinctions between knowledge and innovation. Considerable attention is given to the funding of research and development (R&D) around the world, with the relevance of R&D to different sectors being considered. We also look at some general technologies affecting organisations, including advanced manufacturing technology and information-based technologies. The chapter considers the management of technology, before concluding with a discussion of the effects of technology on organisations, people and society.

Chapter 5 looks at various aspects of the dynamic and multi-faceted social environment. These include: national culture, the demographic environment, population changes and various social changes. In the discussion of national culture, it is argued that this complex area crucially influences all organisational and environmental activity. We also investigate demographic issues at a local, national and international scale and assesses their influence upon organisations. Finally, we take a closer look at a number of critical social phenomena and identify some of the key consequences of social dynamism for commercial and other organisations; issues such as crime, health, the changing nature of the family and work trends are considered.

Chapter 6 looks at environmental and ethical issues in the context of actions and events at global, national and local levels. The basic economic arguments which help us understand how firms are able to pollute the environment are explored and the range of actions which can be taken by governments to monitor and regulate the output of pollutants from economic activity identified. However, it is increasingly being recognised that there are trade-offs between economic growth and development, business activities and profitability and wider ecological and ethical considerations. Environmental campaigners, governments and businesspeople are increasingly recognising the importance of this debate. As we can see that it is often difficult, perhaps impossible, to confine ecological problems to issues that can be dealt with by individual countries, it is becoming increasingly apparent that 'world solutions' need to be sought. The more serious ecological concerns are looked at and the extent of their impact is investigated.. We end the chapter by examining the different approaches adopted by businesses towards environmental and ethical issues, discussing the impact of these upon consumers and noting the extent of consumer power in this respect.

Chapter 7 focuses on key political issues at a variety of geo-political scales, examining the potential impact of such decisions on organisations. Political decisions are made at all geo-political levels, from the global/international scale (such as the United Nations and the World Bank) to regional groupings like the EU, to the national scale and down to local authorities within countries. The role and interaction of these bodies with each other is examined, along with their impact on business and other organisations. We include an examination of different political philosophies regarding the role of government, emphasising especially how the impact of changes in attitudes in recent decades has dramatically changed the international business environment. The chapter concludes by considering the importance of stability and government attitudes to international business and their investment decisions.

Chapter 8 reflects the fact that the business of the twenty-first century operates at a global level. The chapter starts, however, with a discussion of the general idea of law and the various bases upon which it can be made before moving on to consider these issues at the various different levels. The legal environment within which businesses now operate is of necessity far broader than was once the case; they have to be aware of – and comply with – laws at a variety of levels, from national to regional to international. Within these areas we examine various aspects of business behaviour, including issues to do with employees and consumers. The chapter concludes with a consideration of various aspects of international law and legal debates.

Chapter 9 focuses upon the nature of change in the business environment. It has been retitled *Globalisation, challenges and changes* to reflect our belief that the increasingly dynamic nature of the international business environment has resulted in globalisation (in its many forms) becoming *the* crucial issue for debate and discussion. Thus, the chapter notes that the international business environment is increasingly complex, dynamic, and uncertain for many organisations, individuals, groups and governments. Major economic, political, technological and social changes have transformed and internationalised the business environment in the last three decades, necessitating organisational change and increased flexibility. It can be argued that there is a trend towards high profile 'shock events' and non-linear chaotic patterns in many areas of both the natural world and, to some extent, the business world. Climate change and global financial instability are very different problems, but both may have a major impact on businesses around the world. This suggests that organisations might do well to make contingency plans based on a variety of possible future scenarios. Although it is likely that turbulent environments demand government attention and international solutions, the future role of institutions and governments is likely to remain a fiercely debated issue.

Finally, our thanks goes to all those who have helped to put the book together, by providing chapters, case studies, information and advice.

Guided Tour

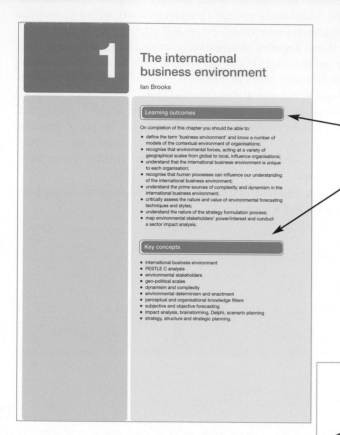

1 The international business environment

Ian Brooks

Learning outcomes

On completion of this chapter you should be able to:

- define the term 'business environment' and know a number of models of the contextual environment of organisations;
- recognise that environmental forces, acting at a variety of geographical scales from global to local, influence organisations;
- understand that the international business environment is unique to each organisation;
- recognise that human processes can influence our understanding of the international business environment;
- understand the prime sources of complexity and dynamism in the international business environment;
- critically assess the nature and value of environmental forecasting techniques and styles;
- understand the nature of the strategy formulation process;
- map environmental stakeholders' power/interest and conduct a sector impact analysis.

Key concepts

- international business environment
- PESTLE C analysis
- environmental stakeholders
- geo-political scales
- dynamism and complexity
- environmental determinism and enactment
- perceptual and organisational knowledge filters
- subjective and objective forecasting
- impact analysis, brainstorming, Delphi, scenario planning
- strategy, structure and strategic planning.

At the start of each chapter **Learning outcomes** and **Key concepts** outline the knowledge and topics which will be covered.

Minicases in each chapter illustrate and elicit analysis of specific issues. These also come with questions to help you take you learning further.

8 The international business environment

Minicase 1.2   UK supermarkets

A few large supermarkets have for many years dominated food retailing in the UK. In recent years many of these companies have also expanded into other areas of business, selling a large number of non-food items in their stores.

The market is dominated by Tesco, as can be seen from the table below.

UK supermarkets, market share November 2008	
Supermarket	**% share of UK market**
Tesco	30.9
Asda	17.1
Sainsbury's	15.9
Morrisons	11.4
Somerfield	3.9
Waitrose	3.8
Aldi	3.0
Lidl	2.3
Iceland	1.7
Netto	0.8

Source: TNS www.tnsglobal.com

Tesco claim that their success is down to many factors. Their 2009 Annual Report (see Tescoplc.com) states that 'Good financial management and leading market positions have served us well this year in the face of a challenging consumer environment. We will continue to pursue our long-term strategy which will put us in an even stronger position once our markets emerge from the economic downturn.' Sales growth for the group is shown as being 15.1 percent for the 2008 financial year.

The company operates some 4,331 stores in 14 countries around the world and employs more than 470,000 people. It is the third largest grocery retailer in the world.

In the UK, it is has almost twice the market share of its nearest competitor, Asda, owned by the American giant Wal-Mart, which is, in turn, slightly ahead of the Sainsbury's chain. This means that, between them, these three have nearly two-thirds of the sales in all UK supermarkets.

Despite this success, many analysts are concerned that the continued growth of these companies, especially Tesco, is bringing problems as well as benefits. These concerns include worries about the impact on suppliers, especially in developing economies, who are unable to stand up to the companies' demands for ever greater efficiencies and ever lower prices. Consumers, on the other hand, clearly welcome lower prices for their everyday shopping, especially at a time of poor economic conditions. There are also concerns about the impact of the big supermarkets on smaller, specialist stores, such as butchers, greengrocers and bakers. These are compounded by the fact that most supermarkets operate from out-of-town sites, which means that the majority of shopping trips are made by car, thus making pollution levels worse. For further information see http://news.bbc.co.uk/1/hi/business/433957.stm

Questions

1 Conduct an environmental analysis of Tesco using the PESTLE C headings and identifying the various stakeholders involved.
2 Should Tesco and the other supermarkets be allowed to continue expanding or should government intervene to limit their growth?

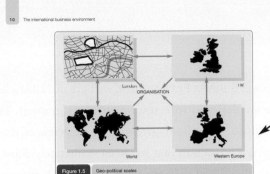

London   UK
        ORGANISATION

World   Western Europe

Figure 1.5   Geo-political scales

| Table 1.2 | Factors operating in Scania's business environment at four geo-political scales |

Geo-political scale	Environmental issues (examples)	Environmental forces
Local	A: Milton Keynes town planning regulations (Scania GB headquarters)	A: Political, legal, social, ecological
	B: Local skilled labour supply conditions	B: Social, economic, competitive
National	A: Value of currencies e.g. Swedish krona/euro	A: Economic, political
	B: Government freight transport policy	B: Political, social, competitive
EU	A: Emissions control and truck size regulations	A: Ecological, technological, political, social, legal
	B: Trading relations and concessions to non-EU countries	B: Political, competitive
Global	A: World Trade Organisation negotiations to pursue free trade agreements	A: Political, legal, competitive
	B: CO_2 emission targets	B: Ecological, social, political

illustrates two influences upon Scania (GB) at four geo-political scales. It also categorises these forces into legal, ecological, political, economic, social, technological and competitive. Many environmental issues, such as EU engine emission regulations, are themselves the outcome of a diverse range of influences acting together. Hence, as illustrated in *Table 1.2*, the nature of the laws governing truck engine emissions within the EU is influenced by a complex interaction of ecological, social, technological, political and legal forces. Conflicting pressures are brought to bear on the European institutions from ecological pressure groups,

---

Figures and tables illustrate key points, concepts and processes visually to reinforce your learning.

The **further reading/source of information** boxes will help facilitate more detailed study and provide many handy weblinks as a starting point for research online.

Each chapter is supported by a list of **References,** directing your independent study to both printed and electronic sources.

Further reading/sources of information

Carbon Trust (www.thecarbontrust.co.uk) Information on efforts to reduce carbon emissions, e.g. using alternative fuels.

Halpern, D. and colleagues (2008) Management and Legal Issues Regarding Electronic Surveillance of Employees in the Workplace; *Journal of Business Ethics*, 80, 175–180.

OECD (www.oecd.org) Organisation for Economic Co-operation and Development. Follow links to science and technology for information on effects on economic development.

Sciliagno, E. (2002) 10 Technology Disasters; *Technology Review*, 105(5), 48–53.

Sustainable Technologies (www.sustainabletechnologies.ac.uk/home.htm) Details of research projects aimed at growth without harm to the natural environment.

Tubbs, M. (2007) The Relationship between R&D and Company Performance; *Research Technology Management*, Nov/Dec, 50(6), 23–30.

UK government (www.innovation.gov.uk/rd_scoreboard) UK government site giving details on R&D.

World R&D Spending Rising (2008) *Research Technology Management*, Jan/Feb, 51(1), 4–5.

References

Adcock, H., Helms, M. and Jih, W.-J.K. (1993) Information Technology: Can it Provide a Sustainable Competitive Strategy? *Information Strategy – The Executive's Journal*, 9(3), 10–15.

Arnold, J., Cooper, C. and Robertson, I.T. (1998) *Work Psychology: Understanding Human Behaviour in the Workplace*, 3rd edn. Harlow: FT Prentice Hall.

Ayres, R.U. (1991) Barriers and Breakthroughs: An Expanding Frontiers Model of the Technology Industry Life Cycles, in Rossegger, G. (ed.) *Management of Technological Change*, Oxford: Elsevier Science.

BBC (2007) Vioxx Settlement to Total $4.85 Billion, http://news.bbc.co.uk Bartel, A., Ichniowski, C. and Shaw, K. (2007) How Does IT Affect Productivity? Plant-level Comparisons of Product Innovation, Process Improvement and Worker Skills. *Quarterly Journal of Economics*, 122(4) 1721–1758. Department for Business, Innovation and Skills (2008) Research and Development Scoreboard, available from www.innovation.gov.uk/rd_scoreboard/

Berry, M.M.J. and Taggart, J.H. (1994) Managing Technology and Innovation: A Review. *R&D Management*, 24(4), 341–353.

Brooks, M. (2009) All Juiced-up and Ready to Go. *New Scientist*, 18 July, 203 2717, 42–45.

Brown, C. and Campbell, B.A. (2002) The Impact of Technological Change on Work and Wages. *Industrial Relations*, 41(1), 1–33.

Burns, T. and Stalker, G. (1961) *The Management of Innovation*. London: Tavistock.

Chan, C. and Lewis, B. (2002) A Basic Primer on Data Mining. *Information Systems Management*, 19(14), 56–60.

Chapman, A.J., Sheehy, N.P., Haywood, S., Dooley, B. and Collins, S.C. (1995) The Organizational Implications of Teleworking, in Cooper, C.L. and Robertson, I. (eds) *International Review of Industrial and Organizational Psychology*, Chichester: John Wiley, vol. 10, pp. 29–248.

Chen, S., Westman, M. and Eden, D. (2009) Impact of Enhanced Resources on Anticipatory Stress and Adjustment to New Information Technology. *Journal of Occupational Health Physiology*, 14(3), 219–230.

Maps

As this book deals with the *International* Business Environment, we have included a series of maps in the following pages. These are designed with several purposes in mind. The first three maps have two different functions. They firstly provide an overview of the world showing countries' relative sizes, using a projection that has been deliberately chosen with this in mind. Many maps, particularly those used in books published in the Northern hemisphere, use a traditional projection that exaggerates the relative size of countries closer to the poles, while simultaneously showing countries near the equator as relatively small. For example, on conventional maps Greenland often appears to be larger in area than India; in fact, it is around 2/3rds India's size. We have also sought to challenge conventional perceptions by including three versions of the World Map. One of these, the most familiar, has the North Pole at the top and is centred on the line of zero latitude, which runs through England and Ghana. (A line of latitude is an imaginary line that runs 'vertically' from pole to pole.) This is followed by two more maps that show a different perspective of the world. The first of these is centred on the line of 180 degrees longitude, which runs through the Pacific Ocean and is roughly equivalent to the international dateline. The second, though centred on zero longitude, has been rotated to show the South Pole at the top and the North Pole at the bottom. The remainder of the map pages show each continent in a little more detail. This allows readers to see the location of the countries and the whereabouts of major cities. We have not included detailed information or statistical data in these pages; this may be found from many sources on the internet or in printed works.

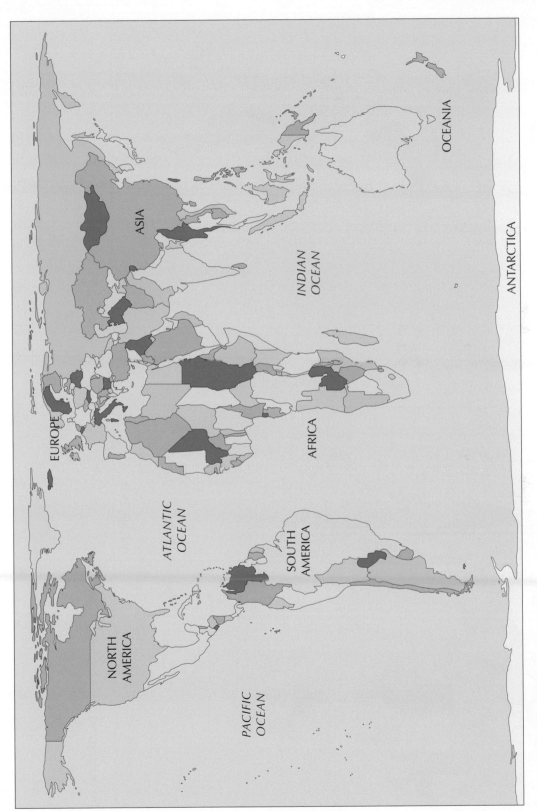

The World centred on the Greenwich Meridian

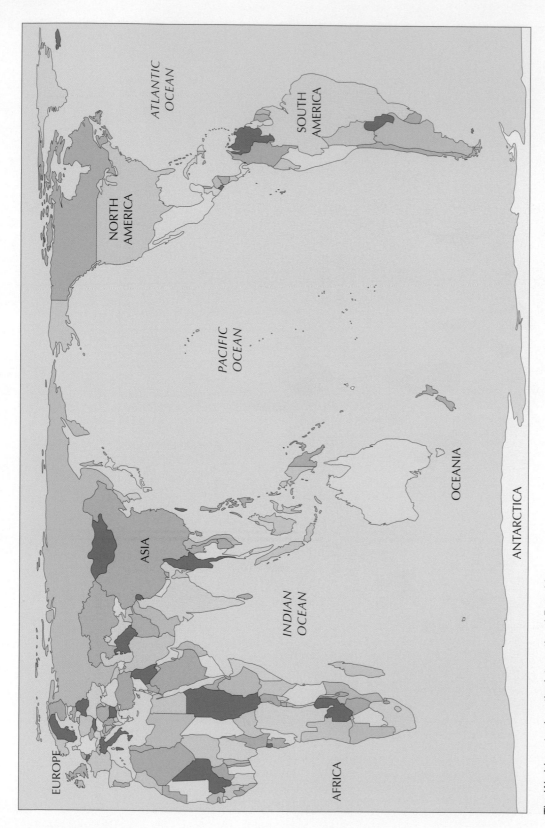

The World centred on the International Date Line

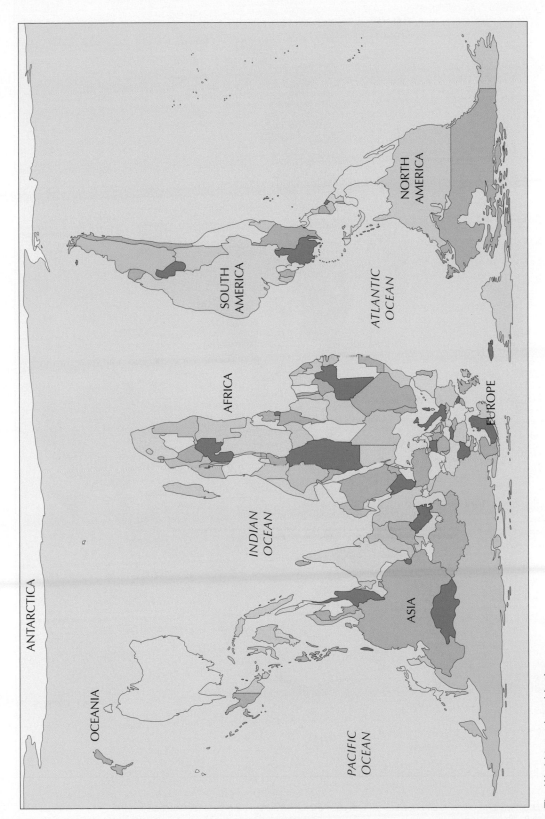

The World turned upside down

Europe

Source: *International Business: Environments and Operations,* 12th ed., Pearson Education (Daniels, J.D., Radebaugh, L.H. and Sullivan, D.P. 2009) p. 39

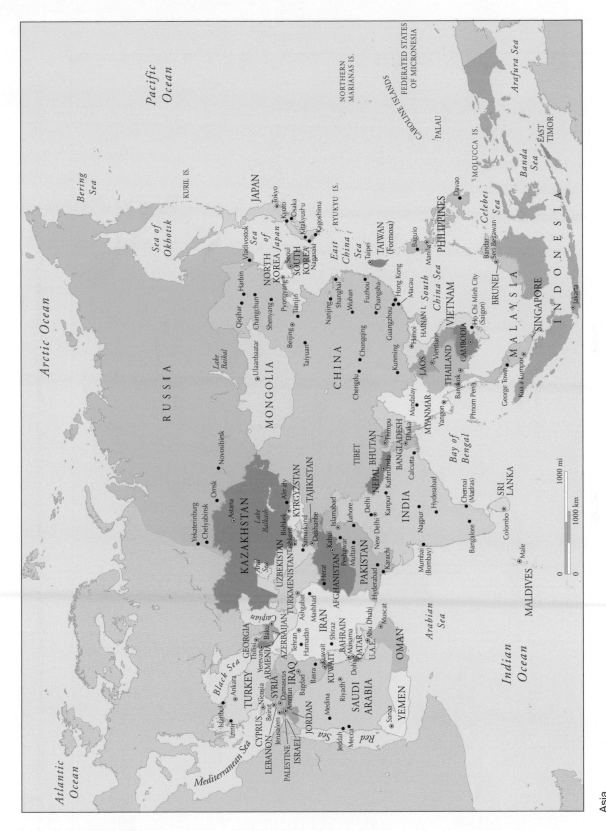

Asia

Source: International Business: Environments and Operations, 12th ed., Pearson Education (Daniels, J.D., Radebaugh, L.H. and Sullivan, D.P. 2009) p. 40

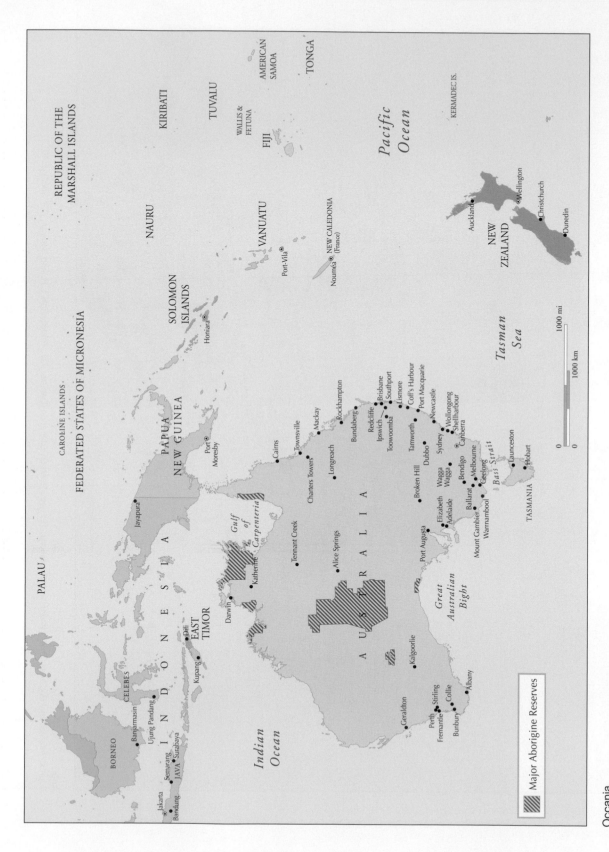

Oceania

Source: *International Business: Environments and Operations*, 12th ed., Pearson Education (Daniels, J.D., Radebaugh, L.H. and Sullivan, D.P. 2009) p. 43

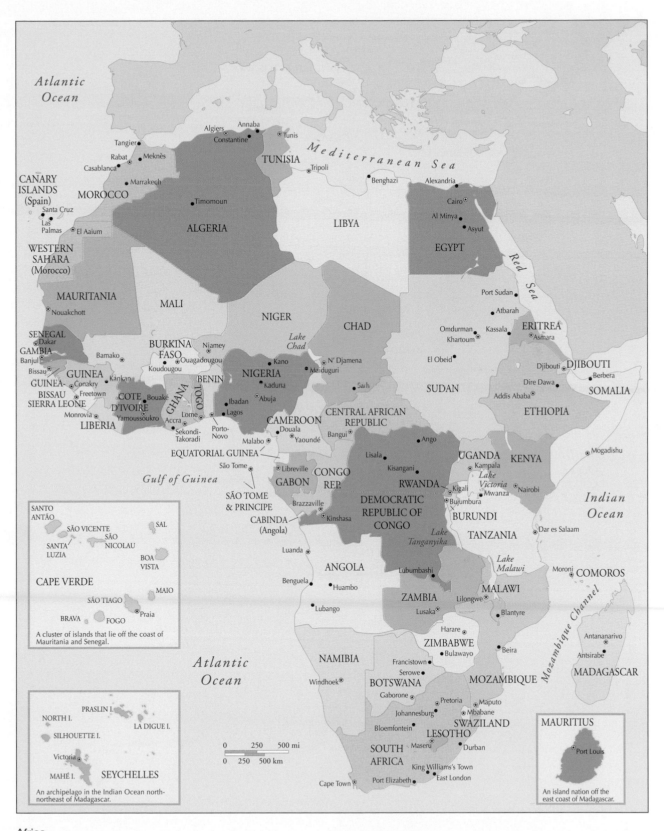

Africa

Source: International Business: Environments and Operations, 12th ed., Pearson Education (Daniels, J.D., Radebaugh, L.H. and Sullivan, D.P. 2009) p. 38

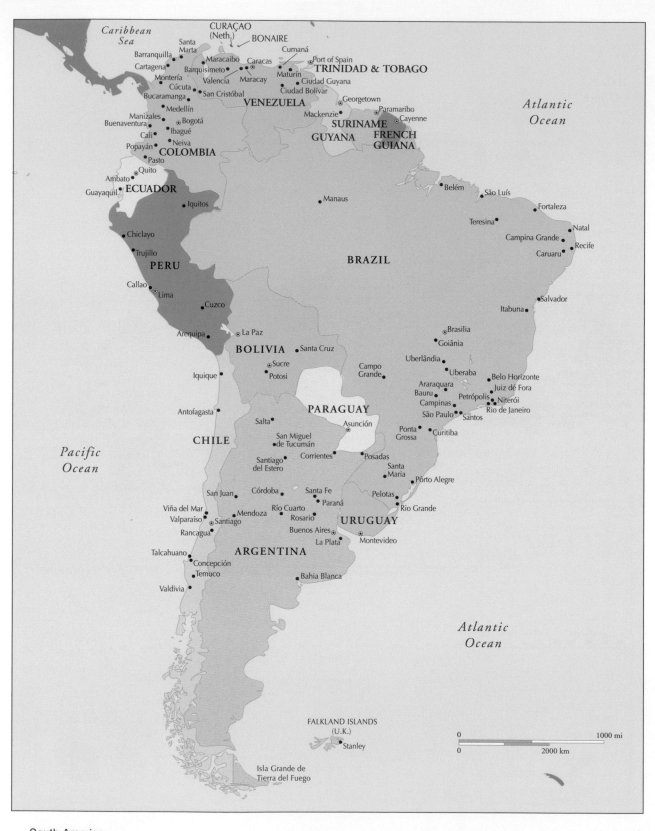

South America

Source: International Business: Environments and Operations, 12th ed., Pearson Education (Daniels, J.D., Radebaugh, L.H. and Sullivan, D.P. 2009) p. 42

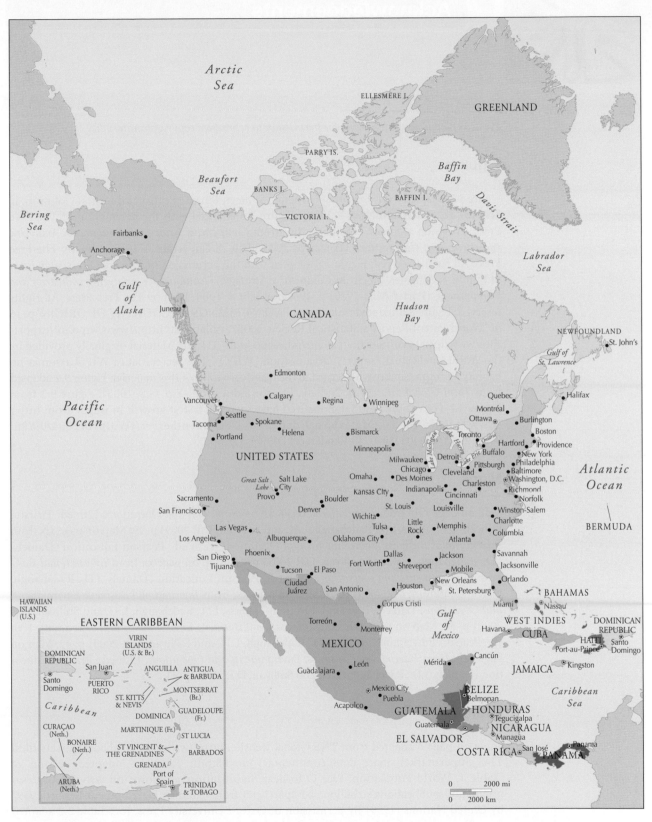

North America

Source: International Business: Environments and Operations, 12th ed., Pearson Education (Daniels, J.D., Radebaugh, L.H. and Sullivan, D.P. 2009) p. 41

Acknowledgements

We are grateful to the following for permission to reproduce copyright material:

Figures

Figure 1.8 adapted from *Exploring Corporate Strategy,* 8th ed., Pearson Education (Johnson, J., Scholes, K. and Whitington, P 2008); Figure 2.6 adapted with the permission of The Free Press, a division of Simon & Schuster, Inc, from *Competitive Strategy: Techniques for Analyzing Industries and Competitors,* (Porter, M.E. 1980) p. 4. Copyright © 1980, 1988 by The Free Press. All rights reserved; Figure 2.8 adapted with the permission of The Free Press, a division of Simon & Schuster, Inc, from *Competitive Strategy: Techniques for Analyzing Industries and Competitors,* (Porter, M.E. 1980) p. 49. Copyright © 1980, 1988 by The Free Press. All rights reserved; Figure 8.5 adapted from 'A.1.3. PATENT FILINGS BY COUNTRY OF ORIGIN' p. 16 of 'World Patent Report a Statistical Review 2008' available at: http://www.wipo.int/export/sites/www/ipstats/en/statistics/patents/pdf/wipo_pub_931.pdf, Material originally provided by the World Intellectual Property Organization (WIPO). The Secretariat of WIPO assumes no liability or responsibility with regard to the transformation of this material; Figure 9.2 adapted from *Total Global Strategy II,* 2nd ed., Pearson Education (Yip, G.S. 2003); Figure 9.3 from Figure 14 'Poor countries that globalized have seen the fastest growth in wages' from http://www.wds.worldbank.org/external/default/WDSContentServer/IW3P/IB/2004/09/28/000112742_20040928090739/Rendered/PDF/wps3333.pdf.

Maps

Map on page xviii from *International Business: Environments and Operations,* 12th ed., Pearson Education (Daniels, J.D., Radebaugh, L.H. and Sullivan, D.P. 2009) p. 39; Map on page xix from *International Business: Environments and Operations,* 12th ed., Pearson Education (Daniels, J.D., Radebaugh, L.H. and Sullivan, D.P. 2009) p. 40; Map on page xx from *International Business: Environments and Operations,* 12th ed., Pearson Education (Daniels, J.D., Radebaugh, L.H. and Sullivan, D.P. 2009) p. 43; Map on page xxi from *International Business: Environments and Operations,* 12th ed., Pearson Education (Daniels, J.D., Radebaugh, L.H. and Sullivan, D.P. 2009) p. 38; Map on page xxii from *International Business: Environments and Operations,* 12th ed., Pearson Education (Daniels, J.D., Radebaugh, L.H. and Sullivan, D.P. 2009) p. 42; Map on page xxiii from *International Business: Environments and Operations,* 12th ed., Pearson Education (Daniels, J.D., Radebaugh, L.H. and Sullivan, D.P. 2009) p. 41.

Tables

Table on page 8 adapted from TNS Global website, http://www.tnsglobal.com/_assets/files/TNS_Supermarket_Share_data_commentary_nov08.pdf; Table 1.5 adapted version of 'Table 1. World Population, Year O to near Stabilization' as shown on www.un.org/esa/population/publications/sixbillion/sixbilpart1.pdf from "Human Development Report 1999" by United Nations (1999) By permission of Oxford University Press, Inc; Table 2.2 adapted from Concentration ratios for businesses by industry in 2004, *Economic Trends,* 635, October (Mahajan, S. 2006), Crown Copyright material is reproduced with the permission of the Controller, Office of Public Sector Information (OPSI).; Table 3.2 from Shadow Economies: Size, Causes, and Consequences, *Journal of Economic Literature,* Vol. 38(1), March, pp. 77–114

(Schneider, F. & Enste, D.E. 2000); Table 3.3 adapted from *National Accounts,* June 2008, June 2009, OECD (2008), and 'Student enrolment in tertiary education' from *OECD Regions at a Glance 2009,* www.oecd.org/regional/regionsataglance; Table 3.6 from *OECD in Figures,* OECD (2008) pp. 59–60, and 'Student enrolment in tertiary education' from *OECD Regions at a Glance 2009,* www.oecd.org/regional/regionsataglance; Table 4.4 from *Economic Trends,* August (2005), Crown Copyright material is reproduced with the permission of the Controller, Office of Public Sector Infoxxivrmation (OPSI); Table 4.5 from *Economic Trends,* 621, August, Table 19 (2005), Crown Copyright material is reproduced with the permission of the Controller, Office of Public Sector Information (OPSI); Table 4.9 adapted from Challenges and priorities for European research: a foresight review, *Foresight,* 3 (4), August, 261–71 (Gavigan, J. Zappacosta, M., Ducatel, K., Scapolo, F and di Pietrogiacomo, P. 2001); Table 4.10 adapted from Successful Industrial Innovation: Critical Success Factors for the 1990s, *R&D Management,* 22 (3), pp. 231–39 (Rothwell, R. 1992); Table 5.1 adapted from *Cultures and Organizations: Software of the Mind". Revised and Expanded 2nd Edition.,* McGraw-Hill, New York, USA (Geert Hofstede and Gert Jan Hofstede, 2005); Table 5.2 adapted from United Nations Population Information Network website, http://www.un.org/popin/data.html; Tables 5.3, 5.4 and 5.5 adapted from United Nations Population Information Network website, http://www.un.org/popin/functional/population.html; Table 6.4 adapted from 'Student enrolment in tertiary education' from *OECD Regions at a Glance 2009,* www.oecd.org/regional/regionsataglance; Table 6.6 adapted from Exploiting green strategies for competitive advantage, *Long Range Planning,* 27 (6), pp. 64–81 (Azzone, G. and Bertele, U. 1994); Table 6.7 adapted from 'Choice: the curse of the green consumer?' from http://www.forumforthefuture.org/greenfutures/articles/602578. This piece originally appeared in Green Futures. Green Futures is published by Forum for the Future and is the leading magazine on environmental solutions and sustainable futures. Its aim is to demonstrate that a sustainable future is both practical and desirable – and can be profitable, too; Table 7.3 adapted from http://www.transparency.org/news_room/in_focus/2008/cpi2008/cpi_2008_table.

Text

Minicase 2.3 adapted from the Office of Fair Trading website, http://www.oft.gov.uk/news/press/2009/114-09; Minicase 3.1 from 'Sarkozy attacks focus on economic growth', *The Guardian,* 14/09/2009 (Davies, L.); Minicase 3.2 from 'German jobs saved by short-term working subsidies, says IMF', *The Guardian,* 1/10/2009 (Elliott, L.); Minicase 3.3 from 'Australia raises interest rates by 0.25% as economy improves', *The Guardian,* 6/10/2009 (Wearden, G.); Minicase 3.4 from 'Europe accused of protectionism', *The Guardian,* 4/05/2009 (Stuart, H.); Minicase 3.5 from 'Sugar the new oil as prices soar', *The Guardian,* 6/10/2009 (Clark, A.).

The Financial Times

Minicase 2.2 adapted from 'Engineer sees big picture', *The Financial Times,* 7/08/2009 (Harding, R.); Minicase 2.4 from 'Little laptops snap at the oligopoly', *The Financial Times,* 16/07/2009 (Gapper, J.), Copyright © The Financial Times Ltd.; Minicase 2.6 adapted from 'Le Big Mac at home in the land of slow food', *The Financial Times,* 3/10/2007 (Yuk, P.K.), Copyright © The Financial Times Ltd.

In some instances we have been unable to trace the owners of copyright material, and we would appreciate any information that would enable us to do so.

1

The international business environment

Ian Brooks

Learning outcomes

On completion of this chapter you should be able to:

- define the term 'business environment' and know a number of models of the contextual environment of organisations;
- recognise that environmental forces, acting at a variety of geographical scales from global to local, influence organisations;
- understand that the international business environment is unique to each organisation;
- recognise that human processes can influence our understanding of the international business environment;
- understand the prime sources of complexity and dynamism in the international business environment;
- critically assess the nature and value of environmental forecasting techniques and styles;
- understand the nature of the strategy formulation process;
- map environmental stakeholders' power/interest and conduct a sector impact analysis.

Key concepts

- international business environment
- PESTLE C analysis
- environmental stakeholders
- geo-political scales
- dynamism and complexity
- environmental determinism and enactment
- perceptual and organisational knowledge filters
- subjective and objective forecasting
- impact analysis, brainstorming, Delphi, scenario planning
- strategy, structure and strategic planning.

Minicase 1.1   Analysing Scania's business environment using the PESTLE C framework

Political

- National and European government transport policies.
- Investment in rail freight terminals and other infrastructure following privatisation.
- Pressure to regulate road haulage companies further, e.g. driver hours, registration requirements.
- Reductions in centrally funded road building; toll roads.
- Excise duty on diesel; levels of road tax on trucks.

Economic

- Effects of economic cycles are pronounced in this industry, dramatically affecting new truck sales which plummeted in 2008/2009, threatening the existence of Scania as a separate branded entity.
- Currency fluctuations: especially of Swedish krona/euro against sterling and non-European currencies.
- Interest rates. Many trucks purchased on financing arrangement often organised through Scania Finance Ltd – the lower the rates, other things equal, the higher the sales.

Social and demographic

- Societal lobby of governments to reduce or control road traffic and congestion.
- Changing shopping habits influencing rates of growth and geographical distribution of retailers.

Technological

- Complexity in truck design and on-board aids, e.g. on-board computers – engine management systems, trans-European navigation, communications.
- Continual improvements in fuel consumption and emissions control as manufacturers seek competitive advantage while complying with euro standards.
- Alternative fuels.
- Alternative transportation systems.
- Improved technologies and quality increasing service intervals.

Legal

- Block Exemption – the EU removed regulation 123/85 so enabling dealers to seek multi-franchises, that is one dealer can market products from different manufacturers. This is also the case in the car industry.
- European Union (EU) transport regulations/harmonisation; working hours directive (drivers); emissions standards (Euro 1, 2, 3, 4, 5); maximum truck sizes.
- Maximum legal truck sizes, likely to increase, may reduce truck demand due to scale efficiencies.

Ecological

- Euro regulations impose increasingly stringent emissions and noise limits requiring costly research and development (R&D) spend on redesign of engines and other parts.
- Environmentalist transport lobby aim to increase rail freight and reduce the numbers of large trucks on the roads.
- Stringent standards require more frequent engine service and emissions checks.
- Increasingly aware and active public concern over health issues, quality of life and road congestion.

Competitive

- Changing customer base: from small haulage operators to large fleet management organisations – increased buyer power.

- Growth of rental market; non-manufacturing suppliers.
- Convergence in design and 'quality' characteristics among main players leads to increasing competition.
- Marque loyalties of declining importance; lifetime cost considerations; aftersales market of increasing importance.
- Whole package concept (e.g. trucks, financing and aftersales services).
- Possible future Japanese or Far Eastern incursion into European truck market.
- New entrants' excursion into large and lucrative aftersales market (as in motor car industry, e.g. KwikFit).

Questions

1 Identify those factors which influence the activity and well-being of Scania, which have their origins in an international context.
2 Which environmental forces facing Scania are confined to just one country such as Sweden, France or the UK?

1.1 Environmental forces

Whether it is an international bank, a university or a multinational motor manufacturer, no organisation exists within a vacuum. It is very likely to have a number of competitors, be subject to international, national and local government regulation and control, obliged to comply with national or international pollution regulations and subject to fluctuations in the fortunes of the global economy. In addition, technology changes almost continually and so too do customers' tastes and preferences. It is clear that the business environment comprises an array of 'forces' acting upon organisations, often with far-reaching implications.

This introductory chapter explains the rationale and scope of the book and demonstrates the fundamental characteristics of the international business environment, its relationship with organisations and the implications for organisational structure and strategy. We start by defining the business environment and by classifying the forces in play. The chapter then develops a model of the international business environment which forms the basis of our approach. We briefly explain the diverse nature of organisations and take a closer look at various approaches to environmental forecasting before discussing the relationship between the business environment and organisational activity. The role of the business environment in influencing the strategic direction of organisations is addressed and some of the complex issues are debated. Naturally, many of the issues raised are further developed in later chapters.

The focus of this book is on the organisation in its environment rather than on the individual, group or government and their external environments. *Figure 1.1* demonstrates that focus.

1.1.1 The international business environment: a definition

The word 'environment' does not merely refer to the natural or ecological environment, although that may be an important consideration for many organisations. It is a general concept that embraces the totality of external environmental forces which may influence any aspect of organisational activity. Similarly, the word 'business' is used to imply any type of organisation, whether it be a commercial profit-making enterprise, a government agency or the not-for-profit 'third sector'. Consequently, we will use the terms 'business' and 'organisation' interchangeably. Hence 'the business environment' is a broad and all-embracing term that encompasses any and all influences which are external to the organisation in question.

In this book, we refer to the 'international' environment suggesting that most, if not all, organisations are influenced by forces often outside of their control: forces which emanate

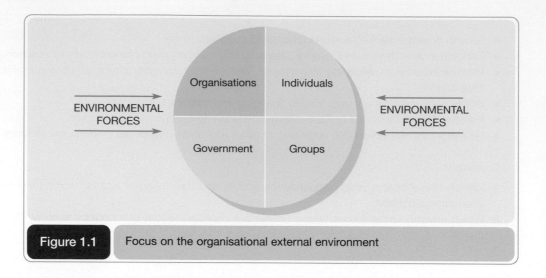

Figure 1.1   Focus on the organisational external environment

from beyond their locality or even the nation(s) in which they operate. Many organisations are, of course, truly global or international in scale, with operations and markets in very many countries. Other organisations are small and largely, if not exclusively, nation-bound or operate only at a local level. All, however, operate in an international business environment and are, to a greater or lesser extent, affected by that environment. For example, the causes and effects of global warming do not respect national boundaries nor the size of an organisation. It is a truly global concern. Similarly, terrorism, even when inspired by narrow nationalistic extremism, is international in its influence: terrorists can strike in any country of the world.

In the commercial world, economic, political or social phenomena in one country can influence the behaviour of organisations in another part of the world, as can be seen from the following two examples. The credit crisis of 2008 onwards originated largely in the USA but very rapidly spread to almost all countries and regions of the world. Virtually no industry in any country has been completely unaffected by the adverse impact of that crisis and its subsequent ramifications. Hundreds of thousands of small and large companies, including one of the world's biggest manufacturing companies General Motors (GM), have become bankrupt or had to make staff redundant and suffer declining profitability. In 2002, a devastating bomb in a Bali nightclub not only claimed victims' lives but also hit the tourist industry in Bali and reduced holiday bookings in many world locations; fewer American tourists visited the UK as a direct consequence of that bomb in a small Indonesian island. Hence, this book takes a holistic view of the international business environment, concerning itself with the range of geo-political scales from global, through international, regional, national and local influences.

Defining the environment has posed an intellectual problem for many decades, although a number of eminent researchers have categorised the different approaches. Wilson (1992) has suggested three broad conceptions of the business environment, each of which is covered in some detail in this book. He argues that the business environment may be viewed as:

- an objective fact, a clear measurable and definable reality;
- a subjective fact, its particular characteristics being dependent on individuals' interpretation and perceptions;
- enacted, where the division between organisation and environment is not clear and where the environment is created and defined by individuals.

This complex argument is explained further in the section on perceptual filters, see section 1.2.1 'Perceptual filters', later. It need not overly complicate our understanding of the international business environment at this stage, although awareness of the role of human perception when defining environmental opportunities or constraints is useful.

It is important for students of business to study the environment and for managers to analyse their organisation's environment for many reasons:

- the nature of the business environment fundamentally influences the activities of business – it affects its markets, technologies, workforce and more;
- operational activities, such as new product launches, staff recruitment drives and changes in manufacturing technology, need to recognise environmental factors and changes in order to better ensure success of the venture;
- it is likely that profit and organisational well-being are fundamentally related to global, national and local environmental conditions;
- strategic planning needs to take into consideration likely changes in the international business environment.

1.1.2 A classification of environmental forces

The simple acronym 'PEST' (standing for political, economic, social, technological) serves well as an *aide-mémoire* when considering the array of environmental forces influencing business activity. In fact if the acronym is enlarged to 'PESTLE' (to include legal and ecological) it encompasses most areas of concern in this field. We add to this consideration of the competitive environment, the interplay between organisations competing, directly or otherwise, with one another, to arrive at the (rarely used) PESTLE C acronym. *Figure 1.2* illustrates this categorisation of the international business environment. This text concentrates on each of these forces and the interaction between them.

PESTLE C analysis enables analysts, including students and managers, to assemble a logical and comprehensive picture of any business's environment. However, it is the interrelationship between the different factors which adds not only complexity and uncertainty but also richness and greater accuracy to the analysis. *Minicase 1.1* illustrates a simple PESTLE C analysis of Scania, a multinational, Swedish-owned truck manufacturer.

There are a number of important aspects of Scania's environment that will influence the company's strategic and operational decision making. Some of these factors lie within Scania's control, such as aspects of truck design to meet Euro standards and fuel efficiency targets, while many others, such as fluctuations in the value of the Swedish krona or the global financial crisis and subsequent economic recession, are beyond its influence.

There are numerous other, sometimes graphic, representations of the business environment; *Figure 1.3* shows the categorisations used by Daft in his 1992 model of environmental forces. This 'dartboard' configuration gives the organisation pride of place in the centre, while radiating from it are eight categories of environmental concerns. This typology is similar to the 'PESTLE' acronym suggesting, as it does, that all environmental forces fall within one or more of these specified categories.

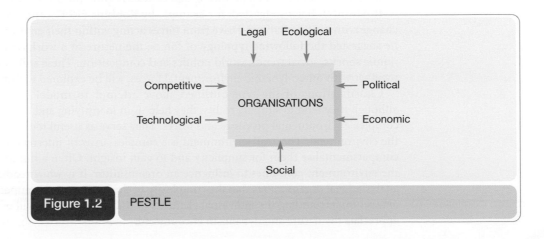

| Figure 1.2 | PESTLE |

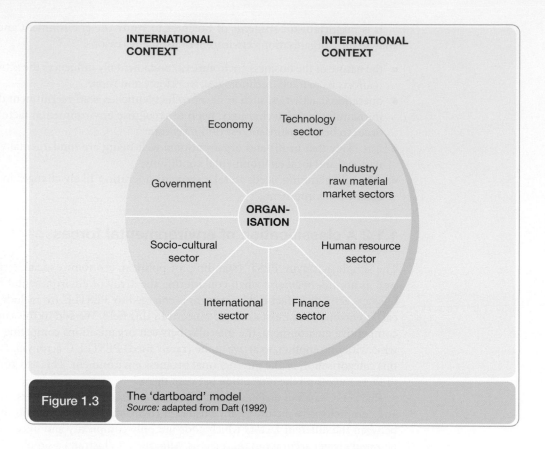

INTERNATIONAL CONTEXT

INTERNATIONAL CONTEXT

- Economy
- Technology sector
- Government
- Industry raw material market sectors
- ORGAN-ISATION
- Socio-cultural sector
- Human resource sector
- International sector
- Finance sector

Figure 1.3	The 'dartboard' model
	Source: adapted from Daft (1992)

Other studies separate a firm's external environment into three categories:

- the 'remote environment', such as global and domestic political, social and technological concerns – this is akin to the contextual environment outlined above;
- the 'industry environment' or its competitive forces; and
- the 'operating environment' which comprises a rather mixed group of actors including suppliers and customers.

It is not the intention of this book to focus, in any detail, on the internal or operating environment of the organisation, although the day-to-day activity of organisations includes interaction with the 'task environment', including an organisation's relationship with its customers, suppliers, trade unions and shareholders. However, this book focuses on the broader contextual environment that permeates and extends beyond the immediate task environment.

It has often been suggested, for example by Robbins (1992), that the prime forces for change within organisations derive from forces acting within their environment. Specifically, he suggested the following typology of forces: the nature of a workforce, technology, economic shocks, social trends, world politics and competition. These still hold true today and, together with other dynamic environmental forces, will be explored within this book.

Classifications of the type outlined above attempt to model the environment and, although they tend to simplify reality, they help us in identifying and understanding what are complex environmental processes and forces. They serve as useful tools to aid our analysis of the environment. The 'real' environment is a complex array of interrelated forces; we merely compartmentalise them for simplicity and to gain insight. Often a number of forces within the environment combines to influence an organisation. It is while reading case studies or analysing real organisations that the complexity of the business environment becomes apparent, yet understanding the individual elements of that environment will enable you to better appreciate the nature and dynamism encountered.

1.1.3 Environmental stakeholders

All organisations, whatever their size, have a number of stakeholders. A stakeholder is a person, organisation, interest group or other body that holds a 'stake' in the business. In addition to having an interest in the activities of the organisation, some stakeholders have power to influence those activities. Institutional shareholders, such as large insurance companies, for example, are powerful stakeholders in many commercial companies and consequently have considerable influence, if they wish to use it, upon the nature of company objectives.

Governments usually hold a controlling influence over public sector bodies and, hence, are vital stakeholders in those organisations. The American government took measures in 2009 to hold a controlling stake in GM, which had been the world's largest company for much of the latter part of the twentieth century; this followed the spending of taxpayers' money by the US government to 'bail out' GM when it appeared it was heading for bankruptcy and possible closure. Similarly, in the UK the government provided support funding for a number of major banks including Northern Rock and the Royal Bank of Scotland and held the majority shareholdings as a consequence. Many countries have a state-funded or national health service whose managers and many medical personnel consider government as a key stakeholder. Whether they, as managers or medical professionals, like it that way is a debatable issue, but the fact remains that the UK government, for example, provides the funds and the legal framework within which hospitals and other public healthcare facilities operate.

However, in addition to government, a general hospital has other 'environmental stakeholders'. These include the local community which the hospital serves. One might argue that this customer base is the most important stakeholder. Of course not all stakeholders will hold equal power or influence over the affairs of the organisation, and the community may have less influence over hospital strategic activities than does the government. *Minicase 1.2* discusses many of these issues as they arise in the UK supermarket sector.

Table 1.1 lists some of the environmental stakeholders of a typical university. It indicates whether the stakeholders have high, medium or low power over the university and whether they have a relatively high, medium or low interest in the activity and strategic direction of the organisation. The analysis involves judgement; however, it can be carried out for any organisation with which you are familiar. It should also be noted that, due to volatility in the business environment, stakeholder power and interest is itself dynamic. *Figure 1.4* shows how one might 'map' stakeholder power and interest in an organisation using the data from *Table 1.1*. This graphically illustrates which stakeholders wield most power and influence. Such an analysis provides a useful analytical tool for managers to assess the relative power and influence of each of their environmental stakeholders. It may prove invaluable in the strategic management process.

1.1.4 Geo-political scales

This book studies the business environment at a range of geo-political scales (see *Chapter 7*). The 'geo' in this case refers to 'geographical' scale while the 'political' implies levels or tiers of government. Hence at the local level in most countries there is a tier of government that is responsible for certain activities within a relatively small area. Similarly there is a tier of government, often very important and influential, at a national scale. In many parts of the world there are also regional groupings of countries, such as the European Union (EU) and the Association of South East Asian Nations (ASEAN) that form a further level of governance. (For more examples and further discussion see section 7.2.2 '*Regional scale*') The EU, for example, has created enormous change, in trading relations, patterns of trade and alterations in product specifications as well as regulations covering many other aspects of the business environment faced by all firms trading within the 27 countries that are now EU member states. It is a dynamic force in organisations across Europe and indeed elsewhere. Furthermore, very many forces acting upon business today have their origins in a global

Minicase 1.2   UK supermarkets

A few large supermarkets have for many years dominated food retailing in the UK. In recent years many of these companies have also expanded into other areas of business, selling a large number of non-food items in their stores.

The market is dominated by Tesco, as can be seen from the table below.

UK supermarkets, market share November 2008

Supermarket	% share of UK market
Tesco	30.9
Asda	17.1
Sainsbury's	15.9
Morrisons	11.4
Somerfield	3.9
Waitrose	3.8
Aldi	3.0
Lidl	2.3
Iceland	1.7
Netto	0.8

Source: TNS www.tnsglobal.com

Tesco claim that their success is down to many factors. Their 2009 Annual Report (see Tescoplc.com) states that 'Good financial management and leading market positions have served us well this year in the face of a challenging consumer environment. We will continue to pursue our long-term strategy which will put us in an even stronger position once our markets emerge from the economic downturn.' Sales growth for the group is shown as being 15.1 percent for the 2008 financial year.

The company operates some 4,331 stores in 14 countries around the world and employs more than 470,000 people. It is the third largest grocery retailer in the world.

In the UK, it is has almost twice the market share of its nearest competitor, Asda, owned by the American giant Wal-Mart, which is, in turn, slightly ahead of the Sainsbury's chain. This means that, between them, these three have nearly two-thirds of the sales in all UK supermarkets.

Despite this success, many analysts are concerned that the continued growth of these companies, especially Tesco, is bringing problems as well as benefits. These concerns include worries about the impact on suppliers, especially in developing economies, who are unable to stand up to the companies' demands for ever greater efficiencies and ever lower prices. Consumers, on the other hand, clearly welcome lower prices for their everyday shopping, especially at a time of poor economic conditions. There are also concerns about the impact of the big supermarkets on smaller, specialist stores, such as butchers, greengrocers and bakers. These are compounded by the fact that most supermarkets operate from out-of-town sites, which means that the majority of shopping trips are made by car, thus making pollution levels worse. For further information see http://news.bbc.co.uk/1/hi/business/433957.stm

Questions

1 Conduct an environmental analysis of Tesco using the PESTLE C headings and identifying the various stakeholders involved.
2 Should Tesco and the other supermarkets be allowed to continue expanding or should government intervene to limit their growth?

Table 1.1	Environmental stakeholders: UK higher education

Environmental stakeholders	Power to Influence strategy	Level of Interest in activities
Government	HIGH	MEDIUM
Students	MEDIUM	HIGH
Quality assessment bodies	HIGH	MEDIUM
Local government	LOW	LOW
Local residents	LOW	MEDIUM
Funding body	HIGH	MEDIUM
Other regional HE institutions	MEDIUM	MEDIUM
Taxpayers	LOW	LOW

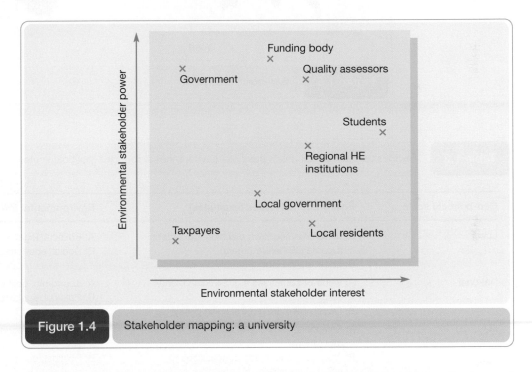

Figure 1.4	Stakeholder mapping: a university

context. Major political disturbances leading to war or terrorism, changes in oil prices and availability, agreements to reduce CO_2 omissions, and innovations in information and communications technology do not respect national boundaries; they are global in reach, operate across nations internationally and influence all organisations directly or indirectly.

Environmental forces operating at different geo-political levels, as illustrated in *Figure 1.5,* influence most organisations. For example, Scania interacts with its environment at a variety of scales. At the local level in the United Kingdom its head office is located in Milton Keynes, England, and a move to an alternative location within the town has been considered. The decision where to locate will be subject to local government planning restrictions, which will in turn be influenced by national laws. Also, Scania employs a large number of skilled, experienced and professional staff who currently live in or near Milton Keynes. Hence, factors within the local environment (i.e. local government and local labour supply) are important to the activities of Scania (GB) in Milton Keynes. However, Scania is also subject to environmental dynamism at the national, European and global scales. *Table 1.2*

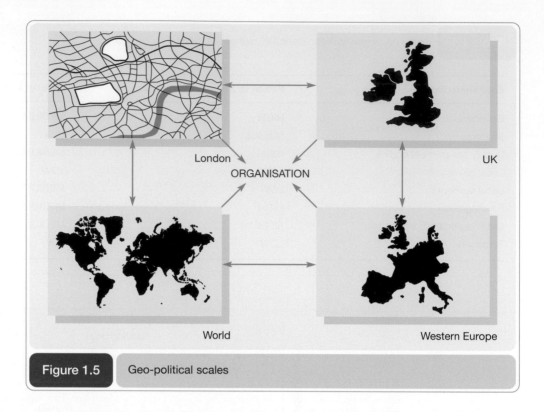

London

ORGANISATION

UK

World

Western Europe

Figure 1.5   Geo-political scales

Table 1.2   Factors operating in Scania's business environment at four geo-political scales

Geo-political scale	Environmental issues (examples)	Environmental forces
Local	A: Milton Keynes town planning regulations (Scania GB headquarters) B: Local skilled labour supply conditions	A: Political, legal, social, ecological B: Social, economic, competitive
National	A: Value of currencies e.g. Swedish krona/ euro B: Government freight transport policy	A: Economic, political B: Political, social, competitive
EU	A: Emissions control and truck size regulations B: Trading relations and concessions to non-EU countries	A: Ecological, technological, political, social, legal B: Political, competitive
Global	A: World Trade Organisation negotiations to pursue free trade agreements B: CO_2 emission targets	A: Political, legal, competitive B: Ecological, social, political

illustrates two influences upon Scania (GB) at four geo-political scales. It also categorises these forces into legal, ecological, political, economic, social, technological and competitive. Many environmental issues, such as EU engine emission regulations, are themselves the outcome of a diverse range of influences acting together. Hence, as illustrated in *Table 1.2*, the nature of the laws governing truck engine emissions within the EU is influenced by a complex interaction of ecological, social, technological, political and legal forces. Conflicting pressures are brought to bear on the European institutions from ecological pressure groups, social and political philosophies, and organisational lobbyists. The outcome is, in this case, a compromise 'solution' enshrined in law.

Unfortunately, it is not always simple or practical to distinguish between the business environment at various geo-political scales, as these influences are often so interrelated and complex that they can only be fully appreciated collectively. Some forces will operate at a number of different levels and manifest themselves in a variety of ways. Hence it may fall to local government to enforce pollution controls that originated at global inter-governmental conferences. Even many small, local companies are increasingly aware that forces operating at the European level, such as product specification directives emanating from Brussels, have a direct and often profound influence on their business. For example, small local butchers' shops in many European countries are finding it increasingly difficult to comply with EU health and safety regulations. For some it is proving to be the proverbial last straw, resulting, perhaps, in the closure of the business.

Not all organisations are influenced equally by the international business environment. In fact what may prove to be a real threat for one organisation could be a wondrous opportunity for growth and profitability for another. For example, the technological advances made in the design, production and marketing of personal computers and the consequent reduction in their cost and improvement in quality have led to enormous increases in their demand for household and business use. These technological forces have, however, virtually proved a death blow to the manufacture of mechanical and electronic typewriters, and have reduced the demand for mainframe computers for certain applications.

In reality, every organisation has a complex array of environmental influences with which it interacts and which are, in their entirety, quite unique. Hence the business environment is a complex array of forces acting, with often unpredictable and unequal force, upon organisations at a variety of geographical and political scales.

1.1.5 The organisation–environment relationship

The relationship and direction of influence between the environment and an organisation are not one-way, simple or static. The belief that the activities of organisations are entirely determined by the environment in which they operate is described as environmental determinism. Although we know that the environment influences business activity, it is by no means certain that absolute determinism is apparent even for the smallest of organisations. Organisations have tentacles of influence which help form and give shape to the business environment. In other words, there is not a one-way causal relationship between environment and organisation. The reality is that many large or innovative companies profoundly shape their own external environment and that facing numerous other organisations in the same industry or sector. The simplest example is that of a number of competing companies in an industrial sector. The activity of one, say the introduction of a new form of retailing, will influence the activity and success of another. For example, the continuing growth of internet shopping will influence the activity and success of high street shops. This in turn will, adversely, impact the demand for retail outlets in city centres, and pose local government and town planners some difficult questions. Furthermore, an economic decision, driven by social change and facilitated by technology will have an impact on other aspects of the social environment. In the example above, city centres may become run-down and witness an increase in unemployment and associated social problems. *Figure 1.6* indicates this two-way influence between organisation and environment.

All organisations form part of the business environment of other organisations, as competitors, allies, suppliers, buyers and so forth. No organisation is isolated and without any influence on its own environment and that of others. Many organisations, especially sizeable and/or influential ones, exert considerable pressures for change in their business environment. Hamel and Prahalad (1994) argue that companies can only control their future if they know how to influence the destiny of their industry. For example, the Direct Line company

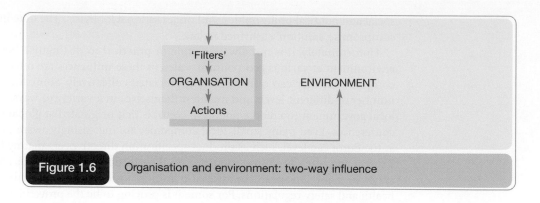

Figure 1.6   Organisation and environment: two-way influence

in the United Kingdom revolutionised the insurance and financial services industries in the 1990s. It effectively marketed and delivered a quick and efficient telephone-line service, enabling customers to contact the company directly (hence the name!). This replaced the then-traditional approach of customers usually finding insurance via a middleman: the insurance broker. This reduced Direct Line's overheads, when compared with normal broker services, and it rapidly increased its market share. In turn this enabled the company to maintain highly competitive rates, which have 'squeezed' more traditional competitors. Direct line, and the numerous companies now mimicking it, has changed the business environment for all insurance and financial services companies, and spawned a new and lucrative business opportunity for price comparison websites. As the technological environment changed, Direct Line also changed, using the internet at least as much as the phone. However, the changing nature of competition in the industry is illustrated by the fact that many customers now prefer to use comparison websites, enabling them to see the prices offered by tens or even hundreds of companies. In effect, this is the job that insurance brokers used to do. Direct Line do not allow such sites to include them in their searches, emphasising once more the 'direct' relationship with (potential and actual) customers.

A similar process has occurred as the internet is increasingly used for marketing and purchasing consumer goods. For example, despite the rapid growth of supermarkets in out-of-town physical locations, there is a widespread view that home deliveries of orders placed on the web (the 'virtual' supermarket) may rapidly lead to fundamental changes in shopping habits in the next decade. This would have potentially enormous knock-on effects on current businesses and their operations. Internet providers of household electrical goods, for example, are already significantly affecting the business of major 'high street' electrical retailers – they may well have to adapt to web-based trading themselves for much of their business or become a thing of the past. For the customer this increased competition is largely welcomed as it tends to lead to reduced prices, but for the retailer it cuts their profit margins and demands greater efficiency in operations. Many retailers are attempting to secure their futures by operating both retail outlets and internet sales simultaneously.

Sometimes organisations within a business sector collaborate with each other in order to maintain a stable environment within known competitive conditions. For example, the various European car manufacturers had for some time succeeded in persuading the EU to allow them a 'block exemption' from some aspects of competition law. This argument was based on the mechanical and electronic complexity of motor vehicles, which, it was argued, required specific expertise to service or repair. The manufacturers long argued that such expertise could only come from dealerships tied to each particular manufacturer. Hence, motor manufacturers maintained control over their distribution channels, which both acted as a strong barrier to entry for any new makes that might want to enter the market and also restricted the effectiveness of competition from independent garages for the servicing and repairing of cars. This situation changed somewhat in 2002, when EU regulations were amended to allow greater competition from independents and for dealerships to offer more than one make of new vehicle for sale. These changes, which are due to be reviewed in 2010, have made major changes to the competitive environment faced by virtually all businesses in the car trade (www.theaa.com).

1.2 A model of the business environment

The model of the business environment illustrated in *Figure 1.7* indicates how the various environmental forces, acting at a variety of scales, pass through what we refer to as 'perceptual filters'. These filters, which are explained more fully below, comprise all the internal mechanisms within organisations that enable managers to construct their own view of environmental realities. For example, an organisation may not have an active environmental scanning capability and hence may miss numerous potential opportunities. Others may be managed by eternal optimists, who are convinced of their organisations' invincibility, even when faced with hostile environmental influences. For all intents and purposes, these perceptual filters actually change and shape 'reality' for organisations. They influence the way organisations look at their environment and what they see. Consequently, we must not underestimate their power and influence. The failure of the UK motorcycle industry, which was virtually wiped out in the 1970s, was in large part due to its inability to accept that the business environment was rapidly changing. Design, product and process changes, largely developed in Japan, were ignored by British manufacturers who failed to perceive and react either to these environmental changes or to evolving customer requirements. The 'new' developments were viewed as distant and faddish: manufacturers were focused on past glories not future realities. The business environment in all countries is littered with similar examples.

Information about an organisation's environment may take a variety of forms: for example, it may comprise sophisticated data from a strategic management information system or, conversely, an apparently minor snippet of information gleaned by a powerful senior manager. There is little evidence to suggest that organisations are more likely to act on concrete data than on the opinion or impression of their senior personnel. Environmental information is always the result of 'human' analysis. It has passed through the complex

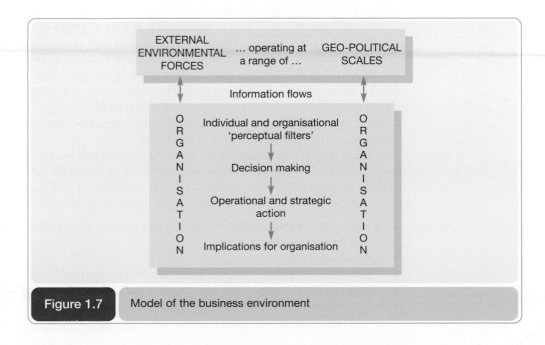

| Figure 1.7 | Model of the business environment |

perceptual filters that exist within every organisation. However, this information will not influence all organisations equally.

Managers at all levels utilise environmental information to help their decision making in order to enable the organisation to operate successfully. A thorough awareness of the nature of an organisation's environment is an essential prerequisite for strategic management. The environment often determines, and always influences, the future course of action of organisations, and acts as a force for change in organisations.

1.2.1 Perceptual filters

Organisations and their employees assist in the 'creation' of their own business environment such that the actual nature of that environment remains as much one of human interpretation as of hard 'reality'. Different organisations in the same industry often view environmental forces quite differently from one another, even though those forces may in fact be very similar. Additionally, organisations filter and interpret incoming information about the environment, and managerial cognition, organisational culture and politics all influence this process. These statements require further explanation.

Decision makers in organisations receive and assimilate incoming data from the environment. That data are, however, incomplete. Even the most sophisticated environmental scanning and forecasting activities can only collect and process a small proportion of all the (potentially) important environmental information. Most strategic decision makers are primarily concerned to learn about those changes which might influence their activity and as such they continuously make decisions regarding the importance or significance of 'new' information. It is quite possible, therefore, that person A will ignore data or dismiss them as unimportant while person B, even in the same organisation, may take this same information on board and 'allow' it to influence his or her decision-making process. This difference in 'reception' may be attributed to differences in the individuals' backgrounds, their beliefs and opinions, their position in the organisation, or how welcome or potentially threatening the information is to the receiver. Just as individuals differ, so do organisations and whole industrial sectors.

Our individual and collective perception only enables us to 'see' and interpret in certain ways. It is these perceptions that drive individual and business actions. Weick (1979) suggests that individual and organisational actions might in turn influence change within the environment. A hypothetical example (*Minicase 1.3*) will help illustrate this phenomenon.

Managers' perception of their environment may have a greater influence on organisational decision making and eventual strategic direction than does more objective information. This raises some major concerns regarding the reliability and validity of managers' perception. It is possible, for example, that managers often make broad generalisations based on a small number of cases. This is perhaps unavoidable. Managers are not entirely objective and analytical; as with all humans, they bring their own beliefs and preferences (and prejudices) to their decision making. As Huber (1985) contends, these shortcomings are inevitable due to the perceptual and cognitive limitations of managers.

Some managers and organisations, in facing an uncertain international business environment, perceive their environment as more certain than it actually is. This is particularly true of those managers who have a low tolerance for confusion or ambiguity.

In summary, the main influences upon individual and organisational perception are:

- characteristics of individuals, such as background, education and duration of employment within the organisation;
- organisational culture;
- organisational politics, structures and control mechanisms;
- history and development of an organisation; and
- industrial sectors and their norms.

Minicase 1.3	Enactment – a self-fulfilling prophecy

Let us assume that *Forefront,* a computer software house, perceives that the competitive environment in which it operates is changing. These perceived changes encourage it to develop a technologically superior Windows™ environment software product. It also perceives that numerous smaller software companies may begin to encroach on its other activities if it does not focus R&D activity in these areas. Faced with a decision, Forefront decides to increase its efforts in R&D in the Windows™ market. This entails reducing both its R&D spend and management attention in those other areas. After two years Forefront has successfully produced and marketed its Windows™ product and remains the market leader. However, there has been a cost. The neglect of its other software products has meant that competitors have overtaken it in market share terms in other product lines.

The company's original perception of its environment led it to a particular strategic management decision. As a result of that decision, Forefront has enacted its environment. That is, its actions have assured that its perceptions became a reality. Its actions, to focus on the Windows™ environment at the expense of other products, have led other 'environmental actors' (that is, its competitors) to adjust their strategic policy to take advantage of the opportunity. Forefront's perceptions and subsequent actions have become a self-fulfilling prophecy.

Questions

1 What is it about Forefront's activity that has made it 'enact' its environment?
2 Discuss why two organisations in the same sector might 'see' their environment in quite different ways.

1.2.2 Dynamism and complexity

Throughout this book we stress the dynamic nature of environmental forces; however, we recognise that the degree or extent of dynamism is not equal for all organisations or environments. For example, at present the extent of environmental flux affecting a funeral director or undertaking business, although not negligible, is less than that influencing General Motors (GM)! Complexity in the environment is a product of a number of interrelated factors and the degree of environmental uncertainty, possibly caused by dynamism, plays a major part. An organisation faced with an uncertain environment is, other things being equal, in a far less advantageous position than one facing stability. However, yet again all is not straightforward, for many organisations become complacent when faced with a set of known environmental parameters. A significant change in one or more of those characteristics often leaves the inflexible organisation unable to cope. Environmental complexity also tends to increase for organisations operating at a variety of geo-political scales. A transnational manufacturing and marketing organisation is likely to encounter dynamic environmental forces at local, national and global scales. *Figure 1.8* can be used to 'map' an organisation's position according to the levels of complexity and dynamism in its environment. By way of illustration we have located the approximate position of a number of 'generic' organisations.

When faced with a complex, uncertain and dynamic environment, some organisations and many individual managers attempt to simplify that environment, at least in their own minds. This is probably not a wise course of action. Researchers have argued that attempts to reduce environmental uncertainty may lead to poor long-term organisational performance. The themes of dynamism and complexity will be developed throughout this book and the consequences for organisations, government, individuals and groups are further explored in *Chapter 9.*

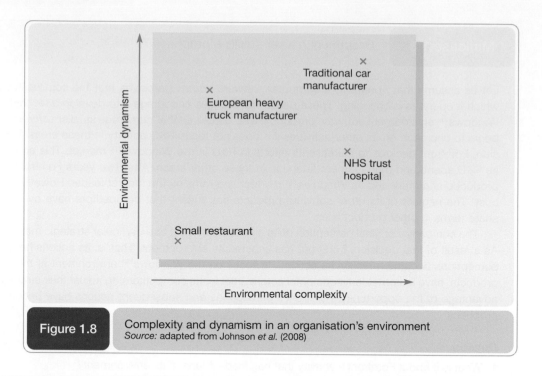

Figure 1.8	Complexity and dynamism in an organisation's environment
	Source: adapted from Johnson *et al.* (2008)

1.3 The organisation

1.3.1 Types of organisations

The term 'organisation' or 'business', as used in this book, embraces a wide range of legal entities with diverse objectives. *Table 1.3* lists, with examples, the main types of organisation in the UK. Clearly, these will vary in different countries governed by different legal practices.

Table 1.3	Types of organisation

Types of organisation	UK examples	Global examples
Government civil service departments and agencies	The Treasury	Ministero Scuola e Educatione (Italy)
Local government organisations	Gloucestershire County Council	California State Legislature
Incorporated by Royal Charter or by Act of Parliament (public corporations)	BBC (by Royal Charter) Post Office (by Act of Parliament)	Air France
Quasi autonomous Non-governmental Organisations (quangos)	Higher education funding council executive (HEFCE)	UMNO (Malaysia
Sole trader	Bombay Palace Restaurant	Kobayashi Electronics (Japan)
Partnership	PricewaterhouseCoopers	PricewaterhouseCoopers
Charity organisations	Oxfam	International Red Cross
Private limited company	Virgin Atlantic	Joe's Garage
Co-operative	Co-operative Retail Society	Cooperativa di Consumatori (Italy)
Public limited company (plc)	Arsenal FC plc	Heineken (Holland)
Building societies and friendly societies	Britannia Building Society	Northwestern Mutual (USA)

As organisations differ fundamentally from one another in their legal status and primary objectives, it is not surprising that the environmental forces that influence them also vary. In fact environmental pressures may encourage some organisations to actually change their legal status and objectives.

Organisational objectives profoundly influence an organisation's activity and strategic direction. Knowledge of these objectives will help determine the importance of different environmental forces and changes. *Table 1.4* gives a flavour of the range of objectives that exists in just three types of organisation.

In addition to the legal status and prime objectives of organisations, there are numerous other factors that may profoundly affect the nature of the organisation–environment relationship. These include:

- organisational structure;
- size of the organisation;
- type of technology used;
- organisational and individual perceptual filters.

These and other factors will, subtly or otherwise, alter the importance of any particular environmental variable. For example, a large and diversified organisation may cope better with a proposed new EU regulation (because of its ability to influence the outcome by lobbying) than a smaller, more specialised firm. Conversely, it is frequently argued that small firms tend to be more flexible and able to cope with environmental uncertainty than large, sluggish organisations.

Table 1.4	Organisational objectives
Type of organisation	**Prime objective**
Commercial company (e.g. Shell plc)	To maximise shareholder value
Charity (e.g. Oxfam)	To relieve poverty, distress and suffering in any part of the world
General hospital (e.g. Leeds General Infirmary)	To provide quality healthcare for the local community

1.4 Environmental forecasting

We have argued that managers' perception influences their vision and assessment of the international business environment. These processes are based on subjective judgements of the environment. However, many organisations attempt to use more objective environmental measures. The following section explores some of these objective, and other more perceptual, measures, while the role that organisational culture and outlook plays in influencing views of the environment is discussed in the final section of this chapter where we briefly explore the 'art' of futurology.

1.4.1 Forecasting in a dynamic and complex environment

Managers with strategic responsibilities in organisations are often frustrated by the difficulty of predicting changes in the environment. It is frequently the case, especially in smaller organisations, that little formal long-term forecasting takes place. It is viewed as such an uncertain science that time is not spent attempting to foresee what is often regarded as the unforeseeable. Instead managers prefer to be influenced by a combination of information resulting from their accumulated experience in business and a variety of perceptual measures of their environment. This may, however, prevent organisations from acting proactively, so that they are often in a position of having to react to a change thrust upon them.

There are many examples of companies that have failed due to their reliance upon incorrect forecasts or the inability of management to react appropriately to environmental evidence. A good example is that of the car industry in the USA in the latter part of the twentieth century. By 1980, over 20 percent of the market (that is an awful lot of cars!) had been taken by foreign manufacturers, which produced smaller, more fuel-efficient vehicles. In the following 20 years or so non-American car manufacturers rapidly improved both their productivity, enabling them to produce low-cost vehicles, and the market appeal of their vehicles. By 2009 two of the three major US manufacturers – GM and Chrysler – were on their knees, while the third, Ford, still struggles to compete in some markets. They are not alone, of course, with some European and even Japanese manufacturers struggling with over-capacity and demanding market conditions. The American auto manufacturers have largely failed to adequately recognise that global economic and political conditions would lead to large increases in oil prices, and that social factors, such as greater female economic and geographic mobility, were 'conspiring' to create a preference for smaller cars.

At best, assessing the potential impact of likely changes in the environment offers organisations an advantage over their competitors by enabling decision makers to narrow the range of options. Measures will always entail some element of subjectivity, if only in the processes involved in collecting the data. The accuracy and, therefore, the value of such forecasts will often depend on the 'richness' of data, itself a product of managers' choice of communication media. Nevertheless, it is clear that, in a dynamic and complex business environment, attempting to forecast sometimes *discontinuous* trends is fraught with difficulty. One need only look at the frequent inaccuracies of Organisation for Economic Co-operation and Development (OECD) and national government forecasts of medium- or long-term economic indicators such as GDP growth despite their 'closeness' to the economy and privileged access to data. Very few senior authorities – the OECD or national governments – predicted the enormous downturn in economic activity since 2008. They got it wrong by an enormous margin! However, to do nothing is also a dangerous course of action for an organisation or government, as is over-reliance on internal sources of information rather than external channels. It is quite possible, under such circumstances, that a state of inertia could set in, which would ill equip organisations to accurately forecast changes in the environment and which may lead to poor quality decision making and organisational underperformance.

1.4.2 An approach to forecasting

One well-known approach to forecasting was suggested by Peace and Robinson in 1994. They suggest that strategic decision makers need to take a step-by-step approach to forecasting (see *Figure 1.9*). Their model outlines five steps:

- selection of environmental variables that are critical to the organisation;
- selection of sources of information about those variables;
- evaluation of forecasting techniques;
- integration of the results of forecasting into the strategic management process; and
- monitoring and evaluation of the critical aspects of these forecasts.

Some variables may be so obviously important to the well-being of the organisation that they become, in a sense, self-selecting. For example, a company which smelts aluminium will be concerned about likely changes in the price of electricity as this forms a major cost in the production process. Other variables will be identified, usually by senior managers with

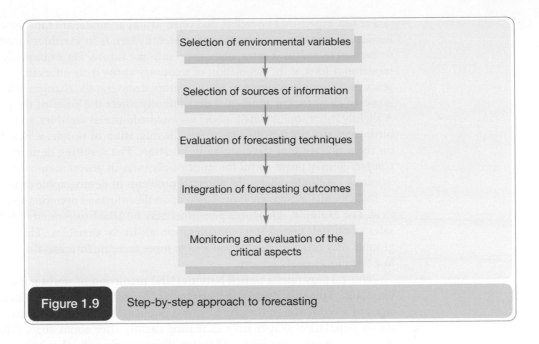

Selection of environmental variables

Selection of sources of information

Evaluation of forecasting techniques

Integration of forecasting outcomes

Monitoring and evaluation of the
critical aspects

| **Figure 1.9** | Step-by-step approach to forecasting |

experience in the organisation and within the sector. However, it is critical to select variables that may be important in the future and not just rely on those which have been critical in the past. It is not a difficult task to select the key variables, although a little lateral thinking may prove useful – and there may be disagreement about which variables are truly 'key'. In order to keep the list of variables manageable it is recommended that you omit factors that have little chance of occurring.

There are numerous sources of information about the international business environment. These include government and international organisations' statistics and forecasts (despite their lack of reliability on occasions!) regarding economic variables such as inflation and growth rates, research findings estimating changes in commodity prices, informed opinions on political, social or technological changes and so forth. A considerable amount of information is merely 'picked up' by managers keeping their eyes and ears open and continually scanning their business environment for opportunities or threats resulting from imminent change. Although quantitative measures of environmental variables carry a certain credibility, more judgemental and subjective approaches are likely to prove practical and sometimes more accurate. You will note from our discussion of perceptual filters that subjectivity impinges on all human activity – not least upon the manager sensing changes in the business environment.

1.4.3 Forecasting techniques

Using sophisticated computer techniques and relying primarily on numerical data, some companies and many governments and international organisations attempt to model changes in the environment. These models often utilise economic data and attempt to estimate future economic variables, such as interest rates and the external value of currencies. There are many private consultancy companies that specialise in developing such models for government and commercial clients. However, as environmental stability is very much a phenomenon of the past, modelling of this type has been subject to considerable 'bad press'. Such models find environmental flux and discontinuity difficult, if not impossible, to predict. For example, models of this nature could not possibly have predicted the terrorist attack on New York in 2001 (9/11) and the catastrophic effect this had on US and European airlines. Nor did they predict the 2008 credit crunch.

Far less expensive to develop, and often just as accurate, are time series and judgemental models. Time series models attempt to identify trends in variables based on historical data or cyclical factors and extrapolate them into the future. For example, a simple time series model may look at the population of a country at five-year intervals over the past hundred years then use this evidence to predict future demographic changes. This method does not, however, allow for environmental discontinuity where the 'rules' of the past no longer apply. A slightly more sophisticated model may add additional variables, such as likely changes in birth rates and predictions concerning the migration of people, which may have a bearing on the population of the country in question. The resulting demographic forecasts (see *Chapter 5*) may prove useful for strategic planners in government and some organisations. *Minicase 1.4* also highlights the potential problems of demographic change.

Judgemental models are those based upon the informed opinion of people in the relevant field. For example, sales-force personnel may be asked to estimate likely future trends in sales potential, taking into consideration all likely variables. Their experience 'on the ground' may prove invaluable and lead to more accurate forecasts than sophisticated modelling techniques could achieve.

Table 1.5 illustrates a United Nations (UN) prediction of world population growth to the year 2150. This prediction combines knowledge of historic trends, including more recent signs of a reduction in the rate of world population growth, with educated guesswork. It shows population growth only increasing slightly after about 2050. Whereas the UN estimate that an extra one billion (1,000 million) people will inhabit the world between 1999 and 2013 (just 14 years), they believe that it will take 129 years for an extra billion people to live between the years 2054 to 2183. Will it be proven correct?

How can anyone predict population growth in the next millennium using 'scientific' means? Well, demographers (those who study population) are luckier than many, as trends in population are partially predictable over reasonably long time periods. For example, if world population growth slows shortly (as they predict), this will mean that there will be fewer young adults in a generation's time, and therefore fewer mothers and fathers to have children.

The UN believes that because world population growth is slowing now, it will continue to do so indefinitely. What they cannot predict is an event or events that cause current trends

---

Minicase 1.4   China's ageing population

China has been emerging from under-development and widespread poverty to become a major economic superpower with rapid economic growth. It has for a generation enforced quite strictly a one-child policy in order to control population growth in what is the world's most populous country. The impact of this is to create an aging population: the 4-2-1 problem where each child often has two parents and four grandparents. Not a problem in many respects but what will this mean in time to come? China remains a relatively young country – median age is about 30 – but rapidly aging. The dependency ratio, that is the number of old and young as a proportion of the number of working-age adults, is currently low – there aren't so many children any more. However, it is now increasing and will by 2050 be as high as in 1975. The big difference is that whereas most dependants in 1975 were children (about 85+ percent) with only about 15 percent of dependants being old adults, in 2050 about 65–70 percent of dependents will be old-aged adults. The trend has begun. In 2015, almost without doubt now, almost 50 percent of all dependants will be older people – by 2020 it will be over 50 percent (unless the one child family policy is rescinded).

Questions

1 How do the needs of older people differ from those of the young?
2 What is the likely impact of these changes on families, organisations and government?

Table 1.5	The growth of world population

Year	Population
1000	310 million
1250	400 million
1500	500 million
1750	790 million
1900	1,650 million
1950	2,520 million
2000	6,060 million
2050	8,910 million (est.)
2100	9,461 million (est.)
2150	9,750 million (est.)

Source: adapted version of 'Table 1. World Population, Year O to near Stabilization' as shown on www.un.org/esa/population/publications/sixbillion/sixbilpart1.pdf from 'Human Development Report 1999' by United Nations (1999). By permission of Oxford University Press, Inc.

to radically alter. For example, there may be dramatic new technological inventions that vastly increase longevity and/or fertility rates or, conversely, there may be new viruses that threaten the lives of billions. However, as suggested, some important demographic factors can be predicted with reasonable accuracy and the predictions are vital to certain business sectors. For example, we know that in most of the Western world, with the possible exception of the USA, the population is ageing. We can make what may be reasonably accurate estimates of the number, even the proportion, of the total population which will be of pension age in the year 2050 – for the simple reason that these people already exist. So, whereas less than 10 percent of the population of the UK in 2010 is of pension age (over 65 years old), it is predicted that that figure will rise to 13.5 percent by 2050. The accuracy of this prediction is highly important for all of us and especially for government and the pension business. It will also have highly significant implications for the healthcare industry; see *Chapter 5* for further discussion on patterns of population change.

Another common, rather creative, method of generating ideas and forecasts is widely known as 'brainstorming'. A number of informed people are encouraged to generate ideas and forecasts in a group setting. It can usefully be employed to estimate future trends in technology development, for example. Many of these ideas may appear fanciful but technological developments often do lead to 'fanciful' outcomes! Such techniques can generate useful judgemental ideas about potential future events.

The Delphi method of forecasting is a more systematic technique than brainstorming. This method attempts to gain consensus among a group of people, such as a senior strategic management group. For example, a company senior management team may meet and aim to forecast their likely competitive position in five years' time. They will discuss all relevant variables and start to agree on as many points and issues as possible in an attempt to develop the most likely and most widely held view. This can then be used in the strategy process.

It is interesting to note some of the predictions made in the past from reputable sources which turned out to be somewhat misguided. *The Quarterly Review* (1825), an English journal, asked 'what could be more palpably absurd than the prospect of locomotives travelling twice as fast as stagecoaches?' In a similar vein, Henry Ford's lawyer advised in 1922 that 'the horse is here to stay, but the automobile is only a novelty – a fad', while an editorial of the *Boston Post* in 1865 wrote, 'well informed people know that it is impossible to transmit the voice over wires and were that it were possible to do so, it would be of no practical value'.

Finally, the Chairman of IBM in 1943 wrote, 'I think there is a market for about five computers'. Refer to section 9.7 *'Future trends?'* for further discussion of 'Futurology'.

Scenario development recognises judgemental and non-quantitative information such as changing fashions. Scenarios are 'pictures' or 'stories' of what might be the case some time in the future. They draw upon both subjective and more objective data. Hence, a company may develop two or three likely scenarios for some future date and take these into consideration in their planning process. They may develop contingency plans to cope with each scenario should it arise. The multinational oil giant, Shell, has made extensive use of scenario 'planning'. An example of this approach, a scenario that hydrogen fuel cells may rapidly replace traditional fossil fuelled engines for road transport, is explored in *Minicase 1.5*.

Finally, a number of organisations and consultancies have developed 'political risk' ratings for countries around the world. These take into consideration the stability and predictability of nations and their governments, terrorist activity, and advise commercial organisations and governments on the risks involved in overseas investment.

1.4.4 Impact analysis

One simple, yet effective, way of forecasting the effect of environmental changes on organisations is to conduct an impact analysis. This involves ascertaining a series of potential environmental changes and assessing the probable effect of these on a range of organisations, usually direct competitors. *Table 1.6* illustrates a simple impact analysis of the truck industry. The effect of a change is first assessed as either a positive (+) or negative (−) influence. Positive influences are those where there will be a benefit to the company financially or otherwise. Changes that may lead to strongly positive effects are given a ++ or even +++ rating. The impact analysis may then involve a brief explanation of the plus/minus score.

It can be seen from the impact analysis in *Table 1.6* that changes in environmental regulations will adversely affect all truck manufacturers; however, some are better prepared due to

Table 1.6	Impact analysis in the truck industry		
Environmental scenario	**Scania (Sweden)**	**ERF (UK)**	**Mercedes Trucks (Germany)**
Ecological	−	− − −	− −
Strict new European Union environmental protection legislation (i.e. Euro standards 4 and 5)	Track record in R&D on environmentally friendly engines and truck design, nevertheless changes will require extra investment	UK company, too small to invest sufficiently in environmentally friendly R&D	R&D expenditure on environment-oriented technology but without outstanding quality reputation of Scania
Economic	+ +	−	+ +
Sweden adopts the euro; UK and sterling remain out of euro	Reduces transaction costs and uncertainty in euro countries	Little effect on UK market but uncertainty and transaction costs remain with exports	Reduces transaction costs and uncertainty in euro countries
Political	− −	− −	−
Governments enforce movement of 'heavy' freight to railways and restrict the use of heavy trucks	Will adversely affect the sale of trucks, servicing and parts sales, as Scania do not produce light trucks and vans	Will adversely affect the sale of trucks, servicing and parts sales, as ERF do not produce light trucks and vans	Mercedes is protected to a degree by having sizeable market shares in motor vehicles of all sizes but heavy truck sales would suffer

Minicase 1.5	The hydrogen economy

Major car manufacturers such as Ford and Toyota are currently embarking on major investments in hydrogen technology and forging alliances in the process with Shell, BP and Exxon. Shell launched a new company in 2003 – Shell Hydrogen – with an initial budget of about US$100 million. Buses powered by fuel cells are already in service in Chicago, Vancouver and Oslo on an experimental basis.

The development has been stimulated by:

- tightening in air quality standards and targets to reduce CO_2 emissions in the light of concern over global warming;
- increasing security threat over oil reserves and consequent fluctuations in oil prices.

The 'obvious' impact of the use of hydrogen fuel cells is a cut in gasoline by up to 100 percent!

Hydrogen is easily made. For example, one large oil refinery, BP's Grangemouth in Scotland, produces about 150 tonnes of hydrogen a day – enough to fuel 500,000 cars. Currently, however, hydrogen is difficult to store and transport. Buses currently being tested are five times more expensive than conventional buses and prices are unlikely to fall until fuel cells can be mass produced. Pure hydrogen is especially difficult to store as it does not liquefy until its temperature reaches absolute zero, and it is highly combustible. Currently, fuel tanks have to be bulky and take up considerable space, and allow only small distances between refuelling. If the technology is to be used in cars it may be necessary to store the gas at around 5,000 psi (an average car tyre 'stores' air at around 30 psi). The technology to do this is yet to be developed. To build a low-carbon economy, governments, investors, businesses and consumers will need to sustain change. Consumers will need to lobby government ('green votes') and engage in 'green purchasing'.

Questions

1 What are the likely implications of this development for: car manufacturers; major oil companies, such as BP, Exxon and Shell; oil-producing countries; and petrol retailers?
2 What is the likely impact upon climate change and global warming?

their scale and a history of concern for such issues. A realignment of exchange rates will not affect all three companies in the same way.

Impact analysis enables managers or analysts to assess the effects of environmental change on an organisation and upon its competitors. Clearly, where such changes are likely to adversely affect an organisation more than its competitors, then contingency planning needs to be considered.

1.5 Environmental analysis and strategic process

1.5.1 Strategy, structure and environmental influence

Most early organisational theory and management research assumed a largely stable business environment. Proponents of the Classical School and of Scientific Management argued that organisations should be machine-like and feature centralised authority, clear lines of command, specialisation and the division of labour, and numerous rules and regulations. However, such mechanised and bureaucratic organisations, typified by hierarchical structures and a fervent adherence to the power-control role of management, are poorly suited to dynamic and complex environments. By the 1940s, in North America and increasingly also in Europe, the deficiencies of the 'classical' organisation became apparent. Technological changes, increasingly complex markets and social, political and cultural changes created new demands on organisations, which many were ill-equipped to manage. Although many of the basic principles identified by classical management theorists, such as Fayol and Taylor, remain entrenched within many 'modern' organisations, other environmentally sensitive changes have occurred. The Human Relations School (late 1930s onwards), typified by the work of Chester Barnard and landmark studies by the Tavistock Institute, together with the Hawthorne studies, signalled change. In the search for greater effectiveness and flexibility within organisations, emphasis shifted towards the consideration of 'people' issues such as motivation and leadership. A better-motivated and well-led workforce will prove to be more flexible and capable of coping with environmental change and complexity.

A study of electronics companies in the UK by Burns and Stalker (1961) attempted to establish why some companies were able to cope with changes in their environment, specifically dynamism in their product markets, while others were inept in this regard. They argued that successful innovators had developed an 'organic' structure while those with 'mechanistic' structures were less able to adapt. Some years later, Lawrence and Lorsch (1967) found a similar relationship between the business environment and the internal structure of the firm in the USA. Where they differed from earlier researchers was that they did not believe that organisations or their environments were uniform or unchanging. They postulated that the more turbulent and complex the environment the greater the degree of difference between sub-parts of the organisation. Hence they argued that successful companies were those that developed appropriate degrees of differentiation between specialist departments while simultaneously promoting integration, calling on common goals.

In environments that are certain and stable, organisations will tend to develop a form and structure which is most efficient in relation to that environment, probably one with a high degree of managerial control and mechanistic structures and systems. If an organisation's environment is uncertain and complex, managers design structures with greater in-built flexibility. However, perception may play a part in this process – that is, managers in organisations which have an organic structure may perceive the environment as being dynamic and uncertain, while those in more mechanistic structures may perceive their environment as being more certain; the reality may be quite different. Nevertheless, there are many firms in the company graveyard whose managers 'perceived' their environments as being stable and certain when in fact they harboured destructive dynamic forces.

There has been research concerning the relationship between groups of organisations and their collective environment. Grinyer and Spender (1979), for example, argued that organisations in a particular industry sector, such as the motor vehicle industry or the higher education sector, have a tendency to develop 'recipe knowledge' about how to operate in that business. This recipe knowledge influences their collective view of the industry environment. They argue, however, that companies which continually develop their recipe knowledge in line with changes in the environment are likely to succeed and prosper at the expense of their more sluggish competitors. The recipe does not imprison these organisations.

As argued in the section above on environmental forecasting, it is often suggested that the success of commercial firms depends on their ability to foresee and subsequently act upon environmental information. Miles and Snow (1978) have identified various types of organisations that possess quite different capabilities and motivations in this respect. Their typology of organisations refers to the 'style' in which they operate strategically. This style influences their relationship with the business environment and is, in turn, influenced by that environment. Hence 'defender' organisations, they argue, attempt to create a stable environment which suits their non-dynamic structure and strategy, while 'prospectors' view their environment as ever-changing and seek continual strategic and structural adjustments to cope with changes. They are continually searching for new opportunities and, in the process, may create change and uncertainty for others within their competitive environment. They identify two other categories of organisation: 'analysers' and 'reactors'. The former are capable of acting in both stable and unstable environments, a quality of considerable value. 'Reactors' act only when environmental change 'forces' them to do so. They are not 'proactive' organisations.

All four types of organisation, it is argued, 'enact' or create their environment. What they choose to see and how they choose to interpret that environment is quite unique to each organisation. Hence a defender may view the same environment as a prospector, yet see stability and continuity all around while the prospector sees only change and opportunity. Clearly each organisation filters data to suit its own capabilities and concerns. Executives selectively misinterpret aspects of their environment. These filters include individual managers' cognitive processes, organisational culture and politics, other group or team factors and the strategic orientation of the organisation. Therefore, as stated above, it is quite possible for two organisations to view the same environmental change as either a glorious opportunity for growth and prosperity or, depending on their perception, a catastrophe threatening organisational survival.

More recently the development of chaos theory has stressed that, because of the unpredictability and constant flux which characterise the business environment, organisational structure and strategy need to be fundamentally reappraised.

1.5.2 Strategic planning

The strategic planning process in organisations is the subject of considerable attention in the field of business and management. The academic and, increasingly, the practitioner worlds are engaged in lively debate over issues such as the nature of strategy formulation. To put it rather simplistically there are two broad schools of thought – the rationalist and subjectivist approaches.

The rationalist approach argues that strategic planning is, or certainly should be, undertaken in a logical and largely linear fashion. It is suggested that organisations monitor their business environment and analyse their internal resource position in order to assess what strengths and weaknesses they have which might facilitate the exploitation of environmental opportunities and the avoidance of environmental threats. A stakeholder analysis is also important at this stage.

PESTLE C analysis, or the many variants upon it described above, is usually undertaken within organisations as a prelude to a more strategically orientated technique – a SWOT analysis. This acronym stands for strengths, weaknesses, opportunities and threats. As part of a strategic process of analysis an organisation may assess its strengths and weaknesses from an internal resource perspective. For example, it may conclude that it is in a sound financial state and that it utilises modern, effective technology. Its weaknesses may, for example, be an under-trained and poorly motivated staff.

It is the latter two elements of this acronym which are of particular relevance here, for it is in the external business environment where both opportunities and threats can be found. As a vital strategic tool, businesses often attempt to identify such opportunities that they may seek to exploit and threats that they attempt to avoid.

Similarly, a popular model suggests that the initial stages of strategy formulation lie in gaining an appreciation of the degree of uncertainty in the organisation's environment. This is preceded by an audit of environmental influences. The strategic planner then conducts a structural analysis of the immediate competitive environment of the organisation before analysing the organisation's strategic position. Johnson *et al.* (2008) explain that the aim of such analysis is to develop an understanding of opportunities that can be built upon and threats which have to be overcome. Organisations can then adapt to their environment and, by actively managing environmental relationships, can in turn shape the changes that are occurring. The task of rational strategic management in this scenario involves reading the environment and then 'creating initiatives that will resonate with the changes that are occurring'

(Morgan, 1989). Senior management generate a series of strategic options from which choices are later made after due analysis and consideration of all parameters. The chosen strategies are then implemented.

Thus it is assumed that actual or predicted changes in the environment lead to planned strategic change in organisations. Strategic planning, therefore, is an attempt to match organisational capabilities with environmental opportunities. Hence the dominant paradigm is that organisations are in a state of 'dynamic equilibrium', continually adapting to their environment. These planning activities, it is argued, are essential for organisations to cope with environmental dynamism.

Strategic planning often tends to adopt a three- to five-year time scale, during which time the business environment of most organisations will alter significantly. However, it should be stressed that proponents of the rational approach do stress the need for 'reality embellishments' such as feedback loops, for example, to enable further environmental scanning to influence decisions at a later stage. They also often stress that factors such as the role of organisational culture, politics and other contextual, non-rational, issues should be included as part of the planning process.

This argument brings us to an alternative perspective on strategy formulation, the subjective approach. This alternative view is often based both on empirical research and intuitive judgement and attempts to explain the actual processes that take place in organisations. They tend to be less prescriptive. As argued above, organisations are not entirely rational or logical in their environmental-sensing or decision-making processes. Organisation-level filters of an intensely 'human' nature disrupt mechanical linear planning processes. They influence the nature and quality of information available and severely limit the range of strategic choices likely to be entertained. They also add an inescapable richness and reality to organisational activity. It is rather pointless to assume, as some traditional rational models imply, that organisational culture, politics and other human processes can, somehow, be easily managed, ignored or stopped from fundamentally influencing organisational activity.

Many academics and management writers question the almost taken-for-granted assumption that successful organisations adapt to or seek to 'fit' their environment. They argue that firms which do seek adaption to their environment are prone to imitation and repetition, as competitors do likewise. Many successful organisations use resources more creatively and challenge environmental assumptions. They are able to influence the environment of their competitors and, in part at least, create their own environment. This process, referred to as 'enactment', is discussed above. However, the simple rational model of strategic planning pays little attention to the notion of enactment or the way in which organisations influence their business environment.

We have argued above that organisations and individuals enact their environment and may view similar information in quite different ways. This is a non-rational process. When we make this assumption we suggest that environments are not fixed and measurable in a strict sense. They are open to multiple interpretations. Additionally, internal processes of strategic planning are not as the Rationalist School would suggest. Often crucial business decisions are based on very limited data, moulded by personal considerations or cultural norms and implemented by political expediency. Some organisations will have sophisticated planning departments; others will be strategically 'led' by a dominant stakeholder such as the managing director. There is not a great deal of evidence to suggest that one style is a guarantee of greater success than the other.

For some time various academics and social analysts have attempted to identify stages in the development of society and to categorise 'types of people' accordingly. One such example is shown in *Minicase 1.6*. The resultant analysis, as well as having interest value, can influence government and organisational decision makers. Businesses and marketers group types of people by all manner of criteria (including where they live), the minicase identifies four broad categories of society applicable to many, largely Western societies.

Minicase 1.6	Types of people

Four broad categories of people can be identified depending on when they were born. They are:

- Builders (born before 1945)
- Baby Boomers (born 1946–1964)
- Generation X (born 1965–1979)
- Generation Y (born 1980–2000)

	Builders 60s & 70s	Baby Boomers 40s & 50s	Gen. X 30s & 40s	Gen. Y 20s
Primary instinct	Think	Think	Feel	Know
Beliefs, values and motivations	Security Work ethic Country Advancement	Variety Freedom Achievement	Lifestyle Fun Community Self-discovery	Class of values No absolute Relational
Learning and leadership styles	Classroom style Control Thinkers	Round-table style Co-operation Thinkers	Unstructured Consensus Feelers	Unstructured Spontaneous Interactive Knowers
Money	Scarce	Earn it	It is not everything	Give it to me
Loyalty to employer	Serve my boss	Working my way to the top	Short cut to the top	Give me Saturday off or I quit
Respecting elders	Seen and not heard	Automatic	Polite	Whatever
Sex	After marriage	On the back seat	Living together	Online
Technology	Ignorant	Aware	Comfortable	Live and breath it
Buying decisions	Price	Choice	Simplicity	Relationship

Source: Shirlaws Business Coaching/Booz Allen Hamilton, www.genconference.net/1366.file.did

Questions

1 Examine the grid above and consider how the differences between age groups have already and may continue to impact how business operates.
2 We await generation Z – what will they be like?

Although interesting, this subject is complex. You are very likely to investigate it in further detail if you are engaged on a structured business or management course which leads to considerations of strategic management or corporate policy. It is, however, wise at this stage to appreciate the arguments of both schools of thought and develop a broad understanding of organisational processes and academic debates.

1.6 Conclusion

It is hoped that you now have a better understanding of the international business environment facing all organisations. That environment is often very complex and rapidly changing. It operates, sometimes, internationally and often nationally, as well as locally. The small local bar or mobile phone retailer, for example, may only employ a few staff and have a small turnover but will be influenced by large-scale changes in the environment. For example, changes in telecommunication and financial transaction technology operate on a global scale and will affect the way these micro companies do their business. Employment laws at a national and international level (such as the maximum working week or minimum wage in EU regulations) will influence the managers' decisions regarding staffing arrangements. Changes in competitors' behaviours and new products will influence what the two micro businesses actually sell; these products and behaviours might originate from the USA or Europe or the Far East, for example. A downturn in the fortunes of the economy will make potential customers think twice about buying a new mobile or going out drinking, particularly if they have become unemployed, and the small business might, in turn, struggle to survive. We have learned that the business environment represents an integrated set of forces operating at a variety of scales and impacting on all businesses. We also know that although attempts to forecast change might prove useful, there are real difficulties in predicting the future and the likely impact of even well-understood changes.

Having set the scene and defined the parameters within which we will study the international business environment, this book now takes a closer look at the individual environmental forces which influence organisations. Chapters 2–8 run through the PESTLE C factors (although not in that order). Each chapter will explore the forces at play and the implications of these for organisations. The final chapter revisits many of these themes in the particular context of the globalisation of the world economy.

Summary of main points

This chapter has aimed to 'set the scene' on the international business environment and to delineate the scope of this book. A number of vital issues and concepts have been covered. The key points are:

- There are a number of interrelated forces acting upon organisations which emanate from the external environment of the organisation.

- For the purpose of analysis, these forces can be placed in distinct categories, but in reality they form an interrelated and complex whole.

- Environmental forces act at a number of geo-political scales, very many at the global or international level.

- The relationship between organisation and environment is not clear-cut, as information flows from the environment to the organisation but also from the organisation to the environment.

- There are a variety of types of organisation which can be differentiated by, for example, their prime objectives or their legal status – the environment influences different types of organisation in different ways.

- Individual perception and organisational filters influence how the business environment is viewed.

- Forecasting the business environment is problematic due to change and complexity, yet many methods exist and are widely used.

- There is a relationship between the business environment and both the structure and strategy of organisations.

- There is considerable debate concerning the nature and process of strategic policy formulation but an understanding of the international business environment is essential for successful strategic management.

Chapter 1 The international business environment   **29**

Discussion questions

1 For an organisation with which you are familiar (e.g. your workplace, university or a case study from this book) identify two environmental forces for each of the PESTLE C categories. Establish the geo-political scale(s) at which each force may operate.

2 Carry out an environmental stakeholder analysis of an organisation with which you are familiar. Place this information on a grid as shown in *Figure 1.4*. What does this tell you about management priorities and their chief concerns?

3 Discuss the range of forces that might act on a small or medium business in your local area, such as a café or fashion clothes shop.

4 Select an organisational case study and identify an array of environmental variables which influence the company.
  a. Which of these variables may management be able to forecast?
  b. What are the likely sources of information to facilitate forecasting?
  c. What approaches and methods of forecasting might be employed?
  d. What would be some of the difficulties in accurately forecasting changes in these variables?

5 Conduct an impact analysis for a sector of industry with which you are familiar.

6 Discuss a scenario and the potential implications for business. The scenario could be (a) a sustained fall in birth rates, such as has been experienced in Italy in the past forty years, (b) an increase in the threat of global terrorism, or (c) a requirement for business to offer flexible working to parents of school-age children.

Further reading/sources of information

BBC (**http://news.bbc.co.uk/**) The BBC website provides up-to-date information on business topics, economics, politics, technology and much more from around the world.

Daniels, J.D., Radebaugh, L.H. and Sullivan, D.P. (2009) *International Business – Environments and Operations,* 12th edn. Upper Saddle River, NJ: Prentice Hall. This American textbook contains much useful information on both the international business environment and businesses' operations.

Dicken, P. (2007) *Global Shift: Mapping the Changing Contours of the Global Economy,* 5th edn. London: Sage. A useful survey of how the global economy has changed in the last 30 years.

European Union (EU) (**http://ec.europa.eu/index_en.htm**) Home page of the European Commission with access to the Directorate General for Competition of the European Union.

Friends of the Earth (**www.foe.co.uk**) The website of one of the main green pressure groups, frequently updated with current issues. You may also want to look at (**www.greenbiz.com/**) which looks at the business end of the debate.

Innovation (**www.innovation.gov.uk/rd_scoreboard**) UK government site giving details on R&D.

Legal information can be found at (**www.statutelaw.gov.uk/**), the UK statute law database which enables you to view UK laws and trace how they have changed over time. You can also consult (**www.law.cornell.edu/world/**) and (**www.jus.uio.no/lm/index.html**), two excellent sources of material on international law and trade law by country.

OECD, The, (http://www.oecd.org/) The OECD website covers the main industrialised countries. It provides a wide range of economic statistics and forecasts on these economies. It is good for most aspects of country data. Follow links to science and technology for information on effects on economic development.

Sloman, J. and Wride, A. (2009) *Economics,* 7th edn. Harlow: Prentice Hall. A good introduction to economics. Wide range of short cases but a book that covers a lot more than just the internal macro-economy.

Stiglitz, J. (2002) *Globalization and its Discontents.* London: Allen Lane. This book, written by a former chief economist at the World Bank, gives a devastating critique of the effects of many of the Bretton Woods institutions' policies in both economic and political terms.

Todaro, M.P. and Smith, S.C. (2009) *Economic Development,* 10th edn. Harlow: Addison-Wesley. A long-established book surveying global issues with an emphasis on a Developing World perspective. Some sections are rather heavy on economic theory for non-economists, but there is still much of value and interest to be found.

Vignali, C. (2001) McDonald's: 'think global, act local' – the marketing mix. *British Food Journal,* 103, (2), p. 97–111. This article focuses on the marketing mix of McDonald's and highlights how the company combines internationalisation and globalisation elements according to various fast-food markets. It illustrates the effect of McDonald's on the global environment and how they adapt to local communities.

Newspapers

Newspapers are a good source of information on many topics. Three of the more important UK papers may found on the following sites:

Financial Times   www.ft.com
Guardian   www.guardian.co.uk
Telegraph   www.telegraph.co.uk

References

Burns, T. and Stalker, G.M. (1961) *The Management of Innovation.* London: Tavistock.

Daft, R.L. (1992) *Organisational Theory and Design.* St Paul, MN: West Publishing.

Grinyer, P. and Spender, J.C. (1979) Recipes, Crises and Adaption in Mature Businesses. *International Studies of Management & Organisation,* 9, 13.

Hamel, G. and Prahalad, C.K. (1994) *Competing for the Future.* Cambridge, MA: Harvard Business Press.

Huber, G.P. (1985) Temporal Stability and Response-order Biases in Participant Descriptions of Organizational Decisions. *Academy of Management Journal,* 28, 943–50.

Johnson, J. and Scholes, K. (2002) *Exploring Corporate Strategy: Text and Cases,* 6th edn. Hemel Hempstead: Prentice Hall.

Johnson, J., Scholes, K. and Whiitington, P (2008) *Exploring Corporate Strategy,* 8th edn. Hemel Hempstead: FT Prentice Hall.

Lawrence, P.R. and Lorsch, J.W. (1967) *Organisation and Environment.* Cambridge, MA: Harvard Graduate School of Business Administration.

Miles, R.E. and Snow, C.C. (1978) *Organizational Strategy, Structure and Process.* New York: McGraw-Hill.

Morgan, G. (1989) *Creative Organisational Theory: A Resourcebook.* London: Sage.

Peace, J.A. and Robinson, R.B. (1994) *Strategic Management: Formulation, Implementation and Control,* 5th edn. Chicago, IL: Irwin.

Robbins, S.P. (1992) *Essentials of Organisational Behaviour,* 3rd edn. Hemel Hempstead: Prentice Hall International.

theaa.com **www.theaa.com/motoring_advice/general-advice/right-to-repair-campaign. html**

UN Secriatariat (1999) The World at Six Billion, available from **www.un.org/esa/population/ publications/sixbillion/sixbilcover.pdf**

Weick, K. (1979) *The Social Psychology of Organizing.* Reading, MA: Addison-Wesley.

Wilson, D.C. (1992) *A Strategy of Change.* London: Routledge.

2

The competitive environment

Jamie Weatherston

Minicase 2.1	Zara: a new model?

The Spanish Inditex group's headquarters is in La Coruna, Spain. It started its international expansion in 1988. Zara, the group's leading chain, opened its first store in 1975. The group now has 4,264 stores in 73 countries (although 83 percent of its outlets are in Europe) and employs over 89,000 people. Zara now has 1,520 stores in 72 countries and contributes 65 percent of the group's overall sales.

The business model that Inditex, and Zara, operates is very different from the traditional model that many of its competitors in the clothing industry follow. The traditional model requires long lead times and limits stores to seasonal collections.

The Inditex model comprises five key elements:

- teams;
- store;
- logistics;
- design and production;
- the main element the customer.

The customer is at the centre of Inditex's business model. All the chains have their own design and sales teams that conceive the collections in their entirety. Their work is not affected by seasons, but is continuous and starts with information processed at the stores on customers' desires and impressions. Once the customers' demand reactions have been analysed, production activity swings into place. This information is communicated directly to the manufacturing facility in real time. This means that if a line is selling well now stock can be sourced very quickly, or if a line is failing it is shelved and replaced. This is unlike the traditional fashion company business model, which starts at the designer's drawing table. Inditex has created a flexible, dynamic and innovative organisation which can take on new trends and tastes in fashion in record time. This enables Inditex to have the shortest possible time to return its latest fashion proposals to the store.

A key part of this organisation is the high-speed production phase, a large part of which is carried out in factories belonging to the group and at centres close to the corporate headquarters of each of the chains. Inditex prioritises time over production costs, thereby reducing the risk involved when manufacturing takes place far from the decision-making centres.

The distribution process is also designed with maximum flexibility and customer orientation to the fore. The Inditex logistics system is designed so that the time between receiving the order in the distribution centre until delivery in the store is on average 24 hours for European stores and a maximum of 48 hours for America or Asia.

All the stores worldwide receive goods twice a week and each shipment contains new products. All employees, regardless of their proximity to the point of sale, share the same customer orientation, from those involved directly in the production process, such as designers, sales or logistics teams, to the professionals in corporate areas such as human resources, systems or finance, among others.

The business model enables Intidex to avoid taking on the risk and capital outlay of developing and maintaining a large back inventory, and it is able to offer substantially more products than other competitors. This means that customers keep coming back, regularly.

Source: Adapted for Intidex Annual Report 2008, available from www.inditex.com/en

Questions

1 Use the price mechanism to explain why Zara has been so successful.
2 In which other industrial markets are you likely to see the same type of business model and why?

2.1 Introduction

In this chapter we explore the competitive environment and determine how its dynamic nature affects both the level of competition that an organisation faces and the future profitability of organisations. It has been suggested by Thompson and Strickland (1995) that when designing an organisation's strategy one of the major tasks facing decision makers is an assessment of the company's external environment, in particular the industry and competitive conditions in which the organisation operates. The structural characteristics of an industry play a key role in determining the nature and intensity of competition within it (Grant, 1995). Using the traditional microeconomic approach we will outline the basic economic problem and the approach of economic systems to that problem, and examine how resources are allocated in differing economies. We will identify the conditions that determine the level of complexity in a market and investigate each of the market structures to which these conditions apply. An exploration of market structures and an understanding of the differences between the structures presented by economists provide a useful starting point for this analysis.

Organisations will always attempt to reduce the dynamism and uncertainty of the market in which they trade. Many tactics – some legal, others not – can be employed to this end. A major part of this chapter will be devoted to the identification and analysis of the tactics exhibited. Examples of the way companies operate legally include: the huge sums of money that pharmaceutical companies need to invest in research and development limits entry by other organisations; while Coca-Cola and Nike partly maintain their market position by their huge advertising spend which acts as a barrier to prevent others from entering that market. Other illegal activities include entering into agreements that restrict competition – a cartel. The European Commission uncovered a cartel of zip and fastener manufacturers, and in 2007 imposed fines totalling €328.6 million on six companies and a German trade association. Japan's YKK group received the highest fine, €150.3 million, followed by Coats from the UK with €122.4 million and Germany's Prym with €40.6 million. The Commission described the zip cartel as 'very serious', both because it went on in some cases for more than 20 years and because it involved the companies' top management, including managing directors, sales directors and board members (Buck, 2007).

On a wider scale, producers of bulk vitamins have pleaded guilty to the US Department of Justice on charges of participation in various cartels in the USA and elsewhere. Canadian and Australian authorities have also imposed fines on certain vitamin producers for cartel activity.

This type of collusive activity may be against the interests of consumers. If that is the case then regulatory authorities need to become involved, as in the cases above. We will examine the role and the activities of these bodies at three geo-political levels: local, national and global. The concept of contestable markets will also provide the reader with an additional interpretation of the market. We will look at these type of activities further.

Michael Porter's (1980) structural analysis of competitive forces (the five forces model) establishes the factors that determine industry profitability and competitiveness. This model originates from the traditional approach and provides a useful basis from which decision makers in organisations can begin to build a picture of their competitive position. Competitor analysis can also be used in conjunction with the five forces model to create a more in-depth analysis of the position. Throughout the chapter we will be identifying the tools and techniques that are needed to carry out an investigation of the competitive environment. The starting point for our analysis is a look at the traditional economic view.

2.2 The traditional economic view

The basic economic problem is how to allocate scarce resources among the almost limitless wants of consumers in society. Choices have to be made about:

- what to produce;
- how to produce;
- for whom to produce.

At this stage an examination of the theory as it applies to two theoretical types of economy – the command economy and the market economy – will be useful.

2.2.1 The command economy

At one end of the spectrum sits a command economy such as North Korea (officially the Democratic People's Republic of Korea). The questions of allocation are really rather simple and are answered by the state. The state decides on the volume of production, the types of goods and services produced, the type of work each citizen will do, the ways in which they will be rewarded, the level of pollution control and many other aspects of life. Individual citizens must accept a large measure of direction in their daily life.

2.2.2 The market economy and the price mechanism

The market economy is at the other end of the spectrum. The traditional view of competition shows us that the market economy is populated by a whole range of different market structures. A different type of market for many things that consumers would like to buy:

> *A market is a set of arrangements by which buyers and sellers are in contact to exchange goods and services.*

> (Begg *et al.*, 1994)

Within this system the consumer is 'king' – consumer sovereignty. Consumers express their choices by the prices they are willing to pay for goods and services. So, if we are willing to buy, at a good price, companies will make things for us. This is the price mechanism (see also *Chapter 6*). This mechanism shows that choices made by consumers directly affect the allocation of resources in the market economy. Consumers aim to gain the maximum satisfaction, or 'utility' (an economist's term) from the goods and services that they purchase. This means that consumers will choose to buy goods or services that give them the most satisfaction.

In the market economy companies choose the methods by which they produce goods and services. They are concerned with the costs of making their products or providing their service and the revenues they receive. This may serve to explain why so many companies have chosen to manufacture in cheaper, overseas markets (see *Chapter 9*). Companies will aim for the greatest return on their investment. Successful competitors will make the best returns and have the greatest chances of survival: see *Minicase 2.1*.

The people who are able to buy the goods and services will also be decided by the market. Those individuals whose services are in greatest demand will receive the greatest rewards, in terms of wages, and so have the greatest buying power. Graduates would come into this category. The preferences of the people with money to spend are registered in the market and companies compete to provide these preferred goods and services.

The consumer is central to the system via the operation of supply and demand. Demand influences price and price influences supply (a fuller analysis of demand and supply is given in *Chapter 6*). Ultimately the use of scarce factors of production – that is, land, labour and capital – is dictated by the demands or wants of individuals. When consumers want more of a product than is being supplied, then price increases, resources are attracted to the industry and supply expands. When demand falls the opposite effect occurs. There is obviously a time lag involved in the operation of the price mechanism. The speed of the effect varies depending on the situation. In a manufacturing context it is very difficult to transfer production quickly from one good to another, in response to a change in consumer demand, because of the specific nature of machinery or the need to re-train labour. However, the situation is not quite so clear cut as it seems, as *Minicase 2.1* shows.

This view of the market economy is based on the structure–conduct–performance (s–c–p) concept. *Figure 2.1* shows us that demand and supply establish the basic conditions of the market. This, in turn, sets the market structure, the conduct of the organisation in the market and its performance, for example its turnover and profit.

You may be unfamiliar with economic theories relating business activity to market structure. As competition is based on these theories it is necessary to have an understanding of some of the concepts raised by microeconomics.

Economists distinguish between various types of market which are classified into four general types: perfectly competitive, monopoly, oligopoly and monopolistic competition. The form that a market will take depends on:

- the nature of the product that is supplied, which in turn is determined by demand and cost conditions facing the market, i.e. the price mechanism;

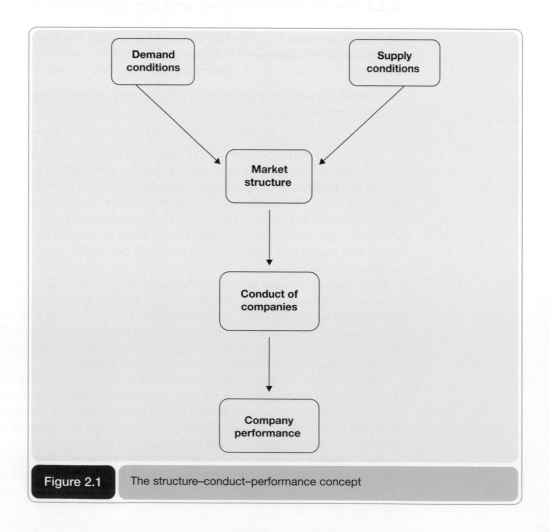

| **Figure 2.1** | The structure–conduct–performance concept |

- the number and concentration of companies in the market; and
- market entry conditions including the existence of barriers to entry and the level of information available to firms and customers.

We will now look at each of these factors.

The nature of the product or service

The nature of the product or service on offer will affect the competition that an organisation is facing, so it is important to explain how products or services can differ. It is usual to distinguish between homogeneous and heterogeneous products, that is, products of the same sort and those of different sorts.

If a number of organisations are selling an identical or homogeneous product, then the ability of producers to set the price of that product is reduced. For example, the price that a sandwich bar can charge for a standard sandwich will be constrained by the price other outlets in the locality are charging. Competitive behaviour is limited because the individual outlet has no market power. If the product is differentiated in some way – for example, organic ingredients – then an outlet has an increased ability to decide the price, and other aspects of competition, because the product is differentiated. Would you pay more for this type of product, over the standard offering? Some customers certainly will.

This ability to differentiate products is recognised as essential and is used widely by organisations. The brewing industry produces heterogeneous products, e.g. different types of beer. Each brew is different, although each still has the fundamental characteristics that distinguish it as a beer. However, even if different beers look and taste very similar, it may be possible for brewers to create a difference through marketing. Marketing is an important differentiating tool that is effective in promoting brand image. Brand recognition and customer loyalty are often important advantages held by incumbents (that is, organisations that already have an established position in the market).

Coffee is a fairly homogenous product but *Table 2.1* shows that the biggest UK coffee chains are still getting bigger. Mintel's own research shows that 65 percent of customers prefer to buy a well-known brand: this goes to stress the importance of effective advertising. The level of competition was so intense that in July 2009 Coffee Republic, the number 6 in the market, was preparing for administration.

Table 2.1	Leading operators in the UK coffee shop market, 2008

	% of outlets
Costa	27
Starbucks	25
Café Nero	13
Sub-total 3 leading chains	65
Others	35
Total	**100**

Source: adapted from Coffee Shops – UK – February 2009 Mintel, a leading market research company. Available from www.mintel.com

Number of firms and concentration

If there is just one organisation in the market then there is no competition. That organisation is a monopolist. This is a rare occurrence. In some cases organisations try to use a range of tactics to enable them to secure a monopoly position. If they are not restrained by regulation, they are capable of making substantial (monopoly) profits.

Intel, the world's largest chip manufacturer by sales, has faced concerns regarding its anti-competitive activities from around the world. In 2005 Japan's fair trade commission ruled that Intel had abused its monopoly power. This was followed in June 2008 when South Korea's fair trade commission fined Intel Won26 billion ($21 million) for abusing its dominant market position and more recently in May 2009, following a nine-year-long case, the European Commission handed down its largest ever fine for abuse of a dominant market position, ordering Intel to pay €1.1 billion (Tait and Nuttall, 2009).

As the number of organisations in a market rises, competition increases and the ability of organisations to protect their profits decline, although some organisations may still be able to protect profits.

Vorley (2003) suggests that large supermarket buyers can extract more favourable terms from suppliers – through bulk buying, playing off suppliers against each other, or threats of de-listing. Using data from the UK Competition Commission's 2000 report on supermarkets, he plotted prices paid to suppliers (relative to the industry average) against market share: see *Figure 2.2*. The largest supermarket, in this case Tesco, can consistently obtain discounts from its suppliers at 4 percent below the industry average, while the smaller players pay above the odds. With retail margins often quite small, these differences in supplier prices have a profound impact on supermarket profitability, and are a frank demonstration of the link between size and buyer power.

At the other end of the spectrum, because of the large numbers of sellers involved, food stalls at any festival or sporting event, or ice-cream sellers on a beach face intense competition as consumer choice is multiplied.

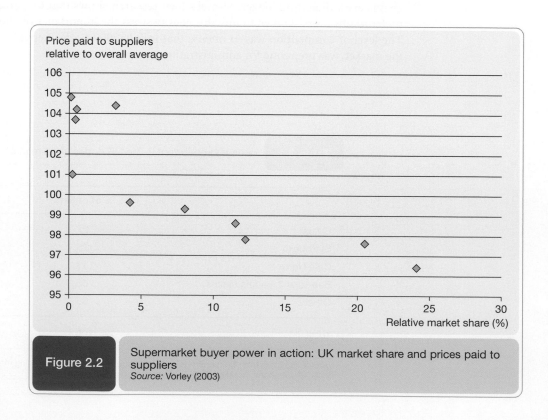

Figure 2.2 Supermarket buyer power in action: UK market share and prices paid to suppliers
Source: Vorley (2003)

Concentration ratio

It is not only the number of organisations that decides the extent of competition in a market. The level of concentration also affects the nature of competition. Concentration measures the share of the total market output that the largest companies have and reveals the extent of the domination by those large companies. Market concentration can be measured by the concentration ratio (CR):

The n-firm *concentration ratio is the market share of the n largest firms in an industry.*

The most commonly used measures are the four-and five-firm concentration ratios. Mintel (2008) estimated that the UK motorcycle and scooter market had sales of £740 million in 2007, with market sales totalling 144,583 machines. The sales of the top four manufacturers – Honda, Suzuki, Yamaha and Piaggio – totalled 75,195 machines. The concentration ratio of the four biggest manufacturers is the output of the four largest firms divided by the total market, that is:

$$75195/144583 \times 100 = 52\%$$

The four-firm concentration ratio is 52 percent, that is CR4 52.

The concentration ratio should give an indication of the amount of competition within an industry. Industries with low concentration ratios may be more competitive because each organisation is competing with a greater number of similarly sized rivals; it may therefore be difficult for one organisation to wield more market power than the others. It is also apparent that the less concentrated an industry, the lower the barriers to entry (and vice versa). If there are few barriers to entry, then new organisations can enter the market relatively easily and capture market share. This effectively increases competitive pressures in that industry (see *'The nature of the product or service' section* for further explanation of barriers to entry).

Alternatively, a high concentration ratio, as in the UK retail sector, may indicate a smaller degree of competition, where it should be possible for each organisation to protect its share. This is particularly likely to occur if the market is still growing. We will analyse this in more detail when looking at the market for goods and services later (see *'Oligopoly' section*).

Evidence suggests that market concentration increased sharply until the 1980s and it appears that this phenomenon is still continuing. One sector which has seen substantial change in market concentration is the US textbook market which is now dominated by three main suppliers. These three now account for approximately 62 percent of the industry, whereas in 1990 it was only 35 percent.

The number of organisations and their concentration is not the only important factor to consider when analysing an organisation's competitive position. *Table 2.2* shows that in the

Table 2.2	CR5 in selected industry groups		
Industry	**CR5**	**Industry**	**CR5**
Sugar	99	Legal activities	10
Tobacco	99	Wood & wood products	9
Oils and fats	88	Construction	5
Confectionary	81	Furniture	5
Soft drinks	75	Plastic products	4

Source: adapted from Mahajan (2006)

UK, there are a number of industries where a few, very large, businesses have dominated their respective industries for several years; these industries have high five-firm concentration ratios. This tells us something about competition in these industries. However, from this data alone we cannot make final conclusions about the level of competition in each industry. The same figures for the sugar and tobacco industries may hide very different stories. *Table 2.2* also shows that some industries have very low concentration ratios. It is likely that these industries will include many small- and medium-sized enterprises (SMEs) and have very different competitive conditions.

The concentration of a market is only one indicator which should be evaluated when assessing the competitiveness of a market. These examples illustrate a basic problem with the concentration ratio measure that it gives no information about inequality or the relative market share within the group of organisations selected.

Herfindahl–Hirschman Index (HHI)

The Herfindahl–Hirschman Index (HHI) is an alternative measure of market dominance and concentration which attempts to overcome the problem of the concentration ratio measure. It was developed in the USA and is used by many regulatory authorities, including the USA and EU, particularly when considering merger activity. The HHI formula is shown below.

$$\sum_{j=1}^{n} (\% \text{ market share})^2$$

The HHI measures not only the number of organisations in the market but also the inequality between them; in terms of market share, the lower the index, the more competitive the market. *Table 2.3* shows the critical levels for both concentration indicators.

The 1992 US guidelines specify that the score on the post-merger HHI has to be less than 1,000 for the merger not to have an adverse effect on competition in the market. So if any proposed merger results in an HHI of over 1,000 it will be looked at closely by the US authorities.

Table 2.3	Critical levels for concentration indicators
Concentration ratio CR	**Herfindahl–Hirschman Index (HHI)**
Market dominance is presumed if:	
CR1 > 33.3%	Unconcentrated market: HHI < 1,000
CR3 > 50%	Moderately concentrated market: 1,000 < HHI < 1,800
CR5 > 66.7%	Highly concentrated market: HHI > 1,800

Market entry conditions

Many markets present severe barriers to entry to prospective competitors, while in others barriers are almost non-existent; *Minicase 2.2* illustrates this situation. It is clearly easier to open a small restaurant than to establish a Formula One racing team! The barriers in each case are very different. Barriers to entry can be categorised into two groups: those deliberately erected to prevent entrants; and so-called innocent barriers.

Minicase 2.2	Trouble at Panasonic

Panasonic, the Japan-based electronics manufacturer, produces a wide range of goods including: televisions, DVD players, portable telephones, air purifiers, lights and air conditioning units. Its success rests on bringing in materials, adding value to them, turning them into a product and then selling them. Panasonic, however, is also a manufacturer much troubled by the global economic downturn – last year it lost Y379 billion.

Under the leadership of Fumio Ohtsubo (president since 2006) and his predecessor Kunio Nakamura, Panasonic has gone further than many of its rivals towards solving the strategic problems that face Japan's electronics industry. It has responded to the global downturn with vigorous restructuring. Its rule of thumb is that any business, factory or product line that loses money for three consecutive years must be closed. The greatest challenge is to the business Panasonic is famous for: consumer electronics. 'It will be hard to earn big profits just by making hardware, as digital has made the barriers to entry smaller for countries such as China and Korea, so on top of our products and technology we need a suitable business model,' Mr Ohtsubo says.

Panasonic plans to grow by its twin focus is on emerging markets and on business-to-business products. This is in spite of the threat of lower-cost competitors such as Samsung, a key competitor from South Korea. Mr Ohtsubo points out that 'there are many buildings going up, especially in developing countries, and they need things like lighting, security and air conditioning, all of which Panasonic can provide'. He also insists that there are still consumer products where the company can prosper, such as white goods, the launch of which, in Europe autumn 2009, was his personal initiative.

Source: adapted from Harding (2009)

Questions

1 How has digital made barriers to entry smaller?
2 Suggest reasons why Samsung may be viewed as a low-cost competitor.

Barriers erected deliberately

In some cases incumbent companies may take action to restrict entry. This could involve increasing expenditure on R&D, the introduction of new technology, advertising, legal action or rewarding customers through fidelity rebates. Barriers founded on reputation – for example, the use of predatory pricing which lowers the price paid by the consumer – can be very effective in making new entrants think twice about the attractiveness of the market or be used to force competitors out.

In 2003 the French internet service provider Wanadoo, owned by France Telecom, was fined €11.5 million by the European Commission for alleged predatory pricing. Wanadoo was accused of selling high-speed internet access at below cost price for over two years, freezing competitors out of the market. 'This practice restricted market entry and development potential for competitors, to the detriment of consumers, on a market which is key to the development of the information society,' the Commission said in a statement (BBC, 2003).

Brand proliferation also acts as a barrier to entry. Multiple brands, produced by the same manufacturer, compete against each other but also present an effective barrier to new products. It is difficult for a new entrant to establish a large market niche with only one product. The world market for soap powders is dominated by two companies: Procter and Gamble (P&G) and Unilever. They do not sell only one homogenous product each, but have a range of differentiated products, targeted at particular segments of the market. This process of differentiation has increased recently. From 1937 to 1980, P&G launched only seven detergents onto the market. This compares with the introduction of 14 new lines from 1989 to 1994. *Table 2.4* shows that, as at 2009, P&G has a total of 33 laundry and fabric care products in the USA.

Table 2.4	P&G laundry and fabric care products in the USA, 2009

Product	No. of variations
Bounce	6
Cheer	7
Downy	8
Dreft	4
Era	7
Total	33

Source: available from www.pg.com/product_card/prod_card_laundry.shtml

Advertising can help to create a stronger brand image and eventually strong brands may create entry barriers, as potential new entrants would be faced with high levels of upfront costs they could not be able to recover. Advertising by food producers helps to create a strong brand image, send signals of quality, differentiate the good from others and thus help to secure consumer loyalty. *Table 2.5* shows that seven of the world's leading food industry and retail companies were in the top 50 advertisers in the USA in 2007, potentially creating a substantial barrier to entry in this industry.

Table 2.5	Leading food industry and retail advertisers in the USA, 2007

Company	HQ	Main activity	Advertising rank 2007
Unilever	UK/NL	Multi-product (incl. food)	10
Kraft foods	USA	Multi-product (food)	18
Anheuser-Busch Cos	USA	Brewing	22
Pepsi Co.	USA	Soft drinks	26
Nestle	CH	Multi-product (food)	27
General Mills	USA	Bakery ingredients/ breakfast cereals	44
Kellogg Co.	USA	Breakfast cereals	45

Source: Bukeviciute *et al.* (2009)

Innocent barriers

Innocent barriers arise when an organisation has absolute cost advantages. In this case the incumbent organisation is able to produce at such a cost that it is uneconomic for another organisation to try and enter the market because its unit costs are, in comparison, much higher (the unit cost is the cost of producing one unit of output). In this situation organisations are said to benefit from economies of scale. We can use the idea of the experience curve to help understand how innocent barriers may be created and to gain additional insight into the problems of entering a market.

Experience curve

The experience curve was first described and popularised by the Boston Consulting Group (BCG), an American consultancy company, in 1968. BCG observed, during studies of company performance, that incumbents in any market segment benefited from the experience that it had accumulated. The study showed a direct and constant relationship between aggregate growth in volume of production and declining cost of production. That is, as production volume increased the company became more efficient at producing the product or service, and the cost per unit of that activity therefore declined. At first cost per unit fell rapidly and then more slowly as learning opportunities were exhausted. This resulted in a progressively declining gradient exhibited in the experience curve (see *Figure 2.3*). It has been claimed that costs fall by around 15 to 30 percent with each doubling of output.

Experience curve savings are particularly important if price levels for a product are relatively similar, because what makes a company more profitable than its competitors is the level of its costs. If an organisation can increase output relative to its competitors, then it will move down the experience curve more quickly, reducing costs and thus widening cost differentials.

BCG put forward three reasons why this fall in unit costs may occur. These are due to economies of scale, specialisation and learning. We will examine each of these.

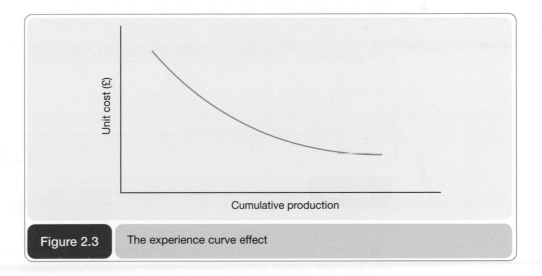

| Figure 2.3 | The experience curve effect |

Economies of scale

Figure 2.4 shows a situation where an increase in size of plant from 10,000 to 30,000 units results in a fall of average total cost (ATC) from £1,000 to £500 per unit (average total cost is total cost divided by output, i.e. TC/O). A large plant with a capacity of 50,000 units reduces ATC even further, to £300 per unit. *Figure 2.4* also shows that costs do not fall at a uniform rate but at a declining rate, and illustrates that costs will eventually rise, producing the typical U-shaped average cost curve in the long run. In this situation the larger the plant, the greater the cost advantage, up to 60,000 units. At an output of over 65,000 units plants suffer diseconomies of scale. When the curve becomes horizontal, between 50,000 and 65,000 units of output, it is known as the minimum efficient scale (MES) of production. Organisations will gain a huge cost advantage by reaching their MES. In some industries economies of scale are substantial, for example in telecommunications and car manufacture. Camillus (1998) suggests that even if SMEs find that they can control overhead costs and maintain a lean organisation, it is likely that this can be matched by well-managed, larger companies that understand and exploit economies of scale and scope. This makes it difficult for SMEs to compete in some sectors.

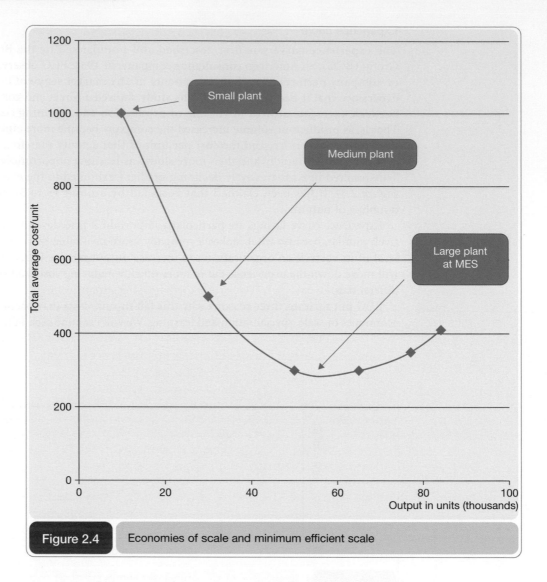

Figure 2.4 | Economies of scale and minimum efficient scale

If the MES is large in relation to the total market demand, then it will be almost impossible for a new entrant to successfully enter the market. An organisation trying to enter the market at lower levels of output, e.g. 20,000 units, would be at a severe cost disadvantage to the incumbents. The prices that the new entrant would have to charge to break even would be much higher than those charged by the incumbent organisations that are experiencing economies of scale, and so it would be very difficult for the new organisation to set a price to attract customers.

The possibility of successful entry into the market is slim: unless the organisation was able to target a particular segment of the market that is regarded as unimportant by the incumbents, this segment could be occupied by an SME. The new entrant would still face a tough struggle as it could be a formidable task to establish a brand image and customer recognition over a very narrow product range.

In the pharmaceutical sector, Simpson (2002) suggests that the MES of organisation needed to discover new medicines has fallen due to a number of factors:

- advances in technology;
- the existence of a pharmaceutical industry with an insatiable demand for such discoveries;
- a capital market, in particular venture capitalists, willing to finance high-risk biotechnology start-ups.

Together, she adds, these factors have provided some research scientists with a new opportunity to establish small biotechnology businesses, outside existing, large pharmaceutical companies and outside universities. Many 'scientist entrepreneurs' have taken this opportunity. From zero in the early 1980s, the USA biotechnology industry, which was the first to develop, had grown to nearly 1,300 companies employing 140,000 people by 1997. The European biotechnology industry, where the UK is the largest player, started up later but has also grown rapidly: to 1,000 companies with nearly 40,000 employees by 1997.

It must also be recognised that capital investment in plant and equipment can lead to overcapacity if market growth is slow. The result could be severe for some companies and industries. The container industry was facing such problems in 2008 as world trade started to slow down prior to the global recession in 2009. New ships were entering into service, but with nothing to deliver. This put a huge strain on a number of the big operators, such as Hapag Lloyd.

Global competition can wipe out previously concrete advantages. Organisations need to be able to respond to change quickly if they are to survive in the fiercely competitive global market. Lean production methods and flexible manufacturing have helped Japanese industry. The importance of innovation to support competitiveness by reducing costs and increasing quality should also be recognised. The technological revolution of the past few decades has transformed retail services. Computerised information technology has facilitated the reorganisation of distribution systems and increasingly efficient stock-handling methods have enabled retailers to benefit from economies of scale.

Specialisation

It usually becomes increasingly possible to design narrow and focused jobs as scale of production grows. Ford's car plants were at the forefront of this move in the 1920s and 1930s. Increasing specialisation through the division of labour should bring advantages. The call centre phenomenon, the modern version of the factory floor, illustrates many of the advantages. These are summarised by Beardshaw (1992):

- increase in skill and dexterity means the task can be carried out more expertly;
- time saving through reduced down time, the time in which a worker is idle, and the time saved on training;
- individual aptitudes can be utilised so individuals can concentrate on what they do best;
- machinery can be further utilised – because of specialisation of the workforce;
- breaking down the process into separate tasks allows for closer management control.

Learning

It is important to understand that organisations, as well as individuals, learn. As tasks are undertaken more frequently, individuals can learn and become more proficient at their work. Labour costs should decline. Similarly, an organisation should be able to learn and put in place efficient systems and procedures which should also translate into cost savings. Learning is likely to be the most important component in the experience curve for organisations in high-technology industries. Maintenance of learning and its conversion into organisational knowledge is a key element of competitive advantage for many high-tech companies. Japanese companies have been at the forefront of the global learning process, adapting the American philosophy of total quality management (TQM) and advancing the ideas. This has led to the development of 'quality circles', 'kaizen' or continuous improvement, 'just-in-time manufacturing', 'right first time, every time' and many more management techniques which some Western companies are still coming to terms with.

The advantages of high volume and rapid movement down the experience curve are advantages that large businesses, by definition, possess. Competitors in the credit card industry – including American Express, Capital One and Providian – have developed customised online offerings and integrated them closely with other delivery channels. They are using their experience as established experts at remote marketing and customer management, swiftly incorporating and utilising client information to hone tailored offerings to select individuals (Olson *et al.*, 2001).

Boeing's domination of the world aircraft market is in part due to learning by experience, gained from early entry into the market, which has been translated into more efficient operations. That Boeing's dominant position in the market seems to be under threat may, in turn, be due to other manufacturers, particularly European competitor Airbus Industrie, having closed the gap on Boeing in terms of learning and experience. The combined effects of experience and economies of scale mean that many big companies gain substantial advantage. Not only are costs lower but visibility in the marketplace is also greater.

The experience curve has been shown to hold for a diverse range of products from:

- photovoltaic solar cells;
- B17-bombers during World War II;
- AT&T long-distance voice tariffs over a 50-year period;
- the Ford Model-T car;
- shipbuilding;
- airframe construction;
- software project management;
- semiconductors.

The ease of entry into a market is probably the major factor influencing competition. If organisations can enter a market at relatively little cost they are likely to seize the opportunity. Various strategies, as we have seen, are available to organisations that enable them to construct barriers that prospective competitors find difficult to overcome. One of the main deterrents to organisations entering a market is the risk of losing valuable funds in the venture. We explore this further by examining the contestable market approach: see *section 'Contestable markets'*.

At this stage it is useful to undertake a closer examination of the market for goods and services. We will build on ideas introduced in this section.

2.3 The market for goods and services

Table 2.6 summarises the characteristics of four different types of market structure.

In the business world almost no organisations operate within perfectly competitive markets, so to explore the market for goods and services we can concentrate our analysis on the monopolies, oligopolies and monopolistically competitive markets.

Table 2.6	Models of market structure			
Characteristics	**Perfect competition**	**Monopolistic competition**	**Oligopoly**	**Monopoly**
No. and size of sellers	Very many, small	Many, small	Few, large	One, no close substitutes
Type of product	Various Homogeneous	Differentiated	Similar	Unique
Freedom of entry	Open unrestricted	Open unrestricted	Limited restricted	Closed restricted
CR (%)	0	Low	High	100
Example	Fruit and vegetable markets	High-street clothing retailers	Airlines, car manufacturers	Saudi Telecommunications Co.

2.3.1 Monopoly

Economists view monopolists as the sole supplier of an industry's output, producing goods and services for which no substitute is available. In this extreme case a monopoly is said to have a concentration ratio of 100, it being the only organisation supplying the market. There are various types of monopolies:

- *legal monopoly*: imposed by statute or under regulation: for example, AT&T in the USA operated as a legal monopoly in the telephone sector until 1982 because it was deemed vital to have cheap and reliable service for everyone. Norway, Finland and Sweden have state monopolies for the sale of alcohol. Railways and airlines have also been operated as legal monopolies in some countries at different times;
- *natural monopoly*: where economies of scale mean that a single firm can supply all purchasers; in this case there is only room for one firm producing at minimum efficient scale, for example water, gas and electricity suppliers;
- *local monopoly*: where, within a small, often rural area, a single organisation is the only source of a product. An example would be a petrol station or a store.

It is possible for the monopolist to make monopoly or abnormal profits in the long run, unlike in a competitive industry where profits are eroded by new organisations entering the market. Indeed, companies which hold monopoly positions, and are able to maintain large profits, are not uncommon. Monopolies can arise because of barriers that prevent entry to competitors. These barriers may be due to actions taken by incumbents or innocent barriers. De Beers' very strong position in the supply of diamonds relies on its central selling organisation controlling 80 percent of world trade in rough diamonds. In Morocco the tobacco market is dominated by the state monopoly, Regie des Tabacs du Maroc (now owned by Franco-Spanish Altadis). The company's monopoly is set to continue until 2010 when other competitors will be permitted to enter.

Monopolists, because of their protected position, need not be overly concerned by the threat of new organisations entering the industry in the short or medium term. However, because of the potentially high market power of monopolies they have to be controlled by regulatory authorities.

The view of the authorities

In the USA federal antitrust policy began with the signing of the Sherman Act in 1890. It was aimed at benefiting consumers and outlawing arrangements 'designed, or which tend, to advance the cost to the consumer'.

In the EU a scale monopoly exists where one firm has at least 25 percent of a market. A complex monopoly occurs where two or more companies totalling over 25 percent of market share or engage in actions which may result in a distortion of competition or which prevents or restricts competition. In 2008 the South African government identified complex monopolies in the fertiliser industry, banking, and the bread and milling industry. At present the threshold for a complex monopoly in South Africa is 45 percent. This is due to change when the Competition Amendment Act becomes law.

Problems associated with monopoly

Lack of competition in the market may mean that there is a danger that a monopolist can take action that may adversely affect the consumer. Results could include:

- restriction of output, as the monopolist can create a shortage, depriving consumers while increasing its profits;
- price fixing, as the monopolist can restrict supply to those who can afford to pay higher prices;

- regulation of terms of supply, as the monopolist can impose harsh terms on customers;
- removal of consumer choice – for example buying cigarettes in Morocco.

Because monopolists may try to manipulate the market against the wishes of the consumer, it is necessary for other forms of control to be applied to the market.

Control of monopoly power

The imposition of strict controls provides a challenge to the monopolist's position and its ability to make profits. Control of monopoly can take a number of forms. In an effort to limit the dangers of monopoly power many monopolies have to be regulated by governments or their agencies. Control of monopolies is not only the province of national government but is increasingly coming under a higher tier of control, i.e. the EU.

EU legislation is based on Articles 81 and 82 of the EC Treaty, implemented by member states 1 May 2004. Article 81 concerns rules on competition concerning agreements, decisions of associations of undertakings and restrictive practices. Abuse of a dominant market position is prohibited by Article 82. The kind of conduct that may constitute an abuse is:

- imposing unfair purchase or selling prices, or other unfair conditions;
- limiting production, markets or technical development to the prejudice of customers;
- applying dissimilar conditions to equivalent transactions with other trading parties thus placing them at a competitive disadvantage; and
- making contracts subject to the acceptance of other obligations which are irrelevant to the subject matter of the contract.

The European Commission may impose fines not exceeding 10 percent of worldwide turnover. The EU (Directorate General for Competition) has exclusive powers to act on certain large mergers with a European dimension. It also has powers to deal with restrictive agreements and anti-competitive practices when trade between members of the EU, or in some cases the European Economic Area (EEA), is affected.

The Competition Commission is the main body regulating markets and mergers in the UK. It was established by the Competition Act 1998. The Act introduced a new domestic competition regime in the UK by outlawing cartels and other anti-competitive agreements and the abuse of a dominant position. The Enterprise Act 2002 introduced a further new regime for the assessment of mergers and markets in the UK. The Competition Commission aims to investigate and address issues of concern in three areas (Competition Commission, 2009):

- In mergers – when larger companies will gain more than 25 percent market share and where a merger appears likely to lead to a substantial lessening of competition in one or more markets in the UK;
- In markets – when it appears that competition may be prevented, distorted or restricted in a particular market.
- In regulated sectors where aspects of the regulatory system may not be operating effectively or to address certain categories of dispute between regulators and regulated companies.

Third-party rights to challenge companies and seek damages are included and alleged anti-competitive agreements and behaviour may be halted during investigation.

The other important body with regard to competition in the UK is the Office of Fair Trading (OFT) headed by the Director General of Fair Trading (DGFT). The OFT's job is to make markets work well for consumers. It is responsible for enforcing the legislation and decides if prohibitions are infringed. The process has three steps:

- *Criteria* – whether either prohibition is infringed is decided upon based on a test on the effect it has on competition.
- *Investigation* – the DGFT has strong investigatory powers, including forcible entry/search powers.
- *Fines* – penalties of up to 10 percent of worldwide turnover can be levied.

However, agreements that provide balanced benefits, shared between consumers and business, are permitted; beneficial effects are assessed by the DGFT for exemption. Appeal is to the Competition Commission. *Minicase 2.3* illustrates a case.

In the UK the privatisations of the 1980s and 1990s also spawned the growth of a number of sectoral regulators (utility regulators and others) that have a specific role to play in promoting or facilitating competition within their sectors. These include:

- Ofgem – in the energy markets.
- Ofwat – in the water industry.
- Oftel – in the telecommunications sector.
- ORR – for railway services.
- CAA – in relation to air traffic services.

Regulation of monopolies can also have a detrimental effect. Joseph Schumpeter (1883–1950), for example, placed particular emphasis on innovation and the ability of

---

Minicase 2.3	Construction firms fined for illegal bid-rigging

On 22 September 2009 the OFT imposed fines totalling £129.5 million on 103 construction firms in England which it found had colluded with competitors on building contracts. The decision follows one of its largest Competition Act investigations.

The OFT concluded that the firms engaged in illegal anti-competitive bid-rigging activities on 199 tenders from 2000 to 2006, mostly in the form of 'cover pricing'.

Cover pricing is where one or more bidders in a tender process obtains an artificially high price from a competitor. Such cover bids are priced so as not to win the contract but are submitted as genuine bids, which give a misleading impression to clients as to the real extent of competition. This distorts the tender process and makes it less likely that other potentially cheaper firms are invited to tender.

In 11 tendering rounds, the lowest bidder faced no genuine competition because all other bids were cover bids, leading to an even greater risk that the client may have unknowingly paid a higher price.

The OFT also found six instances where successful bidders had paid an agreed sum of money to the unsuccessful bidder (known as a 'compensation payment'). These payments of between £2,500 and £60,000 were facilitated by the raising of false invoices.

The infringements affected building projects across England worth in excess of £200 million including schools, universities, hospitals, and numerous private projects from the construction of apartment blocks to housing refurbishments.

Eighty-six out of the 103 firms received reductions in their penalties because they admitted their involvement in cover pricing prior to the final decision.

Simon Williams, the OFT's Senior Director for this case, said:

> . . . bidding processes designed to ensure clients and in many cases taxpayers receive the best possible choice and price were distorted, creating a real risk of increased prices. This decision sends a strong message that anti-competitive and illegal practices, including cover pricing, must cease.

Source: adapted from Construction firms fined for illegal bid-rigging 114/09, 22 September 2009, available from www.oft.gov.uk/news/press/2009/114-09

Questions

1 In this case companies were only fined about 1 percent of their worldwide turnover. Explain the reasoning behind the OFT's decision.

2 How might this illegal activity affect those that had to pay a higher price for their work?

particular types of organisation to achieve technical advances. In this context profits of monopolistic companies can be invested into research and development. It could be argued that Microsoft has used its position to finance R&D, which has helped it to be innovative and create new products.

It is evident from this brief analysis that the authorities worldwide are intent on strengthening competition law by prohibiting anti-competitive behaviour. Monopolists do not have free rein over their market. It is up to organisations within the market to be particularly aware of how changes in the regulatory regime are going to affect them in the future and design organisational responses to meet those changes. Being proactive and implementing self-control, as opposed to being constrained by tight regulation, may be beneficial in the long run.

Schumpeter also recognised the transient nature of the monopolist's position. He suggests that a monopoly will eventually be circumvented by technology and innovation and that barriers to entry are not a serious problem to a competitive market in the long run. Former telecoms monopolies such as BT, AT&T and the Saudi Telecommunications Co. have found out that not only has deregulation resulted in more competition, but also the development of mobile phones, and the internet, has had enormous implications on them as they strive to maintain their competitive position.

2.3.2 Oligopoly

Mahajan (2006) describes an oligopoly as a market dominated by a small number of providers. It has been defined as an industry or market in which the CR4 is above 40 percent (*Table 2.3* shows in more detail when concentration becomes critical). In the USA the term 'shared monopoly' is used by the Federal Trade Commission (FTC) to describe a few firms winning and holding a large share of the business in some product line.

Oligopoly is largely an inevitable consequence of a market system, because as competitive pressures intensify the weaker companies collapse and the industry becomes more concentrated. For example, in 1919 there were 108 car manufacturers in the USA. By 1929 this number had fallen to 44. By the end of the 1950s it had dropped to eight and today there are only three major American car manufacturers (Moore, 2002). How long the big three will last is open to question.

Oligopolies can be found everywhere. There are numerous examples of industries and markets that have, or have moved towards, oligopolistic structures, for example: aerospace, brewing, cameras, cement, steel, supermarket and tobacco industries, to name a few.

The UK grocery market provides a good example of an oligopolistic market in operation. Four organisations account for the bulk of sales. In the USA four appliance manufacturers account for 98 percent of washing machines and four producers supply 85 percent of beef output. *Figure 2.5* shows the position in the non-alcoholic beverages market in the USA in 2008.

The effect of this type of market dominance is also being felt in journalism. Large corporations now have an ability to affect the way people see themselves and others. The concentration of the US media is distorting the public's perception of news and leading them to a false sense of knowledge. By any known theory of democracy, such a concentration of economic, cultural and political power in so few hands – and mostly unaccountable hands – is absurd and unacceptable (Barron, 2000).

In some cases two organisations dominate – for example in the detergent market where P&G and Unilever are dominant, the razor blade market controlled by Gillette and Wilkinson Sword, and the microprocessor market dominated by Intel and AMD. This form of oligopoly is known as a *duopoly*.

Because of the small number of competitors, each organisation has to consider how its actions will affect the decisions of its competitors. Organisations are interdependent, which means that action by one organisation will elicit a response from its competitor(s). This is particularly important in regard to pricing decisions. It is likely that any change in price will be

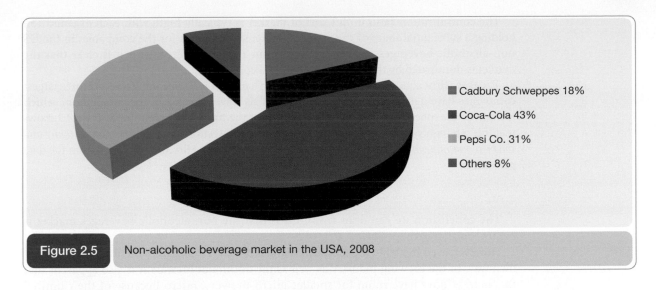

Figure 2.5	Non-alcoholic beverage market in the USA, 2008

copied by competitors, with the effect of reducing profits for all organisations. Freedom of manoeuvre for an organisation is very restricted because of this interdependence of organisations within the market. The consequence of this is usually relative price stability in the market. However, this is not always the case. Augusta (2009) suggests that car insurance in the UK was becoming cheaper as companies compete for business in a very tight economic climate. Also, in December 2008 when British Airways (BA) was offering return flights to New York from as little as £259, Virgin Atlantic responded by lowering its prices to £1 below that of BA. This situation can also be seen across the Atlantic where Kroger, the largest US traditional supermarket group by sales, has been rolling out a 'new lower prices' campaign across its more than 2,400 stores. Simultaneously, its weekly newspaper advertising inserts have been highlighting its low-cost private label goods under the heading 'value for the way you live'. The adverts are part of a price-cutting promotion from America's national and regional supermarket chains – as they compete against Wal-Mart's low-cost supercentres and small hard discounters (Birchall, 2009).

As organisations are reluctant to compete on price, competition in this type of market is often based on quality, branding, advertising and service. This non-price competition has become very important, Phil Knight, the Nike CEO, explained, that 'For years we thought ourselves as a production-oriented company, meaning that we put all our emphasis on designing and manufacturing the product. But now we understand that the most important thing we do is market the product. We've come around to saying that Nike is a marketing-oriented company and the product is our most important marketing tool' (Willigan, 1992). *Minicase 2.6* shows how these competitive tactics have been employed by McDonald's in France.

Advertising has always been and will continue to be an important part of a competitive strategy. Between 1981 and 1998 Walt Disney increased its advertising spend from approximately $100 million to around $1.25 billion. In the same period Coca-Cola's spend increased from $200 million to $700 million and McDonald's rose from $220 million to $1 billion. Between 1987 and 1998 Nike's spend went from $25 million to $500 million (Klein, 2000). This growth continued into the new millennium. However, many analysts forecast a decline in the growth of advertising as consumer confidence was hit by the 2008 credit crunch.

Economists usually distinguish further between those oligopolies that sell homogeneous products, for example oil companies, and those producing differentiated products. In reality all oligopolists try to differentiate their products, either in substance or by marketing, advertising and image creation. In markets where products are differentiated by advertising, for example the cigarette market, it is possible to erect substantial barriers that new entrants cannot overcome.

The concentration ratio in this sort of market is typically high, with each organisation holding a substantial share of the market. Market share figures for the companies in the US non-alcoholic beverages market can be seen in *Figure 2.5*. From this it is clear that the market is dominated by three large international companies.

The three firm concentration ratio (CR3) in this market is 92, meaning that the three largest companies have a market share of 92 percent. This leaves the rest of the competitors, which include all the other brands, with only 8 percent of the market between them. *Table 2.3* shows that this is a highly concentrated market. By referring to section 2.2.2 '*The market economy and the price mechanism*' it is possible to calculate the Herfindahl–Hirschmann Index from the data presented:

$$1(18)^2 + 1(43)^2 + 1(31)^2 = 3114$$

The conclusion we can draw from this is that the non-alcoholic beverages market is highly concentrated: see *Table 2.3*.

However, even in highly concentrated markets the large companies do not have it all their own way. In the brewing industry as well as the dominant brewers it is also apparent that this market does have room for smaller micro-brewers, micro because of their limited capacity and small number of employees. One such organisation is the Mordue brewery in Newcastle-upon-Tyne, renowned for its real ale that is distributed widely in the north-east of England. Other countries, including the USA, have also seen an increase in the number of these micro-breweries.

It is in the interest of firms to erect barriers to entry to make it difficult for new organisations to enter the market. Barriers can be created in many ways (see '*Structural analysis of competitive forces*' section 2.5 below). In some markets it may be possible for organisations to enter and exit at no cost, increasing the effect of competition greatly.

One way organisations can manufacture barriers to entry is by entering into agreements, known as collusion.

Collusion

Organisations in an oligopolistic market may have much to gain from some form of collaboration or collusion. This can be implicit or explicit. The aim is to jointly:

- reduce uncertainty;
- prevent entry into the market; and
- maximise profits.

Collusion has a distorting effect on the market. It allows companies to raise prices and control output, both of which adversely affect the consumer. Because of the likely impact on consumers, both explicit collusion (the operation of cartels) and implicit collusion are illegal. One of the roles of the Competition Commission in the UK and Directorate-General for Competition (COMP) of the EU is to ensure that markets do not operate against the public interest.

Between 2006 and July 2009 the European Commission fined 126 companies from 23 different industrial sectors huge sums for collusive activity. Article 81 of the Treaty establishing the European Community prohibits agreements and concerted practices between firms that distort competition within the single market. Fines of up to 10 percent of companies' worldwide turnover may be imposed on the guilty parties (see section 2.3.1 '*Monopoly*' above.

It is useful at this point to distinguish between explicit and implicit collusion.

Explicit collusion

Under this form of collusion, usually referred to as a cartel, prices are fixed and output or sales are allocated to each member of the cartel. In this situation the cartel is able to act as a monopolist. Allocation decisions are usually the result of negotiation and agreement between the member organisations. Often decisions are made in relation to the sales each organisation has had historically, or on a geographical basis.

Cartels of industries are evident across a wide range. In 2008 the European Commission imposed fines over €1.3 billion on Asahi, Pilkington, Saint-Gobain and Soliver for illegal market sharing, and exchange of commercially sensitive information regarding deliveries of car glass in the European Economic Area (EEA).

These are the highest cartel fines the Commission has ever imposed, both for an individual company (€896 million on Saint-Gobain) and for a cartel as a whole. The four companies controlled about 90 percent of the glass used in new cars and original branded replacement glass for cars at that time, a market worth about €2 billion (European Commission, 2009).

In September 2009 the Office of Fair Trading (OFT) fined 103 of the biggest building companies in the UK £129.5 million for colluding with competitors on building contracts: see *Minicase 2.3*.

Implicit collusion

The distinguishing feature of implicit collusion is the lack of any explicit agreement. According to Game Theory (and the Nash Equilibrium) if there is a payoff for colluding then companies will choose to do this, tacitly. In the case of implicit or tacit collusion a price leader may materialise within an industry and other organisations tacitly follow. Activities include:

- *dominant firm price leadership* – where companies choose the same price as that set by a dominant firm in the industry (the leader);
- *barometric price leadership* – where the price leader is the one whose prices are believed to reflect market conditions in the most satisfactory way. This may be a smaller firm;
- *average cost pricing* – where a firm sets its price by adding a certain percentage on top of the average costs.

The original case for blocking the merger between Sony and Bertelsmann Music Group, creating the world's second largest music company, largely rested on the concept of collective dominance in the industry and tacit collusion in CD pricing. It did not stop the process which lead, in 2008, to the formation of Sony Music Entertainment. Because agreements are often tacit rather than explicit it is difficult to find evidence of such arrangements.

Alternatively, agreements may have some form of official sanction. The price of transatlantic air fares from European destinations has been fixed through the International Association of Travel Agents (IATA). It has been suggested that the existence of this type of system will encourage anti-competitive behaviour.

The breakdown of collusion

Cartels can be vulnerable to competitive pressures. A major problem associated with collusion is the temptation for organisations to 'cheat' and so ignore any agreement. By doing so it is possible for a cartel member to increase profits in the short run, at the expense of other parties to the agreement. As a result it may be difficult to sustain any agreement for a prolonged period, particularly if there is a large number of organisations.

The Organisation of Petroleum Exporting Counties (OPEC), a cartel representing the major oil exporters, was founded in 1960. Its founding objective was to:

> . . . co-ordinate and unify petroleum policies among Member Countries, in order to secure fair and stable prices for petroleum producers; an efficient, economic and regular supply of petroleum to consuming nations; and a fair return on capital to those investing in the industry.

Financial Times (2006) suggests that cohesion within the cartel is the critical ingredient for success. It is a classic case of game theory's prisoners' dilemma: one country cheating and producing more fills the coffers of its treasury because the cheater reaps the benefits of high oil prices (boosted by the production cuts of members that keep to the agreement) and its own high sales volumes. But the cheater's dissension risks causing the scheme to break down as others pile in with greater production and oil prices that collapse as more supply hits the market. This type of cheating has occurred a number of times in the organisation's 50-year history. *Minicase 2.4* shows how an oligopoly might be brought back into a competitive scenario.

Oligopoly is the dominant form of market structure found in all market economies. We have seen that in some oligopolistic industries competition is intense and organisations have to fight hard to maintain their market share. In others the nature of the industry, or the existence of agreements, means that organisations can come close to joint-profit maximisation. However, high profits will attract competitors, so organisations must devote a lot of time to maintaining and defending the barriers to entry. Competition authorities are also active in limiting the amount of collusive activity.

Minicase 2.4	Asustek break laptop oligopoly

In October 2007 Asustek, a Taiwanese multinational, came up with its Asus Eee – a small, light, cheap laptop computer known as a netbook. It was a not-very-powerful device with a tiny screen and a small keyboard. Other manufacturers initially ignored it. 'They thought that the performance was too low and people would not be interested,' says Willy Shih, a professor at Harvard Business School.

However, this new product enabled Asustek to break the grip of a particularly powerful oligopoly. By making a product that many consumers wanted they converted consumers and caused havoc in the personal computer industry. The Asus Eee and rival netbooks made by Acer have reduced revenues and margins at both software and hardware companies. Other computer makers quickly knew the game was up. Acer, Dell and HP surrendered. Everyone except Apple has ended up following Asustek. Apple is now said to be developing a touch-screen tablet without a keyboard as its answer to netbooks.

This, however, leaves a question. If the netbook, which usually runs on Intel's Atom chip, is so appealing, why did it take so long to arrive?

One answer is that USA companies made a mistake. A more cynical one is that it took a long time because some companies preferred netbooks not to succeed. The three-way alliance among Microsoft, Intel and Dell instead preferred laptops to become more powerful and run on fancier versions of Windows.

Microsoft and Intel are still trying to corral netbooks by defining them as a third type of device in addition to desktops and laptops, although it is clear that people are using them almost identically to traditional laptops. Microsoft sets strict memory and screen limits for licences. Microsoft at least recognises that it cannot ignore netbooks, and will tailor Windows 7, its new operating system, for them.

Source: adapted from Gapper (2009)

Questions

1 Why did the computer manufacturers not want to launch a netbook?
2 Is the approach taken by the big manufacturers legal?

2.3.3 Monopolistic competition

Monopolistically competitive markets involve a large number of organisations, which produce similar yet not perfectly substitutable products (differentiated products). Each producer can set its price and quantity without affecting the marketplace as whole; barriers to entry are low. Vietnam, for example, has 2,000 craft villages, 1.4 million craft-producing households and about 1,000 enterprises in production, import and export of a wide range of craft products.

We can see from this example that there is, therefore, freedom of entry into a market, so firms cannot make excess profits in the long run. Each organisation's market share is likely to be small and its actions are of little concern to others. If one organisation changes price, for example, this is unlikely to affect prices throughout the market. The large number of organisations, combined with their correspondingly small size, means that the concentration ratio will be low (see *Table 2.3*) which increases competitive pressures.

The retail trade is often cited as an example of this type of market. Restaurants, hairdressers and builders are all examples of monopolistic competition. A typical feature is that there is only one company in a particular location. There may be many Chinese takeaways in town but only one in a particular street, so consumers may be prepared to pay higher prices rather than go elsewhere. They are not all the same, but differentiated by each seller. A price rise in one store will not always result in price rises everywhere else (although it is suggested that neighbouring shops may respond).

One of the features of monopolistic competition is the high level of advertising as organisations attempt to maintain or improve their position in the marketplace. Product differentiation may exist because of imaginary differences in the mind of the consumer brought about through advertising, branding and the service provided by an organisation. Product innovation is also constantly sought after, as new products may provide a temporary competitive edge and an opportunity to raise prices and increase profit.

The health food industry is dominated by numerous small companies and a few large multinationals with health food interests. Because organisations are small, expensive forms of advertising, for example the use of television commercials, are avoided. Organisations concentrate on below-the-line advertising such as competitions and point-of-sale material. Advertising expenditure has increased substantially in the main sector of this market since 1988.

The real or perceived differences created by advertising and innovation mean that it is possible for an organisation to charge a higher price. If organisations in the market are seen to be obtaining high profits, new organisations can enter the market because of the low barriers to entry. The monopolistically competitive market is therefore liable to see high levels of competition between incumbents and entrants to the market. There will be enormous pressure on organisations to reduce their costs and improve their efficiency as a way of preserving margins and thus profitability.

Many economists maintain that this type of market is almost never found in practice. It is suggested that all organisations in the market have to take account of their competitors at some level.

2.3.4 Summary

We have now applied the traditional economic model of industry structure as a basis of analysing competition. To what extent is this model of use? Caves and Porter (1980) suggest that if structural change within an industry, particularly changes of concentration and entry, appears to be slow then the traditional model will be applicable.

However, in other circumstances the model may present only a partial view of the competitive conditions facing an organisation. In some industries the rate of change may be rapid, with, for example, technology transforming the industry structure by changing both process and products. One only needs to look at the demise of products such as electric typewriters and the changes forced on IBM to cope with the market for personal computers to see the influence of technology (see also *Chapter 4*). It is under these circumstances that the value of using industry structure as a basis for analysing competition may be diminished.

Other economists have also put the structure–conduct–performance approach under the microscope. The Chicago School has taken an alternative view that concentrated markets are not necessarily evil in themselves. Markets that exhibit extremes of concentration may gain benefits such as economies of scale or greater efficiency. The Chicagoans believe that barriers to entry are more apparent than real and that competition is powerful enough to prevent organisations from controlling markets. The conclusion is that conduct and performance of the market are not related to its underlying structure. Competition in a highly concentrated market could be fierce. This obviously has a significant impact on businesses operating in these types of markets.

2.4 Contestable markets

A valuable addition to the theory of industry structure is provided by Baumol (1982). He suggests that it is possible for organisations to enter a market without incurring costs because these costs can be recovered when the organisation exits. There are no sunk or unrecoverable costs. This situation is known as a perfectly contestable market. Sunk costs can include the cost of building, advertising and R&D. If the sunk costs of entry are lower, then the market is more contestable or more competitive. Contestable markets are vulnerable to hit-and-run entry. Supermarkets have been able to establish a major market share in the cola market in recent years. Manufacturing is carried out by a partner and shelf space is readily available. Own brands establish a market partly due to demand for the product being elastic – that is, it is price sensitive, and consumers will increase their demand for the product if the price is sufficiently low. Entry into the market was against a background of increasing consumption of soft drinks. This provides evidence of low barriers to entry and exit for supermarkets and low sunk costs.

It is doubtful whether a perfectly contestable market exists. In most cases some sunk costs are incurred in market entry. It is the scale of the sunk costs which may, or may not, dissuade a potential entrant from attempting a hit-and-run entry.

The risk that Virgin Atlantic took to start an air service from London to Japan was lessened because the sunk costs were relatively low. If the route proved to be unprofitable, aircraft could be transferred to other routes, rental of terminal space could stop and ground equipment could be switched to another airport. Football teams, particularly those in the higher European leagues, face sunk costs when they hire a player or manager on a lucrative long-term contract. If the player or manager under-performs, his contract will still be paid up even if he leaves the club. This clearly is a big risk for the teams and their plcs.

2.5 Structural analysis of competitive forces

Despite criticism, the structure–conduct–performance model may still be a useful foundation for the analysis of a rapidly changing business environment. Porter (1980) argues that 'understanding industry structure must be the starting point for strategic analysis'. Strategic analysis focuses on identifying the basic, underlying characteristics of an industry, which are rooted in its economics and technology. It is these characteristics that shape the competitive environment that the industry faces.

To enhance understanding it is advisable to examine Michael Porter's 1980 model more closely. The model illustrated in *Figure 2.6* brings together many elements discussed above as it is based on the s–c–p paradigm.

Porter suggests that the collective strengths of five forces determine the state of competition and therefore the ultimate profit potential within an industry. The five competitive forces identified by Porter are:

- rivalry among competitors;
- threat of entry;
- threat of substitution;
- bargaining power of buyers;
- bargaining power of suppliers.

Minicase 2.5 shows how this analysis might apply to the games console market.
We will now look at Porter's five forces in more detail.

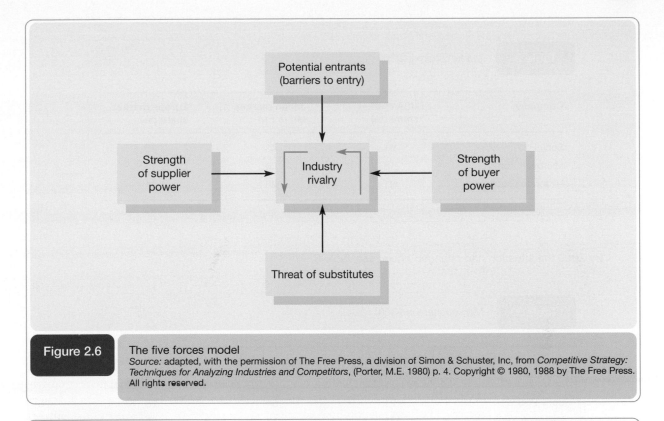

Figure 2.6	The five forces model

Source: adapted, with the permission of The Free Press, a division of Simon & Schuster, Inc, from *Competitive Strategy: Techniques for Analyzing Industries and Competitors*, (Porter, M.E. 1980) p. 4. Copyright © 1980, 1988 by The Free Press. All rights reserved.

Minicase 2.5	A brief structural analysis of the games console industry

Video games achieved almost 50 percent growth (2007 estimated) between 2002 and 2007, making it the high achiever among all leisure sectors (Mintel, 2008).

Competitive rivalry

During the 1990s the market was dominated by three manufacturers: Sony, Nintendo and Sega. The 1995–2000 market share is shown in *Table 1*.

Table 1	Market share 1995–2000

Company	Market share (%)
Sony	47
Nintendo	28
Sega	23
Other	2
Total	**100**

By 2002 *Table 2* shows there were still three key players in the market. Sony was still the leader in the three major markets, Europe, Japan and America, the so-called triad. Nintendo occupied second place, with Microsoft in third. Sega lost its position.

Table 2	Market share in 2002		
Company	**USA market share (%)**	**Japan market share (%)**	**Europe market share (%)**
Sony PS2	61	63	75
Microsoft Xbox	18	4	14
Nintendo GameCube	21	28	11

By 2009 the situation had changed again: see *Table 3*.

Table 3	Market share in 2009		
Company share (%)	**USA market share (%)**	**Japan market share (%)**	**Europe market share (%)**
Sony PS3	21	54	28
Microsoft Xbox	25	18	28
Nintendo Wii	55	27	44

By 2008 Sony had lost the first-mover advantages that it established with its PS2. Capacity to innovate remains a clear key skill in this market. Even Sony's strong brand name has not enabled it to remain as market leader, apart from in Japan. Although Sony will come back strongly.

Nintendo has always been a strong player in the console industry. It has benefited from the big sales of its Wii console which is innovative and designed to attract new game players into the market.

The Xbox 360 has been able to gain ground on the PS3 partly because of the technical problems that delayed the launch of the PS3 and perhaps the fact it was a cheaper, yet comparable package.

Power of suppliers

In the games console market suppliers have little power. They are hardware and software providers who, to a certain degree, rely heavily on the console manufacturers.

Power of buyers

The final consumer also has little power, although prices of the main consoles have come down since launch. Manufacturers can still 'call the shots' when dealing with a distributor.

Threat of substitutes

PC games used to be a strong substitute but sales have fallen year on year; consoles are primarily designed for game play and are the kit choice for most game players. However, social games such as Farmville, Mafia Wars and Pet Society on Facebook, Bebo, MySpace and on iPhone provide a viable alternative to consoles. They are free, widely available and easy to play. Evidence suggests that gamers are leaving traditional consoles. This has spurred revenue growth at Facebook which is now the world's largest games portal. The ten most popular games on Facebook draw over 100 million users a month. Indeed Xbox and Nintendo have already spotted this development and are already moving in. It has been estimated that the social games market could triple to $2 billion by 2012. It is also possible that the demand for consoles could slow down as players move on to other activities, choosing to spend their money completely outside the market.

Threat of entry

The number and impact of potential entrants are not totally clear, but as games consoles are likely to evolve into devices that include gaming, home entertainment and PC capabilities, the dominant players in each of these industries may want to move into the market. Microsoft's success in this respect may point a way forward.

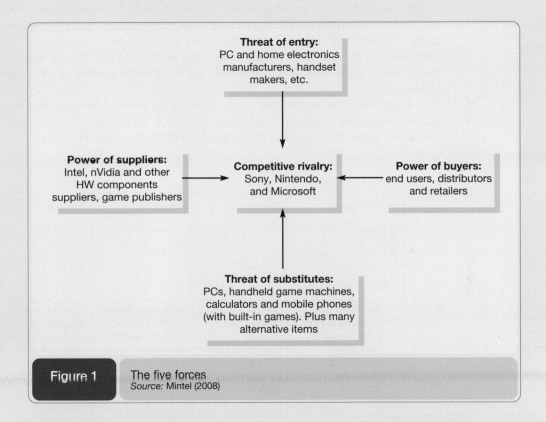

Threat of entry:
PC and home electronics manufacturers, handset makers, etc.

Power of suppliers:
Intel, nVidia and other HW components suppliers, game publishers

Competitive rivalry:
Sony, Nintendo, and Microsoft

Power of buyers:
end users, distributors and retailers

Threat of substitutes:
PCs, handheld game machines, calculators and mobile phones (with built-in games). Plus many alternative items

Figure 1   The five forces
Source: Mintel (2008)

Question

1 Use Porter's five forces model, as we have here, to analyse the competitive environment of an industry of your choice.
2 What other key concepts raised in the chapter could also be useful in this analysis?

2.5.1 Rivalry among competitors

This is Porter's central force. Increased rivalry will lead to increased competition and reduced profits. Intensity of rivalry between competitors will depend on several factors.

The number and relative size of competitors within an industry

If there are many organisations of a similar size, as in oligopoly, then rivalry will be intense. Organisations in the industry are likely to try to gain market share through all possible means, see section 2.3 '*The market for goods and services*'.

The rate of growth in an industry

It is important to recognise that the growth rate of an industry is dependent upon a number of factors and that sectoral differences abound. Market growth in industries where product innovation and displacement are dominant, for example mobile phones, is likely to be very different from that of the more traditional sectors, such as shipbuilding. Geographical differences also need to be taken into account. Cigarette smoking is increasing in some areas of the world and declining in others.

When an industry is growing slowly, competition will be more intense as virtually the only way an organisation can expand is by taking market share from competitors. Competitors of course will fight to retain their own market share. A number of analysts have predicted that the growth of mobile phone sales in the USA and Europe will fall due to the global recession in 2009, although this would be offset by growth in other areas, such as China and India.

It is important for organisations to be aware of the product life cycle that their products face, as competitive conditions can be very different at each phase of the life cycle. *Figure 2.7* shows four stages in the product life cycle, each with its own characteristics.

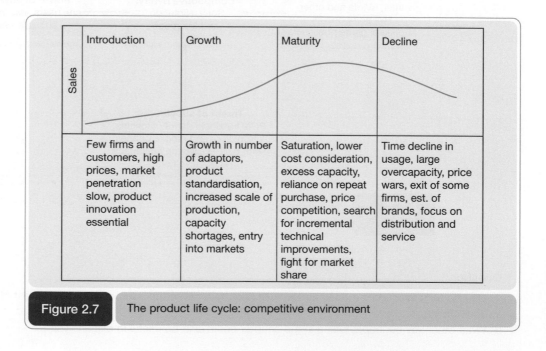

	Introduction	Growth	Maturity	Decline
Sales	Few firms and customers, high prices, market penetration slow, product innovation essential	Growth in number of adaptors, product standardisation, increased scale of production, capacity shortages, entry into markets	Saturation, lower cost consideration, excess capacity, reliance on repeat purchase, price competition, search for incremental technical improvements, fight for market share	Time decline in usage, large overcapacity, price wars, exit of some firms, est. of brands, focus on distribution and service

Figure 2.7   The product life cycle: competitive environment

Cost conditions

The relationship between fixed and variable cost is important. If organisations operate in a business with relatively high fixed costs it will be in the interests of that organisation to cut its prices in order to sell its output. Train operators and discount airlines are willing to reduce prices at certain times of the day and different days of the week to attract customers. Discounts from train operators are on offer to off-peak users and a range of discount cards is often made available for students, families and pensioners. The discount airlines pricing strategy also reflects this problem. They sell tickets at very low prices to enable them to cover at least a portion of their costs. The variable cost of selling a ticket is very low; the fixed cost of operating a railway or an airline is high. Staff have to be employed and planes have to be in service. Organisations in this situation will seek additional business, that is increased ticket sales, as long as the revenue from sales covers the variable costs of those sales. This is why AirAsia and easyJet sell tickets for as little as 10MYR or £1.

Governments also intervene and reduce costs for companies. The battle to attract valuable inward investment from multinational companies is often augmented by substantial offers from governments that cover significant proportions of the start-up cost.

Lack of product differentiation

If there is little to distinguish one product from another, competition will be intense (seethe nature of the product or service in section 2.2.2 *'The market economy and the price mechanism'*).

High exit barriers

Exit barriers can be measured by the costs organisations incur when they leave an industry. Exit barriers are said to be high if the cost of leaving an industry is high. These costs can include high redundancy payments and low scrap value of plant. Exit barriers in the form of emotional barriers and government policy may also be in place. The fact that more football league clubs in England and the rest of the world have not been closed down owes much to the emotional as well as financial support that they receive from their often long-suffering supporters. That more car manufacturers did not close down in the early 1990s may reflect the high cost of leaving the industry. A short period of losses may have been easier to sustain than complete closure. In the case of Renault, financial support was forthcoming from the French government. This situation has been replicated in the crash of 2008.

2.5.2 Threat of entry

New organisations enter a market, attracted by the high level of returns that incumbents receive. New entrants bring new capacity, new resources and a desire to build market share. The result will be more competition and so a fall in profit for all organisations. Threat of entry depends on the strength of barriers to entry: the higher the barriers, the lower the threat of entry. Levy (2005) suggests that car manufacturing has high barriers to entry which include:

- high upfront capital investment in manufacturing equipment;
- compliance with safety and emission rules and regulation;
- access to parts suppliers;
- the need to develop a network of car dealerships;
- the need for big marketing campaigns to establish a new car brand with consumers.

The main sources of barriers to entry are:

- product differentiation;
- economies of scale and absolute cost advantages;
- legal barriers;
- capital requirements;
- access to distribution channels;
- threat of retaliation.

Many of these have been discussed above. We will briefly explore those not already discussed.

Economies of scale and absolute cost advantages

Economies of scale were discussed in detail in section 2.2.2 '*The market economy and the price mechanism*'. No matter what economies of scale exist, other cost advantages may also exist, so-called first-mover advantages, which cannot be replicated by potential entrants. These could include:

- access to raw materials – it is extremely difficult to establish a nuclear industry without access to raw material, as many countries have discovered (for example, Iran, Iraq and North Korea);
- favourable locations – it would be an almost impossible challenge for an overseas bank to set up a wide branch network to compete with the established networks of the home-based organisations, unless, like HSBC, it takes over a UK bank;
- product know-how and experience curve advantages.

Government subsidies can be used to reduce absolute cost advantages. The launch aid received by Airbus Industrie helped it to compete effectively against America's Boeing. The support for sunrise industries, those emerging new industries of the future, may also be a legitimate use of subsidies, as has happened in New Zealand.

Legal barriers

Legal barriers, such as a government licence, charter or a patent, may also be used. A licence is required in many fields of business including the taxicab, banking and broadcasting sectors. E-business is said to offer businesses the opportunity to reduce costs and build new and better relationships with customers. But some businesses, in particular SMEs, are still reluctant to fully engage in electronic transactions. Among the most cited barriers are uncertainties related to e-commerce legislation, in particular for cross-border electronic transactions and the lack of trust and confidence in buying and selling over the internet. Access to simple and practical information on the main legal and regulatory aspects of e-commerce is therefore crucial in order to remove still existing barriers and to help SMEs to 'go digital' (European Commission, 2003).

GlaxoSmithKline and other drug companies are able to protect their new products from competition by use of patents. Environmental and safety standards also place barriers in the way of new organisations entering some industries.

Inefficient public monopolies have in the past been accused of being protected from competition by government funding, especially the power, transport and telecommunications sectors in the UK and telecommunications and postal services in France and Germany respectively. The Japanese government has long been criticised in Europe and North America for imposing barriers that protect Japanese manufacturers and farmers, and drastically limit the import of a wide range of goods, such as rice, cars and Scotch whisky, into the Japanese market. It is clear that, following the recession in 2008, governments around the world, in an attempt to protect vulnerable sectors, continued to push up trade barriers in spite of high-profile pledges at the G20 summit and other forums to resist protectionism (Chaffin, 2009).

Capital requirements

The need for capital is linked closely to our earlier discussion of sunk costs (see section 2.4 '*Contestable markets*'). It may be just too expensive for an organisation to enter a market.

Access to distribution channels

A barrier can be created by the inability of an entrant to gain access to a distribution channel. Manufacturers of designer/branded goods have tried to prevent supermarkets from obtaining goods at a cheaper price on the 'grey market' outside Europe and selling them at lower prices to customers. Tesco, for example, imported Levi jeans direct from the USA. A decision on 16 July 1998 by the European Court of Justice found that this was illegal. It was a blow for retailers such as Tesco. However, in May 1999 the United Kingdom High Court found in Tesco's favour. In a further twist in November 2001, the European Court of Justice upheld Levi's case that the Trademark Directive allows brand owners to restrict access to branded goods and thus enabled them to maintain the high prices of their products as they were sold via dedicated retailers.

Threat of retaliation

The effectiveness of barriers may be in part reliant on the expectations that entrants have of the possible retaliation of incumbent organisations. Porter (1980) suggests that entrants into an industry can be deterred if:

- there is a history of retaliation against entrants;
- established organisations with substantial resources fight back;
- established organisations are heavily committed to the industry and have assets which cannot be employed in other sectors, e.g. car manufacturers can only make cars;
- the industry is undergoing slow or zero growth as new organisations cannot be absorbed so easily (see section 2.5.1 'Rivalry among competitors').

2.5.3 Threat of substitution

Substitutes are those products or services offered by one organisation that can be used in place of the product or service that another organisation supplies. For example, car manufacturers face competition from motorcycle manufacturers and transport providers – bus companies, railways, and airlines – because rather than buying a car it is possible for potential customers to switch to a substitute product that can do the same job. The extent of the threat will depend on the tendency (called propensity by economists) of the buyer to substitute: this could depend on the switching costs and the relative price and performance of substitutes.

The propensity of the buyer to substitute

If the propensity of a buyer to substitute is high then substitutes will present a great threat. Some products have a low propensity of substitution because of the nature of the product, for example cars. People are often reluctant to use alternatives such as public transport. It has proved and will continue to prove difficult to encourage people to switch from cars to other forms of transport. The American Express (Amex) charge card, on the other hand, faces competition from cash, traveller's cheques, chequebooks and credit cards. The threat of substitutes imposes a price ceiling: if Amex charges its customers too much, they have ready alternatives to switch to.

The wider economic environment is also an issue that requires consideration. Car sales across the world have been affected by the recession in 2008; as job losses spiralled consumer demand was subdued and people chose not to spend on these big ticket items. Spending shifted to other goods, or households were choosing to save. Sales in the USA in September 2008 were extremely weak. Nissan was down by 37 percent, sales declined by 34 percent at Ford, 33 percent at Chrysler, 32 percent at Toyota, 24 percent at Honda and 16 percent at General Motors. Overall, industry wide, car sales declined 26 percent (BBC, 2008). This trend continued into 2009.

The situation is further complicated because substitutes may be difficult to identify and hence keep out. What is the substitute for a beer? It is not another brand of beer from another brewer. That is an example of rivalry among competitors: Porter's central force. Substitutes come from outside the industry. Organisations compete for discretionary expenditure, the spare cash that people have. For example, brewers such as Carlsberg are not just competing against Coors, Fosters, Stella Artois and Corona but Coke, Nike, Blossom Hill and Microsoft among others.

Switching costs

The one-off cost that faces a buyer when switching from one supplier to another is important. Where the switching cost is high, then transfer of allegiances is less likely and vice versa. A consumer can quite easily switch to buying a health food product rather than potato crisps, thus reducing the sales of the snack manufacturer. However, the cost of switching from using a car to another form of transport may be substantial and also inconvenience the driver, and so discourage change.

The relative price and performance of substitutes

The profits of postal services in probably all major economies have suffered over the last few years and the postal service could be in terminal decline. Email is cheap and easy, as is using social networking sites such as Facebook. It is becoming less likely that we will use a conventional mail service, as its relative price and performance cannot compete in the market.

2.5.4 Bargaining power of buyers and suppliers

Suppliers are those individuals or organisations from whom an organisation purchases items that are needed to carry out business activities. These are the inputs to the organisation and include raw materials and components. Supplier power can impact on prices, quality and service level demands, all of which will reduce margins. Because of their size and importance, large car manufacturers can probably demand high service levels from their component suppliers and also squeeze prices that they pay to suppliers. Monopoly suppliers are in a very strong position: think about the bargaining power that Microsoft has as its operating system is used in almost all PCs.

Buyers are those individuals or organisations that purchase an organisation's outputs. Bargaining power of buyers can reduce prices, increase quality and increase service level demands, putting pressure on profits. The present downturn in the car market has shown that car manufacturers have a great impact on parts suppliers who may rely solely on one big manufacturer to buy all or most of their output.

The examination of supplier power is comparable with that of buyer power (the factors that contribute to greater buyer power will decrease supplier power) and so we will concentrate on buyer power in this section.

Buyers depend a great deal on the quality and timeliness of information they receive. Full information means that a buyer is in a better position to negotiate a price. Buyers are powerful and more sensitive to price if:

- their switching costs are low – it is easy to go for a drink to the pub next door, no costs are involved (if switching costs are high, supplier power is increased);
- the product is important to the buyer. This could be the case if:
  - the product represents a high proportion of total costs – buyers of major pieces of capital equipment are likely to have a strong hand when it comes to contract negotiations;

- the product is purchased in high volume (see below);
- the profitability of the buyer industry is low which may mean that the buyer will want to reduce the price of goods that are bought in to protect its own margins.

Products are undifferentiated and substitutes are available

We have already outlined the problems that firms face if products are homogeneous and easily substituted (see section 2.2.2 *'The market economy and the price mechanism'*). Buyers can simply play one company off against the other. Competition between suppliers of office stationery is intense. The homogeneous nature of the product means that organisations that want to buy this type of product can shop around for the best prices and, consequently, reduce the sales and profit of the companies they are buying from, so buyer power is increased.

Buyer concentration is high

If your product is bought by only one buyer (a monopsony) then concentration is at 100 percent. In this case buyers have total power, not only over price but also all other aspects of the relationship, including quality and delivery time. Marks & Spencer and some supermarkets have entered into exclusive agreements to buy the whole of the output of some organisations. If they withdraw their order then plant closure may be the result, in this case supplier power is very low.

Threat of integration

In some cases a buyer has the ability to take over the supplier, known as backward integration. If the supplier tries to force a deal, it could find itself being taken over by the buyer, so it has to be careful how it negotiates. A number of fast-food chains and supermarkets, for example, own farms.

Porter's five forces model provides organisations with a model for analysing their competitive environment. Unless a company can analyse its competitors it will never be in a position to compete effectively. The benefits to be gained from having an intelligence-gathering system are immeasurable. A capable system may ultimately ensure survival. *Minicase 2.5* illustrates the use of the model.

2.6 Competitor analysis

The proliferation of different types of washing detergents, such as enzyme-rich, enzyme-free, liquid, automatic, biological and non-biological powders, is not simply a tactic used by the two major manufacturers to put in place a barrier to entry, as described earlier. The multiplicity of types arises from the need of one company to match the innovation of the other. If the companies in the market are unaware of their competitors' direction, then a rival may be able to increase its market share.

Competitor analysis is another way of achieving an insight into the activity of competitors. This type of behaviour exists in industries as diverse as the car industry and software design.

Competitor analysis involves an investigation of competitors' goals, assumptions, strategy, and capabilities (Porter, 1980). Not only do existing competitors need to be examined but there is also a need to put potential competitors under the microscope. Add to this a dose of self-analysis and a picture of the behaviour of the market comes into focus. *Figure 2.8* shows the competitor analysis model.

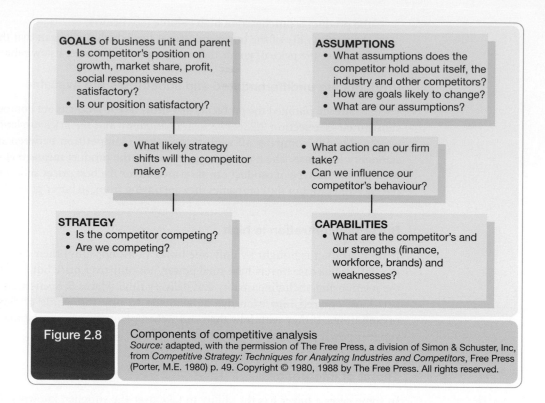

Figure 2.8	Components of competitive analysis

Porter (1980) proposes that competitor analysis can answer questions such as the following:

- What are the implications of the interaction of the probable competitors' moves?
- Are organisations' strategies converging and likely to clash?
- Do organisations have sustainable growth rates that match the industry's forecast growth rate, or will a gap be created that will invite entry?

2.7 Conclusion

We have seen, in this chapter, that the structure of the market has a direct impact on the competition that an organisation faces. It is, however, evident that market structure does not remain static. Today's monopoly could be tomorrow's competitive cockpit. Organisations face a dynamic and changing competitive environment. International competitors are becoming the barometer by which we measure the success of all organisations.

Organisations cannot rest and remain satisfied with their past achievements. It is important to develop and maintain mechanisms with which to sense environmental change. In this chapter we have introduced you to some of the tools and models that can assist organisations in understanding their own position and that of their competitors. We have also shown that there is a role for government at all scales.

Markets left to their own devices may fail and become anti-competitive, so intervention may be needed. This seems more important now in light of the credit crunch and the recession that followed. Governments can also provide support for new, fledgling industries to allow them to grow and become competitive in the international arena.

To help you understand this next stage the following chapter explores the macroeconomic environment.

Summary of main points

Competition is influenced by a wide range of factors. In this chapter we have investigated a range of these factors and introduced you to models to aid your analysis of the competitive environment. The chapter has shown that:

- The basic economic problem, of allocation of resources, is resolved in quite different ways within the command and market economies.
- Competition is influenced largely by the nature of the product, the number of firms and their concentration, and the market entry conditions.
- Some organisations are protected from competition by barriers to entry and may be capable of making above-normal profits in the long run.
- A strong competitive position is likely to be eroded by, for example, the use of technology and innovation.
- Oligopolists are interdependent and must consider the actions of rivals when making business decisions; because of the lack of freedom of manoeuvre, competition is based largely on quality, branding, advertising and service.
- Some organisations act to reduce uncertainty by entering into agreements which may be anti-competitive. Regulations need to be in place to monitor such agreements and to protect the public interest.
- Contestable markets exist where there are no sunk costs of entry. In such markets competition will be intense.
- Porter's five forces are:
  - rivalry among competitors;
  - threat of entry;
  - threat of substitution;
  - bargaining power of buyers;
  - bargaining power of suppliers.
- The collective strengths of the five forces determine the state of competition and therefore the ultimate profit potential within an industry.
- Competitor analysis involves the investigation of organisations' goals, assumptions, strategies and capabilities.

Minicase 2.6   Le Big Mac at home in the land of slow food

France is probably not a country you would associate with a booming trade in Big Macs. Yet nationalist rhetoric has done little to stem the growth of *McDo,* as the Golden Arches are referred to in France. In 2006 it became McDonald's most profitable subsidiary in Europe, with sales hitting €2.7 billion. That is a 9.8 percent increase from the year before and is nearly twice the sales growth seen in the USA during the same period. The group has 1,085 outlets in France. Together, they accounted for 31.5 percent of total operational profit made in Europe, ahead of the UK and Germany.

For Jean-Pierre Petit, chief executive of McDonald's France, the aim was to position the group as a casual diner rather than a fast-food restaurant. The process had begun by establishing a design studio in Paris during the 1990s and spending money creating more congenial and sophisticated environments in its restaurants. In place of the bright fluorescent lights and tacky bolted-down plastic yellow and white furniture universal in the USA, visitors to McDonald's in France find low lampshades, wooden tables, upholstered seating and (imitation) leather banquettes. Some have TV screens, internet connections and iPod stations.

There is not a single Ronald McDonald in sight. In a company that made its fortunes from standardisation and cost cutting, this strategy for McDonald's France was revolutionary.

But the gamble paid off and the result is that in 2006 the typical French consumer spent €9.47 per visit, about twice that spent in the USA.

'French people want quick, affordable food but they also want to be able to sit down and eat a hot meal,' Mr Petit said. 'At the moment, between expensive sit-down bistros where you will spend €20 on lunch and a cold sandwich from the boulangerie, there's not a lot of choices in between,' he added. 'By creating a pleasant environment where customers can stay and enjoy a full meal, we are filling in that gap.'

The menu has also been fine-tuned to cater to local palates. While Big Macs and French fries remain standard fare, the group has added items such as the Croque McDo, its take on the croque monsieur, grilled emmental cheese and ham sandwich, to its offerings. French fries are served with mayonnaise, espresso comes with a piece of chocolate and French pastries such as lemon tartelettes and flan are *de rigueur* at its Starbucks-like McCafés.

A protesting group of sheep farmers led by José Bové became overnight folk heroes after dismantling a McDonald's in the south of France in 1999. This prompted McDonald's to begin a large advertising campaign listing how many French cows, chickens, potatoes and heads of lettuce it uses each year. It also started running an 'open doors' programme where customers are invited to take tours of its kitchens and meet suppliers. The campaign appears to be working. By 2007 cash registers at McDonald's France are ringing up 1 million sales a day.

Source: adapted from Yuk (2007)

Questions

1 Identify each way McDonald's has changed its approach so that it can compete in the French market.
2 Are other companies likely to follow McDonald's lead?

Discussion questions

1 Using the s–c–p concept, think about how monopoly differs from an oligopoly.
2 Using Porter's five forces model explain why brewers such as Carlsberg are competing not only against Coors, Fosters, Stella Artois and Corona but also with Coca-Cola, Blossom Hill, Nike and Microsoft among others.
3 Why are consumers willing to pay extra for a cotton t-shirt that has a swoosh logo on it than one that hasn't?
4 Using relevant sources explain how the car market has evolved and comment on the market structure.
5 In 2009 BMW announced that it was going to withdraw from Formula One racing. Explain the reasoning behind this thinking.
6 Why do the low-cost airlines sell tickets at such low prices?

Further reading/sources of information

The web links below provide the most up-to-date sources. Access to any topic should be possible through the links.

Porter, M.E. (1980) *Competitive Strategy: Techniques for Analyzing Industries and Competitors.* New York: Free Press. This is the original text on competitive advantage and useful if you want to look in more detail at Porter's ideas.

(**www.direct.gov.uk/en/index.htm**) The Treasury site and the Competition Commission here is worth a look.

(**http://ec.europa.eu/index_en.htm**) Home page of the European Commission with access to the Directorate General for Competition of the European Union

(**www.bubl.ac.uk/**) BUBL provides a subject-based service. Subjects can be chosen from a subject tree. Includes discussion lists, news pages and access to other sources. It is designed for use by the higher education community.

(**http://news.bbc.co.uk/**) The BBC website provides up-to-date information on business topics from around the world.

(**http://www.ifs.org.uk/**) Site of the Institute for Fiscal Studies. Includes:

- publications and research;
- budget and pre-budget reports;
- surveys;
- fiscal facts.

(**www.bized.co.uk/**) A website for students and educators in business studies, economics, accounting, leisure, sport and recreation, and travel and tourism.

Newspapers

Newspapers are a good source of information on many topics. They can be found on the following sites:

Financial Times	**www.ft.com**
Guardian	**www.guardian.co.uk**
Observer	**http://observer.guardian.co.uk/**
Telegraph	**www.telegraph.co.uk**
The Times/Sunday Times	**www.timesonline.co.uk/tol/news/**

References

Augusta, I. (2009). Price Wars Have Decreased Car Insurance Rates This Month! 21 July available from **http://ezinearticles.com/?Price-Wars-Have-Decreased-Car-Insurance-Rates-This-Month!&id=2642348**

Barron, J.A. (2000) Structural Regulation of the Media and Diversity Rationale. May, *Federal Communications Law Journal*, 3, 555–560.

Baumol, W. (1982) Contestable Markets: An Uprising in the Theory of Industry Structure. *American Economic Review,* March, 72(1), 1–16.

BBC (2003) EU Watchdog Fines Wanadoo. Wednesday 16 July, available from **http://news.bbc.co.uk/1/hi/business/3070925.stm**

BBC (2008) Car Firms See Sales Plunge in US. 2 October, available from **http://news.bbc.co.uk/1/hi/business/7647708.stm**

Beardshaw, J. (1992) *Economics: A Student's Guide,* 3rd edn., London: Pitman.

Begg, D., Fischer, S. and Dornbusch, R. (1994) *Economics,* 4th edn. London: McGraw-Hill.

Birchall, J. (2009) Supermarkets Adapt Tactics in Price Wars. *Financial Times,* 1 July.

Buck, T. (2007) EU Unravels Zip Cartel. *Financial Times,* 20 September, available from **www.ft.com/cms/s/0/c9f2bb90-6711-11dc-a218-0000779fd2ac.html?nclick_check=1**

Bukeviciute, L. Dierx, A. and Ilzkovitz, F. (2009) The Functioning of the Food Supply Chain and its Effect on Food Prices in the European Union European Commission. *European*

Economy Occasional Papers 47 May, available from **http://ec.europa.eu/economy finance/publications/publication15234_en.pdf**

Camillus, J.C. (1998) Focus! *Praxis Quarterly Journal of Management,* 2(2), August, available from **www.blonnet.com/praxis/pr0202/02020160.htm**

Caves, R. and Porter, M.E. (1980) The Dynamics of Changing Seller Concentration. *Journal of Industrial Economics,* 19, 1–15.

Chaffin, J. (2009) WTO Warns on Barriers to Trade. *Financial Times,* 2 July, available from **www.ft.com/cms/s/0/1a209eda-6665-11de-a034-00144feabdc0,dwp_uuid=2f146ad2-f122-11dd-8790-0000779fd2ac.html?nclick_check=1**

Competition Commission (2009) About Us, available from **www.competition-commission.org.uk/about_us/index.htm**

European Commission (2003) Improving Access of SME's to Information on e-Business Legislation – the European e-Business Legal Portal, available from **http://europa.eu.int/comm/enterprise/ict/policy/legal-portal/**

European Commission (2009) Cartels Questions and Answers, available from **http://ec.europa.eu/competition/cartels/overview/faqs_en.html**

Financial Times (2006) Special Report OPEC: Price Slide Puts Cartel Back in the Spotlight. *Financial Times,* 23 October, available from **www.ft.com/cms/s/1/ae2b9b80-6059-11db-a716-0000779e2340.html**

Gapper, J. (2009) Little Laptops Snap at the Oligopoly, *Financial Times,* 16 July, available from **www.ft.com/cms/s/0/545af572-71a1-11de-a821-00144feabdc0.html**

Grant, R.M. (1995) *Contemporary Strategy Analysis: Concepts, Techniques, Applications.* Oxford: Blackwell.

Harding, R. (2009) Engineers See Big Picture. *Financial Times,* 7 August, available from **www.ft.com/cms/5/0/90c5634c-8396-11de-a24e-00144feabdco.html**

Klein, N. (2000) *No Logo.* London: Flamingo.

Levy, Y. (2005) Michael Porter's Five Strategic Market Forces, available from **www.photopla.net/wwp0503/entry.php**

Mahajan, S. (2006) Concentration Ratios for Businesses by Industry in 2004. *Economic Trends 635 October 2006.* Office for National Statistics, available from **www.statistics.gov.uk/articles/economic_trends/ET635Mahajan_Concentration_Ratios_2004.pdf**

Mintel (2008) Report on Motorcycles and Scooters – UK – July 2008, Mintel, a leading market research company, available from **www.mintel.com.**

Moore, M. (2002) *Stupid White Men.* London: Penguin.

Olson, E., Trascasa, C. and Essayan, M. (2001) Customization: Making Real Money in a Virtual World, available from **http://www.bcg.com/impact_expertise/publications/files/Customization_Making_Real_Money_in_a_VirtuallWorld_Mar_01.pdf**

Porter, M.E. (1980) *Competitive Strategy: Techniques for Analyzing Industries and Competitors.* New York: Free Press.

Simpson, H. (2002) Biotechnology and the Economics of Discovery in the Pharmaceutical Industry. Office of Health Economics, available from **www.ohe.org/biotechn.htm** (No longer available).

Tait, N. and Nuttall, C. (2009) Intel Braced for Billion-euro Fine Under European Antitrust Rules. *Financial Times,* 11 May, available from **www.ft.com/cms/s/0/b5dd5e88-3dc2-11de-a85e-00144feabdc0.html**

Thompson, A.A. and Strickland, A.J. (1995) *Strategic Management: Concepts and Cases,* 8th edn. Chicago, IL: Irwin.

Vorley, B. (2003) Corporate Concentration from Farm to Consumer, available from **www.ukfg.org.uk/docs/UKFG-Foodinc-Nov03.pdf**

Willigan, G.E. (1992) High-performance Marketing: An Interview with Nike's Phil Knight. *Harvard Business Review,* July, 70(4), 90–101.

Yuk, P.K. (2007) Le Big Mac at Home in Land of Slow Food. *Financial Times,* 3 October, available from **http://search.ft.com/ftArticle?queryText=biggest+advertising+spends&aje=true&id=071003000014&ct=0&page=2**

3

The international economic environment

Mark Cook

Learning outcomes

On completion of this chapter you should be able to:

- appreciate the changing nature of production in the major international economies;
- appreciate the role of government in influencing macroeconomic activity;
- recognise the changing nature of growth in the major international economies and the implications that flow from this;
- consider the methods of control and impact of inflation;
- understand the reasons for the changes in unemployment within Europe;
- understand theories of trade;
- understand the development of global trading blocs;
- recognise the importance of international trade between countries and trading blocs;
- understand the interrelatedness between economies;
- appreciate how exchange rate regimes have developed and their possible implications;
- consider the implications for the European economies of the development of a single currency;
- consider the global nature of commodity markets;
- appreciate how corporate social responsibility has grown in importance through the process of internationalisation.

Key concepts

- macroeconomic goals
- the circular flow of income
- growth and structural change
- economic growth
- the costs of growth
- inflation and deflation
- the role of the state
- economic cycles
- unemployment
- international trade and trade theory
- the Single European Market
- the single currency
- commodity markets
- Corporate Social Responsibility (CSR).

| Minicase 3.1 | Sarkozy attacks focus on economic growth |

Nicolas Sarkozy called for a 'great revolution' in the way national wealth is measured today, throwing his weight behind a report which criticises 'GDP fetishism' and prioritises quality of life over financial growth.

Endorsing the recommendations of a report given to him by Nobel prize winners Joseph Stiglitz and Amartya Sen, he said governments should do away with the 'religion of statistics' in which financial prowess was the sole indicator of a country's state of health.

'For years statistics have registered an increasingly strong economic growth as a victory over shortage until it emerged that this growth was destroying more than it was creating. The crisis doesn't only make us free to imagine other models, another future, another world. It obliges us to do so.'

Arguing that gross domestic product (GDP) ignores other factors vital to the well-being of its population, the report proposes a new indicator which would be calculated with GDP but take into account a broader view.

A new indicator would look at issues such as environmental protection and work/life balance as well as economic output to rate a country's ability to maintain the 'sustainable' happiness of its inhabitants.

France, whose economic output has fallen in the decades since the end of the prosperous '*trente glorieuses*' (1945–1975) prides itself on other aspects of life. Its healthcare system has been ranked the world's best by the World Health Organisation, its comparatively short working week is legendary, and its fertility levels are the highest in Europe, along with Ireland's.

Source: Davies (2009)

Questions

1 What other factors, apart from those in the case, does GDP ignore?
2 As developed economies become more focused on services, does this make GDP more difficult to measure?

3.1 Introduction

On one level it is possible to consider organisations as having control over their own actions. They can decide upon the kinds of resources they require, relate these to forecasts of demand, the current goals of the organisation and the organisation's long-term strategy. However, organisations do not exist in a vacuum. They are affected by and respond to changes in both short-term and long-term economic and business conditions. This chapter concentrates on the economic factors that impinge upon business behaviour. This not only includes changes in an organisation's domestic economic environment, but also, more importantly, changes that have taken place in the international economic environment. These changes, such as bilateral and global trading relations, international competitiveness, the EU and the globalisation of markets, affect organisations whether they are involved in international markets or not.

What are the international forces at play and what is their impact on organisations? It is fairly easy to see how interest rates, the level of inflation and competition policy have an effect on organisations, but there are other economic forces to consider. For example, changes in government policy towards training will have a direct impact on organisations both in the short term and the long term and can influence the level of skilled workers available, thereby affecting the organisation's productivity and allowing competitors to gain an increasing share of a previously safe market.

Changes in the external environment with regard to the development of trading blocs such as the EU (see *Chapter 7*) can affect the ability and desire of organisations to be involved in export markets. Economic issues in the home economy can result in governments altering their policies to influence general economic activity. Poor underlying strength in an economy can lead to changes both in interest rates and exchange rates, which may inhibit the performance of the organisations in an economy. Countries/governments/ organisations also may not be independent in their actions but are influenced by global commitments, and rules and regulations pertaining to their own economic or trading bloc. For example, the French government's ability to control its own economy is influenced by its membership of both the World Trade Organisation (WTO) and the EU. This chapter therefore considers the changes that have occurred in both the domestic and international macroeconomic environments. It will consider the structural changes that have taken place in the major economies of the world, the move towards growing international integration, the development of trading blocs, and the role and evolution of international capital flows. In addition, the chapter will address issues such as growth, the co-ordination of macroeconomic policy, the changes in global commodity prices and the changing power structures of the major global economies. Throughout the chapter it is important to bear in mind the impact such macroeconomic environmental changes have upon the organisations that lie therein.

Any account of the macroeconomic environment needs to be selective. In this respect the macroeconomic environment is viewed from a number of perspectives: that of Europe, the OECD, the developing and transitional economies, and the international economy.

3.2 Measures of macroeconomic activity

Governments and organisations are often concerned with the performance of international economies both in absolute and relative terms. But can the levels of economic activity in the major economies of the world be compared? A standard approach is to consider the Gross Domestic Product (GDP) or Gross National Product (GNP), now also known as Gross National Income (GNI), figures of the different countries. GNP/GNI – a measure of the level of economic activity produced in a country in any one year – is a record of the income accruing to a country, some of which may have been produced in the domestic economy (GDP) and some of which may have been produced abroad. GNP/GNI can be measured in a number of ways, but the following have come to be accepted as the traditional approaches:

- all the expenditures that are made on final products during the year – National Expenditure;
- the value of all the output of final products/services produced in that country during the year – National Output;
- all the incomes received by the factors of production in the making of the final products during the year – National Income.

Larger countries tend to have higher total GNPs, therefore GNP per head or GNP per capita is a better inter-country comparison of performance. As *Table 3.1a* indicates, some of the smaller countries, such as Switzerland and Denmark, have the highest GNP per head.

It is useful to contrast the GDP per capita figures of some of the developed countries with those in the developing/third world, shown in *Table 3.1b*.

There are a number of factors to consider when a comparison is made of different countries and on first inspection the developing/third world countries appear to be worse off; for further information and discussion of these comparisons see the UN or OECD websites.

How accurate are these figures? Often income is not reported, being part of what has become known as the hidden or underground economy – activity which does not come to the market for tax purposes (see *Table 3.2*). The inaccuracy of data can pose significant problems for policy-makers. In addition it has been long argued that GDP figures only measure the measurables and do not take into account other aspects of the well-being of the nation (see *Minicase 3.1*)

Table 3.1a	GNP and GNP per capita, various developed countries

Country	GNP 2008 (billions US$)[1] at current prices	GNP per capita 2008 (US$) based on current exchange rates
Austria	315.7	49,596
Denmark	199.7	62,520
France	2,115.0	44,675
Germany	2,927.7	44,363
Italy	1,849.0	38,640
Japan	4,355.8	38,578
Mexico	1,532.5	9,964
Spain	1,456.2	36,061
Sweden	344.0	52,035
Switzerland	332.4	65,200
Turkey	1,013.2	10,031
United Kingdom	2,199.7	43,544
United States	14,096.7	45,230

[1]Current prices and exchange rates.
Source: United Nation, http://data.un.org/Default.aspx OECD (2009)

Table 3.1b	GNP per capita, various developing/third world countries

Country	GNP per capita 2008 (US$) based on current exchange rates
Afghanistan	466
Bangladesh	494
Benin	767
Burkina Faso	522
Burundi	138
Democratic Republic of Congo	181
Eritrea	300
Guinea-Bissau	257
Liberia	219
Malawi	278
Sierra Leone	418
Zimbabwe	314

[1]Current prices and exchange rates.
Source: United Nations, http://data.un.org/Default.aspx OECD (2009)

Table 3.2	Estimates of the underground economy (as a percentage of GDP)

Country/region	% of GDP
Africa	
Sub-Saharan Africa	50–60
Nigeria, Egypt	69–75
Tunisia, Morocco	39–45
Latin America	
Mexico, Peru	40–60
Chile, Brazil, Venezuela	25–35
Asia	
China	20
Thailand	70
Philippines, Malaysia, Korea	38–50
Hong Kong, Singapore	13
Central Europe	
Hungary, Bulgaria, Poland	20–28
Czech Republic, Romania, Slovakia	9–16
Former Soviet Union	
Belarus, Georgia, Ukraine	28–43
Baltic States	20–27
Russia	40–50
OECD	
Belgium, Greece, Italy, Spain, Portugal	24–30
All others	13–23
Austria, Japan, USA, Switzerland	8–10

Sources: Schneider and Enste (2000), Economics Help (2007)

3.3 The role of the state in the economy

Table 3.3 indicates that government expenditure by OECD governments is, in total, around half of their GDP. The five top-spending governments are Sweden, Denmark, France, Belgium and Austria, all of which spend between 50 and 55 percent of GDP. Control of this expenditure has partially come through the Stability Pact of the euro.

Government spending by nearly all EU governments exceeds that of the USA (34–37 percent of GDP), Korea (20–30 percent of GDP) and Japan (32–35 percent of GDP). There is no single reason to explain why some countries have higher proportions of GDP devoted to government expenditure than others, although much of the explanation is to be found in different political attitudes leading to different polices (see *Chapter 7* section 7.4 '*The changing attitudes of governments and institutions*').

In economic terms, a part of the explanation of the differences in spending represents a policy of redistribution of income among citizens. Governments may also play an active role in macroeconomic stabilisation of the economy, using government spending to prevent excessive fluctuations in income and unemployment, thus smoothing out business cycles.

Table 3.3	Total government expenditure as percentage of nominal GDP			
Country	**1990**	**2000**	**2007**	**2008**
Belgium	51.5	51.5	48.2	49.9
Denmark	55.9	53.3	50.3	51.9
France	49.4	51.6	52.4	52.7
Germany	43.6	45.1	43.8	43.8
Greece	44.9	46.7	43.3	45.6
Ireland	42.9	31.5	36.7	41.8
Italy	52.9	46.1	48.5	48.7
Netherlands	54.9	44.2	45.9	45.4
Portugal	40.5	43.1	45.8	45.9
Spain	42.8	39.1	38.7	40.7
UK	41.9	37.0	44.7	47.4
Austria	51.5	51.5	48.2	48.7
Finland	47.9	48.4	47.5	48.8
Norway	53.3	42.3	40.6	39.9
Sweden	59.7	57.0	51.3	53.1
Australia	35.7	35.2	34.7	-
Japan	32.0	39.0	35.8	-
USA	37.1	34.2	37.4	-
Korea, South	20.0	23.9	30.7	-

Sources: adapted from *National Accounts*, June 2008, June 2009, OECD (2008), and 'Student enrolment in tertiary education' from *OECD Regions at a Glance 2009*, www.oecd.org/regional/regionsataglance

Government expenditure is a very important part of total expenditure in most economies. Governments are big consumers, spending around a third of the total that all households spend on goods and services. Like many households they are prone to over-expenditure and are forced to borrow money from the private sector or from abroad. The level of this debt can reach almost unmanageable amounts and, as *Table 3.4* indicates, for some countries, such as Zimbabwe, Japan, Lebanon, Jamaica and Italy, the size of the debt exceeds GDP. Interest payment on these debts is an important problem for countries, particularly those with debts in excess of 100 percent of GDP. In these countries higher taxes, both on the business sector and on consumers, may have to be levied, for a long period, to finance the interest payments and to repay the debt.

Table 3.5 indicates the level of government debt in more developed countries, and shows that it is generally far lower than in many developing countries.

Another way to hold down the rise in government debt is to curtail government expenditure. However, this may be difficult, since as unemployment rises there is often a concomitant rise in state benefits and reduction in tax revenue. It may, of course, be possible to reduce the deficit through increasing tax revenues. *Table 3.6* shows the main sources of revenues for governments in the EU, the tax on labour and businesses, and social security contributions of employers and employees.

The proportion of revenues obtained from the various sources differs from country to country. The average tax on income is higher in Denmark, Germany, Sweden and Australia, and much lower in the Czech Republic, Mexico and South Korea. Social security receipts are very low in Australia, New Zealand and Denmark, and relatively much higher in the Czech Republic, France, Germany and Japan. Taxes on business are on the whole fairly consistent

Table 3.4	Countries with the highest government debt as a percentage of GDP

Country	2008 est.
Zimbabwe	259.4
Japan	173.0
Lebanon	164.3
Jamaica	109.6
Italy	105.9
Singapore	99.2
Greece	97.4
Sudan	93.5
Belgium	89.1
Egypt	85.9
Seychelles	82.1
Bhutan	81.4*
Iceland	80.9
Israel	78.0
Sri Lanka	76.7
Hungary	68.6

*2004
Source: World Fact Book, www.cia.gov/library/publications/the-world-factbook/

between countries, but relatively low in Ireland (which uses them as a means to attract foreign investment) and Switzerland, compared with the EU as a whole (OECD, 2008).

These differences between the burdens of the various forms of taxation can have an impact on company location, level of profits, consumer behaviour and the incentive to work

Table 3.5	General government debt selected developed countries (% of GDP)

Country	1997	2003	2008
Germany	59.7	63.8	65.9
Ireland	64.3	31.1	43.2
France	59.2	62.9	68.1
Luxembourg	7.4	6.1	14.7
Netherlands	68.2	52.0	58.2
Austria	64.4	65.5	62.5
Sweden	71.0	52.3	38.0
UK	49.8	38.7	52.0
US	70.9	62.5	–

Source: Eurostat, http://epp.eurostat.ec.europa.eu/portal/page/portal/eurostat/home

| Table 3.6 | Tax rates and social security contributions, selected countries, 2008 |

Country	Total social security contributions (% of tax receipts)	Highest level of income tax, %	Corporation tax, %	Disposable income (% of gross pay) – married with two children
Australia	0.0	48.5	30.0	89.1
Belgium	27.9	45.1	34.0	77.9
Canada	14.4	46.4	36.1	87.7
Czech Republic	37.1	28.0	26.0	98.3
Denmark	2.2	55.0	28.0	71.2
France	34.2	36.5	35.0	83.1
Germany	36.6	44.3	38.9	76.2
Ireland	13.9	42.0	12.5	104.4
Japan	32.6	47.1	39.5	85.8
Korea	21.0	35.6	27.5	91.3
Mexico	15.7	22.5	30.0	95.4
New Zealand	0.0	39.0	33.0	85.6
Sweden	26.5	51.6	28.0	76.0
Switzerland	22.0	37.8	21.3	90.5
Turkey	17.9	35.6	30.0	69.5
UK	18.2	40.0	30.0	79.7
US	23.4	41.3	39.3	89.1
EU average	25.6	43.4	29.8	82.9
OECD average	22.9	40.4	28.6	84.9

Source: from *OECD in Figures*, OECD (2008) pp. 59–60, and 'Student enrolment in tertiary education' from *OECD Regions at a Glance 2009*, www.oecd.org/regional/regionsataglance

harder. Company location will also be reflected in average living costs abroad, with some of the highest costs being found in London, Iceland, Oslo and Geneva.

3.3.1 Economic cycles

It could be argued that one role of government is to reduce the fluctuations that occur in the economy. Often these fluctuations are not random but follow a cyclical pattern. There are long and short cycles in the economy. The long cycle (the Kondratief cycle) is estimated to have a period of 50 years and is associated with technological breakthroughs. Other cycles are observable, such as the business cycle (trade cycle), a seven- to ten-year economic cycle, and political cycles, cycles of four or five years coinciding with elections. We would expect to find that, in the boom periods of the cycle, economic activity is buoyant and organisations find it much easier to sell their goods and services. At the same time there may be pent-up pressures beginning to appear which serve to drive up prices. At this stage the government may seek to dampen economic activity. Conversely, at the bottom of a cycle, economic activity is subdued; there may be high levels of unemployment and less pressure on prices, and the government may perceive a need to step into the economy more directly and stimulate the level of economic activity.

Over time, markets have become more internationalised and countries have increasingly been involved in closer trading groups so that the phases of their cycles are more concurrent.

Minicase 3.2	German jobs saved by short-time working subsidies, says IMF

Demands by British trade unionists for the government to copy the German system of job subsidies to keep skilled workers employed were given a boost today when the International Monetary Fund (IMF) released its latest overview of the global economy.

While the impact of the worst recession since World War II has been to push up joblessness in every continent and every country, the IMF reported big variations between countries.

America's flexible labour market has not prevented an increase of five percentage points in the unemployment rate, which at close to 10 percent is at its highest level since the early 1980s.

In Germany, by contrast, the sharp contraction in industrial output has led to – so far at least – a rise of only three-quarters of a point in the jobless rate.

Britain's recent unemployment record is slightly better than that of the USA but a lot worse than Germany's. Unemployment averaged 5.4 percent in 2007 and barely moved in the first year of the crisis, rising to 5.5 percent in 2008. Since then, however, the pace of job losses has accelerated and the IMF is predicting unemployment will reach 7.6 percent this year and 9.3 percent in 2010.

Although the crisis began in the financial sector, it has not just been the City that has suffered big losses. There have been large-scale redundancies in manufacturing. And it has been the risk of a permanent loss of skills and industrial knowhow that has particularly concerned the trade unions.

So far, the government has turned a deaf ear to demands that Britain copy the German *Kurzarbeitergeld* scheme, which has extended the availability of subsidies for part-time working from six to 24 months.

Ministers have been put off by the cost – about £1 billion – and have argued that tax credits provide the same sort of support as the German job subsidies.

One area of the UK – Wales – has used the freedom under devolution to introduce a German-style scheme, and Rhodri Morgan, the first minister, told a fringe meeting at the Labour conference in Brighton this week that the initiative was not only saving thousands of jobs but also improving training.

The IMF said today that labour market flexibility cut both ways. Countries such as Britain and the US, which have low levels of employment protection, tended to shed jobs more quickly in a downturn but were likely to see faster jobs growth once the economy recovered.

Source: Elliott (2009)

Questions

1 Can German employment subsidies be considered as unfair for other economies?
2 What benefits does Germany get from subsidising employment?

Thus, when one trading bloc or area goes into recession, it may cause other trading blocs to do the same. One national government cannot, on its own, stimulate its economy while others in its trading bloc do nothing. It is now necessary for groups of countries to co-ordinate economic intervention. For example, the global financial crisis of 2007/9 had its inception in loan markets, particularly the sub-prime housing market where people had begun to carry high debt loads which became untenable as interest rates rose in the USA. The result was that a number of loan companies in the USA began to run into difficulties. In addition many of these sub-prime mortgages were sold on in bundles with other securities to other banks around the world in terms of mortgage-backed securities (MBS) or collateralised debt obligations (CDOs). Other banks outside of the USA began to realise that they possessed large quantities of these MBSs and CDOs. They therefore began to set aside reserves to cover theses bad debts. Moreover, in the UK any one commercial bank could not be sure how sound other banks were and inter-bank lending collapsed. While the housing market was collapsing both in the USA and the UK, there were additional commodity price bubbles to consider. The price of oil tripled from $50 in 2007 to $140 in 2008. Therefore the global economy began to suffer from a two-pronged attack. Commodity pricing was rising and this was feeding through to inflation, causing central banks to raise interest rates while at the same time the banking sector was becoming very reticent about lending. Unemployment began to rise in the USA, UK and the rest of Europe. There was global contagion and stock markets began to collapse. The global economy went into recession. The USA, the Euro Zone and the UK all registered two quarters of negative growth. The Arab world lost $3 trillion, and the recession led to reduced demand for oil. Global co-ordination was needed at central bank level. The global community moved to stimulate the international economy, first through expanding the money supply (through a process called quantitative easing); second, governments purchased huge quantities of government debt and poor performing bank assets (in doing so, the price of gilts rises and the rate of interest on gilts falls); third some banks were nationalised, and finally central banks cut interest rates. Quantitative easing has become a major part of the global stimulus package as, even with exceptionally low interest rates (0.5 percent in the UK in 2009), consumers are not willing to borrow money as they have poor expectations of the future of the economy and are worried about future job losses. Will quantitative easing work? It is a highly risky strategy. If it is not done aggressively enough the banks will still be unwilling to lend. If it is done too aggressively, the global economy runs the risk of the greater amounts of money in the economy causing inflation.

It is relatively easy to see the impacts of economic cycles on international economies, but explaining why they occur is much more difficult. It is too easy to say that it was the financial crisis in the West that led to the global recession. The global economy was beginning to slow down before this. The political cycle can be explained, although not fully, by the behaviour of domestic governments, but the trade cycle is much more difficult to interpret.

3.4 Macroeconomic goals

In general, the governments of most countries have four major economic goals, not all of which are mutually compatible. These are:

- a high level of economic growth;
- a strong balance of payments;
- a low level of inflation;
- a low level of unemployment.

Some of the goals may be conflicting. For example, it may not be possible to have a high level of economic growth and a strong balance of payments. Higher levels of economic growth can lead to increases in the rate of inflation. Thus, in achieving one goal, governments may have to forego others.

Governments have a range of economic policies which they can use to achieve their targets. For example, a government that wishes to improve the sales of its domestic industries could try and stimulate its domestic economy by:

- reducing taxes (fiscal policy), thereby increasing consumer expenditure;
- increasing the amount of money available or lowering interest rates in the economy (monetary policy);
- erecting trade barriers to encourage domestic consumers to buy more home-produced goods.

These policies may result in a short-term increase in business activity in the domestic economy, but the long-term impact may be different. Reducing interest rates may lead to higher levels of inflation in the domestic economy, which then encourages domestic consumers to purchase substitute foreign goods since these products appear to be relatively cheaper. The introduction of trade barriers may lead to other countries imposing retaliatory trade barriers on the country's exports and so damage business sales abroad. Alternatively, the imposition of trade barriers may result in foreign companies seeking entry into the domestic market and producing goods and services there as a means to overcome the trade barriers. This was a strategy adopted by Japanese carmakers both in the UK and the USA. The resulting firms increase competition in the domestic market and this can damage the performance of incumbent firms. What the above indicates is that policies can be implemented to achieve a particular short-term goal, but the long-term side-effects may well be different.

In this chapter we will explore economic growth, inflation and employment, and also refer to the balance of payments as appropriate.

3.4.1 Economic growth

In some countries, GDP has grown at a faster rate than others. This tendency for unequal growth between countries and within trading blocs has implications for government policy, interest rates, exchange rates and the optimal conditions for the growth of businesses within those countries.

Growth brings improvements in real incomes and a greater variety of goods and services to all sectors of the economy. The generation of growth may follow from a highly motivated, skilled and productive workforce, coupled with innovation, quality capital investment, and a high level of skill training and education.

Table 3.7 highlights the poor growth performance of some major Western industrialised nations; it describes growth in real output per worker, a good proxy for growth in real income per person, of five of the world's major industrial countries, and provides a comparison of the post-war years.

The UK has a long-standing peacetime tendency for a slower growth in labour productivity compared with its major competitors. Moreover, *Table 3.7* reveals that there has been a general slow-down in productivity growth since 1973 compared with the two decades after World War II. In fact, by 2008, the productivity of UK workers was only 83.1 percent of those in the USA, measured in terms of GDP per hour worked, Germany 98.2 percent, the G7 nations 89 percent, while the Czech Republic's GDP per hour worked was only 45.3 percent of the USA's, and Hungary 42.3 percent (OECD, 2009).

The pattern of growth has been very uneven since the oil shocks of 1974 and 1979, although it could be argued that some growth rates are coming closer together through global integration. These differences in economic growth rates could also indicate that some

Table 3.7	Growth rate of real output per worker employed (% per annum)				
Time period	**UK**	**USA**	**France**	**Germany**	**Japan**
1937–1951	1.0	2.3	1.7	1.0	−1.3
1951–1964	2.3	2.5	4.3	5.1	7.6
1964–1973	2.6	1.6	4.6	4.4	8.4
1973–1979	1.6	0.3	2.9	3.1	2.8
1979–1997	1.7	0.9	2.2	1.2	2.3
1998–2001	1.4	1.8	2.1	0.6	1.0

Sources: Matthews, R.C.O. *et al.* (1982) p. 31; OECD (1988) *OECD Economic Outlook, April 2002*, www.oecd.org

of the EU economies are in different phases of their economic cycles, and this has been put forward as one of the reasons why the UK opted not to be among the first-wave entrants into the European single currency. Since the beginning of the new millennium, the output per worker in the USA economy has grown partly as a result of its greater level of entrepreneurial activity. Both Germany and Japan now appear to perform relatively less well. The former because of monetary union and the reconstruction of the east of Germany, while in Japan increased saving and a drop in consumer confidence have rapidly slowed the performance of the Japanese economy.

Not all countries have experienced slower growth rates. Brazil, Russia, India and China, known as the BRIC countries, and emerging/transitional economies have performed remarkably well. Even the global slow-down of 2007/8 did not really impact on the growth rates of India and China – see *Table 3.8*.

Table 3.8 also shows how countries have become increasingly integrated into the global economy, with many showing negative growth performances following the world financial crisis of 2008/9.

What factors affect growth rates?

If countries knew precisely which were the important factors affecting economic growth, then remedial action could be taken and we would notice a large number of countries with extremely high and similar growth rates. The factors that are believed to influence growth may have an individual country dimension, or constraints to growth might involve policies at a wider level, such as that of the trading bloc (for example, the North American Free Trade Association – NAFTA) or economic bloc (the EU).

Cook (1996) suggested a range of factors that can be growth-enhancing or growth-suppressing. The growth-enhancing factors are:

- schooling and education investment;
- capital savings and investment;
- equipment investment; and
- the level of human capital.

Table 3.8	Estimates of GDP growth rates for selected BRIC and transitional economies				
Country	**2006**	**2007**	**2008**	**2009**	**2010**
Brazil	3.9	5.6	5.1	−0.8	4.0
India	9.7	9.0	6.5	5.9	7.2
China	11.6	13.0	9.0	7.7	9.3
Czech Republic	7.0	6.1	2.8	−4.2	1.4
Hungary	4.1	1.2	0.4	−6.1	−2.2
Slovakia	8.5	10.4	6.4	−5.0	3.1
Poland	6.2	6.8	4.9	−0.4	0.6
Russian Federation	7.7	8.1	5.6	−6.8	3.7
South Africa	5.4	5.1	3.1	−2.0	2.5
Chile	4.8	4.7	2.9	−1.6	3.0

Source: OECD Economic Outlook, www.oecd.org

The growth-suppressing factors are:

- the level of government expenditure;
- political and social instability;
- trade barriers; and
- the political nature of the ruling party.

More specifically, reasons cited for slower UK growth performance are:

- the short-termism of UK industry – industry favouring projects which give large short-term returns rather than investing for the long term;
- poor labour relations between unions and management;
- its less skilled and less qualified workforce;
- rising exchange rates making its exports less competitive and imports more attractive to purchase;
- its poor record on non-defence research and development.

Porter (2003) noted that the UK appears to have halted its relative decline against its major competitors by becoming more efficient within the constraints of its own economy, but now these efficiency improvements are almost exhausted and the UK needs to look elsewhere to achieve further catch-up. There are still problems with the UK's transport infrastructure, issues with skills and education and although its science base is adequate its private sector and commercial R&D appears to be disappointing (see *Chapter 4*). Porter suggests that if the UK is to become more efficient it needs to:

- move to a higher-value, innovation-driven level where it can create leading-edge products and services;
- change management behaviour;
- target investment in the business environment;
- strengthen areas such as education, industrial clusters and regions.

Structural change

By structural change we mean how the sectors in an economy have changed. It is useful to give some broad definitions of these sectors:

- The primary sector includes activities directly related to natural resources, for example farming, mining and oil extraction.
- The secondary sector covers production industries in the economy such as manufacturing, the processing of materials produced in the primary sector and construction.
- The tertiary sector is made up by services.

In the 1950s and 1960s growth rates of the industrialised economies were at historically high levels. There was an abundant supply of labour, moving from agriculture into other sectors of the economy. Oil discoveries in the Middle East ensured cheap oil supplies, particularly as oil production was in the hands of a few major Western European and North American companies. Further, technology transfer from the USA enabled the relatively backward industries of post-war Europe to make rapid improvements in productivity. Increasing real incomes improved market sizes and, coupled with the removal of trade barriers through the development of the European Free Trade Area (EFTA), the development of the European Community (EC) and the successes of the General Agreements on Tariffs and Trade (GATT), conditions were ripe for high levels of sustained growth.

By the early 1970s conditions were beginning to change. The movement of labour from agriculture to manufacturing had begun to decline: labour relations deteriorated. The 1973/1974 oil price rise led to a period of more expensive and less secure energy, and exchange rate movements led to European commodities losing some of their competitiveness. In addition, there was increasing competition from Japan and the newly industrialising countries

(NICs) – Singapore, Hong Kong, South Korea and Taiwan – in shipbuilding, steel and car manufacture – areas in which the Europeans had regarded themselves as pre-eminent.

At the same time Japan, in particular, had begun to adopt different working practices which implied that the old labour rules needed adjusting, a feature which was heavily resisted by the trade unions in Europe. In other words, inadequate adjustment of its industry had reduced Europe's ability to compete in global markets. Free marketeers believe that the weakness of governments and the strength of trade unions allowed real wage rates (the amount that take-home pay will purchase) to soar. Thus, products became more expensive within Europe, and government policy only served to safeguard jobs rather than improve output. The much more *laissez-faire* approach adopted by the USA and UK governments since the early 1980s has attempted to address the problem of the high price of labour through legislation designed to limit the power of trade unions and encourage private sector involvement through its privatisation policy.

Arguably there has been a convergence of economic activity in structural terms. While many developed economies have become more oriented towards the service sector, developing economies have moved from concentrating on primary products towards more manufacturing and, in some cases, greater investment in services, especially for Western-based companies. As *Table 3.9* indicates, in many developed countries, 66 percent or more of economic activity is in the service sector. For example, in Canada, Australia, France, the UK and the USA it accounts for around 70 percent of economic activity. In some less prosperous European countries, such as Portugal and Greece, agriculture plays a bigger part in the economy, although as *Table 3.9* indicates even for Italy and Japan agriculture plays a relatively more important role in their economies.

The UK has seen a fall in its share of world manufacturing exports and a fall in manufacturing employment. For other countries, such as Japan, the picture is somewhat different. In fact, between 1964 and 1999 Japan continued to see its manufacturing employment grow, while at the same time the UK lost over 43 percent of manufacturing employment (OECD, 2000). In fact, by 2007, the UK had less than 15 percent of its workforce in the manufacturing sector, compared with over 20 percent in Germany, Italy and Japan.

Not only has the overall structure of economies changed, but also, within the various economic sectors, countries have tended to specialise in producing certain products. The UK is more specialised in extractive industries, chemicals and financial services, France in

Table 3.9	Sectoral contribution to GDP and employment, 2007, percentages					
	Agriculture		**Industry**		**Services**	
	GDP	**Employment (1,000s)**	**GDP**	**Employment (1,000s)**	**GDP**	**Employment (1,000s)**
Canada	2.5	422	20.4	3,433	77.1	13,011
Australia	3.4	359	20.7	2,165	75.9	7,946
France	3.5	875	23.0	5,750	73.5	18,375
Germany	2.4	912	31.0	11,780	66.6	25,308
Italy	4.0	920	29.9	6,860	66.1	15,173
Sweden	2.2	101	21.1	956	76.7	3,473
UK	1.3	377	21.5	6,235	77.2	22,388
USA	1.4	2,095	19.8	28,894	78.8	115,058
Japan	4.1	2,580	27.0	17,140	68.9	43,790

Source: US Bureau of Labor Statistics (2009), www.his/gov/

food products, Germany in engineering and chemicals, and Italy in clothing, textiles and footwear.

Consideration of the sectors overall may hide important changes within sectors. Within the secondary sector it is manufacturing which has felt the full force of any structural change, although the impact has been different within manufacturing (the high technology/skill areas have remained very competitive, although the reverse is true for low technology/skill areas). Once again there are differences by country, as *Table 3.9* indicates.

The costs of growth

First, it may be assumed that growth brings only benefits. However, there is a view that growth has a number of negative aspects in terms of environmental damage and that the process of achieving higher growth may not be worth the effort. Growth may cause negative externalities, where the actions of producers or consumers affect not only themselves but also third parties, other than through the normal workings of the price mechanism. It is the developed countries which produce the greatest amount of pollution, including 45 percent of greenhouse gases, and consume around 70 percent of all resources; see *Chapter 6* for a discussion of environmental costs. Many of these costs are likely to be understated, since precise measurements are not available. If, as Meadows *et al.* (1992) suggest, the costs of growth are included in the estimates of real national income, then the benefits of economic growth may be overstated.

Second, to achieve a higher growth rate some consumption expenditure may have to be foregone today and resources switched to investment goods so that future consumption may be higher.

Third, growth also has an impact on resources, particularly non-renewable ones. If growth is stimulated today we are just bringing the day forward when non-renewable resources will disappear. Growth also brings technical progress, which may create jobs but, at the same time, destroy others by making skills redundant. People may be forced to take low-paid, unskilled work or migrate. The results of this process can be seen in the structural changes outlined earlier.

Whether governments should pursue the goal of growth depends, therefore, on the costs and benefits of growth, and how much weight individual groups in society attach to them. Perhaps constrained growth is the solution, where growth is sought but subject to, for example, levels of environmental protection, minimum wages and maximum rates of resource depletion.

There are individuals who suggest that we do not have to worry about using up finite resources. It is their view that as the resource is depleted so its price will rise and consumers will purchase less of it. It is also possible that resources which were not profitable at the old price will come into use, as was the case in the development of North Sea oil and gas reserves. These marginal resources may be used efficiently if technology can provide a means of increasing the capacity usage. Suppose, however, that there comes a point when technology cannot make marginal resources as effective as those that have been depleted. It follows that the prices of materials would rise; this would feed through to inflation, and a wage price spiral would ensue, reducing everyone's standard of living. Alternatively, resources could be rationed.

Although these arguments seem a little improbable on first viewing, the notion of resource depletion did receive support at the Earth Summit in Rio de Janeiro in May 1992 and was considered further at the environmental conferences at Montreal (1996), Tokyo (1998), Johannesburg (2002) and Bangkok (2009). The call was for controlled growth. A constrained growth rate is easier to bear for the developed countries, but for many less developed countries (LDCs) or newly industrialising countries (NICs) the development of indigenous natural resources is seen as a prerequisite for escape from low levels of GDP per capita. The acceptability of this constrained growth scenario to those countries depends upon whether the developed nations provide increased aid to finance any difference between sustainable growth and their 'normal' level of growth.

Even without consideration of the environmental impact of growth, on a macroeconomic level growth can have an important impact on prices. High levels of growth which are coupled with resource constraints can lead to inflation. The Johannesburg conference also called for the diversification of energy supply with a move towards cleaner and renewable technologies. Sustainable development was high on the agenda with the notion of minimising waste, while maximising use and recycling. However, the commitment to the reduction in greenhouse gases and sustainability was not considered a high priority for some countries, notably the USA.

3.4.2 Inflation

Inflation may be defined as a persistent increase in prices over time; in other words, the rate of inflation measures the change in the purchasing power of money.

There are a number of ways in which inflation can be measured. One method is by measuring changes in the Retail Price Index (RPI) (sometimes called the headline rate). The RPI measures the change in prices from month to month in a representative 'basket' of commodities bought by the average consumer. The commodities in the basket are weighted differently to indicate the proportion of expenditure made by the average consumer on various items. As *Table 3.10* indicates, the weights change over time as goods change in relative importance in the average basket of commodities purchased by consumers. Thus in the UK since 1987, clothing and footwear, leisure goods and tobacco account for smaller proportions of the average expenditure of consumers, while housing costs, catering and, to some extent, leisure services have increased.

In the UK, mortgage interest payments are included in the RPI. This means that higher rates of interest will push up mortgage rates and increase the rate of inflation. So if it is the government's intention to reduce inflation by increasing interest rates and thereby reducing

Table 3.10	UK general index of retail prices: group weights				
Category	**1987**	**1994**	**1998**	**2002**	**2009**
Catering	46	45	48	52	50
Food	167	142	130	114	118
Alcoholic drinks	76	76	71	68	63
Tobacco	38	35	34	31	27
Housing	157	158	197	199	236
Fuel and light	61	45	36	31	49
Household goods	73	76	72	73	70
Household services	44	47	54	60	61
Clothing and footwear	74	58	55	51	39
Personal goods and services	38	37	40	43	41
Motoring expenditure	127	142	136	141	121
Fares and other travel costs	22	20	20	20	20
Leisure goods	47	48	46	48	38
Leisure services	30	71	61	69	67
Total	1,000	1,000	1,000	1,000	1,000

Source: Labour Market Trends (1988, 1994, 1998); *Monthly Digest of Statistics,* (2002, 2009) www.statistics .gov.uk/statbase/Product.asp?vink=611

consumer expenditure, the opposite effect will occur. Since the RPI was the index usually used as a basis for wage claims, workers and trade unions could be encouraged to pursue higher wage claims if the RPI increased through increased mortgage rates. These would then increase the costs of industry, causing further price rises.

Other European countries, for example France and Italy, exclude owner-occupation from their consumer price index, while other countries, because of the small size of their home ownership sector compared with their rental sector, will exhibit different changes in their RPI for an equivalent change in interest rates.

In the UK a measure of inflation has been developed which does not include the costs of mortgages, RPIX, now called the underlying rate of inflation. A further method for measuring inflation has also been developed, called RPIY. This measure of inflation excludes both mortgage interest rate payments and indirect taxes such as VAT and excise duty. This is a measure, therefore, of the true underlying rate of inflation. Since 2003, the UK has also switched towards using the Consumer Price Index (CPI) as a measure of inflation. The government has set a target for this of 2 percent per year for the Bank of England. The government cited three reasons why CPI is a better measure for the purposes of setting monetary policy:

- it gives a more realistic characterisation of consumer behaviour;
- it gives a better picture of spending patterns in the UK;
- it is a more comparable measure of inflation internationally and represents international best practice.

Why the concern about inflation?

From 1950 to 1970 prices were fairly stable in Western nations. The first oil price rise in 1973/74 – alongside other factors – changed this. The increase in the price of oil pushed up energy prices and transportation costs, and increased the prices of goods which were oil related. The response of the Western nations was to try to squeeze inflation out of the system. *Figure 3.1* shows how inflation has changed in the UK over the years since 1976, and indicates the price rises following the 1979 oil shock and the further rise in inflation towards the end of the 1980s. During the twenty-first century, inflation continued to be low, but by 2007 inflation began to rise, before falling back again in 2009.

Inflation is said to have redistribution effects. If money wages rise at the same rate as inflation, then real wages remain constant. However, if tax bands and tax thresholds do not

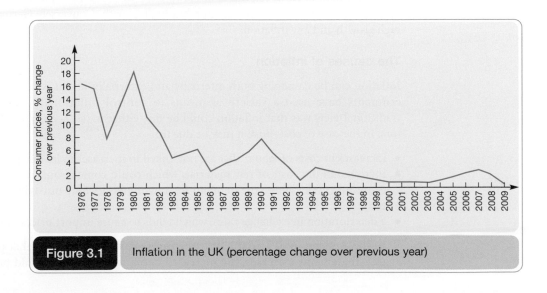

| Figure 3.1 | Inflation in the UK (percentage change over previous year) |

rise in line with inflation, then a greater proportion of income is subject to tax. Inflation also reduces the real value of the debt to the government, thus redistributing income from the people to the state. It also affects individuals and businesses. Inflation favours debtors rather than creditors, as it erodes the value of debt.

Inflation also has external consequences, making domestically produced goods more expensive and less competitive on world markets and imported goods cheaper on the home market. In this case the balance of payments position will worsen and pressure will mount for the exchange rate to fall. As the exchange rate falls it will make imports more expensive and reduce the price of exports, thereby restoring equilibrium in the balance of payments. Governments, however, may pursue a policy of managed exchange rates which prevents the market from restoring equilibrium in the balance of payments. In these cases, controlling the effect of inflation by other means rather than letting the exchange rate do the correction may be a better approach.

During the 1980s, government policies throughout Europe shifted from reducing unemployment to controlling the rate of inflation. Policy-makers who support such an approach argue that this is the correct way since, once inflation is beaten, unemployment will fall. The arguments are stated as follows. High and variable inflation makes future income from investment projects uncertain. Thus firms may reduce investment or may only consider undertaking investment projects which yield a high rate of return in the short term. However, the positive link between inflation and unemployment is somewhat tenuous; Friedman (1977) supports the relationship, while Higham and Tomlinson (1982) find no general evidence.

High inflation may lead to governments imposing wage and price controls which inhibit the working of the market mechanism. Some firms, which may be relatively more efficient or in markets where the demand for their products is rising, may be prevented from offering their employees better rewards because of the controls put in place by government. In addition, the more efficient firms may be unable to offer rewards high enough to entice staff from other sectors of the economy. High inflation may also lead to industrial unrest as unions seek money wage increases in order to prevent a deterioration in their real wages. It may also be expected that high inflation depresses saving, as consumers purchase products from organisations before the prices increase once again.

Inflationary expectations also take time to adjust downwards. A reduction in current inflation may not lead to an improvement in the amount invested since it is possible that investors may feel that the inflation rate will increase again in the future.

Given the problems that can arise from inflation it would be easy to suggest that countries which have relatively higher rates of inflation perform less well than countries with lower levels of inflation. However, this is not always the case. For example, before joining the Euro bloc Spain had relatively high inflation but high growth. Conversely Germany had relatively high growth and low inflation.

The causes of inflation

Inflation can be damaging both internally and externally, and it is not surprising that governments have used a variety of means to control inflationary pressures. The more traditional view was that inflation could be due either to 'cost–push' or 'demand–pull' factors. In the case of cost–push it may be due to:

- increases in costs of labour that are not linked to increases in labour productivity;
- increases in the costs of raw materials which could come about in buoyant stages of the economic cycle, where the demand for raw materials may outstrip supply in the short term;
- a deterioration in exchange rates, which tends to cause import prices to rise.

In the demand–pull scenario, it is the excess demand for goods that pulls up prices. If aggregate demand increases, the increased demand for labour would push up real wage

Minicase 3.3	Australia raises interest rates by 0.25 percent as economy improves

Australia today [6 October 2009] became the first member of the G20 to raise interest rates since the financial crisis began. In a sign that the country has weathered the economic storm better than many other nations, Australia's central bank decided to raise its benchmark interest rate by a quarter-point, to 3.25 percent. It said economic conditions within Australia were stronger than expected, partly thanks to strong growth from China, a key trading partner. Unemployment is lower than feared, and house prices have risen steadily in recent months.

Data released last month showed that Australia's GDP rose by 0.6 percent in the second quarter of the year. The country's interest rates had been at a 49-year low of 3 percent since April. The Reserve Bank of Australia also warned further rate rises are likely in the coming months to prevent the country's economy expanding too quickly. 'With growth likely to be close to trend over the year ahead, inflation close to target and the risk of serious economic contraction in Australia now having passed, the board's view is that it is now prudent to begin gradually lessening the stimulus provided by monetary policy,' the Reserve Bank said in a statement.

Australia was the only advanced country to avoid falling into recession in the past year. Analysts said this is due to the success of official stimulus packages, including increased spending on infrastructure projects and cash handouts to encourage consumers to keep spending.

Source: Wearden (2009)

Questions

1 What reasons might explain why Australia has 'weathered the economic storm better' than other countries?
2 Why has Australia raised interest rates? What might be the consequence of this increase on the Australian economy?

rates. If unions in other sectors of the economy attempted to keep their members' wages in parallel, then it is possible that, even with an excess labour supply in these other sectors, unions would be able to force up wage rates. The overall general increase in wage rates then feeds through into the costs of industry and is subsequently passed on in price increases. This causes real wages to fall, with the possibility that further wage demands could follow. In such circumstances a damaging wage–price inflationary cycle is likely to be established.

Inflation can also be caused by governments 'accommodating' price increases. In this instance, whenever aggregate demand falls, leading to higher levels of unemployment, governments step into the economy directly through changes in either government expenditure or taxation to stimulate the economy. This increase in economic activity would increase national income but can also cause the price level to rise.

Monetarists saw the excessive role of governments during the 1960s and 1970s as being directly responsible for the rise in inflation and argued that this type of intervention would have no long-term impact on output and unemployment. They suggested that the economy would return to some natural level of economic activity but at a higher level of inflation. Does this mean that government activity in the economy may not be worthwhile since it cannot increase output or employment in the long term? From a governmental perspective the long term may extend beyond the lifetime of an elected government; it still might be possible, therefore, to increase employment during the government's term of office! See *Figure 3.2(a)*.

Monetarists argue that if real output and employment are to be increased then governments should intervene not in the demand side but in the supply side of the market. As *Figure 3.2(b)* indicates, the level of output can be increased not only by shifting the aggregate demand curve to the right from AD_1 to AD_2 but also by shifting the aggregate supply curve to the right from $SRAS_1$ to $SRAS_2$. Thus the monetarists advocated the use of policies

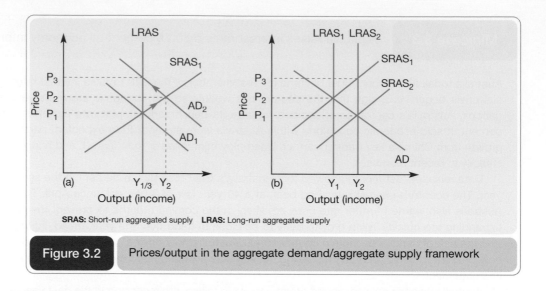

SRAS: Short-run aggregated supply   **LRAS:** Long-run aggregated supply

Figure 3.2	Prices/output in the aggregate demand/aggregate supply framework

to shift the supply curve to the right, so-called 'supply-side measures'. These policies are designed to reduce government involvement and so reduce the frictions they perceive exist in markets (see also *Chapter 2*).

In addition monetarists see the need to control the amount of money in the economy, so would suggest that governments control either the quantity of money (the money supply) or the price of money (the interest rate).

Since government expenditure often exceeds the revenue from taxation, the consequent deficit, the Public Sector Borrowing Requirement (PSBR), was often financed via government printing the extra money. Seigniorage – the printing of money to finance government expenditure – alleviates the government's need to borrow. However, this growth in the money supply increases the amount of money in circulation and could have inflationary consequences. Monetarists suggested that governments seek to reduce the amount of borrowing they undertake. If the monetarists are to be believed then all governments need to do is control the money supply and introduce a series of supply-side measures – policies aimed at improving the quantity and quality of supply – as a means to reduce the level of inflation.

It has been notoriously difficulty to control the money supply. This is for two main reasons. First, we need to define what we mean by the money supply. Is it the notes and coins in circulation (this is defined as M_0); is it notes and coins in circulation plus bank deposits (this is known as M_1) or is it some other definition? The Federal Reserve Bank, in the USA, has over 20 definitions of the money supply.

Second, it was found that, when the UK government targeted a particular measure of the money supply during the 1980s, it had the habit of going out of control, that is exceeding its target rate of growth. If controlling the quantity of money is difficult, what about controlling money through its price (interest rates)?

The monetarist approach of using higher interest rates to control inflation can damage business confidence, increase the costs to industry and raise the costs of borrowing for consumers. In addition, if government expenditure is controlled then this subsequently affects consumer expenditure and business sales.

It has been argued that monetarist approaches to inflation have not been responsible for bringing inflation under control, and that other forces have played a more dominant role. Beckerman (1985) suggests that much of the fall in inflation in the early 1980s can be attributed to the fall in commodity prices that followed from the world recession and the subsequent rise in commodity prices has had the reverse effect (see 'Commodity prices'). The very tight fiscal stance taken by the government also had an influence. Soteri and Westaway (1993) suggest that, for the UK, world inflation, and the exchange rate and its effect on import prices have both played an important part in explaining the changes in its inflation record.

We should also consider the UK's 'temporary' membership of the Exchange Rate Mechanism (ERM). Under fixed exchange rates organisations cannot rely on the exchange rate to restore competitiveness in their prices if their relative inflation rates are too high. In the short term, if labour seeks too high a wage claim, then the loss of competitiveness that follows from any increases in prices would lead to job losses. Thus, the ERM was seen as providing discipline for the labour market. From the middle part of the 1990s until the middle of this current decade inflation was at low levels once again. Some considered that inflation was under control and was not the major concern of the developed nations. Part of the reason was that many Western developed nations have been following anti-inflationary policies and the level of economic activity has not been allowed to grow so rapidly. The outcome of this policy approach is to have unemployment higher than perhaps it should be. The pursuit of targets for entry into the European single currency and the role of the European Central Bank in squeezing inflation out of the system have also led to lower inflation (see *Table 3.11*). At the same time the UK government has given control of its interest rates to the Bank of England, which may have adopted a stronger grip on squeezing inflation out of the system. Moreover, the flow of cheap imports from China (due to their competitive exchange rate) has forced businesses to moderate their price rises.

For some countries, notably a number of those in South America which have historically had high levels of inflation, the approach adopted to reduce inflation was to fix their exchange rates against the USA dollar, and this has successfully reduced their inflationary spiral. It is also worth noting that while inflation has been reduced within Europe, the UK still has a higher inflation rate than many of its major trading partners.

The link between inflation and unemployment may also have changed. The UK, during the opening part of the twenty-first century, has experienced low inflation and low unemployment. This can be partly explained by its highly flexible labour market when compared with continental Europe. Similarly the USA has experienced low inflation and low unemployment.

| Table 3.11 | The UK and European economies since 1997 |

	Inflation (% rate) harmonised indices of consumer prices		Unemployment (% level)		Real GDP (% growth rate)	
	UK	Euro area	UK	Euro area	UK	Euro area
1997	1.8	1.6	6.8	10.5	3.3	3.0
1998	1.6	1.1	6.3	10.2	3.4	2.9
1999	1.3	1.1	5.9	9.4	3.5	2.8
2000	0.8	2.1	5.4	8.4	3.9	3.9
2001	1.2	2.3	5.1	8.0	2.5	1.9
2002	1.3	2.2	5.1	8.4	2.1	0.9
2003	1.4	2.1	5.0	8.8	2.8	0.8
2004	1.3	2.1	4.7	9.0	3.0	2.1
2005	2.1	2.2	4.8	8.8	2.2	1.7
2006	2.3	2.2	5.3	8.2	2.8	3.0
2007	2.3	2.1	5.3	7.4	3.0	2.6
2008	3.6	3.3	6.2	8.0	0.7	0.5

Sources: OECD *Economic Outlook,* December (2002) www.oecd.org, Eurostat (2009) http://epp.eurostat.ec.europa.eu/portal/page/portal/eurostat/home/

Again its flexible labour market plus its higher level of entrepreneurship and business start-ups when compared with Europe may explain this.

At this stage let us consider the arguments. Inflation is costly both domestically and internationally. Many reasons have been put forward to explain why inflation occurs, and almost as many remedies. For the latter there does not appear to be any consensus. However, in seeking to bring down inflation, countries have often deflated their economies and in doing so worsened the conditions for business. For Eastern European countries and emerging market economies the scenario is somewhat different. By the standards of developed economies as shown in *Table 3.12a*, inflation has remained high in many other countries including the BRIC economies. Part of the explanation for the relatively poor inflation performance of many Eastern European countries has been the introduction of market forces into many sectors and the reduction in state management of prices. However, as *Table 3.12b* indicates, there are signs that inflation is being controlled, especially in Slovakia, the Czech Republic and Poland, although high levels of inflation probably have affected business formation and development.

Dealing with deflation

Whereas the 1970s and parts of the 1980s were associated with relatively high levels of inflation, the 1990s and early 2000s have been denoted as a period of low levels of inflation: partly explained by the role of China and other emerging markets producing highly competitive priced products in global markets and forcing domestic supplies to compete with these on prices. Nonetheless, inflation began to rise in 2007/8 due to rising commodity

Table 3.12a	Consumer price inflation (% per annum) in selected developed and BRIC countries									
Year	Brazil	India	China	UK	France	US	Japan	Germany	Italy	EU
2006	3.1	5.2	3.3	2.3	1.9	3.2	0.3	1.8	2.2	2.2
2007	4.5	4.7	7.4	2.3	1.6	2.8	0.0	2.3	2.0	2.3
2008	5.9	8.4	7.2	3.6	3.2	3.8	1.4	2.8	3.5	3.7

Source: OECD Economic Outlook www.oecd.org; *Eurostat*, http://epp.eurostat.ec.europa.eu/portal/page/portal/eurostat/home/

Table 3.12b	Consumer price inflation (% per annum) in selected transition and emerging market countries						
Year	South Africa	Czech Republic	Hungary	Poland	Russian Federation	Chile	Slovak Republic
2006	5.8	2.6	3.9	1.3	9.0	3.4	4.5
2007	7.1	3.0	8.0	2.5	11.9	4.4	2.8
2008	11.0	6.3	6.0	4.2	13.3	8.7	4.6
2009	7.2	1.6	4.5	3.5	8.0	2.0	1.8
2010	5.6	0.3	4.1	1.8	6.5	1.9	1.8

Source: OECD Economic Outlook, www.oecd.org

prices (see '*Commodity prices*' section 3.7). On the other hand, the period after 2008, linked with the world financial crisis, has seen a number of countries experiencing negative price increases, also called deflation. For some countries, for example Japan, deflation is not a new phenomenon: this occurred in 1995 and again from 1999 to 2002.

Deflation sounds like a consumer paradise, but can bring problems to global manufacturers as people put off purchasing today in the expectation that it will be cheaper tomorrow. The fall in prices can be explained by:

- the fall in commodity prices as the global economy slows;
- the opening up of a range of hitherto protected markets to competition;
- the role of technology increasing productivity; and
- the behaviour of organisations which are being threatened by investigation into their pricing practices (supermarkets, over-the-counter medicines, etc.).

The danger for economies is that if consumers believe that prices will fall in the future then they may put off making purchases in the current time period and look to buy in the future when prices have fallen. This reduces current demand, which in turn drives down prices.

For some industries deflation is not bad – industries with rapidly improving technologies and productivity, such as computers. It is the mature industries which have more problems, as they face reduced demand and overcapacity due to lower competitor prices. Lower demand leads to price reductions and lower levels of investment. This, through the circular flow, leads to further demand falls and so the cycle continues. So long as global demand remains relatively sluggish, we may have to get used to living with deflation for some time to come.

3.4.3 Employment

From the end of World War II until the 1970s, control of unemployment was the main goal of most European governments. During the 1970s and 1980s control of inflation assumed greater importance. Phillips (1958) argued that low inflation is not compatible with low unemployment. Nonetheless, a number of governments saw that low relative inflation could lead to higher competitiveness and provide the conditions for improvements in employment, a feature that has appeared once more to be in place during the early part of the twenty-first century.

Although unemployment has fluctuated with the general level of economic activity, there has been a slow upward trend in the natural level of unemployment until the 1990s – the level of unemployment which is consistent with overall equilibrium in the labour market – since World War II. Since the end of the 1990s the UK and USA have experienced almost unprecedented low levels of unemployment (in the UK around 5 percent) until 2007, and this is much lower than the OECD's estimate for the 'natural' rate of unemployment in the UK of 8 percent in 1996. This suggests that some progress on supply-side measures in the labour market has been made (Cook and Healey, 2001). Global economies can never get to a position where everyone is employed. In the UK, 5 percent unemployment is probably the lowest level of unemployment that can be reached given some of the churning effects that arise in the labour market and the failure of people to have the correct skills. *Table 3.13* indicates the differences in employment by gender for selected countries. There has tended to be a rise in employment by both men and women in the labour market but the employment rates of men are generally higher. This suggests something about the skills that women possess and the way society and culture views the role of women in the labour market. However, it also shows that if countries want to draw more people into the labour market, then for those countries, when the activity rates are much higher, this may prove to be more difficult.

Table 3.13	Employment rates (%) by gender, 2000, 2008, selected countries			
Country	2000 – male	2000 – female	2008 – male	2008 – female
EU 27	70.8	53.7	72.8	59.1
Denmark	80.8	71.6	81.9	74.3
Spain	71.2	41.3	73.5	54.9
Italy	68.0	39.6	70.3	47.2
Hungary	63.1	49.7	63.0	50.6
Finland	70.1	64.2	73.1	69.0
UK	77.8	64.7	77.3	65.8
Switzerland	87.3	69.3	85.4	73.5
US	80.6	67.3	76.4	65.5
Japan	80.9	56.7	81.6	59.7

Source: Eurostat (2009) http://epp.eurostat.ec.europa.eu/portal/page/portal/eurostat/home

Burda and Wyplosz (2009) present some further evidence about unemployment levels:

- Where the safety provisions, such as benefits, for the unemployed are more extensive, then unemployment levels are higher. Benefits may allow some people to stay out of the labour market.
- Their skills become inappropriate for the needs of the labour market and they become part of the long-term unemployed.
- Trade unions have been more militant in Europe than in the UK.
- Labour costs consist of more than wages; they include labour taxes (social security and retirement contributions), and these too have risen steeply.
- Regulation of the use of labour, for example length of the working week and dismissal procedures, is also of importance.
- Productivity – output per person – must also be examined. As labour becomes more productive fewer employees are required to produce a given quantity of output.
- Sectoral changes have taken place in a number of European economies as they have moved from labour-intensive manufacturing based industries to service-oriented ones.
- Minimum wage levels may be set higher than the clearing wage in some European countries.
- The European economy is less dynamic than that of the USA, hence fewer jobs are provided.

Job creation in the UK is possible. This is unlikely to come from a simple boost in demand but rather from a longer-term emphasis on investment in infrastructure, training and education (Begg, 1995). Indeed, evidence suggests that there has been a decline in the so-called natural rate of unemployment in the UK since the mid- to late 1990s. This is due to:

- improved labour market skills and a better educated workforce;
- the introduction of back-to-work schemes for the long-term unemployed;
- the continued weakness of trade unions;
- flexibility of the workforce;
- the success of supply-side measures introduced in the previous decade.

For more than a decade the UK government has been acutely aware of the lack of training taking place, a shortage of skills and a general failure to keep pace with the rapidly changing world of work. The world of education has seen the development of a new

National Curriculum and vocationally oriented qualifications. The government's response to the skill shortages that have appeared in UK industry, even though unemployment has been relatively high, includes, for example, NVQs, Investors in People, Modern Apprenticeships and the New Deal.

Nonetheless, Campbell *et al.* (2001) indicated a number of deficiencies that still existed within the UK labour force – and to a large extent still do. There were still skill imbalances in many sectors, the result of which was the driving up of wages with the fastest increases in the managerial, professional and associate professional occupations. There is an oversupply of people with no qualifications. Around 4 percent of employers reported skill shortages and these are more acute in small establishments. Moreover, the skills shortages are sector-specific, affecting manufacturing, construction, wholesale/retail, health- and social care, and more particularly business services. Skill gaps (the difference between the current skill levels of the workforce and the skills needed to meet the objectives of the organisation) affect around 7 percent of establishments. Skill shortages are also regionalised affecting more organisations in the south-east of England. There is also evidence of latent skills gaps – gaps that are likely to emerge if the organisation were to improve its performance relative to its competitors.

In terms of international comparisons, the UK is around the OECD average for the proportion of its workforce qualified to NVQ 2 and 3 or its equivalent. However, it is older workers who are more likely to have these qualifications and younger workers have below-average levels. The UK does have the highest rate of university graduation among the OECD countries, although, both in the case of degrees and NVQs, other OECD growth rates exceed that of the UK (Leitch Report, 2006).

Perhaps more of a problem is in the area of literacy and numeracy. The UK is just below the OECD average for both, yet it is in the older workforce where the shortfall is the greatest. In fact 20 percent of the adult population are proficient at only level one – the sixth worst in the OECD, although at the same time in terms of higher levels of education the UK is ranked highly. Therefore there is a polarisation of skills and education within the UK workforce.

3.4.4 International trade

Since World War II markets have become increasingly internationalised, and it follows that economies have become more 'open', that is more heavily involved in international trade. But why do countries trade? Clearly, much trade takes place because one country is better able to produce particular products and services than its trading partners. For example, a country situated closer to the equator than the UK is better able to produce tropical fruit, while it is possible that, because of its manufacturing base, China is better able to produce some manufactured goods. Countries, by specialising in the products in which they are more efficient, can gain by trading these products for other products produced more efficiently elsewhere. These concepts of efficiency and specialisation lie behind two of the oldest theories of international trade, those of Absolute Advantage (Adam Smith) and Comparative Advantage (David Ricardo).

Absolute advantage

Suppose we have a two country/two good world, where the following holds true.

In *Table 3.14a*, country A is a more efficient producer of cars than country B and country B is a more efficient producer of wool than country A. Country A is said to have an absolute advantage in car production and country B is said to have an absolute advantage in wool production. If both countries had ten units of resource and devoted them equally to the production of wool and cars we would have as shown in *Table 3.14b*.

If the two countries allocate their resources on the basis of their absolute advantage and specialise completely in that product, we have as shown in *Table 3.14c*.

Table 3.14a   Absolute advantage

	Wool		Cars
With one unit of resource country A can produce	10 units	*or*	5 units
With one unit of resource country B can produce	15 units	*or*	2 units

Table 3.14b   Absolute advantage

	Wool		Cars
With one unit of resource country A can produce	50 units	*or*	25 units
With one unit of resource country B can produce	75 units	*or*	10 units
Total world production	125 units	*or*	35 units

Table 3.14c   Absolute advantage

	Wool		Cars
With one unit of resource country A can produce	zero units	*and*	50 units
With one unit of resource country B can produce	150 units	*and*	zero units
Total world production	150 units	*and*	50 units

Using the same amount of resources, total world production of both cars and wool increases through the role of specialisation based on absolute advantage.

Comparative advantage

Suppose, however, that we have the position as shown in *Table 3.15a* with regard to the outputs of countries A and B and their production of cars and wool.

Table 3.15a   Comparative advantage

	Wool		Cars
With one unit of resource country A can produce	20 units	*or*	5 units
With one unit of resource country B can produce	15 units	*or*	2 units

Table 3.15a shows that country A is a more efficient producer of both cars and wool. Is there a role for Country B in terms of trade and production? Ricardo noted that there would be. It all depends on comparative cost ratios. In country A, one unit of resource can produce either 20 units of wool or 5 units of cars. In producing 1 unit of wool in country A, country A would have to give up 5/20 units of cars. In other words, in country A, the production of 1 unit of wool leads country A to give up the opportunity of producing a 1/4 of a car. Similarly in country B, 1 unit of wool production leads to country B giving up the production of 2/15 units of a car. In terms of car production foregone, country B is a lower opportunity cost producer of wool. Looking at the analysis from the perspective of car production, this shows that 1 unit of car production in country A leads to 4 units of wool not being produced. In country B, 1 unit of car production leads to 7.5 units of wool production not being undertaken. We can say that Country A is a lower opportunity cost producer of cars. It has a comparative advantage in car production. Ricardo now suggests that countries should specialise in the commodity in which they have a comparative cost advantage, in this case Country A cars and country B wool.

As before, suppose each country has 10 units of resource and devotes half to car production and half to wool production before trade takes place. We get as shown in *Table 3.15b*.

If countries now specialise in the products in which they have comparative cost advantages we get as shown in *Table 3.15c* (note that country A does not specialise completely in car production).

Once again, total world production, from the same amount of resources, can be increased through the process of specialisation in products in which countries have a comparative cost advantage.

The advantages to the world from both the theories of Absolute and Comparative Advantage depend upon a number of assumptions. First that there are no trade barriers, second the world is characterised by production that is competitive, and, third, that it is easy to switch resources from car production to wool production and vice versa. In reality the world is not dominated by production patterns that are highly competitive but many markets are dominated by oligopolistic or monopolistic suppliers. Krugman (1987) has noted that even

Table 3.15b Comparative advantage

	Wool		Cars
Country A	100 units	*and*	25 units
Country B	75 units	*and*	10 units
Total production	175 units	*and*	35 units

Table 3.15c Comparative advantage

	Wool		Cars
Country A	40 units	*and*	40 units
Country B	150 units	*and*	zero units
Total production	190 units	*and*	40 units

under oligopolistic conditions the world can benefit from free trade. It is important to notice that these theories of free trade means the world is better off, not necessarily that all countries are better off.

In addition, these two theories tell us why trade takes place, but perhaps do not provide us with the complete picture as to why there has been a growth in international trade. The role of mutual benefit is certainly one driving force. Businesses and governments are unlikely to engage, voluntarily, in international trade if they do not expect either to improve their economic situation or achieve any material gain in return. Variations in the costs of production constitute another incentive for international trade to occur. In particular, international trade may lead to domestic firms achieving economies of scale which were not available in their domestic markets alone. Another factor is the globalisation of business through the ability to develop global brands such as Nike, Coca-Cola, Toyota and many others, and the desire by organisations to dominate not only their domestic markets but also global markets.

Changes that have taken place in international markets are of great importance. Many markets have recently become deregulated with reductions in the barriers to trade, and this has enhanced trading opportunities. New patterns of organisation and business location have emerged, including using foreign suppliers, foreign direct investments, joint ventures and international co-operation. These have arisen to obtain better access to markets and enhance competitiveness by exploiting specific local production factors such as favourable labour costs, labour skills and tax situations.

If trade is encouraged, the world may be better off in terms of total production of goods and services, economic growth and in terms of the efficiency with which resources are used. However, countries taking this 'specialisation' route could end up being dependent upon a small range of products or services. For example, many developing countries are dependent upon minerals, natural resources and/or agricultural products not only as their main item of production but also as their main export item. In this case, if another country is able to produce one of these items more cheaply or erects sufficiently strong trade barriers then the first country may see a large reduction in demand for its product or service. This could lead to balance of trade problems, reductions in sales and increases in unemployment. Countries may therefore consider producing items which they are less efficient at providing by using trade barriers.

Before we consider barriers to trade and the attempts made to reduce trade restrictions, let us appraise the importance of trade in the international arena.

Exports by country

The importance of international trade continues to increase, although there are differences between regions in the value of their intra-trade (trade between the members that make up a regional trading bloc) and extra-trade (trade between the members of the bloc and other countries outside of the trading bloc). There is evidence that intra-trade is becoming more important than extra-trade, as *Table 3.16* indicates.

The main target markets for EU exporters and importers are other EU markets and, in particular, those of neighbouring countries. This is especially true for the relatively smaller countries within the EU such as the Netherlands and Portugal. Larger EU members are more likely to possess a greater number of large-scale enterprises which can address global markets, thus their proportion of intra-EU trade tends to be lower. Other smaller EU countries such as Denmark, by being on the periphery of the EU, will have a greater proportion of their trade directed to countries fringing the EU. A similar picture emerges for NAFTA and ASEAN.

On a regional basis, Europe has seen its percentage share of world merchandise exports fall since the early 1990s, although it is still the dominant region (see *Table 3.17*). The share of world merchandise exports for the USA, Latin America, Central and Eastern Europe, Asia in general and more especially China has grown over the past decade. Japan, Africa and the Middle East, like Europe, have seen reductions in their percentage share, although not necessarily in absolute amounts of exports of manufactures.

Table 3.16	Merchandise trade of selected regional integration arrangements – share in total exports/imports			
Region	**1990**	**1995**	**2001**	**2007**
EU				
Intra-exports	64.9	64.01	61.85	68.1
Extra-exports	35.1	35.99	38.15	31.9
Intra-imports	63.0	65.23	60.89	64.9
Extra-imports	37.0	34.77	39.11	35.1
NAFTA				
Intra-exports	42.6	46.06	55.46	51.3
Extra-exports	57.4	53.94	44.54	48.7
Intra-imports	34.4	37.72	39.55	33.7
Extra-imports	65.6	62.28	60.45	66.3
ASEAN				
Intra-exports	20.1	25.52	23.46	25.0
Extra-exports	79.9	74.48	76.54	75.0
Intra-imports	16.2	18.89	22.77	24.5
Extra-imports	83.8	81.11	77.23	75.5

Source: WTO Statistics (2008) www.wto.org/english/res_e/statis_e/its2008_e/its08_toc_e.htm

Table 3.17	World merchandise exports by region, 2006 (percentage share)		
Country/region	**1990**	**2001**	**2006**
USA	11.6	12.2	8.8
Latin America	4.3	5.8	3.6
Western Europe	48.2	41.5	42.1
EU (15)	44.4	38.3	38.5*
Central/Eastern Europe	1.4	2.2	3.6
Africa	3.1	2.4	3.1
Middle East	4.1	4.0	5.5
Japan	8.5	6.7	5.5
China	1.8	4.4	8.2
Asia	21.8	25.0	27.8

Source: WTO (2007)
Note: *EU25.

Trade barriers

The evidence indicates that:

- there has been a growth in trade, especially over the last six decades;
- trade has become increasingly focused on particular trading blocs;

- there should be specialisation through trade;
- some countries may lose from trade as their particular historic advantages are eroded.

With regard to the last factor in particular, and because of the costs of economic change, countries have sought to protect their industries, using such devices as:

- subsidies – payments to reduce domestic prices down to, and sometimes below, world competitive levels;
- tariffs – taxes placed on imports to raise prices up to, and above, domestic prices;
- quotas – limits on the supply of imports into the domestic market;
- Voluntary Export Restraints (VERs) – agreements by an exporter to limit exports into a foreign market;
- using unfair practices such as producer and export subsidies and dumping products below cost to gain market entry;
- non-tariff barriers – these have increasingly come to the fore as trade barriers have been reduced, particularly those on manufactured goods. They include, limiting the free flow of goods on health and safety grounds, planning restrictions for setting up foreign companies, other forms of 'red tape', and limiting points of entry for imports and the like.

In contrast to merchandise exports, *Tables 3.18a* and *3.18b* indicate the importance of commercial services for the developed economies and the small representation of emerging and some transitional economies in this type of trade. It is not surprising that the developed world wants an agreement on services as part of the Doha Trade Round discussed later in this chapter.

All barriers to trade act to prevent the free flow of goods between countries. These types of measures may appear to protect a country's domestic firms but may not bring long-term advantage as other countries may respond. For example, the UK does well in terms of high-technology exports being above the EU average; however, import penetration in other sectors has grown appreciably. Conversely, import penetration into the Japanese market is low. This could imply that the Japanese do not wish to buy foreign imports, but it could also suggest that there are various barriers to entry into the Japanese market. Trade barriers also proliferate when the global economy slows and international trade tensions rise. The growth of tariffs leads to economic inefficiency, companies find it difficult to export their products and world activity levels fall. It was against this background of increased restrictions on

Table 3.18a	World exports/imports of commercial services by selected developed countries/regions, 2006 (world percentage share)

Country/region	Exports	Imports
USA	14.1	10.95
Brazil	0.67	1.11
Canada	1.83	2.56
EU (27)	27.3	24.01
UK	8.28	6.32
France	4.32	4.15
Germany	6.29	8.24
Japan	3.79	4.77
India	2.74	2.49
China	3.63	4.14

Source: WTO (2009)

Table 3.18b	World exports/imports of commercial services by selected emerging and transitional countries, 2006 (world percentage share)

Country/region	Exports	Imports
Algeria	0.07	0.15
Armenia	0.02	0.02
Azerbaijan	0.03	0.11
Bangladesh	0.02	0.09
Bolivia	0.01	0.03
Botswana	0.03	0.03
Cambodia	0.05	0.03
Moldova	0.02	0.02
Ukraine	0.41	0.35
Uzbekistan	0.03	0.01
Zambia	0.01	0.03

Source: WTO (2009)

Minicase 3.4	Europe accused of protectionism

Europe has been accused of going back on world leaders' pledge to avoid exacerbating the recession by throwing up new barriers against international trade, just a month after the London G20 summit.

Brussels will slap tariffs of up to 60 percent on imports of cut-price Chinese candles this month, in one of four measures identified by the World Bank president, Robert Zoellick, on a blacklist of anti-free trade decisions taken since the summit.

Haunted by the example of the 1930s, when leading powers became locked in a tit-for-tat protectionist battle that is widely blamed for precipitating the Great Depression, world leaders at the G20 in London promised to 'refrain from raising new barriers to investment or to free trade in goods and services' and 'rectify promptly any such measures'. But the World Bank believes Europe is among several G20 members, including the USA, Russia and India, which have taken trade-restricting steps since then.

Britain's retailers are furious about the import tax on candles, which will cost up to 60 percent of the value of the products. They say the measure protects German and Polish candle-makers – and estimate that the sanction, which will stay in place for five years, will cost retailers up to £10 million.

The EU has also imposed temporary 'anti-dumping' taxes, which are meant to protect against cut-price subsidised imports, on other products: Chinese wire, iron and steel pipes, and aluminium foil from Armenia, Brazil and China.

Source: Stuart (2009)

Questions

1 Why has Europe introduced a tax on candles?
2 What arguments could Europe use to justify its increased protectionism?

trade that emerged between (and during) the two world wars of the twentieth century that the General Agreement on Tariffs and Trade (GATT) was set up in 1946 in an attempt to reduce the tariff, the main form of trade restriction.

The General Agreement on Tariffs and Trade (GATT) and the World Trade Organisation (WTO)

There were eight rounds of GATT trade talks: the first five concentrated solely on reducing tariffs on manufactured goods. However, since the Geneva (Kennedy) Round in 1964 they had become increasingly complex. *Table 3.19* shows the subjects covered in the later GATT rounds. While GATT has been successful in reducing tariffs generally, countries have still sought to limit the free flow of trade via other means. Methods such as quotas, voluntary export restraints and non-tariff barriers – the use of red tape, government legislation, and health and safety factors – have come increasingly into play. Pivotal to the success of GATT was the most favoured nation (MFN) principle. A trade concession granted by country A to country B must also be granted to all other countries in the trade agreement. Thus one country cannot discriminate between their trading partners.

So was GATT successful? It certainly reduced tariffs, particularly on industrialised goods; world trade grew at an average of around 8 percent during the 1950s and 1960s (WTO, 2007), but slowing economies in the 1970s and 1980s and rising levels of unemployment saw countries seeking bilateral deals and using subsidies to protect sensitive areas such as agriculture. More importantly, the world had also shifted. The Western economies saw the trade in services as being more relevant for them. For the developed world access to the developing world agricultural markets was pivotal. These became the main areas for negotiation in the Uruguay Round.

A final conclusion to the Uruguay Round of GATT negotiations was agreed in December 1993 and involved 28 separate accords devised to extend fair trade rules to agriculture, services, textiles, intellectual property rights and foreign investment. Tariffs on industrial products were cut by more than a third and were eliminated entirely in 11 sectors. Non-tariff barriers were to be converted into tariff barriers which would subsequently be removed. And, most importantly, the members of GATT agreed its abolition and replacement with the WTO, starting from 1 January 1995.

The WTO differs from the GATT in a number of respects:

- The WTO has a greater global membership, now comprising over 153 member countries.
- It has a far wider scope than GATT, considering, for the first time, trade in services, intellectual property protection and investment.

Table 3.19	The later GATT trade rounds		
Year	**Place/name**	**Subjects covered**	**Countries**
1964–1967	Geneva (Kennedy Round)	Tariffs and anti-dumping measures	62
1973–1979	Geneva (Tokyo Round)	Tariffs, non-tariff measures, framework agreements	102
1986–1993	Geneva (Uruguay Round)	Tariffs, non-tariff measures, rules, services, intellectual property, dispute settlement, textiles, agriculture, creation of the WTO	123

- It is a fully-fledged international organisation in its own right, while GATT was basically a provisional treaty by an *ad hoc* Secretariat.
- It includes a package of instruments and measures to which all members are agreed, while GATT included a number of policy measures agreed to by a limited range of countries.
- It contains a much improved version of the original GATT rules.
- It reverses policies of protection in certain sensitive areas such as textiles and clothing, and voluntary export restraints which had been tolerated under GATT.
- It is to be the guardian of international trade, making sure that the agreements at the Uruguay Round are adhered to. It will also examine on a regular basis the trade regimes of individual member countries and try to reduce the level of trade disputes.
- It also provides technical assistance and training for developing countries.

Members of the WTO are also required to supply a range of trade statistics. Perhaps more importantly, it has a speedier trades dispute settlement mechanism, encouraging parties to go for arbitration rather than resorting to their own domestic trade policies. The WTO is not only about liberalising trade: it is possible that it can support trade barriers where there are issues of consumer protection, the restriction of diseases and where the environment needs protecting.

The WTO is currently host to new negotiations begun at Doha in Qatar in November 2001. Initially these talks were to be completed by 1 January 2005 but as yet no agreement has been reached. Part of the reason for the 2005 deadline was that many of the Uruguay Round agreements were due to finish around this time. Moreover, the new trade talks were also designed to consider issues that had arisen since the agreements and accords were signed in the previous (Uruguay) Round. Furthermore, the Doha trade talks give the global community an opportunity to enhance trade flows during a period of global economic uncertainty at the start of the new millennium.

The main areas under discussion at the Doha Round include:

- Agriculture – market access issues, export subsidies, domestic support for agriculture.
- Services – liberalisation of the trade in services.
- Market access for non-agricultural products – reduction of tariffs, reduction in tariff peaks, and tariff escalation.
- Trade-related aspects of intellectual property rights (TRIPS) – issues about generic drugs and the protection of medical discoveries.
- WTO rules on anti-dumping and subsidies.
- WTO rules on regional trade agreements.
- Trade-related investment measures (TRIMS).
- Trade and the environment.

However, the Doha Trade Round has as yet not been completed. At Geneva in 2008 the trade talks collapsed once again, although as of September 2009 there has been a further attempt at reviving these at a meeting in India.

The difficulties facing the Doha Round of trade negotiations are many. They include the fact that many more areas of trade liberalisation are under discussion, that discussion is being undertaken at a time of global economic slowdown when countries are less likely to give concessions, that various groups of countries have formed into broad consensus areas, such as developing countries, and they are refusing to give way on access to their markets for services without reciprocal access to developed country markets for agricultural goods (they also resent the level of subsidies used by the developing countries to protect their agricultural markets). The numbers of countries within the WTO has increased making negotiations more long-winded. Finally, there has been an increase in the number of bi-lateral trade agreements so that for some countries the benefits from trade can be achieved without a global agreement on trade. So what are the current stumbling blocks? One is farm import rules which allow countries to protect poor farmers by using tariffs on certain goods in the event of a price drop or a rapid increase in imports. India, China and the USA could not reach agreement on the tariff threshold when such action would occur.

Trading blocs

The GATT rounds were a series of multilateral trading agreements – trade agreements between different countries at the same time but in different geographical areas of the global community. These multilateral agreements have been paralleled by a process of regional trade agreements (see also *'Regional scale'* in *Chapter 7 section 7.22*). These trading agreements can be of various types such as:

- those that involve reducing tariffs between member countries;
- those that involve reducing tariffs among member countries together with a common external tariff against non-members;
- those that are similar to the second but promote much more commonality than trading arrangements and can cover other rules and regulations, such as common currencies and defence/social policies.

In the period 1948–1994 the GATT received 124 notifications of regional trading agreements relating to the trade in goods. Since the creation of the WTO in 1995, there have been over 300 additional arrangements covering both the trade in goods and services.

The EU is one of the oldest and best-known trading blocs. More recently the USA has become increasingly focused on the issue with the development of the NAFTA, signed in 1993, which includes the USA, Canada and Mexico. Chile has also opened negotiations with the USA. Some forecasters have suggested that, by the year 2010, a free trade area will exist that will cover the whole of the Americas. However, such predictions appear rather optimistic. A further, ambitious project is under way to create an Asia–Pacific Economic Co-operation Forum (APEC) to include America, Japan, China, Taiwan, Malaysia, Australia and other countries with Pacific coastlines. The EU is looking for closer ties with its Eastern European neighbours and there is even talk of a free trade area being set up between the EU and North America. See *Table 7.1*, in *Chapter 7*, for an overview of the membership of some major regional co-operation agreements.

There is some concern from the Director General of the WTO (2007) that the growth of regionalism has both positive and negative effects. On the one hand it increases the trade opportunities of those countries within the regional agreement, but, on the other hand, it may harm multilaterally based trading relationships. One clear complication is that the depth of integration in the various regional trading agreements differs. However, the WTO has also suggested that regional trading arrangements (RTA) can also complement the multilateral trading system, in that some regional agreements have gone further than multilateral agreements and it is this that has resulted in future multilateral agreements. Such was the case in the area of services, intellectual property, environmental standards, investment policies and competition policies. However, regional trade agreements are discriminatory, acting against countries outside the regional agreement, and they depart from the MFN principle which has been pivotal for the multinational trading system.

To what extent do regional free trade areas affect companies? We need to consider the concepts of trade creation and trade diversion. When a free trade area is set up it encourages trade between member countries. This is trade creation, and it occurs because previous barriers to trade will be reduced, giving each of the countries' industrial sectors reduced costs and therefore encouraging inter-country trade within the free trade area. Countries now outside the free trade area may find it more difficult to sell their products to countries which used to be outside the free trade area but are now inside the free trade area, since they often face external tariff barriers. Thus trade is diverted away from the countries outside the free trade area because the price of their products will increase as they face external tariffs, and countries inside the free trade area, which do not face any of these external tariffs, are more likely to trade between themselves. In addition, because a single country can negotiate different regional arrangements with other countries, it has important impacts on its domestic producers, since this increases the costs a firm faces with trying to meet multiple sets of trade rules.

There are also problems with rules of origin. Is a Japanese car made in Europe Japanese or European? The definition may depend on the proportion of parts that are provided by the European country. If it is deemed European then it can be exported to countries within the free trade area subject to no additional tariffs or quotas. On the other, if it is still said to be Japanese, it will face the external tariff barriers.

What appears to be gradually happening is the development of trading areas or zones. These might lead to significant reductions in trade barriers within the trading area that then get transmitted throughout the rest of the world in a kind of domino effect. The result of which is that many firms are likely to be winners. On the other hand trading blocs can lead to some firms being excluded from markets thereby damaging exports. The WTO rules say that trade agreements have to meet certain conditions, but the interpretation of these has proved to be controversial. The Regional Trade Agreements Committee of the WTO has, since 1995, failed to complete all its assessments of whether individual trade agreements conform to WTO provisions. Therefore it is still possible that some trading blocs have damaged the growth in world trade.

3.5 Exchange rate systems

Within the context of the growth (or potential decline) in trade we should consider how different exchange rate regimes affect business behaviour.

3.5.1 Fixed exchange rate

A fixed exchange rate is one which fixes the value of one country's currency against another. The are two key advantages of a fixed exchange rate system:

- The stability that it provides for businesses encourages long-term contractual arrangements between businesses.
- Since the exchange rate cannot be altered to restore a country's competitiveness, if it runs a balance of payments deficit, it imposes a disciplined fiscal and monetary policy, which means a tight grip on inflation.

3.5.2 Floating exchange rate

Alternatively it is possible to have a floating exchange rate – an exchange rate that responds to the market demand and supply of the currency. If there are differences between the demand for and supply of the domestic currency, the price of the currency, the exchange rate, should automatically adjust. Thus one of the great advantages of this type of exchange rate is that it does not require any government intervention; market forces undertake the adjustment. The problems with floating exchange rates are:

- increased uncertainties for traders, which may lead to a greater proportion of short-term contracts; and
- import prices rise then the balance of payments deteriorates, leading to a depreciation in the value of a currency. This restores the competitiveness of exports but further raises the price of imports, and these increased import costs can feed through into domestic inflation levels.

Evidence suggests that fluctuations in the exchange rate are more likely to have harmful effects on business investment. That is, both international investment and domestic investment may be reduced, with concomitant effects on exports, in general, and output in particular.

There are alternative variations on exchange rates such as managed floating – where a currency is allowed to float in the market but governments intervene at some point when a currency becomes too strong or too weak. Alternatively, there are adjustable par exchange rate systems. Here the exchange rate of a currency is fixed against another currency but its rate can be varied if a country runs persistent balance of payments deficits or surpluses. Adjustable par systems have been important since 1945 and two examples are worth mentioning – the Bretton Woods System that existed for most of the Western developed nations between 1945 and 1973 and the European Exchange Rate System that existed in Europe between 1979 and 2001.

3.5.3 The Bretton Woods System

Although widely referred to as being an era of fixed exchange rates, the period from 1945 to 1973 was in reality an adjustable par system. The value of a country's currency was tied (fixed) to the US dollar at a given rate – but some changes were permissible in certain circumstances. For example, the British pound was fixed against the dollar as was the French franc. This meant that the value of the pound sterling and the French franc were also fixed against one another. There was some small variation that a country could get around its fixed value (par value). If a country wanted to alter its fixed value it had to get permission from all the other members of the Bretton Woods System. In addition, the other part of the Bretton Woods System was that it was a gold-backed system, in that $35 could be exchanged for 1 ounce of gold (it is worthwhile noting that the value of gold in August 2009 was $1,000 an ounce).

The Bretton Woods System was characterised by a period of high levels of growth in the developed world economies, but its weakness lies in the fact that by the early 1970s the USA did not have enough gold to back the dollar and that a number of countries began to get into balance of payments difficulties because of their fixed exchange rates, and wanted to move to a floating exchange rate. The collapse of the Bretton Woods System led to a number of European countries such as Germany and France still wanting to retain a fixed exchange rate system – something called the European Snake – and subsequently for the development in Europe of the ERM. The ERM was the dominant exchange rate in Western Europe between 1979 and 1992. However this too collapsed in 1992, due to runs on individual countries' currencies, the problems of inflation that arose through German re-unification, and high levels of capital mobility.

The collapse of the ERM could be seen as another vindication that fixed exchange rate systems cannot work in the long term. Alternatively, the problems that follow from either a fixed or a flexible exchange rate can be removed if countries adopt a single currency – something that will be considered in section 3.6 'European integration', later.

It should be noted that the decision to adopt one exchange rate system in preference to another may not be taken purely on economic grounds, but may be the result of the need for closer political ties.

3.5.4 Current exchange rate systems

Although 16 countries within the EU have adopted a single currency, and more are likely to follow, it has been suggested that, until recently, the world has moved, *de facto*, to what has been called a Bretton Woods 2 exchange rate regime. This is very different from the Bretton Woods 1 System described earlier. It is not a gold-backed system but the US dollar is still pivotal. In Bretton Woods 2, a number of countries have fixed their currencies against the

US dollar to reduce inflationary expectations (many South America economies, such as Argentina, have done this). Others have fixed their currencies against the US dollar at artificially low rates so that they can become export competitive (e.g. China). The result has led on the one hand to an export boom for China and for the USA to have a large trade deficit. To finance this trade deficit (in fact the USA has a twin deficit to finance, that of trade and of public borrowing) the USA needs to issue treasury bills. These have been bought by the Chinese and other South East Asian countries, thereby encouraging the USA to continue to keep importing and for China to have a willing market in which to sell its exports.

Where are the Europeans in all of this? The relative strength of the EU as a trading bloc (its exports exceed its imports), means that the value of the euro has strengthened against the US dollar. If the euro is strengthening against the US dollar then it is also strengthening against all those currencies which have fixed themselves against the US dollar. Increasingly the EU will find itself becoming less competitive in price terms and overseas foreign exports will become increasingly price-competitive in the EU market. To stop this from happening, the EU will need to prevent the euro from strengthening too much against the US dollar. Therefore, the EU/Eurozone is buying into this new Bretton Woods 2. We now have a series of countries that have fixed their exchange rates against the US dollar for a whole variety of reasons. It is because of this that the arrangement has been called the Bretton Woods 2 system. Such a system can be extremely fragile because the purchase of US Treasury Bills (used to finance their twin deficits on trade and their public accounts) can only continue by countries that have been growing through export-led growth. If this falls then their ability to purchase US Treasury bills diminishes and the US economy will go into recession. Whether a soft landing rather than a large re-adjustment is required is a moot point.

3.6 European integration

The establishment of the European Economic Community (EEC) in the late 1950s was a major step towards helping trade within the European 'six' at the time. The widening of membership to the 12 member states by the early 1980s, the further reductions in trade barriers and the setting up and development of pan-European forums appeared to move the major Western European countries to a stronger economic position. In the 1980s there were, however, signs to suggest that the EU 12 were experiencing some difficulties with their economies. First, growth rates had begun to slow and, second, unemployment levels had begun to rise. There was also a distinct lack of co-operation between Community members and a weakness of common policies. Since a number of countries appeared to be pulling in different directions, the European Community appeared to be paralysed. In addition, the massive technological changes that had taken place in the world (see *Chapter 4*) had, to some extent, left Europe behind. It was importing increasing amounts of high technology products. The Community's external position was also, to some extent, weakening and it was becoming increasingly dependent on foreign suppliers. The fragmented home market in the Community was seen by many as a main reason for this development and there was a desire to speed up integration between the various member countries. It was argued that a Single European Market (SEM) would stimulate the scale of production, marketing and R&D, and also strengthen competition, enhancing the efficiency and competitiveness of European industry. However, to get to this stage, the European Community needed to tackle the various barriers that existed within the potential EU market. These included:

- physical barriers such as form-filling and the cost of keeping frontier posts to govern goods and people;
- fiscal barriers – differences in VAT and excise duties distorted trade patterns;

- technical barriers – obstacles to the free movement of goods, services, labour and capital; throwing open to competition the bidding for local or national government contracts (public procurement).

However, it was feared that, once the shackles on markets within the EU had been reduced, this could lead to increased social problems as organisations switched their production to cheaper sites. Therefore, to deal with the social element of the SEM programme, a social charter was drawn up. The Social Chapter of the social charter was originally set to cover a range of social issues including:

- employment rights;
- minimum wages;
- the right to training;
- collective bargaining;
- freedom of association;
- health and safety.

Because of the controversy this raised the final proposal was much watered down, leaving many of the social issues to be decided by the individual nation states, rather than the Commission.

A further condition deemed as necessary for the successful creation of the 'internal market' was a change in the Community decision-making procedures, which until then required unanimous decisions in the Council of Ministers. This condition was met by the adoption of the Single European Act (SEA) in 1987, whereby in matters concerning the internal market qualified majority voting was permitted (see *Chapter 7*).

3.6.1 The impact of the Single European Market

Assessing the overall impact of the SEA is difficult, since there are many dynamic effects to consider, from such diverse sources as changes in the technological and social environments to the expansion of the EU to include many more members. In other words, as Kay (1993) and Swann (1992) noted, it is likely to have effects in the long term as well as in the short term. One major hope was that the removal of barriers between markets was expected to encourage competition.

The EC made an evaluation of the SEM in its report, 'The Impact and Effectiveness of the Single Market', as early as October 1996. It should be noted when considering the results from this report that a number of the pieces of legislation pertaining to the Single Market did not come into force until 1994 or 1995. Even in those early days, however, the report noted the following effects:

- Both intra-EU trade (trade between EU countries) and extra-EU trade (trade between the EU and the rest of the world) had been boosted. Despite predictions that the SEM would lead to 'fortress Europe', this did not appear to have taken place. In addition the SEM appeared to have accentuated intra-industry trade.
- There was an increase in both domestic and cross-border mergers and acquisitions. There is some indication of increasing concentration ratios across Europe, but on a national level the growth in some European countries' industries appears to be much greater relative to other countries. This is particularly the case in Germany and France compared with the UK. Thus the SEM appears to have reinforced different industry structures in some countries rather than equalising it between member countries.
- There has been a growth of FDI into the EU.
- On a macroeconomic level, investment appears to have risen by 1 percent more than it would have done without the SEM, inflation is 1 percent to 1.5 percent less, and income between 1.1 percent and 1.5 percent higher. Employment is estimated to have grown by somewhere between 300,000 and 900,000.

- For businesses, the view was that the SEM had removed a number of obstacles to cross-border transactions and that greater opportunities were apparent. This level of approval was stronger for manufacturers than services, and larger companies compared with smaller ones.

The SEM did appear to lead to a major restructuring of European industry through an upsurge in merger and takeover activity. This is particularly the case for cross-border mergers between EU companies.

Although the SEM has removed a number of barriers, a number still exist through culture, tradition and consumption patterns. At the same time there are still gaps in the legislation, such as the issue of European company law and the harmonisation of taxation. In addition, some of the legislation has still to be enforced, adopted or implemented. To complete the SEM also requires liberalisation and deregulation of markets such as those for airlines, transport in general, telecommunications and utilities. While governments control these sectors or limit competition with domestic firms, then the effects of the SEM may be limited. A further obstacle to a single market is that of different national currencies and it is to this issue that we now turn.

3.6.2 Maastricht and beyond

The SEA of 1987 can be viewed as a major step towards an economically united Europe, but it was not the ultimate step. If Europe is to be truly united then some argue that there is a need for both political and economic union. Some issues relating to political union are discussed in *Chapter 7* of this book. On the economic side, the Maastricht Treaty gave an impetus to the move towards economic union, as it contained a proposal for a Europe-wide single currency. This move towards monetary union sought to co-ordinate both monetary and economic policies of member states. Although a full analysis of the steps in the process is beyond the scope of this book, it is important to note that European Monetary union has in many ways been achieved – although many exceptions and complications remain. Twelve countries completed the step to complete monetary union, with the euro coming into general use in January 2002. Although Sweden, Denmark and the UK met most, if not all, of the criteria, they chose not to be members of the first wave. The number of countries using the European Single Currency has increased since 2002, with Slovenia joining in 2007, Cyprus and Malta in 2008 and Slovakia in 2009. The euro is now the currency of some 329 million people.

There are a number of consequences arising from the adoption of the single currency. National currencies for those member states (the French franc, the Deutschmark, the lire, the drachma and so on) have been replaced by a single currency accepted in each state as its domestic currency. Monetary policy, which was under the jurisdiction of each country, was transferred to the European Central Bank based in Frankfurt – which is responsible for setting interest rates for the whole of the Eurozone. Fiscal policy (taxation) is still in the hands of national governments, but is now subject to some common policies and restrictions – the so-called 'Stability Pact'. It is also notable that each national government has lost the ability to use changes in its exchange rates as a competitive tool. These ideas are discussed in more detail below.

3.6.3 The impact of EMU on government economic policy

Monetary policy has become the concern of the European Central Bank (ECB) rather than being the responsibility of each nation's monetary authority. This means that an individual country will not have the ability to use interest rates for any other economic requirement such as to reduce domestic unemployment or control domestic inflation. However, it is debatable as to how much of a loss this is in reality. To what extent would a country that is not within the single currency have the ability to set interest rates which diverge greatly from those set by the single currency bloc? It was notable that during the ERM crisis in the early 1990s UK interest rates were forced to respond to those being set at that time in Germany. Thus, even if a member of the EU stays out of a single currency its interest rates may well need to respond to those being set by the ECB.

As monetary policy has been lost as a management tool, for each of the individual governments and monetary authorities this leaves fiscal policy as the only form of discretionary economic policy available. The Maastricht Agreement set out targets for fiscal policy expenditure as a prerequisite for joining the single currency and the worry about fiscal mismanagement resulted in 1996 in a proposal to establish a new EU 'Stability Council'. This was confirmed in the Treaty of Amsterdam which set up a council to monitor individual nations' fiscal policy expenditure after entry into a single currency, to make sure that fiscal policy guidelines were not breached. If these fiscal policy guidelines were breached, then the Stability Council would have the power to impose fines on any individual country if it takes more than a year to address its fiscal policy difficulties. Without such a stability pact it is possible that excessive borrowing by one or more of the members of EMU could force up interest rates for all other members.

A third problem with a single currency is that a member country faces a loss of discretionary exchange rate policy – the ability of a country to set its own competitive exchange rate. Before a single currency came into existence a country could use its exchange rate as a 'safety valve' if its economy became uncompetitive, say, due to some internal shock, such as a rapid decline in competitiveness of one sector of its economy. Under a single currency an internal shock of this type could only be solved by the use of massive EU fiscal transfers (regional policy).

Finally, major concerns have been expressed regarding the whole process of moving towards and remaining within the single currency. Concern has been voiced that the financial and monetary elements of the economy have been prioritised and very little emphasis has been given to unemployment. In fact, as mentioned above, in an attempt to hit the targets set out at Maastricht, the European economies have been operating tight fiscal policies which have resulted in growing levels of unemployment and labour unrest. For example, the series of strikes in France and Italy in 2002/3 concerning the financing of pensions can be partly explained by the difficulty both governments were facing through not being able to increase their government expenditure due to the growth and stability pact. In addition, for some countries the role of privatisation has taken on a higher profile as they seek to balance their government accounts. If countries need to be more convergent in their performances, as expressed through the Maastricht criteria, then any fudging of the criteria for entry will make the member countries of a single currency less convergent and thereby weaken the strength of the euro.

3.6.4 The impact of the European single currency on business

The impact on business can be looked at from a number of perspectives: first, from the point of view of businesses in countries within the Eurozone; and, second, from the perspective of businesses in European countries which stay outside of the single currency along with the position of businesses from countries which are non-European but which are active in European markets.

The impact on businesses inside the Eurozone

From a purely economic standpoint, a single currency appears to be attractive for at least some of the larger countries within the EU. A single currency removes transaction costs (the costs of converting one currency into another), which are estimated to average at 0.4 percent of EU GDP. This may be especially important for small and medium-sized businesses. However, it is likely that competitive pressures will increase due to price transparency. This could also lead to organisations reviewing their business strategy and could encourage innovation as companies try to stave off competition. Moreover, such price transparency could force companies to put an end to differential pricing across the EU.

One of the main benefits from a single currency comes through the greater development of intra-EU trade and through its greater certainty this should boost investment (FDI and domestic), growth and jobs. In the case of FDI a single currency should lead to greater market size/potential and this should encourage larger amounts of FDI.

Set against the benefits outlined above were a number of costs of transition to a single currency. There are the costs of conversion (currencies, machines) and the need to change pricing points. Along with price transparency there will also be wage transparency. Therefore, employees will know whether companies in the same sector but in different countries are offering higher wages.

The impact on businesses outside the Eurozone

Countries outside the single currency bloc may suffer from reduced amounts of FDI and the spillover effects this provides to their domestic industries. Companies basing themselves in the UK, for example, will face exchange rate risks not experienced by those in countries within the euro area. In fact it is possible that the pound may become more volatile – it has, during 2009, weakened appreciably against the euro.

Even though the UK was not in the first wave, some foreign companies, notably Siemens and Daimler-Benz, have arranged for their UK suppliers to price and charge for things in euros. The euro has also been pushed through the supply chain in many other organisations. Marks & Spencer will even accept the euro at its cash desks, as will many other major retail stores in most of the popular tourist sites. Thus non-participation will not shield the UK from the effect of EMU. Many companies will have prepared irrespective of the UK government's strategy – in terms of their technical systems, financial systems and even corporate strategy. Moreover, UK companies are affected by the way in which their European competitors change their strategy. The euro is also meant to encourage better integration of national markets and in some industries this will mean restructuring.

The operation of the euro has already led to further co-ordination of economic policies. Nonetheless, in the area of tax harmonisation, the bringing into line of the different tax rates operated by the EU countries is still a long way from fruition, although it is, perhaps, becoming more of a possibility. This may not result in unified rates of tax, but is likely to lead to common tax bands and rules. In this scenario, the UK would be expected to adopt whatever the prevailing rules are among the Euro-27, even without changing to using the euro as its currency.

The development of a single currency for Europe, therefore, poses many opportunities and threats for businesses, the outcome of which will not be equally borne by all sectors of the business community. For countries such as the UK, Sweden and Denmark, the costs to industry of remaining outside the single currency may dent competitiveness.

3.6.5 Enlargement of the EU

Over the decade since the start of the new millennium the expansion of the EU has continued to encompass 27 nations with others such as Croatia, Serbia, Bosnia, Macedonia, Ukraine and Turkey seeking entry in the future.

These new entrants brought a number of costs and benefits to the EU. The economies of the countries of Central and Eastern Europe were twice as agricultural as the EU15 and two and a half times poorer in terms of GDP per head. The combined GDP of the ten countries that joined in 2004 is less than that of the Netherlands; it will take up to 30 years for the newcomers to bridge the economic gap between themselves and the poorest member of the previous EU15.

East–West integration should expand the newcomers' opportunities much more than those for the EU15. Trade with these states (excepting Malta and Cyprus) is dominated by

Germany from the EU, but overall export trade with them accounts for around 5 percent of total EU15 exports. Looking outwards from these countries, the EU15 account for approximately 60 percent of their export trade.

Further costs to the original EU15 can been seen in terms of the level of agricultural and regional support which they hope to gain from the current members. However, proposals put forward by the EU15 in March 1999 and in June 2003 are seen as, first, a way to reduce agricultural expenditure as part of the total EU budget and, second, a way to cope with the costs the new entrants will bring with their large agricultural sectors.

The new entrants also require large amounts of regional funding, given that many, if not all, of their regions have GDPs per head lower than 75 percent of the EU average. The advantages for business may be great. The now 27 member countries total over 500 million consumers in the EU single market. Europe is the world's biggest unified market in trade, services and investment – larger than the USA and Japan combined. However, lower production costs in the new member states could place pressures on manufacturers in the UK, France and Germany. In addition, because it has not always been easy to develop policy agreements for the 15 countries of the EU, the added problems of an EU with 27 countries could mean a move away from the need to get total agreement on policy decisions to one where majority decision making occurs in a much wider range of areas than currently operates. The need to change the rules and procedures can be seen in the issues surrounding and ratifying the Lisbon Treaty (see *Chapter 7*), which was finally ratified in November 2009, almost two years after it was signed.

3.7 Commodity prices

The globalisation of trade, the relative success of GATT and the WTO, changes in technology, the impact of containerisation of freight shipping, and the growth of FDI have resulted in greater consumer choice, many products becoming available all the year round, increased specialisation of production and increasingly lower real prices. All these forces together indicate that the countries of the world have become increasingly inter-linked and dependent on each another. This is most noticeable when we examine global commodity prices. No better example of this can be seen than in the oil market. In July 2008 the price of oil reached US$147 a barrel but has more recently (September 2009) fallen to US$67 a barrel. These fluctuations in oil prices can be seen in the prices of other commodities such as gold and foodstuffs. The IMF (2008) reported that commodity price index had increased by 10 percent in 2008 and by 30 percent over the 2006–2007 period. The World Bank (2009) also noted that between early 2003 and mid-2008 traded food prices increased by 138 percent. So what causes these changes in global commodity prices?

Partly they are reflection of global demand and supply conditions (see *Chapter 6*). In the case of food prices, the growth in the world population is one explanation; if this is coupled with rises in affluence in developing economies the result is a greater demand for higher protein food such as meat and dairy products, and this leads to increases in the demand for grain and protein feeds. On the supply side the higher price of crude oil has increased the cost to farmers in terms of fuel prices and this will also impact on the higher prices for fertilisers. These increases in costs have been passed on to consumers. Higher oil prices will also have added to transport costs, but the price of some foodstuff is linked to the move towards the growth of bio-fuels as a means to reduce oil dependency and to limit global warming. Here some of the most productive land has been taken out of growing foodstuffs and this has reduced supply. In addition, some speculators trying to anticipate what might happen to food prices have bought up future supplies also, increasing demand in the short term. Furthermore, the growth in arable land has not kept pace with the growth in population, crop rate yields are under pressure, and global warming and weather changes have also impacted upon supply. The result is that some developing economy populations may feel squeezed.

It might have been possible that inventory levels of foodstuffs would have compensated for short-term fluctuations in demand and supply, but in many areas of the food market inventories have been eroded. The global recession of 2008/9 may have helped to reduce the prices associated with many foodstuffs; nonetheless, the return of many economies to growth by the start of 2010 will see further upward pressure on food prices.

For other commodities such as minerals, oil and gold, there has been an historic link of their prices with economic activity. Prices tend to decline as global recessions occur and rise during boom periods (IMF, 2008). For example, in the growth period of 2003–2007, the global price of tin and copper soared. However, in the current recession, the price of many minerals has not declined. Why not? Mineral prices do reflect supply and demand conditions; however, there is a dual nature to such commodities. They are also a store of value. Thus, as the US dollar has depreciated in world markets and real interest rates have fallen, the attractiveness of commodities has been enhanced because of their asset properties. The price of gold in September 2009 exceeded US$1,000 an ounce. If this is also coupled with the strength of demand from some emerging economies such as that of India and China, and bottlenecks in rapid capacity expansion, then higher commodity prices may well be here to stay and will impact more unequally on resource-dependent countries, while resource-rich countries will benefit.

For oil, the decline in price down to US$67 a barrel in September 2009, as the world recession took hold, may benefit oil importing countries, and there may have been a change in the buying habits of some countries, such as the USA, switching from petrol-guzzling cars, as the previous price spike in oil prices caused them to switch to smaller cars, but the price is unlikely to fall much further since the Organisation of Petroleum Exporting Countries (OPEC) is attempting to keep supply more in line with global demand.

The further repercussions of higher prices for both minerals, oil and foodstuffs has been for these to impact on domestic country inflation. The risk that this could lead to higher inflationary expectations has influenced global monetary policies, and slowed the growth in some advanced developed economies. Higher commodity prices will also impact on the trade balances of many countries and in the case of foodstuff some countries have reduced import barriers and increased export taxes as a way to maintain adequate domestic food supplies. Thus, commodity prices are a further example of the globalisation of the macro-economic environment and countries need to prepare for a world where global commodity prices are likely to cost a lot more than they did in the past.

Minicase 3.5	Sugar the new oil as prices soar

The price of sugar on global commodity markets has doubled since the beginning of the year and is close to a 28-year high as hedge funds and speculators jostle to bet on the possibility of an international shortage of the world's favourite natural sweetener.

For financiers seeking adrenaline-driven price lurches, sugar has become the new oil. Historically, raw sugar has traded at between 10 and 12 US cents per pound at the New York Board of Trade. But the price briefly touched 24.85 cents last month, its highest since 1981, and sugar is now hovering around the 23 cent mark. The rise has come amid a broader commodity boom. Metals and energy rose sharply today as the dollar weakened and global stockmarkets moved higher.

There are some solid underlying reasons for the upward lurch in the price of raw sugar. Heavy rain has disrupted milling in the world's largest producer of sugar, Brazil, where a sizeable portion of sugarcane has been diverted from food use into ethanol fuel. Meanwhile the biggest consumer of sugar, India, has had a dismal monsoon season and has gone from being a net exporter of sugar to an importer.

'The key premise has really come from Brazil and India,' said Sudakshina Unnikrishnan, a commodities analyst at Barclay's Capital. 'The bulk of the problem lies in inclement weather conditions.' The London-based International Sugar Organisation predicts that global consumption of sugar will outstrip production by 9 million tonnes next year, forcing food companies and governments to dig into stockpiles. In the USA, snack manufacturers including Mars, Nestlé and Krispy Kreme Doughnuts urged the Obama administration to relax import controls, warning the USA could 'virtually run out of sugar'.

Experts say the spectre of a rapidly moving price has attracted the attention of hedge funds seeking to make a short-term speculative buck. Tom Mikulski, a senior strategist at the futures broker Lind-Waldock in Chicago, said: 'When a market starts to heat up like sugar has, you do see a lot of trend-following funds jumping on the bandwagon.' In the City, on the trading floor of the derivatives exchange NYSE Liffe, the volume of trades in white sugar contracts jumped by 40 percent from 145,554 in August to 204,662 in September.

A political outcry over speculation pushing up oil prices last year has encouraged some funds to shift their attention to agriculture futures – in typically lower-profile, less-noticed trading pits. 'It doesn't draw the attention of regulatory authorities like maybe energy does,' said Steve Platt, a futures strategist at Archer Financial Services in Chicago. 'There has been some movement of index funds into a heavier concentration on sugar.'

Source: Clark (2009)

Questions

1 What factors have led to the rise in sugar prices?
2 How might higher sugar costs affect industries and consumers?

3.8 Corporate social responsibility

Increased globalisation, the increasing growth and influence of multinational companies, the reduction in trade barriers, the globalisation of brands and the shifting of global production are not cost free. Often they embody aspects of Corporate Social Responsibility (CSR) at a variety of levels. This was not always the case. (See *Chapter 6 section 6.6 'Organisational agendas'* for further discussion of these ideas.)

Multinational companies may shift production to countries where safety standards and environmental regulations are either very lax or non-existent. The Bhopal incident would be a good example of this. Products that are deemed as hazardous in the West have been sold to third world countries, such as cigarettes with higher tar contents and radioactive milk from the area around Chernobyl. Other aspects of harmful Western company behaviour can arguably be seen with the 'Green Revolution' which raised crop yields but at the same time depressed crop prices. Such a revolution also relied heavily on fertilisers that were produced by Western companies. Even biotechnology may find replacements for traditional third world export crops and the impact of logging, to satisfy the Western demands for hard wood, and its effect on local agriculture and wildlife are well known.

However, by late 1990, multinational companies and Western governments decided (or perhaps they were pushed) into behaving more responsibly with regard to the international environment. For some companies, at least, this move towards greater engagement with the principles of CSR was seen as way of aligning themselves with the changing nature of consumers – and it could be used to provide them with a competitive advantage. Within their domestic economies, regional trading blocks and internationally, they made attempts to recognise their social responsibilities and make CSR a part of their identities. In particular, socially responsible firms sought ways to contribute to social and environmental objectives, integrating these into their business operations in terms of their relations with stakeholders. This might include, addressing issues of 'sweatshop labour', using appropriate technologies, training workers, improving workers' conditions of employment in overseas markets and helping with health and safety issues. In the labour market, CSR may increase labour productivity, reduce days off through sickness, and lessen labour turnover. It may also enhance business profits, leading to further investment overseas. Good CSR makes companies attractive to work for, may make them key organisations for investors who are looking for CSR-friendly portfolios of shares and improve the quality of work produced. Consumers are also looking for social and eco-labelling of products, and may be willing to pay a higher premium for this. Therefore, CSR through its use and the reporting and auditing of this can have a major impact on the success of globalised organisations.

3.9 Conclusion

Business has always been aware of the impact of the economic environment on its performance and behaviour but, whereas businesses would have paid heed to changes in their own domestic economy, the post-war years have increasingly seen markets becoming internationalised so that it is now changes in the international economic environment that may have more impact. Some of these changes, such as alterations in environmental legislation, agreements about the provisions for labour and corporate tax changes, have a direct impact on organisations; other changes alter the environment in which the firm exists and, although not aimed at organisations directly, potentially have greater influence on their behaviour.

Over the last two decades closer co-operation between countries in pursuing macroeconomic policies and the internationalisation of markets has been evident. Such moves require co-ordinated actions among countries. Of course, not all industries are uniformly affected by international macro policy changes – companies which undertake much of their business in the domestic market are perhaps less affected by exchange rate changes than those which are exporting a proportion of their output abroad, but they may be affected by imports. In addition, as discussed in other chapters, the impacts of technology are not equally borne by the different sectors in our society. Nonetheless, businesses cannot ignore the changes that are taking place in their domestic, regional and international environments. If they do so it is highly likely that in the longer term their position in the market will be weakened to such an extent that their businesses are placed at a competitive disadvantage.

Summary of main points	We have seen that organisations are influenced by the many forces at play in the wide economic environment and therefore need to be aware of these forces and to be able to react to any changes. The main points made are that:

- Changes in GDP have been used as a measure of economic growth, although they only measure the measurables.
- Governments have four main economic goals: a high level of growth, a strong balance of payments, a low level of inflation and low unemployment.
- The goals of the government may conflict.
- Governments may steer the economy and smooth economic cycles through the use of fiscal and monetary policy.
- The industrial structure of an economy is not static but open to continual change.

- Many Western industrial economies are seeing a shift away from producing manufactured goods towards providing services.
- Growth can bring with it improvements in real incomes and a greater choice of goods and services.
- Growth also brings with it costs to society.
- Inflation can be caused in a number of ways – through excess demand in the product market, through increased costs of the factors of production and through slack monetary policy.
- Inflation causes both internal and external problems. It may make exports less competitive and therefore imported goods more competitive with domestically produced goods. Internally to the economy it harms those groups on fixed incomes, can cause disruption in the labour market, can lead to even higher levels of expected inflation and favours debtors rather than creditors.
- Government expenditure plays a key role in the functioning of all countries. In the pursuit of the targets for monetary union, unemployment is higher than it would have been in the 12 single currency countries.
- The UK economy still has a number of skill gaps which prevents the economy operating efficiently.
- Countries have become more open, and this has stimulated international trade.
- Evidence suggests an increasing establishment of trade blocs which could both create and divert trade.
- Exchange rates can affect trade volumes and competitiveness.
- Changes in commodity prices often reflect the international forces of supply and demand.
- Internationalisation of both production and consumption raises issues of corporate social responsibility.

Minicase 3.6	Five key points on the road to a new global financial deal

International institutions

While any G20 summit is almost certain not to create a new 'Bretton Woods' System overnight, countries led by Britain and France want an enhanced role for the International Monetary Fund (IMF) to improve surveillance of complex financial markets and help prevent such excesses building up in future. They also favour increased funding for the IMF.

Global regulation

There is a widespread recognition that regulation of financial markets has been far too weak in recent years. Authorities have been increasingly aware of the excesses building up in such markets, like those for mortgage-backed securities, but have failed to increase regulation.

Recapitalisation of banks

This is already happening around the world, with most countries following the British model. The US government announced changes to its $700 billion bail-out for its banking system, under which it will buy fewer toxic mortgage-backed securities from banks and instead recapitalise banks by buying shares.

The G20 meeting on 24 September 2009 discussed a possible response to the problem of banks running out of capital – which could be based on a Spanish-style system whereby banks have to hold a bigger capital cushion in good times, which they can draw upon in bad times.

Fiscal/monetary policy

One aim of the G20 summit was to co-ordinate global action on interest rates in an effort to pump some life back into the world economy and avoid deflation, or falling prices.

New World Order

Recent decades have been dominated by Western industrialised nations grouped together under the banner of the Group of Seven, but the Pittsburgh Summit billed as G20, marked a significant shift. Large-scale economies such as China, India and Brazil now have a place at the table and are demanding a much greater say in global economic oversight because they consider the old 'Anglo-Saxon' free-market dogma to be dead. There is a new world order.

Questions

1 How has the internationalisation of the global economy led to countries to consider Bretton Woods 2?
2 To what extent has the economic power shifted in the international economy? Why?

Discussion questions

1 What can governments do to stimulate growth in their economies?
2 Why is there a difference between male and female participation in the labour market? Will this difference be expected to change over time?
3 Should the UK be worried about its relatively poorly skilled workforce?
4 What are the implications of the growth in trading blocs for export-oriented businesses?
5 What factors lie behind changes in global commodity prices? How do commodity price changes feed through to inflation?
6 Why have the current trade talks (the Doha Round) been difficult to bring to a satisfactory conclusion?

Further reading/sources of information

(www.cia.gov/library/publications/the-world-factbook/) This site provides a useful source of international economics data on a regional and country level.

El-Agraa, A.M. (2007) *The European Union: Economics and Policies,* 8th edn. Cambridge: Cambridge University Press. One of the best texts if you are interested in the European Union. It has some useful statistical tables but on the whole concentrates on policy changes. The book is large but worth the effort.

European Commission (http://europa.eu.int/comm/economy_finance) This website is one of many at the European Commission. Although not always that easy to navigate, it provides a range of important financial statistics.

European Economy, Supplement A – Economic Trends (various years) Produced by the European Commission both in hard copy and online, usually addressing a theme appropriate to the European economies, such as mergers and acquisitions. Supplement C covers issues to do with enlargement.

Griffiths, A. and Wall, S. (2007) *Applied Economics,* 11th edn. Harlow: Prentice Hall. A text that covers a wide range of economics areas from a national, regional and international perspective.

International Labour Organisation (**www.ilo.org/**) The site of the International Labour Organisation (ILO) contains good data on all aspects of the labour market for a wide range of countries. The ILO also produces some good economic analysis of labour market issues.

International Monetary Fund (**www.imf.org**) The International Monetary Fund website provides a range of economic reports and up-to-date economic statistics on the global economy.

OECD (**www.oecd.org/**) The OECD website covers the main industrialised countries. It provides a wide range of economic statistics and forecasts on these economies. It is good for most aspects of country data.

Piggott, J. and Cook, M. (2006) *International Business Economics: A European Perspective,* 3rd edn. Basingstoke: Palgrave. A book that covers not only the main policy issues in the EU but also both European and international business.

Sloman, J. and Wride, A. (2009) *Economics,* 7th edn. Harlow: Prentice Hall. A good introduction to economics. Wide range of short cases but a book that covers a lot more than just the internal macroeconomy.

UK government (**www.open.gov.uk**) This is the UK government's website. It enables you to search both for economic reports and links to their other websites that provide good quality data on the UK economy and sometimes a comparison with other major trading partners.

United States Department of Agriculture (**www.ers.usda.gov/**) Good source of information about the global supply and demand factors behind agricultural products.

World Trade Organisation (**www.wto.org/**) This is the website of the World Trade Organisation. It contains reports on trade disputes, regional trade relations and a wide range of good quality data on trade statistics.

References

Beckerman, W. (1985) How the Battle Against Inflation was Really Won. *Lloyd's Bank Review,* 15 January, 1–12.

Begg, D. (1995) The Anatomy of a Recovery: The UK Since 1992. *The Begg Update,* No. 5, Summer.

Burda, M. and Wyplosz, C. (2009) *Macroeconomics: A European Text,* 5th edn. Oxford: Oxford University Press.

Campbell, M., Baldwin, S., Johnson, S., Chapman, R., Upton, A. and Walton, F. (2001) *Skills in England 2001,* Policy Research Institute, Leeds Metropolitan University.

Clark, A. (2009) Sugar the New Oil as Prices Soar, *The Guardian,* 6 October.

Cook, M. (1996) Economic Growth and the UK Economy. *Economics and Business Education,* Summer, 52–57.

Cook, M. and Healey, N. (2001) *Supply Side Policies,* 4th edn. Oxford: Heinemann.

Davies, L. (2009) German Jobs Saved by Short-time Working Subsidies Says IMF, *The Guardian,* 14 September.

Economic Help (2007) www.economicshelp.org/econ.html

Friedman, M. (1977) Inflation and Unemployment. *Journal of Political Economy,* 85(3), 451–472.

Higham, D. and Tomlinson, J. (1982) Why do Governments Worry About Inflation? *National Westminster Bank Review,* May, 2–13.

IMF (2008) Commodity Price Moves and the Global Economic Slowdown. *IMF Research Magazine,* New York, available from www.imf.org/external/pubs/ft/survey/so/2008/res632008a.htm

Kay, N. (1993) Mergers, Acquisitions and the Completion of the Internal Market in Hughes, K.S. (ed.) *European Competitiveness.* Cambridge: Cambridge University Press.

Krugman, P. (1987) Is Free Trade Passé? *Economic Perspectives,* 1(1), 131–144.

Leitch Report (2006) Prosperity for All in the Global Economy – World Class Skills. HMSO, Norwich.

Matthews, R.C.O., Feinstein, C.H. and Odling-Smee, J. (1982) *British Economic Growth,* 1865–1973. Palo Alto, CA: Stanford University Press.

Meadows, D., Meadows, D. and Randers, J. (1992) *Beyond the Limits.* London: Chelsea Green Publishing.

OECD (1998) *Historical Statistics. 1960–1987.* Paris: OECD.

OECD (2000) *Economics Statistics.* Paris: OECD.

OECD (2008) *Economics Statistics.* Paris: OECD.

OECD (2009) *Economics Statistics.* Paris: OECD.

Phillips, A.W. (1958) The Relationship Between Unemployment and the Rate of Change of Money Wages in the United Kingdom. *Economica,* 25, November, 283–299.

Porter, M.E. (2003) *UK Competitiveness: Moving to the Next Stage.* DTI Economics Paper No. 3, May.

Schneider, F. and Enste, D. (2000) Shadow Economies: Size, Causes and Consequencies. *Journal of Economic Literature,* 38, 77–114.

Soteri, S. and Westaway, P. (1993) Explaining Price Inflation in the UK: 1971–92. *National Institute Economic Review,* 144, May, 85–94.

Stuart, H. (2009) Europe Accused of Protectionism, *The Guardian,* 4 May.

Swann, D. (1992) *The Single European Market and Beyond: A Study of the Wider Implications of the Single European Act.* London: Routledge.

Wearden, G. (2009) Australia Raises Interest Rates by 0.25 Percent as Economy Improves, *The Guardian* 6 October.

World Bank (2009) Historic Commodity Price Boom Ends with Slowing Global Growth. WTO, December, Geneva.

WTO (2007) Proliferation of Regional Agreements 'Breeding Concern'. 10 September, WTO, Geneva.

4

The technological environment

Stephen Swailes

Learning outcomes

On completion of this chapter you should be able to:

- explain the importance of technology and innovation to society and enterprise;
- explain some of the generic technologies that organisations are using;
- appreciate differences in R&D spending by organisations;
- discuss how technology affects organisations, people and jobs;
- identify reasons why organisations do not always benefit from technology investments;
- discuss ethical problems arising from technological change.

Key concepts

- knowledge, technology and innovation
- research and development
- technological change and competitiveness
- technological change and labour
- technology, society and ethics.

Minicase 4.1	Genetic science

Recent advances in the knowledge of human genetics mean that it will soon become possible to develop self-administered screening tests for faulty genes, in the way that pregnancy or blood cholesterol levels can now be tested with over-the-counter kits. These tests will be applicable to unborn babies and to adults to see if there is a gene defect or an increased likelihood of developing a particular condition such as Alzheimer's disease. Furthermore, our improved understanding of genetics will accelerate the production of new drugs to treat conditions such as cystic fibrosis.

Genetic technologies pose some fundamental questions for certain types of businesses, as well as society in general. When each person's genetic fingerprint is identifiable to the extent that their health and even personality can be predicted, then how much of this information will be available to employers? How might insurance companies react to the widespread availability of gene testing? Would people identified as having an increased risk of developing a particular condition be able to get insurance? Under present arrangements they may not, so insurers will need to re-evaluate long-held views about personal eligibility for policies with inevitable consequences for the portfolio of policies offered.

The spread and use of genetic information will need tight control by responsible agencies such as the police and government. At the moment, scientists are ahead of society in the understanding and use of genetics, as the political and media interest in genetically modified foods illustrates. Despite assurances from the scientific community, there can be a long lag between state-of-the-art science and society's acceptance of the technology that results. Society needs to catch up so that restraints and restrictions are enforced and acceptable uses of genetic science become clear.

Questions

1 How could health service providers be affected if a person's tendency towards medical conditions could be predicted by simple tests?
2 How might insurance companies react to technology that allowed simple and quick estimation of a person's future chance of developing a serious medical condition?

4.1 Introduction

This chapter introduces what is arguably the biggest story of the twentieth century that continues into the twenty-first – the proliferation of technology and its effects on organisations. Unlike political, economic and social forces, which are mostly beyond the influence of organisations, managers have much more control and influence over technological forces. After all, technology is developed by organisations for use by organisations but, as we will see, the pace of technological change can pose some difficult problems for society.

The use, or lack of use, of technology has a strong influence upon the competitiveness of firms, sectors and nations. The extent to which technology is adopted can be affected by the attitudes and behaviour of employees, and some organisations fail because they are unable to respond quickly enough to the ways technology is changing. Technology growth and adoption are linked to other macroenvironmental forces such as the health of the economy, which influences the funds that organisations have to invest in using knowledge and developing and implementing new technology. Political decisions have a strong bearing upon the amount and direction of government-sponsored research and upon assistance programmes for industry. Furthermore, governments have to respond to the changes that new technologies bring to society. Politicians have to cope with the near instantaneous spread of news and information in an era of satellite and internet communications and powerful media.

Politicians also have to wrestle with the ethical problems that some new technologies, such as genetic science, create.

While all the primary macroenvironmental forces discussed in this book rise and fall in their intensity and impact over time, the technological environment is currently witnessing a 'new wave' of information-based change. Recent trends towards deregulation in Western markets and intense cost-centred competition have highlighted the central role of technology in helping to maintain and build competitive advantage.

4.2 Why is technology important?

4.2.1 What is technology?

We need a definition of technology to understand the relationship between organisations and their technological environment, and to understand the differences between knowledge, technology and innovation. Knowledge is a theoretical or practical understanding of a subject such as chemistry, mathematics, sociology or language. In the business world our stock of knowledge and understanding about a subject usually increases in small incremental steps as we do more and more research leading to improvements to social situations, procedures, products and manufacturing processes. Technology is the application of knowledge into some practical form, typically applied to industrial and commercial use.

There can be long delays between the early development of technologies and their evolution into widely usable formats. Galbraith (1967) defines technology as 'The systematic application of scientific or other organized knowledge to practical tasks'. Monck et al. (1988) saw technology as 'both a body of knowledge concerned with the solution of practical problems, what we might term know-how, and also the tools and artefacts which are used to achieve those solutions: it is both software and hardware'. Gillespie and Mileti (1977) define technology as 'the types and patterns of activity, equipment and material, and knowledge or experience to perform tasks'. This latter definition suggests that all organisations use a technology and that only the intensity varies. A useful summary of some of the definitions of technology can be found in Berry and Taggart (1994).

Innovation is the spread and diffusion of technology into society and organisations. Freeman (1982) saw technical innovation as the introduction and spread of new and improved products and processes in the economy. This definition includes the design, manufacturing and management activities involved in the marketing of new or improved products. Examples of the links between knowledge, technology and innovation are shown in *Table 4.1*. Knowledge of genetics, for example, has led to the development of tests for specific genes and will, possibly, lead to the widespread use of gene-modifying drugs.

A different view of innovation sees it as more than the spread of technology such that innovation includes changes to existing systems or any new thing or old thing that is used in a new context and may not be scientific or technical. This wider view is based on the ideas of Joseph Schumpeter (1883–1950) who argued that technological and organisational innovations were behind business cycles and thus fluctuations in the state of an economy. Schumpeter (1939, p. 86) observed, 'innovation is the outstanding fact in the economic history of capitalist society'.

Technology has been both attractive and problematic to entrepreneurs and managers for at least the past 200 years. Throughout the nineteenth century, businessmen and workers had a restricted view of technological progress and treated new machinery simply as labour-saving devices (Coleman and MacLeod, 1986). In the nineteenth century the British cotton textile industry had no international competitors, although domestic competition was intense. When the American and Japanese economies became serious threats, British cotton textile companies were unable to respond with appropriate technologies because of the particular

Table 4.1	Examples of knowledge, technology and innovation			
Knowledge discovery	Radioactivity (nineteenth century)	Hydrocarbon chemistry (early twentieth century)	Discovery of the structure of DNA in 1953 and identifying particular genes (1980s onwards)	Storing and processing information in electronic form (mid-twentieth century)
Technology based on the knowledge	X-ray images on photographic plates	Petrol, oils and the internal combustion engine	Tests for specific genes, gene-sensitive compounds	Microprocessor and permanent storage devices (disks)
Innovation from the technology	Improved medical diagnoses and treatment	Automobiles, aircraft	Gene-modifying drugs and genetically modified foods	Personal computers, internet

industry structure that had evolved (Lazonick, 1981; 1983). This example highlights a link between industry structure and the ability to respond to technological change. Structure can impede change, yet we will see later that technology can be a driver of structural change.

From 1929 to 1984 the Japanese economy shifted from mining and light industries to heavy and chemical industries and (after World War II) to automotive and electronics industries. Companies able to absorb Western technology into efficient production systems quickly established market dominance (Yamazaki, 1988). These examples show that technology can create new industries but can also be instrumental in the decline of others.

4.2.2 Technology and modern organisations

While some technologies are associated with harmful effects such as pollution and exploitation of the Earth's resources, the overall benefits of technological change to humanity are well known. Indeed, the technologies behind clean energy are sought to break the links between economic growth and pollution. Governments are anxious to raise national competitiveness and living standards which, in turn, requires a sound economy in terms of job availability, working conditions and public spending. Technology impacts on these factors. It has a large influence on productivity and, in the same way that products pass through a life cycle, so do companies and industries. Sometimes technology accelerates the decline of an industry, as personal computers signalled the end for mechanical typewriters. Technology also adds new sectors – all those employed in the development of information technologies and software, for example.

Faced with intense competition from low-cost countries, some sectors decline in terms of output and employment levels, although often a core of efficient niche producers remains. Leather manufacture is an example where, faced with intense competition from southern Europe and South America, output in North America and northern Europe fell steadily during the 1970s–1990s. In this example, leather manufacturers in high-cost countries have access to manufacturing technologies that improve both the efficiency of the company and working conditions. The long-term problem, however, is that they will also be able to install the same technologies when the manufacturing infrastructure (a network of machinery and component suppliers and distributors) of low-cost producers is more developed. A cycle occurs in which developed countries attempt to stay ahead of developing nations through continual renewal of their technological base and in which the less technologically advanced organisations can catch up through investment.

Thus technology can help to extend the lifetime of certain industries facing strong competition from producers in developing countries. It also contributes to economic development through new sector growth, which may arise because technology contributes to achieving competitive prices in world markets, for example in the telecommunications sector. This could arise from technologies that allow a quick response to orders, consistent quality and cost reduction, but to support regeneration, growth and competitiveness companies need to invest and a large slice of all capital spending is on technology.

One of the biggest trends affecting business organisations is globalisation – the convergence of economic and financial systems as well as consumer tastes and product designs on a worldwide scale and the formation of organisations with global or multinational scale operations (see *Chapter 9*). Consider, for example, the world automobile market, where manufacturers seek scale economies by marketing the same designs, albeit with local variations, across many countries. This reduces costs and so makes good business sense. Technology plays a big part in enabling newly industrialising countries such as Thailand and Indonesia to develop their economic and social infrastructures. Technology is a major change agent in world markets and the pace of technological change is rising.

It is widely believed that investment levels have a strong influence on productivity levels and, in turn, the ability to be competitive in world markets. Arguably, one of the most successful business products, the photocopier which was first introduced by Rank Xerox, was the foundation for that company's domination of the copier market for around 20 years, until patent protection expired. Investment by Canon in copier technology later allowed it to develop its own strong position in the copier market.

We can start to build a picture of technological development underpinning national growth and consumer living standards. However, some emerging technologies present some thorny problems for society, as illustrated by the case of genetic science in *Minicase 4.1*.

4.3 Funding of research and development

4.3.1 National differences

A few discoveries come about by accident or through chance side-effects. Alexander Fleming's discovery of the antibiotic Penicillin is one of the most well known. The effects of Viagra, sometimes used by men in their twilight years, were a happy side-effect of a not very good drug intended to treat a heart condition. TEFLON® the non-stick polymer was an accidental find. However, most new technologies do not evolve by accident; they are the fruits of targeted research and development projects. In our look at the technological environment we need to examine how industrialised nations organise R&D.

R&D can be defined as project work that aims to create new knowledge and understanding with a view to advancing or improving science and technology. It can cover improvements to products and services directly or to the processes and systems used to produce them. In simple terms, R&D advances knowledge, leads to new or better technology and drives innovation.

In 2007, the 1,400 biggest spenders on R&D globally spent £274 billion with about 38 percent of that spending undertaken by companies registered in the USA, 17 percent in Japan, 12 percent in Germany, 6 percent in France and 5 percent in the UK. Spending is targeted at pharmaceuticals and biotechnology (19 percent), information technology (18 percent), automobiles (17 percent), software (7 percent), electrical equipment (7 percent) and the rest of the spending is distributed across other sectors (R&D Scoreboard, 2009).

Governments publish details of the research they want undertaken to meet particular social and technical objectives, and organisations are free to bid for contracts. At national level, governments operate a structure for managing and funding R&D. In the UK, the Department for Business, Innovation and Skills manages the funding of government-held

Table 4.2	Types of research and development

- *Basic or fundamental research* is experimental or theoretical work undertaken mainly to acquire new knowledge. Such work would be undertaken without a particular end use in mind. An example would be the synthesis of new chemical compounds but without any notion of what use they might have.
- *Applied research* is undertaken with some application in mind, for example investigating the usefulness of innovations to medicine or materials technology.
- *Experimental development* is the use of both basic and applied research in the development of materials, processes and synthesis and would typically extend to the prototype or pilot stage.

Source: adapted from Morgan (2002)

research laboratories and non-profit-making research and technology organisations. Funding for projects is also provided through research councils such as the National Environmental Research Council and the Economic and Social Research Council. The main types of research are explained in *Table 4.2*.

The main sources of R&D funding are business enterprises and government, although universities and non profit organisations also carry out some of the work. Expenditure on R&D changes with the general state of the economy. When an economy is buoyant, higher government revenues from taxation support increased public spending, a small part of which goes towards R&D. In a buoyant economy, business enterprises enjoy relatively higher profits which can be invested in R&D. *Table 4.3* shows that gross expenditure on R&D in the UK in 2003 was about £21 billion, having grown steadily since the early 1990s when the UK economy was coming out of recession.

Universities and business enterprises carry out most of the R&D in the UK. Almost all university research is funded by government or business. Businesses also get money for research from government, charities and medical research foundations for some of the work they do.

Table 4.4 shows gross expenditure on R&D from 1998 to 2003 for several countries expressed as a percentage of each country's GDP. The UK spent 1.86 percent of GDP on R&D in 2003 compared with 2.19 percent for France, 2.55 percent for Germany and 2.6 percent in the USA. The UK has decreased the proportion of GDP given over to R&D since the late 1980s when it was about 2.2 percent.

Table 4.3	Gross expenditure on R&D in the UK

Performed by	1996	1998	2000	2002	2003
Business enterprise	11,091	11,431	12,562	13,490	13,687
Higher education	3,324	3,430	3,981	4,544	4,458
Government	1,849	1,659	1,938	1,084	1,222
Research councils	684	667	705	719	788
Private non-profit	211	255		554	669

Note: figures show expenditure by the sector performing the research, and are given in £m, at 2003 price levels.

Table 4.4	Gross expenditure on R&D as a percentage of GDP			
	UK	**Germany**	**USA**	**France**
1998	1.78	2.31	2.61	2.17
2000	1.84	2.51	2.72	2.18
2002	1.87	2.53	2.66	2.26
2003	1.86	2.55	2.60	2.19

Source: Economic Trends, 621, August 2005, www.statistics.gov.uk/articles/economic_trends/1417.pdf

At first glance, the percentages appear very similar, but it is important to recall that gross national product values are huge, e.g. $14,200 billion for the USA in 2008 compared with $2,923 billion for Germany and $2,200 billion for the UK (www.oecd.org/). Small changes to the percentage of gross national product spent on R&D represent very large sums of money in absolute terms. For instance, 0.01 percent of the USA's GDP is around $1.4 billion.

Despite overall reductions in defence-related R&D spending, the US, British and French governments still spend heavily on defence: see *Table 4.5.* In 2003, 56 percent of US government-funded R&D was allocated to defence compared with 32 percent in the UK and 23 percent in France. Germany and Japan spent less than 10 percent. It may be argued that high levels of spending on defence research hinder industrial competitiveness, although defence spending does secure many jobs, for example in aerospace. However, the alternative uses for such large amounts of money, e.g. health and social research, arguably would bring wider benefits to society.

Differences in R&D spending by socio-economic objective shed more light on this point – see *Table 4.5.* While some allowance should be made for the difficulty of categorising different R&D projects in different countries to particular socio-economic objectives, Japan, Germany, France and Italy allocate around 50 percent of government-funded R&D to the advancement of knowledge, i.e. without necessarily having clear practical applications for the research in mind. The US government, in particular, seems less comfortable with the notion of 'blue sky' research given that only 6 percent is for knowledge advancement without clear end uses in mind.

Table 4.5	International comparison of government-funded R&D by socio-economic objective, 2003 (percentages)					
Objective	**UK**	**Germany**	**France**	**Italy**	**Japan**	**USA**
Defence	32	7	23	0.4	4	56
Advancement of knowledge	35	55	45	57	50	6
Industrial development	5.2	12	6	10	7	0.4
Energy	0.3	3.0	4	4	17	1.1
Health	14	4	5	7	4	23
Other (agriculture, environment)	13.5	19	17	21.6	18	13.5

Source: Economic Trends, 621, August 2005, Table 19, www.statistics.gov.uk/articles/economic_trends/1417.pdf

This might reflect political and cultural norms that look to fund projects with clear intended applications for the fruits of research as well as projects with commercial short-term objectives. There are big differences in the amount of R&D directed at energy, which is interesting in the context of concerns about renewable energy sources and depletion of the natural environment. Britain directs 4 percent of government-funded R&D into energy compared with 17 percent in Japan.

The relationship between R&D spending and the performance of organisations is, however, complex. There is no simple 'the more you spend the better you perform' rule. What is clear, though, is that R&D spending is essential for survival – imagine how quickly Microsoft would cease to be competitive if it abandoned research into its software. The same applies to other sectors.

4.3.2 Indicators of scientific and technological progress

National differences in scientific and technological innovation can be tracked in a number of ways that are summarised below. They include patent applications, spending on R&D and employment in technology dependent sectors. A patent is a 'legal title of industrial property granting its owner the exclusive right to exploit an invention for a limited area and time' (Frank, 2003a, p. 7). To qualify for a grant of a patent an invention is evaluated for novelty, usefulness and inventiveness.

The total number of applications to the European Patent Office was around 60,000 each year from 1990 to 1999, but has risen steadily since then to total over 146,000 in 2008 (see *Table 4.6*). By region, the largest contributor was the EU-27 with about 55,000 applications, followed by the USA with 34,500 and Japan with 23,200 applications. The main areas for patent applications are physics, chemistry, electronics and human necessities. To compare nations, the number of applications per million workers is used. This was highest for Germany (585 per million workers) and Holland (466 per million). Spain, in contrast, made 1,200 applications, equivalent to 60 per million workers.

This data show wide variations in the level of scientific and technological development across nations. Germany and Holland lead in terms of applications per worker. The UK and Italy are below average and Spain along with Portugal and Greece (not shown) has the lowest

Table 4.6	Indicators of scientific and technological development, 2004		
Country	**Patents applied for at EPO**	**Number per million workers**	**Annual average growth rate, 1999–2004, %**
USA	34,500	232	3.0
Japan	23,300	351	4.9
Germany	23,300	585	2.1
France	8,000	297	2.2
UK	5,900	200	0.5
Holland	4,000	466	6.3
Italy	4,600	188	4.3
Spain	1,200	60	10.7
EU-27	54,700	241	2.4

Source: based on information contained in Felix (2008)

rates of applications per employee. These differences reflect the different contributions of agriculture and high- and low-tech industries in these countries.

The average spending on R&D by EU-27 countries was 1.8 percent of GDP in 2006, which is considerably less than the percentages spent by Japan and the USA. Over 1.7 million people are employed in the EU on R&D, which is defined as creative work undertaken on a systematic basis to increase the stock of knowledge relating to mankind, society and the development of new uses for such knowledge (Franck, 2003b). Scandinavian countries and Belgium have the highest proportions of R&D personnel in the working population.

4.3.3 Other indicators

Comparing countries by percentage of GNP spent on R&D is a useful measure, but to give a clearer comparison we need to take into account the nature of industry in a country, the extent to which it is labour or capital intensive, and the average size of companies. Some industrial sectors are less research intensive than others and in a labour-intensive business the main source of value added is labour. In a capital-intensive business, plant and machinery are the main sources of value added. Labour-intensive sectors such as footwear and clothing manufacture tend to have low fixed costs and high variable costs. Capital-intensive sectors such as electronics and chemicals have, in comparison, high fixed costs and low variable costs and spend proportionally more on research and development than labour-intensive sectors. Average company size could also play a part in explaining the differences in national spending patterns, as large companies spend more on research than small companies.

How else could we compare firms in this respect? One simple approach is to compare R&D spending per employee across sectors. Employee-based ratios, however, are not the best because employees don't all work the same hours – so the input side of the calculation is flawed. Value-based ratios are much better indicators of performance but are still vulnerable. Since sales revenues from an organisation's many business units are aggregated into a single group turnover figure, it would be problematic to compare a single-product organisation, where all R&D supports all sales, with a multi-product company where R&D might only support some of the product lines. Furthermore, some sectors in the UK such as the labour-intensive footwear and clothing industries, find it more efficient to channel much of their R&D activity through one or two research and technology organisations that serve the whole sector rather than conduct it in-company.

One of the best figures to use when different companies and sectors are to be compared is value added rather than sales. Value added is obtained by subtracting production costs (e.g. materials and services paid for) from sales revenues. This is a better measure of an organisation's performance because it concentrates on the value created by the organisation's activities and can be related to R&D spending to get a good measure of R&D productivity.

Table 4.7 shows the top ten international companies in 2007 according to research spending and the top ten British companies. The international companies are in the automotive, pharmaceutical or computing sectors in comparison with the British companies which mainly serve pharmaceuticals, food, aerospace/defence, telecoms, energy and banking.

Expenditure by business enterprises on research continues to increase and there are three explanations for this (Dussauge *et al.*, 1994):

- The Crisis hypothesis suggests that major technologies, such as petrochemicals, have life cycles. The oil crises of 1974 and 1979, when oil prices increased dramatically, signalled the beginning of the end for oil-based major technologies. Oil prices spiked again in 2008 and, although there is enough oil around for many decades to come, we were reminded of the world's dependency on oil. Increased R&D spending by petrochemicals companies could be a search for cost reductions in the face of rising cost of oil-based products, or searches for replacement technologies.
- The Sustained Progress hypothesis suggests that as societies accumulate more scientific knowledge it becomes increasingly possible to integrate this knowledge into new

Table 4.7	Leading firms by R&D spending, 2007

Top ten global R&D companies	**Top ten UK-owned R&D companies**
Microsoft (£4.1billion)	GlaxoSmithKline, pharmaceutical (£3.2 billion)
General Motors, automotive	AstraZeneca, pharmaceutical
Pfizer, pharmaceuticals	BT, telecoms
Toyota, automotive	Unilever, foods
Nokia, hardware	Royal Dutch Shell, oil production and exploration
Johnson & Johnson, pharmaceuticals	Rolls-Royce, aerospace and defence
Ford, automotive	Royal Bank of Scotland
Roche, pharmaceuticals	Airbus, aerospace
Volkswagen, automotive	Ford, automotive
Daimler, automotive	HSBC, banking

Source: adapted from, Department for Business, Innovation and Skills (2008)

technologies. The time lag between discovery of new knowledge and commercial applica tion is shortening but the funding to sustain the rate of new discoveries is increasing disproportionately.

- The Global Competition hypothesis suggests that, since NICs compete strongly in low-technology industries the more advanced nations concentrate their efforts on researching and creating new technologies in order to keep their competitive lead.

4.3.4 Sectoral differences

Not all business sectors use technology to the same extent, and technology is not equally important to all sectors. Small local service providers or providers of care services, for example, may use little or no technology in meeting their customers' needs although such organisations require considerable know-how to underpin their business operations, for example the know-how needed to care for the elderly and people with special needs.

Table 4.8 shows the research intensity (R&D expenditure as a percentage of turnover) for leading international business sectors. The leading sectors in terms of the amount they spend on R&D are pharmaceuticals and biotechnology, information technology hardware and software, electronics and electrical goods, and aerospace/defence. The USA dominates in four of these sectors with the Japanese leading the field in electronic and electrical goods. The UK is above the international average in funding R&D in pharmaceuticals and biotechnology, aerospace, defence and healthcare, and government policy is likely to try to sustain this position (Tubbs, 2002). These sectors allocate over 5 percent of their turnover to R&D, whereas other sectors, such as food production and oil exploration, invest about 1 percent. It is worth noting, however, that this is sometimes offset by the very large spends needed on capital expenditure – land, buildings, plant and machinery. Consider, for instance, the different demands that oil companies and clothing manufacturers would have for capital expenditure.

The textiles and clothing sectors invest relatively small amounts of turnover in research but this is not to say that they are somehow worse off than sectors with higher levels of spending. Labour-intensive sectors, such as these, are characterised by small companies that individually are not large enough to justify their own research and development department. They have tended to centralise their R&D efforts in industry research centres as this

Table 4.8	Average research intensity in the EU, 2008

Pharmaceuticals and biotechnologies	**15.7**
Technology hardware and equipment	13.5
Computer software and services	9.7
Aerospace and defence	6.6
Technology hardware (fixed line)	6.0
Leisure goods	5.9
Automobiles and parts	4.7
Healthcare equipment	4.4
Electronics and electrical goods	3.7
Industrial engineering	3.1
Chemicals	2.9

Note: Research intensity represents R&D spending by firms divided by sales turnover.
Source: The 2008 EU Industrial R&D Investment Scoreboard, http://iri.jrc.ec.europa.eu/research/scoreboard_2008.htm

has been the most efficient way of conducting research and development for the sector. Developments then transfer from the research centre to individual companies. Technology remains important to labour-intensive sectors but on a different scale. Technology tends to be used for incremental process improvements such as combining two or more manufacturing operations so that labour can be released from the production process, computerising product design, automating some processes such as cutting garment sections and cutting multiple layers of fabric, and developing new fabrics or polymers that can be cut and moulded to give enhancements to the manufacturing process or the final product.

It is partly because of the difficulty of achieving radical technological breakthroughs that some sectors remain labour-intensive. In sectors such as clothing and footwear manufacture, some of the manufacturing operations needed to assemble the products require manual manipulation of components and stitching or sewing together. Until solutions are found to the immensely complex problems of manipulating irregularly shaped components in three-dimensional space and joining them to very high accuracy, such sectors will continue to await breakthrough technologies that will alter the cost structure of the industry. In the meantime, European and US producers, e.g. Nike, carry out research on product development in the USA but sub-contract manufacturing to producers in lower-labour-cost countries, e.g. Asia.

By contrast, in pharmaceutical manufacture, it is through the discovery of new drugs or different ways of making them that companies can gain a distinct advantage over their competitors. Developments of this complexity require dedicated in-house and/or sub-contracted research, for two reasons. First, to keep control over very complex projects so that research spending is managed effectively; second, to keep industrial secrets (intellectual property) within the organisation to retain a competitive advantage.

However, collaboration with other organisations is an important way of supplementing in-company activities. About 37 percent of spending on R&D by UK businesses takes place in the pharmaceutical and biotechnology sectors and 6 percent in aerospace, software and automobiles (R&D Scoreboard 2008). Pharmaceutical research has a large appetite for new compounds with medical applications because success is strongly linked to new products.

Finding these new compounds among the millions of potential molecular structures is costly. Even when drugs have been trialled and approved for use, damaging side-effects can be identified. Drugs company Merck had to withdraw its Vioxx treatment for arthritis in 2004 because of concerns that it raised the risk of heart attacks. Merck was then open to litigation from thousands of people who had heart problems while taking the new drug. In 2007 Merck agreed to pay $4.85 billion in settlement of legal claims against it (BBC, 2007).

Mergers and acquisitions are widely used ways of acquiring technology. Glaxo Wellcome was formed in 1995 from the merger of Glaxo and Wellcome and has since merged again to form GlaxoSmithKline. Part of the rationale for the mergers was a drive for greater economies of scale in R&D in an increasingly competitive sector. Large pharmaceutical companies regularly acquire small companies to bolster their competitiveness.

4.4 Some general technologies

To explain individual technologies in detail is beyond the scope of this chapter. However, some technologies are having a big impact on many business sectors and these are highlighted below along with examples of some specific technologies in different sectors.

4.4.1 Information and communication technologies

It is hard to imagine a business sector that has not had to deal with change brought about by information and communication technology. Even small, local businesses need websites, secure systems of electronic money transfer and computerised inventory control systems. For large businesses the impacts of ICT have had transformational impacts influencing how, for instance, banks and insurance providers interact with customers.

Information and communication technology (ICT) is applied to the capture, storage, manipulation and retrieval of information. Much of the impact of technology has been to accelerate processing times, to replace labour and to change the nature of work that employees need to do and its impact has been revolutionary. Job losses have sometimes been severe and the technology has de-skilled decision processes such that junior staff can be trained quickly to take responsibility for complex customer enquiries. An interesting question about these relatively recent changes, however, is to what extent extensive labour cutbacks cause a loss of organisational knowledge that will have negative effects. In the short term, there are dangers that the quality of decision making can fall, staff loyalty and trust will stay low and customers will be unable to differentiate between providers (see Dopson *et al.*, 1998).

In addition to labour substitution, ICT has blurred the boundaries between formerly distinct sectors (Porter and Miller, 1985). Developments in information technology, coupled with deregulation of financial markets in the 1980s, allowed building societies to enter the market for insurance services and high street banks to offer mortgage products. Because of trends towards longer working hours and busier social lives, many financial services are commonly internet-based giving 24-hour access. In sum, ICT altered the structure of the financial services industry and hence the fundamental competitive forces – ICT changed the nature of competition and thus the business environment.

Decision making in organisations is another broad area bolstered by ICT. Corporate databases allow storage of data about sales, costs and customers on a massive scale, leading over time to the creation of data 'warehouses' and data 'mining' (Kusiak, 2006). Data mining involves statistical analysis of large data sets to find new relationships and patterns in the data. When patterns and relationships are known (e.g. if people who buy product X on Thursdays are likely to buy product Y, then make sure Y, is near X in the store layout), then the information can lead to cost savings or better marketing. Some examples of data mining include (Chan and Lewis, 2002):

- Pharmaceutical companies analysing biological information to find new uses for existing drugs.
- Banks understanding consumer behaviour to see how profitable or risky individual customers are.

4.4.2 Advanced manufacturing technology

Historically, a manufacturing production line contained a sequence of processes arranged so that each separate process added to a product as it passed down the line. Machines were frequently not connected to each other or integrated and often performed one process or, at best, only a few processes. Work-in-progress was carried from one machine to another manually in boxes or by a conveyor belt. When a new product passed down the line substantial time could be needed to change settings on individual machines. For example, changing the die (the

Minicase 4.2	ICT in manufacturing

An illustration of how ICT is used by organisations is shown by looking into a modern food producer. With over 20 bakeries across the UK the company makes about 3 million bread items a day for its own brands and for others. Products are boxed and distributed to customers by lorry and sometimes boxes would be unloaded and loaded on to several lorries if long journeys are needed to get to a destination. Up to 70,000 items a day were being lost or spoiled because of problems with the way paper labels were fixed to the boxes. A new 'track and trace' barcode system which tracks orders right through manufacturing and distribution is saving the company £12 million each year because losses of the product during distribution are much smaller.

ICT also tracks manufacturing processes to monitor efficiency, production volumes and waste. For example, on a specific order, systems in the bakeries are collecting data on how much product is spoiled, the reasons why it was spoiled and how much material (e.g. baking ingredients) is being wasted. Data are generated for management who can act and intervene to make things more efficient.

An 'order to cash' system replaced several systems with the aim of reducing the time taken from the company receiving orders to receiving the cash for those same orders. The system also automatically measures performance against service level agreements. For instance, if the company has an agreement to supply, say, 1,000 bread items to a branch of a supermarket by 7 o'clock each morning, then progress against this target is monitored.

Electronic Data Interchange (EDI) is used to connect the company's bakeries with high street retail outlets. Individual customers can order a specific product, e.g. a customised birthday cake, which is then produced and despatched. The main advantage with this is that individual, small orders have become profitable using EDI. Without EDI there was not enough time to take and process orders and get the product into shops for customers.

A massive database engine is used to analyse sales and marketing data. Many employees in the bakeries are employed on an hourly paid basis and they use a clocking-in system to record when they are in and out of work. Data from the clocking-in system go automatically into payroll systems to calculate the wages of hourly paid employees and generate electronic money transfers.

Questions

1 How has ICT in this case led to higher productivity?
2 How have customers benefited from these changes?

mould) in a sheet metal press to stamp out body parts for cars (doors, wings) might have taken up to a day. Manufacturers have always preferred long production runs of the same product since the unit cost of producing the product falls as volume rises. This occurs through:

- buying materials and supplies in bulk at lower unit costs;
- gaining experience of making a single product so that problems and breakdowns can be quickly overcome;
- operators becoming more skilled and efficient at making the product.

Collectively, these factors combine to produce an experience curve, on which unit costs continually fall as volume output rises. This experience curve effect (see *Chapter 2*) lies behind some decisions made by organisations when they take over or merge with another organisation. By integrating with another organisation's experience, the total experience of making a product is increased and, in theory, unit production costs will fall.

The desire to change product designs in response to the ways markets are changing has traditionally conflicted with the production department's desire for long runs of the same product. Product innovation and renewal are key parts of an organisation's marketing strategy but they do have big implications for production systems. Companies that rely on long production runs to minimise costs may find their cost structures under threat from consumer demand for product innovation. Shorter production runs are required and some organisations are unable to respond to the challenge. Flexible manufacturing systems have helped manufacturers adapt quickly to market demand by allowing them to produce smaller quantities of a product at economic prices. Shorter production runs have become more cost-effective because technology has helped to reduce the costs of setting up a machine to carry out a particular process and the time taken to switch a machine from performing one process to another. Decision making and tooling-up times are also reduced. For example, to tool up for a new product traditionally involved manual design drawing, making patterns for new components or tools, manufacture of tools to cut or mould a new component, and re-tooling of machines to cope with new products or components. Advanced manufacturing technology (AMT), which in simple terms means computer-controlled machines, has opened up new possibilities for manufacturers:

- Machines can be easily re-programmed so that a single machine can cope with changes to processing requirements of different components as they pass through a production line. For example, on a car production line, different fittings are tightened to different levels (torque) by the same machine depending on the model of car being worked upon.
- Machine re-setting is faster.
- Machines can share and exchange information about the specification and processing needs of different products so that a machine informs the next process in the sequence.
- Many different processes can be combined and undertaken by one machine.

AMT can be seen as families of computer-based technologies that are used in manufacturing processes. It is, in a sense, a special case of ICT being applied to manufacturing. Specific examples of AMT are computer aided design (CAD), computer integrated manufacturing (CAM), computer numerically controlled machines (CNC), flexible manufacturing systems and robotics. CAD allows engineering patterns, for example, to be designed on a computer screen and stored for easy alteration and reuse. CAM systems receive and interpret CAD data to co-ordinate the production process.

When computerised designs are confirmed, the digital information is passed on to the next stage so that components are generated from the computerised design and the information used to engineer, for example, new tools or moulds. Designs can be transmitted from European or North American headquarters to offices and factories in lower-labour-cost countries where the products are manufactured. Processes that once took several weeks have been reduced to a few days.

The general thrust of AMT is to improve organisational performance, but getting it to deliver better performance is not easy and there are plenty of examples where AMT has not delivered what was expected of it. This leads to questions about the factors that help make it effective and those that prevent it from giving the expected benefits. Factors that moderate the impact of AMT include size of the organisation, the amount of experience with the technology, and organisation structure. Factors associated with AMT success include the uses of 'lean' manufacturing processes such as just-in-time supply chains, decentralisation of decision making to production teams, teamwork in manufacturing, and training to give experience of a range of production situations in the same organisation (Das and Jayaram, 2003). These findings suggest that AMT will work best when implemented in organisations that are committed to using efficient systems which give employees the freedom to make decisions about things on the shop floor. Not surprising one might say – but worth noting.

4.4.3 Supply chain management and just-in-time

Installation of AMT has also coincided with a major remodelling of the manufacturing supply chain. Traditionally, buyers dealt with many suppliers of materials who tended to be treated in an adversarial way. Suppliers were often switched to enable the buyer to obtain the lowest cost for components. This relationship evolved in the time of long production runs and relatively long product life cycles. When market changes pushed in the other direction, retail and industrial buyers pushed manufacturers to find ways of making smaller quantities of more items and to deliver them much more quickly. This was made possible with AMT and ICT. Point-of-sale data capture in retailers is analysed to identify the quantity of stock items to reorder. These data are transmitted to manufacturers who are able to tool up rapidly to make the products.

Manufacturers have similar links with suppliers so that the materials needed to make a product can be ordered and delivered. Thus time has been eliminated from the total supply chain. Meeting customer needs in a just-in-time (JIT) environment has also altered the relationship between organisations in the chain. One of the many important things that manufacturers have to manage is stock control. This includes stocks of raw materials, partly made products and finished products. Holding stock ties up cash and a basic aim of manufacturers is to minimise the amount of cash tied up at any one time.

Historically, many factories operated with high stock levels and the advent of ICT supporting a JIT production philosophy has allowed stock and work-in-progress levels to be cut and so release cash from the manufacturing processes. JIT, which originated in the Japanese automotive sector in the 1950s and 1960s, aims to eliminate all activities that do not add value to a product and to cut materials usage to a minimum. To achieve this, JIT focuses on several areas:

- Designing products to eliminate any features that do not add value. This requires careful attention to market needs while not over-specifying a design.
- Employees are required to be flexible and participate in actively seeking continuous improvements to processes. Workers often work in small groups to help achieve this and undergo extensive training.
- Set-up times for machines, while necessary, do not add value and so need to be minimised.
- Communication systems are used to ensure that nothing is produced before it is needed. This helps to cut the costs of stocking materials and finished goods.
- The number of suppliers is minimised and they are involved in processes to boost quality and efficiency. They are seen as part of a production system, not simply as detached suppliers of components at the lowest price. Suppliers may need to locate very near to their customers and work closely with them to raise quality and respond rapidly to problems.

Because of the need to share information and better understand the customer's needs (customers are all those in the supply chain, not just the final consumer), organisations have tended to be much more careful about how they select suppliers. Supplier selection is a much more rigorous procedure, with customers seeking assurances that suppliers can consistently meet price, quality and delivery targets. However, once selected, the relationship between suppliers and customer is more secure, organisations work for mutual benefit and long-term relationships are sought. This is in stark contrast with the adversarial and exploitative relationships that once commonly existed. The automotive sector is a good illustration of where supply partnerships have been forged.

4.4.4 Business use of the World Wide Web

In early 2009 about 1.6 billion people or 23 percent or the world's population used the internet; this number has grown by over 400 percent since 2000 (www.internetworldstats.com). Airlines make reservation systems open to passengers who book their flights and purchase tickets online. Companies put their entire product catalogue on the internet and create virtual showrooms. Universities place teaching modules on the internet and make open learning more accessible. Communities of people who share common interests, for example doctors specialising in a particular medical condition, can quickly share new knowledge and information among themselves. The benefits to organisations of maintaining websites include:

- helping to establish a presence, e.g. a small company's website could be more attractive and efficient than that of a well-known large competitor;
- the internet acts as a distribution channel for electronic products (software, music, images) and thus lowers the cost of transactions;
- as transactions are one-to-one, the internet is suited to the advertising and sale of 'embarrassing' or personal products;
- business-to-business transactions are simplified;
- electronic business with small companies becomes viable.

The current limitations of web use include:

- worries over the insecurity of financial transactions and the need for new forms of electronic payment to be developed (despite this, the value of e-commerce is growing fast);
- unacceptable connection times;
- the demographic profile of web users restricts the potential for using it as a marketing medium;
- vulnerability of internet and web servers to hacking, which threatens the security of people and even high security and government installations;
- virtually unrestricted and uncensored access to materials that much of society finds unacceptable and which might, in the long run, alter society's attitudes to such materials.

Other types of communication between organisations are also boosted by the internet. International and global companies require extensive communications between decision makers in various countries. Travelling to meetings is costly and yet alternatives such as video conferencing have achieved only limited use. The internet offers an alternative, through posting information on a website. People in global businesses, for example marketing or design, can communicate ideas, concepts and drawings quickly. Technical and scientific conferences can be held on the internet if authors post their papers on a website for others to see. While this is an important breakthrough, travel to face-to-face meetings will not stop. Humans are social animals after all.

The internet has revolutionised shopping habits by enabling customers to compare and scan a store's product range and order for home delivery. This seems likely to appeal to professional and managerial classes more than to other groups who might have lower motivation to shop electronically and who, conversely, could be motivated to adhere to more social shopping habits. We should take a cautious view of such possibilities, however, as our desire to rationalise the future often fails to foresee other trends that have a bearing on the issue. When computers began to proliferate in business there was much talk of the paperless office. In fact, the opposite has happened because computers made editing and printing much easier, and because business trends moved towards greater documentation to support business objectives, for example in quality management systems.

Minicase 4.3	ICT and crime

Hacking into computers to access sensitive or personal information is a serious problem for organisations and for governments. In the espionage 'game' hackers have exploited weaknesses in networks to steal military secrets. Examples of hacks on USA installations include:

- An Israeli teenager accessing Pentagon systems in 1998.
- Russian hackers stealing information from the US Department of Defense.
- A British man who is currently under investigation for hacking Pentagon and NASA systems in 2001/2, allegedly looking for information on UFO activity.
- Chinese hackers stealing information from a range of USA military systems.

Internet 'warfare' is a big problem and in 2009 there were reports that North Korea was training and using hackers to access systems in the USA and South Korea. Cyber-crime is a constant threat that government security agencies and police are constantly battling. The computer systems of financial institutions, for example, are at risk of attack not only from countries engaging in state-sponsored espionage but also from organised crime syndicates.

Hacking and cyber-crime will be around for the foreseeable future, as they are enabled by the design of the internet itself. Attackers will keep attacking and look for ways to breach security and system designers are constantly identifying the breaches and fixing them.

Sources: Norton-Taylor (2009); Raphael (2009)

Questions

1 How might a cyber attack impact on a business organisation?
2 How could an organisation seek to ensure that its customers remain loyal following such an attack?

4.4.5 Future technologies

A look into future technologies is revealed in *Table 4.9*. As the EU continues to expand and develop, five main areas for science and technology research can be identified.

4.5 Technology and organisations

While technology, particularly ICT, is often seen as a solution to organisational problems, it is becoming clear that ICT requires good and careful management to bring about the expected benefits. Managers need to be clear about the total impact that will come from investment in technologies. Understanding the impact is a complex task because cost–benefit analysis needs to account for much more than changes to incomes and expenditure, yet the non-financial costs and benefits are difficult to estimate. A key problem in managing large technology projects is their vast size and the high numbers of people and organisations involved. Adcock *et al.* (1993) noted that managers can have expectations of ICT that exceed its capabilities. Information technology installations need to be backed up by strategies for other critical factors, such as customer service and distribution.

Information technology in particular has been linked to workplace stress levels (Chen *et al.*, 2009; Korunka *et al.*, 1997) caused by job and workstation redesign, worries about job losses or worries about retraining needs. As well as directly affecting individual jobs, changes caused by the introduction of new technology can indirectly affect other employees. Managers and

Table 4.9	Priorities for scientific and technical research

Key priority area	Example applications
A knowledge society based on ICT	Remote healthcare systems
	Decision systems for agriculture and manufacturing
	Modelling human behaviour in complex systems
Risk and sustainability	Monitoring of natural resources by satellite observation
	Breaking the link between economic growth and environmental destruction – sustaining resources
	Causes and cures of diseases, understanding how economic systems affect health risks
Sustainable energy and transport	Reducing carbon gas emissions
	Expansion of energy from nuclear sources
Health	Development of preventative medicines
	Improved health and safety from a better understanding of health risks
International integration in light of continuing EU enlargement	Greater integration of national databases on health, security and defence

Source: based on Gavigan *et al.* (2001)

supervisors, for example, have to plan and implement change and deal with the human issues arising, including their own fears about loss of control. Because improvement policies are ongoing in organisations, they lead to continuous change and the pressure on employers and managers can seem never-ending. Simons (1986) identified several human resource issues that need reviewing as a result of technological change that are still relevant today:

- job evaluation and grading;
- career development, training (to increase worker involvement in technology and to reduce stress);
- remuneration policies and working conditions;
- personnel planning; and
- labour relations.

4.5.1 Technology and organisation structure

Much research has looked at the ways that technology affects the structure of organisations. Up to about 1950 there was a belief in 'one best way' of managing and organising. This is summed up in Henri Fayol's early twentieth century approach of planning, organising and structuring, commanding through instructions and assistance, co-ordinating and controlling work activities.

In the 1950s an English academic, Joan Woodward, undertook a study to see why British manufacturers varied in structure and how structure affected performance. Her study became a classic of industrial sociology. One of her questions was how can organisation structure be measured and described, i.e. what makes one structure different from another? She looked at many different variables, e.g. the ratio of direct workers (people actually involved in production) to indirect workers (e.g. managers and support staff) and the number of layers of management. From examining about 100 companies the initial results were unclear:

- wages accounted for anything from 3 to 50 percent of total costs;
- the ratio of clerical to direct staff ranged from 3:1 to 1:14;
- the number of levels of management from top to bottom ranged from 2 to 12;
- supervisors' span of control (the number of people under them) went from 7 to 90.

How could these and other differences be explained? Some of the differences could be explained just through the individual preferences of managers but most variance could not be explained in this way. She then focused on the type of work undertaken and realised that a firm that was into mass production could not organise in the same way as a firm building one-off items to order. In sum, organisation structure has to help further the objectives of the organisation rather than conform to some pre-set management ideal. There is no 'one best way' of organising. The 100 firms were then sorted into three broad technical process types: small batch production, large batch and mass production, and process or continuous production.

Firms using similar technical methods had similar organisational structures – the different types of technology employed seemed to dictate the types of structure required to manage it efficiently. Some generalisations were possible from this study. In particular, as technical complexity increased, then:

- labour costs as a percentage of total costs decreased;
- the ratio of indirect to direct labour increased;
- the span of control of top managers increased;
- the ratio of management staff to the total number of staff increased.

The more successful firms had a good fit between their technology level and their structure, the poorer performers showed some departures from the structure that their technology type suggested they should have. Woodward's study sounded the death-knell for the 'one best way' theory of management and opened up a new management approach called *contingency theory* in which structure, management style and organisational success are contingent upon factors such as an organisation's production technology.

However, contingency theory can be criticised on the grounds that technology alone cannot be the only determinant of organisational structure – surely other factors have a role to play? For instance, contingency theory gives insufficient weight to the importance of managerial choice in decisions about how to manage technology and overlooks the tensions between management and employees that might otherwise influence structure. In other words, contingency theory requires that technology is neutral and not contentious for employees. The size of an organisation also has a strong bearing on how it is structured. Woodward's work is very important because it showed how structure, technology and performance can be related, and it marked the start of many more studies into this area.

ICT is associated with moves away from bureaucratic ways of organising to looser, networked organisations where the boundary between one organisation and another is fuzzy. This arises because ICT allows multiple organisations to work around the same database(s) at high speed to create new ways of offering value to customers. Technological changes are seen as a driving force behind internal restructuring, e.g. changes to the number, size and type of departments in an organisation and the reporting relationships among employees. External structuring is also affected, e.g. supply chains and partnership agreements. Partnerships may arise in attempts to spread the costs and risks of business ventures and to pull together areas of different technical and commercial expertise. There is also a view that ICT has enabled a shift from bureaucratic structures to flatter structures, to matrix structures, to networks and to shadow structures (Dibrell and Miller, 2002). When it was first adopted, ICT supported existing structures but has since become, in some organisations, a substitute for structure (i.e. a shadow structure). While there is a formal structure of departments, divisions and reporting relationships, alongside this sits a shadow structure enabled by ICT.

Table 4.10	Characteristics of organic and mechanistic organisations

Organic	Mechanistic
No rigid rules	Many rules/low individual freedom
Participative/informal	Bureaucratic/formal
Views aired openly	Restricted/suppressed use of voice
Face-to-face communication	Written communication
Interdisciplinary teams	Functional separation
Creative iteration	Long decision chains
Outward-looking	Slow decision making
Flexible adaptor	Rigid, slow adaptor
Non-hierarchical	Hierarchical
Information flows up and down the organisation	Information flows up the organisation Directives come down the organisation

Source: adapted from Rothwell (1992)

An assumption of the classical approach is that organisational efficiencies are best achieved through specialisation of tasks and subdivision into specialist units. This notion extended to individual jobs being clearly defined and distinct. Many people might have done the same job, but there was little overlap between jobs. By the early 1960s this form of organisational structure was recognised as being a significant barrier to the innovation process. Burns and Stalker (1961), in another classic study, called the traditional organisational structure 'mechanistic' and argued that a different, 'organic', organisational structure was much more conducive to innovation. The main differences between mechanistic and organic structures are shown in *Table 4.10*.

In essence, organic structures are less burdened by rules and restraints upon employees, tasks are less rigidly defined and creativity is assumed to come from co-operation and exchange of ideas and information, facilitated by a less hierarchical chain of command. Managerial control is present, of course, but the climate is one of involvement, participation and sharing, rather than close supervision and demarcation. Horizontal co-operation across an organisation, rather than vertical authority relationships, is stressed.

Burns and Stalker (1961), however, also related organisation structures to the organisation's environment. Where environments were essentially stable – that is, the past tended to repeat itself, and predictions could be made with high degrees of confidence – the mechanistic form of organisation could be successful. Confectionery and insurance companies, at the time, fitted this category. Where environments were more dynamic – that is, less easy to understand and harder to predict – organic structures were more successful at supporting innovation processes.

We might now begin to expect that organisation structure needs to change with the business environment, to continually evolve to cope with fresh demands upon it. This idea of constant metamorphosis has been advocated by Greiner (1972). Whether environmental change is driven by new technology or not, Greiner's notion is worth remembering. Over short periods (up to a few years) organisational restructuring may be small and incremental in nature. During this time there will be periods when structure will not change at all. Every few years, however, a major transformational change is needed to realign the organisation with its fast-moving environment.

4.5.2 Technology and industry structure

The finding that mechanistic organisation structures could be successful in stable environments is probably still true today. However, far fewer sectors still enjoy a stable business environment. Deregulation of financial services markets in the early 1980s had major impacts upon the stability of business environments for banks and insurance companies. Privatisation of the UK water, gas and electricity utilities has dramatically increased the rate of change and degree of uncertainty in those sectors.

Industry structure is typically seen in terms of the number of firms in a sector, their relative size, their interrelationships and the concentration of market share (e.g. oligopoly or monopoly). Industry structure is thought to have a strong bearing on industry profitability (see *Chapter 2*). Although there are other influences, industry structure is thought to explain about 17–20 percent of industry profitability (Sampler, 1998). In contrast, theories that focus on how organisations use their resources, i.e. how they uniquely configure resources to add value, have attracted interest as ways of explaining performance.

For some sectors, it is relatively easy to assess structure, e.g. the product is easily classified. Different car manufacturers can be identified and their market positions and market shares calculated, for instance. Other sectors, particularly information-based sectors such as financial services, are much harder to analyse with a much bigger and diverse base of organisations providing them, e.g. high street banks, supermarkets and internet-based providers. The boundaries of the competition are harder to define (Sampler, 1998).

Technology and industry structure are related. It seems clear that technology is a cause of structural change but also we can argue that industry structure influences technological progress. Organisations merge, are taken over and enter into joint ventures to help develop knowledge and technology. Technology and industry can be seen as evolving together (co-evolution) (Nelson, 1995). *Minicase 4.4* shows how technology has influenced the structure of the music industry.

4.5.3 Technology, jobs and skills

It is true that technological change leads to loss (or displacement) of jobs, although it is preferable to see a bigger picture of how change affects jobs. Job losses do occur but, simultaneously, new jobs can be created that require the skills to work with new technologies as well as jobs in companies making and supplying them. We saw above how technology influences structure, and another main focus for research on technological change looks at the implications for the skills that organisations need, pay levels, types of working contract and gender issues such as the link between gender and job type in addition to job displacement.

The American sociologist Harry Braverman contended that new technology in the workplace would, under capitalism, continually de-skill jobs and lead to increasing polarisation of the workforce into skilled and unskilled workers. Lewis (2007), however, points out that a problem with this view is that it is difficult to get agreement on what skill is and how it can be measured to see if there is more or less of it around. Furthermore, studies of technology and skill produce mixed results – some find technology leads to up-skilling whereas others find evidence of de-skilling. Bartel *et al.* (2007), for instance, found that the adoption of computerised manufacturing technology increases skill requirements of people operating machines, in particular their technical knowledge and ability to solve problems. General claims of the type that technology de-skills or technology decentralises decision making are not very helpful it seems. It is better to ask under what conditions (i.e. what work situations and contexts) technology leads to de-skilling or up-skilling or centralisation/decentralisation (Liker *et al.*, 1999).

In general, the skills that are linked to increased use of flexible technologies include problem solving, interpersonal skills such as team working, computer skills, reading and mathematics (Gale *et al.*, 2002). Other generalisations are that the impact of technological

Minicase 4.4	Technology and the music industry

Faulk *et al.* (2005) analysed how technology and government policy affected the music industry in the USA. The main legal foundation protecting song and music writers is through copyright legislation which gives writers exclusive rights to perform the work. Sound recording was first achieved in 1860 and was developed commercially by Thomas Edison in the 1870s and 1880s. Further technical breakthroughs in movies (talkies), radio and TV fuelled outlets for music and allowed music writers to benefit from royalties obtained through copyright protection. Revenues from music grew further on the back of tape recordings and better quality records such as the long playing (LP) albums and stereo sound. In the USA an oligopoly had formed in which five record labels (e.g. A&M) controlled over 50 percent of record sales in the album charts.

In the 1970s, however, consumers could easily copy from one tape cassette to another or copy from record to tape, so technology was beginning to reduce the control that the big record labels had over music distribution. People copying music for friends hit sales, as did organised piracy on a large scale. While organised piracy could be pursued through the law, it was not feasible to pursue individuals doing it privately as was the case with copying film from TV to video. The USA copyright law changed in 1976 to allow individuals fair use of music that they had obtained legally and this included copying for their own convenience. It was very difficult to prevent piracy, short of banning the ownership of certain recording equipment (in the same way that ownership of certain types of guns is prohibited) – and it didn't happen.

The next phase in the story of technology and music started with cable TV, digital recording and transmission, and the internet. Cable TV eventually led to monthly subscription as the predominant way of watching TV and led to greater viewing choice and a boost for music. CDs improved the quality of music and for a short time most people could not copy them, but it soon became easy to burn (copy) CDs. The internet allowed people to swap music and burn to CD, having a big impact on industry revenues.

New legislation was introduced in the USA to tackle the problem of internet music swapping, although digital music exchanges continued. On the plus side, music producers started to offer 'digitally wrapped' music, i.e. music delivered not via CD but via subscription-based downloads. This opened up a completely new distribution channel and cut packaging and distribution costs.

The music industry case neatly shows how technology can create new distribution channels, how it can change industry structure (i.e. change the balance of power among different organisations and stakeholders), and how it can trigger legislation to protect artists and companies.

Postscript: The *Guardian* reported that an estimated 95 percent of music available online is downloaded illegally (Swash, 2009).

Questions

1　Do you share the industry's concerns over illegal downloading?
2　Can legislation be used to solve this problem?

change at the level of the firm, e.g. on competitiveness, is much larger than at national level and wage increases for people working with advanced technologies are higher at the national level than the firm level (Brown and Campbell, 2002). Suppose an organisation has an urgent need to adopt new technologies, then it may have an increased demand for higher skilled workers. If it needs these workers in greater proportion to their availability in the labour market, wages for higher skills will increase relative to lower skills (Dunne and Troske, 2005). The level of impact on wages depends upon how quickly the supply of skilled workers increases, e.g. through education and training. In simple terms, skills can be seen as something that organisations buy through wages. Basic laws of supply and demand (see *Chapter 6*) would suggest that high demand for scarce skills, e.g. certain types of ICT professionals, will raise the wages paid and reducing demand for a skill in plentiful supply, e.g. semi-skilled production workers, will lower wages.

4.5.4 Technology and productivity

Conventional wisdom holds that technological change is a driver of productivity improvements, although it is not the only one. The USA is usually placed at the top of international productivity leagues, but these comparisons obscure the fact that different countries can lead the field in certain sectors. The UK, for example, has competitive advantage in pharmaceuticals and agriculture. Until recently, the UK had some embedded features of its business environment that were thought to impede progress (Lorenz and Smith, 1998), including:

- a naturally smaller market than the USA and Japan, which both enjoy large domestic markets that make capital investment more attractive;
- a national culture that is thought to devalue manufacturing and production in favour of services, and which inhibits the training and development of engineers who can compete internationally;
- relatively poor management skills that fail to capitalise on creativity and productivity of employees; and
- insufficient development of companies operating in high-growth sectors, such as electronics and electronic engineering, and reluctance to cast off declining and low-growth sectors, such as brewing and textiles.

Apart from the smaller market problem, the impact of the other factors listed above is debatable. Even when technology is available to a sector, organisations may not enjoy fully all the potential benefits from it. A study of the UK footwear manufacturing industry in the 1980s found that while technological change was a source of productivity growth, the industry had been slow to exploit the gains available to it and technology had not diffused fast enough (Guy, 1984). Footwear is historically a low-profit industry, and a brief consideration of the sector using Porter's (1979) five forces model (see *Chapter 2*) shows why. Putting pressure on profits are low barriers to entry, scale economies occur at low volume, and there are many competitors who use price as the basis of competition. Much of the output is purchased by large retail chains with high power. In contrast, supplier power is weak and there is no substitute for footwear. The continuing low profit levels that this position brings to most footwear manufacturers act as a brake on investment which tends to be sporadic, following relatively good profit years, rather than part of a long-term investment strategy. The returns on investment in these circumstances are limited (Guy, 1985).

Investment in ICT by the financial services sector (e.g. banks) has been extensive, although studies show that ICT investment has often not delivered the expected benefits (Harris, 2001). In the context of the banking sector, the main reasons put forward for this are:

- ICT is available to other organisations, e.g. large food retailers, who have entered the market in efforts to offer new services to their large customer bases.
- Banks had a poor grasp of how to measure the effectiveness of the ICT projects that they had implemented.
- Banks had not learned from unsuccessful ICT projects in ways that helped reduce the chance of repeating the mistakes made.
- Responsibility for project management was sometimes 'fuzzy' and so it was difficult to hold people accountable for a lack of success.
- There was a tendency to try to integrate ICT into existing structures and processes rather than 'focus upon innovation and business transformation'. Organisations tended to let old knowledge influence the extent of new knowledge that projects generated.

These, and other, factors are used by Harris to explain an 'IT productivity paradox' in which the predicted benefits of technology investments do not always come to fruition.

4.5.5 Technological change and job stress

Stress is not an easy concept to define but does relate to the physiological reactions (e.g. tiredness, headaches) and psychological reactions (e.g. irritability, fear of failure) that people have to the situations that they get into.

Why do people get stressed? Conservation of Resources Theory (Hobfoll, 2001) basically says that people seek to obtain new resources and protect existing resources. Resources are broadly defined to include things, personal relationships, and social and working conditions. Psychological stress occurs when these resources are threatened or depleted or when a person thinks (anticipates) that their resources will be diminished. Research on stress often makes the distinction between things that provoke stress (stressors) and the responses to them (strains) (Arnold *et al.*, 1998; Ganster and Murphy, 2000). Workplace stressors include high workloads and pressure to meet deadlines. It was not too long ago, 25 years perhaps, when most jobs were, relative to today, fairly predictable in the way they were carried out. Since then, and due to political, competitive and technological changes, expectations put upon employees have changed.

Although different people have different capacities to cope with job stressors, there seems little doubt that levels of workplace stress are much higher than they were. Reasons for this include:

- Regular change to work systems requiring new learning and adaptation.
- Many organisations operate continually, such that the pressure to perform and deliver is ever present.
- The amount of information that employees have to process has increased and this is closely linked to ICT.
- There is greater pressure on employees to manage their own careers rather than rely upon a benevolent organisation to provide life-long work.
- There is greater regulation of working methods from political insistence and technological systems, such that employees have less control over what they do and how they do it.

Chen *et al.* (2009) studied the implementation of a new computer system in an organisation. They found that people who had participated in additional workshops, aimed at getting them to think about their resources and how they could support each other through the implementation, reported lower stress, lower dissatisfaction and higher confidence than work colleagues who had not attended the workshops.

An eighteenth-century proverb said that, 'it's not work that kills, but worry' and herein lies the problem. Recent information-based technological changes have coincided with rising stress levels, although they are by no means the only cause.

4.5.6 Teleworking and working from home

Teleworking (telecommuting) is a system in which employees use ICT to perform work away from the organisation for which it is carried out. It is a form of flexible working which is discussed more fully in *Chapter 9* (see section 9.6 *'Flexible working'*).

The simplest form is where teleworkers work from their own homes for an employer or client. Teleworking is applicable to many sectors and the type of work undertaken includes information analysis, data processing, financial services, sales, journalism and publishing. Basically, teleworking represents a trend towards remote working (e.g. at home) that is enabled through ICT, in which information is exchanged between teleworkers and another organisation. When the impacts of ICT on businesses were first recognised there were predictions that it would help to solve some of society's problems such as road congestion but it has not been adopted as widely as thought at first (Clear and Dickson, 2005).

During the recessions of the early 1980s and early 1990s, organisations looked closely at the cost of overheads such as human resource services and data processing. There was a general trend to eliminate these functions from corporate structures and to buy in the services as needed. Often, displaced employees would sell their services back to their former employer. Having made some savings on overheads, organisations turned their attention to the remaining employees. Some organisation structures were 'flattened' by moving away from pyramid-like structures containing several layers of management. The number of layers was reduced such that the remaining managers had larger spans of control, and there were fewer grades of employees. For some employees, job security declined as the number of fixed-term and part-time contracts grew.

The rise of factories in the nineteenth century meant that, instead of working at home, large numbers of workers travelled to organised workplaces. This became, and remains, the normal working pattern today, but teleworking is perhaps enabling the beginning of a reversal to the patterns of past times. However, not all home-workers are teleworkers. Furthermore, some people work where they live, often performing manual, low-technology work, and others have the option to regularly work from home even though they are normally working elsewhere. One difference between these groups is that those who have the option to work from home tend to be well educated and well paid, in higher status occupations and satisfied with their jobs. In a way, choosing to work from home, say one day a week, is a job perk to those already in good positions (Felstead *et al.,* 2002).

The main drivers for teleworking include:

- cost reductions for employers arising from lower overheads (savings on space, facilities and employment costs);
- potential access to a larger and more flexible workforce that helps employers cope with sudden rises and falls in demand;
- teleworkers may prefer the flexibility and freedom relative to regular attendance at a remote site.

While teleworking seems to offer advantages to both employers and employees, it does bring about changes to the relationship between teleworkers and organisations that need careful management (Chapman *et al.,* 1995; Teo *et al.,* 1998). These include:

- reduced promotion prospects caused by the 'marginalisation' of teleworkers, i.e. falling victim to the 'out of sight, out of mind' problem;
- reduced opportunity for peer interaction and professional development;
- reduced job security;
- confusion over the boundaries between home and work that influence social relationships;
- greater feelings of social isolation that can lead to low motivation;
- the need for a particular management style which is task-focused and relies on trust and shared responsibility.

These and other issues need to be managed if teleworking is to spread. It does not suit hierarchies or management styles based on subordination (Clear and Dickson, 2005). Managers will have to learn how to manage without close control and supervision, and this will require a revolution in the mindset of many managers. Employees will need to take responsibility for their own careers and act as if self-employed, looking after their own pension and sickness arrangements. Professional isolation is a potential consequence of teleworking. Golden *et al.* (2008) defined this as feelings of being left out, of missing opportunities for mentoring and missing the interaction with others. They found that the more teleworkers feel isolated, the lower their job performance is, and that the more they telework the more they feel isolated. Yet the extent of teleworking seems likely to grow and it is a reasonable supposition that many more employees could carry out some of their work from home, even if not by teleworking. Given the infusion of ICT in homes and workplaces and the changing patterns of work, Wilks and Bilsberry (2007) question whether continued use of the term 'teleworking' is appropriate. They propose 'home anchored workers' to better describe working patterns, although the phrase doesn't quite slip off the tongue so well.

4.6 Managing technology

4.6.1 Technology development

Before the industrial revolution and the growth of the large organisation, important technological developments, for example metalworking, watermills and windmills evolved over hundreds of years as experience accumulated. Accidental or random discoveries of important new knowledge such as Alexander Fleming's discovery of antibiotics are now very much the exception. In the main, discoveries and the innovations that spin off from them are not random processes. Scientific and engineering know-how are usually deliberately focused on a problem in response to societal pressures or needs (see *Table 4.9*).

Yet we should not expect technological progress to be in simple proportion to the amount of R&D invested. Barriers exist to advances which can prove particularly troublesome to overcome. Nuclear fission reactors which produce electricity were developed soon after the first fission (atom) bomb was exploded in 1945. The controlled nuclear fusion reactor once thought to be imminent after the invention of the fusion H-bomb in the early 1950s and which could provide clean energy remains a very long way off and may never be seen (Roberts, 2002).

The state of related and supporting technologies also affects the rate of progress in an area. Consider, for instance, the growth in computerised travel booking systems and the increase in demand for air travel. This simple example shows how progress in one area can accelerate change in another. Recently, motor manufacturers have used advances in electronics to produce engine management systems to help maximise fuel economy. Catalysts are now used to clean up exhaust gases. But are the limits of efficiency and cleanliness from the internal combustion engine being approached? Breakthroughs in vehicle engine technology await advances in fuel systems or radically new engine designs. Cars powered by electric motors have been produced but their low speed and limited range hinder their commercial attractiveness. The technological barrier is battery chemistry and design, and, until we can produce batteries that deliver much more power, all-electric cars seem a very long way ahead (Brooks, 2009). However, we are now seeing hybrid vehicles such as the Toyota Prius which combine petrol and electric power.

Ayres (1991) suggested that important innovations occur in clusters after a scientific breakthrough that opens up new territories for process and product development. Researchers can be imagined pushing on a particular door until it begins to open. They may need to push for years, even decades, until the breakthrough emerges. If this vision of the technical environment is representative, then it raises some important questions for managers of research-dependent organisations:

- How to decide what projects are the most promising?
- How to determine how much money to invest in an area?
- What is the best way of organising research, e.g. internally or in collaboration with others?
- How is progress with particular research projects measured?
- When should particular projects be stopped or run down?

The clustering of innovations was one of five causes of innovation identified by Rothwell and Wisseman (1991). They noted the connections between social, economic and technological developments as follows:

- There is a need for technological change – simply stated this says that technologies are developed when there is a need for them, as with the development of radar in the late 1930s to respond to the emerging role of air power in war.

- Very often, major inventions are not single advances, but rely upon clusters of related technologies to make them work. There may be a time lag between one breakthrough and a breakthrough in an important related area.
- Social resistance to change is well known, although it varies across cultures, ages and religions. As we have become acutely aware, the spread of Western culture into some Islamic states is a cause for concern in some quarters.
- In addition to technical capability (including expertise, finance and organisation), driving force and dogged perseverance are needed to see projects through to marketable ends, such as new processes or products. The few years between President Kennedy's announcement of a space programme and Neil Armstrong's walk on the moon testifies to the power of a national driving force.
- Social objectives are important. At any point in time, a society will have objectives for its development. These objectives in turn influence the direction of technology development. Volvo's pioneering work with semi-autonomous work teams in the 1970s may have reflected a general Scandinavian preference for group decision making (see *Chapter 5*).

Rothwell and Wisseman (1991) argue that there is a reciprocal relationship between technology and culture: technology follows culture and culture follows technology. Both statements seem to be true.

4.6.2 The organisation of research and development

There are several ways of organising the ways that R&D is performed. The simplest and traditional approach is to centralise in-house facilities in an R&D division that serves other business units. The alternative is to decentralise R&D so that each business unit carries out its own activities. Both approaches give full control over projects and sensitive information is relatively secure. Problems with this approach have surfaced, however, as it can be slow and inward-looking.

Given the trend towards shorter product life cycles and expanding legislation covering products, working conditions and the environment, shorter development times are needed. To accelerate idea generation and development, organisations actively seek collaborative projects, spin-offs, joint ventures, mergers and acquisitions to supplement in-house research: see *Minicase 4.5*. To gain access to knowledge and skills, organisations are increasingly internationalising their R&D activities. R&D intensive organisations (see '*Other indicators*', in this chapter), for instance, have R&D centres across Europe and the USA, with some in Japan also. This raises challenges through (Gassman and von Zedtwitz, 1998):

- the need to develop managerial and technical standards;
- developing managers who can work across cultures;
- developing R&D scientists who can transfer knowledge across borders;
- managing virtual projects and teams.

4.7 Technological change and society

4.7.1 Ethical aspects of technological change

The subject of ethics deals with the moral issues arising from decisions open to individuals and groups, including business enterprises. In the simplest terms, ethics deals with the rights and wrongs of things. Throughout history, technology has changed human society – from the first use of flint axes as weapons, through the discovery of farming practices and the working of metal into art, tools and weapons. Modern society is very aware of the ethical issues of technology such as ICT, the science of cloning and the science of genetically modified (GM)

Minicase 4.5	BP – reducing carbon emissions through collaboration

The demand for energy will continue to rise as populations grow and economies industrialise. With most energy production based on the use of fossil hydrocarbons (gas, oil, coal), we have become acutely aware of the effects that carbon emissions are having on the atmosphere and on climate change and global warming. Energy sources and energy production are scattered across the world yet we share the same breathing space. Tackling carbon emissions is far beyond the scope and abilities of any single government or organisation and so we have seen many collaborations and ventures that pool resources and expertise. The international oil companies are at the forefront of developing technologies that, for example, access new gas and oil supplies with less impact on the environment or lead to more efficient transportation of oil and gas.

Collaborative ventures between governments, energy companies and scientific organisations are a common feature of the energy business. BP, for example, has ventures in Angola on a deep-water site, Abu Dhabi on hydrogen fuels with the Chinese Academy of Sciences among others. BP also collaborates with engineering company Sumitomo and with software companies to produce new systems. It also works with chemical companies on the materials that are pumped back into underground reservoirs after oil or gas has been extracted. The company is investing $500 million in biotechnology institutes in the USA, for example, to better understand how energy can be taken from crops and how bacteria can be used to recover carbon.

Source: Eyton (2009) www.bp.com

Questions

1 Given the pressures to raise living standards across the world, how realistic are prospects for reductions in pollution from industrial processes?
2 What are the main barriers to major cutbacks in pollution?

foods. These developments raise ethical questions, for instance, about the working conditions in call centres, the amount of information that organisations hold on people and the effects on the natural environment.

One big area of concern relates to approaches to risk. In the 1950s and 1960s when nuclear power was a focus of government policy there were (and there still are) serious questions about the health and safety risks to people living close to power stations and about the best ways of dealing with highly radioactive wastes. A more recent example concerns the supposed risks to regular users of mobile phones of brain damage from frequent exposure to radio waves. The key question surrounding technology boils down to whether the benefits arising from using a new technology outweigh the known or hypothesised disadvantages. A common approach to resolving this question examines whether a majority of people will benefit from a technology even though some will be disadvantaged, perhaps seriously. This idea of greatest benefit for the greatest number is called a utilitarian approach to decision making.

A current and future ethical problem concerns the issue of privacy in light of the near limitless capacity of ICT to store information about individuals from their internet usage, motor insurance and credit card transactions among others. In the UK, government departments such as the Revenue and Customs, Vehicle Licensing Authority, the police and social services hold information on individuals, and questions have been raised about whether the type and amount of information held goes beyond what is needed for the operation of government in a free society.

The Vehicle Licensing Authority holds records of registered vehicles and it is easy to identify vehicles that are not taxed. Number plate recognition software, installed in police cars and on the roadside, checks the numbers of passing vehicles and where unlicensed vehicles are observed this provides irrefutable evidence for a court that an unlicensed vehicle was used on a public road. At a very simple level of analysis it seems reasonable that technology should be used to identify major offences. For serious crimes few would disagree with this principle but, for less serious offences, how much should the routine journeys of people be monitored in order to identify breaches of the law? How far should this principle be taken?

For decades, the police have stored items, e.g. clothing, from serious crime scenes. The recent technology of DNA profiling, which produces a person's unique 'DNA fingerprint', has allowed DNA samples from old crime scenes to be matched against fresh DNA samples taken by the police. In the UK, the police take DNA samples (a mouth swab, usually) from people arrested, regardless of whether they are later charged or convicted and profiles are compared with all DNA profiles obtained from unsolved crimes. Several people have been convicted of murder and other serious crimes using this evidencing technique, as well as lesser crimes. DNA has also been used to clear the names of a few people wrongly imprisoned for crimes they could not have committed.

At a simple level of analysis one could argue that society benefits from such a policy. But look more closely. A proportion of people arrested are never charged and of those charged some are not convicted. Up till March 2008, for instance, 65 percent of people arrested in the UK for terrorist offences were not charged and this ratio 'is similar to that for other criminal offences' (Home Office, 2009, p. 1). Is it right that people who have not been found by a court to have broken the law should have a DNA sample, taken by force if they refuse, on permanent record and have it compared with databases of DNA samples from scenes of crime? Is it right that people arrested for minor offences should be evaluated as potential rapists, robbers or murderers?

How long will it be before the government deems it in society's interest that a DNA sample be taken from all people on reaching the age of 16? The rationale that the innocent have nothing to fear is seductive but can be used as a licence for security services to monitor people without limit, in the name of safety and justice, such that the freedom of the individual is seriously curtailed (see *Minicase 5.6* in *Chapter 5*). It is arguable that issues of privacy and freedom are fundamental concerns in a society that feeds on information storage and exchange. The way our attitudes to the collection and use of information about people change in the future has the potential to alter the relationship between individual and state.

Another technology presenting serious ethical problems concerns GM foods, given the sometimes uncertain effects upon humans who consume them and upon plant and animal species that interact with them in their natural environments. Ethical problems are also raised by the technologies that support cloning. For instance, research upon human embryos which, while appearing distasteful to many, may have the potential to lead to breakthroughs in medical sciences and hence produce benefits to mankind.

4.7.2 Workplace surveillance

Workplace surveillance has become an issue for employees and researchers (Kidwell and Sprague, 2009). What can be monitored?

- website connections;
- the content of emails sent and received;
- employee behaviour via CCTV;
- time spent on a keyboard and even keystroke analysis;
- badges can record where people are in a building at any point in time;
- random drugs testing, e.g. where there are threats to safety;
- recording of telephone calls (for your protection and for staff training);
- placing global positioning devices in mobile telephones and company vehicles.

Employers advance sensible reasons for this, for example to ensure that employees are not abusing the organisation's resources and to help prevent theft and sabotage or to protect employees from assault or abuse (closed circuit television – CCTV). One of the challenges for employers is to balance the extent of their surveillance with employees' attitudes and feelings about the reasons why their actions are being monitored. If trust is a casualty of a workplace surveillance strategy, then the employer will suffer through poorer relationships and potentially lower creativity and higher staff turnover. It falls on employers, therefore, to be explicit about what is being monitored and to give the reasons for it. A company may argue that CCTV is used to protect employee safety yet employees may feel it is because a control-oriented management mistrusts its people and wants to squeeze the last bit of productivity from them or to victimise individuals. Employees want and expect some privacy, even though they are on their employers' premises and using their resources.

4.7.3 Technology and safety

The industrial revolution in the UK (about 1760 to 1830) led to large numbers of people working in factories as well as an improved transportation system involving canals and railways. At that time, and in the decades that followed, safety hazards were largely seen as an accepted part of working life. Working conditions were poor and hazards were ever-present. In the UK, about 4,750 people were killed in industrial accidents in 1900 compared with the lowest ever annual figure of 180 in 2008. Hazards came from crude production processes, e.g. in mining and heavy industry, and others came from a lack of knowledge about the effects of materials, such as lead, mercury, gases, solvents and fibres, on the human body, leading to many industrial diseases. The first Act of Parliament relating to health and safety at work (The Factory Act) was passed in 1802 and gave some protection to children working in cotton mills. Other Acts in the 1800s specified working hours, working times and minimum ages of employees, and extended to include other industries and the mines. In the UK, worker safety was brought under a comprehensive system of law through the Health and Safety at Work Act of 1974. This imposes duties on employers and employees to uphold safe practices. This is discussed further in *Chapter 8*.

Accident rates are inevitably linked to the extent of exposure to hazards and the potential consequences of those hazards. Trawler fishing is far more dangerous than writing software. While technology-intensive sectors seem less hazardous, when high-technology systems go wrong the effects can be disastrous (see *Minicase 4.6*).

An example of the widespread use of a technology to improve safety stems from the UK government's targets for reductions in casualties from road traffic accidents. Speed cameras are a well-known method but it is already possible to fit cars with devices that either record speeds for later analysis or, via satellite positioning, 'know' a road's speed limit and control the engine so that speeds cannot be exceeded. Such controls are not yet socially acceptable but are possible.

4.7.4 Technological change and vulnerability

Although human societies have been adopting new technologies for thousands of years, communities remained largely self-sufficient until recently. If some disaster befell a community, the impact was contained and the bulk of society carried on unaffected. Recent technologies based on oil and electronics have led to extensive integration of communities such that they, we, are highly dependent upon others. Indeed, we are highly dependent upon a small number of providers of essential services. Imagine, for instance, the effects of a large-scale shutdown of electricity supplies. All ICT-based work would cease. Financial systems would be thrown into chaos given the volume of electronic transactions. Air and rail transport would stop, emergency services would be paralysed, and factories and hospitals would stop functioning. The effects would be virtually instantaneous.

While leading to great advances, these same technologies have made the developed (and developing) countries very vulnerable to industrial action and to terrorist acts. It has been argued that part of the explanation for America's occupation of Afghanistan and Iraq lies in eliminating threats to vital technologies.

| Minicase 4.6 | Technology disasters |

Thalidomide – a drug marketed in the 1960s to treat morning sickness. Unknown to its developers, Thalidomide has a horrible side effect if taken during a short period in early pregnancy. If taken when the limbs of a foetus are forming the drug interferes with normal limb development. Thousands of babies were born with missing or deformed limbs. It was taken out of use when its effects were discovered. Very recently, new uses for Thalidomide have been found but its use must be very strictly controlled to prevent use by pregnant women.

Three Mile Island – a nuclear power plant in the USA where, in 1979, a small amount of radioactive material was released into the atmosphere when safety systems failed. Although a major radiation incident was avoided, the US authorities were sufficiently concerned about what might have happened that government policy on nuclear power was re-evaluated.

Chernobyl – in 1986 this nuclear power plant in the Ukraine was the site of a major (non-nuclear) explosion that released radioactive material into the atmosphere. There was an immediate effect whereby hundreds died of radiation poisoning. People living in the region are still affected as long-lasting radiation entered the food chain.

Bhopal – the site in India of a chemicals plant that, due to failures of safety procedures, released deadly methyl isocyanate gas killing thousands of people living around the plant (see *Minicase 6.5* in *Chapter 6*).

Dow Corning and breast implants – Dow made silicone breast implants in the 1970s and 1980s and most implant operations were done for cosmetic rather than medical reasons. There was strong evidence that, for some women, the implants had led to major medical problems including inflammation, excessive scarring and problems with the immune system. Legal proceedings rumbled on into the 1990s, with concerns that information showing that implants could lead to health problems had been suppressed alongside medical opinion that the link between implants and the observed symptoms was inconclusive.

Exxon Valdez – in 1989 this loaded oil tanker ran aground in one of the world's unspoilt natural environments in Alaska. Major damage to marine and shore life occurred plus disruption to the livelihoods of a working community based on the sea. Tanker spills are all too common, and while they are not directly caused by technological failures (more likely bad weather, incompetence, mistakes) oil is an indispensable part of energy and transport systems.

Questions

1 How should an organisation react to a crisis arising from its own operations or products?
2 What systems and procedures should organisations have in order to deal with major crises caused by their own activities?

4.7.5 Technology and waste

Although technology has delivered many great steps forward, it also has a dark side. How many PCs are scrapped each year – many containing usable components and their only problem being too slow? How many hi-fis, TVs, fridges and cars are scrapped each year? A combination of technical progress coupled with clever marketing (especially branding) has created societies in which the interval between production and disposal of goods can be very short. This has led to serious impacts on the amount of waste being produced and the call on the Earth's resources to maintain production (e.g. forests and land use). Recycling technologies help but we are a long way away from being in an equilibrium state in which new goods are produced out of recycled materials.

This pattern of 'progressive obsolescence' began with mass production in the 1920s (Slade, 2006) and created, in the USA to start with, a climate of conspicuous consumption. Mass production combined with built-in 'planned obsolescence' (e.g. cars remodelled every three to four years) fuelled the throw-away society that seems to exist in many parts of the world.

4.8 Conclusion

Technology represents an environmental force so strong that it can affect the competitive advantage of nations and shape the attitudes of society. Technology-intensive organisations must continuously manage the organisation of R&D and the production of new knowledge on an increasingly international scale. Managers need to understand how emerging technologies could affect their organisation so that it responds to threats and opportunities in the best way. Managing technology into the organisation is difficult and there are many examples of project failure. This calls for a sound understanding of the benefits technology can offer and of the people management issues created inside the organisation. ICT and genetic science are posing complex ethical problems for organisations and for government.

<table>
<tr><td>

Summary of main points

</td><td>

This chapter introduces key aspects of technological change that relate to business organisations. Specifically:

- Knowledge and technology evolve, usually in small steps but occasionally in large jumps. We are witnessing such a jump in information-based technologies at present.
- Innovation is a key feature of business organisations and has been for 200 years.
- ICT is having a revolutionary impact upon governments, business organisations and individuals.
- For optimum performance, organisations need to find the best fit between technology available to them, the socio-economic environment and their choice of strategy.
- Where technology is a major factor in determining organisational performance (in some organisations and sectors it is a minor factor) it must be seen as central to organisational decision making.
- Technological change affects jobs, skills and productivity.
- Technological change offers the only prospect of sustainable economic growth on a global scale.
- Technological change is creating controversial decisions about personal privacy and interference with plant and human biology.

</td></tr>
</table>

<table>
<tr><td>

Discussion questions

</td><td>

1 What areas of research do you feel should be priorities for government funding?

2 How can Europe and North America sustain a technological lead ahead of newly industrialising countries? Will the NICs eventually catch up?

3 Think of a range of goods and services – what characteristics of these goods/-services support sales over the web? What characteristics impede sales on the web?

4 What are the legitimate interests of employers and employees in relation to workplace surveillance?

5 What factors should an organisation think about when it wants to introduce new technology in the workplace?

6 How might knowledge workers such as scientists and engineers differ from unskilled and semi-skilled employees in their attitudes to work, to their managers and to their organisations?

</td></tr>
</table>

Further reading/sources of information

Carbon Trust (**www.thecarbontrust.co.uk**) Information on efforts to reduce carbon emissions, e.g. using alternative fuels.

Halpern, D. and colleagues (2008) Management and Legal Issues Regarding Electronic Surveillance of Employees in the Workplace; *Journal of Business Ethics*, 80, 175–180.

OECD (**www.oecd.org**) Organisation for Economic Co-operation and Development. Follow links to science and technology for information on effects on economic development.

Sciliagno, E. (2002) 10 Technology Disasters; *Technology Review*, 105(5), 48–53.

Sustainable Technologies (**www.sustainabletechnologies.ac.uk/home.htm**) Details of research projects aimed at growth without harm to the natural environment.

Tubbs, M. (2007) The Relationship between R&D and Company Performance; *Research Technology Management*, Nov/Dec, 50(6), 23–30.

UK government (**www.innovation.gov.uk/rd_scoreboard**) UK government site giving details on R&D.

World R&D Spending Rising (2008) *Research Technology Management*, Jan/Feb, 51(1), 4–5.

References

Adcock, H., Helms, M. and Jih, W.-J.K. (1993) Information Technology: Can it Provide a Sustainable Competitive Strategy? *Information Strategy – The Executive's Journal*, 9(3), 10–15.

Arnold, J., Cooper, C. and Robertson, I.T. (1998) *Work Psychology: Understanding Human Behaviour in the Workplace*, 3rd edn. Harlow: FT Prentice Hall.

Ayres, R.U. (1991) Barriers and Breakthroughs: An Expanding Frontiers Model of the Technology Industry Life Cycles, in Rossegger, G. (ed.) *Management of Technological Change*, Oxford: Elsevier Science.

BBC (2007) Vioxx Settlement to Total $4.85 Billion, **http://news.bbc.co.uk** Bartel, A., Ichniowski, C. and Shaw, K. (2007) How Does IT Affect Productivity? Plant-level Comparisons of Product Innovation, Process Improvement and Worker Skills. *Quarterly Journal of Economics*, 122(4) 1721–1758. Department for Business, Innovation and Skills (2008) Research and Development Scoreboard, available from **www.innovation.gov.uk/rd_scoreboard/**

Berry, M.M.J. and Taggart, J.H. (1994) Managing Technology and Innovation: A Review. *R&D Management*, 24(4), 341–353.

Brooks, M. (2009) All Juiced-up and Ready to Go. *New Scientist*, 18 July, 203 2717, 42–45.

Brown, C. and Campbell, B.A. (2002) The Impact of Technological Change on Work and Wages. *Industrial Relations*, 41(1), 1–33.

Burns, T. and Stalker, G. (1961) *The Management of Innovation*. London: Tavistock.

Chan, C. and Lewis, B. (2002) A Basic Primer on Data Mining. *Information Systems Management*, 19(14), 56–60.

Chapman, A.J., Sheehy, N.P., Haywood, S., Dooley, B. and Collins, S.C. (1995) The Organizational Implications of Teleworking, in Cooper, C.L. and Robertson, I. (eds) *International Review of Industrial and Organizational Psychology*, Chichester: John Wiley, vol. 10, pp. 29–248.

Chen, S., Westman, M. and Eden, D. (2009) Impact of Enhanced Resources on Anticipatory Stress and Adjustment to New Information Technology. *Journal of Occupational Health Physiology*, 14(3), 219–230.

Clear, F. and Dickson, K. (2005) Teleworking Practice in Small and Medium-sized Enterprises: Management Styles and Worker Autonomy; *New Technology, Work and Employment,* 20(3), 218–233.

Coleman, D.C. and MacLeod, C. (1986) Attitudes to New Techniques: British Businessmen. *Economic History Review,* 39(4), 588–611.

Das, A. and Jayaram, J. (2003) Relative Importance of Contingency Varaibles for AMT. *International Journal of Production Research,* 41(18), 4429–4452.

Department for Business, Innovation and Skills (2008) Research and Development Scoreboard, available from **www.innovation.gov.uk/rd_scoreboard/**

Dibrell, C.C. and Miller, T.R. (2002) Organization Design: the Continuing Influence of Information Technology. *Management Decision,* 40(6), 620–627.

Dopson, S., Ruddle, K. and Stewart, R. (1998) From Downsizing to Revitalization. *Financial Times,* 27 February, 12.

Dunne, T. and Troske, K. (2005) Technology Adoption and the Skill Mix of US Manufacturing Plants. *Scottish Journal of Political Economy,* 52(3), 387–405.

Dussauge, P., Hart, S. and Ramanantsoa, B. (1994) *Strategic Technology Management.* Chichester: John Wiley.

Eyton, D. (2009) Expanding Wings in the Hydrocarbon Sector – the Era of Collaboration, **www.bp.com.**

Faulk, G., Lambert, R.P. and Rolston, C.P. (2005) The Effects of Changing Technology and Government Policy on the Commercialization of Music. *Journal of Non-Profit and Public Sector Marketing,* 13(1/2), 75–90.

Felix, B. (2008) Patent Statistics, Statistics in Focus, 17/2008, Eurostat, available from **http://epp.eurostat.ec. europa.eu/cache/ITY_OFFPUB/KS-SF-08-017/EN/KS-SF-08-017-EN.PDF**

Felstead, A., Jewson, N., Phizacklea, A. and Walters, S. (2002) The Option to Work at Home: Another Privilege for the Favoured Few? *New Technology, Work and Employment,* 17(3), 204–223.

Frank, S. (2003a) Patent Applications to the EPO Continue on an Upward Trend 1990 to 2001. *Statistics in Focus,* 4/2003, Eurostat.

Frank, S. (2003b) R&D Expenditure and Personnel in Europe: 1999–2001. *Statistics in Focus,* 4/2003.

Freeman, C. (1982) *The Economics of Industrial Innovation.* London: Frances Pinter.

Galbraith, J.K. (1967) *The New Industrial State.* Harmondsworth: Penguin Books.

Gale, H.F., Wojan, T.R. and Olmsted, J.R. (2002) Skills, Flexible Manufacturing Technology and Work Organization. *Industrial Relations,* 41(1), 41–79.

Ganster, D.C. and Murphy, L. (2000) Workplace Interventions to Prevent Stress-related Illness: Lessons from Research and Practice, in Cooper, C.L. and Locke, E.A. (eds) *Industrial and Organizational Psychology,* Oxford: Blackwell Publishers, pp. 34–51.

Gassman, O. and von Zedtwitz, M. (1998) Organization of Industrial R&D on a Global Scale. *R&D Management,* 28(3), 147–161.

Gavigan, J. Zappacosta, M., Ducatel, K., Scapolo, F and di Pietrogiacomo, P. (2001) Challenges and Priorities for European Research: A Foresight Review. *Foresight,* 3(4), August, 261–271.

Gillespie, D.F. and Mileti, D.S. (1977) Technology and the Study of Organizations: An Overview and Appraisal. *Academy of Management Review Symposium: Organizations and Technology,* 4(1), 7–16.

Golden, T.D., Veiga, J.F. and Dino, R.N. (2008) The Impact of Professional Isolation on Teleworker Performance and Turnover Intentions. *Journal of Applied Psychology,* 93(6), 1421–1431.

Greiner, L.E. (1972) Evolution and Revolution as Organizations Grow. *Harvard Business Review,* July, 37–46.

Guy, K. (1984) Footwear, in Guy, K. (ed.) *Technological Trends and Employment, 1: Basic Consumer Goods.* Aldershot: Gower.

Guy, K. (1985) Paper, in Clark, J. (ed.) *Technological Trends and Employment, 2: Basic Process Industries*. Aldershot: Gower.

Harris, L. (2001) 'The IT Productivity Paradox – Evidence From the UK Retail Banking Industry. *New Technology Work and Employment,* 16(1), 35–48.

Hobfoll, S. (2001) The Influence of Culture, Community and the Nested Self in the Stress Process: Advancing Conservation of Resources Theory. *Applied Psychology: An International Review,* 50(3) 337–369.

Home Office (2009) Statistics on Terrorism Arrests and Outcomes in Great Britain, *Home Office Statistical Bulletin,* 04/09, 13 May.

Kidwell, R.E. and Sprague, R. (2009) Electronic Surveillance in the Global Workplace: Laws, Ethics, Research and Practice. *New Technology Work and Employment,* 24(2), 194–208.

Korunka, C., Zauchner, S. and Weiss, A. (1997) New Information Technologies, Job Performance and External Workload as Predictors of Subjectively Experienced Stress and Dissatisfaction at Work. *International Journal of Human–Computer Interaction,* 9(4) 407–425.

Kusiak, A. (2006) Data Mining: Manufacturing and Service Applications. *International Journal of Production Research,* 44(18/19), 4175–4191.

Lazonick, W. (1981) Competition, Specialisation and Industrial Decline. *Journal of Economic History,* 41(1), 31–38.

Lazonick, W. (1983) Industrial Organization and Technological Change: The Decline of the British Cotton Industry. *Business History Review,* 57(2), 195–236.

Lewis, T. (2007) Braverman, Foucault and the Labor Process: Framing the Current High Skills Debate. *Journal of Education and Work,* 20(5) 397–415.

Liker, J.K., Haddad, C.J. and Karlin, J. (1999) Perspectives on Technology and Work Organization. *Annual Review of Sociology,* 25, 575–596.

Lorenz, A. and Smith, D. (1998) Britain Fails to Close Competitiveness Gap. *Sunday Times,* 11 October, section 3, pp. 10–11.

Mattheus, R. (2002) Here Comes the Sun. *New Scientist,* 9 February, 173, 2329, 36–39.

Monck, C.S.P., Porter, R.B., Quintas, P. and Storey, D.J. with Wynarczyk, P. (1988) *Science Parks and the Growth of High Technology Firms*. London: Routledge.

Morgan, J. (2002) Research and Experimental Statistics 2000. *Economic Trends,* 585, August, 32–56.

Nelson, R.R. (1995) Co-evolution of Industry Structure, Technology and Supporting Institutions and the Making of Competitive Advantage. *International Journal of Economics and Business,* 2(2) 171–184.

Norton-Taylor, R. (2009) GCHQ Steps-up Strategy to Combat Cyber Attackers; Brown Announces. *Guardian,* 25 June.

Porter, M.E. (1979) How Competitive Forces Shape Strategy. *Harvard Business Review,* March–April, 137–145.

Porter, M.E. and Miller, V.E. (1985) How Information Gives you Competitive Advantage. *Harvard Business Review,* July–August, 149–160.

R&D Scoreboard (2008) Department of Business Innovation and Skills, available at **www.innovation.gov.uk**.

Raphael, I.R. (2009) Fighter Jet Hack Far From First Government Breach. *PC World,* 21 April.

Roberts, M. (2002) Here Comes the Sun. *New Scientist,* 9 February, 173, 2329, 36–39.

Rothwell, R. (1992) Successful Industrial Innovation: Critical Success Factors for the 1990s. *R&D Management,* 22(3), 231–239.

Rothwell, R. and Wisseman, H. (1991) Technology, Culture and Public Policy, in Rosegger, G. (ed.) *Management of Technological Change*. Oxford: Elsevier Science.

Sampler, J.L. (1998) Redefining Industry Structure for the Information Age, *Strategic Management Journal,* 19(4), 343–355.

Schumpeter, J.A. (1939) *Business Cycles: A Theoretical, Historical and Statistical Analysis of the Capitalist Process,* Vol. 1. New York: McGraw Hill.

Simons, G.L. (1986) *Management Guide to Office Automation*. Manchester: National Computing Centre.

Slade, G. (2006) *Made to Break: Technology Obsolescence in America*. Cambridge, MA: Harvard University Press.

Swash, R. (2009) On-line Piracy: 95 Percent of Music Downloads are Illegal. *Guardian*, 17 January.

Teo, T., Lim, V. and Wai, S. (1998) An Empirical Study of Attitudes Towards Teleworking Among IT Personnel. *International Journal of Information Management*, 18(5), 329–344.

Tubbs, M. (2002) *Research and Development Scoreboard – Analysis*. London: Department of Trade and Industry.

Voola, J. (2006) Technological Change and Industry Structure: A Case Study of the Petroleum Industry. *Economic Innovation and New Technology*, 15(3), 271–288.

Wilks, L.J. and Billsberry, J. (2007) Should We Do Away With Teleworking? An Examination of Whether Teleworking can be Defined in the New World of Work. *New Technology, Work and Employment*, 22(2), 168–177.

Yamazaki, H. (1988) The Development of Large Enterprises in Japan: An Analysis of the Top 50 Enterprises in the Profit Ranking Table (1929–1984). *Japanese Yearbook on Business History*, no. 5, pp. 12–55.

5 The international cultural, demographic and social environment

Jon Stephens and Tony Purdie

Learning outcomes

On completion of this chapter you should be able to:

- understand the concept of national culture and its link with globalisation;
- have increased awareness of differences in national cultures and the reasons for this;
- identify differences in business cultures through the work of Hofstede and Trompenaars;
- appreciate the key factors that determine changes in a country's population;
- understand how demographic changes can be significant for both businesses and governments;
- have a clearer understanding of some of the key social trends in terms of family, lifestyle and crime;
- appreciate how the nature of organised labour has changed.

Key concepts

- national culture
- the convergence/divergence debate
- Hofstede's five dimensions of national culture
- Trompenaars' dimensions of national culture
- culture shock and culture shift
- national culture and business practices
- the rate of natural population change
- birth rate and death rate
- replacement fertility rate
- population pyramids
- dependency ratios
- international migration
- patterns of family development
- lifestyle trends
- organised labour
- changing work trends.

Minicase 5.1	The new Ford Fiesta

In 1993 Ford Europe launched a new car, the Ford Mondeo. As the name implies, this was intended to be Ford's 'world car' that, with minor changes, would be sold by all Ford's regional businesses. The aim of this ambitious global strategy was primarily to reduce the cost of new product development by removing duplication of activities throughout the company. Why design a new car four or five times, when a single design could be sold everywhere?

Sadly, while the Mondeo sold well in Europe, it was not successful anywhere else. It was too small for the North American market and too large for the Far Eastern market. Furthermore, the design was deliberately bland so that it would be reasonably acceptable in all cultures – and ended up being considered unattractive compared with more stylish competitors.

After this relative failure, it might have been surprising to many when in 2008 Ford launched a new version of the smaller-sized Fiesta as part of its 'One Ford' strategy – in other words, another attempt to build a 'world car'. The new model, with small changes, was to go on sale in China in 2009 and America in 2010. Why should this venture prove more successful than the last one? An article in the *Economist* (2008) magazine gave an insight into the company's thinking.

The company believed that this smaller car (classed as a 'supermini') would be suitable for Far Eastern markets. In America, higher fuel prices and the approaching recession were encouraging buyers to trade down from the traditional 'gas guzzlers' to more fuel efficient cars, especially in urban areas. But the greatest change in thinking was the styling of the new car which was described as 'kinetic' and quite different in nature to the dull, staid look for which Ford had been known. The aim was to make the car into a 'fashion item' – to be 'drop-dead gorgeous' both inside and outside. The target market was to be young, prosperous, style-conscious adults – what the *Economist* calls the 'iPod' generation. As the global success of the iPod shows, this demographic group exists in most regions of the world.

If Ford has got its market research right, the new Fiesta will be the car that drags the company away from the threshold of bankruptcy.

Questions

1 Find out the latest sales figures for the new Fiesta in Europe and other regions of the world. Has the car been successful?

2 Can you identify other products which have been designed to appeal to this demographic group? What risks does a company face when it targets this group?

5.1 Introduction

This chapter covers some of the wider factors present in the increasingly complex business environment facing firms in the twenty-first century. It will start by examining the national cultural environment which is becoming more and more important as the process of globalisation continues and companies have to deal with and operate in different countries. This may be through direct investment or through joint ventures or strategic alliances but it will mean that management styles and practices that are used in the home country may or may not function efficiently in a different cultural environment. If these issues are not addressed by companies it could even lead to a 'culture shock' which can have a damaging impact on their overseas performance.

The first section of this chapter will identify some of the issues that determine cultural differences, making use of some key theoretical studies such as those by Hofstede and Trompenaars, and then will show how cultural differences can create problems within the business environment, before seeking to show how some of these cultural differences can be overcome and even turned into competitive advantage for companies that handle cultural differences effectively.

The second part of the chapter will look at the demographic environment and many of the issues arising from the demographic structures faced by organisations when they are operating internationally. Demographic changes are some of the most predictable changes in the business environment and the first section will look at some of the key components of natural population growth and the factors that influence these with examples drawn from many countries. The issue of international migration has also become more significant in determining population size and both legal and illegal migration will be looked at in this context. While the absolute size and the change in size of population will be very significant, it is also important for organisations to examine the changing structures of populations as this may have important implications for market attractiveness. One way of looking at changing populations is by using population pyramids and these will also be examined in this chapter. The structure of the population may have very important implications for governments as well as business organisations. One of the major issues facing governments in Western Europe is the impact of ageing populations and particularly the implications of this trend for public pension provision in the future.

The final part of the chapter will explore the social environment and again look at some of the implications of these changes for the business environment. There are more and more studies of changing social trends and there is such a wealth of data (see *'Further reading'*) that one can analyse information at local and regional level as well as at national and inter-country levels. One of the factors that links with the previous section on ageing population is the issue of the changing nature of the modern family both in terms of family size and the changing relationships and lifestyles within families. Within the context of lifestyle changes we will look at changes in trends of consumer behaviour, in smoking and drinking, and also in crime trends. The changing nature of work is also explored, especially in terms of the impact of new technologies and the resultant trend to more flexible working practices and some of the implications of these changes for organised labour. Wider social trends such as education and crime trends are also explored as both of these may be of significance for companies and managers who may be operating outside their home country.

5.2 The national cultural environment

The examination of the national cultural environment presents us with an opportunity of understanding differences and similarities between different cultures. We start this analysis by looking at what we understand national culture to be.

5.2.1 Definitions of national culture

One of the immediate problems faced when looking at national culture is to find an acceptable definition of what it is. Kroeber and Kluckhohn (1985) found over 160 definitions when they were researching this issue. The culture of countries was originally examined from an anthropological or sociological one as opposed to a business one, although the development of globalisation has thrown the national cultural issue much higher up the agenda for businesspeople who are working in countries other than their own. One of the most commonly used definitions is that of Hofstede and Hofstede (2005) who defines national culture as:

The collective programming of the mind which distinguishes the members of one group or category of people from others.

Hofstede and Hofstede go on to point out that values form the core of culture.

This definition highlights the significance of values and the fundamental taken-for-granted assumptions that are held by a large group of people in the country and which in turn will influence their behaviour. It is often differences in these sets of values that will drive differences in national culture and perceptions of what is acceptable and not acceptable behaviour in the culture. This can obviously be of great significance for business operations in countries other than your own, an issue that will be explored later in the chapter. Development psychologists believe that by the age of ten most children have their basic value system firmly in place and that after this age changes are more difficult to obtain.

Figure 5.1 shows that national cultural values will be influenced by a range of factors and the degree of difference between these factors may well determine the degree of difference between national cultures.

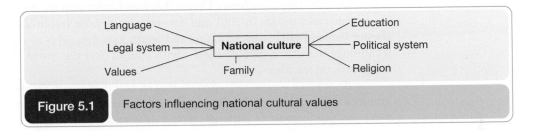

| Figure 5.1 | Factors influencing national cultural values |

One of the most significant factors is that of language and thus countries that speak the same language tend to be closer culturally than where there are strong linguistic differences. It could also explain why there can often be significant sub-cultures in a country built around different languages. An example in Europe would be Switzerland where citizens might speak either French, German, Italian or Romansch. Sometimes there might be a shift in languages taught in countries, which might have some impact on cultural attitudes; an example here would be the shift towards Mandarin Chinese from Cantonese Chinese in Hong Kong since Hong Kong was returned to China in 1997. Sometimes these language changes can be fiercely resisted as has been seen in France where there has been some resistance from the *Academie Française* to the new 'pop culture' words which are mainly English in origin.

One should not discount the impact of religion upon culture, especially where the political systems and religious systems are closely intertwined, as in many countries in the Middle East where the impact of Islam and Judaism has been very strong and has conditioned cultural attitudes strongly as it directly affects the value systems of individuals which we have seen is a central factor influencing culture. One of the main reasons why Eastern cultures are significantly different from Western ones is the impact of Confucianism on the region.

It should be stressed that whereas country analysis does suggest certain national behavioural patterns, there do still remain significant sub-cultures in many countries where the national pattern may be modified. These sub-cultures can be because of historical factors and may be enhanced by different religious or linguistic patterns.

5.2.2 National culture and globalisation

The role of national culture and potential national cultural differences has become an increasingly important part of the business environment as a result of the increase in globalisation, with more and more countries looking to operate outside their home base and thus finding that they are coming into increasing contact with different cultures. One of the key questions companies have to ask themselves when they internationalise is the extent to which they need to adapt to the new culture they are operating in. This could mean adaptation of things such as:

- marketing;
- human resource management;

- the product itself;
- management styles used in the company.

This reflects a wider debate called the convergence/divergence debate which has been a key feature of understanding the globalisation process.

The convergence perspective (Kerr *et al.*, 1960; Levitt, 1983) suggests that globalisation is inevitably leading to more and more standardisation as consumers become aware of global brands, and companies realise the advantages of having standardised products or practices that can be used throughout the company, no matter which country they are operating in. Brands such as Coca-Cola, Nike and Nokia are recognised globally, which means the potential global market is enormous and opens up opportunities for economies of scale through global advertising campaigns and standardised manufacturing. Even football clubs are seeking global identities; Manchester United developed links with the New York Yankees for the North American market in 2001 and devotes considerable resources to building the Manchester United brand name in China and South East Asia. This is a good example of how technology has driven globalisation – with fans all over the world able to watch the club every week on television.

The divergence perspective suggests that in reality it is not always that easy to transfer brands across countries and that companies may face difficulties when transferring management practices because of national cultural differences. This may be especially so where the company has an ethnocentric perspective in which it assumes that the practices used in its home country will work in any other country (the opposite is a polycentric perspective, where different strategies may be adopted if significant local differences occur). As can be seen, the degree of national cultural differences may well determine whether practices can be easily transferred from the home company to its overseas business units. A close cultural fit (for example the USA and UK) would probably suggest that little adaptation is needed and therefore the convergence perspective might be a valid one to follow, whereas if there were significant cultural differences, then adopting an ethnocentric approach might be a high risk strategy.

One of the most famous examples of this was the early stages of the operation of the EuroDisney theme park in France in 1992. The early stages of the project were fraught with problems both in terms of customer retention (the French were not happy about wine being unavailable in the Park) and in keeping staff (in the early days there was a very high rate of staff turnover) with the result that the project nearly failed. It has been argued that one of the main problems here was misunderstanding between managers (mainly American and Canadian) and staff (predominantly French). It was only with the appointment of a French CEO that things began to turn around to the point that the park (now renamed Disneyland Paris) is now well established. Having learned from this experience, the company took great care to work in partnership with local government during the planning and construction of Hong Kong Disneyland which opened in 2005. *Chapter 9* discusses a number of other issues around globalisation.

5.2.3 Identifying differences in national culture

As can be seen from the convergence/divergence debate, the cultural fit (or difference) between two countries is an important factor in the international business environment. While we can make various generalisations arising out of historical, linguistic, religious and other factors, we need some more precise criteria to evaluate the differences in national culture from a business perspective. Here we shall turn to two of the most significant writers about national culture who both provided frameworks against which we could test a country's national culture in order to see how closely it fits with other countries' patterns.

One of the most significant writers on national culture is Geert Hofstede who wrote *Culture's Consequences* in 1984 and updated in Hofstede and Hofstede (2005). This provided a useful framework by which we can measure national cultures. A significant limitation in

Hofstede's work is that it was based solely on the responses of staff from a single company (IBM). This meant that it might have been influenced by the corporate culture of IBM and also that it was limited in its scope, because in 1984 IBM did not have offices in certain countries such as China and Russia. However, the research is still important because it identified certain dimensions around which one can examine cultures and these remain valid.

Hofstede and Hofstede (2005) identify, four variables or dimensions around which one could begin to evaluate differences in national culture and some of these are identified in *Table 5.1.*

The first of these dimensions is power distance which represents the social distance between people of different rank. If we look at a country with a high power-distance score (Malaysia for example), this would suggest that there is a clear gap between superiors and subordinates in this country. This would be reflected in the way that superiors are addressed (formal or informal) and the willingness or unwillingness to question any decision made by a superior, i.e. in a high power-distance country superiors' decisions are more likely to be accepted without discussion and superiors would carry great respect. This is very common in Asian cultures where this is underpinned by the Confucian philosophy, which encourages respect for superiors and elders. Low power-distance countries would suggest cultures where managers may be challenged more openly and where respect may draw more from ability than seniority.

The second dimension identified by Hofstede is individualism which reflects the extent to which an individual relies on a group or collectivist approach to issues (a low individualism score) or the extent to which the individual takes individual initiatives to solve problems or make decisions (a high individualism score). *Table 5.1* shows the high score for the USA, one of the most individualistic cultures in the world, whereas Singapore reflects a much more

| Table 5.1 | Selected examples of cultural dimensions taken from Hofstede and Hofstede |

Country	Power distance (PDI)	Individualism (IDV)	Masculinity (MAS)	Uncertainty avoidance (UA)	Long-term orientation (LTO)
Denmark	18	74	16	23	46*
Sweden	31	71	5	29	33
Japan	54	46	95	92	80
Singapore	74	20	48	8	48
UK	35	89	66	35	25
France	68	71	43	86	39*
Germany	35	67	66	65	31
Italy	50	76	70	75	34*
Spain	57	51	42	86	19*
Brazil	69	38	49	76	65
Australia	36	90	61	51	31
USA	40	91	62	46	29

Note: 1. The figures show the relative positions of each country – the closer the values, the closer is the cultural fit for that dimension.
2. The LTO scores are taken from the Chinese Culture Connection (1987) article, except for those marked (*) which were based on replications.
Source: Hofstede and Hofstede (2005)

collectivist approach (hence a low individualism score), which again is quite common in Asian cultures.

The third dimension identified by Hofstede is uncertainty avoidance, which essentially reflects people's attitudes towards ambiguity in a society or country. When there is a high score for uncertainty avoidance it suggests a culture where people are unhappy with ambiguous situations and prefer more direction. It also suggests that in these countries it will be hard to undertake rapid changes in the organisation because this would probably cause anxiety and stress, as the nature of rapid change is that it does lead to uncertainty. According to the Hofstede data, Greece has a high level of uncertainty avoidance whereas in a country such as Sweden uncertainty would be much more tolerated and thus change programmes might be likely to receive less resistance.

The final dimension identified by Hofstede was that of masculinity, which is probably one of the more complex of his variables. It reflects values that are widely considered to be more 'masculine', such as assertiveness, competitiveness and the need to achieve results. A low masculinity figure suggests a higher degree of co-operation and more caring approaches to dealing with people in the organisation. This value can also reflect the level of discrimination against women in the organisation, i.e. it might be hard for a female manager to progress in a high-masculinity culture or to have the same degree of respect as a male manager. A good example in this context is Japan, which has the highest masculinity index in Hofstede's survey and where it is seen as very difficult for female managers to progress up the corporate ladder.

Although there were only four dimensions of culture in his original work, Hofstede identified a fifth dimension through work carried out with Bond and the Chinese Culture Connection Group (1988) which was evaluating the Asian context of national culture. The main outcome of Bond and Hofstede's later work was evidence that most Asian cultures seemed to have a long-term perspective about work and relationships as opposed to a much shorter-term perspective found primarily in Western cultures. This might explain why Asian companies prefer to build relationships with Western companies through joint ventures and strategic alliances rather than attempting mergers.

A further development from Hofstede's work is the idea that you can place countries in clusters of those showing similar patterns of the dimensions just described. If, for example, we look at the two variables of power distance and uncertainty avoidance we could end up with a pattern as suggested in *Figure 5.2*.

It is interesting to note here that although countries may be geographically close (e.g. France and the UK) they may have very different cultural characteristics which might be significant when managers of these two countries are working together. *Figure 5.2* suggests that

Denmark	UA:23 PD:18		
Sweden	UA:29 PD:31		
UK	UA:35 PD:35		
USA	UA:46 PD:40		
		Italy	UA:75 PD:50
		France	UA:86 PD:68
		Greece	UA:112 PD:60
		Japan	UA:92 PD:54
		Spain	UA:86 PD:57

Figure 5.2 Cultural clusters

Spanish managers would be much more at ease with their French counterparts than with, say, Swedish managers, because of the different perceptions about how to deal with subordinates and how much direction to give to other managers.

The second key writer on cultural differences is Fons Trompenaars, who drew on the work of Hofstede and others such as Kluckhohn and Strodtbeck (1961). Following a questionnaire survey of 15,000 respondents, he identified seven areas where cultural differences could occur. The seven areas identified were:

- universalism vs. particularism;
- affective vs. neutral;
- collectivism vs. individualism;
- specific vs. diffuse relationships;
- achieving vs. ascribing status;
- time as sequence vs. time as synchronisation;
- inner directed vs. outer directed.

The first of these, universalism vs. particularism, is where a universalist approach suggests that culture should be driven by rules and that there are universal rules that should be respected, whereas a particularist culture tends to have a more flexible interpretation of rules and draws more on people relationships. Universalist cultures tend to be found more in the UK and USA, whereas particularist cultures are more common in Asia. This may cause problems in negotiating between these countries as managers may have different conceptions as to what rules of business behaviour will apply.

Affective vs. neutral cultures relates to the extent to which emotion is used and is acceptable in a culture. In some countries people keep emotions under check (the 'stiff upper lip' approach), whereas in others emotional behaviour would be expected and condoned within a working environment. The implications for the successful operation of international teams are self-evident.

Collectivism vs. individualism reproduces the dimension previously identified by Hofstede, whereas specific vs. diffuse relationships relate to the extent to which managers separate their work relationships from other relationships. In a specific culture the manager–subordinate relationship may be observed at work but is not necessarily replicated in their relationship outside work, whereas in a diffuse culture (as is often found in Asia) the relationship at work influences all other relationships.

The issue of status is also identified in terms of achieving vs. ascribing status. In a culture with an achieving status, status is seen very much as something that is achieved by individuals through their own actions. In an ascribing culture, status might be ascribed to an individual through factors such as age or gender. You would find achievement status cultures in Scandinavia; ascribing status cultures are found in Asian countries as well as Argentina and Egypt.

Another dimension identified by Trompenaars was how time is perceived in a culture and he identified time as sequence vs. time as synchronisation. Time as sequence suggests a rational linear approach to issues where one issue is dealt with before another begins (one step at a time approach). Time as synchronisation suggests that time is seen as circular in the sense that a number of parallel activities can continue at the same time. A sequential time approach is found in Germany. The French tend to have a more synchronic approach which again may have implications for joint projects or team working between these two cultures.

The final dimension is inner directed vs. outer directed. This contrasts those countries such as the USA and Switzerland where there is a belief that the individual can determine events and control situations (inner directed) with those countries where the belief is that the individual's actions are determined by other forces such as the need for harmony with nature. This belief is central to both Confucianism and Buddhism and thus colours attitudes in Asian cultures (outer directed).

Through looking at the frameworks provided by Hofstede and Trompenaars it can be seen that there are a number of dimensions against which differences of national culture can be measured. We have also seen how some cultures have a relatively close fit with each other, whereas others have significant cultural differences where the divergence theory becomes more significant. Sometimes the differences in culture can lead to the phenomenon of culture shock where businesspeople operating in a different culture may suddenly find themselves disoriented as they realise they are having problems adapting to the local culture. Torbiorn (1982) suggests that businesspeople working overseas usually have an initial 'honeymoon period' where the excitement of working in a different country outweighs any initial problems encountered. It is only later, as cultural misunderstandings and confusion occur, that this initial positive dimension fades. There might also be the problem of language, which means that communications do not run smoothly, which again leads to confusion and stress. This is where the culture shock begins as the manager realises that cultural misunderstandings are undermining their effectiveness and their confidence.

Much will depend upon the ability of the individual manager to overcome this and the support given by the manager's organisation through cross-cultural training and support. Without this there is the danger that the manager will reject the culture they are operating in and turn very negative against it. Sometimes they may seek other expatriates and create an expatriate 'bubble' in terms of seeking to surround themselves with other people from their own culture and thus restrict contact with the local culture. The other extreme is that they will completely adapt to the local culture and 'go native', which has advantages but might affect their loyalties when difficult decisions have to be made on a corporate basis. In the twenty-first century the demand is for managers who are culturally aware and who can operate in a range of cultures, as opposed to the traditional expatriate who might work for many years in one base overseas.

5.2.4 The impact of national culture on business practices

If one accepts that national cultural differences can be significant in terms of affecting the international business environment, then the question arises as to identifying some of the key areas of business practice where some cultural adaptation may be necessary (especially when there is a significant gap in the cultures of the countries concerned). This idea can be explored further in *Minicase 5.2*.

With increased globalisation there has been a significant increase in international mergers, alliances and joint ventures, where the successful adaptation to national cultural differences

Minicase 5.2	American investment in China: some cultural dimensions

By 2001 the People's Republic of China (PRC) had become the primary location for global foreign direct investment with over US$47 billion being invested, with a large amount of that figure coming from corporate investors in the USA, which remains the base for a majority of the world's largest multinational corporations. Although there is some direct investment in China, the preferred method of market entry is by forming a joint venture with a Chinese company. This has the advantages for the investing firm that the Chinese company will have useful contacts and an existing distribution system, while the Chinese company can benefit from using improved management techniques and technology transfer. Given the significant increase of Chinese–US joint ventures, there will be increased pressure on managers from the two countries to work together in order to make the joint ventures or direct investment work effectively.

This is where the issue of national culture comes increasingly important as it will be necessary for managers to identify and adapt to national cultural differences if they are to work together effectively. We can use the data from Hofstede and Hofstede (2005) and Trompenaars (1997) to have a look at cultural characteristics of China, Hong Kong and the USA.

Table 1	Cultural characteristics		
	PRC	**Hong Kong**	**USA**
Hofstede and Hofstede (2005) ranking			
Power distance	20	15	38
Uncertainty avoidance	1	49	43
Individualism	23	37	1
Masculinity	54	18	15
Trompenaars (1993) ranking			
Achievement	32	20	2
Universalism	39	38	7
Internal control	19	8	7
Specificity	34	16	17
Affectivity	41	38	20

From the table we can immediately see that there are significant cultural differences between the PRC and USA. It is interesting to note the position of Hong Kong. It is close to the PRC in some respects and close to the USA in others. This reflects the phenomenon of culture shift in that Hong Kong has been exposed to both Eastern and Western business cultures over many years, and so its cultural behaviour may have changed in some respects. Thus an American company would probably find less of a culture clash if setting up in Hong Kong than in mainland PRC. However, since its handover from the UK back to the PRC in 1997 it is possible that Hong Kong's culture may be changing again.

There remain, however, significant differences in management styles, reflecting some of the cultural differences and so the ability of managers to adapt to each other's cultures will appear to be a significant factor in the potential success of American–Chinese joint ventures.

Questions

1 Imagine an initial meeting taking place between Chinese and American managers concerning a new joint venture. Using material from the case and above, try and imagine potential problems that might arise in this meeting through cultural misunderstanding – look at it from the perspective of both the American and Chinese manager.
2 You have been asked to lead the American delegation in the negotiations above. How would you brief them in terms of the management style to be adopted with the Chinese? Should you adapt or not?

may be an important factor in determining their effectiveness. Any such venture would require a number of meetings where negotiations would take place. This is where issues such as effective communication between the prospective partners would be significant and where cultural factors could come into play, e.g. in a German business culture humour is not usually used in business discussion whereas it is much more common in British business culture and therefore the use of jokes by the British managers may be misunderstood by German managers. Humour is also acceptable in Chinese business cultures, although Chinese humour may differ from British humour. The issue of power distance would also come into communications in terms of how people are addressed, i.e. formally or informally, and certain forms of non-verbal communication might be frowned upon in different cultures. In China this rather formal approach can be observed in unlikely situations. Part of the ritual at meals invariably requires toasts to be made to each other – often downing *Moutai,* a highly potent liquor. Visitors must be on their guard if they are to get through the evening! In recent years, the *Moutai* has been replaced by beer or even a soft drink – this may be a sign of greater acceptance being shown by hosts. It is also evident that the culture of younger Chinese managers, especially those who have been educated at universities in America, Europe and Australia, is slowly changing. In Malaysia the smile can mean many things. A smile and a nod may suggest that your opinion is respected but it does not mean that the person agrees with you; or a smile may be a cover for extreme embarrassment when the person wants to avoid losing face.

One consequence of international mergers, joint ventures and alliances is the increased use of international teams and, again, issues of how the team works together might be significant, e.g. when there are different perspectives on time (sequential vs. synchronic), attitudes to hierarchy in the group (power distance) and the way the group handles ambiguity (uncertainty avoidance).

We can look at these cultural differences in more depth by comparing American and Chinese management styles. We have already seen that the American management style is very individualistic in nature and there is relatively low uncertainty avoidance – individuals will be expected to make decisions and to react to change effectively. It is certainly a hard-working culture where excessive working will be encouraged and where the practice of the business breakfast is well established. Americans like decisive leaders and new ideas are generally welcomed. Communication is generally informal in nature with the use of first names between senior managers and their subordinates. The American manager will tend to be short-termist in nature and will be looking for instant results from a meeting, and status in the organisation is more likely to be based on salary size than age.

If we contrast this with the Chinese management style we might notice a few differences. The Chinese manager will be influenced by the Confucian influence that pervades many aspects of Chinese life. Thus there will be great respect for more senior people in the organisation (linked to high power distance), respect for elder people, and especially the need for politeness and harmony in their working life. The Chinese manager will also be a hard worker and a lot of time will be spent on developing relationships (*guanxi*) with people both inside and outside the organisation. Communication will usually be very formal and often top-down and great effort will be made that no one loses 'face' in discussions or negotiations, although the Chinese manager may not be expecting an instant decision from the meeting – it may be more about building up the *guanxi* with new partners. The Chinese manager might also be more comfortable about working in groups rather than on an individual level, although less happy about close physical contact with other people and they would not be happy about any personal disclosures, preferring to talk solely about the business in hand. Meals will be an important part of negotiations and humour is very acceptable in these situations. *Minicase 5.2* poses some further questions.

There will also be functional areas of business that will be affected by cultural differences, most notably in marketing and human resource management (HRM). From the marketing perspective there will be the discussion of whether to go with global marketing campaigns (the convergence perspective) or whether there is a need to adapt the product for the particular cultural needs of the country concerned. The attractions of following the convergence approach would be in terms of economies of scale in that the same advert could be used on a global basis, thus reducing costs and also developing a global brand image. The divergence approach might be needed if the product needs adapting for particular markets. For example, the British tend to use a lot of humour in their advertising, but this humour might not be seen as humour in other countries and thus there is a need to adapt the campaign according to local demands. Although McDonald's in many respects follows a convergence perspective in terms of common approaches to layout, design and a common brand, it still adapts its product range in different countries, especially in countries where certain foods may be banned for religious reasons, for example cows are sacred to Hindus in India and elsewhere, so lamb is served as an alternative.

From the HRM perspective, national culture may be very significant when looking at areas such as training, appraisal and recruitment. In terms of training, it may be dangerous to use direct training approaches such as direct discussion/questions or role-play situations when you are working in an environment where there is a high power distance and people prefer to be told what to do rather than discussing it with the trainer. It may also be difficult to get responses in Eastern cultures where there is the fear of loss of face. Performance appraisal might also have to be adapted as it suggests an appraisal of a subordinate by a superior, whereas modern styles of appraisal such as 360-degree appraisal would also include assessment by fellow workers and subordinates as well as their line manager. This might be difficult to translate into a culture where there is traditionally a high power distance. The issue of recruitment might also be significant in terms of whether you employ expatriate managers (from your home country) or local managers (who will know local conditions but may be less familiar with the corporate culture of the company). Daniels *et al.* (2009) suggest that it is getting harder to find managers willing to spend long periods abroad. The trend is clearly towards managers spending shorter periods abroad but in a variety of countries, and many of these managers will become more culturally sensitive through training and experience.

5.3 The demographic environment

Demography concerns the study of population and population change and can be seen as another important factor that will affect the business environment. Whereas many of the environmental indicators such as social and technology trends are hard to forecast, the impact of demographic changes can be more confidently predicted, i.e. if we know the number of 5-year-olds in a country in 2010 we will have a pretty clear idea of the number of 15-year-olds there will be in 2020 and 25-year-olds in 2030 and this may be useful when predicting potential markets.

This section will examine some of the key drivers of population change and explain some of the main trends that are affecting population change worldwide and then look at some of the implications of population change for individuals, businesses and government.

5.3.1 Key drivers of population change

The two main indicators of natural population change are birth rate and death rate. Birth rate can be defined as:

> the number of live births per thousand of the population.

The death rate can be defined as:

> the number of deaths per thousand of the population.

When these two figures are put together you will get the natural increase or decrease of the population, again measured per thousand of the population.

However, there is another factor that has to be taken into account when looking at population change. This is the net migration per thousand of the population, which reflects the difference between immigration (into a country) and emigration (out of a country). If we add this figure to the natural change in population we will see the overall increase or decrease in the population. Information on population change in selected European countries between 2010 and 2015 is shown in *Table 5.2*

From the information in *Table 5.2* we can see that there are some significant differences in population patterns in Europe. Ireland has a birth rate which is far in excess of its death rate, and also has a lot of inward migration which means that its population is increasing

	BR	DR	NC	NM	TC
Bulgaria	9.6	14.6	−5.0	−1.4	−6.4
France	11.4	9.0	2.4	1.6	4.0
Germany	7.9	11.0	−3.1	1.3	−1.8
Greece	9.1	10.4	−1.3	2.7	1.4
Ireland	14.8	6.5	8.3	4.2	12.5
Italy	8.6	10.5	−1.9	3.6	1.7
Poland	9.8	10.5	−0.7	−0.6	−1.3
Portugal	9.2	10.5	−1.3	2.3	1.0
Sweden	11.5	9.8	1.7	2.7	4.4
UK	12.0	9.8	2.2	3.0	5.2

Table 5.2 Estimated population change in selected European countries 2010–2015

Key: BR = birth rate/thousand; DR = death rate/thousand; NC = natural population change (BR − DR)/thousand; NM = net migration (immigrants − emigrants)/thousand; TC = total rate of population change/thousand.

Source: adapted from United Nations Population Information Network website, http:www.un.org/popin/data.html

relatively quickly. This could be contrasted with the figures from Germany where the death rate exceeds the birth rate, meaning that the natural population is declining. This is only partially offset by inward migration, meaning that the total population in Germany is forecast to decline in the future. A further example can be seen with the case of Bulgaria where not only does the death rate exceed the birth rate but there is also a net outflow in migration, all leading to a rapid decline in the population. The EU has carried out forecasts of population change by 2050 based on current trends and, whereas strong population growth is expected in Ireland (increasing 31 percent), the UK (increasing 13 percent) and France (increasing 10 percent), population decline is anticipated in other countries such as Germany (declining 4 percent), Spain (declining 8 percent), Italy (declining 22 percent) and Russia (declining 30 percent). These trends obviously have significance for businesses which will be exploring potentially high-growth markets against those where demand is likely to fall as a result of population decline.

To understand why these changes are taking place we need to understand why birth rates, death rates and migration rates are changing.

5.3.2 Birth rate factors

Birth rates tend to be more volatile than the death rates and thus may have more short-run impact on population changes. Birth rate may be affected by many factors such as attitudes towards family size. The trend seen in most of Europe is a decline in family size. The usual quick test in this respect is to look at your family size and then compare it with your parents' family size and grandparents' family size and so on. One undoubted factor here is the fact that more women wish to follow their own careers before having children and so delay the age at which they have children. The cost of having children might also be taken into account as well as the degree of flexibility in the labour market which determines the extent to which women (or men) can follow more flexible work patterns in order to look after children while continuing in work. Other determinant factors could be the values of the country or the impact of religion on attitudes towards children or the availability and use of

Table 5.3	Forecast total fertility rates, 2010–2015
India	2.52
Sri Lanka	2.22
USA	2.02
UK	1.85
France	1.85
Sweden	1.85
China	1.79
Spain	1.56
Bulgaria	1.50
Russian Federation	1.46
Italy	1.41
Greece	1.41
Germany	1.34

Source: adapted from United Nations Population Information Network website, http:www.un.popin/functional/population.html

contraception in a country. These factors may come together to account for the remarkably high birth rate in Ireland, for example.

A critical indicator which will reflect all these factors is the total fertility rate which reflects the average number of children per female. Even more significant is the replacement fertility rate, the fertility rate needed if a population is to replace itself. The recognised replacement rate needed for this is 2.1 children.

If we look at *Table 5.3* we can see some of the current predicted figures for total fertility rates as suggested by the UN.

From *Table 5.3* we can see that Sri Lanka has a figure which just exceeds the desired replacement rate, while the USA is almost exactly at the desired rate. France and the UK have relatively good rates, which are reflected in their higher birth rates and their predicted population growth. The lowest figures seem to come from either Eastern European countries, where generally weaker economic performance may be a factor in smaller family size, or the Mediterranean countries (such as Italy, Spain and Greece) where the cause is less easy to define but may be linked to inflexible labour markets and changing attitudes among women. The notable exception is Germany; comparison with data from previous years suggest that its fertility rate is almost exactly the same as ten years ago, while that of the other countries in *Table 5.3* has increased. Certainly this decline in the number of children in these areas may be having a significant impact not only on the future population size of these countries but also on the future age structure, as this trend will (other factors remaining equal) lead to a rapid ageing of the population with all the implications that has for businesses and government (see section 5.4 '*Patterns of population change*' and *Minicase 5.4*).

5.3.3 Death rate factors

As has been previously suggested, the death rate tends to be more stable than the birth rate and it usually reflects the changing age structure of the population. A higher concentration of older people will tend to lead to a gradual increase in the death rate. Death rates have come down in many parts of the world as a result of better medicines and improved sanitation and healthcare, although there are still significant discrepancies between the developed and the developing world. In many parts of the developing world people generally have very basic diets which might make them more vulnerable to epidemics or illnesses, such as those illnesses linked to poor drinking water. These factors help explain the higher death rates and lower life expectancies in these countries.

There is also the impact of armed conflict which may have an impact on the death rate if there is a prolonged civil war, as has been seen in several countries in Central Africa. With globalisation and improvements in transport, diseases can travel much more quickly as can be seen with a number of health scares in the last ten years. In 2003 the SARS outbreak spread very quickly from Guandong province in China to Hong Kong and thence to several places, most notably Toronto in Canada. In 2005 a variant of the H5N1 influenza virus known as Bird Flu spread rapidly in the Far East (although with relatively little impact on other regions). Most recently, an H1N1 variant known as Swine Flu was declared to be a worldwide pandemic by the WHO but, at the time of writing, was not expected to cause a significantly high number of deaths, thanks to better living conditions and improved healthcare.

A much more significant epidemic in terms of its impact has been the spread of the HIV/AIDS virus. While this virus has spread throughout the world, its most serious effects are being felt in sub-Saharan Africa as *Minicase 5.3* illustrates.

Minicase 5.3	Life chances in the UK and Malawi

When looking at population change it is usually considered that birth rate is more volatile than death rates and that change in population is primarily driven by changes in birth rates and replacement fertility rates. Sometimes, however, the key driver affecting a country's rate of population change can be a dramatic change in the death rate. A region that has been devastated by an epidemic is sub-Saharan Africa where the HIV/AIDS virus has spread alarmingly in some countries and has led to severe changes in mortality rates.

We can highlight these changes by contrasting life chances between Malawi and the UK using data published by the United Nations in 2007 (http://esa.un.org/unpd/wpp2008/index.htm). Malawi is a much smaller country in population terms than the UK (13.9 million in Malawi compared with 60.7 million in the UK) and is also a much poorer one; the healthcare spend per capita in Malawi was $19 compared with $2,900 in the UK.

This has meant that Malawi was poorly positioned to deal with the HIV/AIDS virus. If we look at the UK we can see that HIV prevalence was about 0.2 percent of the population which meant that in 2005 there were about 68,000 people with HIV. AIDS deaths in that year were less than 1,000. While these figures are significant, they have not had a major impact on mortality rates in the UK; in fact life expectancy in the UK is gradually rising and was estimated in 2007 as being 79 years.

The impact of HIV/AIDS has been much more devastating in Malawi with over 14 percent of the population being affected by the illness and with AIDS deaths in 2005 being estimated at 78,000. The effect of the epidemic has been to leave many children orphaned (550,000 in 2005) and many of those, in turn, may carry the virus. This is having a significant effect on life expectancy; the UN estimated that if HIV/AIDS did not exist, the typical life expectancy of a Malawi child would be 64; this has been reduced to 48 by the virus. One in five children in Malawi does not make it past their fifth year.

Even much more advanced countries such as South Africa have been seriously affected. With a population of 48.5 million, there were 320,000 deaths from HIV/AIDS in 2005 and life expectancy for those with HIV/AIDS was only 50 years compared with 67 years for those without HIV/AIDS. There has been severe criticism of the South African government for its inappropriate and ineffective policies towards the epidemic.

Questions

1 What can Malawi do to control and eradicate the HIV/AIDS epidemic in the country? What resources are needed for this to happen?

2 Do you feel that the ease with which viruses spread (e.g. H1N1 and HIV/AIDS) is linked to increased globalisation or can they be controlled locally?

5.3.4 Migration factors

Migration of people across borders has long been a feature of history and in the modern globalised economy it seems that migration is seen as a global issue rather than a regional one. An economic migrant from Afghanistan would now look as much at migrating to Western Europe as to moving to the countries adjacent to Afghanistan. Historically there have been many great shifts of population. In the nineteenth century there was great movement from Western Europe to the USA, Canada, Australia and Argentina where there were new prospects for economic development and there were more opportunities. People migrating in search of new opportunities for work are seen as economic migrants, whereas those migrating to escape oppression and persecution in their home country could be seen as political migrants. Many of the people who migrate are younger and more ambitious. They can enrich the economy into which they move in terms of providing new skills and filling gaps in the labour market.

The Republic of Ireland has for a long time experienced significant outward migration, predominantly to the USA, UK and Australia. It is said that there are more people of Irish descent in New York than there are in Ireland – it is believed that there are 44 million Americans of Irish descent. The horrific potato famine in 1845/46 was a significant spur to migration, primarily to the 'New World', and continual waves of outward migration occurred as younger people looked for new opportunities away from the depressed economy. This is obviously a loss for the country as the younger people are the most flexible in terms of taking up new job opportunities and in learning new skills. Irish migrants were seen as an asset to the UK where many worked in the construction industry. What is interesting now is that the economic resurgence of Ireland in the 1990s, (the 'tiger economy' of Europe), has led to greater opportunities for young Irish people within Ireland and this has considerably reduced the flow of young Irish people abroad. Indeed, we can see from *Table 5.2* that a strong inflow of migrants to Ireland is forecast for 2010 to 2015, suggesting that the traditional outward flow has reversed itself. Unfortunately the Irish economy has been hit relatively hard by the recession in 2008/9 with companies such as Dell Computers shifting European production to low-wage rate countries such as Poland. It is quite possible that the migration trend will reverse if the Irish economy fails to recover quickly.

If we look at the same table we can see the case of Germany where the inward migration is partially offsetting the decline in natural population growth. Germany has traditionally been a magnet to economic migrants because of its successful economic growth record, which has encouraged inflows of migrants, predominantly from Turkey and Eastern Europe. However, the result has often been political and social tensions manifested by racial attacks and have encouraged the growth of far-right political parties, a feature found across Europe. Migrants also face other problems with some of them finding themselves in areas characterised by low-quality and poorly maintained housing with all the resulting social problems that follow from that. In 2005 riots broke out in a *banlieu* (suburb) in northeastern Paris which had a high concentration of immigrants and high unemployment. Unrest rapidly spread to other parts of Paris and other cities throughout France, and has recurred occasionally. So, whereas the influx of migrants can be a boost for a country's labour supply and can improve mobility of labour, it can result in some of the tensions identified above.

One of the biggest challenges faced by the EU in the twenty-first century is that of illegal migration, which constitutes mainly economic migrants looking for new opportunities and deriving mainly from developing countries. An example of this is the influx of Albanians coming illegally into Italy with some moving on to other countries and some staying in the 'hidden economy' of Italy where they don't have to declare their earnings. It often poses a quandary for governments as to how tight their restrictions should be. One could look at Italy with its predicted 22 percent fall in natural population by 2050 and question whether, in fact, inward migration might be necessary for the country to maintain its current economic structure.

Another migration issue that can be seen throughout Europe and many developing economies is the shift from rural locations to urban locations, leaving many villages in the more remote regions populated mainly by older people. However, this in turn causes problems in cities with uncontrolled urban sprawl and increased congestion. Some major urban areas continue to suffer from poor housing and education, overstretched services, increasing crime and general social and economic hardship. The better-off tend to move to the affluent suburbs leaving the very old, the unskilled and certain ethnic minority groups concentrated in inner-city areas. This leads to a range of social problems allied to high crime rates which pose additional problems for governments.

A similar challenge has faced the Chinese government with migration from impoverished rural areas to the many huge and growing cities. The trend is unlikely to be reversed without great investment in rural economies and in early 2009 Xinhua, the official Chinese news agency, reported a statement by President Hu Jintao that the promotion of stable agricultural and rural development would be a priority for the government.

5.4 Patterns of population change

At this stage it will be useful to look at some of the issues surrounding population change.

5.4.1 The impact of population growth

Table 5.4 shows how the world's population has changed together with the predicted population figure for 2050.

It took 123 years for the world's population to increase from 1 billion to 2 billion but only another 33 years to increase from 2 billion to 3 billion, with the last landmark of 6 billion being passed in October 1999, a mere 12 years after reaching 5 billion. This does reflect a

Table 5.4	World population growth 1950–2000 and forecast for 2010–2050
1950	2.5 billion
1960	3.0 billion
1970	3.7 billion
1980	4.4 billion
1990	5.3 billion
2000	6.1 billion
2010	6.9 billion
2020	7.7 billion
2030	8.3 billion
2040	8.8 billion
2050	9.1 billion

Source: adapted from United Nations Population Information Network website, http:www.un.popin/functional/population.html

quickening of population growth, driven primarily by population growth in developing countries where high birth rates have been accompanied by falling death rates (through improved medicine and sanitation), thus creating population growth. This high rate of growth, if unchecked, will continue to put extreme pressures on the world's resources unless they could be developed at a commensurate rate (e.g. increasing agricultural production through more use of genetically modified crops).

In some countries high population growth could be seen as a real inhibitor to economic growth and development. In Bangladesh, for example, the population was 123 million in 1998, is now 160 million and is predicted to grow to 210 million by 2020. It is characterised by a high birth rate and low death rate and 45 percent of the population are currently under 15 (compared to only 13 percent of the EU's population being under 15 in 1998). Bangladesh has some fertile countryside but is prone to flooding and there is limited room for further agricultural expansion, with the result that the increasing population is putting tremendous pressure on existing resources. The country needs to double agricultural output by 2020 to stand still and already 50 percent of the population are below the poverty line, so the need for more control on population growth is very clear in order to reduce the existing pressure on resources. One country that has managed this very well is China with its 'one-child policy' where significant social pressure is brought on couples to have just one child, with the result that the recent surge in economic growth in China is not being held back by too rapid a population growth.

However, *Table 5.4* shows that world population, although still increasing, is forecast to grow at a slower rate (the increase from 2040 to 2050 is around 4 percent compared with a 20 percent rise from 1950 to 1960). This is because of the effect noticed earlier (in *Table 5.2*) of many countries (especially European ones) where population growth is practically static or is even declining through the very low fertility rates identified in *Table 5.3*. This does suggest in the future something of a redistribution of world population away from areas such as Europe towards areas such as East and South East Asia and this may have implications for businesses' long-term investment plans and development strategies.

5.4.2 The distribution of population

While it is interesting to look at actual population changes, it is also important to look at the structure of the population in terms of the relevant age structures as this will also give us clues as to how the population is evolving and some of the implications of this for both businesses and governments. The distribution of population can be looked at both within a country and between countries.

The age structure of a country or region can best be illustrated by a population pyramid and an example of such a pyramid is shown in *Figure 5.3*, which shows how the age structure of the EU will change between 1990 and 2020.

If the birth and death rates for men and women are similar and remain constant, then one would expect to see the widest bars of the pyramid at the bottom and a smooth reduction in width all the way to the highest age groups. But short-term and long-term trends will distort this picture. For example, World War II (1939–1945) caused the deaths of many people, especially young men born between 1915 and 1930, which probably accounts for the asymmetry of the pyramid at the highest ages.

What is most interesting for us are the effects of longer-term changes in birth and death rates. This population pyramid clearly shows that the population of the EU is ageing. At all ages greater than 45 the numbers (as a percentage of the population) will increase by 2020, whereas at all ages below that they will decrease. This is because of the 'baby boom' in the 1980s followed by a forecast reduction in births. We shall see more and more older people and relatively fewer younger people than at present. We have already seen the very low replacement fertility rates in many European countries and this is a prime causal factor for this change, allied to the fact that older people are living longer. If we look at the global picture we see that in 1950, 27 percent of the world's population

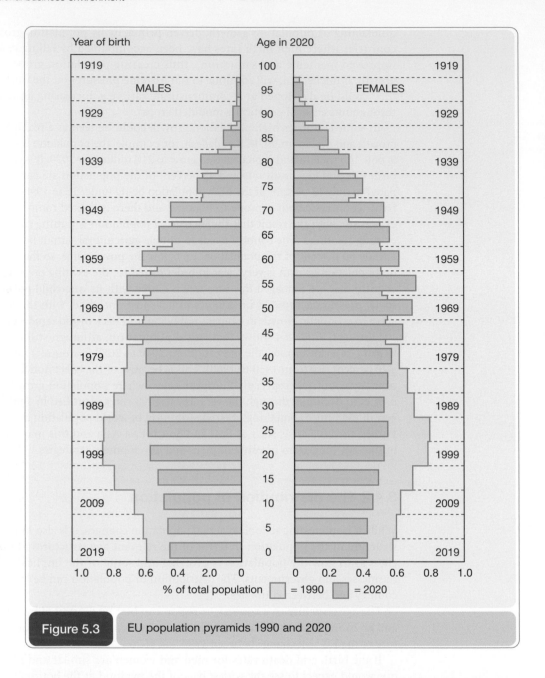

Year of birth | Age in 2020

MALES | FEMALES

% of total population ☐ = 1990 ☐ = 2020

| **Figure 5.3** | EU population pyramids 1990 and 2020 |

was under 15 and only 12 percent above 60. By 1998 the figures were nearly level with 19.1 percent of the world's population under 15 and 18.8 percent over 60, and by 2050 the predicted figures are much more dramatic with 15 percent of the world's population predicted to be under 15 and 33 percent over 60. It is perhaps these figures that are more significant than the figures for overall population growth as they show a relatively rapid ageing of the world's population. The predicted figures for Europe in 2050 are even more extreme with only 13 percent of the population predicted to be 15 or less compared with 39 percent being over 60. This will also be reflected in changes in the average age of the population. The average age in the UK in 1950 was 35, which had risen to 38 in 2000 and is predicted to rise to 44 by 2050. In rapidly ageing countries such as Italy it will rise even higher to 52 in 2050.

These rapidly ageing populations (unless they are changed by significant influxes of young migrants) may pose problems for companies who operate in these markets and for

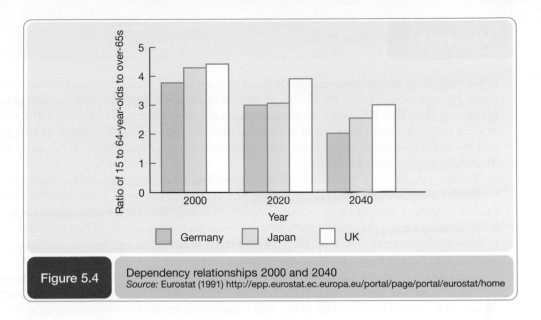

Figure 5.4	Dependency relationships 2000 and 2040
	Source: Eurostat (1991) http://epp.eurostat.ec.europa.eu/portal/page/portal/eurostat/home

governments faced with a significant increase in older people. One critical ratio that is affected by these changes is the Dependency Ratio, which reflects the number of 15 to 64-year-olds to the rest of the population as it is from this group that the taxes will be raised which will support the schools, hospitals and other support services that are needed for groups outside that age range.

Figure 5.4 shows the ratio of 15 to 64-year-olds to the over-65s in the UK, Germany and Japan. These last two countries have a much more rapidly ageing population than the UK, and it can clearly be seen that there will be fewer and fewer numbers of people available to support the over-65s, which has many significant implications for governments, not least the issue of how to support these people with pensions without resorting to massive tax increases.

In sectors where demand for products is based around younger age groups, the rapidly ageing population may have important strategic considerations. A company, such as Mothercare, started out in 1961 by serving the needs of mothers-to-be and very young children, then extended its product ranges to older children, up to age eight, partly as a result of a decline in the number of children being born. The brewing industry depends for a significant part of its sales on the male age group from 18 to 30, with a male in this group on average consuming 70 percent more beer than males in the over-40s group. With a prospective fall in this age group across Europe, brewing companies have to think up longer-term strategies which can accommodate this. Hence, there has been a shift towards speciality beers and drinks which might be attractive as alternatives to traditional beer and also the shift by companies into catering in pubs which would appeal to more mature adults and families. The brewing companies have also sought to diversify into other sectors such as hotel ownership and recreation facilities.

On the other hand, the growth in the proportion of older people throws up opportunities for businesses which seek to target this group (see *Minicase 5.4*). Examples of this would be travel firms which seek to cater to the needs of the older consumer or the potential for pharmaceutical companies producing drugs which are much more likely to be used by this age group. Numerous financial services groups target this sector offering products at those who are retired or are about to retire. There has also been a significant increase in the number of registered nursing and retirement homes which cater for the older citizen and which provide more sheltered housing for older people. Older people tend to prefer wine to beer and there is evidence of a gradual increase in wine drinking in the UK.

Minicase 5.4	Saga Group

In the mid-1950s, entrepreneur Sidney De Haan decided to offer cheap holidays to retired people at off-peak times. He took advantage of the low prices offered by hoteliers who were only too willing to see their poor occupancy rates rise. Fifty years on, Saga (now a subsidiary of Acromas Holdings) had a turnover in excess of £700 million in 2007, offers holidays, financial services and magazines to the over-50s. Saga recognised that the special needs of older customers represented a market opportunity. It has even started an online messaging service for older people.

Retired people have grown progressively wealthier and Saga now offers holidays trekking in the Himalayas and round-the-world cruises costing up to £30,000 per head. It has expanded in the lucrative US market. It has also developed its 'product' portfolio to include financial services such as insurance brokering. It can negotiate many preferential rates for its low-risk customers, since, for example, older people tend not to drive great distances hence reducing the probability of being involved in a car accident. They also spend more of their time in their houses, so reducing the opportunity for burglars to strike.

Saga employs around 2,000 staff in its travel business with approximately the same number in the financial services side of the business. What is more, it has found its business is virtually recession-proof, as a decline in a national economic cycle has little influence on the income of retired people. What is damaging, however, is a decline in interest rates which does adversely influence the incomes of its clients.

An unexpected threat to the business was posed by the UK Government's Equality Bill which went through Parliament in 2009. As written, this would have forced Saga to make its services available to all age groups. In a written submission to Parliament in June 2009 Saga stated '. . . the Bill as it stands risks negatively affecting our customers' ability to buy the holidays they want and the financial and other services they need at a competitive price.' The reason for this is that the company would lose some of the financial advantages mentioned earlier if it had to offer its products to people of all ages.

Questions

1 Saga has been one of the most successful companies in terms of catering to the needs of the older population. What other companies and industries have responded to the increased demand from this group?
2 Which types of companies have suffered from the ageing of the population and what strategies can they follow to counteract these problems?

5.4.3 Wider implications of population change

As has been previously suggested, population change is relatively slow and is the most predictable aspect about the business environment. At the same time it will have important wider implications, which can be seen at individual, corporate and governmental levels.

At the individual level the changes we have looked at will be reflected in the sort of life people can expect to live in the twenty-first century. One of the key indicators will be that of life expectancy as that reflects the changes of lifestyle and medical improvements, which means that people can generally expect longer lives than in previous times. *Table 5.5* shows some examples of life expectancy for people born in the period 2010–2015.

From this it can be seen that women usually outlive men by some years, which explains the relatively high number of women found in the older age ranges of the population pyramid (see *Figure 5.3*). However, the trends of life expectancy have seen a gradual increase to the extent that more people are living to 100 years of age. Against this generally positive picture one should not forget that average life expectancies can also decrease as in sub-Saharan Africa (see *Minicase 5.3*). Another indicator of improvements in living standards is the decline of the infant mortality rate, which shows that children have a much stronger chance of survival in their first year as a result of medical and sanitary improvements, particularly

Table 5.5	Selected examples of life expectancies, 2010–2015

Country	Men	Women	Both
France	78.6	85.1	81.9
Germany	77.8	83.1	80.5
Greece	77.7	82.5	80.1
Italy	78.6	84.6	81.6
Switzerland	80.2	84.7	82.5
Bulgaria	74.3	70.9	74.3
China	72.3	75.9	74.0
Poland	72.3	80.4	76.4
Russian Federation	61.9	74.1	67.9
UK	77.8	82.3	80.1
India	63.7	66.9	65.2
Singapore	78.5	83.4	81.0
South Africa	51.8	53.8	52.9
USA	77.7	82.1	79.9
Brazil	69.9	77.2	73.5
Zimbabwe	50.4	49.8	50.4

Source: adapted from United Nations Population Information Network website, http:www.un.popin/functional/population.html

in developing countries. However, one should not forget that there are still serious global discrepancies in this respect as in 2009 approximately one-sixth of the world's population does not have access to safe water and approximately three-fifths of the world's population do not have adequate sanitation.

At the corporate level we have already seen how businesses in markets with ageing populations may have to refocus their selling strategies. This is particularly relevant when the older age groups have more spending than previously, which has led to the concept of 'grey power'. In developing countries, where there is still a high birth rate and a significantly higher proportion of younger people, companies may find substantial markets for products which are wanted by this age range – this could apply to certain global products with strong brand images that are associated with younger people and may sometimes be seen as essential fashion accessories. An example here would be the effect that satellite television has had on the merchandising of football clothing linked to well-known global clubs such as Manchester United and Real Madrid, especially in South East Asia.

Another factor that might be significant for companies when considering overseas investment decisions is the geographical mobility of labour, which reflects the ease with which labour can move around the country in search of employment, and also the occupational mobility of labour, which reflects the ease with which labour can move between jobs and how quickly they can be retrained. It is usually the case that younger people are more mobile both in terms of geographical and occupational mobility and so a younger age-profile might be attractive to some companies, especially those who invest in labour-intensive industries. It has been noticeable that many large organisations have been moving their labour-intensive call centres to developing countries where there is an established pool of young, educated people who are available for work.

Perhaps the most challenging dimension of demographic change is that faced by governments. When there is high population growth (as we saw in the case of Bangladesh), there are enormous pressures on governments to provide adequate resources for the growing population. While the prime requirement is for food and water, there will also be requirements for educational and medical facilities which will be very difficult to fulfil without help from other sources. In the situation of Europe and Japan, where the trend is essentially that of an ageing population, the governments will face other issues. One factor will be a gradual decline in the number of younger people. This might mean that in some cases schools have to be closed down, especially in areas where natural population decline has been exacerbated by migration. On the other hand, with a significant increase in the number of older people there will be a significant increase in the demand for medical services, especially as older people generally require significantly more medical support than younger people. Thus the demand for hospitals and medical support provided by the government will grow and governments will have to become increasingly aware of the needs of older people when determining their political programmes.

5.5 Social dynamics

The final part of this chapter will examine some of the social trends that have occurred over the last years and assess some of the implications of these for the way we live and how they might be significant for the business environment.

Social dynamics will be looked at from three perspectives, with current trends identified in each case. The first dynamic of social change relates to changes in the changing family. The family is the basic building block of society and yet it has been influenced by many factors over the last 20 years. We have already seen how the falling birth rates might be significant for family size, although we will also examine changes in family structure and changes in the patterns of relationships. A very good source to identify such trends is the National Census in the UK which first took place in 1801 and has taken place every ten years since that date with the next census due in 2011. An additional source is the General Household Survey which began in 1971 and which is carried out each year based on a sample of 9,000 households. The second social dynamic we will examine will be the change in lifestyles. This will reflect some different aspects of how we live and how we spend our leisure time and what we spend our money on. It will also reflect how healthy our lifestyle is and our educational needs as well as looking at trends in crime in our society. The third social dynamic to be examined will be the change in work and the extent to which the nature of work is changing in the twenty-first century and will also cover other work-related issues such as the minimum wage and changes in organised labour.

5.5.1 The changing family

Statistics from various UK sources have been widely used in this section. However, it must be recognised that in this section we are describing a trend that is evident in many more countries than the UK.

Using information published by the UK Office of National Statistics, we can learn about many social changes in the past 40 years. We have already identified that falling birth rates have tended to lead to a reduction in family size. In the UK, household size has declined in a fairly consistent pattern from a figure of 2.91 persons in 1971 to a figure of 2.48 in 1991 and then again to 2.4 in 2003/4. Many of the reasons for this have been discussed above; also more people are living alone than at any previous time. One-person households have increased from 17 percent of all households in 1971 to 30 percent in the census of 2003/4 (a total of 6.5 million households). There are always a number of older people who live alone, but the figure for this group has remained stable, with the big increase in single households occurring in the 25–44 age group. This may be significant for companies who might target this age group and might be one of the factors behind the significant increase in demand for satellite television in the UK. The 'traditional' family pattern, where there exists a married or cohabiting couple with dependent children, has changed; the number of dependent children living in such a family declined by 1 million between 1998 and 2008 (70 to 63 percent). The proportion of children living with one-parent families increased 22 to 23 percent over the same period. Companies might have to start thinking about non-traditional targets when they target their markets.

Another area of change in the family is that of changing family relationships. One key issue here is that of marital status. In 2006, the majority of people were married (52 percent of men and 50 percent of women). However, the proportion of unmarried people cohabiting rather than marrying has increased significantly (24 percent of men aged 16 to 59 in 2006 compared with 11 percent in 1986 and 25 percent of women compared with 11 percent in 1986) and this trend appeared to be stronger in the younger age ranges. This is reflected by the fact that people seem to be marrying at a later age as they seek to develop their careers or move through the cohabiting phase previously identified.

A factor influencing this is the changing role of women in society and the increased career expectations of women. More women want to develop their own careers before having children and the increased availability of flexible working allows them to return to work on a full- or part-time basis much more easily than in the past. One consequence of this is the massive increase in demand for child-caring facilities, such as nurseries, where the demand has mushroomed, despite there being a gradual decline in the birth rate.

There are also some changes in traditional family roles, where the roles may be shared more between the household members. There are increasing cases where the female partner or wife may earn a higher income than her husband/partner and so we see the development of the 'househusband'.

Another factor that has contributed to the increase in single households (especially in the 25–44 age group) is the increase in divorce in the UK. Over the period 1973 to 1993 the number of divorces rose by nearly 60 percent although many divorced people re-marry. The latest figures suggest that the number of divorces has fallen to the lowest number since 1977– but this probably reflects the greater number of couple cohabiting rather than marrying.

There are significant differences in divorce rates across Europe which reflect different religious, social, legal and cultural factors, with the countries in Northern and Western Europe typically having higher divorce rates than Southern Europe. In 2005 the EU average for divorce was 2 per thousand people and the highest rate in 2007 was in Belgium (2.8 per 1,000) with the UK also above the EU average (2.4 per 1,000). Not surprisingly, the lowest rates in 2007 were found in Ireland and Italy where the rate was 0.8 per 1,000.

The role of the family in society also varies across Europe. Vogel (1998) suggests that there are three clusters of European Society:

- the Nordic countries, comprising Denmark, Sweden, Norway and Finland;
- the Southern European countries of Greece, Italy, Spain and Portugal (although Ireland could also be included in many respects);
- most of the continental countries in between, which show characteristics of the first two clusters but not as strongly – this group would include France, Germany and the Netherlands.

The differences between these clusters would be determined by religious, social, political and cultural factors but might also be linked to the labour market and the role of the state. The Nordic cluster operates in a climate of large government spending on social programmes and high rates of labour market participation (through full-time and part-time work). There is less financial dependence on the traditional family unit and more opportunities for people to follow their own course and live independently (another factor contributing to the increase in single households).

The Southern European countries tend to have less comprehensive social programmes and more rigid labour markets with less opportunity for flexible working. There tends to be a higher financial dependence on the traditional extended family that is familiar in Italy, for example. While the traditional extended family undoubtedly has many benefits, such as emotional security and personal identity, it might also account for fewer younger people leaving home until a much later age and having some degree of social control and psychological constraints being placed upon them. It might be particularly difficult for women in these cultures to enter the labour market and reduce their financial reliance on the family. This will certainly create different lifestyle experiences within these countries and might also be significant for companies planning European marketing campaigns. In Southern Europe, advertisements would be much more likely to revolve around the 'traditional family' than in Northern Europe.

5.5.2 Changing lifestyles

Whereas the earlier population censuses focused on demographic factors, more recent ones have begun to explore much more about lifestyle in order to measure how lifestyle may have changed over time. One aspect of this might be to look at how our use of consumer durables has changed over time. In the 1950s, televisions were extremely rare and seen as a luxury item, whereas a television is now seen as almost as a necessity by many people and there is practically 100 percent saturation in the UK. In the UK in 1972 only 37 percent of households had central heating and 42 percent a telephone. In 2007, according to the UK Expenditure and Food Survey, the corresponding figures were 95 percent for central heating and 89 percent for telephones. While the figure for telephones might seem surprisingly small (and has actually fallen in the last few years), it should be remembered that between 2001 and 2007 ownership of mobile phones rose from 26 percent to 78 percent so almost all homes have one way or another of communicating via telephone. Companies operating in such saturated markets may find it difficult to achieve high rates of growth unless they can convince consumers to upgrade their products (possibly as a result of new technological breakthroughs). An example here would be in the saturated television market where there is a move to flat-screen and digital technology – this switch has been so marked that Dixons, a major high street retailer, announced in 2008 that it would no longer sell traditional cathode ray tube televisions.

What the surveys do show is that there was still considerable market growth potential in new products, particularly in new technology and home entertainment. The percentage of UK homes with computers has risen from 49 percent of households in 2001 to 67 percent in 2007 and 61 percent of households had internet access. For higher income homes, the percentages are approaching 100 percent, suggesting that there may still be opportunities for lower priced computers for lower income households. The increase in home entertainment had been equally rapid with sharp increases in the number of satellite, cable and digital television receivers (up from 29 percent of households in 1998 to 77 percent of households in 2007) and 88 per cent of households had a video recorder or DVD player (18 percent in 1983).

We also appear to be much more mobile than 30 years ago. In 1972, 48 percent of households had no car whereas the figure in 2007 is 25 percent, which may reflect improved income levels stimulating the demand for cars. Interestingly, the number of one-car households has hardly changed (43 percent in 1972 to 44 percent in 2007) but the most significant change is in households with two or more cars, which has increased from 7 percent in 1971 to 26 percent in 2007. This might be a reflection of more dual-income households where two cars are needed for work purposes or it might reflect greater affluence. What it certainly shows is a greater concentration of cars which has boosted the car market but it also implies that there is a likelihood of increased pollution and overcrowding on the road system as a result of this trend.

These changes in spending are obviously of great significance for companies operating in these sectors but they also can suggest a picture of how lifestyle has changed in the twenty-first century from previous decades with the wider implications of that.

5.5.3 Health

Another aspect of lifestyle is the issue of health and how healthy our lifestyle has become. One way of looking at this is to look at healthcare systems. The amount spent on healthcare systems varies considerably with high rates of spending in the USA and Germany contrasting with much lower rates of spending in countries such as Ireland, the UK and Turkey. There are also some contradictory trends occurring which reflect differing attitudes towards having a healthy lifestyle and some of these issues are covered in *Minicase 5.5*, which contrasts the increasing evidence of obesity in Europe with the massive explosion of health and fitness clubs.

Minicase 5.5	Calorie wars: couch potatoes or fitness fanatics?

An article in *The Observer* in June 2003 (Revill, 2003) identified the potential problems of increased obesity in the UK population and the potential health risks that the population faced as a result of this. The UK health and fitness industry grew very quickly in the early 2000s; about 12 percent of the UK's population belonged to a fitness club in 2007. So it appears that one part of the population is getting increasingly unhealthy in terms of their eating and fitness habits and adding on the calories, whereas another part is rushing off to the gym to burn some calories. These 'calorie wars' seem to reflect changing social trends in our society.

If we look at the obesity issue first, according to the WHO *Atlas of Health in Europe* (2008), the proportion of overweight adult males in the period 2000–2006 varied from 67 percent in Greece to 45 percent in Switzerland. During the same period the proportion of obese male adults varied from 26 percent in Greece to 7.4 percent in Italy. Surveys suggest that the differences between regions in Europe are reducing – that is, even in the countries where the prevalence of obesity is historically low, the trend is upwards.

Curiously, the UK is not included in the WHO publication, but other studies suggest that it is near the top of the scale with one in five adults classified as obese and also one in nine children. The reasons usually quoted are to do with changing lifestyles in terms of increased consumption of 'junk' foods and a lack of physical exercise for many people, with people staying at home more for their entertainment (the couch-potato lifestyle). The main concern is with children, with 9 percent of boys and 13 percent of girls classified as obese, a figure that quadrupled between 1984 and 1994. When children become overweight it vastly increases the risk of them developing diabetes – and the rate of diabetes has increased considerably. There have been government initiatives to try and counter this trend, such as encouraging families to eat five portions of fruit and vegetables a day and to make it easier for people to walk to work, although one could question how effective this will be when addressed to the socio-economic groups which are most obese.

At the same time we see more and more people joining health clubs with a significant expansion in this area. The drivers for this are obviously health-linked but it has also become a lifestyle trend, even to the extent of individuals having personal trainers. When surveyed on why they had joined health clubs, the majority had joined to get fit, although 30 percent had also joined to lose weight and 31 percent had joined to relax and relieve stress, with 10 percent joining for social purposes. Fitness chain operators such as Fitness First and David Lloyd Leisure grew at a rate of up to 10 percent per annum in 2004, despite the relatively high cost of some of these clubs. However, growth has slowed in recent years with a lot of consolidation in the industry.

Questions

1 How can you explain the fact that we have a trend towards increasing obesity and a trend towards increased use of health clubs at the same time?

2 Many developed countries face a similar situation. Should all governments do more to tackle the problem? How could they do this?

5.5.4 Smoking and alcohol

Two key areas which link both health and consumer spending are the trends in drinking and smoking. Both of these areas reflect lifestyle decisions made by people and they are also both multi-million pound industries and yet at the same time there is a health dimension involved because of the specific diseases linked with these two products.

In the UK, the trend in the 1990s was for a slight increase in overall alcohol consumption for men, but a much more marked increase for women, especially younger women. UK consumption is still relatively low by European comparisons (see *Table 5.6*). The reason for this is that many Central and Southern European countries are wine producers and it is much more normal to drink with a meal than is the case in Northern Europe. There are signs of changing drinking habits, however, with a decline of beer drinking in Northern European countries as many people have switched to wine and other beverages. In the traditional wine-growing countries the reverse effect has been noticed with less consumption of wine, especially among younger people. This has implications for beer and wine producers who may diversify into new areas.

There are also significant differences in the pattern of alcohol consumption across Europe. In Southern Europe daily drinking will be most common and yet the quantity consumed per drinking occasion is much higher in Northern Europe. This has been linked to the concept of 'binge drinking' (Institute of Alcohol Studies, 2002), which is defined as 'the consumption of five or more standard drinks in a single drinking occasion'. This has been found to be particularly prevalent in Northern Europe, especially Finland, Sweden and the UK and even more prevalent in teenagers and young adults where British, Irish and Danish teenagers have been identified as the heaviest drinkers in Europe and are more likely to get drunk and report problems associated with drinking compared with their counterparts in other European countries. This raises ethical questions about drinks companies who target this age group in these countries.

Table 5.6	Alcohol consumption by country (1997–2006)			
Country	**1997**	**1999**	**2000**	**2006***
Luxembourg	11.4	12.2	12.3	15.6
Romania	9.8	12.2	12.1	9.7
Portugal	11.3	10.3	11.7	11.5
Republic of Ireland	9.7	11.0	10.8	13.7
Czech Republic	10.5	10.5	10.6	13.0
France	10.9	10.7	10.5	11.4
Germany	10.8	10.6	10.5	12.0
Spain	10.2	9.9	10.0	11.7
Denmark	9.9	9.5	9.5	11.7
UK	8.2	8.4	8.4	11.8
Greece	8.3	8.2	8.0	9.0
Latvia	6.9	7.7	7.4	9.6
USA	6.6	6.7	6.7	8.6
Japan	6.4	6.6	6.5	7.6

Note: Measured in litres of pure alcohol per capita consumption.
Source: IAS (2001) www.ias.org.uk *Data in this column from the WHO and may not be strictly comparable with the IAS data (www.who.int/)

When looking at the trends in smoking it can be seen through the General Household Survey results that the prevalence of cigarette smoking fell substantially in the UK in the 1970s and 1980s and, to a lesser extent, in the 1990s and 2000s. The decline has been strongest in men, from 51 percent of men smoking in 1974 to 22 percent in 2007, although it has also declined among women with 20 percent of women smoking in 2007. The highest rates of smoking are found in the 20–24 age group.

When looking at the European picture on smoking the decline observed in the UK is not so common and there is increasing debate about the effectiveness of tobacco control systems in Europe. Ashraf (2003) comments on the disappointing results from the WHO for its third action plan, which covered the period 1997 to 2001 and was aimed at reducing the level of smoking within Europe through stronger anti-smoking measures. The WHO report identified that 30 percent of adult Europeans are smokers (38 percent of men and 24 percent of women), although it noticed an increasing gap between Western and Eastern Europe with regards to cigarette consumption in that 34 percent of men in western Europe smoked compared with 47 percent of men in Eastern Europe. More recent data suggest that the gap remains very wide: the WHO *Atlas of Health in Europe* (2008) shows that around 60 percent of males smoke in the Ukraine and the Russian Federation compared with around 14 percent in Sweden. This might reflect response of the tobacco companies who, faced with stronger anti-smoking legislation in Western Europe, are targeting the new high-growth markets of Eastern Europe. The prevalence of smoking among young people was 30 percent and the report noted that there had been no decrease in cigarette consumption for this age group over the period of the report. The health dimension linked to smoking is the occurrence of lung cancer and here the death rate for men in Western Europe has stabilised at a rate of 73 per 100,000. Another trend identified by the report was the massive increase in cigarette smuggling in order to avoid paying government duty on cigarettes. It is now estimated that one-third of cigarettes traded worldwide are smuggled, although the figures are slightly lower in Europe, where the UK government has estimated that about 20 percent of the cigarettes consumed in the country are smuggled. There is undoubtedly a move towards more tobacco controls through taxation, advertising bans and protection of the rights of non-smokers but this is only leading to different strategies from the big tobacco companies.

5.5.5 Crime

Another area of changing lifestyle is the issue of crime: see also *Chapter 8*. Heidensohn (1991) suggests that the quite dramatic change that continues to affect family life and gender roles may have an impact on crime. She points out that a growing number of children are being raised in one-parent households, often poorly housed in the worst areas. It seems that these children may be more likely to be 'pushed' into criminal activity.

On the other hand, UK government statistics from the British Crime Survey (BCS), which is an annual survey based on a sample of 40,000 people and which began in 1995, have shown a gradual decrease in crime in the UK and they suggest that there has been a 36 percent fall in crime for the period 1997 to 2008/9. Studies, such as that by Barclay *et al.* (2001), who carried out an international comparison of criminal justice statistics for the Home Office, show that during the period 1995–1999 recorded crime fell by 10 percent in the UK compared with the EU average of a 1 percent decline.

More recent international comparisons suggest that, where data are available, in 2007 the highest levels of homicide in Western and Central Europe during this period were found in Switzerland with a rate of 2.26 per 100,000 followed by Finland on 2.17. The figure for England and Wales was 1.37, well down the list – yet Scotland's most recent figure of 2.13 points to remarkably wide variations even within fairly small geographical areas. Some of the highest figures came from Honduras (48), South Africa (37.3), Russia (16.5), while the USA (5.8), though well down the list, seems to be still a more violent country than most of Western Europe. These figures might be significant as high levels of violence and homicide may be a factor influencing the willingness of executives to live in these cities, and could be a deterrent to inward investment. South Africa, in particular, has a serious image problem with crime which the government has failed to tackle effectively.

Computer crime is a new area of crime that seems to be on the increase and which is becoming a major concern to governments and business corporations. A 1995 study of 1,200 American companies by the management consultants Ernst and Young showed that over half the companies in their survey had suffered financial losses related to computer security. The theft of computers and computer parts, rather than the theft of information, seems to be one of the major problems facing small businesses. No one is exempt from the risks associated with computer crime. However, as Wall (2007) points out, it is very difficult to find accurate statistics about what he calls 'cybercrime'. This is because different groups use different terminology, many firms and individuals do not report cybercrime for various reasons and finally because computer security firms have been known to publicise dubious statistics, that are designed to frighten businesses into buying their products or services. But the potential for serious crime is shown by the well-publicised theft, in 2008, of credit card details of over 38,000 online customers of Cotton Traders, a UK-based clothing firm, by a hacker. With the rapid growth in electronic commerce, the potential for such crime is growing, which contributes to concerns about the security of e-commerce transactions and thus inhibits growth in the sector.

5.5.6 Terrorism

The last aspect of crime that we shall briefly consider is that of terrorism, also examined in *Chapter 7*. This is not a new form of crime, but before 2001 it was generally regarded as 'local' in that terrorist acts took place mostly in regions with political, social, religious or ethnic problems – for example, the 'troubles' in Northern Ireland during the latter part of the twentieth century. The 9/11 attack on New York in 2001 marked a new trend – the threat of terrorist acts in places that do not have the problems referred to above, but are somehow associated with conflicts taking place in other countries. Terrorists are now aiming at economies and businesses – for example, by choosing targets associated with travel and tourism. After 9/11 transatlantic air travel in particular declined sharply and this brought to an end the mergers and acquisition boom in the first years of the twenty-first century. A number of airlines collapsed due to the global reduction in air travel.

Although air travel recovered after a few months, the much more intensive security measures introduced at most airports have made international travel much more time-consuming. In addition, companies may be less inclined to do business in areas affected by unrest in case they become targets of local terrorist and kidnappers, and where insurance costs may be prohibitive. For a recent review of the challenges posed by these threats see the chapter by Andrew Lee in Ibeh and Davies (2009). *Minicase 5.6* shows how criminal and terrorist activity is impacting more and more on the daily life of ordinary citizens.

5.5.7 Education

We shall now consider briefly the worldwide trends in education. This is an important part of the international business environment because of the close relationship between education levels and economic prosperity. As Porter (1990) pointed out, a nation's knowledge and skills resources are a key factor affecting national competitive advantage. A well-educated workforce leads to growing levels of economic prosperity which in turn leads to greater availability and demand for education in that country – a virtuous circle. Conversely, a weak economy means that a nation cannot afford to invest in education – and so the nation is unable to develop its economy – a vicious circle. From the perspective of international business, growing economies offer new markets; and an educated workforce means that companies can set up subsidiaries in these growing markets making use of the local workforce rather than expatriates. But how can the vicious circle be broken?

Minicase 5.6	The surveillance society

Criminal and terrorist activity means that citizens are now under closer scrutiny than ever before. Listed below are some of the actual and potential mechanisms for monitoring your movements and activities:

- Credit card details show exactly what you purchased, where and when. Supermarket loyalty cards do the same.
- Mobile phones act as tracking device that pinpoint where they are. Your location when you make a call is known and mobile calls and text messages can easily be recorded.
- Email traffic is probably being intercepted and read, for security reasons, on a sampling basis. Past connection, albeit innocent, to a person or organisation deemed by security services to be of interest could put your email traffic under scrutiny – just in case. Your employer can monitor your email and web usage.
- Computer records show all the websites that you have visited.
- On your shopping trips, you are filmed in most shops that you enter and some CCTV cameras in public places can compare faces with facial recognition software against databases of people of 'interest' to the authorities. Facial recognition software needs to be more accurate than it is now if it is to be more widely used – but these times will come.
- On your drive to work, cameras can record registration numbers fixing a vehicle in place and time and, potentially, run the number against databases such as motor insurers.

Questions

1 To what extent should routine surveillance of normal, law-abiding activities be tolerated in a free society?
2 How will society benefit from routine surveillance and database checking of people going about their everyday life?

In 2000, a meeting sponsored by UNESCO and attended by governments from 164 nations, established a 'collective commitment to dramatically expand educational opportunities for children, youth and adults by 2015'. A mid-term report on the Education for All programme was published by UNESCO in 2008. Progress has been made, but there is still a long way to go – but there is no doubt that, if reasonably successful, this initiative will be one of the main drivers behind the global shift in economic power from the developed nations to the less-developed world, with new threats and opportunities for businesses everywhere.

5.5.8 Work trends

Finally we need to look at changing work trends which will affect people in society, although many of these themes are developed in more depth in *Chapter 9*. One of the trends we have already identified is the increased possibility of part-time working in countries with more flexible working practices where there are opportunities for part-time working, teleworking, job-sharing and outsourcing of labour to specialist agencies. This throws up new opportunities for part-time work, especially for women. It is interesting here to compare data for part-time and full-time working for women with the society clusters suggested earlier by Vogel (1998). In the Northern European cluster of countries such as Scandinavia and the UK, the most recent figures show that female employment has increased dramatically since 1997 and is gradually approaching the level of male employment as more opportunities through flexible working, better childcare facilities and greater independence have seen more opportunities for working women. Much of the growth, however, has been in part-time jobs. At the lower end of the scale we see again the cluster of Southern European countries and Ireland, all of which have large proportions of traditional families with full-time housewives. In Italy, for example, 47.2 percent of females were in employment compared with 70.3 percent of males in 2008 and the proportion is fairly static. This may be a problem when companies try to introduce more flexible working patterns in certain countries and can lead to rigidities in the labour market.

Another aspect of labour is the extent of organised labour in countries, usually reflected by membership of trade unions. The general trend in trade union membership has been for a steady decline in numbers. Metcalfe (1990) argues that the decline in union membership is the result of an interaction of five factors:

- the macroeconomic environment;
- the composition of jobs and the workforce including the relative decline in manufacturing industry;
- the policy of the state;
- the attitudes and conduct of employers;
- the stance taken by employers.

For example, in the UK one of the main factors was the big increase in legislation during the 1980s' Thatcher government which significantly changed the behaviour and practices of trade unions. The trend can clearly be seen in the UK where trade union membership fell from 13.3 million in 1979 to 7.6 million in 2006. It is very interesting to look more closely at these figures. If we look at the union membership density (i.e. the proportion of employees belonging to a recognised trade union) then we can see that for men, the density fell from around 35.4 percent in 1995 to 27.3 percent in 2006. Over the same period, the density for women has reduced from just under 30 percent in 1995 to 28.5 percent in 2001 and has since risen back to 28.8 percent in 2006. This marked difference probably reflects the decline of UK manufacturing industries (which tended to employ males) and the growth in service industries.

In Germany and Belgium there are works councils, which have the right to be consulted over closures or prospective merger activities, and European legislation has also seen the introduction of minimum wage levels to protect the lowest-paid sectors of the community. The minimum wage was finally introduced in the UK in April 1999 when it was set at a basic level of £3.60 an hour. In 2009 the UK minimum wage was £5.80 compared with Portugal's £2.59 an hour and Belgium's £8.32 an hour. This may be a factor that would need to be taken on board in industries which depend on low-paid and largely unskilled labour.

Hillman (1996) has examined the wider trends in the working environment and how we will work in the twenty-first century and he suggests that there will be a transformation in social life and the way we work. He suggests that the key trends in the twenty-first century will be:

- increasingly footloose economic activity;
- fierce global competition, fuelled by advances in information and communication technologies;
- shifts in occupational patterns in favour of managerial, professional and technical jobs in the service sector and a shift to knowledge workers;
- a growth in the importance of small and medium-sized enterprises, reflecting changes in the nature and organisation of work as many large organisations are forced to restructure;
- more flexible labour markets in many countries, with part-time and temporary work, weaker relationships between employers and employees and the threat of recurrent unemployment and underemployment;
- fractured career patterns and work/leisure boundaries, with training increasingly the responsibility of individuals themselves;
- increasing dangers of exclusion for socially and economically disadvantaged groups.

Many of these trends are already becoming clearer in the years since Hillman (1996) wrote about these issues and make the way we will work in the future much more complex than in the past. The likelihood of staying with one employer for the bulk of your working life is becoming increasingly remote, with more emphasis being placed on the individual to develop their skill base to cope with more flexible working environments of the future. One could argue that this is making the working environment much more stressful than in the past but also more challenging and potentially rewarding.

5.6 Conclusion

This chapter has covered a number of cultural, demographic and social aspects of the business environment which may have significance for companies. We have seen that when companies have an international dimension then they are much more likely to be influenced by exposure to other cultures and it may well be the success with which the company handles these differences that will determine its success in any overseas activities, although the extent of the problem may be determined by the closeness or otherwise of the cultural fit between countries.

We have also seen that companies and governments have to pay increasing attention to changes in the demographic structure within the business environment. Population changes may be gradual, compared with other areas such as technological change, but their significance is becoming increasingly recognised and nowhere more than in those countries that are facing rapidly ageing populations, as we have seen in Europe and Japan.

Finally we have examined a number of social changes in terms of family changes, changing lifestyles and the changing nature of work, all of which may be very significant for businesses in certain sectors in terms of identifying developing or declining markets and developing strategies to deal with these.

Summary of main points	

- When businesses operate internationally, they will need a clearer understanding of national cultural differences.
- Hofstede and Trompenaars give us frameworks for understanding differences in national business cultures.
- The extent of cultural adaptation will depend upon the closeness of the cultural fit between countries.
- Businesses may have to alter their management styles, their marketing policies and their HRM policies to take cultural differences into account.
- Demographic changes can be easily identified and easily predicted.
- The pattern of falling fertility rates is leading to a rapid ageing of the population in Europe and Japan.
- The increased pressure on the working population to support the retired population will put severe pressures on governments.
- The nature of the family and family relationships is changing rapidly in the UK.
- The role of the family varies across Europe.
- Changing lifestyles are leading to changing consumption of tobacco and alcohol, although there is clear evidence of increased obesity – especially among younger people.
- The level of criminal activity may influence international investment decisions.
- Trade union membership has continued to decline against a background of more flexible working patterns in the country.
- There is a close relationship between education levels and economic prosperity.

Discussion questions

1 By using data from Hofstede in the text, compare the national culture of France and the USA. How might the differences you identify have affected the relationship between American managers and French workers in the early days of Disneyland Paris?

2 Imagine that there is a proposed merger between your Italian company and a British company and you have been appointed to lead a team made up of managers from both countries to examine any cultural problems linked to the proposed merger. How close would the cultural fit be and how might you seek to improve cultural understanding between the two groups of managers?

3 Critically assess the extent to which some companies would benefit and some face a crisis through the ageing of the population. Look for examples in your own country of companies who will be affected by this trend and suggest strategies they could follow in response to this.

4 To what extent do you agree with Vogel's (1998) views about the three clusters of European society? To what extent does your own country fit into the family behaviour suggested in this analysis?

5 To what extent do you feel that the level of crime (or perception about crime) is becoming a bigger factor in the social environment? To what extent will it influence investment decisions by companies?

6 Assess the extent to which the overall decline in trade union membership is likely to continue into the twenty-first century. Are there any factors that might reverse the current trends?

Further reading/sources of information

The web links are some that have been found useful when researching this chapter.

Census (www.ons.gov.uk/census/index.html) The next UK national census will take place in 2011. This site gives access to data from the last national census of 2001 as well as summary data from previous censuses.

EU (http://epp.eurostat.ec.europa.eu/portal/page/portal/eurostat/home) This is the home page of the EU's statistics services through which you can find a wide range of materials on the EU.

Executive Planet (www.executiveplanet.com/index.php?title=Main_Page) This website will give you a fascinating range of information on business culture in many countries – including how to greet people and how to behave in business situations.

UK Natural Statistics (www.statistics.gov.uk/hub/index.html) This site is the gateway to UK national statistics covering a very wide range of social and demographic areas. You can even get information down to the level of your local neighbourhood and compare this with UK averages.

UN (www.un.org/popin/) This is the home page of the United Nations Population Information Network from which you can find any material you need on population as well as special reports.

Up my street (http://upmystreet.com) This website will give you lots of socio-economic information down to the level of individual postcodes.

Halsey, A.H. and Webb, J. (2000) *Twentieth Century British Social Trends*, 3rd edn. Basingstoke: Macmillan. Covers all the main social changes that occurred in the twentieth century, although it is a lengthy book.

McFarlin, D.B. and Sweeney, P.D. (2006) *International Management: Strategic Opportunities and Cultural Challenges,* 3rd edn. Boston, MA: Houghton Mifflin Company. A useful book which examines cross-cultural communication and the management of intercultural groups.

Stephens, J. (2009) National Culture, in Brooks, I. *Organisational Behaviour: Individuals, Groups and Organisations,* 4th edn. Harlow: FT/Prentice Hall, pp. 283–320. The chapter gives a good general overview of the main theories and issues concerned with national culture.

Tayeb, M. (2003) *International Management: Theories and Practice.* Harlow: FT/Prentice Hall. Another book which is very good on the management implications of national cultures.

United Nations Department of Economic and Social Affairs (2006) *Demographic Yearbook,* New York: United Nations Publications. Lots of fascinating data from around the world – in English *and* French.

References

Ashraf, H. (2003) European Tobacco Control Reaches a Critical Phase. *The Lancet,* 359, 585–586.

Barclay, G., Tavares, C. and Siddique, A. (2001) *International Comparisons of Criminal Justice Statistics 1999,* Home Office Statistical Bulletin, Issue 6/01.

Chinese Culture Connection (1987) 'Chinese values and the search for culture-free dimensions of culture', *Journal of Cross-Cultural Psychology* 18 (2), pp. 143–64.

Daniels, J.D., Radebaugh, L.H. and Sullivan, D.P. (2009) *International Business: Environments and Operations,* 12th edn. Upper Saddle River, NJ: Prentice Hall.

Economist (2008) Ford's European Arm Lends a Hand. March.

Heidensohn, M. (1991) *Crime and Society: Sociology for a Changing World.* Basingstoke: Macmillan.

Hillman, J. (1996) *University for Industry: Creating a National Learning Framework.* London: Institute for Public Policy Research.

Hofstede, G. (1984) *Cultures Consequences: International Differences in Work-related Values,* abridged edn. Beverley Hills, CA: Sage.

Hofstede, G. and Bond, M.H. (1988) Confucius and Economic Growth: New Trends in Culture's Consequences. *Organisational Dynamics,* 16, 4–21.

Hofstede, G. and Hofstede, G.J. (2005) *Cultures and Organisations: Software of the Mind,* 2nd edn. New York: Mcgraw-Hill.

Ibeh, K. and Davies, S. (eds) (2009) *Contemporary Challenges to International Business.* Basingstoke: Palgrave Macmillan Institute of Alcohol Studies (2002) **www.ias.org.uk/**

Kerr, C., Dunlop, J.T., Harbison, F. and Myers C.A. (1960) *Industrialism and Industrial Man: The Problems of Labour and the Management of Economic Growth.* Cambridge, MA: Harvard University Press.

Kluckhohn, F. and Strodtbeck, F. (1961) *Variations in Value Orientations.* New York: Peterson.

Kroeber, A. and Kluckhohn, C. (1985) *Culture: A Critical Review of Concepts and Definitions.* New York: Random House.

Levitt, T. (1983) The Globalisation of Markets. *Harvard Business* Review, May–June, 92–102.

Metcalfe, D. (1990) Union Presence and Labour Productivity in British Manufacturing Industry: A Reply to Nolan and Marginson. *British Journal of Industrial Relations,* 28, 249–266.

Porter, M.E. (1990) *The Competitive Advantage of Nations.* New York: Free Press.

Revill, J. (2003) Fat Chance. *The Observer,* 8 June.

Torbiorn (1982) *Living Abroad: Personal Adjustment and Personnel Policy in an Overseas Setting.* New York: Wiley.

Trompenaars, F. (1993) *Riding the Waves of Culture.* London: Nicholas Brealey.

Vogel, J. (1998) *Three Types of European Society,* available at **www.nnn.se/n-model/europe3/europe3.htm**

Wall, D.S. (2007) *Cybercrime.* Cambridge: Polity Press.

World Health Organisation *Atlas of Health in Europe,* available at **www.euro.who.int/Document/E91713.pdf**

6

The ecological environment

Jamie Weatherston

Learning outcomes

On completion of this chapter you should be able to:

- understand some of the ecological and ethical effects that arise because of business activity;
- appreciate the basic economic arguments which underlie the operation of the marketplace (including the law of demand and supply and the concept of externalities) and which underpin any analysis of how business organisations are able to pollute the environment;
- outline the range of actions which can be taken by governments to monitor and regulate the output of pollutants from economic activity;
- appreciate the range of organisational responses to ecological issues in general and to environmental legislation in particular;
- recognise the impact of economic activity, and of different regulatory regimes, on consumers, and appreciate the extent of consumer power in respect of ecological issues;
- be familiar with the importance of corporate social responsibility;
- set the above outcomes in the context of actions taken at global, national and local scales.

Key concepts

- environmental pollution
- climate change
- theory of demand and supply
- price determination
- equilibrium
- market failure
- externalities
- the principle that the polluter pays
- sustainable development
- Corporate social responsibility
- BATNEEC
- environmental impact assessment
- environmental contexts
- environmental options
- the consumer and the environment
- ethics.

Minicase 6.1 | Aviation answers to climate change

Evidence suggests that most industries will have to cut their emissions to 10 percent of their current level by 2050 to meet the government's climate change targets. The UK has signed up to an 80 percent cut in greenhouse gas emissions by 2050 compared with 1990 levels. Aviation is one industry that is having an impact on climate change.

It has been estimated by the IPCC (International Panel on Climate Change) that aviation accounted for 4.9 percent of man-made climate impacts in 2005 (AEF, 2009a). In the UK, in answer to a Parliamentary Question on 2 May 2007, aviation minister Gillian Merron said that 'emissions from flights departing the UK contributed approximately 13 percent of total UK emissions in 2005' (AEF, 2009b).

Demand for air travel has been increasing steeply. According to Airbus, passenger traffic is increasing at 5 percent a year – requiring more than 24,000 new passenger and freight aircraft by 2026 (Jaggi, 2006). At the same time the industry is working on a number of different solutions to limit its environmental impact.

Jaggi (2006) proposed that airlines are looking at turboprop engines, in recognition of their fuel efficiency – most turboprop-powered aircraft, although slower than jets, can fly 35 percent further for the same amount of fuel. In 2007 easyJet unveiled proposals for a short-haul airliner powered by turbine engines with open-fan blades, for greater efficiency and therefore better economy. The aircraft could produce 50 percent less CO_2 and 75 percent less nitrogen oxide than Boeing's 737 and Airbus's A320 aircraft. BA is considering adding turboprops to its jet fleet for short-haul work. In February 2008 Virgin Atlantic became the first airline to operate commercially running partly on biofuel. Looking further forward, advances in fuel cell and battery and electric motor technology used for road vehicles will find their way into aircraft.

Questions

1 Is there any downside to operating planes using biofuel?
2 What impact will the economic recession of 2009/10 have on the aviation industry?

6.1 Introduction

Many of us are aware of a range of environmental problems facing people and the planet. In this chapter we look at some of the most serious ecological and ethical concerns, and the extent of their impact, investigate the economic arguments which help us analyse how organisations, through their everyday business activities, are able to pollute the environment. We will explore the range of actions which can be taken by governments to monitor and regulate the outputs from economic activity.

Over recent years the basis of much environmental regulation has been via market-based mechanisms. Therefore, the introductory part of this chapter examines the economic arguments which underpin the operation of market-based economies. The areas covered include the laws of demand and supply and the price mechanism. This section also has a wider purpose: it links to the coverage of competition in *Chapter 2,* as demand theory underpins much of the work related to market structure (please note that this section features general, rather than environment-related, examples to explain the ideas).

The chapter moves on to consider externalities and different approaches to regulation. We end by examining the different approaches adopted by organisations towards environmental issues, examining their views regarding corporate social responsibility and by discussing the impact of these upon consumers and noting the extent of consumer power in respect of ecological issues. This analysis is set in the context of actions taken at a global, national and local scale.

Environmental pollution has an impact on a number of areas which affect us all. In order to assess the nature of this impact we need to distinguish between renewable resources, those that can be replaced and non-renewable resources, those when used are lost forever.

There has been considerable concern about global warming and the effects of acid rain, loss of biodiversity, sea pollution, depletion of natural resources such as tropical rainforests, and the destruction of the Earth's protective ozone layer. CFCs have been banned due to their adverse effects on the ozone layer. In Stockholm in 1972 the international community met for the first time to consider global environment and development needs.

The 'Earth Summit' (the UN Conference on Environment and Development) was held in Rio de Janeiro in 1992, marking the twentieth anniversary of the Stockholm Conference. At Rio, Agenda 21 and the Rio Declaration were agreed. Since then a number conferences have been held, including Berlin in 1995 and Kyoto in 1997, which produced the Kyoto Protocol. Indeed each year since 1995 a conference has been held under support of the United Nations Framework Climate Change Convention (UNFCCC). The latest conference was held in Copenhagen in 2009 where a successor to the Kyoto Protocol was under discussion. This chapter explains the impact of these on organisations and governments. Agenda 21 elements and issues are shown in *Table 6.1*.

Without naturally occurring greenhouse gases such as carbon dioxide, methane, nitrous oxide and water vapour, human life would not exist. However, industrial development has necessitated the burning of significant amounts of coal, oil and methane, and the felling of more and more forests resulting in excessive carbon dioxide (CO_2) emissions. Greenhouse gases including carbon dioxide and methane are said to contribute to the greenhouse effect. Most commentators agree that the greenhouse effect brings a rise in global temperatures.

The increase in the Earth's temperature has, in turn, caused sea levels to rise. It has been predicted that, at current rates of increase, sea levels could rise by another 50 cm by the year 2100 (Radford, 1997). This would have a serious impact on coastlines, particularly those in East Anglia, Holland, Egypt, India and Bangladesh, as well as imperiling many small low-lying islands such as the Maldives in the Indian Ocean and the Marshall Islands in the Pacific Ocean (Brown, 1995). Effects would clearly be felt in communities near the coast and have severe consequences for agricultural areas such as the Ganges Delta, an area already prone to flooding.

Table 6.1	Elements of Agenda 21

Elements	Issues
Social and economic dimensions to development	Poverty, production and consumption, health, human settlement, integrated decision making
Conservation and management of natural resources	Atmosphere, oceans and seas, land, forests, mountains, biological diversity, ecosystems, biotechnology, freshwater resources, toxic chemicals, hazardous radioactive and solid wastes
Strengthening role of major groups	Youth, women, indigenous peoples, non-government organisations, local authorities, trade unions, business, scientific and technical communities, farmers
Means of implementation	Finance, technology transfer, information, public awareness, capacity building, education, legal instruments, institutional frameworks

Source: www.earthsummit2002.org/Es2002.PDF

Whatever one's view of the seriousness of the problems of global warming and destruction of the ozone layer, it is clear that environmental problems result from economic activity. The growth of business activity is often at the expense of the environment.

The balance of power between business organisations, particularly large multinationals, on the one hand, and individuals and environmental groups on the other, is grossly unequal. Government has a role to play regarding the potentially polluting activities of organisations. Regulation proceeds, essentially, from a knowledge of how markets operate. It is therefore appropriate to examine the theory of demand and supply and of externalities in order to appreciate the debate on environmental regulation and the role of government intervention. For the global economy to become ecologically sustainable, it may be necessary to organise business and industry along ecologically sound principles. This will require the transformation of corporations, their products, production systems and management practices (Shrivastava, 1995). We will take the chance to explore the role and activities of each of these actors and their effects, both positive and negative, on the environment.

6.2 The impact of the marketplace on the ecological environment: an economic perspective

The two extremes of economic management (see *Chapter 2*), the free market and the command economy, are not evident in their purest form within any country. For example, Hong Kong, which used to closely resemble a pure market economy, has, from 1997, had to follow the lead of the Communist government in China to some extent. The final years of the twentieth century saw the fall of command economies in, for example, Poland, Bulgaria and the former Soviet Union. Market forces have been allowed to become more active in these economies to alleviate the worst excesses of state control.

Within all Western-style market economies, government influences the allocation of goods and services. It does this for a number of reasons:

- to moderate the trade cycle by demand management and supply-side policies to promote such things as employment, investment and direct structural change (see *Chapter 3*);
- to restrain unfair use of economic power by, for example, monopolies (see *Chapter 2*);
- to correct inequalities through the redistribution of wealth via taxation or regional policy to support industry (see *Chapter 3*);
- to manage price levels, employment, balance of payments and growth rate in accordance with social objectives (see *Chapter 3*);
- to provide public goods, such as defence, law and order, roads and parks; such things are socially desirable, but unprofitable, and it is generally not possible to directly charge for them; and, of specific relevance to the subject of this chapter,
- to remove socially undesirable consequences of commercial activity. The private profit motive does not always ensure that public wealth will be maximised; it can create environmental problems, such as pollution and resource depletion.

Society has to find a way of resolving the primary economic issues of:

- what to produce;
- how to produce;
- for whom to produce.

In many economies we have seen that these questions are now more commonly being answered by market forces (see *Chapter 2*). It is important to understand the problems that industrial activity causes to the environment. However, in order to understand how market forces can result in environmental problems and to appreciate the viability of potential solutions it is also necessary to understand the foundations of the market system, that is, the concepts of demand and supply.

6.2.1 The theory of demand

Demand is the quantity of a commodity which will be demanded at a given price over a certain period of time. By 'demand' we mean demand backed by money, or effective demand. Common sense says for most goods (normal goods) a lower price will mean that more will be purchased (even if this increase in consumption leads to an increase in pollution or environmental damage) and at a higher price less will be purchased. This is the law of downward sloping demand. For any commodity it is possible to use market data to construct a demand schedule, showing how many units of the commodity would be demanded at various prices. In reality this is difficult to do. However, King (1972) did try to estimate the demand relationship for beer in 1960s' America, based on the wholesale price of beer, and it did show an inverse relationship between price and quantity demanded.

However, it is easier for our purposes to work with hypothetical data. *Table 6.2* shows how the demand schedule for a box of chocolates may look.

Table 6.2	Demand schedule for boxes of chocolates

Price/unit (£)	Quantity demanded/week (000s)
6	0
5.5	1
5.0	2
4.5	3
4.0	4
3.5	5
3.0	6
2.5	7

The data in *Table 6.2* can be presented in the form of a graph. Price is plotted on the vertical axis and quantity on the horizontal axis. This is the demand curve as shown in *Figure 6.1*. The demand curve tells us the quantities which would be demanded at each price. From the area of the rectangle 0XYZ we can calculate the total revenue received by the seller at the given price, as the area of the rectangle is equal to price multiplied by quantity ($P \times Q$). As the price of the box (P_x) changes there will be extensions or contractions of demand (changes in the quantity demanded) as shown in *Figure 6.2*.

As the price of a box of chocolates (P_x) decreases from £5.00 to £4.50, demand extends along the demand curve to three thousand boxes. The opposite effect is evident, as can be seen from *Figure 6.2*, as price rises there is a contraction of demand. In this example we can see the effect that a price change has. Low-cost airlines throughout the world use a pricing strategy that takes advantage of this phenomenon. However, it is not only price that determines or influences the demand for a product. The other determinants or conditions of demand are:

1 *Price of other related goods* (P_r) – changes in the price of other goods will affect the demand for airline tickets. Substitute goods are competitively demanded. For example, if you plan to take a trip and the price of train tickets or long-distance bus tickets rises, then some consumers may decide that it is better to buy airline tickets for their journey. So in this case a rise in the price of a substitute good (train and bus tickets) will lead to a rise in demand for airline tickets. Complementary goods, in comparison, are jointly demanded: if the price of hotel rooms fall, for example, then more people may be encouraged to fly, boosting demand for airline tickets.

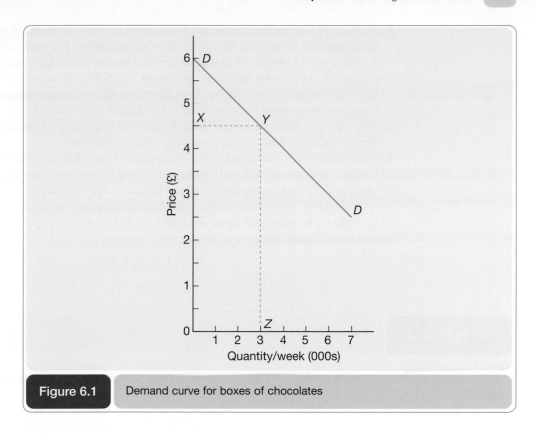

Figure 6.1   Demand curve for boxes of chocolates

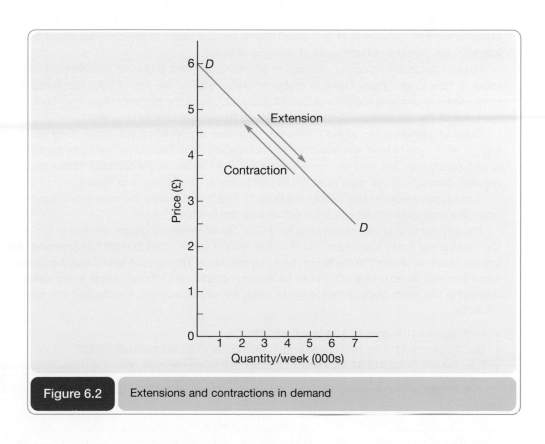

Figure 6.2   Extensions and contractions in demand

2 *Income* (*Y*) – a rise in income will result in more goods demanded, whatever the price. Your spending on airline tickets is likely to increase when you begin to earn more money. A reduction in income will obviously have the reverse effect. However, in the case of inferior goods, an increase in income will result in a fall in demand. For example, spending on food staples such as rice has been shown to fall in developing economies as people earn more money and are able afford to buy higher quality items.

3 *Taste* (*T*) – a change in taste or fashion (perhaps influenced by advertising) will alter the demand for a product. Think about your own experiences!

4 *Other factors* (*Z*) – these include seasonal factors that affect the prices of food items, government influences such as legislation limiting the sale of firearms, the availability of credit and changes in population size or structure: see *Minicase 6.2*.

So demand is influenced by all of these factors, in some way: putting all these elements together mathematically gives us the demand function:

$$D_x = f(P_x, P_r, Y, T, Z)$$

Minicase 6.2 **Tourism in Greece**

In the summer when you have a break you may be considering a trip to recover from the rigours of student life.

The choice of where you go depends on a number of factors. The price that you have to pay is clearly a prime consideration. You may also have to consider the price of other goods that you buy. Will a trip to the sun be offset by the low price of food and drink when you arrive at your destination? The relative strength and value of currencies will play a part here as well. Your income will be another factor. Can you afford to go? Do you have to work during your break to pay off debts or loans? Do you need to work to save money for the new semester? Other people's views may also be paramount. Is your planned destination a 'good' place to see and be seen in or is it stale? These are just some of the considerations that need to be taken into account (see the determinants of demand above).

Greek islands are a popular destination providing sun, sea and sand. The first decision that you need to make is how to get there. Flying is probably going to be at the top of your list. Budget airlines offer very cheap fares to destinations all over Europe. easyJet, one of the pioneers, flies from London direct to Athens, the price of the ticket depending on the day you fly and the time of your flight.

Ferry offices are open at the Eleftherios Venizelos airport when you arrive. See where you fancy going and on what type of boat and buy a ticket. No haggling here. Those in a hurry can take the hydrofoil or high-speed catamaran, but they are more expensive. Deck class on the ordinary ferries is cheaper. A bus runs regularly throughout the night from the airport to the ports of Piraeus or Rafina.

The islands are very busy in July and August. This is particularly the case in the first two weeks of August when the population of Athens spills out all over the islands

On arriving at a Greek island on a ferry you can immediately gauge the amount of accommodation by the numbers of hotel, apartment and domatia owners waving their boards to catch your attention. Domatia are the Greek equivalent to the British bed and breakfast. Timing your arrival may be crucial: leave it too late and there may be no rooms left. Prices for accommodation are officially fixed; every room has a guest notice displaying the room price. Three levels of price are available: high, middle and low season. Typical prices could be:

- High season (1 August to 31 August) €80.00.
- Middle season (1 June to 30 June and 1 September to 30 September) €50.00.
- Low season (1 April to 31 May and 1 October to 31 October) €35.00.

Are the prices really fixed? A little bargaining can secure a room for €45.00, less than the mid-season rate.

If any of these determinants of demand, apart from price, changes then the demand curve will shift to the right or the left. For example, if there is a rise in disposable income (a change of Y in the equation) demand for boxes of chocolates will increase (at every price) and the demand curve moves to the right. If income falls in the future, other factors remaining constant, fewer boxes will be demanded so the demand curve will move to the left (see *Figure 6.3*). Note that we need to qualify this by stating that we expect this to happen *ceteris paribus* – other things being equal.

To summarise, it is important to distinguish between movement *along* the demand curve, due to change in price of a good, and movements *of* the demand curve, due to change in one of the other determinants of demand.

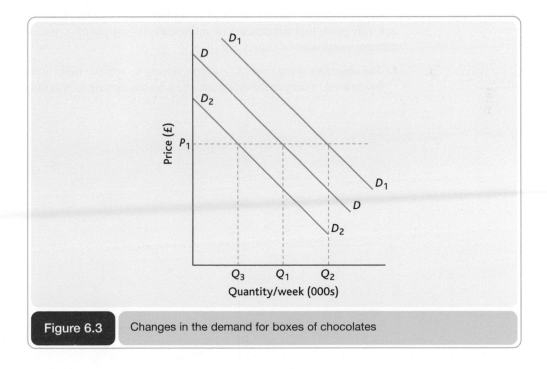

| Figure 6.3 | Changes in the demand for boxes of chocolates |

6.2.2 The theory of supply

The market for goods and services is determined not only by demand. The demand which consumers express, through their willingness to buy, needs to be met by the willingness of producers to supply goods and services. Supply is the propensity (or tendency) of producers to sell the commodity at a given price over a certain period of time.

More goods will be supplied at a higher than at a lower price. This law of the upward sloping supply curve can be explained by the aim of producers to maximise their income.

Table 6.3	Supply schedule for boxes of chocolates

Price/unit (£)	Quantity price/unit supplied/week (000s)
6.0	8
5.5	7
5.0	6
4.5	5
4.0	4
3.5	3
3.0	2
2.5	1

We know from our earlier discussion of the demand side that the data can be presented either in the form of a schedule or graphically, as shown in *Table 6.3* and *Figure 6.4*.

As price changes there will be extensions or contractions along the supply curve (changes in the quantity supplied). For example, if the price of a box of chocolates moves from £4.50 to £4.00 the quantity supplied falls from five thousand boxes to four thousand boxes per week, as shown in *Figure 6.5*.

In this example we see the effect of a price change only. However, as with demand, it is not only price that determines or influences the supply of a product. The other determinants or conditions of supply are:

1. *The objectives of the firm (B)* – a firm aiming to achieve maximum profits will have a different level of output (lower) from one which is aiming to maximise sales.

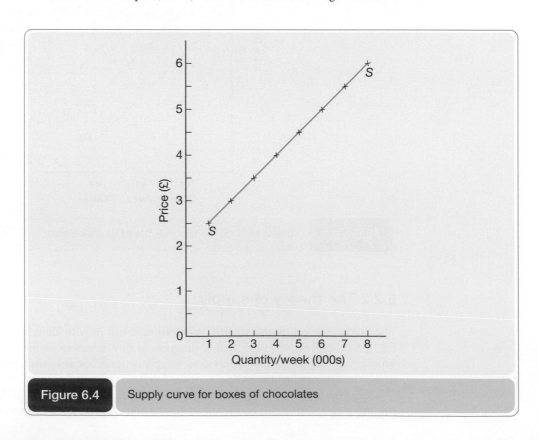

Figure 6.4	Supply curve for boxes of chocolates

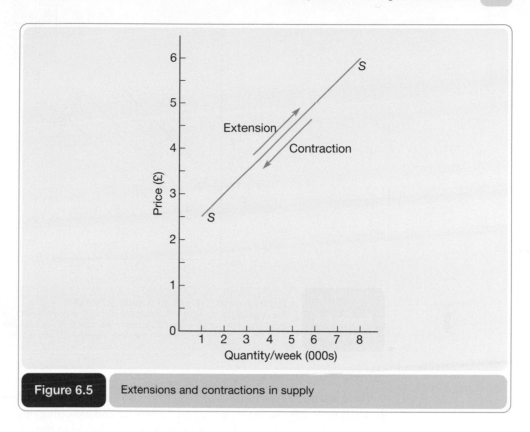

| Figure 6.5 | Extensions and contractions in supply |

2 *The price of certain other goods* (P_g) – where goods are jointly supplied, they are said to be complements in production, such as beef and leather; a decrease in the price of one good will lead to a decrease in the quantity of the other good which will be supplied. If the price of beef falls, then farmers are less likely to supply it to the market. The result may be a reduction in the supply of leather. Goods that are substitutes, such as beers at a brewery, are said to be competitively supplied. A brewer could probably switch production from one brew to another, for example from bottled beer to draught if the price of draught beer were to rise while the price of bottled beer was unchanged.

3 *Price of the factors of production* (P_f) – the cost of production will rise if the price of a factor of production increases. For example, if raw materials were more expensive and the price of a good remains unchanged, then its output becomes less profitable, and less will be produced. In this scenario it may be better to look for an alternative source of supply. Other costs, such as labour costs and the cost of capital, are also important to companies and influence their output decisions.

4 *The state of technology* (T) – technology can be used to improve productivity and so increase supply. However, changes in technology can pose challenges. The widespread use of the internet and downloading of music has created serious problems for the music industry worldwide. Profits for the six major companies continue to fall.

5 *Other factors* (Z) – although this heading acts as a 'catch-all' it is important in its own right. An organisation can be influenced by its expectations of what is likely to happen in the future or the number of new companies entering the market. Changes in government practices with regard to taxation, subsidies or regional policies have a substantial impact.

Supply of a product can be influenced by all of these factors. We can express this by the supply function:

$$S_x = \int(P_x, B, P_g, P_f, T, Z)$$

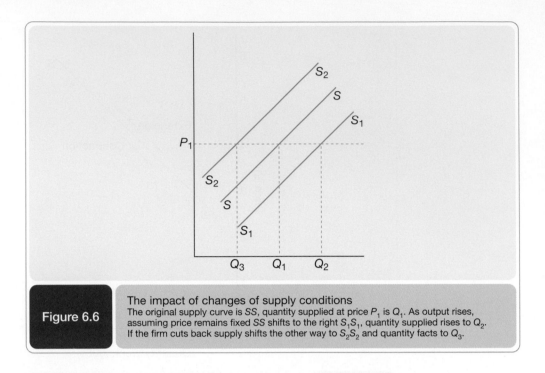

Figure 6.6

The impact of changes of supply conditions

The original supply curve is *SS*, quantity supplied at price P_1 is Q_1. As output rises, assuming price remains fixed *SS* shifts to the right S_1S_1, quantity supplied rises to Q_2. If the firm cuts back supply shifts the other way to S_2S_2 and quantity facts to Q_3.

The rules that apply to the demand curve also apply here. If there is a change in one of the conditions influencing supply, apart from price and assuming other factors are held constant (*ceteris paribus*), then the supply curve may be shifted to the right or left. For example, a business organisation may seek to supply more to the market by investing in new technology. As a result the supply curve will move to the right because the firm has increased its output. The reverse situation will also be true (see *Figure 6.6*).

To summarise, it is important to distinguish between movement *along* a supply curve, due to change in price of a goods, and movements *of* the supply curve, due to change in one of the other determinants of supply.

6.2.3 Price determination

Economists use the term 'equilibrium' to describe a state in which internal forces, or variables, are in balance and there is no tendency to change. Market price is determined by the price at which consumers are willing to buy and producers are willing to sell. This is called the equilibrium price. The corresponding quantity is called the equilibrium quantity. In the case of the market for boxes of chocolates, in our example, the equilibrium price is £4.00 and the equilibrium quantity is four thousand boxes per week. The point of intersection is called the equilibrium point in the market (see *Figure 6.7*).

If there are changes in the conditions of demand the demand curve moves and changes in the conditions of supply result in the movement of the supply curve. Both market price and quantity will change. The extent of the changes depends on the price elasticity of supply and price elasticity of demand, that is the extent to which demand and supply are sensitive to changes in price. However, in general we can state that:

1 An increase in demand causes an increase in the equilibrium price and quantity.
2 A decrease in demand causes a decrease in the equilibrium price and quantity.
3 An increase in supply causes a decrease in the equilibrium price and a rise in the equilibrium quantity.
4 A decrease in supply causes an increase in the equilibrium price and a fall in the equilibrium quantity.

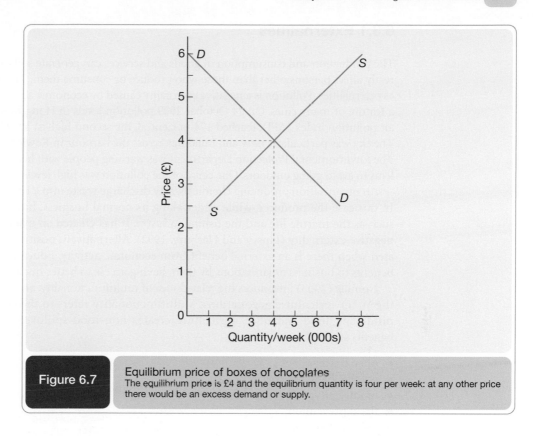

Figure 6.7	Equilibrium price of boxes of chocolates
	The equilibrium price is £4 and the equilibrium quantity is four per week: at any other price there would be an excess demand or supply.

6.3 Market forces and the environment

When every person's standard of living is maximised, market forces can be said to be an efficient mechanism for the allocation of resources. In this case the market can operate free from any regulatory control. This scenario is unrealistic; it is unlikely that a market can ever achieve such an allocation and so be completely free from intervention. The release of CFCs from, for example, aerosol containers, refrigerators and air conditioning units, was thought to be having a serious impact on the ozone layer. Resources, in this case, were being used to the detriment of society in general. The market did not act to reduce the impact of CFCs and adopt less-polluting propellants until put under substantial consumer and political pressure (e.g. the 1987 Montreal Protocol). This example shows that, although the market may act to reduce the harmful impact that it has on the environment, it is frequently an incomplete response. Action is often in response to stakeholder pressure, discussed in section 6.63 'The influence of stakeholder power'. In this case governments had to play a role in reducing the use of CFCs; on 1 January 1995 the production and import of CFCs was banned in the EU.

It is likely that market forces will not bring about the best or optimum allocation of resources. It is beyond the scope of this book to look in detail at all aspects of the failure of markets, but it is vital for us to assess how this failure can result in damage to the environment.

It is not only in market systems that high levels of pollution have been experienced. The former Communist states have also suffered. In east-central Europe considerable pollution may be the result of four decades of central planning by Communist governments, which failed to adhere to declared priorities for sound environmental management; instead, there was serious ecological damage of the sort previously attributed only to Western capitalist regimes (Carter and Turnock, 1993). The same scenario can also be seen in parts of China now.

6.3.1 Externalities

The production and consumption of goods and services can generate spillover effects that indirectly affect persons other than those who produce or consume them. These effects are known as externalities. Pollution is a negative externality caused by economic activity that appears to be a feature of many cities. On 24 October 2009 pollution levels in Hong Kong, measured by the air pollution index (API), reached 174 in Central, the second highest level in the city's history. The sky was particularly hazy and buildings across the harbour in Kowloon were barely visible. The Environmental Protection Department was warning people with heart or respiratory problems to avoid going outdoors. One cause of the pollution was high levels of nitrogen dioxide.

An organisation producing chemicals may discharge waste into a river, causing fish to die. In this case the producer, while undertaking its normal business, has harmed third parties such as the marine life and the fishing industry. It has created an external cost known as a negative externality (Lipsey and Harbury, 1992). Alternatively, positive externalities are created when there is an external benefit from economic activity. Education provides spillover benefits to business organisations by them having access to better quality staff.

Nomille (2003) introduces the related idea of multifunctionality, an issue that has arisen in the WTO agriculture negotiations. Multifunctionality refers to the concept that, besides producing food and fibre, agriculture creates non-food spillover – multifunctional – benefits such as:

- open space;
- wildlife habitat;
- biodiversity;
- flood prevention;
- cultural heritage;
- viable rural communities; and
- food security.

Organisations do not, generally, fully consider the wider social costs or benefits of their business activities. For example, a company may argue that it is not in its economic interest to invest in anti-pollution systems and so may economise on the provision of anti-pollution controls (this will be discussed in section 6.6 '*Organisational agendas*' later in this chapter). In this case 'private costs' and shareholder returns are of uppermost concern to the organisation. This type of judgement may lead to higher levels of harmful emissions into the environment.

However, if the organisation were to take stock of all of the costs involved in its activities, it would have to include external costs, that is, the cost to society of the externalities caused. Adding external cost to private cost gives us the social cost and shifts the supply curve to the left. Price would rise and quantity demanded would fall. The resulting lower output should reduce the externalities. This new level of output is the socially efficient level of output with no welfare loss to society.

It is clear that negative (and positive) externalities arise under specific circumstances. Companies do affect individuals and vice versa. We can examine this situation under four main headings:

- actions by companies which affect other companies;
- actions by companies which affect individuals;
- actions by individuals which affect companies;
- actions by individuals which affect other individuals.

6.3.2 Actions by companies which affect other companies

Industrial waste from production processes can enter the sea and so impact on commercial fisheries. The gradual pollution of Japan's inland sea, between Honshu and Shikoku, in the

1950s and 1960s severely damaged fish stocks. A similar situation can be seen now in China and in many of Europe's rivers. In these cases private costs have predominated, as it is not in the economic interests of those industries producing the waste to reduce pollution caused by their activities. In these cases a negative externality has arisen.

Positive externalities can be of great benefit. The success of some sports, for example football clubs, can enhance business activity in any town or city. With over 40,000 spectators at some games the knock-on effect on shops, restaurants and bars is substantial. The 'feel good' factor is also felt by supporters, who, as employees, may even bring benefits to their own organisations. It has even been suggested that sporting success can help to attract inward investment.

6.3.3 Actions by companies which affect individuals

A common example is the case of a firm polluting an air or water source as a by-product of production. Examples here include the production of refrigerators using CFCs, a coal-burning electricity plant with nitrous oxide and sulphur oxide by-products, or a paper mill, which dumps chlorine bleach into a river as a by-product of producing white office paper. China's rapid industrialisation has been pressing on at a huge environmental cost, with up to 70 percent of its waterways polluted and air quality in its biggest cities among the world's worst (*Asia News*, 2007). A further dramatic illustration of producers affecting individuals was illustrated by the Union Carbide disaster in Bhopal, India in 1984 (see *Minicase 6.5*).

However, actions by companies can have a positive impact on individuals. International experience confirms that education and training are positive externalities. In 2000 Unilever Tea Kenya, a Unilever subsidiary, began a tree-planting project: Trees 2000. One aim of the project was to improve the efficiency of water catchments – a direct business benefit to rain-dependent crops such as tea. However, the project has involved local people to extend awareness. Books on trees have been given to primary schools. Another aim was to increase biodiversity, complement existing conservation and environmental protection programmes, and provide an amenity for staff and the neighbouring community. Altogether, by the beginning of 2008, Trees 2000 has contributed 620,000 trees to Kenya's landscape. It has also provided beneficial habitats for birds and insects, shade for animals, and medicines and recreation areas for local people (Unilever, 2009).

6.3.4 Actions by individuals which affect companies

Worldwide road traffic has been growing substantially and is likely to continue for the foreseeable future. If individuals continue to use their cars, then costs are likely to be inflicted on businesses as increasing congestion raises transportation costs for companies which may have direct repercussions on the price of goods in the shops. This example of traffic congestion illustrates how individuals do not consider their full impact on road conditions. *Minicase 6.3* shows the situation facing Bangkok in Thailand.

There is a clear positive benefit to industry of a better trained and more highly qualified workforce. However, it is increasingly difficult for organisations, particularly in times of recession, to fund in-house training. This training gap is now being filled by individuals taking the initiative for their own training. Student numbers have grown substantially in many countries since 1976. The number of students enrolled in tertiary education is an indicator of a country's future potential for its skilled labour force. A highly educated labour force is a major factor in determining regional competitiveness in the knowledge-based economy (OECD, 2009). *Table 6.4* shows student enrolment in selected OECD countries.

OECD (2009) recognises that a university education is not sufficient for a professional career spanning three or four decades. Lifelong learning is a learning opportunity given at all ages and in different contexts: at work, at home and through leisure activities. It is often accomplished though distance learning or e-learning, continuing education, or correspondence

Minicase 6.3	Traffic congestion in Bangkok

Eighty-two percent of Bangkok's journeys during the early 1990s were by bus, car, motorbike or taxi, (average vehicle speeds in the centre dropped to as low as 10km/h (6mph)); this caused appalling traffic congestion and the resulting air and noise pollution has proved a constant headache for the city's population and the Thai government.

Thailand's government has considered road pricing, as in cities such as London, and also introduced several other measures aimed at improving traffic congestion. These include fines handed out by police to speeders and jaywalkers, and the threat of increased insurance premiums for repeat traffic offenders; encouraging vehicles to use compressed natural gas, a cheaper, cleaner and odourless alternative to petrol or diesel.

In December 2001 a two-month pilot scheme was launched in Silom Road, in the heart of the city's commercial district. An 800m part of the road was closed every Sunday, an action which led to thousands of rural Thais flocking to the the area, which had previously been flooded with traffic. Figures, quoted by the AFP news agency, indicated that about 70 percent of Bangkok residents approved of the closures, saying they hoped it would improve air quality.

Thailand's tourism authority praised the scheme as one where people could finally walk around 'in an atmosphere of clean air and total comfort'. Following the success, authorities halted weekend traffic along four more roads, including the infamous Khao San strip where backpackers congregate.

Bangkok has two main problems. First, there is a severe shortage of roads – a mere 8 percent of its surface is covered with roads compared with 16 percent in Tokyo and 20 percent in the majority of other major cities. Second, there was a lack of viable alternatives for Thais wishing to travel. The first scheme designed to tackle this issue was the Bangkok Transit System (BTS) – widely referred to as Skytrain – opened in December 1999. However, the high price of fares, at up to three times the parallel bus service, and the system not covering main commuter arteries beyond the central district did little to motivate would-be regular passengers. Despite the system being laden with serious debts and lower-than-expected ridership, further extensions to the Skytrain network were announced in September 2006. The second scheme, Bangkok's new subway system (the Blue line) opened in July 2004. The metro runs in a semi-circle from the north to the south of the city. Although the 18 stations on its route are still out of reach for many people who live in Bangkok's suburbs, the network penetrates much further than the above-ground Skytrain. The authorities plan to build another 60km of tunnels within the next six years, which the government hopes will cut Bangkok's legendary traffic congestion by 50 percent. It is planned that, eventually, three metro lines will cover all of the major areas of Bangkok.

The measures together have had a noticeable impact. According to Bangkok's Pollution Control Department, the city has seen a 47 percent decrease in the amount of harmful small dust particles since 1997. Bangkok's air quality has improved considerably over the past two decades.

Sources: Bangkok to Combat Traffic Congestion, Friday 21 December 2001, 22:17 GMT, available from http://news.bbc.co.uk/2/hi/asia-pacific/1723804.stm; Bangkok Skytrain Transit System, Thailand, available from www.railway-technology.com/projects/bangkok/; Cheung (2004); Bangkok's Air Pollution Slowly Evaporating, 25 October 2007, available from http://afp.google.com/article/ALeqM5igofs7w3nkCpf mcg3-NRTBLB3fJg

Questions

1 Using the four headings in the section 'Measures available to limit externalities' below, categorise the measures that the Thai government has put in place, and identify and evaluate other measures to help reduce congestion.

2 Identify the negative externalities that may result if the situation is not improved.

courses. It is now an important part of the education path. While it is undertaken by individuals, it enables companies to be in a better position to be able to react to a rapidly changing economic climate. Participation in lifelong learning varies among countries, with the UK, Finland, Sweden and the Netherlands showing higher participation rates than the rest of the European countries.

Table 6.4	Percentage of population enrolled in tertiary education 2005

Country	% enrolled
Portugal	3.61
Greece	5.82
Ireland	4.51
Japan	3.16
Iceland	5.13
Australia	5.02
UK	3.80
Mexico	2.29
OECD average	4.19
Norway	4.63
USA	5.84
Denmark	4.29
France	3.59
Turkey	2.92
Italy	3.47
Netherlands	3.46
Germany	2.75
Korea	6.67

Source: adapted from 'Student enrolment in tertiary education' from *OECD Regions at a Glance 2009*, www.oecd.org/regional/regionsataglance.

6.3.5 Actions by individuals which affect other individuals

Concerns have long been raised by communities across the world arising from higher volumes of tourism which can have an impact on their environment and culture. This is clearly an example of a negative externality where the activity of individuals affects other individuals. On the other hand, a positive externality is created when individuals improve their driving habits or maintain the area in which they live. Immunisation is also an example of a positive externality. Not only are those who have been immunised protected from the disease, but others in the wider community, who have not received the treatment, also benefit as there will be fewer carriers of the disease overall.

6.3.6 Summary

Negative externalities are a direct consequence of economic activity. If private producers exclude the costs imposed on other people from their output calculations they will produce more of the good than is socially desirable. The direct result will be negative externalities, as outlined earlier, and a welfare loss to society. Some pollution, however, may be socially acceptable because the enormous cost of reducing many types of pollution to zero may pose even more limits on society.

It has been suggested that it is in the economic interests of individuals and companies to accept the consequences of these negative externalities. This view, which encourages negative externalities, may be blinkered. Short-term benefits of having more and cheaper products to consume may not be in the wider long-term interests of the community and the environment. However, organisations in some parts of the world are often encouraged to take this short-term view by their shareholders as they strive for greater returns. Having considered the difference between the private and social optimum output, we now need to examine the role of the government.

6.4 Measures available to limit externalities

There is a disincentive for organisations to develop or install new, more environmentally friendly equipment, because the cost of so doing is likely to be a reduction in their competitiveness. Organisations competing across industries throughout Europe face a dilemma regarding the harmful effects of their production. The extra cost of pollution control equipment will increase costs overall and, perhaps, result in an inability to compete with cheaper, less environmentally conscious, competitors from the developing world. However, taking no action may mean that stricter legislation is imposed on the industry.

Governments do not have to let all negative externalities persist. They can intervene in the market through a range of means, including adopting policies that use, or improve, the price mechanism, or by employing extra-market policies. Cost is a key consideration for government and the organisations when deciding upon the appropriate type and timing of intervention. In this section we discuss limiting externalities under four headings:

- property rights;
- market solutions;
- tradeable permits;
- regulation and legislation.

The principle is designed to encourage businesses to improve processes and is achieved by setting standards and controls which companies have to comply with in order to avoid incurring any extra costs through taxes or fines.

Organisations will usually try to pass on their increased costs to the consumer. Some consumers will refuse to pay the increased price and consumption of the good will fall. As was noted earlier in the chapter, this will reduce the level of externalities, for example pollution, and result in a more socially efficient level of production.

6.4.1 Property rights

For some negative externalities, such as pollution, if somebody had ownership rights to the air, sea, etc., then they could take the polluters to court and sue for compensation. If it is possible to identify the legal rights of the parties involved then bargaining may be viable. For example, a paper mill producing pulp may be willing to compensate a fishing club that owns a stretch of water if the latter accepts a certain amount of pollution. In return the mill will save money on its waste treatment.

Four problems arising from the use of bargaining are evident:

- it is difficult to establish the legal rights involved;
- it would be impossible to list everyone who is affected by harmful emissions from a particular factory for the purpose of compensation;
- there may be no bargaining machinery in place;
- the costs to an organisation of administering such a system, even if agreements were reached, could be enormous.

Because of these problems, bargaining is unlikely to be successful. As the market finds it very difficult to respond to the problem, many argue that there is a need for government intervention.

6.4.2 Market solutions

The aim here is to change the costs of the activity to account for the negative externality. This usually involves the use of charges, taxes or subsidies.

The tax mechanism can be used to impose extra costs on both producers and consumers. Welford and Gouldson, (1993) suggest that the increased use of financial instruments, such as regulatory charges, landfill levies and fines, are all manifestations of the 'polluter pays' principle (PPP), which requires that the costs of pollution be borne by those who cause it.

The European Union's Environmental Liability Directive (2004/35/EC) came into force in April 2004 with a requirement that it should be implemented into national law by all member states by May 2007. It aims to prevent significant environmental damage by forcing industrial polluters to pay prevention and remediation costs. The effect of the measure is to increase the costs of production for manufacturers and reduce the output of pollutants.

The PPP also applies to car buyers in Singapore, where car buying permits are necessary before anyone can purchase a car. Additionally, high import duties, which increase the purchase price of a car, high road tax and road pricing in the central business district all serve to reduce demand for cars. However, to compensate for this Singapore has a very efficient public transport system.

If a tax reflects the full external environmental cost then the externality has been fully internalised. This is a very big 'if', since the issue is whether the tax can ever accurately reflect the external cost. The aim is to impose a tax that will result in the socially efficient level of output. In such situations organisations have a choice: they can continue to pollute and pay for it or invest in anti-pollution measures which will, in the short term, reduce their tax liability and, possibly, save them money and/or offer competitive advantages in the long term.

Grants can be provided to polluters as an incentive to reduce the amount of discharge and encourage environmentally friendly forms of behaviour. European farmers can obtain subsidies under the Common Agricultural Policy (CAP) for land improvement schemes that enhance the environment. One key reservation is that the use of grants or subsidies flies in the face of the 'polluter pays' principle.

6.4.3 Tradeable permits

A more recent development in the area of controlling negative externalities has been the use of tradeable pollution permits to enable emissions trading. These permits limit the degree of structural change necessary and focus on tackling the worst culprits. In the USA the majority of laws concerning the environment rely on this system. For example, clean air legislation sets a limit on emissions of nitrous oxide and sulphur dioxide from power stations, and the government issues a fixed quantity of permits giving authorisation to emit a certain amount of these gases. It is therefore in the interests of power stations to reduce their emissions, if possible. If they pollute at a level higher than their permit allows, they have to buy permits from another company. If they pollute less than they are allowed to, they can sell their permit.

Tradeable permits allow those companies which find the cost of pollution control to be relatively low to sell their rights for a fee or allow those which have invested in long-term 'clean-up' measures to sell their permits to those whose emissions exceed their permit. Having such a market means that resources are used more efficiently to control the overall level of pollution.

Organisations will buy rights to discharge, as long as the cost of the permit is below the cost of the pollution control measures they would otherwise have to undertake.

This type of tradeable system is also evident at a global level. The 1997 Kyoto Protocol binds most developed nations to cap and set up a system to trade in the major greenhouse gases. The European Union Emission Trading Scheme is the largest multinational, greenhouse gas emissions trading scheme in the world.

6.4.4 Regulation and legislation

A common method of intervening in the market to force organisations to address negative externalities is by regulation, usually by imposing a set of legal obligations upon organisations or individuals. Regulations are commonly used to impose external costs on producers. Regulations can take many forms which include (Lee, 1994):

- prohibiting the abstraction, use or disposal of particular substances, products and processes which are considered to be environmentally damaging (e.g. CFCs have been banned because of the damage they cause to the ozone layer);
- setting maximum limits for the abstraction of particular natural resources (e.g. water from rivers);
- setting maximum limits for discharges of pollutants to air, water or land (e.g. exhaust emission standards are being applied in many countries);
- prescribing the technology which may be used for particular processes of production or the materials which may be used in particular processes (e.g. catalytic converters must be used on cars to cut emissions);
- establishing ambient quality standards.

Regulations are used because they are easier than other types of intervention to administer. Taxation of, for example, CO_2 discharge into the atmosphere such as that discussed above requires sophisticated and costly monitoring. Regulations may not require this level of monitoring as spot checks may be enough. Through regulation an organisation could be prohibited from producing more than the socially efficient level of output.

All regulation in EU countries takes the lead from EU environmental legislation, which is grouped into seven fields. Regulations can be applied that relate to all these areas:

- general environmental policy regulations;
- air;
- chemical, industrial risks and biotechnology;
- nature conservation;
- noise;
- waste;
- water.

For example, directive 2006/66/EC of the European Parliament and of the Council on batteries and accumulators and waste batteries and accumulators entered into force on 6 September 2006. The deadline for implementation of the legislation in the member states was 29 September 2008. The objective of the directive is to reduce the amount of mercury and cadmium allowed in batteries and to encourage recycling of spent batteries. Disposing of the waste from these products pollutes the atmosphere (in the case of incineration) and contaminates ground-cover and water (in the case of landfill or burial). The directive aims to reduce the environmental pollution from this waste. In addition, recycling the waste enables the recovery of thousands of tonnes of metals, including precious metals such as nickel, cobalt and silver (Europa, 2009).

The amount of materials that are recycled is increasing, partly due to this type of legislation. Some European countries are much better placed than others. Recycling rates in Germany and Denmark are around 80 percent. In Germany, for example, householders sort waste into separate containers to facilitate recycling.

However, regulations do cause problems. Because the legislation is often uniformly applied it tends to be costly for the industries affected to keep up with the changes. This may mean that the law makers are under pressure from lobbyists to 'tone down' legislation or that there is no incentive for organisations to improve performance beyond compliance with the regulation. It has even been suggested that trying to make industry cleaner, by applying tighter standards, may protect old, dirty technology already in place and discourage cleaner innovation.

Regulations, however, may also be able to promote business activity. Opportunities will flourish in the waste clean-up industry, giving export opportunities as other countries adopt similar regulations that tend to minimise waste. Porter (1990) argued that environmental regulations can create new jobs. It is possible that the imposition of strict regulations can actually improve the ability of a firm to compete. Stringent standards for product performance, product safety and environmental impact can stimulate companies to improve quality, upgrade technology and provide features that respond to consumer and social demands. Easing standards, however tempting, may be counterproductive (Porter, 1990). The environmental technologies industry could be losing as much as £2 billion in annual sales due to the weak regulation and enforcement of legislation requiring these safer processes on the rest of industry (Environmental Industries Commission, 1996).

Environmental standards can also act as a barrier to entry (see *Chapter 2*): those car manufacturers which had already fitted catalytic converters on cars for sale in the USA lobbied in favour of their adoption in the European market.

Organisations that are based in countries with substantial regulations, such as Sweden, may be in a position to gain competitive advantage over organisations operating under a more lax regime. As legislation changes and converges throughout Europe and the world, those organisations that have worked under the strictest regimes could have a distinct competitive advantage. Scania, the multinational truck manufacturer, has used the strict legal environment in Sweden to compete successfully in the truck industry. Murray and Fahy (1994) suggest that the advantage to the early movers is most likely to arise from:

- positive consumer perceptions and attitudes which become attached to companies and their brands;
- the accumulated experience of dealing with new materials, technologies and processes;
- the ownership of proprietary design, recovery and recycling technologies and processes.

It may be difficult for organisations that are left behind to catch up.

Anti-monopoly legislation may be used to prevent the abuse of monopoly power (see *Chapter 2*) which could include infringement of environmental regulations. Firms could also be taken into public ownership and their output controlled to take into account both public and private costs. How ineffective this may be can be judged by reference to the high levels of pollution in the former Soviet Union. One of the key foundations of environmental policies adopted by the Conservative government in the UK from 1979 was that effective regulation did not require legal ownership of industries.

6.5 Government regulation at different geo-political scales

Government at various geo-political scales, from international to local, oversees the marketplace. Increasingly, much of the development of policy relating to environmental issues is taking place at global and regional scales. Nation states, which will have participated in the formulation of policy, will then often have to give domestic effect to such things as international treaties or European directives via legislation and appropriate executive action. Various global and regional institutions monitor activities in different nation states. This activity makes it vital for organisations to understand their environmental impact: see *Minicase 6.4*.

6.5.1 Regulation at global level

At the global level, regulation is primarily concerned with nations agreeing to environmental protection initiatives via international summit meetings. The United Nations Framework Convention on Climate Change (UNFCCC) shows how progress at this global scale is slow.

Minicase 6.4	Carlsberg social responsibility and environmental affairs

Following the acquisition of Scottish and Newcastle and Heineken in 2008, Carlsberg was the 4th largest brewer in the world, with more than 45,000 employees, in 150 markets, and over 500 beer and soft drink brands.

	2004	2005	2006	2007	2008
Sales volumes (million hl)					
Beer	92.0	101.6	100.7	115.2	126.8
Soft drinks	19.4	19.1	20.2	20.8	22.3

Note: (hl: hectolitres).

Almost from the beginning, in 1847, Carlsberg has been aware of its responsibilities. The new millennium saw further changes. In 2002 Carlsberg expanded its principles for Corporate Social Responsibility (CSR). This was soon followed by a Code of Responsible Management that included reference to business ethics and labour standards. Furthermore, a so-called 'legal compliance' programme was also implemented to ensure that competition regulations were always observed. In 2002 it was also decided that Carlsberg Breweries' environmental activities would undergo improvement through internationally recognised standards for environmental management, ISO 14001.

In 2008, Carlsberg became a signatory member of the United Nations Global Compact, through which it committed to supporting and advancing the ten principles of this organisation. At this time Carlsberg's CSR policies were revised in order to strengthen their commitment to minimising the environmental and social impacts of their products and production methods. These goals include:

- Environment: focusing on the carbon and water footprint of the entire value chain;
- Responsible consumption: to minimise problems related to misuse of alcohol;
- Responsible supplier management: to encourage them to comply with Carlsberg's requirements.

The need to do this was highlighted when Carlsberg was fined £25,000 in 2006 by the UK's Environment Agency for allowing a company that did not have a waste management licence to dispose of its waste (Harvey, 2006) and by Carlsberg's 2006 inclusion on a Chinese Water Pollution Map for discharging waste from a brewery in Tianshui in the north-western Gansu province (Lau and Dixon, 2007). In 2010 Carlsberg will publish its first Global Compact Communication on Progress.

Sources: adapted from Carlsberg A/S Annual Report 2008, available from www.carlsberggroup.com/Investor/DownloadCentre/Pages/annualreport2008.aspx; Harvey (2006); Law and Dixon (2007)

Questions

1 Explain why Carlsberg is so enthusiastic to develop its CSR agenda?
2 What are the ten principles of the United Nations Global Compact?

At the Earth Summit in June 1992, 172 of the world's governments met to adopt three agreements:

- Agenda 21;
- the Rio Declaration on Environment and Development;
- the Statement of Forest Principles.

And two legally binding conventions:

- the United Nations Convention on Biological Diversity;
- United Nations Framework Climate Change Convention.

The Convention entered into force on 21 March 1994. As of 22 August 2007, 192 countries had ratified the convention.

The Convention divides countries into two main groups. Annex I has a total of 40 industrialised countries currently listed, including the relatively wealthy industrialised countries plus countries with economies in transition (the EITs), including the Russian Federation, Turkey, the Baltic States, and several Central and Eastern European States. Annex I countries agreed to reduce their emissions of greenhouse gasses to targets that are mainly set below their 1990 levels. The OECD members of Annex I are also listed in Annex II, which comprises 23 developed countries that pay for costs of developing countries.

All other countries, mostly the developing countries, are known as non-Annex I countries. They currently number 145.

The text of the protocol to the UNFCCC was adopted in Kyoto, Japan, on 11 December 1997. The Kyoto Protocol and its rulebook set out in the Marrakesh Accords consist of five main elements (UNFCCC, 2003):

- *Commitments* – at the heart of the Kyoto Protocol lies a set of legally binding targets on greenhouse gas emissions for industrialised countries. These amount to a total cut among all Annex I countries of at least 5 percent from 1990 levels by 2008–2012. All countries are also subject to a set of general commitments.
- *Implementation* – to meet their targets, Annex I countries must put in place domestic policies and measures that cut their greenhouse gas emissions. They may also offset their emissions by increasing the removal of greenhouse gases by carbon sinks. Supplementary to domestic actions, countries may also use the three mechanisms – joint implementation, the clean development mechanism and emissions trading – to gain credit for emissions reduced (or greenhouse gases removed) at lower cost abroad than at home.
- *Minimising impacts on developing countries* – the protocol and its rulebook include provisions to address the specific needs and concerns of developing countries, especially those most vulnerable to the adverse effects of climate change and to the economic impact of response measures. These include the establishment of a new adaptation fund.
- *Accounting, reporting and review* – rigorous monitoring procedures are in place to safeguard the Kyoto Protocol's integrity, including an accounting system, regular reporting by countries and in-depth review of those reports by expert review teams.
- *Compliance* – a Compliance Committee, consisting of a facilitative and an enforcement branch, will assess and deal with any cases of non-compliance.

The protocol entered into force on 16 February 2005, the 90th day after the date on which at least 55 countries, incorporating Annex 1 countries that account for at least 55 percent of the total carbon dioxide emissions in 1990, have ratified, accepted, approved or acceded to the protocol. As of 14 January 2009, 183 countries had ratified the Kyoto Protocol. The total of carbon emissions that these Annex 1 countries represent is 63.7 percent. *Table 6.5* shows the carbon dioxide emissions of the main Annex 1 countries (UNFCCC, 2009). As the protocol has now been ratified a surcharge for exceeding the target can now be enforced.

At this global level the chief guiding concept is sustainable development assuring that, for the sake of generations to come, the amount and quality of what has been called 'natural capital' – for example, atmosphere, water, tropical rainforest and biodiversity – are not reduced by economic development. From the early 1980s onwards a range of key reports from institutions, such as the World Commission for Environment and Development and the World Bank, made pleas for integrating environmental considerations into policy-making on economic development.

Table 6.5	Percentage carbon dioxide emissions of main Annex I countries, 2009

Country	Percentage
Australia	2.1
Canada	3.3
France	2.7
Germany	7.4
Italy	3.1
Japan	8.5
Poland	3.0
Russian Federation	17.4
Spain	1.9
UK	4.3
USA	36.1
Other Annex 1 countries	10.2
Total	100.0

Source: adapted from UNFCCC (2009)

6.5.2 Regulation at regional level

We turn now to the regional scale to discuss the role of the EU in respect of environmental regulation. The signatories to the Treaty of Rome (1957), which created the EEC, were not particularly concerned with environmental issues. This oversight was rectified by the Single European Act (SEA) 1987 which adopted the specific environmental objectives in Article 130R, namely:

- to preserve, protect and improve the quality of the environment;
- to contribute towards protecting human health;
- to ensure a prudent and rational utilisation of natural resources.

These objectives were extended by the Treaty of European Union (1992) (the so-called Maastricht Treaty) to include:

- sustainable and non-inflationary growth respecting the environment;
- promotion of measures to help resolve global environmental problems.

EU policy intentions are set out in its Environmental Action Programme. The first was from 1973 to 1976. The European Commission (EC), through Directorate General (DG) XI, is responsible for the environment. DG XI takes the role of initiating and implementing EU policies on the environment. The policy has, over the years, changed in its scope. In the past, European environmental initiatives tended to be reactive and based on regulation; they are now becoming more market-driven and voluntary. The 'polluter pays' principle, discussed above, is now at the centre of much EU legislation.

Towards the end of 1993 it was agreed that a long-planned European Environment Agency (EEA) should be set up in Copenhagen, Denmark. One of the major tasks of the EEA has been to set up a European Information and Observation Network (EIONET) to provide objective, reliable and comprehensive scientific and technical information at a European level. The aim is to provide data to enable the European Union to 'take the steps necessary to protect the environment as well as to assess the results of their actions' (data are available from http://ec.europe.eu/index_en.htm).

The EEA co-ordinates a system of national networks to enable it to achieve its objectives. Collaborative activity is important in order to avoid duplicating work being carried out by other bodies. It published its first report on the environment in 46 countries in 1995, the Dobris Assessment, which uses a wide range of headings to analyse the extent of any progress, including:

- climate change;
- stratospheric ozone depletion;
- acidification;
- tropospheric ozone;
- chemicals;
- waste;
- biodiversity;
- inland waters;
- marine and coastal environment;
- soil degradation;
- urban environment;
- technological and natural hazards.

A second version followed in 1998. Conferences of European environment ministers, such as those in Sofia in 1995 and Aarhus in 1998, aim to use these assessments to help to develop principles and policies designed to bring about environmental improvement and convergence upon a more sustainable pattern of development in Europe. The EEA has an ongoing programme of assessments available on its website.

The 6th EAP was adopted on 22 July 2002 by the European Parliament and the Council. It sets out the framework for environmental policy-making in the EU for the period 2002–2012. The programme identifies four priority areas for urgent action (Europa, 2008):

- climate change;
- nature and biodiversity;
- environment and health and quality of life;
- natural resources and waste.

The new programme stresses the need for member states to better implement existing environmental laws, and the Commission announced that it will bring increased pressure to bear on member states by making implementation failures better known. Another theme in the new programme is working with business and consumers to achieve more environmentally friendly forms of production and consumption.

As we turn to consider regulation at a national level, it is important to note that the environmental laws of EU member states are increasingly determined by the Union, 'while the mechanisms through which these objectives are to be reached are determined nationally' (Welford and Gouldson, 1993). Furthermore, as industries are becoming increasingly globalised, organisations need to comply with varying environmental legislation and respond to action from cross-border pressure groups which may differ widely from those in their home market.

6.5.3 Regulation at national level

Many nations now place a great deal of emphasis on the environment. The essential task for governments is to update regulations to control health and environmental issues and provide support for organisations. The underpinning UK legislation in this field is the Environmental Protection Act 1990 (EPA) and the Environment Act 1995 (EA). Other countries and states have their own legislation. For example, in the Australian State of

Queensland it is the Environmental Protection Act 1994 (amended on the 1 January 2009) and the Environmental Protection Regulation 2008. The UK is currently working towards a long-term goal of reducing CO_2 emissions by at least 60 percent by 2050 and in the budget in 2009 the Chancellor committed to cut emissions by 34 percent by 2020, against 1990 levels. The Climate Change Act 2008 commits the government to fixed and binding five-year carbon budgets. The evidence now suggests that as part of an international agreement the UK may have to reduce emissions by 80 percent.

In the UK, regulatory activity largely stems from the Department for the Environment, Food and Rural Affairs (Defra). Other ministries, such as the Department for Business, Enterprise and Regulatory Reform (BERR), whose Business Link scheme provides advice on environmental issues for small firms in particular, also provide support. Legislation will usually come in two forms:

- Primary legislation, that is Acts or Orders to understand the major principles;
- Secondary legislation, that is regulations to find out about details and updates.

Chien (1991) suggests that legislation is based on the 'four Rs':

- reduction of the amount of waste produced;
- reuse of durable items;
- recycling of natural resources;
- regeneration of discarded products for use as new materials or products.

There is a wide variety of means available for the enforcement of environmental law. Criminal prosecution may impose a fine or imprisonment. Injunctions or claims for damages may prevent some harm from occurring or compensate for injury sustained. Licences or contracts may regulate and set standards. Enforcement agencies (such as the UK's Environment Agency) have wide powers to inspect, report and take action over pollution (Hartshorne, 2003).

If organisations produce waste they have a duty of care in respect of that waste under the EPA 1990. Managers in such businesses need to be aware that breach of this duty of care can lead to fines and prison sentences in addition to civil liability for causing damage to environmental or human health by waste. The EPA 1990 is designed to achieve the 'best practicable environmental option'. The EPA 1990 can grant authorisation to make emissions from any 'prescribed processes' but the process must use the 'best available technique not entailing excessive cost', the BATNEEC test. This test obliges organisations which are polluting to adopt cleaner technologies providing they are not 'excessively' costly. Welford and Gouldson (1993) note that organisations which have developed self-regulation schemes such as EN ISO 14001 'will be at a considerable advantage when gathering the information and applying the criteria of BATNEEC'.

Enforcement notices may be served if an organisation is in breach of the terms of its authorisation to emit. More serious risks which cannot be dealt with in this way will result in the issue of a prohibition notice, which can force the closure of a facility until an organisation complies with its authorisation.

The Environment Agency (EA) was established in England and Wales by the EA 1995 and came into existence in April 1996. It is a key body in respect of enforcement issues in the UK. It is responsible for issuing discharge consents for companies wishing to discharge wastes into rivers. The EA 1995 established the principal aim of the agency to protect or enhance the environment as a whole and make a contribution towards attaining sustainable development. In an attempt to approach environmental issues from a holistic perspective the EA has identified nine key themes in environmental management:

- addressing climatic change;
- regulating major industries;
- improving air quality;
- managing waste;

- managing water resources;
- delivering integrated river basin management;
- conserving the land;
- managing fresh water fisheries;
- enhancing biodiversity.

All other EU governments are also moving forward on this agenda. To improve environmental performance and to incorporate EU directives Ireland has introduced the Protection of the Environment Act 2003. The Act covers integrated pollution prevention and control, a licensing system and new waste management measures. Under the legislation local authorities have more powers and tougher laws against those breaching environmental regulations. The result is more licences being revoked or suspended and larger fines, up to €3,000 for a conviction or a €600 daily fine.

The approach of governments within the EU, as we can see, closely follows EU directives and guidelines. We turn now to examine regulation at the local level.

6.5.4 Regulation at local level

Regulation at a local level is important; indeed, it is vital as it helps to ensure EU directives are properly put in to place. When Bulgaria joined the EU in January 2007 it was clear that it did not possess the administrative capacity at a local level to meet environmental protection requirements. A project was put in place in January 2008 to strengthen the administrative capacity and improve investment in planning skills.

The position of the UK is rather more advanced. Local authority environmental health departments have regulatory responsibility for a number of areas, including food hygiene, health and safety (together with the Health and Safety Executive), pest control, and air and noise pollution. They are also responsible for planning, licensing and trading standards.

Legislation underpins activity at this level. The Clean Neighbourhoods and Environment Act 2005 provides local authorities, parish and community councils and the Environment Agency (EA) with more effective powers and tools to tackle poor environmental quality and anti-social behaviour. It deals with many of the problems affecting the quality of the local environment and is backed by 17 principal regulations. (Defra, 2007).

In summary, it is true to say that progress at the global level in taking ecological regulatory action is often slow. However, since most serious ecological concerns tend not to be confined within particular geographical boundaries, the ability to make progress at this global level is critical to the effective tackling of many of the Earth's ecological problems. Action at regional, national or local levels often stems from these wider global initiatives.

6.6 Organisational agendas

There has been a long and hot debate as to whether organisations have responsibilities to society, with more pressure being placed on organisations to give something back. For the past two decades corporate social responsibility (CSR) has been gaining in importance and visibility. What was once a relatively invisible phenomenon has become a highly publicised marketing tool for companies (Basil and Weber, 2006).

6.6.1 Corporate social responsibility

Wood (1991) describes CSR as 'a business organisation's configuration of principles of social responsibility, process of social responsiveness, and policies, programmes, and observable outcomes as they relate to the firm's societal relationships'.

CSR requires that an organisation does more than just what is expected of it. In recent years, customers, employees, suppliers, community groups, governments, and some shareholders have encouraged firms to undertake additional CSR investments (McWilliams and Siegel, 2007). Indeed, Orlitzky *et al.* (2003) point out that CSR and CSP (corporate social performance) help the firm build a positive reputation and goodwill with its external stakeholders.

It is with this in mind that we now turn our attention to looking at the impact of organisations.

All organisations cause environmental problems and disasters as a direct result of their activities. Taylor *et al.* (1994) identify three categories of company:

- High penetration companies have the greatest impact on the environment. They include agriculture, chemicals and plastics, and metals and mining.
- Moderate penetration companies have some impact, and can save money by cutting wasteful practices. They include electronics, leisure and tourism, and packaging and paper.
- Low penetration companies feel that environmental matters do not concern them. These include advertising, education and local government.

A well-documented example of a high penetration incident occurred in March 1989 when the oil tanker *Exxon Valdez* ran aground in Alaska. By 2007 it was estimated that Exxon Mobil Corp. had paid $3.7 billion in clean-up operations and fines related to civil and criminal charges, resulting from the oil spillage. The number of cases of this type of violation is still substantial. One of the biggest fines, $23.5 million, was levied on the Cunard Line for the damage sustained to a coral reef in the Gulf of Aqaba when it was hit by the vessel *Royal Viking Sun*. It is not only the fines that damage organisations. Cannon (1994) has estimated that loss of market share, disruptions to supplies, compliance with new regulations and the effect on share price, cost Exxon a further substantial sum – between $8 billion and $15 billion. Rebuilding consumer confidence in such cases may prove very difficult.

Even the most environmentally aware organisations can have problems. Unilever states that its core value is a commitment to sustainability: for this it has received a number of awards and plaudits (Unilever, 2008). However, despite this commitment, Unilever has incurred a number of penalties for infringement of environmental regulations. In one such case Unilever China's plant in Hefei (Anhui) was found by the State Environmental Protection Administration to have discharged waste containing banned chemical substances. The company was fined 150,000 yuan and ordered to remedy the situation (*Asia News*, 2007).

According to Taylor *et al.* (1994) this may be an example of moderate penetration. However, Unilever has an improving record in environmental management and its aim is to reach 100 percent compliance.

Even organisations, which may be labelled as low penetration such as universities, are taking action to reduce the impact that they have on the environment. A number of institutions are taking action to reduce the number of inputs they use and are putting in place effective recycling policies.

It is evident that organisations also have responsibilities. Hutchinson (1996) outlines four responsibilities of business, which are shown in *Figure 6.8.*

Given the nature of the business environment facing them, it is clear that organisations throughout the world realise that there is a wide range of responses available to meet the changing environmental agenda. More are discovering that they need to be seen to be responding to this changing context. Hamel and Prahalad (1994) suggest that radical change is necessary if lasting solutions are to be found, and government, business and individuals have a role to play. The future is about sustainability. Companies are competing for the future but can only do so if they are far-sighted, regenerate their core strategies, innovate and use new ways of thinking to transform their organisations. Of importance to this agenda are changing stakeholder views, which we will explore in the next section.

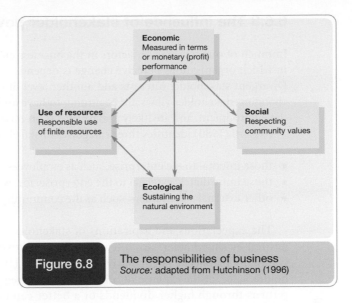

Figure 6.8	The responsibilities of business *Source:* adapted from Hutchinson (1996)

6.6.2 The environment and stakeholders

Stakeholders are groups or individuals who have a stake in, or an expectation of, the organisation's performance (see *Figure 6.9* and also *Chapter 1*). The environmental stance of an organisation is influenced by the perceptions of its stakeholders and the relative power which each possesses. *Minicase 6.5* demonstrates such a case. Many organisations, such as The Body Shop, believe that 'good ethics' and consideration of wider stakeholder interests will pay in the long term.

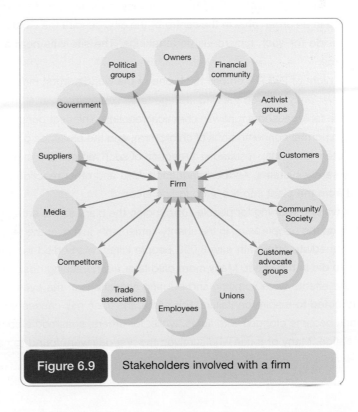

Figure 6.9	Stakeholders involved with a firm

6.6.3 The influence of stakeholder power

In much of our coverage of factors in the business environment we have noted that the way in which organisations perceive change is dependent upon their unique 'perceptual filters'. Divergent stakeholder interests add another level of complexity. It must be recognised that changing stakeholder views are beginning to have an impact on how organisations perceive the environment, and are likely to have effects on business and profit.

Argenti (1980) identifies three categories of stakeholder:

- those internal to the enterprise, such as employees/management and shareholders;
- those immediately external to the enterprise, for example suppliers and customers;
- other external stakeholders, such as the community and pressure groups.

The expectations and aspirations of stakeholder groups differ. The short-term profits desired by shareholders are often given priority over the interests of other stakeholders. Company managers, particularly in the UK and USA, have traditionally managed shareholder value, at the expense of other stakeholder requirements, by maximising shareholder returns through higher dividends or a better capital return from the sale of shares that have increased in value. This requirement frequently conflicts with the adoption of more socially and environmentally sound policies. This approach is not as visible in Europe or Asia.

| Minicase 6.5 | The Bhopal disaster |

In 1977, Union Carbide India Limited (UCIL) set up a manufacturing facility in Bhopal, a city of some 900,000 inhabitants in Madhya Pradesh, India. It was licensed by the state government to manufacture phosgene, monomethylamine (MMA), methylisocyanate (MIC) and the pesticide carbaryl (Sevin). The plant was located in an urban area in the centre of the city, despite the existence of an industrial area which had been set aside for such hazardous undertakings. The site was near a lake which provided an essential water source.

On the night of 2–3 December 1984, one of the world's worst industrial disasters occurred at the plant. Water inadvertently entered the MIC storage tank, containing over 40 metric tonnes of MIC. The addition of water to the tank caused a runaway chemical reaction. The heat generated by the reaction, the presence of higher than normal concentrations of chloroform, and the presence of an iron catalyst (from corrosion of the stainless steel tank wall), resulted in a reaction of such momentum that the gases formed could not be contained by safety systems. As a consequence, MIC and other reaction products, in liquid and vapour form, escaped from the plant into the surrounding areas.

There was no warning for people surrounding the plant as the emergency sirens had been switched off. The effect on the people living in the shanty settlements just over the fence was immediate and devastating.

The immediate aftermath saw 8,000 people killed. Many died in their beds or staggered, blinded and choking, to die in the street. Many more died later after reaching hospitals and emergency aid centres. The early acute effects were vomiting and burning sensations in the eyes, nose and throat. Most deaths have been attributed to respiratory failure. For some, the toxic gas caused such massive internal secretions that their lungs became clogged with fluids, while, for others, spasmodic constriction of the bronchial tubes led to suffocation. Many of those who survived the first day were found to have impaired lung function.

Follow-up studies on survivors have also reported neurological symptoms including headaches, disturbed balance, depression, fatigue and irritability. Abnormalities and damage to the gastrointestinal, musculoskeletal, reproductive and immunological systems were also frequently found.

The factory was closed down after the accident. The accident also led to intensive experimental and epidemiological research into the toxicity of MIC and the tissue damage it could cause. Prior to the Bhopal accident, practically nothing was known and, therefore, since 1984 numerous human health investigations and laboratory toxicity studies have been conducted. However, among the controversies regarding blame and accountability, and the research into the toxicity of MIC, the fate of the redundant former UCIL site was largely overlooked.

The survey conducted for the Bhopal Legacy report by Greenpeace International has demonstrated substantial and, in some locations, severe contamination of land and drinking water supplies with heavy metals and persistent organic contaminants both within and surrounding the former UCIL plant. There is an urgent need for a more detailed and extensive survey if the full extent of ongoing contamination from the plant is to be determined.

Source: adapted from What happened in Bhopal?, available from www.greenpeace.org.uk/toxics/what-happened-in-bhopal

Questions

1 Identify the stakeholders in the Bhopal case and comment on their power to influence decisions.
2 Identify other instances where consumer pressure has forced an organisation to re-think its actions. Comment on the impact on the organisation.

The expectations of the local community may substantially differ from those of a company, resulting in a conflict of interests. How do these wider social needs for more jobs, improvements in local amenities and minimum pollution correspond to the aims of a company? A major problem for the external stakeholders, such as the local community, is that they have insufficient power to influence company strategy because of their fragmented nature (see *Minicase 6.5*). Ansoff (1984) suggests that the dominant coalition, those in positions of power, such as the board of directors, can bias strategy toward their own preferred course of action. In this way senior management can initiate strategies to support shareholders' wishes, which may be to the detriment of the environment and the local community. It would be unusual for external stakeholders to be part of the dominant coalition, so their influence is rarely felt.

Pressure in respect of environmental performance can be applied on the organisation by pressure groups, media and insurers (Welford and Gouldson, 1993). Thilo Bode, then head of Greenpeace International, stated at the Rio Summit in 1992, 'Big corporations today have a responsibility that goes beyond their aim to make a profit. The focus is on social, moral and ethical considerations'.

Becoming shareholders in a company, to drive the environmental issues, is a tried and tested tactic. In 2001 Friends of the Earth bought shares in Balfour Beatty and tabled a resolution in relation to its involvement in the controversial Illisu Dam project in Turkey. It was claimed that its construction would displace thousands of Kurdish people. Balfour Beatty did eventually withdraw from the project. Friends of the Earth contended that 'Balfour Beatty's decision to drop out of the project shows the power of shareholder pressure and publicity campaigns' (EIRIS, 2009).

A survey by Entec in 1996 suggested that green issues were moving up the corporate agenda (Caulkin, 1996). Forum for the Future (2003) reported a survey of mainstream fund managers in the UK and USA, which revealed the increasing importance of social and environmental issues. The majority of fund managers interviewed in the UK and USA now see social and environmental performance as part of the 'non-financial' risks facing their investments. They are integrating engagement on these issues with companies into their mainstream corporate governance process, and the number of large institutional investors engaging on these issues has grown substantially. Green issues are also important for small businesses. A survey of small business owners in the USA by PayCycle (McHenry, 2009) found that:

- 63 percent say environmental issues are just as important;
- 35 percent were worrying more about the environment this past year than ever before;
- 88 percent feel it is important for their businesses to be green.

Evidence, including that from the World Resources Institute, is rapidly accumulating that companies who best manage risks and opportunities related to the natural environment gain durable competitive advantages. This fact elevates environmental topics from an operational concern handled by engineers, lawyers and specialised environmental staff to a front-line, strategic imperative for all business units of the firm – and their managers. As environmental and sustainable development pressures inexorably intensify, managers in the twenty-first century will need a much thicker, more adaptive 'playbook' than their predecessors.

It is open to organisations how they respond to environmental issues. In the next section we will examine the range of alternatives.

6.6.4 Environmental options

Roome (1992) sets out a continuum of five possible environmental options for organisations:

- non-compliance;
- compliance;
- compliance plus;
- commercial and environmental excellence;
- leading edge.

The first three options may be taken by businesses whose primary reference point is legislation.

Non-compliance

An organisation that adopts a non-compliance position may, because of lack of resources or managerial inertia, be unable to satisfy legal requirements. It may also be the case that an organisation makes a business decision not to satisfy basic legal requirements. Some may make a policy decision not to comply with the regulations in order to secure lower costs. Either or both of these scenarios can sometimes be found in the small and medium enterprise sector, although not exclusively. In many cases organisations are 'found out'.

In 2007 American Electric Power (AEP) agreed to end a year-long federal lawsuit by investing $4.6 billion to reduce pollution and clean up smokestacks at its coal-fired power plants. The Environmental Protection Agency called it 'the single largest environmental enforcement settlement in history by several measures.' The settlement also fined AEP an additional $15 million in civil penalties and another $60 million in clean-up and mitigation costs (msnbc.com, 2007).

Compliance

The compliance standpoint is clearly a minimal response and focuses efforts upon the action required to satisfy the minimum legal requirements.

These two stances are essentially reactive. By adopting a reactive stance it is possible that a company may fall behind competitors that are developing products and processes to meet future tougher environmental conditions.

In fact it is becoming evident, because of the objectives of governments worldwide, that organisations cannot take decisions without reference to environmental consequences (see above). This may limit the options that organisations have in response to the environment and cause a change in direction for many organisations. It is likely that all policies will have to have an environmental dimension at the early stages of formation. So organisations will move from being reactive to a more proactive stance, as described by the final three of Roome's (1992) options.

Compliance plus

During the 1980s a shorthand reference to environmentally concerned organisations – and consumers – was use of the word 'green'. 'Green' organisations, such as The Body Shop, were said to have a positive and proactive stance toward environmental and ethical issues. The compliance-plus option demonstrates that a proactive stance towards legal standards can benefit the organisation. The reduced probability of fines associated with non-compliance and the reduced likelihood of bad publicity leading to a loss of market share are demonstrable benefits of taking this option (see above).

Nike, Gap, Adidas and Wal-Mart continue to be high-profile targets of non-government organisations (NGOs) and consumer activists seizing on the latest whiff of worker exploitation and environmental scandal. During the 1990s one global consumer brand after another was hit where it really hurts: on its balance sheet. Many were badly hurt and have since learned that a serious commitment to CSR is central to improving the bottom line (see earlier).

The clamour for corporate righteousness has led to an explosion of corporate social responsibility literature on websites belonging to Gap, Coke, McDonald's and Nike to name but four (Lopatin, 2002). In 2006 the environmental communication guidance standard, ISO 14063 (see www.iso.org/iso/catalogue_detail.htm?csnumber=34676) was launched to offer guidance on what should be considered in developing an environmental communication programme. Evidence shows that by 2008 two-thirds of the world's leading public companies report formally on sustainability (Spada, 2008). Internal and external pressures are also said to have prompted over 50 percent of companies to go beyond compliance with existing legislation and 75 percent have begun developing environmental management systems and so moving toward compliance plus. Such an organisation might aim to integrate an environmental management system into its overall business strategy via a standard such as EN ISO 14001 (see www.iso14000-iso14001-environmental-management.com/iso14001.htm).

Commercial and environmental excellence and leading edge

Roome's (1992) two remaining options incorporate Kleiner's (1991) approach, which identified three key components of green companies:

- They will have developed a mechanism for placing a monetary value on the complete life cycle of their products, from raw materials through production to distribution, consumption and disposal. Such 'cradle-to-grave' or 'life-cycle cost' accounting will assist in the development of products and limit environmental impact.
- They will record and publish environmental data, possibly thereby averting environmental disasters and improving community relations.
- They will be committed to reducing waste at source, for example via some form of total quality management (TQM) programme.

A business focused on 'commercial and environmental excellence' would ensure that its core corporate and managerial values always take account of environmental management issues; 'leading-edge' businesses set the standard for a particular industry through the adoption of 'state-of-the-art' environmental management systems. Some companies have put in place ecological strategies that seek to eliminate emissions, effluents and accidents through preventative action and continuous improvement at every step of the production process

(Shrivastava, 1994). This more proactive stance can be illustrated by the systems adopted by 3M in *Minicase 6.6*.

A brief examination of a range of company Annual Reports suggests that shareholder expectations in respect of a company's environmental record may be increasing. This may partly be due to pressure groups, which have sought to purchase shares in order to gain

---

Minicase 6.6	3M

Over recent years 3M is one company that has prided itself on taking a longer-term view with regard to environmental issues. 3M has a diversified portfolio of businesses, based largely on its wide expertise. It has a strong reputation for product innovation, an example being 'Post-it notes. From 1970 a number of steps have been taken to support policy on the environment.

- 1970 Environment department established.
- 1973 Energy management programme.
- 1975 Environmental policy adopted.
- 1975 Pollution Prevention Pays (3P) programme launched.

The Pollution Prevention Pays (3P) programme was designed to apply pollution prevention on a company-wide basis and document the results. The programme helps prevent pollution at source, in products and manufacturing processes, rather than removing it after it has been created. 3M employees worldwide have initiated more than 4,820 3P projects.

- 1989 Pollution Prevention Plus (3Pi).
  3Pi committed 3M to stricter environmental controls and increased R&D expenditure.
- 1990 global environmental goals established.

A greenhouse gas emissions reduction goal of 50 percent was set from a 1990 base year. 3M achieved a 54 percent reduction from 1990 to 2006.

In 2005, 3M set a new group of goals for the period of 2005–2010. The current goals, which are indexed to net sales, are as follows:

- – Reduce volatile air emissions by 25 percent.
- – Improve energy efficiency by 20 percent.
- – Reduce waste by 20 percent.
- – Complete 800 3P projects (not indexed to net sales).

- 1998 product life-cycle management introduced.
  Product life-cycle management is an integral part of 3M's sustainability strategy. The spotlight is now on products throughout their entire life cycle, from manufacturing through to customer use and disposal.

- 2002 Pollution Prevention Pays updated.
- 2007 environmental solutions catalogue introduced.

3M Environmental Product Solutions enables 3M to offer their customers a portfolio of products to help them reduce their impact on the environment.

Source: adapted from 2008 Sustainability Progress www.3M.com/sustainability available from http://solutions.3m.com/3MContent RetrievalAPI/BlobServlet?locale=en_US&univid=1046797127668&fallback=true&assetType=MMM_Image&blobAttribute=ImageFile& placeId=7BC6E48B1800BAE180A88E492700005E&version=current

Questions

Using Roome's (1992) continuum:

1 Where does a company stand that uses end-of-pipe pollution control? Explain your answer.
2 Assess and comment on the environmental option 3M follows (visit the 3M website for up-to-date further information).

access to annual general meetings and be in a formal forum to put over their views. There is evidence, also, of the increasing popularity of 'green' investment funds.

A proactive stance may require substantial amounts of initial capital investment and put an organisation at a cost disadvantage in relation to more reactive competitors, for example those located in developing or transition economies. However, there are a number of cases of organisations who justify investment in, for example, waste minimisation schemes as making hard-headed, if long-term, business sense. The increasing cost of landfill dumping may cause more organisations to make such decisions.

6.6.5 The importance of the organisation's environmental context

The environmental context in which an organisation carries out its business may be a major factor influencing the environmental stance that it adopts. Organisations need to respond to the question of how the environment is viewed in the country or market in which they operate.

Multinational companies are key players in the economic development of LDCs as they are 'footloose', meaning that they are free to choose any location in the world for their business. The proliferation of legislation in Europe and the USA, as well as increasing costs, has caused the development of 'pollution havens' as some organisations have relocated to less regulated developing countries in order to escape tougher environmental legislation in their home markets (*Croner Guide*, 1996). There is a clear trade-off between business growth and concern for the environment as these companies exploit the less stringent environmental controls of many LDCs. This may be an example of organisations trying to shirk their environmental responsibilities. It has been reported that the swine flu virus that was launched on the unsuspecting world in 2009 may have been 'born' in an industrial pig plant, belonging to an American corporation, in Mexico, where fewer checks and controls allowed the virus free reign to develop and grow.

We can examine the environmental context facing organisations with reference to the work of Azzone and Bertele (1994), who outline five environmental contexts which relate either to national context or to the situation prevailing in certain product/service markets:

1. *Stable context* – here there may be either slow changes or no changes in environmental legislation. There may be a of lack of public perception of environmental issues or an almost complete lack of consumer power. Organisations in these circumstances will find it easy to ignore legislation and adopt a non-compliance stance. This could be the case in developing countries of Latin America, for example the *maquiladora* zone in Mexico is home to blue-chip American companies such as DuPont, General Electric and GM.

2. *Reactive context* – here environmental problems are known by small groups, consumer interest is limited and legislation evolves slowly. In this context, organisations may comply with legislation, responding only slowly when the pressures build up. Many UK organisations in the past opted for this approach to dealing with environmental problems.

3. *Anticipative context* – here the public are more aware and have the ability to move issues on to the political agenda. It is more difficult for firms to influence the political process. Legislation and regulations become more demanding and organisations need to develop a compliance-plus strategy, anticipating changes and using technological developments to ensure that new standards can be met. The regulatory regime in the EU is increasingly encouraging this approach.

4. *Proactive context* – within this context 'green' consumers are said to have a major impact. Organisations may need to demonstrate more concern for the environment if they are to prosper. Commercial and environmental excellence may provide a competitive advantage in the short term but may be indispensable if an organisation is to compete in this type of environment in the long term.

5 *Creative context* – here public opinion is extremely aware of environmental problems but there is a lack of accepted technological solutions to problems. A leading-edge company will be at the forefront of the technological push for the optimal solution. The cost of this could be substantial, but the rewards from developing and controlling a proprietary technological development can be enormous.

Clearly organisations need to be aware of the context in which they operate and need to be able to respond to changes. Organisations that adopt a stance which is out of line with the context in which they operate may not survive in the long term.

Organisations with some of the 'greenest' credentials tend to be engaged in self-regulation schemes of one type or another. Clearly, such companies are in the category of 'compliance plus', or beyond, in Roome's (1992) classifications.

6.6.6 Self-regulation

Global, European and national voluntary self-regulation schemes are having a considerable impact. These self-regulation schemes require organisations to 'sign up' to regimes which typically involve making information available to the public, principally via a corporate responsibility statement, together with clear targets and objectives needed to meet the policy. In such schemes, considerable stress is placed on plans to achieve continual improvements and of integrating environmental issues with those concerns of general management. Environmental audits and further statements on the progress made in respect of environmental objectives tend to be the final pieces of the jigsaw. The concept of environmental audit, in particular, requires organisations to monitor and collect detailed information in order to judge whether improvement has been achieved.

At the global scale there is an extensive range of such self-regulation schemes sponsored by the International Chamber of Commerce (ICC) and the International Standards Organisation (ISO), among others. The ICC's 'Business Charter for Sustainable Development', for example, outlines a range of actions to integrate the management of environmental issues with the general policies and activities of organisations. Perhaps the best-known scheme is EN ISO 14001 – introduced in September 1996 as *the* international standard for environmental management.

The Eco-Management and Auditing Scheme (EMAS) is an example of self-regulation at a European level requiring voluntary eco-audits. EMAS came into operation in April 1995. EMAS is based on a standard environmental management system, as embodied in the EN ISO 14001 standard. The most common benefits of EMAS implementation (EMAS, 2009) are:

- reduced costs, namely in the purchasing process through minimising materials, energy consumption, water consumption and other business resources, in turn raising companies' profit margins;
- reduced environmental risks, which can also turn into financial benefits resulting from trust by shareholders, investment companies, insurance companies and financial institutions;
- maintained and/or increased competitiveness by being able to satisfy the environmental management requirements of a growing number of customers;
- improved ability to comply with environmental legislation;
- greater credibility – the EMAS logo and the verified environmental statement are proof of sound environmental management and concern for the general welfare of the community;
- increased staff commitment – the involvement of employees in the implementation of the environmental management scheme is likely to reinforce the identification of staff with the company and increase their participation in the long-term development of the organisation.

Table 6.6	Organisational implications of environmental stances

	The context				
	Stable	**Reactive**	**Anticipatory**	**Proactive**	**Creative**
Environmental problems	None	Problems addressed when defined	Anticipates new legislation	Examines opportunities for products and company	Searches for new technology
Activities involved:					
• R&D	No	No	Yes	Yes	Yes
• Production/logistics	Limited	Yes	Yes	Yes	Yes
• Marketing/sales	No	No	No	Yes	Yes
• External relations	No	Limited	Yes	Yes	Yes
• Legal	No	Limited	Yes	Yes	Yes
• Finance	No	No	No	Yes	Yes
• Environmental department	No	No	Usually	Usually	Usually
• Top management	No	No	Sometimes	Yes	Yes

Source: adapted from Azzone and Bertele (1994)

In 2001 EMAS was revised and again in July 2008 the EC proposed to revise EMAS to increase the participation of companies and reduce the administrative burden and costs, particularly for small and medium-sized enterprises (SMEs). It is expected that a revised EMAS regulation will be adopted in 2009 and will enter into force at the beginning of 2010 (EMAS, 2009).

Although schemes are voluntary, in the future consumers and business customers are likely to place considerable pressure on supplier organisations to 'sign up'. In 2009 there were 4,095 EMAS registered organisations: 1,471 were in Germany, which has the largest number.

Whatever the response to the environment that an organisation adopts, it is likely that an increased level of activity will be necessary as the environmental context moves from stable, at one end of the continuum, to creative, at the other. It is important to recognise the extra costs that will be incurred by an organisation as it moves from one stance to another (see *Table 6.6*).

To summarise, it is evident that there are many non-legally binding reasons why organisations need to be aware of their impact on the natural environment and, perhaps, to take action to improve the situation. The sort of environmental agenda which an organisation adopts will be influenced by both its environmental context and the extent of stakeholders' power and interest.

6.7 The position of the consumer

Environmental issues are becoming increasingly important in consumers' buying decisions Research shows that some consumers are ready to reward companies. Creyer and Ross (1997) suggest they may be prepared to pay a higher price or actively seek out those companies which they believe to be ethical. People want reasons to reinforce their relationship with brands, and more ethical standards of operation are one method of encouraging consumer loyalty (Lopatin, 2002).

The BBMG Conscious Consumer Report (Bemporad and Baranowski, 2007), finds that nearly nine in ten Americans say the words 'conscious consumer' describe them well, and if products are of equal quality and price they are more likely to buy from companies that:

- manufacture energy efficient products (90 percent);
- promote health and safety benefits (88 percent);
- support fair labour and trade practices (87 percent);
- commit to environmentally friendly practices (87 percent).

Further, Purvis (2006) reports that a range of environmentally sounder alternatives are gaining consumer acceptance in the UK (see *Table 6.7*).

However, Malcolm Baker, global director of Research International Qualitatif, estimates that only 5 percent of consumers actually buy goods on ethical grounds. A November 2002 survey by advertiser WPP, of 1,500 consumers across 41 countries, concluded that consumers were happily married to their brands and would *do anything* to preserve this special material bond (Lopatin, 2002).

Evidence also suggests that ethical consumerism is affected by a slowdown in the economic cycle as consumers have to consider whether they can pay premium prices for ethical products. Key Note (2008) estimates that ethical consumerism in the UK was worth £35.4 million in 2007, although growth is forecast to slow between 2008 and 2012 due to economic slowdown and consumers being obliged to base their purchase decisions on price alone. However, the growth rate is expected to pick up again in 2011 and 2012, as economic conditions become more favourable.

It is interesting to examine the collective power that consumers can exert on businesses and governments in respect of ethical issues. Consumer boycotts can be effective campaigning tools, and can raise people's awareness. The Ethical Consumer (2009) lists a number of UK boycotts, including those against:

- Adidas for using kangaroo skin to make some types of football boots;
- Burma which is ruled by one of the world's most brutal regimes and has used forced labour to prepare the country for tourism;
- Chevron Texaco for dumping billions of gallons of toxic waste in the Ecuadorian Amazon and failing to clean it up;
- Coca-Cola for its repression of trade union activity in Colombia and its depletion of groundwater resources in India;
- Nestlé for its irresponsible marketing of baby milk formula which infringes the International Code of Marketing of breast milk;

Table 6.7	Market share of leading ethical products

This piece originally appeared in Green Futures. Green Futures is published by Forum for the Future and is the leading magazine on environmental solutions and sustainable futures. Its aim is to demonstrate that a sustainable future is both practical and desirable – and can be profitable, too.

Product	Market share(%)
Lead-free petrol, catalytic converters, condensing boilers	100% market share soon
Dolphin-friendly tuna	90
A-rated, energy-efficient washing machines	85
A-rated cold appliances (fridges, freezers)	76
A-rated dishwashers	74
Free-range and barn eggs	40
Fair-trade coffee	20% of ground coffee market

Source: adapted from 'Choice: the curse of the green consumer?' from http://www.forumforthefuture.org/greenfutures/articles/602578

- Proctor and Gamble for its continued use of animal testing;
- Starbuck's because for every cup of coffee that it sells, farmers in coffee-growing countries such as Ethiopia earn about 2p;
- Tesco due to its escalating use of Radio Frequency identification.

However, primary effects may be small and many boycotts may be judged not to have succeeded. Trowell (1998) identified secondary effects that may be more long term and have a greater impact:

- changes to regulations;
- lasting change in industry practices;
- allowing substantial growth or entrance of ethical players into the market;
- effects on decisions of similar organisations to the target.

There is some suggestion that consumer power is starting to be influential in respect of products made using child labour. Adverse publicity has caused many companies to amend their sourcing arrangements and seek assurances about the circumstances of manufacture. A shift to 'ethical consumption' and 'ethical investment' may be the next step from 'green consumption'. Ethical funds such as TSB Environmental, AXA Sun Life Ethical and Standard Life Ethical screen out, for example, companies which produce pollutants, pesticides or arms, and those which test on animals. In 2007 EIRIS estimated that the latest SRI/ethical retail total fund value stood at £8.9 billion (EIRIS, 2009).

Of even greater significance is the growing number of organisations 'sleeping with the enemy'. Partnerships between organisations and environmental groups are aimed at promoting organisational goals by adopting 'market-based environmentalism' to reduce costs and create product differentiation. Hartman and Stafford (1997) identify a number of green alliances involving McDonald's, The Body Shop and Friends of the Earth.

Clearly, consumers can only act in a 'green' way if they possess reliable information about the relative effects of a range of products on the environment.

Azzone and Bertele (1994) suggest that as eco-labels with third-party certification are developed, such as the Blue Angel in Germany, 'green' qualities of products will become more obvious and 'green' consumers will become more important. It is easier for consumers in Germany to adopt 'green' purchasing habits because they have a comprehensive system of eco-labelling. This provides them with better quality information about products and the effects which their production, use or disposal might have on the environment.

To summarise, it is clear that individual consumers have limited influence either upon the environmental stance of organisations or upon government policy but as the environmental context develops more companies are responding in this regard. However, there is increasing evidence to suggest that consumers can, when mobilised by environmental pressure groups, have considerable influence upon organisations, most particularly via the threat of a mass product boycott.

6.8 Conclusion

Since it is often difficult to confine environmental and ethical problems within individual countries it is becoming increasingly apparent that 'world solutions' need to be sought. There is also an increasing recognition that in order to address ecological problems it is no longer possible for environmental campaigners and businesses to snipe at each other from entrenched positions. Both sides are recognising the importance of agreeing trade-offs between economic development, which is important in terms of providing people with the means to live, and environmental protection, which seeks to ensure that the natural environment is used sensibly. The essence of this 'trade-off' is encapsulated in the principle of 'sustainable development' – the notion that we need to protect the natural environment for the sake of future generations.

In this chapter we have identified some of the issues that are important to the well-being of the planet and models that enable us to compare the different stances of organisations with respect to ecological issues. The main points are:

- The Earth is facing a number of serious environmental issues, including the green-house effect.

- The operation of the market is based upon the law of supply and demand.

- The concept of externalities describes the situation where an organisation has not fully internalised its costs. Most polluting emissions are, therefore, seen as nega-tive externalities.

- Governments can use a range of actions to monitor and regulate the output of pollutants from economic activity: property rights; market solutions; tradeable per-mits; regulation and legislation.

- Progress at the global level in ecological regulation action is often slow since it operates via a series of International Summit meetings, such as that at Rio in 1992. However, since most serious ecological concerns tend not to be confined within geo-political boundaries, the ability to make progress at this global level is critical to the effective tackling of many ecological problems.

- The viewpoints which organisations can adopt in respect of ecological regulation range from non-compliance and compliance, through to some more proactive stances, and culminate in the use of state-of-the-art processes by what have been called 'leading-edge' organisations.

- The ecological viewpoint adopted by an organisation is likely to be strongly influ-enced by the nature of its business environment and by its perceptions of the interest and power of stakeholders and its view of corporate social responsibility.

- The extent of individual consumer power in respect of ecological and wider ethical issues is clearly weak. However, there is an increase in single-issue action taken by environmental pressure groups which is capable of having a serious effect on how organisations view their stakeholders.

- Many companies are taking note of wider ethical considerations.

1 Find and examine the figures for the sale of cars in 2007, 2008 and 2009. Explain using the language of the theory of demand why demand changed.

2 How does your own education provide a provide a positive externality for the soci-ety in which you will live?

3 Why is the process of setting and agreeing to environmental targets take such a long time? What are the consequences of targets not being agreed?

4 Should businesses take note of the views of all of their stakeholders when making commercial decisions?

5 Select a country that fits each of Azzone and Bertele's (1994) five environmental contexts contexts. Explain the reasoning behind your choice.

6 Taylor *et al.* (1994) identified three types of company: high, moderate and low pen-etration. Using appropriate sources, identify three high-penetration companies and comment on their environmental impact. How has their business performance been affected?

Further reading/sources of information

The web links below provide the most up-to-date sources. Access to any topic should be possible through the links.

Business and Human Rights Resources Centre (<u>http://www.business-humanrights.org/ Home</u>) A collaboration between Amnesty International and a number of academic institutions. Many resources available including access to business sectors, countries, regions and key issues.

Earth Summits (<u>www.earthsummit2002.org/</u>) The stakeholder forum is an international multi-stakeholder organisation on sustainable development which promotes the outcomes from the first Earth Summit in 1992 and the Johannesburg Summit in 2002.

Ethical Consumer (<u>www.ethicalconsumer.org/</u>) A UK alternative consumer organisation. Researches the social and environmental records of companies.

EU (<u>http://ec.europa.eu/environment/index_en.htm</u>) Home of the EU environment site.

Friends of the Earth (<u>www.foe.co.uk</u>) Friends of the Earth website, frequently updated with current issues.

Greenbiz (<u>www.greenbiz.com/</u>) Site which looks at the business end of the debate. Includes a news centre, business toolbox, reference desk and some good links.

Greenpeace (<u>www.greenpeace.org/international/</u>) Home page of Greenpeace. Includes a whole host of environmental issues and links with other organisations.

OECD (<u>www.oecd.org/department/0,3355,en_2649_34421_1_1_1_1_1,00.html</u>) OECD's Development Co-operation Directorate. Provides access to work on enhancing the coherence of OECD country policies in the areas of environment and development co-operation.

World Resource Institute (<u>www.wri.org/</u>) Home page of the World Resources Institute (WRI) of New York. WRI is an environmental research and policy organisation. Provides access to sites covering a variety of environmental issues around the globe.

References

AEF (2009a) Aviation Now Contributes 4.9 percent of Climate Change Worldwide, available from <u>www.airportwatch.org.uk/news/detail.php?art_id=3230</u>

AEF (2009b) Available from <u>www.aef.org.uk/?p=109</u>

Ansoff, I. (1984) *Implementing Strategic Management*. Englewood Cliffs, NJ: Prentice Hall.

Argenti, J. (1980) *Practical Corporate Planning*. London: Allen and Unwin.

Asia News (2007) China Fines Hitachi and Unilever Over Pollution, available from <u>www.speroforum.com/site/article.asp?idarticle=11073</u>

Azzone, G. and Bertele, U. (1994) Exploiting Green Strategies for Competitive Advantage. *Long Range Planning*, 27(6), 64–81.

Basil D. and Weber, D. (2006) Values Motivation and Concern for Appearances: The Effect of Personality Traits on Responsiveness to Corporate Social Responsibility. *International Journal of Non profit and Voluntary Sector*, 11(1), 61–72.

Bemporad, R. and Baranowski, M. (2007) Conscious Consumers Are Changing the Rules of Marketing. Are You Ready?, available from <u>www.bbmg.com/pdfs/BBMG_Conscious_Consumer_White_Paper.pdf</u>

Brown, P. (1995) Global Warming Summit at Risk'. *Guardian*, 25 March.

Cannon, T. (1994) *Corporate Responsibility: A Textbook on Business Ethics, Governance, Environment: Roles and Responsibilities*. London: Pitman.

Carter, F.W. and Turnock, D. (1993) *Environmental Problems in Eastern Europe*. London: Routledge.

Caulkin, S. (1996) Tarmac Melts Under Pressure. *Observer*, 26 May.

Cheung, T. (2004) Subway Cheers Bangkok Commuters, available from **http://news.bbc .co.uk/1/hi/world/asia-pacific/3866145.stm**

Chien, E. (1991) Working Towards Environmental Quality in the 21st Century. *Environmental Protection Administration*, January.

Creyer, E. and Ross, W. (1997) The Influence of Firm Behaviour on Purchase Intention: Do Consumers Really Care About Business Ethics? *Journal of Consumer Marketing*, 14(6), November/December, 421–433.

Croner Guide (1996) *Environmental Management*. Kingston-upon-Thames: Croner Publications.

Defra (2007) Clean Neighbourhoods and Environment Act, available from **www.defra .gov.uk/ENVIRONMENT/localenv/legislation/cnea/**

EIRIS (2009) A Brief History of SRI/Ethical Investment, available from **www.eiris.org/**

EMAS (2009) What is EMAS?, available from **http://ec.europa.eu/environment/emas/ index_en.htm**

Environmental Industries Commission (1996) **www.eic-uk.co.uk/main.6fm**

Ethical Consumer (2009) Current UK Consumer Boycotts, available from **www. ethical consumer.org/Boycotts/currentUKboycotts.aspx**

Europa (2008) The Sixth Environment Action Programme of the European Community 2002–2012I: Introduction to the 6th Environment Action Programme (6th EAP), available from **http://ec.europa.eu/environment/newprg/intro.htm**

Europa (2009) Disposal of Spent Batteries and Accumulators, available from **http://europa .eu/scadplus/leg/en/lvb/l21202.htm**

Forum for the Future (2003) Ethics Go Mainstream: Social and Environmental Performance Closely Linked to Good Corporate Governance, Say Fund Manager', available from **www.forumforthefuture.org.uk/aboutus/default.asp?pageid=338**

Hamel, G. and Prahalad, C.K. (1994) *Competing for the Future*. Boston, MA: Harvard Business School Press.

Hartman, C.L. and Stafford, E.R. (1997) Green Alliances: Building New Business With Environmental Groups. *Long Range Planning*, 30(2), 184–196.

Hartshorne, J. (2003) UK Law and the Environment, available from **www.naturenet.net/ law/envlaw1.html**

Harvey, F. (2006) Environmental Fines on Companies Branded 'Tiny'. *Financial Times*, 26 July, available from **www.ft.com/cms/s/0/87c6d1f4-1c42-11db-bd97-0000779e2340.html**

Hutchinson, C. (1996) Integrating Environmental Policy with Business Strategy. *Long Range Planning*, 29(1), 11–23.

Jaggi, R. (2008) Aircraft: The Future is Fuelled by Innovation, *Financial Times*, 20 April, available from **www.ft.com/cms/s/0/9ff95994-0cfb-11dd-86df-0000779fd2ac.html**

Key Note (2008) *Green and Ethical Consumer November 2008 Market Assessment*. London: Key Note Ltd.

King, W. (1972) Example of the Demand Relation, available from **http://william-king.www.drexel.edu/top/prin/txt/SDch/SD6.html**

Kleiner, A. (1991) What Does it Mean to be Green?' *Harvard Business Review*, July–August, 4–11.

Lau, J and Dixon, L. (2007) Chinese Website to Expose Air Polluters, *Financial Times*, 14 December, available from **www.ft.com/cms/s/0/c177f1aa-a9cf-11dc-aa8b-0000779 fd2ac.html**

Lee, N. (1994) Environmental Policy, in Artis, M. and Lee, N. (eds) *The Economics of the European Union*. Oxford: Oxford University Press.

Lipsey, R.G. and Harbury, C. (1992) *First Principles of Economics*. London: Weidenfeld & Nicolson.

Lopatin, M. (2002) 'Discredited' Labels Have Most to Gain from Ethics. *Observer,* 8 December.

McHenry, J. (2009) 63% of Small Business Owners Say Environmental Issues as Important as ..., available from **www.topix.net/content/prweb/2009/04/63-of-small-business-owners-say-environmental-issues-as-important-as**

McWilliams, A. and Siegel, D. (2000) Corporate Social Responsibility and Financial Performance: Correlation or Misspecification? *Strategic Management Journal,* 21(5), 603–609.

msnbc.com (2007) Power Firm Agrees to Record Pollution Cleanup, available from **www.msnbc.msn.com/id/21198255/**

Murray, J.A. and Fahy, J. (1994) The Marketing Environment, in Nugent, N. and O'Donnell, R. (eds) *The European Business Environment.* London: Macmillan.

Nomille, M.A. (2003) Multifunctionality: Options for Agricultural Reform, available from **www.ers.usda.gov/publications/aer802/aer802j.pdf**

OECD (2009) OECD Regions at a Glance 2009, available from **http://titania.sourceoecd.org/vl=2546199/cl=24/nw=1/rpsv/regionsataglance2009/01/05/index.htm**

Orlitzky, M., Schmidt, F. and Rynes, S. (2003) Corporate Social and Financial Performance: A Meta-analysis. *Organization Studies,* 24, 403–441.

Porter, M.E. (1990) The Competitive Advantage of Nations. *Harvard Business Review,* March–April, 73–93.

Purvis, A. (2006) Choice: The Curse of the Green Consumer?, available from **www.forumforthefuture.org/greenfutures/articles/602578**

Radford, T. (1997) Glowing, Glowing . . . Gone? *Guardian,* 25 November.

Roome, N. (1992) Developing Environmental Management Systems. *Business Strategy and the Environment,* Spring, part 1, 11–24.

Shrivastava, P. (1994) *Strategic Management: Concepts and Practices,* Cincinnati, CT: South-Western.

Shrivastava, P. (1995) Environmental Technologies and Competitive Advantage. *Strategic Management Journal,* 16, 183–200.

Spada (2008) Environmental Reporting: Trends in FTSE 100 Sustainability Reports November 2008, available from **http://www.spada.co.uk/wp-content/uploads/2008/11/environmental-reporting-spada-white-paper.pdf**

Taylor, B., Hutchinson, C., Pollack, S. and Tapper, R. (1994) *The Environmental Management Handbook.* London: Pitman.

Trowell, J. (1998) Secondary Effects of Consumer Boycotts, available from **www.i-way.co.uk/~jtowell/2bcthome.htm#references**

UNFCCC (2003) Marrakesh Accords, available from **http://unfccc.int/resource/guideconvkp-p.pdf**

UNFCCC (2009) Kyoto Protocol Status Ratification, available from **http://unfccc.int/files/kyoto_protocol/status_of_ratification/application/pdf/kp_ratification.pdf**

Unilever (2008) Sustainable Development 2008: An Overview, available from **www.unilever.com/Images/Unilever_Sustainable_Development_Overview2008_v3_tcm181-163522.pdf**

Unilever (2009) Kenya: Tree Planting Raises Biodiversity Profile, available from **www.unilever.com/sustainability/casestudies/environment/kenyatreeplantingraisesbiodiversityprofile.aspx**

Welford, R. and Gouldson, A. (1993) *Environmental Management and Business Strategy.* London: Pitman.

Wood, D.J. (1991) Corporate Social Performance Revisited. *Academy of Management Review,* 16, 691–718.

7
The international political environment

Graham Wilkinson

Learning outcomes

On completion of this chapter you should be able to:

- identify political activity at global, regional, national and local levels;
- understand different systems of government and representation;
- recognise different political viewpoints regarding the role of governments;
- understand the rapidly changing nature of the political environment;
- outline the role of key international institutions;
- consider the issues surrounding political risk and stability;
- recognise the importance of global political threats.

Key concepts

- political economy
- levels of government
- democratic and authoritarian government
- attitudes to the role of government
- regional co-operation and integration
- international institutions
- political risk and stability
- liberalisation and intervention.

Minicase 7.1	The credit crunch and international political co-operation

The rapid deterioration in the global economy from late 2008 onwards is, arguably, the most important change in the international business environment for many years. Although the crisis started in the USA, its rapid spread around the globe has been a clear indicator of just how closely the countries of the world are connected with each other, both economically and in many other ways. The credit crunch, as these events became known, has had an impact to varying degrees throughout the developed and developing countries of the world. Although it is primarily an economic phenomenon, the effects of these events go far beyond the money markets into much of the rest of society. There is a social impact, as unemployment rises in many countries. There is a technological aspect as communications technology allows us all to become more rapidly aware of global events and enables rapid cross-border transfers of resources. There are legal implications regarding job losses and responsibility for damage caused by the financial institutions' allegedly reckless investments. There are certainly competitive considerations, as banks were encouraged to merge with each other to avoid their collapse or were taken over by governments.

Possibly most notable, however, is the fact that political leaders in every country, led by President Barack Obama in the USA and Gordon Brown in the UK, have been calling for a global response to a global problem. This implies that these leaders have realised that it is necessary for greater political co-operation to occur, so that there is a co-ordinated policy response throughout the globe. Action by one or two countries, however well-meaning or large in scale, is not thought to be sufficient to solve – or alleviate – the problems posed.

It is also notable that discussions have extended well beyond the traditional international institutions. Whereas in the past it is undoubtedly true that the developed economies of the West would have dominated, the response to recent events has seen a recognition that the balance of power in the world is shifting. In part this is because the political landscape of the globe has changed. Since the fall of the Berlin Wall in the autumn of 1989 and the subsequent collapse of communism in Eastern Europe and the then Soviet Union, the world has not been divided into two politically opposed camps: one capitalist, the other communist. There has been a change of ideology away from the idea of intervention and government control to one of liberalism and a *laissez faire* approach to economic management. At the same time it has become evident that 'Third World' countries such as China, India and Brazil have started to play – and have wanted to play – a much greater role in world affairs. This is partly because they have become much more integrated into the global economy and partly through a recognition of that fact by the Western powers. The sheer size of these countries is also a factor. China and India together account for around 40 percent of the world's total population: too big to be ignored.

The most notable political impact of all this has been the announcement that the G20, not the G8, will become the 'usual' forum for discussions. As shown below, see section 7.2.1 titled '*Global scale*', the G8 includes only the traditional rich, industrialised economies of North America, Western Europe and Japan plus Russia; the G20 includes those eight, plus many developing economies, including China and India. The balance of power is changing.

Questions

1 The G20 does not have any formal powers. Why, then, do its discussions and debates have important affects on international political relations and the global economy?
2 Should global institutions such as the G20 be given more power or should they remain simply as 'talking shops'?

7.1 Introduction

Political decisions affect all aspects of the business environment. Decisions about economic policy, competition policy, legal frameworks, ecology, technology, globalisation and more are taken by national governments, local governments and international institutions. Politics is also important in itself. This is because political (and other) decisions are based on underlying ideologies or beliefs. In other words, different people and societies view things in different ways, possibly based on different cultural or religious beliefs. For example, some people believe that governments can and should actively intervene in many aspects of a country's economic life, influencing or controlling what goods and services are produced; others believe that government should, as far as possible, leave these decisions to the market mechanism. Furthermore, these ideas or philosophies change over time.

The main aim of this chapter is to examine this complex area of the environment, considering both the structures of governments and institutions and also the philosophies that shape their thinking and decision making. As stated above, it is necessary to remember that the ideas discussed in this chapter are closely linked with other elements of the business environment and are taken at a variety of levels. This means that the processes involved are very complex, with decisions and policies at any one level both being affected by and affecting policies and decisions at the other levels. Political changes are likely to create opportunities or present threats to organisations. In this chapter we consider a number of such changes in different parts of the world, and look, in general terms, at their impact upon business.

The structure of the chapter reflects this complexity. Following the introduction, the next two sections deal largely with questions of what the various levels of political institutions are designed to do. The next section then examines how attitudes to these roles have changed over time, particularly in the period since the end of World War II, while the final sections consider the impact of these attitudes and policies on international business.

7.2 The different geo-political levels

Decisions that affect business organisations are made at all geo-political levels – global, regional, national and local. For example, competition policy in the UK (see *Chapter 8*) is determined at national and regional level (by the UK government and the EU) and is monitored at a local level by local authorities – and all this takes place against a background of global trading rules set by the WTO. Political decisions at all these levels, such as those on economic policy, social policy, the control of pollution and support for technology (each of which is examined elsewhere in this book) all have an impact on business activities. The business environment is liable to change as a result of radical political shock, gradual shift or a combination of the two.

It should also be noted that political and economic ideas and actions are closely interlinked. As can be seen elsewhere in this book, (see, for example, *Chapter 9*), the national business environment in any one country is now closely linked to events in many others. For example, the so-called 'credit crunch' beginning in 2007/2008 had its roots in economic/financial decisions in the USA, but quickly spread to many other countries around the globe. These events clearly had economic consequences for many governments, businesses and individuals. In turn this meant that the governments of many countries were faced with difficult political decisions as to how they should attempt to deal with the crisis, decisions that affected not just economic factors but also the wider life of the country, such as spending on healthcare, education, transport infrastructure and foreign affairs.

It is evident that decisions and actions made at any of the political level can have an impact on organisations, both large and small. Organisations will perceive political change differently; some may feel threatened, others may see the changes as offering business opportunities. This is the context of our analysis of the political environment covering all four political scales mentioned above: global, regional, national and local. Many people regard the national level as the most important of these and for this reason, the role of the nation state is discussed in more detail below (section 7.3 '*The nation state*'); in this section, however, we start with the largest scale, that of global institutions, and work our way via regional and national matters to the lowest, local, level.

7.2.1 Global scale

The changing international scene, with its powerful interests, has an enormous impact on the operating activities and strategies of many organisations. The international agenda is increasingly being set by international protocols and transnational bodies. There are many institutions that have been set up with some political power over sovereign, independent nation states, particularly since the end of World War II. Most of these bodies, if not all, require the states that are participating in them to give up some of their independent, sovereign rights, often by signing a treaty. This is a document which binds two or more countries to do something together: that is, a collection of commitments which are negotiated, agreed upon and signed. Treaties do not come into effect, however, until the governments concerned have ratified them; in other words, until each nation state has agreed to give up some of the sovereign rights it has in favour of closer co-operation. Only once the treaty is ratified – that is to say, all the countries that have signed the treaty agree that it should be implemented – will its provisions take effect. These types of institutions can be usefully split into two types: international (or global) institutions (discussed here) and regional co-operation agreements (discussed below).

International institutions

The United Nations

The most well-known of the international institutions is the United Nations (UN). This body officially came into existence on 24 October 1945. Its purposes, as set out in its Charter, are 'to maintain international peace and security; to develop friendly relations among nations; to cooperate in solving international economic, social, cultural and humanitarian problems and in promoting respect for human rights and fundamental freedoms; and to be a centre for harmonizing the actions of nations in attaining these ends' (www.un.org). There are six major bodies that are the core of the organisation. These are the: General Assembly; Security Council; Economic and Social Council; Trusteeship Council; International Court of Justice; and Secretariat.

However, it should be noted that there are many more programmes, agencies and bodies which are part of the UN's overall presence and activities. These include such well-known institutions as UNICEF (the UN Children's Fund) and the UN Development Programme (UNDP), as well as many less high-profile organisations.

The original UN Charter was signed by 51 nations. Many more states have joined over the years and the number has also fluctuated as the identity of member states has changed (see *Figure 7.1*). For example, both the former German Democratic Republic (communist East Germany) and the Federal Republic of Germany (capitalist West Germany) were admitted as separate members in 1973; the two states were reunified (as the Federal Republic of Germany) in 1990 and thus became a single member of the UN. Conversely, the splitting of the former Yugoslavia into five, then six, separate states has caused an increase in the number of members. By 2006 the total number of states in UN membership had become 192, with the admittance of Montenegro in its own right, following its split from Serbia (which itself had formerly been a part of Yugoslavia). The previous additions were in 2002, when Timor-Leste (East Timor) was admitted after its independence from Indonesia, and so

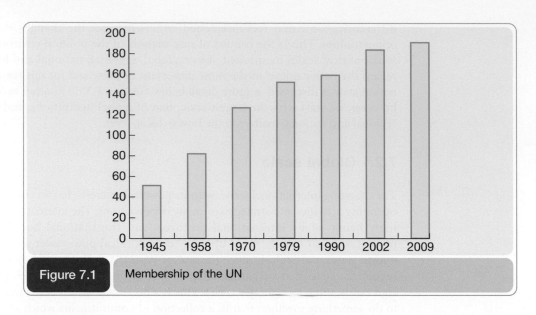

Figure 7.1	Membership of the UN

was Switzerland, after that country decided to end a long period of non-involvement with international organisations.

As can be seen from its charter, the UN has a wide-ranging mandate to involve itself in many aspects of global life. The main, original, purpose was the promotion of world peace by providing a forum in which disputes between the governments of sovereign states could be settled by discussion rather than resorting to military means. In addition, if military intervention is thought to be necessary, the UN has powers to send in peace-keeping forces. It does not have its own troops, relying instead on member countries volunteering forces for specific instances of duty.

The main forum for discussion is the General Assembly (in which all 192 member states are represented) and the Security Council, both based at the UN buildings in New York City. The Security Council has 15 members in total. There are five permanent members: the USA; the UK; France; the Russian Federation; and China. The remaining ten seats on the Security Council are occupied by other member states for a fixed period before others take their place. At the time of writing, these ten are: Austria; Burkina Faso; Costa Rica; Croatia; Japan; Libya; Mexico; Turkey; Uganda; and Vietnam.

The five permanent members play a dominant role in proceedings and wield the most power. However, their role and power has been increasingly criticised, not least because of the view that there is no valid reason for only these five to be permanent members. That they are the five permanent members is partly because of historical accident (they were the countries that were victorious at the end of World War II, just prior to the founding of the UN); they were also the first five states to possess nuclear weapons. Their dominance comes from the fact that each one has the right to veto resolutions that would otherwise be passed by either the General Assembly or the Security Council. This means that they are in a position to exert greater influence on the UN's policies and priorities than any of the other members. In turn, that means that they play a vital role in all decisions, but especially those that are con- troversial in some sense. Critics argue that the five permanent members should no longer play such a dominant role simply because of historical accident – the fact that they were powerful over 60 years ago when the UN was founded. They argue that the balance of power in the Security Council should be changed to reflect changes in the global political environment in the period since then, not least the relative importance of large countries in Asia, Africa and Latin America compared with smaller European countries such as France and the UK.

It is rare for the UN to play a direct role in influencing the business environment. Its influence is usually felt indirectly in influencing the actions of governments of member states, whose legislatures may, in turn, affect business more directly. However, there have been some instances where the UN itself has played a major role in influencing, if not determining, the political environment in which business operates. For example, the UN General Assembly has agreed on various occasions that sanctions should be imposed to prevent (or discourage) business from investing in and/or trading with particular countries. This was the case for Vietnam for some years in the 1970s after the end of the US/Vietnam war and for South Africa, while that country was controlled by the whites-only government during the apartheid years that ended with Nelson Mandela's election as President in 1994. More recent examples include sanctions to do with the military government in Burma/Myanmar and in late 2009 sanctions against the regime in the Democratic People's Republic of Korea (usually called North Korea) in response to that country's resumption of the testing of potential nuclear capability.

A major example of the controversy surrounding this area of the UN's activities can be seen in the build-up to the war in Iraq in early 2003. Following the first Gulf War in the early 1990s, in which Iraqi forces were compelled to relinquish their occupation of Kuwait, the UN had become increasingly concerned about the nature of the Iraqi regime under Saddam Hussein and the possibility that it was developing what became known as 'weapons of mass destruction' (chemical, biological or nuclear) and the missile technology to deliver them over great distances. The General Assembly and the Security Council of the UN passed a series of resolutions concerning Iraq throughout the 1990s. These were mostly concerned with applying trade sanctions unless the country co-operated fully with weapons inspection teams appointed by the UN. President Saddam did co-operate, to some extent, for some years but not after 1998. The heightened tensions in the year after the events of 11 September 2001 caused many countries, especially the USA under President George W. Bush and the UK led by Prime Minister Tony Blair, to become increasingly concerned that Saddam's regime was developing weapons in defiance of UN resolutions. The Security Council unanimously passed a further resolution in the autumn of 2002, requiring Iraq to co-operate fully with UN inspection teams and threatening unspecified further action if it did not. As 2002 turned into 2003, the USA and UK continued to build up their military forces in the vicinity of Iraq in anticipation of war. At the same time, attempts were made to secure a further UN resolution that would specifically authorise the use of military force. However, when it became clear that various countries, including China, Russia and France, would not support such a resolution – indeed, France said it would use its veto – the UN found itself sidelined as the USA and British forces attacked Iraq without specific UN authority, but with the support of what was termed a 'coalition of the willing'.

The significance of these events is still being debated and they may still come to be seen as a significant turning point in the history of the UN. The USA (and UK) have argued that for the UN to be effective it must be able and willing to back up its resolutions with actions and that by failing to do so in the Iraqi case it has lost much of its authority and power in the world of the early twenty-first century. Critics of the US and UK stance, on the other hand, argue that it is the actions of those two countries that are *causing* the UN to become sidelined and ineffective. They say that when it became clear to the USA and UK that their argument would not be accepted by the rest of the Security Council, those two governments simply did what they wanted to do. Critics, therefore, are convinced that this 'unilateral' action by the USA and UK creates a dangerous precedent whereby countries may feel that they can act without the authority of the UN.

It is apparent that the disagreements caused by these events linger on after the end of the war in Iraq, even though all the governments concerned are rebuilding their relations in the post-war period – and all are still involved in the workings of the UN. It should be noted that the personal element in all of this should not be underestimated. Many of the leaders on both sides of the argument at the time of Iraqi invasion – George W. Bush in the USA and Tony Blair in the UK on the one hand and Jacques Chirac in France on the other – are no longer in power. The relationships between their successors are not shaped by the same forces in the same way.

The Bretton Woods institutions

A further important influence on international politics – and economics – is provided by the trio of institutions originally proposed just before the end of World War II at a conference held in the mountain resort of Bretton Woods in New Hampshire, USA. The motivation of the participants was based in economics, as they wished to set up a system of regulation of world trade, exchange rates and international flows of capital. This was based on the belief that the isolationism and retreat from open trading that had occurred in the 1930s had not improved living standards for citizens in countries where there was depressed economic activity but had, in fact, worsened the situation. To avoid such disastrous political and economic decisions being taken again, three new bodies were proposed. These were the IMF, the International Bank for Reconstruction and Development (IBRD), and the International Trade Organisation (ITO).

In the course of the negotiations and the subsequent ratification of the treaties it became evident that several countries harboured reservations about signing over powers that they held as sovereign states to these institutions. Although the treaties regarding the IMF and the IBRD – now known as the World Bank – were ratified and those institutions came into being, there were more problems regarding trade. In particular, the USA did not ratify the treaty setting up the ITO, fearing that there would be too great a loss of sovereignty and too little control over its own economy if it were to sign. As a result, the ITO was replaced by a different sort of body, the General Agreement on Tariffs and Trade (the GATT). This was a looser collection of states, in which all decisions had to be taken by agreement of all the members via a complex series of negotiations. The IMF and World Bank, in contrast, had their own powers assigned to them, meaning that they were able to adapt policies and take actions without continually having to get the agreement of all their members for each decision.

As globalisation and technology have progressed and political thinking has changed, so too has the role and impact of these organisations. The GATT negotiated itself out of existence in a lengthy series of meetings, known as the Uruguay Round, that lasted from 1986 to 1993. It was replaced by the WTO, a body much more akin to the ITO originally proposed at Bretton Woods. Meanwhile, the World Bank and the IMF continue to play a major role in regulating the world economy, in particular having a major impact on the processes of development in Asia, Africa and Latin America (see *Minicase 7.2*). However, it is important to realise that economic decisions are also political decisions in many ways. For example, one of the functions of the IMF is to lend money to countries suffering from international debt problems, to enable them to pay back some of the debt, to pay for essential imports or to spend on development projects (such as schooling or healthcare). Over the years, the IMF's approach to how this should be done has changed. As its political thinking has moved from an interventionist to a more free-market/liberal stance, so the economic policies it champions have also changed to reflect that liberal political agenda. Before lending money to countries, it requires a process of structural adjustment to take place. This usually involves reducing government spending, particularly on subsidies, so that prices more closely reflect market prices, the privatisation of state-owned businesses, encouraging inward investment by foreign multinational companies and reducing regulations on business. All these do have an economic effect – but all are also political in nature, reflecting the views of politically liberal/conservative economists who favour free-market approaches to government intervention.

This approach has also become known as the 'Washington Consensus', partly because it represents the general policy approach of successive US administrations (regardless of whether they have been run by the Democratic or Republican party) and partly because the IMF headquarters and World Bank headquarters are in adjacent buildings in Washington, DC. Although detailed analysis of the impact of these institutions is beyond the scope of this book (see, for example, Stiglitz, 2002; Todaro and Smith, 2009; World Bank, 2003), there have been many criticisms of the way policies have been devised and implemented. (The economic impact of IMF/World Bank policies is also examined in *Chapter 3*.)

Minicase 7.2	Tanzania and the IMF

After independence in 1961, Tanzania under President Julius Nyerere adopted a socialist approach to politics, in which development priorities reflected the needs of ordinary people. Policies were designed not with economic growth in mind, but rather that the basic needs of the population should be the priority. This meant that policy was to concentrate on the provision of water supplies, sanitation, healthcare and basic education, all based around the rural nature of what was (and still is) a largely agricultural society. Tanzania should be self-reliant, socialist and egalitarian. Nyerere also wanted to reject money from foreign sources, so that Tanzanians could shape their own agenda for the future. The emphasis was to be on rural development, where production was to be based on communal ownership of land and any profits were to be used for the benefit of the entire community.

Thus, the political philosophy was that the government should – and would – supply basic infrastructure and services, such as a primary school and teacher, basic healthcare via a resident paramedic, electricity and clean water. Overall, Nyerere believed that the population would benefit, living standards would improve and development (and wealth) would gradually result. These policies were put into effect from the late 1960s onwards. Initially there is little doubt that they were was some degree of success and many people in the more remote and poorer rural areas were keen to embrace the new approach. Looking at the statistical evidence it can be seen that there were certainly successes in the field of social development.

However, problems slowly became apparent. As government attempted to extend the programme to more prosperous regions, resistance increased. At the same time, it was becoming apparent that there was increasing corruption, that earnings from agriculture were not as high as had been hoped or expected and that other parts of the economy, notably industry, were being neglected. The lack of economic growth also meant that it became increasingly difficult for the government to fund the social services which were meant to be the cornerstone of development.

By the mid-1980s, however, it was evident that major changes were needed. Nyerere's successor as president, Ali Hassan Mwinyi, embarked upon a new direction. He approached the IMF for assistance. In response, the IMF, after long negotiations, agreed to the release of funds to Tanzania, subject to various conditions, particularly regarding the control of the economy. In line with its usual approach, the IMF's Structural Adjustment Programme required reducing government involvement in the economy. Success was defined as more rapid economic growth. Government subsidies were reduced and fees for schooling and medicines introduced. Spending on installing and maintaining clean water supplies and sanitation was cut. The value of the Tanzanian shilling was reduced on international money markets, making exports cheaper for foreign buyers and increasing the cost of imported goods. The government reduced the amount of regulation faced by business and encouraged the investment of foreign capital by multinational companies. Political changes saw the development of multi-party politics and Western-style elections by the mid-1990s. In short, the whole emphasis of Tanzanian development changed from one of socialism to a more conventional, market-oriented approach.

Defenders of the current approach argue that it will bring long-term benefits to the population and that the old, socialist, system was simply unsustainable. Without economic growth the money to sustain welfare spending simply was not there.

Questions

1 Outline the socialist policies and development priorities of Nyerere when he was President of Tanzania. What impact did these have on the environment for business during that period?
2 Discuss the effects of IMF-devised Structural Adjustment Programmes on development and the business environment in Tanzania (and other developing countries).

Other institutions

In addition to the major institutions just discussed, there are many other international organisations with varying memberships and aims. Many of these have economic or commercial objectives, but others are based more on cultural or historic links. Some have little, if any, formal powers, but arc nevertheless important as discussion forums where ideas are debated and policies formulated. Indeed, it can be argued that meetings of, for example, world leaders or finance ministers have a greater influence on the world's politics (and business environment) than many of the more formal organisations and institutions discussed above.

There are many examples of such organisations. Perhaps the most important is the G20, discussed below, but others can certainly exert a major influence on global politics and economics through their discussions and actions. For example, the 13 countries that are members of OPEC (the Organisation of Petroleum Exporting Countries), can have a major influence on the volume, and thus the price, of oil around the world. A different kind of link underpins the Commonwealth, now made up from 53 independent states, most of which were formerly British colonies. Despite their independence, they (and the UK) are now part of what their website describes as a 'voluntary association of 53 countries that support each other and work together towards shared goals in democracy and development' (www.thecommonwealth.org). A third example is the Organisation of the Islamic Conference, made up from 57 countries united by the common faith of most of their inhabitants. Its website (www.oic-oci.org) describes its as being the 'collective voice of the Muslim world' with the aim of 'ensuring to safeguard and protect the interests of the Muslim world in the spirit of promoting international peace and harmony among various people of the world'. Many other examples of influential international organisations may be found.

The G20 and its predecessors

The origins of this body go back to the 1970s when a regular series of meetings, usually three or four times a year, of the finance ministers of the seven largest non-communist industrial economies began in response to the destabilising events then occurring in the world economy. As there were seven countries concerned, namely Canada, France, (West) Germany, Italy, Japan, the UK and USA, they quickly became known as the Group of Seven or the G7. Although the group had (and has) no formal powers as such, it can be seen that the comments made and opinions formed in such meetings would – and do – lead directly to policies being implemented by the governments of the countries represented. A similar series of meetings, although less frequent, usually annually, is also held involving the heads of state of those countries. Following the fall of communism and the break-up of the Soviet Union, Russia joined proceedings in the early 1990s and the G8 was born.

The end of the twentieth century also saw volatile economic conditions in much of the world. There was also increasing concern that the G8 represented only the older industrial countries, while the rapidly growing and populous developing economies were excluded from its discussions. It is beyond the scope of this book to detail the various steps and permutations of invitations to various countries that have been made to correct this imbalance. Two of the more important are the initial invitations to Brazil, China, India, Mexico and South Africa to attend as observers, sometimes leading to the use of the term G8+5, and the more recent expansion of the organisation. In 1999 it was recognised that membership should include more developing nations, in recognition of their increasingly important role in the world. This expansion has meant that membership taken together includes the countries that have over 80 percent of the world's population and who are responsible for around 85 percent of the value of world trade. The membership is technically made up of the finance ministers and/or central bank heads from the participating nations, but in practice heads of state (prime ministers, presidents) are often involved. There are 19 countries in the group, namely Argentina, Australia, Brazil, Canada, China, France, Germany, India, Indonesia, Italy, Japan, Mexico, Russia, Saudi Arabia, South Africa, South Korea, Turkey, the UK and USA plus the EU. It is, thus, known as the G20. The importance and influence of this organisation can also be seen from the fact that representatives of the World Bank, IMF and other institutions regularly attend its meetings. Its role has become particularly important in the twenty-first century, as governments have sought to co-ordinate their responses to global challenges, such as climate change and the economic downturn resulting from the credit crunch.

It is clear that the role of the G20 is becoming increasingly important and that there is a recognition of the growing impact of developing economies on global political discussions and decisions. This can be clearly seen in the announcement at the G20's September 2009 meeting that it, not the G8, will in future be the main forum for inter-governmental discussions. The fact that the meeting concerned, held in Pittsburgh in the USA, was attended by USA President Barack Obama is further, if symbolic, evidence of the change in global political attitudes.

7.2.2 Regional scale

Regional co-operation agreements

In addition to the UN and the Bretton Woods institutions, there are many other international bodies and systems that have been agreed by various governments around the world. One development that is becoming increasingly important is the growing tendency of countries to engage in closer co-operation at a regional level. Although this progressive integration is important economically (see *Chapter 3*) it is also important politically. Although there is no real economic reason for co-operating countries to be geographically close to each other, the vast majority of co-operation agreements are based on regional trading blocs, most likely for political reasons. Probably the best known (and longest established) of these is the EU, which is discussed in some detail below. Many other groupings are in existence in many different parts of the world and with varying degrees of political, legal and economic integration among their membership; some – but not all – of these are shown in *Table 7.1*.

Table 7.1	Selected regional co-operation agreements and member countries
Regional organisation	**Member states**
The Association of South East Asian Nations (ASEAN)	Brunei Darussalam, Cambodia, Indonesia, Laos, Malaysia, Myanmar, Philippines, Singapore, Thailand, Vietnam
The Caribbean Community (Caricom)	Antigua and Barbuda, the Bahamas, Barbados, Belize, Dominica, Grenada, Guyana, Haiti, Jamaica, Montserrat, Saint Lucia, Suriname, St Kitts and Nevis, St Vincent and the Grenadines, Suriname, Trinidad and Tobago
The East African Community (EAC)	Burundi, Kenya, Rwanda, Tanzania, Uganda
The European Union (EU)	Austria, Belgium, Bulgaria, Cyprus, Czech Republic, Denmark, Estonia, Finland, France, Germany, Greece, Hungary, Ireland, Italy, Latvia, Lithuania, Luxembourg, Malta, Netherlands, Poland, Portugal, Romania, Slovakia, Slovenia, Spain, Sweden, UK
Mercosur	Argentina, Brazil, Paraguay, Uruguay
North American Free Trade Area (NAFTA)	Canada, Mexico, USA
Southern African Development Community (SADC)	Angola, Botswana, Democratic Republic of Congo, Lesotho, Madagascar, Malawi, Mauritius, Mozambique, Namibia, Seychelles, South Africa, Swaziland, Tanzania, Zambia, Zimbabwe

There are also many other groupings of states co-operating in various ways, some of which overlap with each other either in function and/or in membership. It should be noted that all these agreements are very different from each other and involve very different levels of political co-operation and integration. At the simplest level there are the free trade agreements, like NAFTA, whose members are solely interested in the increased wealth generated by the increased efficiency that can result from reducing or eliminating trade restrictions. At the other extreme, we have the EU, whose members are committed to growing political, as well as economic, integration.

The European Union

The origins of the EU can be traced back to the Treaty of Paris in 1951, which established the European Coal and Steel Community (ECSC). There were six signatories to the treaty: Belgium, the Federal Republic of Germany (West Germany), France, Italy, Luxembourg and the Netherlands. The aim of the Treaty of Paris was to establish a unified market in those two commodities, within which all the countries could prosper from reduced barriers to trade. An important benefit, which should certainly not be overlooked, is that the establishment of the ECSC also had political effects, binding former wartime enemies more closely together.

Six years later, in 1957, the same six countries signed the Treaty of Rome. This created the European Economic Community (EEC) and the European Atomic Energy Community (Euratom). The Treaty extended economic ties by creating a customs union and common market. These three communities came together to establish the European Community (EC) in 1965. The first enlargement was in 1973 when Denmark, Ireland and the UK became members. Greece joined in 1981, followed in 1986 by Portugal and Spain. Further developments took place with the creation of the European Economic Area in May 1992 – the world's biggest free trade area. Austria, Finland, Norway, Iceland and Sweden joined the EC 12 and established an integrated economic entity with a population of 372 million and enormous opportunities for trade and commerce. In 1995 Austria, Finland and Sweden became full members of the EU; Iceland and Norway remained outside, preferring economic co-operation only to the increasingly political nature of the EU.

In the twenty-first century, the EU has shown it is politically committed to enlargement, as it has embraced 12 new members, the majority of them formerly part of the Soviet Union or former Communist states. Ten joined on the same date in 2004: Estonia, Latvia and Lithuania (all formerly part of the Soviet Union); Poland, the Czech Republic, Slovakia, Hungary and Slovenia (all formerly Communist states); Malta; and Cyprus. The newest members, since 1 January 2007, are Bulgaria and Romania, again both former Communist states. This has brought the total EU membership to some 27 states with a total population of a fraction under 500 million, making it the largest single trading bloc in the world.

The EU has evolved largely through amendments to the original treaties, notably via the Single European Act of 1987, the Treaty of European Union 1992, more commonly known as the Maastricht Treaty, and the Treaty of Amsterdam in 1997. More recently, the Treaty of Nice paved the way for further enlargement of the EU by countries from the former Soviet bloc and the Mediterranean, mentioned above; it came into force on 1 February 2003. The most recent of these is the Treaty of Lisbon signed by the 27 Heads of State of EU member countries on 13 December 2007. On 3 November 2009 the Czech Republic became the 27th and last member state to ratify the treaty, allowing it to come into force in December that year. It is designed to increase the efficiency and effectiveness of decision making and policy implementation in the enlarged community. As such it is to replace the failed 'European Constitution', which was designed, said its proponents, to simplify and streamline the administration of the enlarged community. We now look at each of these major developments in the EU's political processes in a little more detail.

The Single European Act of 1987 changed decision-making procedures within the Community. Prior to its adoption, decisions had to be agreed by a unanimous vote; this condition was replaced by the ability to adopt decisions subject to qualified majority voting, clearing the way for speedier decision making within the community. The Treaty of Nice extended this process to more areas and has also redesigned the rules relating to exactly how the 'Qualified Majority Voting' procedures will operate in the future. This is to take account of the fact that as the number of member states continues to increase (from the original six to a total of 27 in 2007 and maybe even more in the future), the decision-making processes of the Union must be simplified and streamlined to avoid the entire system becoming paralysed in bureaucratic arguments.

The Single European Act of 1987 also required that the Single European Market should be in place by the end of 1992. Its objectives were to improve the environment for business by providing for the free movement of labour, capital, goods and services within the Community and to facilitate closer co-operation between countries on a range of other matters. It was anticipated that the benefits would include increased growth, higher employment, lower prices and wider choice for consumers as the free movement of goods and services took effect throughout the Union. This development of the Single European Market not only led to increased competition within the EU, but has also enhanced the ability of European business to compete in world markets by increasing the efficiency of EU-based businesses.

When the Treaty of the European Union, the Maastricht Treaty, of 1992 came into force on 1 November 1993 the nature of cooperation changed as the EU came into being, comprising the EC, a Common Foreign and Security Policy, and a common approach to Justice and Home Affairs: the so-called three-pillar structure as outlined by Thomson in 1995. The Maastricht Treaty was the focus for much internal disagreement throughout the countries of the EC. In the UK, there was much debate within both the Conservative and Labour parties. There were similar discussions in Denmark and France, where it was only ratified following referenda. Perhaps the most contentious issue of the treaty, as far as the UK and Danish governments were concerned, was the Social Chapter, which included minimum requirements on: health and safety; consultation between management and employees; working conditions and the working week; equality between men and women regarding job opportunities and treatment at work.

The idea of applying regulations to the labour market was totally contrary to the supply-side approach that the Conservative government had adopted since 1979 (see *Chapter 3*) and it felt that the costs to business would result in substantial job losses. By opting out of this part of the treaty the government hoped that the lower-cost business environment it created within the EU would prove attractive to inward investment. As a result of the opposition by the UK government the Social Chapter was only included as a protocol annexed to the treaty. The UK Parliament ratified the treaty in 1993, although the UK (and Denmark) secured an opt-out clause on significant parts of the treaty, opt-outs that still exist. This included not just the Social Chapter provisions but also the section on Economic and Monetary Union that has led to the adoption of the euro in place of national currencies by 15 of the EU's current member states.

A part of the negotiations included an agreement that was made to revise the treaty around the middle of the decade, providing for a conference to be convened in 1996. The inter-governmental conference lasted more than a year, ending with the Treaty of Amsterdam. This had four main objectives: to place employment and citizens' rights at the heart of the Union; to sweep away the last remaining obstacles to freedom of movement and to strengthen security; to give Europe a stronger voice in world affairs; and to make the Union's institutional structure more efficient with a view to the future enlargement of the Union (as has now occurred).

This process continued with the Nice Treaty, which came into effect early in 2003. As well as changing the areas and rules relating to qualified majority voting, as noted earlier, this treaty also changes and streamlines the political processes of the EU. The number of seats that each state has in the Parliament has been reduced, so as to allow for members from the new entrants to take their place without unduly increasing the size – and cost – of the institution. However, the number of parliamentary seats held by each state is still proportional to its population as a percentage of the total EU population. In addition, there were changes in the number of commissioners and the way they were appointed, meaning that larger states lost their previous automatic right to have two individuals serving on the Commission at any given time. Finally the powers of the EU president were somewhat enhanced, although the position was still to be filled on a rotating basis, by each country in turn, for a six-month period.

This process was to be taken a stage further with the report of the Convention chaired by former French president Valéry Giscard d'Estaing. This was set up to investigate and propose changes to three areas of activity in the EU, in the process producing what many, including those writing the report of the Convention themselves, regarded as a draft EU constitution. The heads of state of the then 25 EU members signed the relevant documentation in 2004 and the process of ratification began. Critics, however, argued that this proposal gave far too much power to the centralised European institutions and thus made decision making increasingly remote from the citizens of the member states. In other words, it was argued that the power of (democratically elected) national governments to control their own affairs was being replaced by control from an unelected, centralised bureaucracy. These fears caused voters in referendums in the Netherlands and France to reject the treaty establishing the constitution. There was also passionate debate and opposition evident in many other countries of the EU. This was enough to cause the abandonment of the original proposals for the constitution.

However, many of the original aims of the constitution were incorporated in the Treaty of Lisbon. As noted above, the 27 heads of state of EU member countries signed this on 13 December 2007 and, following ratification by all the states, it came into force nearly two years later. Supporters argue that the enlargement of the EU to 27 members requires that its processes and procedures be modernised if the EU is to function efficiently and effectively. Opponents argue that the Lisbon Treaty is merely the (rejected) EU Constitution, with all of that proposal's weaknesses and faults.

The changes included in the Treaty of Lisbon cover a variety of areas of EU life. They include, say proponents of the treaty, greater powers for the (democratically elected) European Parliament; greater emphasis on subsidiarity, i.e. enhancing the role of national parliaments; ending the rotating presidency; increased efficiency in the institutions; the incorporation of the Charter of Fundamental Rights into law and various other changes. Critics argue that while many of these changes may seem reasonable, they in effect move power away from the sovereign member states to the centralised institutions of the EU. In other words, they are, from this perspective, a further, undesirable, step towards the creation of a federal 'United States of Europe'. The changing nature of the EU is evident from these objectives. Remember that the original treaty dealt solely with trade in coal and steel; now the organisation is concerned with political, legal and social matters as well as economics. Both the global environment and the political aims and objectives of EU member states – and the EU itself – continue to change. As such, it seems likely that the future development of the EU will require further agreement – either on the lines suggested above and/or in other ways. More treaties are, it seems, inevitable, even if the length of time and the difficulties involved in ratifying the Lisbon Treaty mean that many politicians will be wary of attempting such an exercise in the near future.

The policies and ideas set out in, and stemming from, the various treaties are translated into policy and practice by a variety of EU institutions. Their powers, roles and, to some extent, conduct are set by the treaties, although there is plenty of room for interpretation in many instances. It should also be noted that as the scale and aims of the EU have changed over time, so too have the power and influence of the various institutions. The five most important such bodies are: the European Parliament; the European Council; the Council of the European Union; the European Commission; and the European Court of Justice. Readers should be aware that many more bodies, each with a specific role, do exist. Many of these are less well known, but still play an important role in the political and economic life of the EU. Examples of these include: the European Investment Bank; the Economic and Social

Minicase 7.3	The Lisbon Treaty

The EU was founded in 1957 with six member states. Following the admission of Bulgaria and Romania in January 2007 there are now 27 member states. The organisation has evolved largely through amendments to the original treaties, notably via the Single European Act of 1987, the Treaty of European Union of 1992, more commonly known as the Maastricht Treaty, the Treaty of Amsterdam in 1997 and the Treaty of Nice in 2003. The proposed European Constitution was not ratified by member states. It has since been replaced by the Treaty of Lisbon, signed in 2007 by all 27 member states and finally ratified by all of them by November 2009, allowing its provisions to take effect.

These treaties have been largely concerned with streamlining and simplifying the operation of the Union, often by changes to the powers of the various institutions. For example, the Single European Act changed decision-making procedures within the community. Prior to its adoption, decisions had to be agreed by a unanimous vote; this was replaced by the ability to adopt decisions subject to qualified majority voting, clearing the way for speedier decision making. This is to take account of the fact that as the number of member states continues to increase, the decision-making processes of the Union must be simplified and streamlined to avoid the entire system becoming paralysed in bureaucratic arguments. The same Act also provided the framework for the Single European Market, aiming to improve the environment for business by providing for the free movement of labour, capital, goods and services within the EU.

More recently, the failed Constitution and the Treaty of Lisbon, which replaced it, have sought to extend the role and influence of the EU, to give the organisation a stronger voice in world affairs, as well as revamping some internal arrangements.

Questions

1 Examine the views of the UK's main political parties on closer European integration. What are the arguments in favour? And against?
2 What functions should the EU devolve to the national governments of the member states and which should be retained under EU control?

Committee; the European Training Foundation; the Agency for Health and Safety at Work; the Committee of the Regions; the European Environment Agency; the European Monetary Institute; and the Court of Auditors. The inter-governmental conference (IGC) is another important EU forum. It is necessary for an IGC to prepare the ground for a new European treaty. Although a detailed analysis of these institutions is beyond the scope of this book, it is important to remember that, individually and collectively, they help shape many policies that affect not only business but also the day-to-day lives of citizens of member states.

7.2.3 National scale

The national level of political decision making, based on the sovereign rights of the independent nation state has long been regarded as the most significant level of decision making. This belief is based on several characteristics which states in general possess:

- sovereignty;
- territoriality;
- authority; and
- legitimacy.

These four concepts together define the basis of the modern nation state. Sovereignty means that the state has control over its own affairs (unless power is ceded voluntarily when it joins international bodies, as discussed in section 7.2.1 '*Global scale*' section). This control is limited to a defined area (territoriality) over which the government exercises authority. The fourth concept, that of legitimacy, is perhaps harder to define. Broadly speaking, it is taken to mean that the government of a given country is regarded – either within that country and/or by the outside world – as having the right to exercise power and authority within its territory. The political systems adopted within each country vary as a result of independent evolution over hundreds of years. It is important to recognise that these national political systems will have an important impact on the operation of business in any given nation state.

It can thus be seen that in the modern world each nation state (for example the UK, Russia, Brazil, Spain, Kenya or India) has control over affairs within defined boundaries – and no direct control over affairs beyond its borders. The government of each country is free to pass laws that reflect the priorities and beliefs that reflect its particular culture and are thought to reflect the particular priorities of the society they represent. Although culture may be hard to define (see *Chapter 5*), there is no doubt that there are different values and beliefs that distinguish one society from another. The shared values and beliefs within nations also allow the coherence of these societies.

It should, however, be noted that such common beliefs and values are not always reflected in the boundaries of any given state – and that those boundaries can and do change over time. For example, Catalan people may be regarded as having a distinctive culture – as being a nation – but politically they are in either France or Spain, the nation states which control the territory where the Catalan peoples live. Similarly, the Maasai in East Africa are split between the modern territories of Kenya and Tanzania.

This disparity between peoples and nations, coupled with a strong desire on the part of many to control their own society, has led to many conflicts and wars in the past – and seems likely to continue to do so in the future. For example, the state of Yugoslavia as created at the end of World War II has since fractured into the separate, sovereign, states of Slovenia, Croatia, Serbia, Montenegro, Bosnia-Herzegovina and Macedonia; furthermore, Kosovo has declared its independence from Serbia, although this is only recognised by a few countries. These states are, to a large extent, based on cultural groupings, in turn based on factors such as language and religion. In Asia, the people of East Timor won independence from Indonesia in 2002 after a long and bitter struggle. In other areas independence is still being sought by a variety of means, from political campaigning to war and terrorism. These include places such as Kashmir (where control is currently held by India in one part of the territory and Pakistan in the other), various republics of the Russian Federation who desire complete independence from Moscow, the former colonial area of Spanish Sahara currently controlled by Morocco and territory in Western China, including Tibet.

Nevertheless, despite the changes in boundaries and the apparently transient nature of many states, it is still these countries that form the most powerful political entities. International and supranational bodies such as the UN and the World Bank are set up by the nation states and, generally, can only be effective in their work with the consent of nation states. At the other end of the scale, local governments within the territory of a sovereign state are subservient to its national government.

The power of national governments to control affairs within their boundaries is, therefore, based on an acceptance by citizens of their right to do so. In other words, governments can only function effectively when those they govern accept their authority. In such instances government may be regarded as legitimate. If this relationship breaks down, for example if an elected government is forced from office by a military coup (as happened, for example, in Chile in 1973, Pakistan in 1999 and, more recently, in Honduras in 2009), the resultant government may be regarded by many as not possessing any legitimacy; others, however, may simply accept – or even support – the change. These relationships and the powers of national governments are discussed in more detail in section 7.3 '*The nation state*'.

Increasingly, however, the closer integration of economies throughout the world means that the balance of power has, to some extent, shifted away from this level of government. Some commentators, for example Kenichi Ohmae as long ago as 1995, claimed that the increasing globalisation of markets means that 'Nation states are no longer meaningful units in which to think about economic activity. In a borderless world they consign things to the wrong level of aggregation.' Ohmae lists a number of what he calls 'natural economic zones', which do not recognise geographical or political boundaries. These include: Northern Italy (as a separate entity from the rest of Italy); Hong Kong and Southern China; British Columbia in Canada and the adjoining states of the North-Western USA; and Singapore and its neighbouring Indonesian islands.

7.2.4 Local scale

The lowest of the levels of government with which we are concerned is local government, that is any authority which is subservient to national governments and whose decision-making power derives from the national government. These vary greatly in both size of population and in the powers they possess. For example, the state of California may be regarded as a local government in as much as the state is just one of the 50 states of the USA and federal law has priority over many local decisions, yet the population of California – around 37 million – is greater than that of many sovereign states. Furthermore, there are other levels of government – city and county – below that of the state.

In the UK, local government varies widely in different parts of the country and between urban and rural areas. Scotland now has its own parliament, Wales and Northern Ireland their own assemblies, and the English regions have also been given a little power of their own. All these areas do, however, continue to send MPs to the UK's national parliament at Westminster. Below these levels, local government is made up from a patchwork of county councils, district councils and unitary authorities, usually large cities or conurbations, each with its own powers and policies.

In the UK, as in many other countries, elected councillors, under powers laid down by parliament, run local authorities. They provide services and have regulatory responsibilities. A further change attempted in the UK was made in 1998 when the national parliament passed an Act which allows cities to elect executive mayors, as is done in many other countries, for example the USA. The idea was to reform local government, encourage greater public participation and provide stronger leadership at a local level. However, the measure has not proved popular and few areas have decided to take up the option of having a directly elected mayor. One exception is Greater London. The first elected mayor there, in 2000, was the high-profile figure of Ken Livingstone. His tenure as mayor and leader of the Greater London Authority resulted in some notable changes to local government in the UK capital, notably the imposition of a Congestion Charge on all cars entering the central area during the working day on Monday to Friday. The aim was to reduce congestion and pollution by encouraging people to use public, instead of private, transport. The policy is certainly controversial – but it is widely regarded as successful. Nevertheless, partly because of opposition to the scheme in some areas and also for other reasons, Livingstone lost the 2008 election for the Mayor of London and was replaced by the equally flamboyant figure of Boris Johnson.

7.3 The nation state

7.3.1 Systems of government

It may be seen that the power of governments can be based on a variety of sources and that citizens participate in government to different degrees. The traditional view is that political systems can be arranged along a spectrum, from democratic systems on the one hand to totalitarian dictatorships on the other. Although there are many different forms of democracy, the common theme throughout is that government should represent the will of the people. In general, this is taken to mean that elections should be held periodically. In this way voters may express their desire to return the same individuals or political parties to office or to elect a different government to represent their interests. In countries with totalitarian governments or dictatorships, however, there are no such rights. There are no elections, opposition is often banned and political activity that opposes the government is suppressed. In short, the citizens of the country have no power over when a government leaves office or its policies while in office.

In the industrialised countries of the West, the common belief is that democracy is the best form of government. The detailed analysis of the variety of voting systems and ways of representation is beyond the scope of this book but some major systems may be identified. As regards voting: in many countries the 'first past the post' system is employed, whereby the candidate with the largest number of votes wins the election, regardless of how large, or small, a percentage of the votes cast has been received. In other countries, there is a requirement that the winner must receive at least 50 percent of the votes cast. A further variation is that seats in parliament are allocated to parties in the same proportion as votes cast. This has the advantage of accurately reflecting the voters' preferences, but may well mean that the parliament is made up from a large number of small parties with no one party having anything approaching a majority. Even from this short section it can be seen that there are still considerable differences between systems which share democratic governments. The proportional representation system in Italy has, for example, created a much more volatile environment for business than the system in use in the UK. Italy has had a succession of unstable coalition governments for most of the post-1945 period. In the UK, a 'first past the post' system is used to elect members of parliament (MPs) to serve in the House of Commons and has provided a much greater degree of stability. The Electoral Reform Society in the UK identifies three main types of voting system, each with sub-categories (Electoral Reform Society, 2003). These are shown in *Table 7.2*.

However, democracy (of whatever sort) is not to be found in many of the world's nation states. In these countries governments' power and authority are based not on the consent of citizens as expressed through the ballot box, but rather on the power of the military and other forces the government controls. This was, arguably, particularly evident in the then-communist countries of the Soviet Union and Central Europe until their governments fell, often without much of a struggle, in the years after 1989. Such governments still hold power in some parts of the world, from the communist dictatorships in North Korea, China and Cuba to the military governments of Guinea and Burma/Myanmar, the theocratic governments of some Middle-Eastern countries such as Saudi Arabia and the (*de facto*) one-party states of Eritrea, Turkmenistan and Syria.

Table 7.2	Voting systems	
Type of system	**Main characteristic**	**Variations used**
Single-member systems	One representative is elected for each seat contested	• First past the post • Supplementary vote • Alternative vote
Multi-member systems	Two (or more) representatives elected for each seat contested	• Single transferable vote • Party list systems
Mixed systems	A combination of the two systems above	• Additional member system • Alternative vote plus

Source: adapted from Electoral Reform Society (2003)

There is often (but not always) a close correlation between these forms of political environment and the economic environment within a country. Democratic governments have tended to favour free-market, *laissez-faire* economic policies, allowing individuals, businesses and markets to function freely within some regulatory framework. Dictatorships, however, have tended to favour planned systems, whereby the economic activity of the state is prescribed by government, not left to the market mechanism. It should also be noted that totally free markets and totally planned economies are theoretical extremes. In practice, free-market, liberal economies impose various laws and rules which businesses and individuals must follow; that is to say, there are limits to freedom of action. Conversely, most planned economies have left some economic activity in private hands, even if the vast majority of production has been controlled by the state.

A further difference is to be found in the relationship between central and local governments. In many countries (such as Ireland, Uganda, Jamaica and New Zealand) there is what is known as a unitary system. This means that the central (national) government retains strong decision-making powers for itself and allows only limited freedom of action to local governments. An alternative is the federal system, in which the central authority is relatively weaker, as much power is devolved to a lower level of government often known as states. Examples of federal systems include the USA, Australia, Germany and India.

7.3.2 Functions of government

Constitutions and the legislative, judicial and administrative functions of government

This section considers the formal basis of (democratic) systems of government. It looks, in particular, at the ways in which the three main functions of government are carried out. These are commonly regarded as the *legislative* (law-making), *judicial* (law-applying) and *executive* or administrative functions. All three play crucial complementary roles within all systems of government – although the ways in which they are separated from each other, if at all, varies widely from country to country. Indeed, many consider that the separation of these powers is a crucial aspect of democratic governance. In particular, the independence of the judiciary from other branches of government is widely regarded as a necessary pre-requisite for free political activity in any given country. Or, to put it another way, a state in which the judiciary simply and always follows the government line is unlikely to be one in which political freedom is highly regarded by the authorities.

Constitutions form the basis of this system, outlining the powers and rights of governments, the judiciary and individual citizens. In many countries, but not the UK, the constitution is a formal, written document, in which these rights and responsibilities are (clearly) stated. These documents may cover such things as the timing and frequency of elections, the role of the head of state, the areas of responsibility of the different branches of government, as well as allowing or prohibiting various specific actions.

In the UK, as just stated, there is no written constitution. Instead, the powers of the head of state and the other parts of government have evolved over centuries, being modified as time goes by on the basis of parliamentary legislation (statutes) and judicial rulings. It is therefore evident that case law, as decided in the courts, has a major impact on the UK's system of government.

In the UK the head of state is Her Majesty the Queen, fulfilling a role that is now largely symbolic – although many centuries ago the monarch was in effect a dictator. Nowadays, however, political power is held by the Prime Minister as the effective leader of the nation. He or she is the person who, as the leader of the largest political party after a national (or general) election, is normally, appointed as the head of government. Other Members of Parliament from the winning party are appointed as Ministers and placed in charge of various departments, such as Transport, Education, Defence, Health and so on. (It should be noted that the actual names of the departments and the specific policy areas for which each is responsible are not fixed: indeed, they are frequently changed.) Policy is made after discussions among the Prime Minister and other ministers in what is known as the Cabinet. Much of the work of both Houses is in reviewing and debating the contents of such proposed legislation. The resultant legislation is then debated in Parliament and, once approved by both the House of Commons and the House of Lords, passes on to law and becomes an Act of Parliament (or statute) when given the Royal Assent. Every year a large number of new Acts is added to the statute books. Policy is then traditionally implemented administratively by civil servants in government departments. Increasingly, however, that role is being taken on by quangos, which are semi-autonomous bodies set up to specifically implement and control particular aspects of policy, e.g. the Financial Services Authority (FSA) which regulates financial services to ensure companies are complying with government requirements and relevant legislation. The UK, however, for many decades, centuries in fact, did not ensure that there was a rigid separation of powers – and still does not do so. It can be seen that the three functions overlap in may areas of parliamentary activity, for example Law Lords are both members of the House of Lords and of the judiciary. This situation was modified, to some extent, by the introduction of a UK Supreme Court in the autumn of 2009.

A different system is evident in the USA, which has a written constitution. This was written in such a way as to ensure that there was a clear 'separation of powers'. The roles of the elected President, the elected Representatives and Senators in the two Houses of Congress and the appointed Supreme Court judges are clearly stated and a system of 'checks and balances' is in place to allow each to limit the power and freedom of action of the other parts of government. In this way the legislative, judicial and administrative functions are kept distinct. It is often thought that such checks and balances are important for the effective operation of a democracy.

These examples perhaps show some of the complications inherent in this area. Few would dispute that the UK and the USA are, by most indicators, democratic states in which there is a great deal of freedom for individuals to pursue political aims, criticise governments and for politicians to be voted out of office. But it is also the case that many believe that one of the hallmarks of a totalitarian regime is the lack of a clear separation of the judicial function from the legislative and executive functions.

In summary, one of the key features of a democratic system of government is the ability of the judicial, legislative and administrative functions to operate in a reasonably autonomous way so as to be able to provide a system of 'checks and balances' – but the degrees of separation and the formality of such structures vary widely from one country to another.

7.4 The changing attitudes of governments and institutions

7.4.1 The role of government

As noted above, there is often a close link between the amount of political freedom in a country and the amount of economic freedom. And there are a variety of political views as to how big a role government should play in economic affairs.

Democratic governments that allow oppositions to form, campaign and come to power have largely favoured the *laissez-faire* approach. Such governments are usually also in favour of limited or minimal regulation of business and economic activity. For example, the industrialised countries of North America, Western Europe, Japan and Oceania have been among the leaders in liberalising their political and economic systems. This does not mean that they have totally abandoned all regulation of business activities – far from it. Indeed, many commentators (and governments) now believe that the credit crunch of 2008 and beyond is evidence that deregulation may have gone too far, that the authorities failed in their duty to ensure efficient functioning of the financial system by allowing banks and other financial institutions too much freedom of action. But it does mean that there is a belief among those governments that political and economic freedom go hand-in-hand to bring benefits of increasing affluence via rapid economic growth to their citizens – although the question of how those benefits are distributed is one that may need further discussion. For international business this usually means that these governments welcome foreign investment and are happy to create a climate in which business is willing to invest. Indeed, many governments offer incentives to foreign businesses, so keen are they to attract the investment to their country, rather than seeing it go to a rival nation.

On the other hand, many governments that seek to limit individuals' freedom of action politically are also interventionist in nature regarding their economies. In both Cuba and China, for example, business activity is subject to considerable regulation and government involvement. However, even in these countries – and many others – attitudes to business have changed in the last 15 to 20 years (see *Chapter 9*). Few countries, North Korea is one, now actively discourage foreign investment, even if many governments, particularly in Africa, Asia and Latin America, remain suspicious of the role of multinationals and wary of the power they wield. Indeed, even in the industrialised economies, the increasing power of multinational companies to influence policy is being increasingly questioned.

Thus it can be seen that different individuals and indeed different cultures (see *Chapter 5*) have different attitudes to the role of government in controlling a country's affairs, in particular, how its economy is owned, controlled and regulated. What is notable over the last 30 years or so is how attitudes have changed within various countries and how this change is spreading around the world. In particular there has been a general move away from an interventionist/Keynesian approach towards *laissez-faire*, away from state planning and ownership of enterprises to the free market. This is reflected in the privatisation of many former state-owned enterprises and an increasing welcome for inward FDI. However, in most cases, despite these global pressures, nation states still possess considerable autonomy and the capacity to 'do things differently'.

The extent of government intervention in the economy thus varies enormously between countries – and in all cases the state still has an important role to play. The importance of government through public spending on infrastructure, such as roads, railways, educational establishments (such as schools and universities) and hospitals, is still very significant. In countries throughout the world this sort of public expenditure supports a significant amount of economic activity. In Europe the EU is seeking to secure equality of treatment and opportunity for organisations bidding for public works contracts. Cuts in government expenditure are likely to have a significant adverse impact on businesses that supply those sectors. Increased private sector investment in projects may partially offset the loss of public works. Large companies are, increasingly, not limited by national boundaries and, therefore, by individual government decisions. When one government makes a decision to cut expenditure it is important for companies to look elsewhere for business. Key projects such as building new infrastructure (such as airport runways, rail lines, schools, hospitals, roads) provide opportunities for companies from many countries to bid for business and gain valuable contracts. The international nature of the market has never been more evident, and nor has the need for effective monitoring of the wider environment. The changing attitudes in the UK (and around the world) are examined in more detail below (and also in *Chapter 3*).

7.4.2 Changing attitudes in the UK

Political priorities 1945–1979: interventionism

The political thinking of governments and the resultant priorities can be most clearly seen in their attitudes to economic policy and the degree of intervention in the economic activity of the country they control. In line with the thinking and policy decisions taken at Bretton Woods, governments in the UK and in many countries around the world adopted interventionist policies following the end of World War II. They turned away from the pre-war traditional economic thinking to a Keynesian approach, to controlling the economy by adopting a more proactive stance in dealing with economic and business affairs. The Keynesian approach rests on the assumption that the economy is inherently unstable and in need of active government intervention, largely through fiscal policy (see *Chapter 3*), to control demand in the economy. It is believed that the level of activity in the economy can be controlled, business cycles smoothed out, peaks and troughs eliminated and unemployment limited. For some 20 years or so it seemed that this policy was – and would remain – successful. In the world's developed economies, economic growth continued year after year at very satisfactory levels, while unemployment and levels of inflation remained low. International trade flourished, growing at unprecedented rates, largely thanks to the stability offered by a system of fixed exchange rates. All of this meant that governments were politically popular with electorates and there was little desire for change.

However, as the 1960s continued, it became apparent that all was not well. Fixed exchange rates were causing some problems to international trade and competitiveness, while in many countries (such as the UK), inflation and unemployment were both rising and growth was slowing. The 1970s saw increasingly high levels of unemployment and inflation, which many argued could not be explained by Keynesian theory or solved using traditional interventionist polices. As the economy in the UK and elsewhere stagnated it was argued that a new approach to economics and other policies was needed, one which reflected a different political philosophy.

Political priorities 1979–2008: liberalism

As it became apparent to many that the interventionist approach was unable to still deliver a strong economy, Keynesian theory was open to criticism, especially from free-market/liberal politicians, who advocated a different economic approach. They argued that the general well-being of society was best served by less government intervention, allowing private enterprise and individual entrepreneurs to make more decisions based on the wishes of consumers. The role of government was to provide a minimal legal and regulatory framework to allow such activities to flourish. The 1979 general election in the UK proved to be a significant political milestone, as the new government moved to an approach that was said to involve much less government 'interference' in running the economy (and the country). In other words, the interventionist approach that had characterised government policy since 1945 was replaced by a more liberal agenda, based on a philosophy known as Monetarism.

There is no doubt that this approach caused rapid change in society in the UK – and around the world. Ronald Reagan, who was elected President of the USA in 1980, held a similar philosophy of 'small government'. As that decade progressed, these ideas gained greater acceptance (alongside considerable resistance) around the world. Many countries that had previously been averse to a liberal approach gradually (or rapidly) adopted liberal policies. Such an approach became fashionable, the new orthodoxy. One reason why that was the case is that the statistics clearly show that countries that pursue liberal policies do have faster economic growth, often much faster, than countries that follow an interventionist philosophy.

However, critics argue that while the country may be richer, the benefits of that wealth are far from equally shared. In fact, they say, such an approach may result in greater inequality, in the rich getting richer and the poor being ever more exploited. This, they say, can be seen at different political scales, both within countries and globally. Such an approach, they concede, may be good for businesses that can locate their activities wherever they find the environment most to their liking, but it is not necessarily good for workers.

Political priorities 2008 onwards: back to Interventionism?

The events of 2007 and 2008 leading to the credit crunch, recession and a much more volatile business environment have, perhaps, shown that critics of the liberal approach have been correct. It is now widely believed that deregulation has gone too far, that more government intervention is needed to ensure that it is not just a few people who benefit from economic activity but a larger number. The bailout of failing banks and other financial institutions, particularly in the UK and USA, represents a major change in political thinking. Indeed, several of the major banks in the UK are now effectively nationalised: that is, they are (largely or completely) owned by the government. Such an approach would have been unthinkable in the early years of this century. It should, however, be noted that government regards this as an extreme and temporary measure; the banks will be sold back to private companies or entrepreneurs when they have returned to profitability and stability in the future. There is no desire to intervene so directly in the long term. Nevertheless, there is widespread acceptance that greater government regulation is needed, certainly in the financial sector and possibly elsewhere in society.

Minicase 7.4	Deregulation and bankers' bonuses

Following the credit crunch of 2008 and the subsequent recession, there has been much debate as to the role government should play in regulating the economy, in particular the amount of action is should take in the banking sector. This debate has been particularly vocal in the UK and USA. Both countries have large financial sectors and both have actively pursued policies of deregulation in recent years. In other words, they have followed a process of dismantling regulations governing the activities of business organisations.

Deregulation has opened markets to greater competition with the aim of increasing innovation and thus benefiting both consumers of financial services and the economy as a whole. The capital market and financial sector is the market to which companies and the government turn when they need medium- and long-term funds. A whole range of controls have been abolished in the UK capital market, most notably with the 'Big Bang' in 1986, which increased competition in the stock market, especially from foreign securities houses, and allowed non-banking financial institutions to provide services previously closed to them. These changes were seen as a way of encouraging competition and, therefore, improving the efficiency and competitiveness of UK businesses.

One side-effect of these changes was to change the culture of financial services organisations, so that the amount of risk-taking, leading to potentially great profits, was encouraged. In particular, such risk-taking behaviour by individuals was to be rewarded with huge bonus payments, of hundreds of thousands or even millions of pounds per year for many individuals working in UK and US financial institutions. Many argue it is this culture, coupled with deregulation, that led to excessive risk-taking in pursuit of such bonuses. That behaviour by individuals led, in turn, to the spectacular financial failures of 2008 when both UK and US governments had to intervene to prevent the collapse of financial service organisations. In the UK, Northern Rock was taken fully into public ownership and the government also acquired a majority stake in the Royal Bank of Scotland and HBOS, as well as putting in place further financial support for other banks. The total cost to the taxpayer at the time was estimated to be around £50 billion.

At the time, October 2008, it was widely reported that the pay and bonuses of individuals were felt to be excessive. The most famous example is that of Sir Fred Goodwin, who was Chief Executive of the Royal Bank of Scotland from 2000 until shortly after its takeover by government, to prevent its bankruptcy, in October 2008. During his leadership of the bank, it had grown dramatically, becoming one of the largest financial institutions in the world, with assets reported to be worth a little under £2 trillion. This growth was, however, based on great risk-taking, risks that left the bank facing a loss of £24 billion in 2008 – hence the need for it to be nationalised to prevent its collapse. Sir Fred, however, was seen to leave his post in January 2009 with a substantial lump sum and pension, much to the anger of many MPs and much of the public. Some figures in the City argued that there was no problem, as the sums had been agreed in advance and were legally enforceable. Sir Fred himself took a similar view. Eventually, however, public pressure forced some amendments to his entitlements, leaving him with a lump sum of around £2.7 million and an annual pension of over £300,000.

This incident in particular, and the credit crunch in general, has led to something of a rethink in government, and elsewhere, as to how much regulation and intervention there should be. Many argue that if government has to have a role in running the financial sector, then it should regulate not just the activities of the institutions but also the levels of pay and bonuses awarded to them.

Questions

1 Do you think that the deregulation of the financial sector in the UK and USA (and around the world) has improved the quality of service to businesses and/or made the industry more efficient?

2 How actively, if at all, should governments intervene to regulate or control bonus payments to individuals in the financial service industry in the UK and USA?

7.4.3 Regulation, deregulation, markets and planning

The changes in the UK outlined above have also been seen, to a greater or lesser extent, in many countries around the world. In the vast majority of countries, the liberal agenda has now been adopted, as countries have embraced the political and economic freedoms offered. There are, of course, exceptions to this general rule and wide variations remain between different countries. However, the scale of the changes is apparent when we consider the collapse of communist systems in the former Soviet Union and throughout Eastern Europe. In all these countries, both political and economic models have moved from statist planning approaches to more open, more liberal, more free-market approaches. Some countries have, of course, advanced further and faster in this process than others.

Major changes are apparent in other parts of the world. Many developing economies have undergone a profound change of direction, from suspicion of foreign governments and multinational companies, to embracing liberal ideas. Notable examples are India and Tanzania. India has changed from a system of running a (largely) planned economy within a democratic political system to a markedly free-enterprise approach, especially at a federal level. The change in Tanzania has been, if anything, even more remarkable, from a one-party socialist state to a country in which free-enterprise is, arguably, flourishing (see *Minicase 7.2*).

One exception to the general linking of economic and political freedom is the People's Republic of China. The last 30 years have seen major changes economically. Under the leadership of Mao Zedong following the 1949 communist revolution, China pursued a policy of collectivisation, in which free-enterprise economics was banned, production was planned by the state and, politically, the Communist Party tolerated no opposition. The country thus fitted very closely the idea that political dictatorship and economic planning were closely intertwined. Following Mao's death, however, a different approach became apparent. His successor as leader, Deng Xiaoping believed that China needed to become richer – and quickly. Thus, from being virtually closed to the outside world China changed direction. Foreign companies were allowed access to invest in China, initially in the special economic zones such as Shenzhen and then increasingly into other areas. This was attractive to many multinational companies, who saw the possibility of cheaper production with reduced labour costs enabling them to become more competitive on a world scale (and also the longer-term possibilities offered by selling to the citizens of the most populous country on the planet). As these companies prospered and the Chinese economy did indeed grow much more quickly, other companies followed. In short, it is at the least arguable that China has now largely adopted a liberal, free-enterprise economic system, in which businesses (both domestic and foreign) make decisions with only limited government involvement.

Politically, however, there has been little change. There is still only one political party, the Communist Party, that controls all of China's affairs. Some argue that its control is relatively loose and that there is, effectively, freedom of speech and action in China, even if no opposition parties are allowed to form. Proponents of such a view argue that China does not have Western-style democracy, but that there is no need or desire within China for it to do so. Opponents, particularly in the West, see a different picture. They argue that there is a major contrast between the economic openness that has developed over the last 20 or so years and the tight state control of political activity that remains in place, with censorship of the media and suppression of dissent an everyday event. Whichever view one takes, it is evident that there is a disparity between the changing economic attitudes and the rigidity of the political system that show China *is* an exception to the general 'rule' discussed earlier.

From the discussion above it is apparent that the world has changed, that there has been a movement away from planning and regulation to markets and deregulation. The pace and extent of these changes have varied around the world from country to country, but there has been little dispute about the general direction of change. The change of emphasis and thinking in the 'corridors of power' has had some influence on the values and assumptions held by managers of businesses. In turn, this has affected the way managers consider customers, employees and other groups with an interest in their organisation (the stakeholders). In essence, the role of government intervention in the economy has been reduced and the importance of self-reliance emphasised.

More recently, however, it has become more apparent that this system too has flaws. Critics have long argued that, while the embrace of liberal political and economic philosophies may have brought more freedoms and faster economic growth, these benefits came at a price. To put it rather simply: they argued that the rich got richer and the poor got poorer. And that this was apparent both within countries, where income distribution became more unequal, and around the world, where the gap between rich countries and developing economies widened. Some supporters of liberalism acknowledged some truth in these allegations – but argued that such changes were a temporary but necessary step on the road to prosperity. Others, arguably, simply believed that such changes were inevitable.

It is undoubtedly true that countries which have pursued such liberal polices have seen their economies grow more quickly than those which have not embraced them so readily. But there have increasingly been those, particularly in the richer countries, who have come to question the morality of such policies. There is, they say, a difference between growth as a policy in itself and the question of just who is benefiting from that growth. Such objections have been seen in the increasing number of demonstrations when leaders of the world's economies (the IMF, World Bank, G20) meet to discuss future policies. However, recent events have led to a revival of the debate, not just among 'anti-capitalists', but also in the 'corridors of power'. The near-collapse of the global banking system following the failure of the sub-prime mortgage market in the USA in 2008 has caused many to reconsider the role of the state in regulating economic affairs. Whereas the years after 1979 saw a continual reduction in regulation, there is now a political change becoming apparent, with policy-makers in many countries re-introducing greater government involvement in economic and business life. While we may support or oppose political decisions, depending on our political leaning, these important changes will have a lasting effect on business and consumers around the world.

7.5 The impact of governments and institutions

As we have seen elsewhere in this chapter, there are a great number of influences on the political process and many different forms of government. What is most important from a business perspective is, arguably, the degree of risk that organisations may face when undertaking investment, particularly, but not exclusively, in countries that are not their home. All firms have limited resources – they cannot do everything, sell or produce everywhere, that they may wish to. What influences the decision? The answer is a combination of many factors, one of which is how different stakeholders within the organisation perceive the various risks incurred in any given investment decision.

Risk is difficult to define precisely. It includes the policies and attitudes of international institutions, regional organisations, national governments and local authorities to business investment. This may be in the form of tangible factors, such as legislation that governs working hours, wage rates, health and safety conditions, trade union representation, the repatriation of profits from investments abroad and so on. Or it may be less tangible: does government welcome foreign investment? Or is its attitude hostile and unwelcoming? It must be remembered that firms, especially when investing internationally, are faced with choices, particularly the choice of where to invest. This is discussed in more detail below.

The second part of this section highlights three major concerns: corruption, terrorism and climate change and the potential changes to the regulatory regimes in various countries. This is clearly a complex area, where detailed discussion of policies and arguments is beyond the scope of this book. However, it is important to remember that these factors are the subject of political debate, political will and political decisions – and that those policies will impact on businesses and individuals, potentially in a huge number and variety of ways.

7.5.1 Political risk, stability and the attitudes of policy-makers

One factor that is undoubtedly important for all organisations, however, is certainty. In other words, the fewer unknowns with which a firm is faced, the better. Firms like stability. It can certainly be argued that business does not care if a government is democratic or totalitarian, if it is liberal or communist, if it is legitimate or not. As long as the government is stable – and investment, therefore, safe – most businesses are happy. It is for this reason that many firms continued to invest in South Africa during the time of apartheid, the white minority rule period that ended with the election of Nelson Mandela as President in 1994. Similarly, the widespread reports of human rights abuses by the Chinese government have not stopped firms from taking advantage of that country's welcoming attitude to foreign investment in recent years. Indeed, the liberalisation of the Chinese economy (if not its political system) has been one of the major developments in the international business environment over the last 20 years.

Countries, particularly developing ones, may be attractive because they are potential sources of important natural resources, less regulation and lower labour costs. It is, however, also important to assess the stability of the political, financial, social and cultural systems when evaluating a potential investment in any given country. If companies export, or have production facilities outside their home bases, action by foreign governments may present both opportunities and threats.

Historically, the most important threat has usually been seen as that of nationalisation, that is the takeover of a firm's assets by the government. In some cases, for example when the UK Labour government nationalised the coal and transport industries in the late 1940s, compensation was paid to the organisations or individuals that had owned the assets before they were taken into state control. In other instances, for example, after the Cuban revolution in 1959, assets may be simply seized by the state, leaving their former owners out of pocket. Although the risk of nationalisation is nowadays perceived to be small, it is one that cannot be ignored, as can be seen from events in Russia (see *Minicase 7.5*) and Venezuela in recent years. In the twenty-first century, the power of the communists in the Russian parliament has waned somewhat, but companies are still fearful that the tide may turn again in the future. In other instances, governments may freeze assets, curtail overseas sales contracts or impose exchange controls, which can reduce the amount of money organisations can draw out of profit-making overseas subsidiaries, particularly when there is a downturn in the domestic economy.

Conversely, and much more commonly in recent years, the privatisation of former nationalised industries may present opportunities for investment and trade. This phenomenon began in the UK in the 1980s under the government of Margaret Thatcher when many state-owned

Minicase 7.5	Political risk in Russia

In 1998 the economic and political unrest in Russia following the devaluation of the rouble and the collapse of the Russian stock market resulted in a considerable undermining of confidence in the Russian economy. The outcome of this was a rise in the popularity of the Communist party. The party, under the leadership of Gennardy Zyuganov, was at the time the largest in the Duma (the Russian parliament). The Communist party pointed to serious consequences following the collapse, including hyper-inflation, mass unemployment and economic collapse.

With the election of Vladimir Putin as President, in 1999, support for the Communist party fell, but it remains the largest opposition party in the Duma. Zyuganov, still the leader, has pointed out that the 2008 credit crunch is likely to have adverse effects on the Russian economy and state. He has criticised the approach adopted in the West, supporting the banks and other industries, and has called for a more 'socialist' solution. In particular, he argues that under a Communist leadership the nationalisation of private businesses should be a priority. This would allow the government to control their activities.

Although such views are unlikely to find widespread favour with President Medvedev and Prime Minister Putin, there have been signs that some greater political control over the activities of firms, especially foreign firms, is desired. For example, in 2006 the Russian government required Shell to give up its controlling stake in a US$20 billion liquefied natural gas project in Sakhalin in favour of domestic companies There has also been pressure placed on BP in relation to alleged environmental concerns about its activities in Siberia. These developments are clearly of concern to foreign businesses and may alarm investors in the City of London and other Western financial markets. These and similar developments are likely to have serious ramifications for both home-based and foreign-owned businesses.

Questions

1 How could companies reduce the threat of nationalisation?
2 Should the Russian government pay more attention to the demands of the communists and modify its policies to take some account of their concerns?

industries were sold to private-sector investors. This action was based on the ideological belief that greater business efficiency and, thus, a better service for customers can be gained from placing organisations in a competitive environment rather than their being a state monopoly provider. This change in political thinking, from interventionist to free-market, was followed in many economies around the world, including much of Africa, Asia and Latin America, and opened up opportunities that were previously not available.

Although the specific conditions that attract investment will vary from firm to firm and decision to decision, the attitude of governments is a major factor in determining the level of inward investment. In Asia, the Indian government, after decades of being suspicious of foreign investment, has, since the early 1990s, been much more welcoming. This has resulted in many foreign companies taking advantage of the highly educated but relatively low-cost Indian workforce to establish themselves on the sub-continent. Many of the investments have been in manufacturing (for example, Suzuki took a major stake in the Indian car manufacturer Maruti in the early 1990s). However, the major growth in recent years has been in the service sector as Western companies have taken advantage of the changes in technology to locate data processing facilities and call centres in India. This means that, for example, dialling a local number in the UK to enquire about an insurance claim or quote may result in the call being handled by an Indian call centre in Chennai or Delhi.

More recently, the situation has changed again. Some larger Indian firms have started to invest in foreign production facilities, reversing the flow of investment. A major example of this is seen in the activities of the Tata conglomerate, which own the steel-maker Corus (a part of which was once the government-owned British Steel Corporation) and who bought the Jaguar and Land Rover car business from Ford in 2008.

It is notable that not-for-profit organisations are also affected by – and are seeking to affect – changes in the international political environment. Campaigning groups such as Greenpeace and Oxfam are increasingly international in their outlook and activities. This is partly because the major problems that can be identified around the world, problems that demand political decisions if action is to be taken to solve them, are global or international in nature. The major challenges of climate change and terrorism, for example, are not limited to sovereign states. Climate change, in particular, has a global impact regardless of whether or not individual states are contributing substantially to the cause of the problem. Indeed, it is arguable that it is the effects of pollution and carbon production in developed (rich) economies that are already causing problems for developing (poor) economies. In these circumstances, it is clear that only a global political response has any chance of addressing the problem effectively. It is, therefore, logical that organisations such as Greenpeace and Oxfam should be campaigning globally for global political action to be taken.

Both organisations can point to successful campaigns in the past, when governments have taken action that has changed the business environment facing companies are has caused them to follow a specific course of action. For example, back in 1995 Greenpeace successfully campaigned against Shell's decision to sink a redundant oil platform – the Brent Spar – at the end of its working life, by organising consumer boycotts of Shell's products. Nestlé, too has been the target of a campaign based on its selling of powdered baby milk in developing economies where clean water is in short supply. Oxfam continues to lobby governments in an attempt to get them to legislate to improve living standards, by exposing what it sees as corrupt practices such as low minimum wages or long hours in 'sweat shops' producing goods for the multinationals.

7.5.2 Global challenges – corruption, terrorism and climate change

At a national level, one of the major deterrents to business investment is the level of corruption in a country. That is not to say that the simple existence of corruption will, in itself, deter firms from investing. But it does make a location both more expensive and less stable – and therefore less attractive compared to possible alternatives. Transparency International, an independent agency based in Berlin, conducts annual surveys of perceptions of corruption, producing an index based on a variety of other surveys. This ranks 180 of the world's countries (they regard the data on the remaining countries as insufficiently reliable to be used) on a scale of ten (totally free from corruption) to zero (totally corrupt). *Table 7.3* shows the results of the 2008 survey for a selection of countries; for the complete results and a full explanation of the methodology used visit www.transparency.org.

Recent years have seen the emergence of a further destabilising influence, the increasing risk from terrorist activity. Since the al-Qaeda attacks on New York City's World Trade Center and the Pentagon outside Washington, DC on 11 September 2001, the worldwide climate has undoubtedly changed. The USA, in particular, with its so-called 'War on Terror' sees itself as both the main victim of such attacks and also as the main defender of the 'free world' against the terrorists. It should be remembered, however, that terrorism is not a new threat, even if the scale of the September 11 attacks was unprecedented. Many people and businesses in many countries have suffered from terrorist attacks for many years. Since 2001, attacks have taken place in various parts of the world, notably on the Indonesian island of Bali, in Saudi Arabia, Moscow and Morocco. In Europe, commuter trains were bombed in Madrid in March 2004, while in the UK London's transport system suffered a series of attacks on 7 July 2005. More recently, some ten targets including restaurants, cinemas, a railway station and luxury hotels in the Indian city of Mumbai, were attacked in November 2008. All of these resulted in a heavy loss of life.

Table 7.3	Corruption perceptions Index 2008, selected countries

Rank	Country	CPI score	Rank	Country	CPI score
1=	Denmark, New Zealand, Sweden	9.3	54	South Africa	4.9
4	Singapore	9.2	55=	Italy, Seychelles	4.8
5=	Finland, Switzerland	9.0	62=	Croatia, Samoa, Tunisia	4.4
7=	Iceland, Netherlands	8.9	65	Cuba, Kuwait	4.3
9=	Australia, Canada	8.7	72=	Bulgaria, China, Mexico, Peru, Swaziland (and others)	3.6
12	Hong Kong	8.1	80	Saudi Arabia	3.5
16=	Ireland, UK	7.7	85=	Albania, India, Montenegro, Panama, Senegal (and others)	3.4
18=	Belgium, Japan, USA	7.5	92=	Algeria, Bosnia-Herzegovina, Lesotho, Sri Lanka	3.2
21	Saint Lucia	7.1	102=	Bolivia, Lebanon, Tanzania (and others)	3.0
23=	Chile, France, Uruguay	6.9	109=	Argentina (and others)	2.9
26	Slovenia	6.7	115=	Egypt, Malawi (and others)	2.8
27	Estonia	6.6	121=	Nigeria, Vietnam (and others)	2.7
28	Qatar, St Vincent & the Grenadines, Spain	6.5	126=	Indonesia, Libya (and others)	2.6
32	Portugal	6.1	145=	Kazakhstan, Timor-Leste	2.2
33	Israel	6.0	147=	Bangladesh, Kenya, Russia, Syria	2.1
35	UAE	5.9	151=	Cote d'Ivoire, Ecuador, Laos, Papua New Guinea, Tajikistan	2.0
36	Botswana	5.8	166=	Cambodia, Turkmenistan, Uzbekistan, Zimbabwe	1.8
40	South Korea	5.6	178=	Iraq, Myanmar	1.3
47=	Cape Verde, Costa Rica, Hungary, Jordan, Malaysia	5.1	180	Somalia	1.0

Source: adapted from Transparency International (2009)

It is clear that the combined effect of terrorist attacks and the USA-led response, particularly under former President George W. Bush, (especially given the lack of UN involvement, see '*Global scale*', above) is to make the world a more dangerous place. While it would be facile to suggest that business is the major loser in these developments, it is nevertheless important to note that business does play a major role in society in countries around the world – and that terrorism (or the potential threat of terrorism) is one major determinant of investment decisions by multinational companies. In turn, those investment decisions help to shape not only production patterns, but also the distribution of jobs, incomes, consumption and standards of living. For example, many of the world's airlines have seen a sharp downturn in passenger numbers as a result of terrorist activity in the aftermath of the 9/11 attacks. Other events, such as the SARS epidemic in 2003 or spread of swine flu from early 2009 also had adverse affects. The downturn in the world's major economies following the credit crunch is also likely to adversely affect businesses around the world, causing not just economic but also political responses. This change in the public's desire to travel has an impact not just on the airlines, but also on the economies and living standards of the many countries whose tourist income has dropped as a result.

One final problem that faces all sectors of society including business – and one that demands a political dimension if it is to be solved – is climate change. As we have seen above and in *Chapter 3*, there is now increasing concern that human activity is causing – or, at the very least, helping to cause – a significant increase in global temperatures. A global average rise of two degrees Celsius has been widely predicted to occur over the course of the twenty-first century. Although this may not sound a great deal, many scientists have pointed out that it may have a devastating impact on sea levels, rainfall patterns and the ability of land to sustain agricultural production. As business activity is, it is argued, directly responsible for much of the rise, it is business – and consumers – that need to react to reduce the rise in temperature that is currently predicted.

The burning of fossil fuels, in particular, is a major cause of rising levels of carbon in the atmosphere and the resultant warming. As all manufacturing, service provision and transportation involves the use of some form of energy, it is argued that companies (and individuals) must find ways to become more efficient in their energy consumption, use other less-polluting forms of energy – or change the entire basis of our society. It is, therefore, argued that companies should, for example, produce goods nearer to their markets to cut down on transportation and the resultant energy use. It is further argued that governments need to take co-ordinated decisions to ensure that all countries are acting together to reduce the threat. But there are problems with this. Developing countries such as China, India, Brazil and South Africa argue that since most pollution has been caused by the richer countries, especially the USA, it is the richer countries that should make the greatest cuts. The developing economies point to the fact that increasing living standards for their citizens – in other words, development – means increasing production so that goods and services which citizens of the richer countries take for granted become increasingly available in poorer countries. There is, thus, a great deal of debate about what political changes need to be made, how rapidly and how business should respond to these concerns (see *Chapter 6*).

7.6 Conclusion

7.6.1 Change and stability, liberalisation and privatisation

It is evident that organisations around the world are having to cope with rapid changes in the political (and other) environments that help shape their activities. It is only a quarter of a century or so ago that the rival political philosophies of capitalism and communism, generally represented respectively by the USA and the Soviet Union, were dominating the global political environment in the so-called Cold War. This meant that hegemony, or influence, was split between these two superpowers and their respective political philosophies. The two vied for influence around the world, encouraging newly independent countries in the developing world to adopt a particular path, either statist/interventionist or based on a liberal/free-market political philosophy.

All that changed, amazingly rapidly, at the start of the 1990s, with the collapse of communism and the break-up of the Soviet Union. This seemed to leave the USA dominant as the world's only true superpower. Arguably, however, this situation is now changing again, with the USA no longer so dominant. Some would see the rise in importance of Muslim ideas, *perhaps* connected to the terrorism discussed above, as the major change. This has been called a 'clash of civilisations'. Others see the growing wealth and power of China as the dominant force challenging American (or Western) supremacy. As can be seen elsewhere in this book, these changes have been accompanied by many others, In the political sphere, the stability (albeit often tense stability) of the Cold War years has been replaced by a much more volatile situation. Political philosophy has, for the moment at least, changed from frequently interventionist to being more *laissez-faire* in virtually every country around the globe. This increasing liberalisation has had profound consequences for business. On the one hand, it means that new opportunities for expansion into new markets or new locations for production have arisen. On the other hand, as firms have scrambled to take advantage of these opportunities, the level of competition has undoubtedly increased.

Furthermore, it is notable that the role of governments and politics has changed. This is partly because of the changing attitudes already mentioned. But it is also to do with the actions that have resulted. Many governments have – and are still – privatising many formerly state-owned enterprises, thus providing yet more opportunity for private capital. The role of government, then, is changing from one of owning assets to one of regulating how those assets are used. However, the effects of what may be called excessive deregulation, as shown by the credit crunch and its aftermath, have changed thinking yet again. Many analysts and politicians are now calling on the state to take a more active role once more, moving back a little way – but only a little way – from *laissez-faire* liberalism towards greater state involvement.

Alongside these changes in thinking, there have been changes in institutional arrangements, with the power of national governments arguably decreasing as the international institutions (such as the IMF, World Bank and WTO), together with the increasing importance of regional co-operation (most notably the EU), have become increasingly involved at political and other levels. At the global scale a large range of interactions takes place, involving such groupings as supranational bodies, governments, multinational companies and international pressure groups. The activities of these groups will often result in new law or policy being formulated, which will have implications for organisations. Some of the political pressures which manifest themselves at the national and local scale will have their origins at this global scale. Clearly, therefore, it is important for managers in organisations to understand the levels (global, regional, national and local) at which different political decisions are taken in order that lobbying can be carried out effectively.

Organisations are increasingly operating in a diverse range of countries. As we have seen, a large variety of factors are relevant when making decisions about the countries in which to locate any business activity. Many of these are specific to the company involved, as they assess their environment in the light of their stakeholders' aims and objectives. Clearly, for multinationals in particular, an awareness of political issues and tensions within all the countries in which a firm operates – or is considering operating – is of crucial importance. Such organisations will, therefore, want to ensure that appropriate staff have a good general idea of the multiplicity of factors that need to be taken into account in investment decisions, including people skilled in assessing the political risks involved in different countries or regions.

Taken together, all these changes mean that the environment in which organisations operate has become much more demanding, much more volatile – and, perhaps, potentially more rewarding.

Summary of main points

This chapter has examined a range of political issues important to the context of the book as a whole. The main points made are that:

- Political change can and does occur at all levels which we have identified: global, regional, national and local.
- At the global scale there is a huge variety of organisations, some with formal powers, some simply influential. In either case, their activities will impact on the lower political levels and affect the activities of all organisations to a greater or lesser extent.

- There needs to be awareness by organisations which wish to produce and/or sell in a range of countries that the interests of those countries may, on occasions, conflict with their own goals. As a result they must be prepared to respond flexibly when local political factors demand.

- Organisations can, and do, try to influence political decisions at all levels, seeking to limit any threats posed by political change and to enhance their business opportunities.

- At a regional level, the roles of key institutions and the evolving nature of such co-operation agreements need to be clearly understood by organisations.

- At a national level, the relationship between the judicial, legislative and administrative functions of the state varies from country to country – but, once again, organisations need to be aware of the importance of decision making in each of these areas.

- It is important to recognise how corruption impacts on business in many countries and industry sectors.

- There are key challenges that transcend national boundaries, in particular terrorism and global warming.

Minicase 7.6	Climate change

One of the major developments in recent years has been increasing concerns around the world about the effects of climate change and global warming. The impact of such changes is likely to be felt in every country and have effects an all aspects of society, including the way business operates. Indeed it is widely believed that for some countries, notably those in the hotter parts of the planet, the effects of climate change are already becoming worryingly apparent.

One country that is particularly concerned is the Maldives, a collection of small islands in the Indian Ocean. Using data from the CIA's *World Factbook* we can see that the country is relatively wealthy, with a GDP per head of almost US$4500 (calculated using the purchasing power parity method), a figure that has been growing at over 5 percent a year in recent times. However, the unemployment rate is relatively high at nearly 15 percent. The government is, therefore, keen for the economy to grow even more quickly, a point emphasised by President Nasheed, since his election in November 2008. Although the country is an Islamic Republic, the legal system is based on a mixture of Islamic and English legal principles. (The country was formerly a UK colony before its independence in 1965.) The main source of employment and revenue is tourism. Based around the country's many idyllic beaches, it accounts for over one-quarter of GDP and around 60 percent of foreign exchange receipts.

What, then, is the problem? Simply this: the highest point in the country is a mere 2.3 metres above sea-level. With the expected rise of 2 to 4 degrees Celsius by the end of this century, it is widely expected that sea levels will rise sufficiently to wipe the country off the map.

Questions

1 How could international political cooperation reduce the impact of climate change on the Maldives?
2 What steps could the government of the Maldives take on its own to tackle the problem?

Discussion questions

1 Does a *laissez-faire* (free market) approach to politics and economics necessarily bring benefits to all the citizens of a country?

2 Do bodies such as the G20 play a useful role in setting global political priorities or should individual governments have a greater role to play?

3 How important are the activities of groups such as Greenpeace and Oxfam in influencing the political decisions that shape the international business environment?.

4 As some countries join together in supra-national organisations such as the EU and others fragment into smaller units, how important is the nation state in the twenty-first century?

5 Research the impact of the IMF's policies on three developing countries. Compare and contrast the results of those policies.

6 When investing into foreign countries, should businesses be concerned about the social policies of the host government or merely its stability?

Further reading/sources of information

The Bretton Woods institutions

The three organisations each have their own website. Although much of the information can be complex and technical in nature, there are also more accessible commentaries on the work of the organisations and many potentially useful statistics. The websites for the three organisations are:

International Monetary Fund: **www.imf.org**

World Bank Group: **www.worldbank.org**

World Trade Organisation: **www.wto.org**

European Union (**http://europa.eu.int**) This is the EU's official website. As with the UN and the Bretton Woods institutions, it provides access to a large mass of information, some of which is, again, complex and/or technical. Nevertheless, it is a useful source of information on many aspects of the EU, such as: historical development; institutions; policies; documents; political agenda; publications; news; governments online (which gives web addresses for member states); updates on issues relevant to the EU; and a search engine to help you find specific EU-related information.

You should also be aware that the other regional institutions mentioned in the chapter also have a great deal of information available online. For example, the Southern African Development Community website can be found at **www.sadc.int**, while that for ASEAN is at **http://aseansec.org** (not at **www.asean.com**, which was a shopping site!).

Office of the e-envoy (**www.open.gov.uk**) This site is run by the Office of the e-envoy, part of the UK government's Cabinet Office. It aims both to promote internet access in the UK and provide links to government department and local authority websites. As such it is a good starting point when searching for information and statistics relating to policies and priorities at various levels of UK government.

United Nations (**www.un.org**) This is the official homepage of the UN. It provides access to the full text of many archived documents as well as providing links to the sites covering the work of the UN's various agencies and departments.

Media sites

The websites of many magazines, journals, newspapers and broadcasters provide valuable sources of information on many developments in the global political economy. However, it is important for you to remember that (virtually) all publications are not neutral in their approach. Although data may well be reported factually, articles will be based on the particular perspective of the publication concerned.

To see articles framed in a way that is generally supportive of a free-market, *laissez-faire* approach to economics and politics visit *The Economist,* a journal published weekly in the UK, at **http://economist.com.** For a different perspective on world events, one that is largely critical of current economic polices and political trends, see *The New Internationalist* (published monthly in the UK) at **www.newint.org.**

The broadcast media sites can be particularly valuable as a source of up-to-date news on political and economic events. Also, their archive material of stories from the (recent) past is often a major source of information and data. The BBC site is particularly useful; it can be found at **http://news.bbc.co.uk**

Kegley, C.W. and Wittkopf, E.R. (2001) *World Politics: Trends and Transformations,* 8th edn. Boston, MA: Bedford St Martins. This is a comprehensive look at world politics, political systems, priorities and problems, from a US viewpoint.

Stiglitz, J. (2002) *Globalization and its Discontents.* London: Allen Lane. This book, written by a former chief economist at the World Bank, gives a devastating critique of the effects of many of the Bretton Woods institutions' policies in both economic and political terms.

Todaro, M.P. and Smith, S.C. (2009) *Economic Development,* 10th edn. Harlow: Addison-Wesley. A long-established book surveying global issues with an emphasis on a Developing World perspective. Some sections are rather heavy on economic theory for non-economists, but there is still much of value and interest to be found.

World Bank (2003) *World Development Report 2003.* New York: Oxford University Press/The World Bank. This is a useful edition of the World Bank's annual publication relating to global development trends and priorities. Each year's edition focuses on a different theme.

References

Commonwealth, The (2009) **http://thecommonwealth.org**

Electoral Reform Society (2003) **www.electoral-reform.org.uk**

Ohmae, K. (1995) Putting Global Logic First. *Harvard Business Review,* January–February, 119–125.

Organisation of the Islamic Conference (2009) **www.oic-oci.org**

Stiglitz, J. (2002) *Globalization and its Discontents.* London: Allen Lane.

Todaro, M.P. and Smith, S.C. (2009) *Economic Development,* 10th edn. Harlow: Addison-Wesley.

Transparency International (2009) **www.transparency.org**

United Nations, The (2009) **www.un.org**

World Bank (2003) *World Development Report 2003.* New York: Oxford University Press/The World Bank.

8

The legal environment

Chris Jeffs

Learning outcomes

On completion of this chapter you should be able to:

- understand the purpose of laws and how they are modified over time;
- be familiar with the sources of difference between legal systems in different countries;
- recognise how EU law is incorporated into national law;
- describe how to form a new business entity;
- be able to recognise the impact of personal liability;
- recognise the importance and relevance of different laws and how they may affect business;
- understand the importance of contracts in defining the terms and conditions of a business transaction;
- be familiar with the range and purpose of consumer protection laws;
- understand the purpose of competition law and its role in regulating cartels and monopolies;
- recognise the importance of protecting intellectual property rights in business and the mechanisms to achieve this;
- outline the key legislation behind employer–employee relationships, and how these are stipulated in contracts of employment;
- appreciate the business implications of health and safety legislation;
- outline the difference between laws that are generated by nations in order to control foreign trade and ownership, and international laws and treaties;
- recognise the importance of international treaties, the organisations that create them and how they are governed;
- outline several key international treaties, the purpose of them and the mechanisms of enforcement;
- outline the risks that businesses undertake when they do businesses internationally;
- describe the forms of international dispute resolution and the purpose and mechanisms of international arbitration.

Key concepts

- law and morality
- public and private law
- court hierarchy
- liability
- national law systems

- supranationality and the influence of European law on member states
- business liability
- contracts
- negligence and the law of tort in relation to business
- criminal law and business
- consumer protection
- competition law, cartels and monopoly regulation
- forms and laws relating to intellectual property rights
- employment law
- health and safety
- sanctions and embargoes
- nationalisation, expropriation and confiscation
- constraints on FDI
- role of international organisations and treaties
- role of international courts
- inadequacies of treaties and conventions
- international business risks
- importance of international contractual terms and conditions
- international dispute resolution
- mechanisms of international arbitration.

Minicase 8.1   The Danone–Wahaha feud

The longest lawsuit in Chinese history, which become known as the 'Danone–Wahaha feud', may be close to being resolved. The dispute has been running for three years and involves the Paris-based global dairy foods group Danone and Wahaha, the largest beverage company in China. Danone–Wahaha formed a partnership in 1996 and for ten years it was considered to be a highly profitable, rapidly growing alliance. In 2006 a disagreement escalated into a complex legal dispute which was to be played out in many countries. The main issues behind the legal dispute are the 'status' of Wahaha's other business ventures and the ownership of the Wahaha trademark.

There are actually five joint ventures (JVs) between Danone and Wahaha, all of which use the Wahaha brand. Danone has investments in each and Wahaha is responsible for the operation and management of them. Under their JV contract, Wahaha promised not to undertake any production or operations which competed with the JV companies, and Danone agreed not to damage the status of the JV. In April 2006, Danone alleged that Wahaha had infringed the contract by setting up other ventures in competition with the Danone–Wahaha JVs. As compensation for these actions, Danone demanded that Wahaha give them a 51 percent ownership in the new ventures, valued at 4 billion yuan (approx. 400 million euros). Wahaha rejected the request considering that it amounted to a hostile takeover.

In addition, Danone claims that the Wahaha trademark belongs to the Danone–Wahaha joint venture, and that Wahaha's use of the trademark in other ventures constituted an infringement of the JV contract. However, the Wahaha Group disagrees, claiming that it is the true holder of the trademark and the use of the trademark by other Wahaha ventures was legal.

Danone has since filed more than 37 lawsuits against Wahaha for violating the JV contract and the illegal use of the Wahaha trademark in countries such as France, Italy, the USA and China. Danone has even taken the wife and daughter of the Chairman of Wahaha to a US court, accusing them of co-plotting the actions that led to 'damaging Danone's interests'. This was despite the daughter being at a US school at the time of the alleged action. So far, all the indictments and court cases both in China and abroad have ruled against Danone.

Mediation has been tried on a number of occasions; the French president Nicolas Sarkozy has also been involved, but on each occasion no agreement could be found. The Danone–Wahaha JV contract stated that any disputes that might arise should be submitted to the Stockholm Chamber of Commerce (SCC) for arbitration. In May 2007, Danone filed a number of arbitration applications to the SCC accusing Wahaha of unlawful competition and fraud, claiming compensation of up to 890 million euros, which is the expected loss of profit during the remaining 39 years of the contract term. In response, Wahaha claimed that the ventures had no production or operations business and were therefore not in direct competition; they also stated that these companies were known to Danone from the start. In retaliation, Wahaha also claims that Danone has breached the JV contract by acquiring the Chinese beverage company Robust, which in 2000 was the largest competitor of Wahaha.

In its indictments Danone has tried to avoid Chinese law; contractually, however, their dispute is to be governed under Chinese law and, in accordance with international laws, the SCC will also consider the outcomes of the previous rulings. At the time of writing the companies are still waiting for a final judgment.

Questions

1 Why was the Stockholm Chamber of Commerce (SCC) cited in the original contract for dispute resolution?
2 Why do you think that Danone wanted to avoid legal action in China?

8.1 Introduction

The opening case describes the legal complexities of trading across borders with local disputes ending in global litigation. This chapter will discuss the purpose of laws and their influence on the operation of national and international business.

Increasingly, laws governing supply, transportation, investment, human rights, environmental protection and e-commerce are becoming internationally regulated. It is therefore vital that multinational companies are aware of all the international and national legislation in the regions that they manufacture, transport through and trade with. For example, a US company conducting business in Poland will have to comply not just with Polish law, but also regional EU as well as US federal and state law. Fortunately much of this legislation overlaps and so long as there is an awareness of unusual legal issues, and steps are made to abide by the most stringent laws, most organisations will manage.

8.2 The law

Laws consist of a set of rules imposed upon members of society. In a democracy these laws are defined, modified and enforced through an elected assembly with a separation of powers between the political body and the judiciary. Laws can be viewed as a form of contract; we obey the laws and in return the government (aided by the police, courts and penal system) agrees to protect us from those who break the law. Anyone that disobeys the law in effect breaks that contract and can be penalised under the rule of law.

National law can be subdivided into that which is public and that which is private:

- Public law regulates the relationship between the public and the state.
- Private law regulates the relationship between members of the public.

A car crash involving two members of the public is an example of where private law might be used. The collision may result in action being taken against one of the parties for negligent driving.

International law can also be subdivided into public and private categories:

- Public international law is concerned with establishing the rules to be followed by nation states, particularly in relation with each other.
- Private international law is concerned with establishing which national law is to be used in the case of an international dispute.

Private international law may be used if, for instance, a dispute arises between a Chinese company and an American company.

8.2.1 The law and morality

Issues of morality are of great importance to law making, society and business. Morality is a form of informal rules and codes of conduct that are embedded in and generally accepted by the majority of people in society.

Morals are formed from the culture, upbringing, religious beliefs, education and behaviour of the population. Indeed, over time morality has formed the basis of laws in most countries. However, due to the fact that each individual has a different set of moral codes, some people will be more likely to infringe laws. For instance, many people have broken the law by driving at speed in a restricted area or have illegally downloaded music or video files, but do not consider themselves as acting illegally; whereas they would never break the law by stealing from or harming another human being.

As morals change, laws also have to change to reflect the expectations of the citizens. Examples of laws which have been decriminalised include those banning homosexuality, abortion and the distribution of hard-core pornography, all of which were illegal in the UK less than 50 years ago. The smoking of cannabis and the use of brothels have been legalised in the Netherlands, and the personal use of hard drugs is no longer illegal in Portugal. In June 2009, the 148-year-old law prohibiting homosexual activity, which dated back to British colonial rule in India, was overturned under human rights legislation in a Delhi court. In business the word 'morality' is not commonly used; however, you will find the terms '*business ethics*' and '*corporate social responsibility*' which broadly equate to the same thing and are discussed in detail in *Chapter 6*.

8.2.2 The law and national boundaries

Within the EU there is increasing trade, and political and legal integration. This has a direct impact on national law-making bodies, because, as national laws become inadequate, transnational laws are created to bridge the gap. Legislation has therefore become highly complex; however, for clarity, we will subdivide the types of law into the following categories: national, regional (e.g. EU), business and international laws, although you will see as the chapter progresses that these classifications are somewhat arbitrary.

8.2.3 National law

On a national level a transparent and well-regulated legal system is important to ensure that businesses can thrive. Any systems of government which offer fully separate powers between the political leaders and the legal system will provide a set of checks and balances which reduce the likelihood of bribery, coercion and corruption.

National legal systems are often very different from one another due to historical, cultural, religious and political reasons. However, all of the world's legislative systems share two components:

- that of legislation or law-making; and
- adjudication or dispute settlement.

International businesses have to be aware of not only the major differences between national legal systems but also the subtle differences between them; hence lawyers are always required for their specialist and local knowledge.

It is useful to categorise the different types of national legal systems that are found around the world by their historical foundations. The following types of national legal system are commonly recognised:

- common law;
- civil law;
- theocratic (religious) law;
- bureaucratic law;
- mixed law (combination of civil and common laws).

Common law

The common law process is the basis of the legal systems in the UK and many of its formal colonies including the USA, Canada, Australia, India, Barbados and Malaysia. The common law tradition dates back to 1189 which is prior to that of the establishment of the English parliament. The distinguishing feature of common law is that it is based on the cumulative judgments of individual court decisions. On occasion, judgments can create new legal precedents which must be followed by other judges hearing similar cases. As the common law system is continually evolving, it creates different legal precedents in different common law countries: for instance, there are many important differences in areas of patent law between the USA and UK.

Civil law

Civil law is an older form of law than common law and is based on the documentation (or codification) of what is legal and what is not. The Romans first implemented this form of law-making and spread it throughout their empire into the Western world. Subsequently, Napoleon Bonaparte implemented his civil law codes (French Civil Code, 1804) in countries conquered by France in the late eighteenth and early nineteenth centuries, thus embedding this method of law-making in Western Europe. It is for this reason that civil law is also sometimes called Napoleonic law. Countries that use civil law include: France, Germany, Greece and Italy; the South American countries of Argentina, Brazil and Chile, and other countries such as Japan and Sweden.

Historically the civil code was focused on private law, but in modern times it has been supplemented by commercial and civil codes. There are some important differences in civil law over common law. For example, the fact that there is only one single source of pre-coded law means that it is anticipatory in nature, rather than being reactive, as in the common law system. Another important difference between civil and common law is that of the role of the judge. In civil law cases the judge decides on the breadth and depth of the evidence to be submitted to the court, whereas in common law courts this is for the lawyers to decide. Civil laws can also be rushed through quickly and may often be done so in the name of political expediency. For example, in February 2009, the Italian government of Silvio Berlusconi decreed a new law allowing the authorities to detain immigrants for six months while their requests for asylum were being processed (BBC, 2009a). This was in response to public pressure following a spate of rapes which had been blamed on immigrants.

Theocratic law

Theocratic law is similar to that of common law in that it is not a written law. A theocracy is a country that applies religious law to both civil and criminal cases. Iran, Afghanistan (under the rule of the Taliban) and the Vatican City are well-known examples of theocracies where religious leaders pass judgment through their interpretation of the Koran or Bible. In each case the religious leaders have the power of veto in all legal matters. This was demonstrated in 2009 when Iran's Supreme Leader Ayatollah Ali Khamenei vetoed calls for an annulment of the June election (Fathi, 2009). Islamic law is based on the Sharia law (God's rules or path) and provides guidance on many aspects of day-to-day life, including economics, banking, contracts, hygiene and sexuality.

Islamic practice can be aligned largely to the dominant Sunni or Shi'ite schools. The Sunni school itself comprises a number of schools of thought, ranging from the most orthodox Hanbali school (practised in Saudi Arabia and by the Taliban) to the more liberal Hanafi school (dominant in Central Asia, Egypt, Pakistan, India and Turkey). Shia Muslims follow the Ja'fari school, which is dominant in Iran. These differences have more impact on the legal systems in each country rather than how individual Muslims live their lives. For example, Sharia law prohibits the paying or charging of interest on loans and deposits which could be restrictive for business enterprises. In order to conform to the law, Muslim banks offer alternative leasing arrangements with fees payable up front, while depositors receive shares in lieu of interest payments.

Bureaucratic law

The legal system in countries ruled by dictatorships is often called bureaucratic law. Examples of bureaucratic countries include North Korea, under the dictatorship of Kim Jong-il, and Myanmar, ruled by the dictator Than Shwe. Under bureaucratic law dictators and their bureaucrats may change the rules of the law, or previous contractual agreements, with little notice, regardless of what is stated in the constitution. This provides numerous problems for companies dealing in such countries where there is a lack of consistency and often poorly defined appeals procedures. Increasingly the political situation in Zimbabwe is that of a dictatorship that is ruling under bureaucratic law. In May 2009 President Robert Mugabe enacted a law which forces foreign companies, including mines and banks, to sell a 51 percent ownership to members of the Zimbabwean black community; alternately the government can seize 25 percent of shares without paying (Dzirutwe, 2009). In response to these laws and the unpredictable political situation, international mining companies have reduced investment and wound down operations in the country.

Mixed law

Mixed law systems are usually combinations of common law and civil law systems, where there is an element of codified legislation and new precedents set by judges. The EU is gradually moving towards a mixed system, with the combination of civil and common law across its member states. Other examples of mixed systems include Quebec, South Africa, Botswana, Sri Lanka and Scotland. Despite the fact that the Scots and English have close geographic proximity and shared political systems, there are some significant differences between Scottish and English laws particularly in the areas of criminal, property, inheritance and family law. One obvious difference is in the legal 'age of majority' or adulthood, which is 16 years in Scotland but 18 in England. However, the two countries are broadly similar in areas of taxation, business and consumer law.

It has been demonstrated that there are significant differences between legal systems in different countries. However, national laws of member states of the EU are also influenced by European legislature. To illustrate this, this chapter will look at how the English and the EU legislatures work together in partnership.

8.3 The English system of law

Despite the law in England being historically based on common law principles, in reality most new laws are set by parliament via statute law, which are otherwise known as 'Acts of Parliament'. However, many criminal laws in England and Wales, such as that of murder, are still legislated through common law and are not actually illegal under statute law. One of the earliest statutes was that of the Magna Carta (1215), with the revised version of 1297 still on the statute books of England and Wales. Nowadays statutes are created in a long process involving readings, debate and amendment, the bill passing through both the House of Commons and the House of Lords. Once finalised and approved, the bill passes to the Queen for Royal Assent. Increasingly, however, statutes originate from EU directives which demonstrate a convergence with civil law.

English law can be classified into public and private (civil) law. Civil law in this context should not be confused with the civil (Napoleonic) form of law, as it is only concerned with civil procedure and not, for example, criminal law. *Figure 8.1*, provides examples of the areas jurisdiction (cover) for England and Wales.

Civil law (private law) provides legal rights to individuals or corporate bodies and exists primarily to govern their relationships. If a case goes to court it is typically heard in a county or high court and the claimant must prove that the defendant is liable on the balance of probability. However, most civil law claims never get to court as they are more often settled by agreement before the trial begins. If a party is found guilty, the penalties are usually in the form of damages which may be covered by the defendant's insurance policy. Disputes between private citizens and the state are usually heard by tribunals. The tribunal service in England and Wales hears approximately 1 million cases per year and deals with a wide range of disputes including social security, income tax, mental health, special needs education, care standards, asylum support and specialist military and employment tribunals (Tribunals Service, 2009).

Criminal law is a form of public law. The enforcement of these laws is usually by the police rather than an individual. If the police charge someone with a criminal offence the

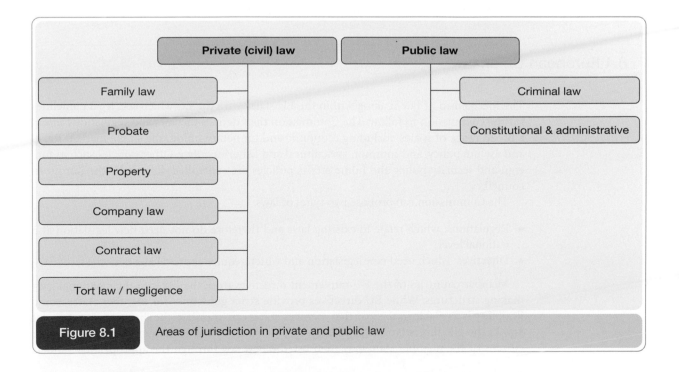

| **Figure 8.1** | Areas of jurisdiction in private and public law |

Crown Prosecution Service (CPS) in England and Wales has to decide whether there is enough evidence to proceed with the case. Depending upon the severity of the crime, it is either heard in a magistrates' or a crown court. In a crown court the prosecution must prove that the subject is guilty and, if so, the penalties may include fines, rehabilitation or prison sentences. It is worth remembering that businesses are also capable of committing criminal acts, for instance by not complying with health and safety legislation. Since April 2008, the law of Corporate Manslaughter (killing through negligence) has been enacted in England and Wales, and can now be used to hold senior management personally liable for corporate negligence. In June 2009, a director of Cotswold Geotechnical Holdings was the first to be charged under the new gross negligence legislation following a mud landslide that killed a 27-year-old company employee (Morris, 2009).

8.3.1 Courts in England and Wales

The criminal court structure in England and Wales is based on a pyramid of hierarchy with:

- the magistrates' court at the bottom (accounting for 95 percent of all criminal offences);
- the crown court;
- the court of appeal (criminal division); and
- the Supreme Court at the top.

Cases that start in a low court such as the magistrates' court can if necessary be passed up to a higher court. Decisions of superior courts are binding on the lower courts.

Magistrates' courts handle routine and petty cases such as environmental health, shoplifting and acts of criminal damage. They also have the power to grant alcohol licenses and enforce payment of council bills. The Justice of the Peace (JP), who presides over the court, can sentence with penalties of a maximum of 6 months imprisonment or £5,000 fine. Crown courts are adversarial in nature with the judge presiding over the case to ensure that the rules of evidence are obeyed and to decide, usually with the aid of a jury, who the winning party is. Under this system the burden of proof is on the accuser and it is they that have to produce the most convincing evidence. Unlike many European countries, under English law the judge cannot be involved with the drawing out of the evidence.

8.4 European Union law

The mechanism of law-making within the EU starts with the EC which sets legal guidelines for the commission to follow. The Commission then defines the laws and regulations across a broad range of issues, including economic and monetary union, the single market, social and asylum policy, and common agricultural and fisheries policy. Other policies such as foreign and security policy and home affairs policies are controlled directly by the European council.

The Commission can propose two types of laws:

- Regulations: which relate to existing laws and therefore do not need new legislation at a national level.
- Directives: which need new legislation and which require approval at a national level.

Member countries of the EU implement directives from the EU into their national law-making structures. While EU directives provide strict guidelines for member states, some flexibility is available in the way that member states can 'translate' the directive into national law. In the UK this is typically achieved by passing an Act of Parliament. Once passed, the citizens of the member state may then use the new law through the appropriate channels

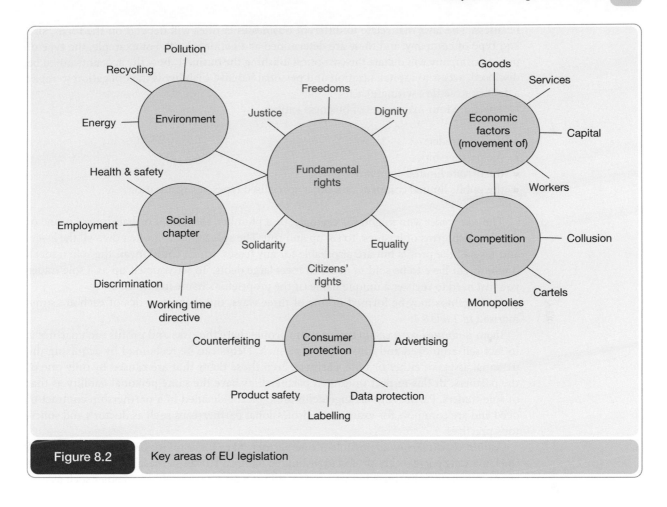

Figure 8.2	Key areas of EU legislation

through their own national legislature. In many areas of law the EU has brought harmonisation to what was otherwise a somewhat diverse collection of national laws.

The most significant EU legislation is bound into treaties and charters; some of the key areas are highlighted in *Figure 8.2,* and are discussed later in this chapter.

The European Court of Justice (ECJ) is the legal authority responsible for ensuring that EU laws are implemented. It has the power to take legal action against a member state if it is not fully complying with EU legislation. As the EU has a higher authority in these areas of law, these are often called *supranational laws.*

The legal relationship between the EU and its member states is a complex one. For example, in Britain in 1972, Parliament recognised the *European Communities Act* through which European Community law was incorporated into UK law. Under this and subsequent legislation the Supreme Court has ultimate authority over domestic matters, and the ECJ has overall authority on EU laws. However, it is still disputed, in some areas of law at least, which law-making authority should be supreme.

8.5 Business law

8.5.1 Forming a business entity

Business law may be characterised as those laws that are related to the formation and running of a company (the business entity) and those that have to be followed when conducting business. The laws that relate to different businesses entities will depend on the focus, size and type of company, and these are determined at a national level. For example, the type of private company will dictate the cost of establishing the business, how the accounts are to be disclosed, access to capital, taxation and personal liability. Liability is the obligation to repay a debt or to settle a wrongful act.

There are four main types of business entity:

- the sole trader;
- the partnership;
- the private limited company;
- the public limited company and other specialised types of organisation.

The *sole trader* who might, for example, be a plumber, electrician or hairdresser is one of the simplest forms of business to set up and run. The sole trader will often own all the assets and take all the profits but are also liable for any losses, which could mean the sole trader's house might have to be sold in order to meet large debts. To set yourself up as a sole trader you just need to register a unique name (if the proprietor's name in not used).

Partnerships may be formed in one of three ways, the characteristics of each are summarised in *Table 8.1*.

In an *unlimited partnership* two or more people share the risks and profits each partner is in fact self-employed and must register as such. Debts can be reclaimed by acquiring the personal assets of either or both partners, even those debts that are caused by only one of the partners. In this respect unlimited partnerships have the same personal liability as that of sole traders. Partnership arrangements are typically detailed in a partnership contract of deed and are common, for example, in professional partnerships such as doctor's and solicitor's practices.

A *limited partnership* is possible if one partner takes full liability for any accrued debts, the remaining partners are protected by limited liability. However, these partnerships are not commonly used in business but they are found in finance management schemes such as unit trusts.

A *limited liability partnership* (LLP) is a relatively new form of partnership in the UK (Limited Liability Partnership Act, 2000): it occurs where each of the partners (or members) contribute to the business but are not personally liable beyond what they have invested.

Table 8.1	Characteristics of partnerships		
Partnerships	**Liability/risk**	**Legal requirements**	**Examples**
Unlimited	Share risks and profits Both equally liable for debts	Register as self-employed. Partnership contract	Doctors Dentists Architects
Limited	Share risks and profits One partner takes full debt liability	Register as self-employed. Partnership contract	Financial management schemes
Limited liability (LLP)	No liability beyond what is invested	Register as self-employed. Partnership contract or deed	Solicitors Accountants
		Register & submit annual accounts to Companies House	

The LLP has proven to be particularly popular with solicitors and accountants, where personal negligence claims against the company may be high (see the football league *Minicase 8.2* as an example). Like other forms of partnership, each member has to register as being self-employed; however, the LLP must also register and submit annual accounts to Companies House.

In law a company has its own legal identity, separate from that of its owners (shareholders). This means that the shareholders do not have any liability for debts beyond what they have invested, i.e. the company's finances are separate from its personal finances. A registered limited liability company requires shares to be distributed to the owners in proportion to the amount contributed. In the case of *private limited companies,* such as the Virgin Group Ltd, shares are not offered to the public but are sold or gifted to private individuals. With the example of the Virgin Group the majority of shares are owned by Richard Branson. *Public limited companies (plcs)* such as British Airways plc are freely traded through the stock exchange and require a minimum of £50,000 of shares to be available. Both types of limited company must register a memorandum and articles of association with Companies House and submit annual reports for external audit. Profits are distributed to the shareholders in the form of dividends and of course shareholders are keen to see their share value increase. In order to maintain appropriate procedures (governance), it is usual for companies to have a secondary or non-executive board, whose purpose is to ensure transparency and accountability to the shareholders.

In order to encourage a healthy investment in stocks and inflate the value of the company, plc executives will often do their best to 'talk up' the future prospects of the company. This was demonstrated in 2004 when the oil company Royal Dutch Shell was maintaining a healthy share price with a 20 percent exaggeration of its oil reserves. Once it was known that the company had deliberately misled the shareholders and an indictment of fraud was being considered, the stock value plummeted by £3 billion (BBC, 2004).

The principle of limited corporations is common around the world but there are different systems in use. *Table 8.2* provides a list of company limited liability suffixes and their approximate equivalents; different countries apply different prerequisites to these business entities.

In addition to the laws that govern the setting-up and running of the business, there is a whole range of additional laws that relate specifically to the act of doing business. These may be categorised as to whether the legislation is predominantly national, regional or of international origin. Historically these laws have been designed and enforced at a national level, but increasingly there is an international dimension with legislation occurring at a regional level or through conventions and treaties at an international level. This has left many areas

Table 8.2	Company liability suffix in different countries

Country	Limited liability suffix	Translation
UK, USA, S. Korea	Ltd or Plc	Private limited company or public limited company
Brazil	Ltd or SA	Limitada or Sociedade Anônima
Denmark	Ap/S or A/S	Anpartsselskab or Aktieselskap
France	Sàrl or SA	Société à responsabilité limitée or Société Anonym
Germany	GmbH or AG	Gesellschaft mit beschrankter Haftung or Aktiengesellschaft
India	Pvt. Ltd or Ltd	Private limited company or Public limited company
Netherlands	BV or NV	Besloten Vennootschap or Naamloze Vennootschap
Spain	SL or SA	Sociedad Limitada or Sociedad Anónima

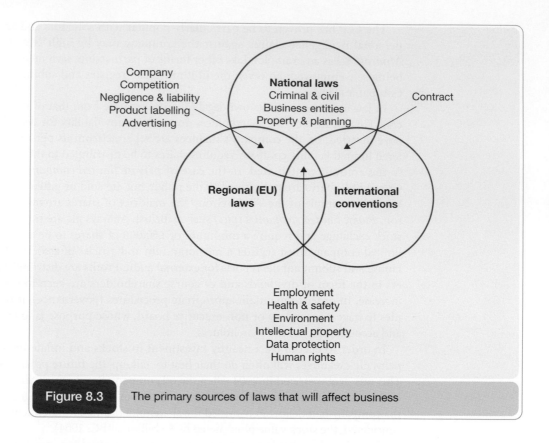

| Figure 8.3 | The primary sources of laws that will affect business |

of law with overlapping jurisdictions. Examples of laws that might affect businesses and the primary sources of these laws are illustrated in *Figure 8.3*.

8.5.2 Contract law

Businesses that enter into negotiations will usually formalise the deal in a mutually acceptable, legally binding contract. These contracts can be in written or verbal form, depending on the historical precedent in the country concerned; however, a written contract is easier to contest in a court of law. Contracts come in different forms but are mainly used to govern relationships between buyers and sellers or between organisations and their employees. Regardless of the purpose, all contracts detail the terms and conditions of the agreement such as price or salary, timescales, warranty, delivery, etc. If the contract conditions are not met over a specified timescale, one party will be in breach of contract and can be legally challenged. For example, in 2008 the clothing store Primark cancelled orders with three of its Indian suppliers after being informed that they were sub-contracting work to other suppliers that used child labour. Primark claimed that unapproved sub-contracting was in breach of their contract (Arnott, 2008).

8.5.3 Tort – Negligence and liability

Business tort law is concerned with damage to a reputation or damage as a result of deliberate action or negligence. It covers areas such as patents and counterfeit goods, defective goods, data protection and poor advice or duty of care, such as in medical, accounting or legal cases (see Football League *Minicase 8.2*). The international law firm Fulbright and Jaworski found, in their fifth annual survey, that the type of litigation which is of the greatest concern to UK

| Minicase 8.2 | The English Football League sues its legal advisers for professional negligence |

Following the collapse of ITV Digital in 2002, the English Football League made one of the largest claims for professional negligence in British legal history (Harris, 2006).

Without the broadcasting deal the Football League was significantly out of pocket and initially sued Carlton and Granada, the owners of ITV Digital, in an attempt to recover the £132 million in broadcasting fees it was owed. However, the High Court ruled that the owners were under no legal obligation to repay the debts of their subsidiary.

Following this ruling, the Football League sued their solicitors for professional negligence for failing to stipulate payment guarantees when negotiating the broadcasting deal with ITV Digital.

In the High Court in June 2006, Mr Justice Rimmer ruled in favour of the legal advisers finding them liable in only two minor counts of breach of duty, for which they were fined a token £4. Summing up, Mr Rimmer said, 'Is the solicitor supposed to review the whole range of commercial considerations that underlie a particular deal, work out which ones he is concerned the client may not have given sufficient thought to and remind him about them? ... in my opinion the answer is no.' The High Court decided that the Football League already knew about the risks when they signed the contract and were ordered to pay the defendants legal costs in the case. Not surprisingly the defendants agreed, saying, 'This decision confirms that solicitors cannot be expected to underwrite the success of their clients' commercial transactions nor to advise them of things they know already' (Harris, 2006).

Questions

1 Why do you think the Football League decided to sue the solicitors that acted for them?
2 How would liability insurance have helped the defending solicitors in this case?

and US companies is contracts litigation, followed by labour and employment. Personal injury and product liability are concerns to only one in five of the companies surveyed (Fulbright, 2008).

Negligence indictments are usually for relatively minor claims, for example customers suing businesses for accidents such as slipping on wet floors or claiming for damage to cars in a car wash. A number of small cases may also build into a much larger case that may reveal persistent negligence. This occurred in the famous case of *Liebeck* v. *McDonald's* in 1994. The McDonald's restaurant chain stipulated that beverages should be served at between 83 and 88 degrees, more than 20 degrees hotter than most other coffee providers and hot enough to cause third-degree burns. After 700 previous complaints to McDonald's had been demonstrated and a particularly severe case of burning was proven, significant damages amounting to hundreds of thousands of dollars were awarded to the plaintive (Public Citizen, 1999).

Class actions are lawsuits against particular companies on the behalf of many, possibly hundreds, of individuals or companies. In the USA, liability through group or class actions is common in the pharmaceutical, oil and chemical industries, and includes claims for environmental damage, side-effects of drugs and disease resulting from exposure to asbestos and tobacco. Specialist legal companies advertise potential class actions and promise to act on the individual's behalf on the basis that it will be easier and cheaper to settle claims in one large court case rather than hundreds of individual ones. A recent class action in a case of tort was settled in New York in 2008 in the favour of 153 water companies based across 17 states, after it was found that drinking water was contaminated with a the potential carcinogen MTBE. The settling defendants included the oil companies BP Amoco, Chevron and ConocoPhillips (US Legal 500, 2008).

Class actions are less common in the UK or the EU, but tort cases are on the increase. In 2007, GMTV, which is part-owned by ITV and the Disney Corporation, were accused of gross negligence in television phone voting over a period of four years. It was found that the telephone lines were often held open in order to raise additional revenue, despite the fact that the competition had closed. The UK media watchdog Ofcom fined the broadcaster GMTV a record £2 million for gross negligence (Sabbagh, 2007).

Fortunately, insurance companies offer various types of liability insurance, such as employer, public and product liability insurance, which are designed to protect businesses against these costs. In many parts of the world it is compulsory for businesses to have employer liability insurance; however this can be very expensive, so many large companies prefer to 'manage the risk' rather than pay high premiums. Companies that are aware of their stakeholders and their impact on the environment are thought to be less likely to be indicted in tort claims. See *Chapter 6* for more information on corporate social responsibility.

8.5.4 International business law

Recognising the significant differences between business laws in nation states, the UN Commission on International Trade Law (UNICITRAL) adopted a Convention of Contracts for the International Sale of Goods (CISG) which came into force in 1988. These regulations have resulted in significant moves towards harmonising the terminology, rules and obligations documented in contracts. At the time of writing, the CISG has been ratified by 76 countries, including all the major trading nations with the notable exception of the UK (UNCITRAL, 2009). The CISG exists in six different languages (Arabic, Chinese, English, French, Russian and Spanish) and aims to reduce the confusion over translation and wording disputes in contracts.

8.6 Criminal law

Obviously businesses can protect themselves from criminal legal action by conducting their activities according to national and international laws. However, it is still surprising to note the high number of indictments against companies or their executives for criminal acts. These indictments are typically the result of not complying with national laws on health and safety, financial reporting, bribery, money laundering, fraud, mis-selling of goods, unsafe products, environmental damage, counterfeiting, unlawful importations, corporate manslaughter, etc. The 2001 case of Enron is a well-known example of where the criminal laws of money laundering, fraud, insider trading and making false statements, were found to be broken (BBC, 2003). The scandal not only led to Enron's senior executives being jailed, but it also brought down Enron, at that time America's seventh largest company. Arthur Andersen, which at the time was one of the largest accounting and consultancy companies in the world, was also broken up after they were found to have destroyed evidence relating to the case. Cases such as this highlight the need for transparent practices, efficient governance and an awareness of business ethics and corporate social responsibility.

8.7 Consumer protection

Laws protecting the consumer have been used since the Middle Ages; however, additional legislation has been drafted in more recent times and now covers issues such as:

- defective products;
- misleading advertisements;
- doorstep and distance (also internet) selling;
- cancellation of contracts;

- returns and warranties;
- safety of food and medicines;
- weights and volumes;
- advice and labelling of products;
- as well as specific regulation on, for example, package tour holidays, data protection and safety standards.

The UK Trade Description Act (1968) was drawn up to protect consumers from goods or services that have been given a false description or a wrong price. Local authorities may enforce this Act under criminal legislation and following a conviction a magistrate can fine or imprison the culprit. In addition to this Act, stricter consumer protection laws are to be introduced into the UK as a result of changes in EU legislation. For example, since May 2009, EU legislation includes previously excluded trades, such as fortune tellers, spiritualists and astrologists. These service providers now have to clearly state in writing that what they offer is for entertainment only and that they cannot guarantee the accuracy of their predictions. Those that break the new law will be liable to fines up to £5,000 or two years in jail (Gibb, 2008).

Safety and quality standards are often created by government bodies in order that companies can show that their product or service meets the required standard and they can then advertise this fact in their product information. This is particularly useful to those organisations that act in a socially responsible manner and wish to demonstrate this (see *Chapter 6* for more on CSR). Examples of safety standards certificates include the British Standards Institute (BSI) KiteMark and the European CE mark which cover products as diverse as electrical appliances, fire safety extinguishers, soft toys, crash helmets and concrete. China has also made great strides in this area of law and has now amalgamated its previous schemes into a single China Compulsory Certificate (CCC) which applies in particular to electrical, mechanical and safety products.

Safety and quality marks may be a useful differentiator in a market and essential if you wish to export to other markets but in some sectors legislation regarding packaging and labelling is also important. Food, medicines and potentially hazardous products have to conform to each nation's requirements, which is why on international products consumers are now used to seeing multiple languages and different international symbols on the packaging.

In the USA, the Food and Drug Administration (FDA) regulates and enforces laws that protect consumers in the areas of food, medicines, medical devices and cosmetics. The EU also legislates in this area with the aim to standardise practice across the region. In the UK the Food Standards Agency is the government department which protects public health and consumer interests. As part of its role it checks the correct labelling of food products according to the appropriate legislation. The Food Safety Act (1990) also lays down compositional rules for products such as bread and flour, chocolate, fruit juice, infant formula, jams, sausages, mineral waters, spreadable fats, etc. *Figure 8.4* provides a list of details that must be clearly shown on food products in the UK (Food Standards Agency, 2009).

While food labelling regulations are in place in most parts of the world, regulations for food labelling are less stringent in some regions, for example China requires only a small number of the above items to be displayed. However, as in most countries, if a product arrives without the appropriate information it will be refused entry or confiscated. Inappropriate labelling can also cause confusion. For example, it was alleged that a Chinese supermarket placed the German children's cereal Brugel among the pet foods. The store and customers were clearly unable to determine what the product was. This was perhaps understandable as the cereal package had no Chinese writing on the label and was printed with cartoon animals such as dogs, cats, birds and monkeys.

Advertising laws also differ widely from country to country, especially with regards to the content and placement of advertisements. For example, tobacco advertising is banned on radio and television in the USA but the EU also bans tobacco advertising in print and on the internet. The advertising of alcohol is also a contentious issue and has wide variations in how legislation is applied. The laws range from weak 'industry regulated' advertising in Australia,

> 1 The name of the food.
> 2 A list of the ingredients.
> 3 The amount of an ingredient which is named or associated with the food.
> 4 An appropriate durability indication (sell by/use by dates).
> 5 Special storage conditions.
> 6 The name of business and manufacturer.
> 7 The place of origin (depending on the product).
> 8 The process used in manufacture (depending on the product).
> 9 Instructions for use (depending on the product).

Figure 8.4   UK requirements for food labelling

to strict bans on all forms of alcohol advertising and consumption in Saudi Arabia and Libya as Sharia law dictates. In order to produce some harmonisation across the EU, in 2005 a framework of guidelines was implemented for member states. To comply with these regulations advertisements should not be directed to minors or be linked with higher performance, or indicate that a higher alcohol content is preferable to a lower one. Implementation of these laws has ironically meant that Sweden, who previously had a total advertising ban on high alcohol drinks, has now relaxed its laws and applies health warnings instead.

With increasing ease and reducing costs, organisations routinely store and share information about individuals, whether they are employees, suppliers or customers. There is hardly a business, bank, credit card company, telephone provider, utility supplier, medical or educational institution or other government body that does not hold data on most individuals. This does not even start to consider the freely available information and photos that you provide for the world to see through your favourite social networking site! Consider, as an example, the grocery retailer Tesco. Via your store card they not only hold your personal details, but from your buying patterns they could also determine:

- how much alcohol you drink;
- if you are a heath food fanatic;
- if you have any children;
- if you are trying to lose weight;
- if you have a medical condition;
- if you have a pet.

It is likely that, as customers, we would want to keep this information confidential, and in this case, because it provides Tesco with a distinct competitive advantage, it is unlikely that it would be shared. However, in different circumstances the selling of databases to other organisations is a common, lucrative and legal source of income. Companies are prepared to purchase this information as it can be used to help to target marketing campaigns or, for instance, be used to filter appropriate candidates for interview.

Legislation to protect personal information has been slow to develop, especially when set against the rapid changes in information technology. There has, however, been some progress, for example under EU legislation all personal data should be protected in a number of ways (ICO, 2009). With regard to stored data it should be possible for an individual to stop the data being used for the purposes of direct marketing. Furthermore stored data should:

- be processed in an appropriate manner that is relevant to a specific purpose;
- only contain information that is selected for a specific purpose;
- be accurate, secure and regularly updated;

- be kept for no longer than is necessary and then destroyed;
- be available so that individuals can ask what information is held on them;

Data protection legislation has numerous implications for business as it impacts what information can be stored and shared across organisations, between organisations and between countries. It also requires significant resources to manage the database and comply with requests for information. Businesses are also struggling to clarify the legal perspective in 'grey areas' such as their right to covertly monitor employees' telephone calls and web activities while at work. Also banks, call centres and government departments have found themselves open to charges of providing poor data security when their systems have been open to hacking and poor practice has allowed data to fall into the wrong hands.

8.7.1 Competition law

In most parts of the world businesses are governed by anti-competitive laws which aim to protect consumers, encourage entrepreneurial development and help to ensure a fair and open competitive market. In the UK this is the job of the Competition Commission and the Office of Fair Trading. In the USA it is the Antitrust Division of the Department of Justice that regulates the competitiveness of industry. In August 2008 China established its own anti-trust laws; however, outside China there are initial concerns that these might not be thoroughly or equally enforced. In the EU competition law relates to three main areas:

- cartels;
- monopolies and mergers;
- government assistance.

Forming a cartel is highly tempting to some business sectors as it can reduce competition and optimise profits. In order to protect consumers from this abuse of power, cartels have been made illegal in many parts of the world, including the USA, Europe and more recently in India (2008) and China (2008). In order to combat cartels, the EC encourages whistle-blowing, or the exchange of information in return for leniency, and can impose fines of up to 10 percent of the company's worldwide revenue. Indeed in many parts of the world, including the USA, France, Japan and Brazil, criminal sanctions can be applied, resulting in the imprisonment of company executives. During 2008, the Antitrust Division of the Department of Justice in the USA imposed more than US$1 billion in criminal fines, typically averaging at more than $100 million per company (*Global Competition Review,* 2009). In 2008, the UK's Office of Fair Trading brought criminal charges against three former and one current BA executives under the Enterprise Act (2002) for allegedly fixing prices with respect to air passenger fuel surcharges (Prosser, 2008). *Table 8.3* lists the ten highest cartel fines in Europe since 2000.

Table 8.3	Ten highest cartel fines per undertaking		
Year	**Undertaking**	**Case**	**Amount in €**
2008	Saint Gobain	Car glass	896,000,000
2009	E.ON	Gas	553,000,000
2009	GDF Suez	Gas	553,000,000
2007	ThyssenKrupp	Elevators and escalators	479,669,850
2001	F. Hoffmann-La Roche AG	Vitamins	462,000,000
2007	Siemens AG	Gas insulated switchgear	396,562,500
2008	Pilkington	Car glass	370,000,000
2008	Sasol Ltd	Candle waxes	318,200,000
2006	Eni SpA	Synthetic rubber	272,250,000
2002	Lafarge SA	Plasterboard	249,600,000

Source: Europa (2009a)

Monopoly legislation is another means to prevent a company from getting into a dominant market position. If there is only one or a small number of competitors they are more likely to either abuse their position by charging high prices or alternatively put their rivals out of business by undercutting their competitors' prices. Either way, in the long term it is not good for the customer. A high profile case was that of Microsoft and Netscape and their competitive internet browsers. See *Minicase 8.3* which discusses *AOL Time Warner* vs. *Microsoft*. *Chapter 2* provides further details regarding anti-competitive activities.

The European Competition Commission also regulates proposed mergers to ensure that they will not significantly reduce the level of competition and will also investigate a proposed merger if it is referred to them by the national regulatory body of a member state. For example, in May 2009 the Commission approved Lufthansa's proposed takeover of BMI. This was on the basis that it would not significantly affect competition across the EU as the two companies had already co-operated with each other through the Star Alliance (Europa, 2009b). However, if the EC decides that competition could be distorted, then mergers might be refused or only given conditional approval. Conditional approval might, for instance, be granted if parts of the new business are sold off or specialised technologies are made available to other companies, possibly though licensing deals. For example, when My Travel and Thomas Cook merged in the summer of 2007, the Commission found that the merger would cause a monopoly situation in Ireland, as it

Minicase 8.3	*AOL Time Warner* vs. *Microsoft*

In the early 1990s, AOL Time Warner's Netscape was the most used internet browser, commanding an 80–90 percent worldwide market share (Market Share, 2009). However, by the mid-1990s it was losing ground and under severe competitive pressure from Microsoft's Internet Explorer. In 1996, AOL Time Warner accused Microsoft of abusing its near monopoly market position by bundling its Internet Explorer software with the Windows operating system, which meant that the majority of the world's PC users had a copy of Internet Explorer. In its defence, Microsoft claimed that the Internet Explorer product was a result of innovation of the Windows operating system and the two products should be considered as one: the product was a feature of Windows and was provided for free. These claims were refuted by AOL Time Warner, who stated that the internet browser was not integral to the operating system, as the operating systems could run without it.

In parallel to this dispute, Microsoft was also in the courts having been indicted by the Department of Justice and 20 USA states for unfair competitive practices and abuse of its dominant market position in operating systems and internet browsers. In April 2000, the judge pronounced that Microsoft was guilty of the charges and suggested that Microsoft was split into two companies: one selling the operating system the other selling applications. Following an appeal by Microsoft, the verdict was overturned and in September 2001 the Department of Justice claimed to no longer be looking to split up Microsoft and was instead seeking an alternative resolution. In November 2001, the Department of Justice settled, with Microsoft having agreed that it would share its application programming interfaces with other third-party developers. This ruling at the time was widely condemned as being weak and ineffective as it did not tackle the key anti-competitive issues in the case.

In 2003, the legal dispute between AOL Time Warner and Microsoft was finally resolved. AOL Time Warner was awarded $750 million in compensation and a seven-year free licensing option for Internet Explorer (HU, 2003). While this deal provided useful finance to AOL Time Warner, it was widely perceived in the industry as a win–win resolution for Microsoft, who could easily afford to pay compensation at this level. Since the deal there has been a significant decline in sales of the Netscape browser, which resulted in the withdrawal of the Netscape product in 2007.

In 2009 the global consumer still has a limited choice of internet browsers. In the world market, 65.5 percent use the bundled Internet Explorer which comes with Microsoft Windows, and 22.5 percent of the world market uses Mozilla's Firefox as an internet browser. Between them the companies command a monopoly position with an 88 percent share of the web browser market (Market Share, 2009).

Questions

1 Why do you think that these court cases have taken so long to come to a resolution?
2 Do you think that the Netscape–Microsoft deal has benefited consumers in the long run?

would control more than 50 percent of the travel market in this region. To counter these concerns, Thomas Cook offered to divest its Irish business, Budget Travel. The conditional merger was approved and the combined group is now the largest travel company in Europe (Europa, 2009c).

Increasingly, global organisations such as the WTO, the UNCTAD and the OECD have been investigating the implementation of anti-trust legislation. However, it is doubtful that, even if it happens, the LDCs will not have the necessary legislative and enforcement procedures to effectively implement the new legislation.

Free competition can also be compromised by governments that provide unfair inducements in the forms of state aid, low taxation or 'free loans'. However, regulations that protect the principle of fair play are somewhat unique to the EU and do not apply within other regional trade agreements. During the 2008 financial crisis these rules were severely tested, as more than 50 banks across Europe and the airline Alitalia were spared bankruptcy through support of their respective governments. It was argued by some that, during the global economic slowdown, rules sometimes have to be adapted as the consequences of denying state aid might be disastrous. For example, in May 2009 General Motors in Europe was looking for 3.3 billion euros in financial assistance to avoid bankruptcy (Massey, 2009). It was estimated that a total of 300,000 jobs were at risk across the EU, in Germany, Belgium, Great Britain, Poland, Spain and Sweden. Under EU rules, state aid might be permitted if the company is in danger of going out of business. However, other European automobile manufacturers might consider that if aid were provided then it would amount to unfair practice and a distortion of free competition.

8.8 Intellectual property rights (IPR)

Another area of law that concerns businesses is that of the protection of *intellectual property* (IP). The benefit of IP protection is that it encourages innovation and entrepreneurship which are both important features of a growing economy: see also *Chapter 4*. If an invention is protected, the owner has the right to sue the infringer under civil law. It is for this reason that companies prefer to trade in regions that provide stringent enforcement of IPR. Intellectual property rights oversee a number of different areas of the business, including trademarks, copyrights, design registration, licensing, patents, etc.

The purpose of a trademark is that it provides instant recognition of the origin, design and quality of the product. Trademarks are typically a word, phrase, company logo or brand, and, like patents, they should ideally be registered in order to be protected. One of the oldest trademarks is Stella Artois which has reportedly been in use since 1366. This example demonstrates a characteristic of trademarks in that they do not expire so long as they remain in use. Trademarks can be recognised by the suffix ™ when they are unregistered, or ® when they have been formally registered. Many large organisations such as Microsoft have registered many hundreds of trademarks, such as the original MS-DOS® (operating system), Calibri® (font name), Brute Force® (video game), Excel® (spreadsheet) and the Xbox® (gaming system). Trademarks are often rigorously defended, as was the case in June 2009 when Psion successfully defended its trademark rights over Intel's use of the word 'NetBook®' (Meyer, 2009).

Legislation in this area has had to be adapted in order to protect trademark use and regulation on the internet. This was partly in response to 'cyber-squatting', 'land grabbing' or 'domain name parking'. This practice occurred in the 1990s when familiar web names were purchased with the intention of either selling them on at profit, or alternatively making financial gains from misdirected pay-per-click advertising. Recent legislation has meant that large companies have been able to sue over infringements of trademarks in order to protect the continuity of their web content. Previous 'cyber-squatted' domain names such as www.kodak.ru and www.bbcnews.com have been successfully defended by the parent corporations (Lynn, 2009). Following this ruling you might like to see what happens when you attempt to connect to these sites.

Copyrights differ from trademarks as they automatically apply to most forms of literary, artistic and musical works across all forms of media, and can be recognised by the symbol ©. One of the oldest copyrights might be the tune 'happy birthday to you' which was composed in 1859 and copyrighted in 1935. The copyright was due to expire in 2010, 75 years after registration, but it has now been extended until 2035 by the owners AOL Time Warner. Music copyright is currently in the news as the music industry is struggling to keep up with the rapidly changing world of file sharing, through both illegal and legal means. Napster was one of the first, and certainly the most high profile, internet sites which offered free peer–peer copying of music. However, in 2007 they lost a seven-year battle for copyright infringement brought by the large record labels (Kravets, 2007). European sound recordings are currently protected by copyright for 50 years, which means many of the original recordings by, for example, Elvis Presley, the Rolling Stones and the early Beatles albums are due to expire. In order to combat the loss of income the record companies are pushing for an extension of the copyright term, beyond the current 50 years. The music and lyrics, rather than the recording, is protected for 70 years after the songwriter's death. Many industry watchers feel that it is time for the songwriters and composers to make some direct financial returns. The BBC provides some useful information on how to ensure that you can prove copyright ownership which, among other things, involves posting the new material to yourself by recorded delivery. (BBC, 2009b).

In the UK, businesses can also protect a new product design by registering the design for a maximum of 25 years. This is a simple and inexpensive process but one that is not much more robust than that of the automatic copyright of design drawings. However, should the company wish to license its design to other companies it may make the licensing process easier.

Unlike trademarks and copyrights, patents must be formally registered and are thereafter typically protected from copying for a period of 20 years. Patents may then be renewed for shorter periods of time but this tends to be a very expensive process and may require a modification to the invention. Copying a product is, of course, made easier once the patent design is registered and published. Despite the legal protection of a patent it is quite often only a matter of time before a competitor either finds a legal way around the patent, or sells counterfeit products in parts of the world that are not covered by the patent or where patent enforcement is weak. To get around this problem some organisations license the IP to other companies in order to maximise their returns in as short a time as possible. *Minicase 8.4* provides more detail on the mechanism and issues behind the patenting of pharmaceuticals. Examples of patent infringement are also described in the *Minicase 8.5*.

Traditionally, patents have been the preserve of national legislation; however, the registration of international patents across many countries has been made simpler since 1980 when the European Patent Office started granting patents which can now cover as many as 38 countries. Nevertheless, there are still significant differences between the European Patent

Minicase 8.4 — Patenting pharmaceutical products

The pharmaceutical industry is particularly keen to optimise patent life, as the cost of drug development can run to hundreds of millions of dollars and take 8–10 years. As the patent is applied for early on in the drug development process, often 5–8 years of the patent life has already expired before the drug is marketed. In order to overcome this limitation, pharmaceutical companies are keen to quickly license the manufacture and marketing of the drug around the world, to maximise their returns in as short a time as possible. At the same time the pharmaceutical industry spends vast amounts of money defending its patents from counterfeit products and illegal generic substitutes which are commonly sold through the internet.

Generic drugs are licensed drugs that are marketed without their original brand name. They are generally less expensive than brand-name drugs, they are chemically identical and meet the same regulatory standards demanded by the FDA (US Food and Drug Administration) and other regulatory bodies for safety, purity and effectiveness. Generic drugs can be authorised and licensed by the original patent holder or unauthorised and manufactured by a competitive company.

Pharmaceutical companies spend significant resources in changing the purpose (use), chemical structure or formulation of the drug with the aim of being granted a patent extension, a process that is called ever-greening. The expiration of a patent removes the monopoly of the patent holder on drug sales and it is particularly at this time that generic manufacturers enter the market. For example, Valium is the brand name of a tranquiliser or sedative that was first patented by Roche in 1981. Since the expiry of its patent in 2002, it has been marketed by many other companies, often at significantly reduced prices, under its generic name Diazepam. Roche has since ceased to manufacture and market the product as it sees little profit in the generic market.

Questions

1 Why do you think that generic pharmaceutical manufacturers watch to see when patents are due to expire?
2 Is it possible for generic companies to apply for a patent on their generic drugs? If not, why not?

Office and, for example, the USA Patent and Trademark Office in the way patents are applied for and what is considered patentable. Some of these differences are highlighted in *Table 8.4*.

Table 8.4 — Major differences between US and EU patent laws

US patents	EU patents
Protection in the whole territory of the USA	Protection across 38 European countries
Patent office will investigate logbooks, publications, prototypes and other evidence before making a decision as to who invented it first	The first to file and be awarded a successful patent is considered the inventor
The inventor has a one-year grace period after making the invention known before a patent must be applied for	Patents will not be granted if the information was first made public or disclosed to another person without a non-disclosure agreement
Requires the inventor to include details on the best way to use the invention	A means of use must be stated but this may not be the best way to use the invention
Computer software and business processes can be patented	These are only patentable if they have a 'technical effect' (i.e. a company can patent an operating system but not a game – this will be protected by copyright)

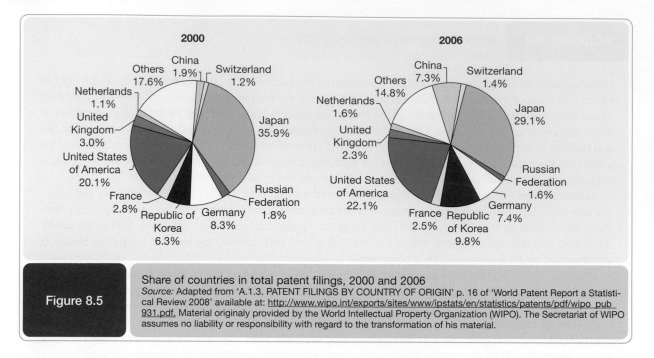

Figure 8.5

Share of countries in total patent filings, 2000 and 2006
Source: Adapted from 'A.1.3. PATENT FILINGS BY COUNTRY OF ORIGIN' p. 16 of 'World Patent Report a Statistical Review 2008' available at: http://www.wipo.int/exports/sites/www/ipstats/en/statistics/patents/pdf/wipo_pub 931.pdf. Material originaly provided by the World Intellectual Property Organization (WIPO). The Secretariat of WIPO assumes no liability or responsibility with regard to the transformation of his material.

To try to overcome these differences there have been encouraging attempts to standardise patent protection and simplify the patent application process across a broader range of countries. Following on from the 1970 Patent Co-operation Treaty (PCT), the World Intellectual Property Organisation (WIPO) has worked as a specialised agency of the UN and, in 1996, entered into a co-operation agreement with the WTO. WIPO is now able to grant international patents in 141 countries from Afghanistan, Brazil and China to Zimbabwe. The applicants do not have to register in all member countries; they can stipulate which countries they wish for their patents to apply. In 2007 WIPO handled 158,400 international PCT patents, of which 33.6 percent were filed from the USA, with Japan filing the next largest number of patents accounting for 17.5 percent of the total (WIPO, 2008). *Figure 8.5* displays the patents filed through WIPO plus the patent filings in the country of residence. Note the decrease in total patent findings from Japan and the increase over the same six-year period of total patent filings from China and the Republic of Korea.

It is worth noting that a comparison of the number a patent submissions is often used as a crude mechanism to evaluate how innovative a country is. However, a comparison of this sort does not take into consideration the size or the litigious nature of the country, or the quality of the submitted patents. Also, when a patent is granted it does not always represent a technological or commercial breakthrough, so this form of comparison should be treated with some caution.

8.9 Employer relationships

There are many laws that govern the relationship between an employee and an employer and these include the following:

- contract law including termination of contract;
- health and safety and liability;
- anti-discrimination (gender, sexual orientation, race, disability, age);
- wrongful dismissal and redundancy;
- minimum wage;
- working time regulations (including holiday entitlement);

- sick pay entitlement;
- maternity/paternity leave;
- recognition of trade unions;
- employment of minors.

In Western democracies many of these laws are taken for granted, almost as a citizen's right. Indeed, in some social democracies, like Sweden, employment benefits such as those of paternal leave are more generous than those that are detailed in European legislation. Many organisations will also routinely exceed the legal minimal requirements in an effort to demonstrate their credentials as a socially responsible company. *Chapter 6* provides more information on corporate social responsibility. With the aim of ensuring that EU member states enforce European legislation, the EU will on occasion take nations to court. In 2006, the EC brought a case against the UK government in the European Court of Justice, after the UK had failed to enforce the EU daily and weekly rest rules (Eironline, 2006).

Not surprisingly, the employee and employer relationship is based on the contract of employment. In the UK changes in the law have enhanced the rights of employees. Employers can no longer selectively recruit and fire staff at will. Recruitment and dismissal must be demonstrated to be non-discriminatory by race, age, gender, disability, religion and sexual orientation. In the USA in 2005 there was widespread media coverage of a dispute at Dell Computers in Tennessee, when Somali Muslim shift workers were sacked after they sought to perform the Maghreb prayer each day after sunset. It was concluded that this case breached the US Civil Rights Act of 1964 which requires an employer to accommodate religious practices, unless it causes 'undue hardship'. The employees were reinstated and the mangers at the plant were given extra training on religious practices and employment law (Spooner, 2005).

Like the contract of sale, the contract of employment also states terms and conditions of the contractual arrangement. In the UK these conditions must fall within the national legislation guidelines found in the Working Time Regulations Act (1998). In the contract of service an employee should expect to see details of pay, sick pay, holiday, pension rights, length of notice to be given on termination (by both parties), a job description, a place of work, etc.

As with all contracts there must also be a level of goodwill between both the parties and so, while they may not be explicitly stated, under common law the employees are expected to undertake their work with reasonable care and obey reasonable orders. The emphasis here is on the word 'reasonable'. For instance, if a manager told an employee to falsify records and the employee refused, the employee will not be breaching his or her contract of employment. From the employer's perspective it must pay the employee on time (at a rate of the minimum wage or above), provide safe working conditions and implicitly must not undermine the employees' trust and confidence.

Despite having the appropriate legislation and being a signatory to the United Nations Convention on Child Rights, the laws are not always enforced. Of the many employment laws in India there is one specifically dealing with child labour, the Child Labour (Prohibition & Regulation) Act 1986. This states that children under the age of 14 are not permitted to work in mines, factories or other hazardous environments. According to Indian government statistics, India has 17 million child labourers, the highest number of child labourers in the world (Khattar, 2009). Some children are even forced to live at their workplace, in 'bonded labour', which is also illegal in India. The law is there but the resources to enforce it are not, a situation that the Indian government is very keen to rectify. Whether Western businesses choose to work with companies that are breaking national and international law may be down to their ethical stance, a topic that is discussed in *Chapter 6*.

8.9.1 Health and safety

The health and safety of all employees should be paramount to all employers regardless of the local criminal law legislation. However, this legislation is not solely the remit of the employer, the employee also takes some responsibility to ensure legislation is being followed.

In the UK, the Health and Safety at Work Act 1974 has been regularly updated and influenced by EU legislation. Although not a comprehensive list, health and safety legislation in the EU broadly applies to the following occupational issues and facilities:

- mechanical, electrical, construction, dangerous substance, noise pollution, gas and fire safety hazards;
- product safety, including food and drink;
- the lifting and moving of heavy goods;
- working at height and in confined spaces;
- stress in the workplace;
- the correct use of computer screens;
- appropriate and well-maintained tools and equipment;
- provision of first-aid facilities and documented emergency procedures;
- provision of protective clothing, hazard warning signs and appropriate training.

In the UK preventable accidents which lead to stress, physical injury or death are referred to the Health and Safety Executive (HSE). The HSE will investigate to ensure that the correct procedures have been followed, for example, by checking that work has undergone an appropriate risk assessment and that the subsequent health and safety plan has been implemented. If the guidelines have not been followed and a preventable accident occurs, the company may be fined, or, in the circumstances of corporate manslaughter, the directors could be imprisoned. In June 2009 PFG Plant Hire in Omagh was charged with not completing an adequate risk assessment and was fined £30,000. This related to a fatal accident in January 2008 when an employee died after a wall he was demolishing collapsed upon him. After the verdict a spokesperson for the Health and Safety Executive in Northern Ireland said, 'It is vital that all companies properly identify and address hazards within the workplace and implement systems to minimise and control risks' (BBC, 2009c).

Health and safety legislation can also be applied to cases where poor internal practices endanger the public. In 2007, Cadbury Schweppes was taken to court over a salmonella outbreak, during which it had to recall 1 million chocolate bars. A leaking pipe was the cause of the incident. After pleading guilty, the company was fined £1 million under health and safety legislation (Herman and Jordan, 2007). Cadbury Schweppes was found liable for placing unsafe goods on the market, inadequate testing during the manufacturing process and for the delay in notifying the authorities of the outbreak. Counterfeit medicines and toys can also lead to a breach of health and safety legislation, as is described in *Minicase 8.5*.

8.10 International law

International law can be sub-divided into two areas:

- nationally legislated laws affecting international business;
- international laws which are agreed by nation states through international organisations.

8.10.1 Nationally legislated laws affecting international business

Laws are sometimes implemented in order to limit trade and put pressure on rogue states, oppressive regimes or those with nuclear ambitions. These laws are usually politically motivated and may also be driven by foreign policy and military objectives. They include:

- sanctions and embargoes;
- extraterritoriality;
- constraints on foreign ownership;
- nationalisation, expropriation and confiscation.

Minicase 8.5	The dangers of counterfeiting

While globalisation and the lowering of trade barriers are generally considered to be good things, these have also created new opportunities for illegal trade. According to the EC (European Commission, 2008) the sale of some counterfeit goods is now more profitable than that of drug trafficking. The bogus product is produced on an industrial scale, with false papers and changed origins implying that the pirated goods are authentic.

The counterfeiting of goods is a multifaceted issue. Not only does it create a black market where consumer protection and taxation do not apply, it also undermines the intellectual property rights and the profitability of legitimate businesses. A recent EC report (European Commission, 2008) claims that counterfeiting is an increasing problem for Europe, with the majority (60 percent) of all the counterfeit products coming from China.

Counterfeit seizures of medicines in the EU increased by 50 percent in one year (2006–2007) with fake drugs coming in from Switzerland (40 percent), India (35 percent) and the UAE (15 percent). In one case customs officials in the EU seized counterfeit 'heart medication' which consisted of a mixture of brick dust and yellow paint coated in varnish (European Commission, 2008). The risks of counterfeiting drugs are not just financial, the counterfeiters may also put lives at risk. The WHO claims that in some countries fake medicine may account for 30 to 50 percent of pharmaceutical sales. This has led to a number of disasters, for instance in Niger fake meningitis vaccines killed 2,500 people, fake cough syrup killed 89 people in Haiti and fake anti-malarial tablets killed 30 in Cambodia (WHO, 2006).

Counterfeit toys are also a major health and safety issue due to inflammability, mechanical and electrical safety, toxicity, sharp edges and small parts which can be swallowed by children. In 2007 millions of Chinese-made toys were recalled by the EU and the USA following health and safety concerns. Most notably 1.5 million wooden toy trains were recalled as they had been decorated with paint containing lead (Lipton and Barboza, 2007).

There is, however, evidence that China is trying to stop the production of counterfeit products. In 2006 China held up several high-profile examples where it had successfully prosecuted Chinese companies that had been infringing intellectual property (IP) laws. One case was that of the *Sony Corporation* vs. *Guangzhou Top Power Electronics*. Guangzhou Top Power Electronics was found to be manufacturing counterfeit Sony camcorder batteries. The Guangzhou Intermediate People's Court ordered Top Power Electronics to cease infringement of the Sony trademark and patents rights and ordered stocks and moulds to be destroyed. Sony was awarded 600,000 yuan (approx. 62,000 euros) in compensation (Lawfuel, 2007).

Questions

1 Why is counterfeiting so harmful to:
   a) other legal business?
   b) the consumer?
   c) the economy?
2 What additional measures can be taken to protect against counterfeit goods?

8.10.2 Sanctions

Sanctions are restrictions in trade with a specific country. They may include the restriction of or the withdrawal of trade deals. This can be achieved:

- by increasing tariffs;
- by boycotting goods from the country;
- by banning imports;
- through the cancellation of technology transfer arrangements.

A sanction may be unilateral, with just a single country participating, or multilateral, with several participating countries. The UN and other regional bodies, such as the EU, have the power to stipulate multilateral sanctions against trade with specified countries. The Ivory Coast (officially Republic of Côte d'Ivoire), currently has UN sanctions applied against all forms of diamond trade. This follows decades of violence and human rights violations, funded in part from the illegal sale of 'conflict diamonds'. The UN has made it clear that these sanctions will be reviewed once the country holds a free presidential election.

The EU also applies sanctions 'on behalf' of its members: Myanmar (Burma) has had EU trade sanctions applied against it since 2006. These will be in place until democratic progress has been made, which includes the freeing of the political prisoners, such as the opposition leader Aung Suu Kyi, who has spent 13 of the last 19 years under house arrest (CNN, 2009). EU sanctions against Burma include a travel ban on the country's top officials, a trade ban on timber, metals and precious stones, an arms embargo and a freeze of Burmese assets in Europe.

8.10.3 Embargos

An embargo is a complete ban against all trade with a specified country. Since February 1962, following the 1959 revolution when Fidel Castro seized power in Cuba, the USA has had a unilateral trade embargo against Cuba. It was originally imposed in response to Castro's forced nationalisation of American-owned companies. The intention was to deprive Cuba of foreign currency and bring down the Communist regime. The embargo was further strengthened in 1996 by new laws which punished US companies that traded with Cuba. However, in March 2009, USA President Barack Obama eased some sanctions by allowing Cuban-Americans to travel to the island once a year and to send money, food and medicines to relatives there (Carroll, 2009). However, it has been made clear by President Obama that the remaining trade embargo will stay in place until democratic elections are held in Cuba.

Sanctions and embargoes are often ignored by countries and businesses that are looking to show solidarity with the country concerned, or by those wishing to make the most of a business opportunity. Countries such as China, South Africa and Russia are often accused of breaking embargoes, for instance the arms embargo against the Democratic Republic of Congo (BBC, 2006). Embargoes come with a predefined list of what is and is not permitted. However, some items for export may have a dual purpose, one legal and the other illegal, and it is this loophole that is often used to circumvent the embargo. In June 2009 three men were jailed in the UK after buying military parts on eBay for fighter jets in Iran. They denied that they were breaking the UK arms trading embargo, claiming that the equipment was to be used in the Iranian health sector as ambulance breathing apparatus (BBC, 2009d).

8.10.4 Extraterritoriality

Countries also attempt to control legal activities outside their own national border. This practice is called *extraterritoriality* – the exemption from national legal jurisdiction. It provides a mechanism where the state is exempt from local law and is commonly applied to foreign diplomats and civil ships in foreign waters. In the reverse situation, extraterritoriality can also be applied to citizens when they have committed a crime overseas. In 2005 an Afghan warlord was convicted in the UK and jailed for 20 years after being found guilty of kidnap and torture in his own country (BBC, 2005). Faryadi Zardad had been found working in a pizza restaurant in London.

Extraterritoriality can sometimes be used as a means to abdicate responsibility for the rule of law, as is the case for the US naval base of Guantanamo Bay in eastern Cuba. From 2002 the base was used to house suspected terrorists from Afghanistan and Iraq. The US government initially claimed that the detainees had no legal rights as the base was not subject to US law as it was outside its jurisdiction. Additionally, as 'unlawful combatants', the USA stated that the prisoners were not entitled to protection under the Geneva Convention.

However, in 2004, a US Supreme Court ruled that, despite the base being in Cuba, it was entirely controlled by the USA and therefore the detainees were subject to a defence under the Fifth Amendment. In January 2009, President Obama signalled his intent to close the camp and release or transfer the prisoners elsewhere (Goldenberg, 2009).

Businesses are also obliged to fulfil local contractual obligations even when their customers are overseas. In October 2007 the British House of Lords ruled that credit card companies were still required to insure and refund their customers should they purchase goods or services that are undelivered, damaged or otherwise misrepresented. Tesco Personal Finance and Lloyd's TSB had been appealing against the decision of a previous appeals court that the insurance-backed guarantee should only apply to UK purchases. However, the Law Lords said that under the 1974 Consumer Credit Act, there was no territorial limitation that excluded foreign purchases and that the standard insurance protection should also be offered on foreign transactions (BBC, 2007).

Extraterritoriality is increasingly common in international trade, as countries often lack confidence in other nations to regulate business with appropriate law, especially in areas such as taxation, competition laws (e.g. cartels), security, organised crime, corporate governance and data protection. Extraterritoriality causes additional complications for international businesses that already have to negotiate complex and often conflicting legal systems in different countries. For this reason organisations such as the International Chamber of Commerce (ICC) are encouraging nation states to harmonise national laws and to recognise equivalent standards.

Concerns around the world are frequently raised over foreign companies controlling key domestic industries. In order to counter this, many governments have placed constraints on the levels of foreign ownership, or *foreign direct investment* (FDI) as it is also known. This is achieved in one of four ways, as illustrated in *Figure 8.6*.

Limits to foreign ownership can be found in most countries and industries: for instance most European and North American airlines, newspaper ownership in Canada and the telecommunications industry in Japan restrict FDI. Total bans of foreign ownership in

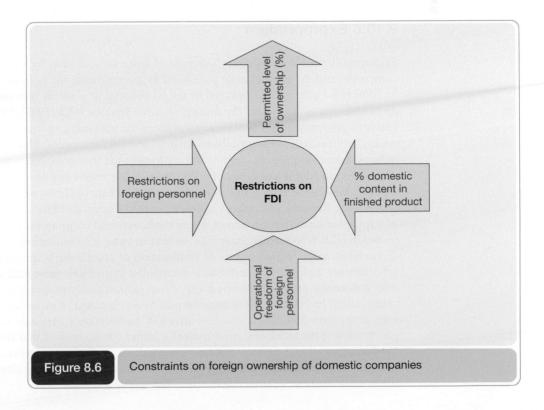

| Figure 8.6 | Constraints on foreign ownership of domestic companies |

domestic industries are effectively state monopolies and these include critical industries such as the fishing and energy sectors in Iceland and the oil industry in Mexico. The UK is one of the least restricted countries in the world with significant foreign ownership in power generation, utilities, media and telecommunications. Multinational companies have to consider the consequences of limited foreign investment. Even if major ownership is not part of their long-term strategy, circumstances might change which could frustrate their ownership ambitions in the future.

Nation states have the right to decide on their own macro economic policy agenda. The degree of public ownership (whether foreign or domestic) is often the result of the political leanings of the government. Major industries are more likely to be state or publicly owned under socialist or communist governments, whereas capitalist governments will be more in favour of free market trading. Under free market systems even key utilities, such as electricity generation are privately owned perhaps even by foreign companies. The process of taking a business from private to public ownership is called *nationalisation*. Expropriation and confiscation are types of compulsory nationalisation.

8.10.5 Nationalisation

Nationalisation is the transfer of ownership from the private to the public sector. Large industries such as mining, energy, water, steel, chemicals, oil production, etc. are often targets for nationalisation on the basis that the industries are key to the economy, and that they are a useful source of income. However, nationalisation is not just the preserve of socialist states, it also occurs in more free market economies. Recent nationalised companies include the financial institutions AIG, Northern Rock and Hypo Real Estate by the US, UK and German governments respectively. All these companies are now majority owned by their governments and in these instances it is not because of political ideology, but in order to save a wider financial collapse and national panic following the economic crisis of 2008.

8.10.6 Expropriation

Expropriation is the compulsory purchase of a private company by a government. Foreign companies may be compulsorily purchased by governments for political or financial ends. In 2005 H.J. Heinz was encouraged to sell its processing plant in Venezuela to the government after troops had seized the disused factory (*Business Week*, 2005). Since then President Chávez's government has continued to expropriate national and foreign industries such as energy, utilities, telecommunications, cement and oil companies. This trend towards compulsory nationalisation, in conjunction with steep tax increases, has persuaded companies such as Exxon Mobil and ConocoPhillips to leave Venezuela and to seek international arbitration. Venezuela is not the only country that expropriates private companies; the Democratic Republic of Congo, Guinea, Ecuador, Mexico and Zimbabwe all have a history of expropriation. The concern of many multinational companies is that the worldwide recession is likely to further encourage nationalism and nationalisation.

Fortunately the blatant seizure or confiscation of companies is uncommon. Even if governments are inclined to compulsorily nationalise businesses, most tend to take ownership with at least the pretence of some form of negotiation and expropriation rather than direct confiscation. In 2000 the Mexican government was accused of expropriation against a foreign company: Metalclad who had invested heavily in a Mexican waste facility. The government introduced new environmental buffer zones, insisted that the company had to fund local social and medical welfare systems, declared the area a protected environmental zone and finally refused permission for its use as a landfill (DePalma, 2000). In summary, it made what was once a promising business financially unviable.

8.11 International laws and treaties

The chapter now turns its attention to international laws which are agreed by nation states through international organisations such as the UN. It is important to recognise that, unlike nation states, in the international arena there is no legislature, written constitution or international court to which countries are legally bound to submit.

National disputes can, however, be voluntarily submitted to the International Court of Justice (ICJ), which is based in The Hague under the jurisdiction of the UN. Countries are encouraged to take this route in order for international disputes to be resolved in a non-confrontational and peaceful manner. The ICJ is composed of 15 judges who have been elected by the UN General Assembly and the Security Council each for a maximum period of nine years. The ICJ has been asked to arbitrate on a wide variety of national disagreements, ranging from navigational rights between Nicaragua and Costa Rica, to passing judgment over Georgian charges of racial discrimination against the Russian Federation following the attacks and ethnic expulsion of Georgians in the region of South Ossetia (ICJ, 2009).

As there are no predefined forms of international law, the ICJ derives its legislation from the sources listed in *Table 8.5*.

8.11.1 International conventions

An international convention is the signed agreement between several and often many nation states that establishes a relationship governed by international law. Many conventions are subsequently registered with the UN in order that they can be regarded as a binding treaty. The principle of treaties was developed by the International Law Commission over a 20-year period. In 1980 it resulted in the Vienna Convention on the Law of Treaties (VCLT) which details the essential elements of international treaty law and has since been ratified by 109 states. Treaties come in two forms, either bi-partite as between two nations or multi-partite between several nations. *Table 8.6* lists some of the important administrative areas for international treaties. They have been categorised as having either external or internal jurisdictions and are reviewed in this chapter. A full list of UN treaties can be found on the UN Treaty Collection web page (UNTC, 2009).

Territory is definable as the area that a nation state regards as its own and exercises sovereignty over. This includes all water, subsoil, the airspace, the territorial sea and land under the territorial sea. Conquest is the taking of territory by military force; however, the use of force is

Table 8.5	Sources of legislation for the ICJ	

Legal sources	Examples of other influences
International Conventions and Treaties	Equity and fairness
International Custom (generally accepted legal practice)	Other international organisations such as:
The decisions of highly qualified layers of different nations, e.g. the International Law Commission	The Council of Europe
	The European Union
	The African Union
	The Organisation of American states

Source: ICJ (2009)

Table 8.6	Key areas of international legislation

External responsibilities	Internal responsibilities
Territory, conquest and the use of force	Treatment of foreign nationals
The law and the sea	Environmental protection
	Human rights
	Terrorism and security
	Data protection

no longer legal under international law as stipulated in a series of UN charters, such as the 1970 Declaration of Principles of International Law. The UN has ruled that the Israeli invasion of Palestine in 1967 and the Iraqi invasion of Kuwait in 1990 have both involved the forceful taking of territory and were condemned as illegal by the UN Security Council at the time.

Disputes over territory in the Polar Regions have been common for many years, with Denmark, Norway, the Russian Federation and Canada making claims on the Artic and the USA, Argentina, Chile, France, Australia, Norway, the UK and New Zealand, claiming territorial rights in Antarctica. However, two main treaties, the Antarctic Treaty of 1961 and the 1991 Madrid Protocol on Environmental Protection, have designated the region for peaceful and scientific purposes, and prohibit all military incursions and activities relating to mineral resources until the year 2041. Dispute settlements in this area must be referred to the ICJ.

These conventions were primarily defined in 1982 with the Convention on the Law of the Sea which details the responsibilities of the nation state to:

- a territorial sea limit of 12 nautical miles;
- a delineation of territorial sea between adjacent states (for example, the Anglo-French division of the Straits of Dover);
- a peaceful passage through territorial waters;
- 'freedoms of' high seas (non-territorial);
- deep sea mining;
- nuclear testing
- confirmed nationality of ships; and
- the protection of the marine environment.

During 2008 the Laws of the Sea were a regular feature in news articles, highlighting acts of piracy in the Gulf of Aden and the Indian Ocean. Somali pirates held ships and crews for ransom until they were paid by the ship owners. It is estimated that in 2008 the owners of the hijacked ships handed over about $80 million in ransom payments (BBC, 2009e). Piracy is specifically covered in the Laws of the Sea and dictates that nation states may seize pirate ships and arrest the persons on board. This has lead to several nations sending their warships to patrol the area and capture pirate ships in the region.

State responsibility is the requirement of one state to another to observe international law. Hence if one nation state or one of its officials breaks an international law, the state may be liable. These laws also cover the treatment of foreign citizens in that they should be treated in a civilised manner and their human rights should be respected. For instance, the Organization of American States, the EU and the Organisation of African Unity have agreed on common criteria to be applied to refugees and asylum seekers.

Nation states have a responsibility for the environment both in their own territory and that affecting the neighbouring territory, and in recent years regulation in this area has increased dramatically. The Rio Declaration on the Environment (1992) declares that nation states must implement policies which protect and enhance the natural environment. One of the most notable agreements in this area is the Kyoto Protocol which came into force in 2005. Under this agreement, developed nation states are required to reduce their greenhouse gas emissions according to individual targets (UNFCC, 2009). Environmental issues are discussed more fully in *Chapter 6*.

Since the advent of global sourcing, living and working conditions, health and education have become international issues. Together they can be categorised under the title of human rights. A number of international human rights treaties have been adopted since the signing of the United Nations Universal Declaration of Human Rights in1948. Unfortunately the UN Declaration of Human Rights was only a resolution, so while the content was well-meaning it was not legally binding. However all the declarations, principles, guidelines, rules and recommendations produced by the UN do at least provide moral guidance to nation states. They also serve as a blueprint for regional (e.g. EU) and national legislation, and provide a comprehensive body of legislation to protect individual and group human rights. The human rights covenants, statutes, protocols and conventions are, however, legally binding for those nations that ratify them. Nevertheless, putting the principles into practice is not always easy; developing countries, for instance, often have other pressing priorities such as sustaining food supplies and encouraging economic growth. Some of the key human rights UN treaties are listed in *Table 8.7*.

Another important legacy of the Declaration of Human Rights (1948) was the creation in Strasbourg of the European Court of Human Rights. Over the past 50 years this court has heard over 10,000 cases. Its rulings have been binding on the member states and have

Table 8.7	Major UN human rights treaties and instruments

Core international human rights treaties and instruments

Racial discrimination

Political and civil rights

Rights for economic social and cultural reasons

Rights against cruel treatment, punishment and torture

Rights against discrimination of women

Rights of the child

Rights of migrant workers

Rights of persons with disabilities

Rights of protection against enforced disappearance

Right of self-determination

Rights of indigenous peoples and minorities

Rights of older people

Rights in the administration of justice

Right to health

Fair condition of employment

Freedom of association

War crimes and crimes against humanity

Rights of migrants and refugees

Source: UN (2009)

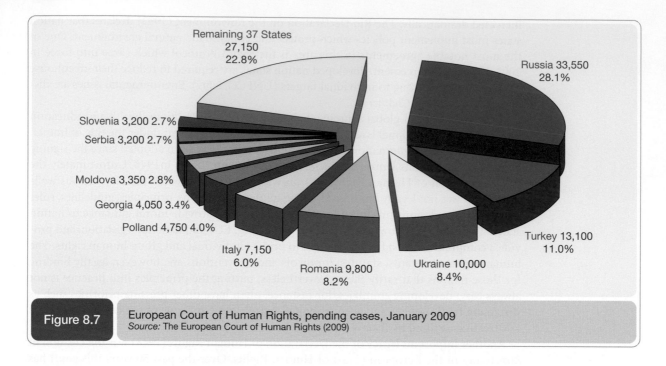

Figure 8.7	European Court of Human Rights, pending cases, January 2009
	Source: The European Court of Human Rights (2009)

resulted in many changes in legislation. In January 2009, there were more than 97,000 cases pending, more than half of these cited Russia, Turkey and Romania: see *Figure 8.7*. Most of the violations related to complaints on the fairness or the length of legal proceedings in the host country; 64 per cent of violations were concerning a right to a fair trial and the protection of property, and approximately 8 per cent concern the right to life or the prohibition of torture and inhuman or degrading treatment (The European Court of Human Rights, 2009). The cases range from the torture of an opposition leader in Azerbaijan (2007), to the compulsory isolation of an HIV-infected person in Sweden (2005). The UK is often indicted, for example in the case of a prohibition on marriage between father-in-law and daughter-in-law while their former spouses were still alive (2005). All these instances have violated the terms of the human rights Acts.

Currently, within the UN there is no equivalent court to that of the European Court of Human Rights, although a 'world court of human rights' that would try cases against member states and multinational corporations is often called for.

Unfortunately, despite the regulations and courts judgments, serious human rights violations still commonly occur. The death penalty is prohibited for juveniles under international treaty and in most national legislatures; the USA for example banned the execution of juveniles in 2005. However, since January 2005, five countries–Iran, Saudi Arabia, Sudan, Pakistan and Yemen – have confirmed that they have executed juvenile offenders. Iran has executed more juveniles than any other nation and, according to human rights lawyers in Iran, there are at least 130 juveniles on death row. For some offences, in Iran, the death penalty can be imposed on girls as young as 9 and boys from the age of 15, but the minimal age can also be determined by the court's judgment on when the child has reached puberty (Human Rights Watch, 2009).

Businesses can also come under scrutiny when it comes to human rights legislation. In May 2008 Google was under shareholder pressure to justify why it had submitted to pressure from the Chinese government to censor areas of the search engine in China (Google.cn). Pressure groups such as Amnesty International claim that censorship restricts freedom of information and therefore impacts on human rights. Pressure groups have called on Google to at least notify users that the content has been restricted due to legal pressure from the government. Google argued that it was better to comply with the Chinese government legislation and provide a somewhat restricted service to the Chinese population than to provide no form of service at all. It is unclear if this form of censorship is illegal under the terms of human rights legislation or if it is more of an ethical issue. However, Google became increasingly concerned by events in China and, in early 2010, was considering revising its position and withdrawing from the Chinese market. See *Chapter 6* for more on business ethics.

8.12 Terrorism and security

Increasing cross-border terrorism has resulted in a rush of new national and international legislation in the areas such as intelligence sharing, illicit weapons trading, nuclear proliferation, money laundering, etc. As an example see *Minicase 8.6* on money laundering. Global security is also controlled through arms treaties and the Nuclear Non-Proliferation Treaty (1970). Since it came into force it has been ratified by 189 nations, including those that possess nuclear weapons, the USA, UK, France, China and Russia. All the signatory nations support disarmament, non-proliferation and the use of nuclear energy for peaceful means only. However, despite international pressure from non-nuclear nations, the nuclear countries still have substantial nuclear arsenals. It is estimated that Russia and the USA still own 23,000 active

Minicase 8.6	Money laundering

Money laundering is the means by which criminals conceal from investigators the source and original ownership of funds that are generated from illegal activities. The criminal intent is to convert income whether it is from embezzlement, fraud, bank robbery, smuggling or the drug trade into 'legitimate funds'.

Money can often be made to 'disappear' through, for example, the Caribbean and Pacific islands which have strict privacy laws and less than transparent banking systems. The Pacific island of Nauru, for instance, has 400 registered banks, despite only having a population of a few thousand citizens, and is widely considered to be the money laundering route of choice for the Russian mafia (BBC, 2001).

Tracking illegal funds can be a likened to looking for a 'needle in a haystack'. With millions of electronic transactions every day the investigators rely on 'tip-offs' from financial institutions whenever there is a suspicious transaction. Investigating only major transactions encourages the criminals to move money around in smaller amounts. The funding of terrorist activities is particularly difficult to trace: the sums used are often very small, e.g. $50,000, and are relatively easy to hide within legitimate business transactions. There are also suspicions that some charities might be used as fronts for money laundering. For example, in May 2009 the two founders of a Dallas-based Islamic 'charity' were given 65-year prison sentences after they were found guilty of illegally funneling $12.4 million to the Palestinian militant group Hamas. The 'charity' was claiming to be providing legitimate disaster relief aid to Palestinian refugees (Reuters, 2009).

If it is difficult to trace illegal funds through Western financial systems, it is harder still to trace laundered money through informal money transfer networks, such as those in the Middle East, India, Pakistan, Afghanistan and China. Many of these systems are hundreds of years old and are also used for legitimate purposes. Fortunately for the criminals, records are often not held and money is transferred by the use of tokens or passwords, with financial transactions being made predominantly based on trust.

Questions

1 Why is it so important that money laundering is stopped?
2 What actions can governments implement in order to make it easier to trace illegal funds?

warheads, sufficient to destroy the world many times over (BBC, 2009f). Nevertheless these same countries put pressure on nations such as India, Pakistan and North Korea who openly test their nuclear weapons and who are not signatories to the treaty.

8.12.1 Legal risks

Multinational companies are exposed to a wide range of potentially damaging risks as they trade in many different countries. The main risks can be categorised as legal, cultural or political and economic. The main legal risks are listed below:

- a general respect for the rule of law;
- level of enforcement, e.g. of intellectual property;
- contract enforceability;
- degree of corruption;
- impartial legal systems;
- efficiency of legal systems;
- transparency and governance;
- liability for sub-contractors.

Legal risks may be based on the differences in legislature, the way that the legal system works, the relative lack of legal enforcement, corruption and the lengthy delays and bureaucracy of the legal system. India is renowned for its corrupt officials and the backlog of untried cases which, according to the Chief Justice, at the current rate could take 466 years to clear. The UN development programme estimates that there are 20 million cases waiting to be heard in India, 646 of these are over 20 years old (Associated Press, 2009). The legal system in Japan does not have these problems and the legislature is broadly similar to European countries as it is based on the civil code of Germany and France. However, unlike these countries, Japan, prior to May 2009, did not even conduct severe crimes by jury (*Taipei Times,* 2009). Also in Japan, negligence cases are also more likely to be tried under the criminal system, even though a Western company might consider the circumstances to be relatively minor. Japanese contracts also tend to be light on detail, relying instead on the honesty of their business partners. However, when contracts are used, most of the terms and conditions should be familiar to European companies.

Corruption is a serious issue, particularly in many less developed countries. It causes problems to business by circumventing the legal processes and tends to protect the wealthy and powerful rather than the deserving. It may also slow down or subvert legal cases, making them too time-consuming and costly to administer. From a competitive perspective it may produce an unbalanced competitive market with bribes being paid for the award of contracts or the preferential distribution of goods. *Table 7.3* in *Chapter 7* is an extract from the corruption perceptions index which is annually published by Perceptions International, and provides a perspective on the relative levels of corruption in countries around the world (Transparency International, 2009).

Some risks, such as those connected with politics and currency, are outside the control of the company. Civil unrest, curfews, currency crises, terrorism, expropriation or confiscation of assets can also lead to unmanageable risk and significant financial loss. For those that require it, businesses can insure against specific political risks. For example, Western oil companies based in Nigeria may request insurance cover against acts of terrorism on their pipelines. As with all forms of insurance, the bigger the risk the larger the premium will be.

8.12.2 International dispute resolution

Disputes between transnational businesses cannot always be resolved in a national court. So when an international business dispute occurs, the complexity of the different jurisdictions and types of law make the legal process a difficult one to manage. As a starting point towards a resolution, the answers to the following five questions have to be agreed, some possible alternatives have also been listed:

1 Which countries' law should be used?
   a. The domestic law of one of the companies
   b. A country neutral to both parties
2 In which country (forum) should the hearing be resolved?
   a. The home country of one of the companies
   b. A country neutral to both parties
3 Which system should be used to resolve the dispute?
   a. Negotiation
   b. Mediation
   c. Arbitration
   d. Litigation
4 Will both parties be bound by the resolution?
5 How shall it be enforced?

Fortunately, in anticipation of possible disputes, most of these details are already agreed and stipulated in the terms and conditions of the contract. However if a company has not specified a choice of law to resolve disputes, then under the 1980 Rome Convention on the law applicable to contracts, the contract is governed by the law of the nation that is most closely connected to the company that is implementing the contract. In this chapter's opening *Minicase 8.1* (The Danone–Wahaha feud), the JVs were all based and managed in China, therefore Chinese laws mainly applied to the dispute resolution. The outcomes of this decision are important to international businesses, as different national jurisdictions will apply a more or less favourable history of litigation with larger or smaller compensation rulings. For instance, US law typically awards higher settlements in product defect cases than courts in European countries.

Expensive, time-consuming and potentially embarrassing litigation through the courts is only one mechanism to achieve a resolution to a business dispute. Many international business disputes are actually settled without litigation and outside of a court of law. Mediation or arbitration are the alternative means to achieve a resolution. Mediation is a simple and relatively informal process where a neutral mediator supervises the process, provides advice and works with both parties to find agreement. It is important to note that the mediator is a facilitator in this process rather than a judge. Under arbitration, however, the process is more akin to an informal court case where an arbiter acts as a judge, or 'neutral' as they are known. The lawyers for each side present their arguments and the neutral proposes a solution to resolve the dispute. This judgment can be legally binding if the parties have agreed this in advance, but even non-binding arbitration can often provide a means towards constructive negotiation.

There are a numerous organisations that are willing to act as arbiters in order to resolve business disputes. These include the International Center for the Settlement of Investment Disputes (ICSID), which is a part of the World Bank in Washington, and the Paris-based International Chamber of Commerce (ICC), which provides international dispute resolution services to over 500 businesses a year. Dispute resolution may be managed through the ICC's Amicable Dispute Resolution (ADR) service, dispute boards or the International Court of Arbitration.

In the Danone–Wahaha opening case, the Stockholm Chamber of Commerce arbitration service was stipulated in the contract and is being used to resolve the long-running dispute.

8.13 Conclusion

Businesses are increasingly interconnected by international trade which is regulated by national, regional and international laws and treaties. International businesses need to be aware of the differences between legislatures and other risks of conducting businesses overseas. When international disputes occur between companies, it is prudent to stipulate in a contract the arbitration services and the forms of law which are going to be used, so that a resolution may be achieved as soon as possible. Most disputes are the result of poor initial communication or unrealistic expectations. Businesses that are based on long-term partnerships are built upon trust and are the least likely to require legal intervention.

Summary of main points

In this chapter we have identified some of the issues in the legal environment that are important to countries, companies and individuals. The main points are:

- Laws are created and enforced at national, regional and international levels.
- National laws are based on historical precedents and culture and are used to regulate society.
- Different countries have different legal systems.
- The English legal system is based on a hierarchy of courts and is increasingly influenced by EU law.
- Significant EU legislation is bound into treaties and charters, covering fundamental rights, trade, consumer protection, social welfare and the environment.
- Business ownership is highly regulated and is based on differing liabilities.
- National, regional and international laws often have overlapping jurisdictions.
- Contract law governs both internal and external relationships.
- Contracts stipulate the terms and conditions of the agreement.
- Negligence and liability indictments range from small claims to large class actions and are pursued particularly vigorously in the USA.
- Criminal law can also be applied to businesses and the owners of businesses.
- Consumer protection is an old concept and aims to protect the consumer from poor quality goods and services and forms of mis-selling.
- Quality may be assured by the use of quality standards, accurate labelling and government enforcement.
- Proper use of personal data is unlikely to breach data protection laws, but organisations must manage the data appropriately.
- Governments and the EU protect the consumer by ensuring that businesses are not acting in collusion or are in a position to abuse monopoly power.
- Protecting intellectual property is vital in encouraging innovation and entrepreneurship.
- There are a number of organisations, such as the World Intellectual Property Organisation (WIPO) that provide multiple country patent protection services.
- Counterfeit goods create black markets which undermine product investment and reduce tax revenues.
- Employers have the legal responsibility to look after their employees in terms of their welfare and health and safety.
- Nation states can legislate to nationalise and control foreign ownership of domestic companies, and through sanctions and embargoes they can apply international pressure on other countries.
- International laws are agreed by nation states though international organisations such as the UN.

- The role of the International Court of Justice is to resolve disagreements between nations in a non-confrontational manner.

- The Declaration of Human Rights was the forerunner of a broad series of international treaties which have been incorporated into the legislature of many nations.

- The European Court of Human Rights pronounces on violations of human rights in its member states.

- State-sponsored violations of human rights occur in many nations regardless of international legislation or the nation's constitution.

- All international business involves some risk as there are many different and unknown variables, such as those in law.

- There are a number of international mediation services, such as the International Chamber of Commerce (ICC), to which companies can apply to in order to resolve international disputes.

- Negotiation, mediation, arbitration and litigation may all be used to solve disputes.

Discussion questions

1 With the use of examples, describe the main differences between common law and civil law.

2 Illustrating with examples, describe the different forms of tort law and demonstrate how liability might effect businesses.

3 List, with examples, six different areas of law concerned with consumer protection.

4 Which regulators govern competition law in the USA, EU and the UK?

5 Discuss three types of national laws which will impact international business ownership and trade.

6 In the case of international disputes, which questions do the companies have to answer before the dispute resolution process starts and which organisation(s) might they turn to for assistance?

Further reading/sources of information

The web links below provide the most up-to-date sources. Access to any topic should be possible through the links.

Data Protection (**www.guardianedge.com/resources/data-protection.php**) Worldwide interactive data protection laws map, podcasts and datasheets.

EU Commission (**http://ec.europa.eu/competition/index_en.html**) EU Commission, competition rulings and past cases by industry.

Human Rights Watch (**www.hrw.org/en/home**) Human rights watch, news, podcasts and videos from around the world.

International Centre for the Settlement for International Disputes (**http://icsid.worldbank. org/ICSID/Index.jsp**) World Bank, International Centre for the Settlement for International Disputes (ICSID), details of current and past disputes.

International Chamber of Commerce (**www.iccwbo.org/id96/index.html**) How the International Chamber of Commerce (ICC) works.

International Court of Justice (**www.icj-cij.org/homepage/index.php?p1=0**) The International Court of Justice (ICJ) home page, cases and rulings.

International Law (**www.law.cornell.edu/world/** and **http://www.jus.uio.no/lm/index.html**) For two excellent sources of material on international law and trade law by country.

Statute Law (**www.statutelaw.gov.uk/**) The UK statute law database enables you to view UK laws and trace how they have changed over time.

Strange Court Cases (**www.paralegaltraining.net/blog/strange-court-cases**) A fun website with examples of strange court cases from around the world.

United Nation (**www.un.org/en/rights/** and **http://www2.ohchr.org/english/law/index.htm#core**) The United Nations (UN) human rights home page, news, cases, humanitarian affairs and international law.

UN treaties (**http://treaties.un.org/Pages/UNTSOnline.aspx?id=1**) Listing of current UN treaties and who has ratified them.

World Intellectual Property Organisation (**www.wipo.int/pct/en/distance_learning/**) World Intellectual Property Organisation (WIPO) free internet course on the patent co-operation treaty (PCT).

World Intellectual Property Organisation (**www.wipo.int/portal/index.html.en**) How the World Intellectual Property Organisation (WIPO) works and the services it provides.

Adams, A. (2006) *Law for Business Students,* 4th edn. Harlow: Pearson Education.

Keenan, D. and Riches, S. (2005) *Business Law,* 7th edn. Harlow: Pearson Education.

Wallace, R.M.M. (2005) *International Law,* 5th edn. London: Thompson.

References

Arnott, S. (2008) Primark Drops Three Indian Suppliers for Using Child Workers. *The Independent,* 17 June [online], available from **www.independent.co.uk/news/business/news/primark-drops-three-indian-suppliers-for-using-child-workers-848564.html**

Associated Press (2009) It Would Take Delhi HC 466 Year to Clear the Backlog: CJ (sic), *Express India,* 13 February [online], available from **www.expressindia.com/latest-news/It-would-take-Delhi-HC-466-yrs-to-clear-backlog-CJ/423127/**

BBC (2001) Tiny Island Talks Tough on Tax Havens, available from **http://news.bbc.co.uk/1/hi/business/1496492.stm**

BBC (2003) The Enron Affair, available from **http://news.bbc.co.uk/1/hi/in_depth/business/2002/enron/default.stm**

BBC (2004). Oil Giant Shell's Investors Shocked, available from **http://news.bbc.co.uk/1/hi/business/3890045.stm**

BBC (2005) Afghan Warlord Guilty of Torture, available from **http://news.bbc.co.uk/1/hi/uk/4693239.stm**

BBC (2006) DR Congo Arms Embargo Failing, available from **http://news.bbc.co.uk/1/hi/world/africa/6055864.stm**

BBC (2007) Card Companies Lose Refund Case, available from **http://news.bbc.co.uk/1/hi/business/7070720.stm**

BBC (2009a) Italy Passes Emergency Rape Law, available from **http://news.bbc.co.uk/1/hi/world/europe/7902107.stm**

BBC (2009b) One Music – How to Copyright, available from **http://www.bbc.co.uk/radio1/onemusic/legal/copyrightp03.shtml**

BBC (2009c) £30k Fine After Employee Death, available from **http://news.bbc.co.uk/1/hi/northern_ireland/8097373.stm**

BBC (2009d) Iran Air Part Sales Trio Jailed, available from http://news.bbc.co.uk/1/hi/england/berkshire/8083791.stm

BBC (2009e) Somali Pirates Seize Another Boat, available from http://news.bbc.co.uk/1/hi/world/africa/7994980.stm

BBC (2009f) Obama Seeks Thaw in US–Russia Ties, available from http://news.bbc.co.uk/1/hi/programmes/from_our_own_correspondent/8133457.stm

Business Week (2005) Chávez' Oil-fueled Revolution. *Business Week* 10 October [online], available from www.businessweek.com/magazine/content/05_41/b3954088.htm

Carroll, R. (2009) Obama Will Use Spring Summit to Bring Cuba in From the Cold *The Guardian,* 8 March [online], available from www.guardian.co.uk/world/2009/mar/08/cuba-obama-administration

CNN (2009) Court Grants Appeal in Suu Kyi Case. *CNN.com,* 17 June [online], available from http://edition.cnn.com/2009/WORLD/asiapcf/06/17/myanmar.suu.kyi/index.html

DePalma A. (2000) Mexico Is Ordered to Pay a US Company $16.7 Million. *The New York Times,* 31 August [online], available from www.nytimes.com/2000/08/31/business/international-business-mexico-is-ordered-to-pay-a-us-company-16.7-million.html?scp=1&sq=metalclad%20mexico&st=cse&pagewanted=2

Dzirutwe, M. (2009) Mining Firms in Zimbabwe Challenge Ownership Law. *Reuters,* 8 May [online], available from http://uk.reuters.com/article/idUKL7100933320090508

Eironline (2006) European Court Finds UK in Breach of Working Time Directive, available from www.eurofound.europa.eu/eiro/2006/10/articles/UK0610029I.htm

Europa (2009a) Latest Figures on Fines, Statistics, available from http://ec.europa.eu/competition/cartels/overview/index_en.html

Europa (2009b) Mergers: Commission Clears Proposed Takeover of SN Brussels Airlines by Lufthansa, available from http://europa.eu/rapid/pressReleasesAction.do?reference=IP/09/974&format=HTML&aged=0&language=EN&guiLanguage=en

Europa (2009c) Mergers: Commission Approves Proposed Acquisition of MyTravel Group by KarstadtQuelle, available from http://europa.eu/rapid/pressReleasesAction.do?reference=IP/07/614

European Commission (2008) Customs: Commission Publishes 2007 Customs Seizures of Counterfeit Goods at the EU's External Border, available from http://europa.eu/rapid/pressReleasesAction.do?reference=IP/08/757

Fathi, N. (2009) Iran's Top Leader Dashes Hopes for a Compromise. *The New York Times,* 19 June [online], available from www.nytimes.com/2009/06/20/world/middleeast/20iran.html

Food Standards Agency (2009) Understanding Labeling Rules, available from www.food.gov.uk/foodlabelling/ull/

Fulbright (2008) Fifth Annual Litigation Survey Findings, available from www.fulbright.com/index.cfm?fuseaction=news.detail&article_id=7637&site_id=286

Gibb, F. (2008) Fortune Tellers Targeted in New Consumer Protection Regulations. *Timesonline,* 23 May [online], available from http://business.timesonline.co.uk/tol/business/law/article3987725.ece

Global Competition Review (2009) Getting the Deal Through, Cartel Regulation, available from www.gettingthedealthrough.com/narrative_pdf.php?id=126

Goldenberg, S. (2009) With One Draft Order, Obama Signals the End of Guantanamo. *The Guardian,* 22 January [online], available from www.guardian.co.uk/world/2009/jan/22/obama-ends-guantanamo

Harris, J. (2006) Hammonds Wins Football League Claims, but Pays £4 Damages. *The Lawyer,* 23 June [online], available from www.thelawyer.com/hammonds-wins-football-league-claim-but-pays-%C2%A34-damages/120618.article

Harris, N. (2006) Football League Sues its Solicitors Over ITV Digital Collapse. *The Independent,* 9 February [online], available from www.independent.co.uk/sport/football/football-league/football-league-sues-its-solicitors-over-itv-digital-collapse-465976.html

Herman, M. and Jordan, D. (2007) Cadbury Fined £1 Million Over Salmonella Outbreak. *Timesonline,* 16 July [online], available from http://business.timesonline.co.uk/tol/business/industry_sectors/consumer_goods/article2083030.ece

Hu, J. (2003) AOL, Microsoft's Peace a Sign of Times (sic). *Cnet news,* 23 May [online], available from http://news.cnet.com/AOL,-Microsofts-peace-a-sign-of-times/2100-1026_3-1011700.html

Human Rights Watch (2009). Secret Execution of Juvenile Offender, available from www.hrw.org/en/news/2009/05/01/iran-secret-execution-juvenile-offender

ICJ (2009) List of Cases Referred to the Court Since 1946 by Date of Introduction, available from www.icj-cij.org/docket/index.php?p1=3&p2=2

ICO (2009) Data Protection Act: The Basics, available from www.ico.gov.uk/what_we_cover/data_protection/the_basics.aspx

Khattar, S. (2009) Education is Key to Abolish Child Labour (sic). *The Times of India,* 15 June [online], available from http://timesofindia.indiatimes.com/Education-is-key-to-abolish-child-labour/articleshow/4656555.cms

Kravets, D. (2007) Napster Trial Ends Seven Years Later, Defining Online Sharing Along the Way. *wired,* 31 August [online], available from www.wired.com/threatlevel/2007/08/napster-trial-e/

Lawfuel (2007) Hong Kong, June 11, 2007, available from www.lawfuel.com/show-release.asp?ID=12984

Lipton, E. and Barboza, D. (2007) As More Toys are Recalled, Trail Ends in China. *The New York Times,* 19 June [online], available from www.nytimes.com/2007/06/19/business/worldbusiness/ 19toys.html

Lynn, J. (2009) Cybersquatting Cases Hit Record in 2008. *Reuters,* 15 March [online], available from www.reuters.com/article/technologyNews/idUSTRE52E22G20090315

Market Share (2009) Browser Market Share, available from http://marketshare.hitslink.com/browser-market-share.aspx?qprid=0

Morris, S. (2009) Company Director Faces First Corporate Manslaughter Charge. *Guardian,* 17 June [online], available from www.guardian.co.uk/uk/2009/jun/17/mudslide-corporate-manslaughter-charge

Massey, R. (2009) Mandelson Mulls Vauxhall Rescue After GM Warning. *This Is Money,* 6 March [online], available from http://www.thisismoney.co.uk/markets/article.html?in_article_id=480172&in_page_id=3

Meyer, D. (2009) Psion Settle Netbook® Trademark Dispute. *Cnet news,* 1 June [online], available from http://news.cnet.com/8301-1001_3-10253210-92.html

Prosser, D. (2008) BA Chiefs Charged in Price Fixing Case. *The Independent,* 8 August [online], available from www.independent.co.uk/news/business/news/ba-chiefs-chargedin-price-fixing-case-888370.html

Public Citizen (1999) Legal Myths: The McDonald's 'Hot Coffee' Case, available from http://www.citizen.org/print_article.cfm?ID=785

Reuters (2009) Islamic Charity Leaders Get 65 Year Jail Terms, available from www.reuters.com/article/domesticNews/idUSTRE54Q6AP20090527

Sabbagh, D. (2007) GMTV Fined Record £2 Million by Watchdog Over Phone-in Scandal. *Timesonline,* 26 September [online], available from http://business.timesonline.co.uk/tol/business/industry_sectors/media/article2536674.ece

Spooner, J.G. (2005) Dell: Dispute Over Muslim Prayers Resolved. *Cnet News,* 21 March, available at http://news.cnet.com/Dell-Dispute-over-Muslim-prayers-resolved/2110-1047_3-5628889.html

Taipei Times (2009) Launch of Japanese Jury System Arouses Concern, available from www.taipeitimes.com/News/world/archives/2009/05/22/2003444186

The European Court of Human Rights (2009) Some Facts and Figures: 1959–2009, available from www.echr.coe.int/NR/rdonlyres/65172EB7-DE1C-4BB8-93B1-B28676C2C844/0/FactsAndFiguresEN.pdf

Transparency International (2009) 2008 Corruption Perceptions Index, available from **www.transparency.org/news_room/in_focus/2008/cpi2008/cpi_2008_table**

Tribunals Service (2009) Home page, available from **www.tribunals.gov.uk/**

UN (2009) The Universal Declaration of Human Rights, available from **www.un.org/en/documents/udhr/**

UNCITRAL (2009) Status: 1980 – United Nations Convention on Contracts for the International Sale of Goods, available from **www.uncitral.org/uncitral/en/uncitral_texts/sale_goods/1980CISG_status.html**

UNFCC (2009) Kyoto Protocol, available from **unfccc.int/kyoto_protocol/items/2830.php**

UNTC (2009) United National Treaty Series, available from **http://treaties.un.org/Pages/UNTSOnline.aspx?id=1**

US Legal 500 (2008) Mass Tort and Class Action: Toxic Tort, available from **www.legal500.com/c/us/litigation/mass-tort-and-class-action-plaintiff-representation-toxic-tort**

WHO (2006) Counterfeit Medicines: Fact Sheet, available from **www.who.int/medicines/services/counterfeit/impact/ImpactF_S/en/**

9 Globalisation, challenges and changes

Ian Brooks, Jamie Weatherston and Graham Wilkinson

Learning outcomes

On completion of this chapter you should be able to:

- understand the impact of globalisation;
- understand the move towards greater dynamism, complexity and uncertainty (turbulence) in the international business environment of most firms;
- speculate about the future prospects for organisations, individuals, governments and groups in society as a result of environmental turbulence;
- outline the nature of chaotic and turbulent environments and the implications of these for long-term planning and flexible working;
- reflect on the differences between predictable and unpredictable change and the implications of this for organisations;
- understand the characteristics of the advantages and drawbacks of flexible working;
- discuss the influences that the changing international business environment and, in particular, the trend towards flexible working, have upon individuals and groups in the social community;
- explore environmental scenarios;
- discuss the future role of government and understand the environmental forces acting on public sector organisations.

Key concepts

- dynamism, complexity, uncertainty and turbulence
- predictable and unpredictable change
- chaos theory
- futurology
- long-term planning
- environmental scenarios and planning
- flexible working
- demographic time bomb
- social inclusion and exclusion
- interventionist and *laissez-faire* government.

Minicase 9.1	Dealing with unexpected changes

Twice in the last decade events have shown how vulnerable an advanced society can be. On both occasions fuel prices in the UK had risen substantially above the general price index due to government tax policies and global price increases. Businesses, in particular farmers and hauliers, for whom fuel costs are especially important, protested against continuing rises by picketing fuel refineries. The normal flow of tankers to petrol stations was affected. In some areas many stations ran dry as consumers fearful of long-term shortages filled up. The sudden rise in demand for fuel made the supply situation worse. Supermarkets reported 'panic' buying of foods. The government was suspicious that the oil companies were not doing all they could to get tankers out, in the hope that the government might cave in and reduce taxes, something it pledged not to do. Oil company executives were summoned to Number 10 and the Cabinet's emergency committee met regularly. Troops were on standby to move fuel supplies. After about a week the protestors gave up their picketing and normality resumed. The Home Secretary was quoted as saying, 'as a consequence of these protests, essential services, the basic fabric of our society and national life, were brought to the brink'.

Such is the extent of the integration of critical resources and concerns about vulnerability that the UK government created the Centre for the Protection of National Infrastructure. The Centre advises on the security of essential services such as food, water, energy and other services that if compromised would lead to severe economic or social consequences. The threats, they say, are largely from terrorist groups or espionage by foreign powers. Terrorism is not just about bombs and bullets; electronic or chemical attacks are capable of causing massive disruption and harm.

Questions

1 Identify the ways in which businesses and consumers may be affected by industrial action or terrorist attacks.
2 How might governments deal with this increased vulnerability to global events?

9.1 Introduction

This final chapter will, in significant measure, depart from the format of the bulk of this text. It is more exploratory in nature, focusing to some extent on the future. It is hoped that you will develop your imagination and differentiate between the more certain and the speculative aspects of the future world. We look at both reasonably predictable changes, such as the aging of many societies, as well as more speculative change. The pace of change is also discussed. However, whether predictable or not, the greatest challenge is actually coping with change. The chapter explores various responses to macro-environmental change, such as flexible working. It examines the impact of change on organisations, groups, individuals and government.

We are constantly reminded that the pace of change is speeding up and, by other commentators, that 'we' are moving in unpredictable directions. Of course if we fully accept the 'unpredictable thesis' then there would be little point in attempting to plan for change and we would just have to accept whatever came our way! Futurology is the name often given to the art of imagining or at least reflecting upon likely future scenarios for change. Ironically, futurology is probably one of the oldest arts we have – people have attempted to predict the future, no doubt, since the origins of our species, with varying degrees of success. Some cultures adopt a broadly accepting position regarding the future, suggesting that, for example, it is God's will, while others have a greater tendency to believe that mankind can forge its own future. We will not enter that particular debate here. Instead, we will explore some of the previous ideas and reflect on more current visions of our future. These visions for change in the business environment may have a profound impact on organisational activity and our social and work lives.

9.2 Globalisation

Globalisation can be referred to as a phenomenon, a process, a state or a concept. It has evolved partly due to the trend for increasing international trade across national boundaries and the conduct of business activities in more than one country – and because of the changes in the various aspects of the international business environment discussed throughout this book. Put simply, it is a process that refers to the growth of inter-dependencies between national markets and industries on a worldwide scale. This growing interdependence between national economies has resulted in a trend towards global markets, global production and global competition. There are many theories and models that try to explain the process of globalisation; we will look at some of them.

Many commentators take the view that globalisation probably started some way back in the nineteenth century. From this perspective, it is possible to identify four phases of globalisation. The first phase, which peaked in about 1880, was mainly due to improvements in transportation and automation that enabled reliable long-distance trade. Telegraph and telephone communication in the late 1800s facilitated information transfer, which many firms found to be especially useful in managing their supply chains.

Phase two reached its height in the first decades of the twentieth century, when territories under the control of European colonial powers were seen as sites to establish multinational subsidiaries. This period also saw some overseas expansion by American corporations into profitable European markets. This phase is perceived to have ended with the economic crash in 1929, which caused a global depression and a move to inward-looking polices by many governments.

The third phase was based on the lowering of tariff barriers and the resultant increase in international trade after the end of World War II. As individuals, particularly in the richer economies, became wealthier and the austerity of the war years faded, there was massively increased demand for consumer goods. As the largest and least war-damaged economy post 1945, it was, perhaps, inevitable that the USA would become the most dominant power in terms of globalisation.

The fourth (and final) phase of the process has depended largely on two of the changes discussed in this book. These are, first, changes in technology, such as the widespread availability of the personal computer (PC) linked to the internet/world wide web, the increasing use of mobile communications and the development of robotics both for tracking components and finished goods and in the automation of production. Bear in mind, also, that these factors have not only affected manufacturing industry; the service sector, for example banking and tourism, have also benefited from these changes. Distance is no longer an issue – the world has shrunk to a manageable size. The second factor is the change in political attitudes and economic policies that have allowed companies (and consumers) to take advantage of these technological advances. It is apparent that there has been much convergence of global economic thinking, with many more countries moving towards an acceptance of liberal, free-market ideas. Social trends changed, too, as consumers apparently became less concerned with products' national identities. *Table 9.1* shows these phases.

Figure 9.1 shows some factors in the macro-environment that have had an impact on globalisation.

Theodore Levitt (1983) was one of the first academics to write about globalisation. In 1983 he said that technology is the driving force behind the globalisation of markets and, thus, a 'converging commonality' in countries around the planet. He suggested that:

- communications (e.g. TV);
- transport;
- travel;
- products; and
- processes;

Table 9.1	Four phases of globalisation

Phase of globalisation	Period	Trigger	Characteristics
First phase	1830–1890	Rail and ocean transport	Automated manufacturing; cross-border trading of commodities
Second phase	1900–1930	Electricity and steel production	Emergence of European and American manufacturing and extracting industries
Third phase	1948–1970s	GATT, end of World War II rebuilding	Efforts to reduce trade barriers. Rise of Japanese multinationals, triad nations and branded products
Fourth phase	1980–Current	ICT, automation, consultancy, privatisation	FDI fuelling growth in LDCs, technology and transport innovations, global media and branding

were all leading to an 'irrevocable homogenisation' of demand. Levitt's key assumption or hypothesis was that local tastes and preferences will vanish if the product is cheap enough. The implication of this is that:

- identical products will be sold in all markets; and
- industries will be dominated by global corporations benefiting from huge economies of scale.

An alternative view is put forward by writers such as Douglas and Wind (1987) and Ohmae (1989) who suggest that some products are 'global', others are not. They point out that there are many barriers to standardisation and that companies cannot ignore local consumer needs. Indeed, companies can gain considerable benefits by making minor changes to suit different national markets. That is not to say companies should ignore the attractions of standardisation. If companies can standardise, even to a small extent, then they will be able to avoid duplication of effort in, for example, research and development and provide the same products in markets where this is acceptable. The emphasis is, perhaps, best summed up by Kenichi Ohmae's famous phrase 'Think globally, act locally'. In essence, this can be seen to mean that companies should regard the globe as one market, but should make changes to their products and services when necessary, to better serve each local market.

It is clear that some markets are in line with Levitt's 'converging commonality' e.g. designer clothing where consumers are more than happy to buy the latest exclusive design. A second example would be CDs, which are produced to identical technical specifications the world over. Other markets are, however, locally differentiated. This can be seen in the variation in menus that McDonald's, for instance, offer around the world, even while the core image and branding of the company remain constant. While it is possible to recognise both of these viewpoints, one thing is clear: customer needs are becoming more complex and so are markets. This so-called convergence/divergence debate is also discussed in *Chapter 5*.

George Yip's (2003) model provides further insight into the forces driving globalisation. It helps us to understand the pressure that industries are under to globalise: see *Figure 9.2*.

Yip also says that an understanding of the global forces assists a company to identify the critical success factors in a global industry and market.

Market drivers:

- similar customer needs and tastes;
- the existence of global customers;
- transferable marketing between different countries.

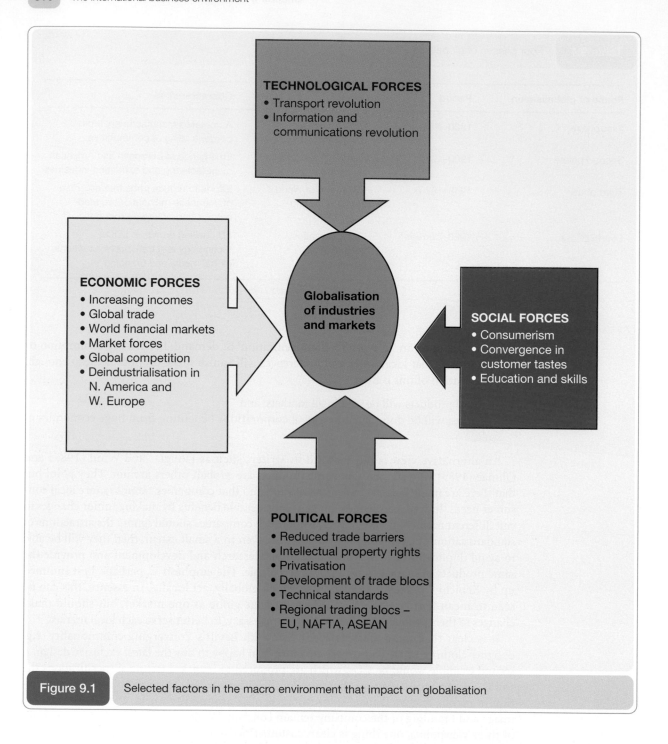

TECHNOLOGICAL FORCES
• Transport revolution
• Information and
  communications revolution

ECONOMIC FORCES
• Increasing incomes
• Global trade
• World financial markets
• Market forces
• Global competition
• Deindustrialisation in
  N. America and
  W. Europe

**Globalisation
of industries
and markets**

SOCIAL FORCES
• Consumerism
• Convergence in
  customer tastes
• Education and skills

POLITICAL FORCES
• Reduced trade barriers
• Intellectual property rights
• Privatisation
• Development of trade blocs
• Technical standards
• Regional trading blocs –
  EU, NAFTA, ASEAN

Figure 9.1   Selected factors in the macro environment that impact on globalisation

Competitive drivers:

• competitors' global strategies;
• country interdependence.

Cost drivers:

• scale economies and scope including product development costs – experience curve;
• favourable logistics;
• country-specific differences.

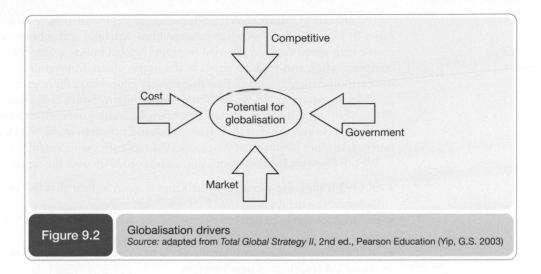

| **Figure 9.2** | Globalisation drivers
Source: adapted from *Total Global Strategy II*, 2nd ed., Pearson Education (Yip, G.S. 2003) |

Government drivers are numerous and include:

- trade policies; tariff barriers; subsidies to local companies; ownership restrictions;
- local content requirements; controls over technology transfer; intellectual property regimes; currency and capital flows;
- marketing regulations; host government concerns; technical standards.

Overall, then, it can be seen that there is a great deal of evidence that globalisation has been on the rise, increasingly rapidly as the twentieth century came to an end and the twenty-first began. Even the turbulence and the problems of the 2008 credit crunch have not stopped the process. It may have slowed some international expansion by companies, indeed, that is certainly the case, but there is little evidence of any reversal of the trends of the previous three decades. On the contrary, policy-makers around the world have called for a global response to a global problem, acknowledging the inter-connected nature of the global economy (and global societies). As we have shown throughout this book, it is possible to use the PESTLE C model to look at these forces driving globalisation (and some of the obstacles too).

At a political level the formation of world institutions such as WTO, UN, the World Bank, OECD and IMF have been necessary to facilitate globalisation. We can also see global legal entities such as the International Court of Justice based in The Hague, as well as countries becoming more willing to share criminal intelligence to fight against global crime. The increase in the number of global standards including patent protection and electrical standards also break down barriers to international trade.

At an industry level the emergence of worldwide markets, including new businesses based on internet trading, is a good indicator. Global production, global competition and global brands, e.g. McDonald's, Coca-Cola, Toyota and Adidas, are now commonplace across all the continents, not just the richer parts of the world. There has also been an increase in cross-border mergers and acquisitions throughout the 1990s and beyond until the economic downturn of 2008 has (temporarily, perhaps) slowed the process. Even so, this activity has resulted in even more global corporations, some (such as India's Tata) based in developing economies. World financial markets have developed to support all this activity.

Technological change, often based on developments in information technology and the fall in the cost of computer processing (widely accepted to have fallen at around 30 percent per year for 20 years), have been vital in pushing globalisation. IT developments allow companies to produce new goods and reduce production costs through advances in CAD and robotics. Now even the smallest SME (e.g. a musician in a bedroom) can reach a global market. This in turn alters industry structure and markets.

The increase in information flows between geographically remote locations has been made easier by high-speed global telecommunications. Satellites and submarine fibre-optic cables enable high-speed data transfer vital to support global business. Satellites are vital for mobile communication and tracking goods in the supply chain. Innovation has provided access to information through search engines that provide information for huge numbers of people and provides for more rapid research and development. Some countries are clearly further advanced in this process than others. For example, South Korea, which has almost 100 percent internet access and some of the fastest broadband networks in the world, could be in a position to take more advantage of the changes than countries with less fully developed systems.

We can illustrate how communication has speeded up over the centuries:

- in 1492 it took five months for the King of Spain to hear that the voyage of Christopher Columbus to the Americas had been a success;
- in 1865 two weeks passed before news of the assassination of Abraham Lincoln in Washington, DC reached Europe;
- in 2001 it took two seconds for the world to *witness* the collapse of the twin towers of the World Trade Center in New York City.

Social and cultural developments, such as the increased amount of travel by citizens of many nations with low-cost flights and fewer restrictions, have increased awareness, interaction and the desire to experience foreign cultures; Levitt's idea of converging lifestyles may be getting closer. And to this can be added the increase in personal connectivity, e.g. MySpace and Facebook give the impression of a globalising world.

Ecological awareness is also developing a global reach with international treaties. For example, the Kyoto Protocol agreed in 1992 and ratified by the majority of the world's national governments (but not the USA) indicated a growing international agreement to recognise and combat the threat to humanity from increasing economic activity. This, and the meeting at Copenhagen in December 2009 to discuss and decide upon a replacement for Kyoto, have been criticised by environmental campaigners as being insufficient to tackle the problems that exist. Nevertheless, the very existence of such agreements and conferences indicates an increasing recognition of the problems and a desire, however limited in some cases, for action – internationally agreed and co-ordinated action – to tackle those problems.

In short, it can be seen that there are both costs and benefits, and advantages and disadvantages, in the process of globalisation. That is why the topic is one that arouses much passion and much debate. Supporters of globalisation see it as being of benefit to all, if not now, then at some point in the future. Opponents worry about the inequalities they perceive as being inherent in the process (the rich get richer, the poor get exploited) and nationalists are concerned about what they see as the diminishing power of the nation state. These issues are discussed in a little more detail in the next section.

9.3 The consequences of globalisation

As can be seen from *Tables 9.2* and *9.3,* there are many contentious issues involved and much debate about the consequences of globalisation. Much has been written about the consequences of globalisation – both good and bad. *Table 9.2* outlines some advantages of globalisation for businesses, customers and countries; *Table 9.3* some disadvantages.

Let us begin this part of the discussion by concentrating on one of the main worries expressed by many governments (and individuals) around the world, the view that globalisation can threaten a country's national sovereignty and capacity for independent action in a number of ways. These may include such issues as:

- the size and scale of multinational companies, which gives them significant influence over policy making of governments;

Table 9.2	Advantages of globalisation for businesses, customers and countries		

To business	To customers	To countries
Access to mass markets – increased sales	Lower prices	Improved standards of living in both developed and developing countries
Economies of scale and reduced costs	Wider choice	Increased democracy – fall of communism
Access to resources	Improved quality	
Access to finance and tax savings		

Table 9.3	Disadvantages of globalisation for businesses, customers and countries		

To business	To customers	To countries
Increased competition	Standardisation	Exploitation
More demanding consumers		Loss of national culture and identity
Increasing volatility		Uneven benefits
		Environmental factors

- increased international competition may necessarily mean that some countries miss out;
- the increasing number and variety of international laws and standards may be difficult for some countries to keep up with;
- governance issues are coming to the fore, which may cause problems for some countries with less developed legal frameworks.

A second area of concern for government is that companies may take advantage of changes to move their activities to cheaper locations, an activity known as offshoring. However, it must be remembered that offshoring can also create employment. Offshoring is typically defined as the establishment of a business or part of a business overseas. We can see it in the relocation of manufacturing from more developed economies to those that are less developed, or in the transfer of call centres from the UK to India or from the USA to Puerto Rico. Offshoring will inevitably involve the loss of employment in the country that the business leaves. As costs increase in one country then companies can move their operations to cheaper and cheaper locations as they chase lower costs. The result is that new jobs could be only temporary.

The effect on the workers, who in many less developed nations may be poor, needs to be taken into account. A number of multinational companies have been accused of offering very poor rates of pay and forcing employees to work in sweatshop conditions. Some have also been accused of employing child labour, which means that these children could be missing out on education. There is pressure on global companies such as Gap, Next, Nike and Matalan to enforce rigid standards throughout their supply chains.

It is not all bad news. Conditions do seem to improve in many countries over time. In Vietnam it has been estimated that wages have increased five-fold in recent years. Developing

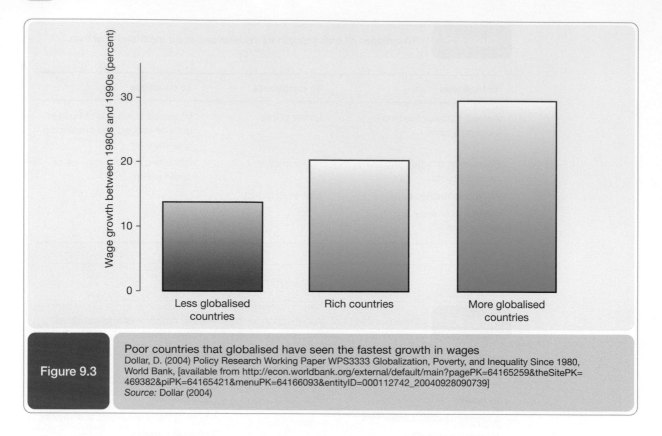

Figure 9.3

Poor countries that globalised have seen the fastest growth in wages
Dollar, D. (2004) Policy Research Working Paper WPS3333 Globalization, Poverty, and Inequality Since 1980,
World Bank, [available from http://econ.worldbank.org/external/default/main?pagePK=64165259&theSitePK=
469382&piPK=64165421&menuPK=64166093&entityID=000112742_20040928090739]
Source: Dollar (2004)

countries such as India, China, Vietnam and Bangladesh have all benefited from global production. The World Bank (Dollar, 2004) found that wages have generally been rising faster in
globalising developing countries than in rich ones, and faster in rich ones than in non-globalising
developing countries: see *Figure 9.3*. The point is that the fastest wage growth is occurring in
developing countries that are actively increasing their integration with the global economy.

The impact on the environment is rather more difficult to accurately quantify. Growth
brought about by increased economic activity does have a negative impact: see section 6.3.1
'*Externalities*'. Pollution is some countries is reaching critical levels; at certain times of the
day it may be dangerous for some people to leave their homes. China's economy has grown
at a spectacular rate over the last 15 years. Rising energy needs led to the building of the
Three Gorges Dam, used to produce hydro-electric power. While this is a spectacular
achievement, it has been at the expense of flooded agricultural lands, flooded cities, the displacement of millions of people and the loss of vital habitat for wildlife. Increased carbon
emissions could in the medium to long term have a catastrophic impact on the planet,
which we are already starting to see now.

The impact on national cultures will vary from country to country. Writers warn of the
'McDonaldisation' of society and Western companies and brands gaining a dominant position. There is even a chance that familiar national foods could be replaced by their global
counterparts and even languages may be affected by the global use of English.

9.4 Changes in the international business environment

Here we identify, by way of a summary or stock-take, a number of dynamic environmental
issues that have been raised in this book. These critical environmental trends include:

- globalisation in manufacturing and service provision;

- large-scale geographical changes in the distribution of manufacturing (e.g. vast increase in parts of South East Asia and stable, even declining, outputs in much of North America and Europe);
- some economies specialising in manufacturing while others specialise in service industry and consumption;
- global recession and vastly differential national economic growth rates creating rapidly shifting patterns of global wealth and income distribution;
- growth in the power and influence of economic and political unions, such as the EU, and countries, such as the BRIC economies – Brazil, Russia, India and China;
- the spread of nuclear weapons capability;
- religious fundamentalism;
- the threat of international terrorism;
- changing emphasis from multilateralism (e.g. power lying with the UN) to unilateralism (e.g. power with the USA or others);
- increasing debate on the future role of government;
- failed states;
- the prevalence of long-term unemployment and under-employment;
- the continuing integration of Europe and of other regional blocs;
- atmospheric, water, space, land and noise pollution, resource depletion and water shortages;
- global warming;
- increasing availability of information and ease of communication;
- technological advances, including ICT, biotechnology, genetics, robotics, virtual worlds;
- the demographic transition typified by declining fertility rates and increasing life expectancy leading to an ageing population in most countries – the so-called 'demographic time bomb' – with serious long-term implications for caring for the old, levels of taxation and government and individual indebtedness;
- dynamic national and international cultures, mass migration and cultural interaction, tolerance and intolerance; and
- changing attitudes towards the family, health, crime and society.

This list provides ample food for thought. Many of the issues raised have crucial implications for all governments and organisations, groups and individuals. Collectively, these environmental forces are fundamentally influencing, and being influenced by, patterns of economic growth, employment and investment.

9.5 The nature of the international business environment

The first chapter of this book identifies dynamism and complexity as two key factors in the business environment of many organisations. These are the prime characteristics of a turbulent environment (see *Minicases 9.1* and *9.6*). The models discussed in *Chapter 1* help us to categorise environmental influences (using the PESTLE C model) and to devise lists of key organisational opportunities or threats (the 'O' and 'T' in SWOT analysis). However, Johnson *et al.* (2008) argue that organisations need to understand the *nature* of their environments before they audit the individual environmental factors. Such an analysis might be expected to help an organisation decide upon the sorts of systems which are required to monitor and respond to environmental change.

New technologies and increased globalisation of many markets encourage environmental turbulence, such that organisational planning cannot be seen as a continuous 'rolling out' of previous plans. Merely from scanning a quality daily newspaper, it is possible to catalogue a range of increasingly 'commonplace' surprises which threaten today's organisations, such as major global accidents, terrorism, kidnappings, hostile company takeovers, sabotage via product tampering, investigative journalism, equipment breakdowns, political upheaval and pressure group activity.

If environmental factors are less predictable, then planning needs to be seen as a more flexible, adaptive and responsive process. It is these two key areas, that is, the planning process and the need for organisational flexibility, which are given considerable attention in the next section. However, during this discussion we should be aware of the impact an organisation can have on its environment and the operation of the market by way of its strategic, tactical and operational actions. If dynamism and complexity are key factors in analysing the nature of an organisation's business environment it seems reasonable to ask whether there are any academic models which may be of assistance to us. Miles (1980) devised a useful series of questions for evaluating the nature of an organisation's environment. The suggested process involves mapping an organisation's environment using a series of continuums, for example, from simple to complex and static to dynamic.

There is a growing field of literature on crisis, chaos and shock event management. Underlying analysis of such 'shock events' in the business sphere, however, is the developing body of knowledge about the concept of chaos. Gleick (1987), in a seminal work, offered some fascinating insights into the discoveries about the behaviour of things in the natural world. These included the graphically termed 'butterfly effect' in global weather forecasting: the notion that a butterfly stirring its wings today in one part of the world might transform weather systems next month in another far-off area. He also said that these ideas have begun to 'change the way business executives make decisions about insurance, the way astronomers look at the solar system, the way political theorists talk about the stresses leading to armed conflict'.

A number of largely American researchers have looked for such chaotic patterns in the movements of the stock market, in an attempt to predict its behaviour. However, this work has been criticised because:

- any small errors made at the start of the process would be likely to result in huge forecasting errors over time;
- huge amounts of data are required to model chaotic systems and these were unavailable in most markets; and
- the ability to spot chaotic patterns is small given the large number of variables which influence the markets – particularly if we think that new factors are now affecting performance.

Writers such as Stacey (2007) have looked at the business impact of chaos theory. He notes the tendency in many business cycles towards the sort of 'non-linear feedback loops' observable in the natural world. Although the value of chaos theory may be questioned, it is possible that the mathematical models designed to explore non-linearity will generate useful analytical tools for managers in the future.

9.5.1 Implications for individuals and groups

When environmental change demands organisational change, as it almost continuously does, then we as individuals have to respond. It is becoming increasingly uncommon for people to work within a stable environment and undertake similar tasks and responsibilities for any length of time. Individuals are required to change at least as rapidly as the business environment if they are to remain effective. They need to continually develop their capabilities in order to function effectively within changing organisations. As the now clichéd saying goes: 'standing still is not an option'. We have to develop new skills and behaviours and, perhaps more importantly, new attitudes and ways of thinking, as the environment demands flexibility and the capacity and willingness to seek personal development opportunities.

Moves towards greater flexible working and the growth of the flexible firm are of direct relevance to individuals in the workplace. It is individuals who are being made 'flexible' and it is they who will, or will not, cope with the changes in working patterns outlined above. In developing economies, many people who work in factories are on short-term contracts and/or fear for their jobs as costs increase or demand drops. In developed economies, many people in higher-paid jobs now have what has been called a 'portfolio career'. This is multi-faceted and may include holding a number of 'loose' employment contracts, with a number of employers. For example, a management consultant might work on a few short-term projects with a number of organisations, undertake to write a management textbook for a publishing company and work for a university business school as a part-time lecturer.

Most individuals (particularly in the richer countries of the world) have been accustomed to regular 9 to 5, permanent, pensioned employment, so that new developments present personal challenges in balancing work and life patterns. Changes in employment and career patterns have important and far-reaching consequences for pension provision and some welfare payments. With an ageing population, government fears the rising burden of pension and welfare demands upon the public purse. The picture is more pronounced in some Western countries. By 2030, people over 65 in Germany, the world's third-largest economy, will account for almost half the adult population, compared with one-fifth now. Unless the country's fertility rate recovers over the same period, its population of under-35s will shrink about twice as fast as the older population will grow. The total population, now 82 million, will decline to 72 million while the number of working age will fall by a quarter, from 40 million to 30 million. The pattern is similar in Japan, Italy, France, Spain, Portugal, the Netherlands and Sweden. Curiously, perhaps, China faces a similar concern due to its long-standing 'one-child' policy (see *Minicase 1.4* in *Chapter 1*).

Increasing numbers of middle-aged and older people are having to adjust to changing employment patterns. The OECD has calculated that only just over a third of UK citizens aged over 55 years are in paid work. The equivalent figure for France is 27 percent while for Italy it was just 15 percent. Redundancy, early retirement opportunities and the lack of employment prospects for those over 55, together with youth unemployment and increasing numbers in higher education, ensure that the vast bulk of the workforce in Western Europe is between 25 and 55 years old. Many people's working life is restricted to just 30 years, which seems at odds with the much reported increases in life expectancy and the demographic time bomb most countries are facing. *Minicase 9.2* explores these quite contrasting demographic trends.

Increasingly governments and commentators are suggesting that people (especially in European countries with aging populations) will in fact have to consider working into their 70s in order to continue to enjoy an acceptable standard of living. This may be taking us back a generation or two. In the 1960s in the UK, for example, the majority of young adults started work aged 15 or 16 and were expected to retire at 65 (male) or 60 (female) – a working life of up to 50 years (albeit one which started at an earlier age than is likely to be the case in the future). For some people changes in this regard have been unwelcome and have led to a reduction in their standard of living. Many have had to adjust their work-life expectations. Increasingly, the lack of adequate pension provision for vast numbers of now young and middle-aged people suggests that early retirement, or indeed retirement at all, may not be an option in the near future. Whereas retirement has not been an option for many in developing countries, increasingly, especially in the USA and even Europe, more are opting to work post-retirement age (and age discrimination legislation is supporting this trend).

Previously predictable life-cycle patterns have, in the last two decades, changed considerably. The Sigmoid Curve, see *Figure 9.4*, is an analytical model for depicting a person's working life cycle. It is often suggested that people start life falteringly, then make steady and consistent progress before peaking and enjoying a 'decline' during retirement. However, the timeframe for the Sigmoid Curve, rather like many product life cycles, is now being squeezed. This means people need to develop new options for a second or even third career during their working lives. Evidence suggests that an increasing number of people (especially in developed economies) switch careers at least once during their working life and undertake a seemingly different occupation (e.g. from executive to management lecturer). *Figure 9.4* shows this secondary curve superimposed on the Sigmoid Curve, indicating that many people can sustain personal growth by developing a second career.

Minicase 9.2   A parting of the ways

Demographic forces are pulling America and Europe apart. If the trend continues America's strong position in the world may grow further. The population in the USA is rising faster than many had expected. The fertility rate in the USA remains buoyant while in Europe it is low and decreasing. Even America's immigration rate is higher than in Europe and immigrants are reproducing faster than native-born Americans. The population of Europe is ageing rapidly; in the USA its median age is far more stable. It is estimated that the median age of Americans in the year 2050 might be 37–40 (very close to the current state at about 35) while in Europe it could easily be over 50 (currently it is about 39). This represents a stunning difference largely accounted for by the ageing of Europe's population. To move within just 40 years to a difference in median age of about 15 years represents a major parting of the ways with far-reaching cultural, social, economic and political implications. If the trend continues, America's population will overtake that of Europe (excluding Russia) well before 2050. Unlike Europe, America's older people, their 'seniors', will remain a more stable proportion of the total population than in Europe.

The fertility rates in most of Europe are below replacement level which is about 2.1 children per woman. In some countries, for example Germany, it is only 1.3, meaning that natural population change in Europe is rapidly downwards (the population of Germany and Italy, for example, is in decline). Inward migration does reduce such falls to an extent. Immigrant populations usually have higher fertility rates. For example, in the USA the non-Hispanic whites' fertility rate is 1.8 (below replacement levels) while for the black population it is 2.1 and 3.0 for the Hispanic population. In many areas in the south of the USA (e.g. Los Angeles and Houston) Latino groups account for well over half of the under-14-year-olds. Whereas traditionally America's cultural ties with Europe have been strong, things might change. The majority of immigrants come from Latin America or South and East Asia and this might, in time, pull America's attention away from Europe.

Questions

1 Discuss the likely implications of these changes on richer economies (e.g. Europe, the USA, Japan and Australasia) for organisations, individuals and governments.
2 Discuss the likely implications of these changes on the poorer economies of Asia, Africa and Latin America for organisations, individuals and governments.

This discussion has highlighted a trend in society towards greater life and employment uncertainty. For many people flexible working improves choice and freedom while for others it constrains or sidelines them. Unfortunately, as individuals we are powerless to change societal trends or governmental policy. Globalisation and technological change conspire to transform our social and working worlds. What we can do is exercise some control

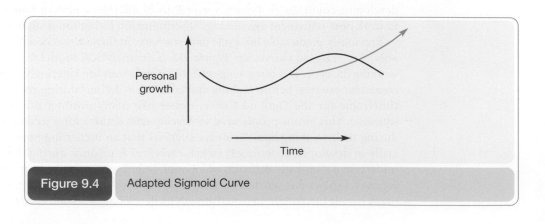

Figure 9.4   Adapted Sigmoid Curve

over our own patterns of living. The paradox is that fragmentation and flexible working can offer new freedoms for those able to take advantage of them.

One further aspect of this needs to be discussed: the impact on groups of people as distinct from individuals. Over a generation ago, Pawley (1974) considered that Western society was withdrawing from 'the whole system of values and obligations that has historically been the basis of public, community and family life'. He was of the opinion that technological developments such as televisions in children's bedrooms, computers, games consoles and MP3 players which he termed 'socially atomising appliances', were fuelling a retreat into 'private lives of an unprecedented completeness'. During the 1980s the then UK Prime Minister Margaret Thatcher famously denied that there was such a thing as society, as distinct from groups of individuals. Pawley's assessment has, perhaps, proved to be particularly pertinent, especially in Western countries in the twenty-first century.

Concern has been expressed about the degree to which young people feel 'disconnected' from the political and social system and about the generally acknowledged scale and growth of an underclass of permanently or long-term unemployed, poorly educated, living on benefits and surviving at the fringes of society. Many other, particularly young, people have been attracted by single-issue campaigning on such matters as animal rights and environmental protection. The mainstream political parties have struggled in many democracies to energise people and motivate them even to vote. Election turnout in the European parliament elections held across the EU every four years, has progressively fallen in the last two decades to below 50 percent. However, this is not always the case, as demonstrated by the enthusiastic participation of many in the 2008 USA presidential election that brought Barack Obama to power.

9.5.2 Implications for organisations

Whatever their objectives and legal status, organisations have, almost without exception, changed over the last decade. Very many have restructured internally, realigned their business processes to improve customer service, made focused strategic changes to their management control systems, developed their staff, improved their technological positioning to achieve competitive advantage and adjusted their product market portfolio. Most of these changes reflect a conscious response to turbulence in the business environment, including recession, and a deliberate effort to influence that environment. Many organisations have undergone fundamental change because the environment has itself transformed. The global forces for change really are profound.

A number of researchers, among them some notable management 'gurus', have attempted to predict the ways in which organisations will change in the next decade and beyond. Such predictions are often based on current trends and collective expectations together with a pinch of 'educated' guesswork. To a large extent it is the changing nature of the international business environment that will dictate the nature of these changes and, in turn, the way organisations respond to change will alter the nature of the environment for all. The next section will first look at the implications of the changing business environment for long-term planning and will then explore one particular organisational response to environmental turbulence, that is the growth of flexible working, touching on its different forms in different countries.

Operational plans have always been distinguished from strategic plans on the basis of the time period they cover and the scope and detail they contain. Strategic plans have tended to imply a planning horizon of about five years and to cover the organisation as a whole. To be able to plan over this sort of period implies a reasonable level of certainty about the environment in which the organisation operates. However, turbulence in the environment leads to an increasing lack of stability and predictability which, in turn, makes long-term strategic planning hazardous. This has led many writers on strategy to question whether organisations should adopt long-term, centralised approaches to planning. Mintzberg (2000) believes that incremental and emergent approaches to the process of strategy formulation should increasingly be considered by organisations. Increased environmental turbulence also suggests that systems of planning which devolve responsibility to individual business units are likely to make organisations more adaptable and responsive to environmental change.

Stacey (2007) questions many of the underlying assumptions used by firms in the process of long-term planning. He points out that many of these assumptions are based upon a range of quantitatively based analytical techniques. These techniques contribute to an underlying assumption, on the part of some theorists and many managers, that there is a 'best way' to plan. However, as noted above, long-term organisational planning is becoming less and less reliable or valid in today's turbulent environments.

Perhaps we should not over-react; after all, Mintzberg (2000) reminded us that each succeeding generation tends to perceive its present situation as more turbulent than its predecessors. He suggests the key factor is whether organisations can learn to think strategically and avoid inappropriately formal processes of planning. He reminds us that:

> changes that appear turbulent to organisations that rely heavily on planning may appear normal to, even welcomed by, those that prefer more of a visionary or learning approach. Put more boldly, if you have no vision but only formal plans then every unpredicted change in the environment makes you feel that the sky is falling.

Mintzberg also suggests that the perceptual filters discussed in *Chapter 1* may operate differently in different countries. However, turbulence demands an organisational response. One such 'reaction' has been for organisations to attempt to develop far greater flexibility; hence the growth of the concepts of the 'flexible firm' and of 'flexible working', discussed in section 9.6 *'Flexible working'*.

9.5.3 Implications for governments

This section explores some of the implications for government of environmental change before looking at the ongoing debate concerning the role of government; see also *Chapter 7*. Government at local, national, regional and global levels is a powerful environmental force which influences the business environment of all organisations. However, there is a range of environmental phenomena which are themselves of major concern to governments at various levels. Many of these are listed in the introductory section of this chapter. We will look at just two of these changes and briefly assess the consequences for governments; these are international competitiveness and technological change.

International competitiveness

As we have seen, progress towards the globalisation of production and trade has been rapid in recent decades. It has been hastened by the successes of the GATT, replaced in 1994 by the WTO, by market and political union between countries, and by many genuine attempts on the part of world leaders to reduce 'distance' between nations and communities. Moreover the growth of reasonably unfettered capitalism has made the world a very different place today than it was just a couple of decades ago. *Figure 9.5* shows the estimated GDP of the top ten economies in 2050. Note the enormous growth of China and India, significant growth in Brazil and Mexico, and the *relative* decline in most Western economies such as the USA. The recession from 2008 to date will only serve to hasten the change in world order.

Despite the volatility in economic growth, the last two decades have witnessed large increases in global income and in levels of international trade in both goods and services. Many protective barriers have been removed or reduced, such that competition between nations and companies is, by and large, more fierce than in previous decades. It is now important for companies and governments to consider the level of national and regional competitiveness. Undoubtedly, some countries enjoy political, social, technological and economic advantages which encourage multinational, transnational or global companies to invest in them. A number of organisations and researchers have attempted to calculate

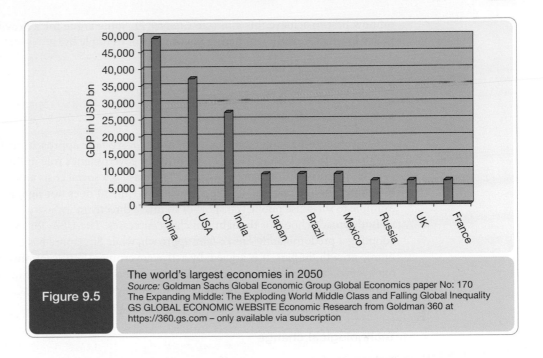

Figure 9.5

The world's largest economies in 2050
Source: Goldman Sachs Global Economic Group Global Economics paper No: 170
The Expanding Middle: The Exploding World Middle Class and Falling Global Inequality
GS GLOBAL ECONOMIC WEBSITE Economic Research from Goldman 360 at
https://360.gs.com – only available via subscription

national competitiveness and produce 'league tables'. They consider such things as average wage rates, workforce skills and capabilities, income and corporation tax rates and the degree of political stability. The World Economic Forum Global Competitiveness Index (GCI) ranking for 2006–2007 and, for comparison purposes, 2001–2002, are shown in *Table 9.4*.

Many individuals, groups and organisations in most countries argue that government should play a major part in attempting to maintain or improve their national competitiveness. By so doing they may facilitate the achievement of comfortable economic growth rates, better and secure employment opportunities and improvements in standards of living. Although most governments actively pursue policies which they believe will enhance the competitiveness of their country and its organisations, there is considerable disagreement

Table 9.4   World Economic Forum GCI ranking

Top 10 rankings 2001–2002		Top 10 rankings 2006–2007	
1	Finland	1	Switzerland
2	USA	2	Finland
3	Canada	3	Sweden
4	Singapore	4	Denmark
5	Australia	5	Singapore
6	Norway	6	USA
7	Taiwan	7	Japan
8	Netherlands	8	Germany
9	Sweden	9	Netherlands
10	New Zealand	10	UK

on how best to achieve this aim (see *Chapter 7*). Some argue for a heavily 'interventionist' policy in which government plays a major role, for example by:

- directly investing in industry;
- providing training;
- building state-of-the-art infrastructure;
- facilitating international trade.

Conversely, other arguments favour a more *laissez-faire* approach, such as was traditionally the case in the USA or Hong Kong. Broadly, government's role in this scenario is to 'free' private enterprise from many 'constraints', such as high social costs and taxes, and to allow it to compete in free markets. In this scenario government does not significantly intervene, for example to subsidise public transport or to invest directly in industry.

Both broad schools of thought can claim successes. The USA, for example, flourished by adopting a predominantly *laissez-faire* approach, while Singapore has experienced rapid economic growth, in part, it is argued, by active government interventionist policies. Whatever one's views, it is clear that national and/or regional competitiveness is increasingly becoming an important determinant of the material well-being of a population. Consequently, government has an obligation to its citizens to ensure they share in global successes.

Technological change

Technological change has a significant influence over economic growth (see *Chapter 4*). Government, therefore, has a role to play in the development of conditions suitable for technological advances to be made and transformed into economic wealth-creating opportunities. The approach governments adopt will largely depend on their ideological stance, as indicated above. One government may, for example, invest a significant element of revenue collected from taxation into research which might lead to economic wealth-creating opportunities largely for private industry. Another may prefer to allow market mechanisms to dictate research and development spending levels within industry. Clearly, the role of government, although crucial, varies considerably across the world. It is reported, for example, that in Hong Kong multinational organisations have for decades been invited to invest, irrespective of the technological benefits they might bring to the province. However, the government of Singapore has been somewhat more vigilant and active in encouraging companies which bring transferable technological advances to their country.

Although there is often government involvement, private sector organisations are the major sources and users of new technologies. The extent of their involvement varies from industry to industry. One notable example is discussed in *Minicase 9.3*. which illustrates the impact of technological developments in the petroleum industry.

In addition to creating the 'right' conditions for technological development and diffusion, government also has a regulatory role to perform. This role may involve prohibiting, or otherwise regulating, potentially unethical research and technological development. Many countries are currently debating issues concerning the advances in genetic engineering which have been made in recent years. There are important and far-reaching ethical consequences of many technological advances. Although self-regulation, by researchers and professional bodies for example, is important, many people expect governments to adopt an ideological and regulatory stance in this regard.

9.6 Flexible working

Given the dynamic nature of the business environment outlined throughout this book, it is clear that there has been, and will continue to be, a major impact on all the actors discussed,

Minicase 9.3	Making the earth move – seismic shifts in the petroleum sector

Companies in the oil exploration business look for oil. One way of finding it uses a relatively new technique of three-dimensional seismology. This uses sound waves to map underlying layers of rock to create a picture of what it is like deep underground. Seismology helps explorers to find deposits that previous exploration methods would not have discovered. It therefore improves the success rate for drilling oil wells, which is an expensive business, especially if the bores turn out to be either dry or don't produce enough oil to make them worthwhile. Shell, Amoco and Exxon among others all use three-dimensional seismology to cut the costs of exploration that have to be recovered in prices per barrel. Other effects of the technology of the industry are:

- The formation of new companies that assist in collecting data from three-dimensional seismology surveys and also companies that support them.
- Sophisticated computing systems are needed to analyse data and specialist software, and hardware companies have evolved to fill this niche. *Earth Vision* is one such system.
- The fast pace of technology development and investment costs catalysed consolidation among companies providing seismic surveys – the numbers of companies declined.
- Mergers among big oil exploration companies brought about a more concentrated industry. Mergers were a way for big firms to maintain their relative standing in the industry. The big seven firms of the 1960s reduced to four, e.g. Exxon Mobil combined as did BP and Amoco.

Source: based on Voola (2006)

Questions

1 How has the use of technology changed in the oil/ petroleum industry in the last 30 years?
2 What are the costs and benefits to society of the widespread use of these techniques to discover ever more remote sources of oil?

that is governments, organisations, groups and individuals. We need to look at one of the most common responses to these pressures in the environment, the move towards greater flexibility in working practices.

There are a number of highly contentious issues associated with flexible working. For example, government policy may favour a reduction in the legal restrictions on the hiring and dismissal of workers, which would most certainly increase flexibility. However, this could have significant, often harmful, consequences for many groups and individuals. This is a key issue for many developing and advanced economies. Many countries have a legally enforceable minimum wage, but the consequences may be higher unemployment levels among low-skilled, particularly young, people. In many countries governments are considering age-discrimination legislation, in particular to prevent discrimination in the employment of older people. Although it is recognised that government has a role to play, the impact of often unintentional consequences of government intervention, can be damaging. Getting it 'right' is rarely straightforward.

It is evident that this real or perceived need for flexibility is increasingly influencing employment conditions. Within organisations, people are both the most vital and the most costly resource. Traditionally, however, people have often been seen, rightly or wrongly, as being prone to inflexibility and inertia. As a consequence many organisations have sought to achieve greater flexibility in employment conditions in recent decades. Both employers and employees lead the trend, with governments often regulating, sometimes supporting, developments via legislation. That said, 'flexibility' often means different things to individuals as opposed to businesses. It is also true to say that the concept has an ethnocentric quality so that the very concept of flexible working and the flexible firm is more familiar in, say, the

UK than in France, whereas the term is far less in common usage in China or India than in Western countries. Nevertheless, globalisation has a tendency to ensure that methods of coping with turbulence are replicated across national boundaries and cultures. For example, despite the cultural resistance to flexible working in France, many forms of such working, outlined below, are increasingly practised. The same may well be true of practices in the developing world in the coming decades.

In the richer Western economies, the old 'industrialised' scenario of reliable employment, which allowed families shared times for shopping, travel and leisure, together with patterns of work and retirement within the nuclear family, is metamorphosing into what some have called a 'post-industrial' age. Alvin Toffler (1985), a well-known writer about the future shape of work and of organisations, termed such a society a 'super-industrial' age or a 'third wave'. More and more countries are now moving into this new phase of development. Toffler suggests that this new wave follows on logically from the 'first wave' – the Agricultural Revolution and the 'second wave' – the Industrial Revolution. Others have referred to it as post-Fordism – that is, following Henry Ford's mass-production era. In this evolutionary phase certain types of work are in decline as other types of work are emerging. However, it is at least arguable that newly industrialising economies in the developing world are still in the process of entering the second wave as they industrialise, usually on the basis of mass-production techniques.

It is clear that as new waves occur it can cause us to think again about our underlying assumptions about the nature of work. Key characteristics of this new age are expectations on the part of employers that workers will be very flexible (examined in some detail below) and be able to adapt products and services, almost at will, to meet the particular needs of individual customers. The enhanced capabilities of many organisations to customise products and services have been strongly influenced by developments in, for example, microprocessor technology and management techniques. Computers enable us to process and communicate data and information extremely rapidly. Advances in telecommunications technology have delivered significant improvements in the quality of data about life and work throughout the globe. These technologies have been harnessed by organisations which wish to operate in a range of countries.

As long ago as 1995, Bridges identified some rather ruthless 'new rules' which are still evolving but apply to many parts of the global economy today. The rules are divided into three key points:

- everyone's employment is dependent on the organisation's performance and, as a result, employees need to continuously prove their worth to the organisation and to behave more like an external supplier than a traditional employee;
- workers should, therefore, plan for career-long self-development by taking primary responsibility for their development, their pension and by renegotiating their compensation arrangements with each organisation when, and if, the organisation needs to change; and
- wise companies will need to work closely with these new-style workers to maximise the benefits for both parties and to bring a range of projects to satisfactory completion.

9.6.1 Forms of flexible of working

Having looked at some of the assumptions which underlie recent trends we can now examine the different forms of flexible working which may be found. All of these are driven by external forces. First, we can identify various types of 'numerical' flexibility, which generally affect employees' hours of work. These include long-standing practices such as:

- overtime;
- home working;
- shift work;
- part-time work;

- flexi-time;
- teleworking;
- annual hours contracts;
- zero hours contracts;
- the use of temporary staff;
- job-sharing.

A few of these require some further explanation.

Some companies offer employees work as and when required by the employer, these 'zero-hours' contracts enable the organisation to adjust staff levels in line with customer demand. Employees on these types of contract are likely to be less than satisfied with this arrangement as it introduces considerable uncertainty into their working lives. Another market-driven change is apparent in the electricity generating business. One company encourages some employees to engage in 'winter/summer stagger', where they work longer hours in the winter to accommodate increased demand. Hence people are employed on an annual hours basis. There has also been an increasing number of people employed as temporary and agency labour over the last few decades in many developed economies.

The hours employees in different countries work vary considerably, although increasingly legislation has been put in place to restrict excessively long hours working in most developed and many developing economies. Throughout the twentieth century many developed economies established firstly a 48-hour working week, as the norm, reducing to a 40-hour week. This 'rule of thumb' remains today. In 1995 the People's Republic of China adopted the 40-hour week as its recommended 'normal' working week. Most developing economies in Asia have now adopted a 40- to 48-hour working week. The European Union Working Time Directive of 1993 established a maximum working week as 48 hours, with the added intention of restraining the use of overtime above this limit. There are of course many exceptions to these practices. In both Pakistan and Thailand, for example, it is suggested that over 40 percent of employees work in excess of 48 hours a week. Hours worked impacts on individual and family life directly and is particularly significant in considerations of work–life balance. This is true of all employees but particularly significant to many women who also find that they are 'required' to assume a major role in the provision of unpaid work in the home. Female participation in paid work has increased significantly, especially since the 1980s, in most countries with the lowest participation rates being in the Middle East, North Africa and South Asia.

Home working is not new, although the scale of this activity is increasing. However, teleworking goes a step further by connecting home-based employees by the use of computer modems to the organisation and/or other teleworkers. The availability of communications technology has also led to the 'virtual office' where laptop computers, the internet and mobile phones enable people to work in any location. Linked with this is the practice of 'hotdesking' where employees 'touch base' at the office and use whatever workspace is available, picking up messages on email. 'Telecottaging', where a local venue acts as a central point for teleworkers, may be one way of solving the problem of isolation. From an ecological perspective an increase in teleworking, which is particularly commonplace among management consultants, computing and sales personnel, may help reduce rush hour traffic and air pollution.

A second form of flexibility, referred to as 'distancing', is where employees are replaced by subcontractors and employment contracts are replaced by contracts for service. Again this has been commonplace in many industries, such as construction and manufacturing, for many decades. However, the process is increasingly popular in other types of activity, including service industries, and in the public sector.

A third form of flexible working is broadly termed 'functional flexibility'. Although in many organisations strict lines of demarcation exist between jobs, these are seen as offering little flexibility and often prove obstacles to effective teamwork and subsequent productivity gains. Hence multi-skilling, where individuals are trained to undertake a broader array of tasks, is becoming more commonplace.

A fourth form of flexibility, pay flexibility, is increasingly commonplace. This may involve the harmonisation of terms and conditions, including the removal of artificial barriers between white-collar and blue-collar workers, such as differences in pension, sick pay and holiday entitlements.

Many flexible working practices find their ultimate focus in the concept of a virtual business or virtual enterprise. Amazon.com was an early example of a virtual business, competing with traditional high-street booksellers without such a physical presence, relying purely on electronic, internet interaction with its customers. Clearly, however, there is also a physical location, for the various warehouses store the items and a physical distribution system is used to deliver to the consumer. Despite some early doubts about the viability of such a business model, Amazon has survived, prospered and expanded its activity to include CDs/DVDs and an ever-wider range of consumer goods. Of course, it still operates without a shop presence. Other businesses rely even more heavily on the virtual world, as consumers move from buying physical products that need to be delivered to their homes to simply downloading items over the internet. Apple's iTunes uses just such a system – although Apple does still retain a high-street presence in many cities to sell the devices onto which music, games, photos and so on are downloaded.

Finally, there are a number of related concepts including career breaks, paternity and maternity leave, secondments, domestic leave for careers, childcare assistance and school holiday leave. Many of these measures may be considered as 'family-friendly' and are intended to help motivate and retain staff.

Minicase 9.4 explores the two-tier 'flexibility' found in Spain.

About 17 percent of the workforce in the EU works part-time, growth in this respect being most notable in Germany, while rates have always been well above average in the UK (refer to *Figure 9.6*).

Minicase 9.4	Spanish two-tier flexibility

There is strong evidence to suggest that flexible work practices are on the increase, although less agreement concerning whether this is part of a strategically planned reaction to changing environmental circumstances, including employee needs/wants, a result of short-term economic expedience or the outcome of a shifting balance between capital (employers) and labour (employees). Recent studies into flexible working in Europe suggest that, although there is an overall trend towards greater use of flexible working patterns, there is considerable variation in practice between countries, sectors and sizes of organisation.

In very broad terms there are two tiers of employees or workers in Spain. About two-thirds of workers have very secure permanent contracts while the rest simply do not. Unemployment in Spain is among the highest in Europe (around 20 percent in 2010) and increased significantly throughout the recession in 2008 onwards. The vast bulk of those losing their job were employees on short-term, non-permanent employment arrangements. Employers have been wary of employing new staff on permanent contracts or of training or developing these people. They provide flexibility in the system – a source of labour that can be turned on or off at short notice. Meanwhile those on secure contracts continue to be shielded from the harsh economic environment. They are usually highly unionised and continue to enjoy pay rises despite the recession. But, for how long?

Questions

1 Is a unionised system of working sustainable in rapidly changing global circumstances where competitive forces for change are significant?
2 What benefits could flexible working bring to employers and employees?

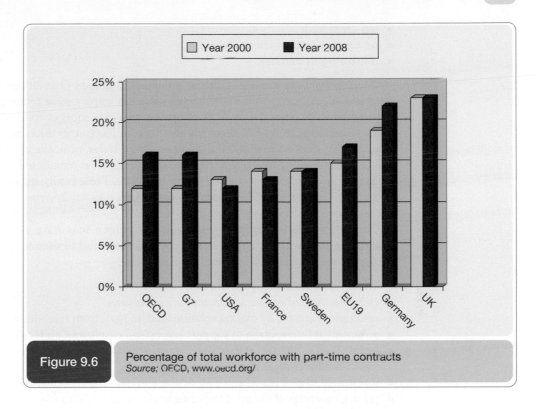

Figure 9.6	Percentage of total workforce with part-time contracts
	Source: OECD, www.oecd.org/

Non-permanent employment has increased as has subcontracting. *Figure 9.7* highlights the vast differences in this regard within the EU with Spain (see *Minicase 9.4*) having almost a third of its workforce on temporary contracts. The majority of part-time workers are female. Around 50 percent of women employees in the UK work part-time; the EU average is just 30 percent.

The UK has the most flexible workforce in the EU with over 10 million people (almost 40 percent of all employees) either:

- part-time workers;
- temporary workers;

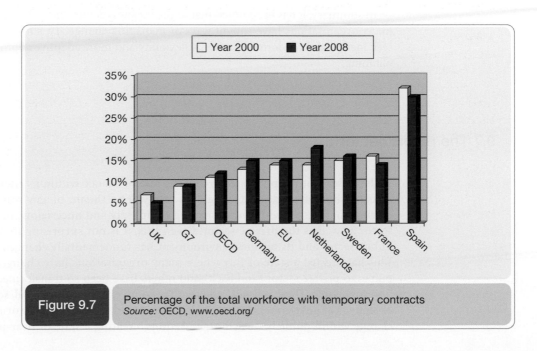

Figure 9.7	Percentage of the total workforce with temporary contracts
	Source: OECD, www.oecd.org/

- self-employed;
- on a government training scheme;
- unpaid family workers.

This represents an increase of almost 2 million in a decade. Over 80 per cent of all medium-sized and large organisations in the United Kingdom employ some temporary staff. The BBC, for example, now offers the majority of new recruits only short or fixed-term contracts, as do many universities. In the UK there has also been an increase in the number of men working flexibly, from 23 per cent in 1994 to about one-third today, while the proportion of women in this category remained stable and high at 50 per cent. Over a million employees work school term-time only while about 200,000 people job-share. These family-friendly measures attempt to motivate employees and help parents balance work and family demands. They also facilitate the retention of competent and well-trained staff.

Changes in the international environment, which may have encouraged the moves towards flexible working, ensure that the flexible firm and flexible working will become an increasing reality. Summarised here, they include:

- increased national competition;
- globalisation and consequent competitive pressures;
- uncertainty created by market volatility and, in part, from recessionary periods;
- government intervention to support and extend employees' and/ or employers' rights;
- technological change, particularly in information technology and communications, which facilitates some forms of flexible working;
- investment in new plant requiring new and ever-changing skills;
- greater awareness of the need to pursue active policies and practices to ensure environmental sustainability (and to reduce the traffic congestion on many roads and in most cities!);
- a move from Fordism to post-Fordism, from mass production to flexible specialisation;
- continued emphasis on costs and budgets and financial stringency in the public sector;
- political influence, particularly in the public sector;
- reductions in trade union power;
- increasing numbers of women and other employee groups 'demanding' alternative employment conditions; and
- a change in attitudes to work and life, to levels of organisational loyalty (both ways) and responsibility for personal and career development.

In summary, it has been noted that as the business environment becomes more turbulent many organisations have sought ways of managing change. This has encouraged them to seek increased short-term operational flexibility and more adaptive approaches to long-term planning.

9.7 The public sector

Both the scale of the public sector and the rate of change within its environment make it a valuable but often neglected field of study. The theme of environmental change or dynamism, together with ever-increasing complexity and uncertainty, prevails in the public sector as well as the private sector. Given this, it is not surprising that the nature of the public sector and its business environment has fundamentally changed in recent decades. This has created a state of flux where many organisations have changed ownership from public to private sector (and back) and others have been so transformed as to be virtually unrecognisable. There is little doubt that the complex range of political, social and economic objectives of governments over the last two decades has created enormous pressures for change within publicly owned organisations, creating a state of near-permanent tension between different interest groups. *Minicase 9.5* illustrates how these forces impact on a public sector organisation in the UK.

Public sector organisations often conduct government business, are largely funded from the public purse via taxation and are usually accountable to government at some level. As a result it is the duty of government to ensure that proper care is taken when allocating resources. Hence, government at local, national and international levels has an all-encompassing and powerful influence over public sector bodies.

The environmental changes are themselves part of a global transformation in the nature of public sector organisations. In most countries the public sector is a major employer and service provider. Governments wishing to cut back on their spending face substantial difficulties. An ageing population, as discussed in *Minicase 1.4* in *Chapter 1* and in *Chapter 5,* continues to put increased demands upon healthcare, state pension and welfare systems, necessitating increased government expenditure. What is more, as the population ages there will be fewer people working and potentially fewer taxpayers.

9.7.1 The changing scope of the public sector

It can be argued that the existence of the public sector is due to the failure of the free-market system to provide all the services required by the general public and by government. However,

---

Minicase 9.5	Change in a National Health Service hospital

An objective expressed in the hospital's plan is to 'produce a multi-skilled workforce', more specifically, 'to introduce teams of generic hotel service assistants at ward level so as to improve flexibility and responsiveness to patient needs by combining the role of porters, domestics and catering staff'.

At the hospital all domestics, unqualified nurses and ward clerks are to be based at ward level, a relocation which is involving severing many existing formal and informal relationships. Most of the 260 personnel are being trained in patient care, cleaning and portering skills in order to develop multi-skilled competencies. Staff will then undertake a wider array of tasks and be required to embrace flexibility and teamwork. There may be reduced role certainty. They will need to manage the interface with clinical and other staff groups on the ward. All existing formal status and pay differentials between the hitherto separate groups will be removed. Some staff will be required to change their shift pattern and the total hours they work within any one week.

It is argued that successful implementation will help to 'provide good value for money' and 'make cost savings'. It will ensure, for the time being at least, competitiveness with external commercial players. The single grade and pay spine will reduce status differentials and simplify the highly complex bonus schemes that had evolved. From an operational point of view it will bring benefits of flexibility and simplify work scheduling. It will serve to even out the workload for staff and improve efficiency by avoiding waiting-for-action time and duplication of effort. Managers believe it will improve worker motivation as people will feel part of a team. They will, it is believed, take a pride in their work at ward level.

In conclusion, the philosophy underpinning the care assistant concept is a familiar one. A multi-skilled, flexible workforce is thought to facilitate operational planning and enhance both the efficiency and effectiveness of service provision. The assumption is that employees benefit from the resultant job enrichment and co-operative teamwork, cost savings are there for the making, via enhanced efficiency, and patient care is improved.

Questions

1   What are the benefits and drawbacks to the *employer* of these changes?
2   What are the benefits and drawbacks to the *employee* of these changes?

both the scope and scale of the public sector in any country are in part the result of prevailing political ideologies, or those that prevailed in the past (see *Chapter 7*). A multitude of other factors also influence both the level of government involvement in the economy and the scale of public expenditure. However, there is no indisputable law of economics which argues that the public sector should, for example, operate the wide range of services found in most developed countries. Neither is there, at any time, a 'correct' or indisputable level of government expenditure.

There are a certain, strictly limited, number of services which most politicians, academics and the general public agree should be delivered by the government or at least be under its tight scrutiny. Relatively uncontroversial examples include the judiciary, the police and the armed services. However, there are a large and growing number of activities which are the subject of considerable public debate in many countries regarding the most appropriate form of ownership and operation.

Throughout the nineteenth and twentieth centuries, the trend towards a mixed economy (see *Chapter 3*), where economic activity is shared via both public and private ownership, proceeded apace in the developed industrialised world with the introduction and growth of government-owned services. The scope of government activity in most countries grew to include responsibility for education, health, law and order, defence and more. Additionally, many industrial organisations were nationalised, meaning that they were not owned by private shareholders but by government on behalf of the nation, e.g. the coal-mining, steel, gas, railways, electricity and water supply businesses.

There has been a major reversal of this trend since the 1980s. In the last two decades of the twentieth century there was a tendency in many countries, both developed and developing, for governments to move away from direct provision of goods and services towards a focus on regulating more and producing less. The range of mechanisms which governments have employed includes:

- privatisation;
- deregulation;
- contracting-out public sector services;
- establishing non-governmental-organisations (NGOs – often paid for by government) in order to perform a service;
- quality charters, league tables and published performance targets;
- tougher and more independent inspectorates; and
- private/public sector financial partnerships.

Many politicians, businesspeople and academics still believe that private markets are capable of providing some services that are (or were) more usually regarded as 'public goods'. They would argue that in many circumstances the market is a sound and appropriate mechanism for the allocation of scarce resources (see *Chapter 6*). As such the marketplace, via the price system, allocates goods and services to individuals and organisations. These include healthcare (supported by private insurance) and education (backed with means-tested student loans and private schools). Although the market economy is far from faultless, the alternatives are not necessarily guaranteed to be more efficient or effective in servicing the needs of society or individuals.

Others argue that the marketplace would lead to a multi-tiered system and a restriction of access to high-quality services for a significant section of the community. Additionally, objectors to the idea of a pure market economy argue that competition in the provision of many public services, such as healthcare, is morally unacceptable and practically unworkable.

Although the move to more market-friendly policies was pursued vigorously in many countries, the global recession of 2008 onwards has caused a rethink by policy-makers in many quarters. This is based on the belief that deregulation has gone too far, particularly in respect of the banking sector, which has seen a number of nationalisations and other public involvement, especially in the UK and USA.

The political forces outlined above are themselves driven by powerful economic, social and technological changes within the global arena. Wider environmental changes inform political agendas and mould ideologies. However, the mechanism of influence between the wider environment and political activity is two-way as government decisions profoundly influence those environmental forces. For example, whereas changing social needs create dynamism to which government and public organisations have to respond, those same social changes are, in part, the result of government policy and behaviour. The relative poverty of some groups has contributed to many social problems such as urban deprivation, long-term unemployment, crime, drug abuse and social exclusion and unrest. As a result government and public sector organisations are faced with a social environment which is, in part, a consequence of their previous activity.

9.8 Future trends?

Let us start this look forward by looking backwards. By going back 30 years, approximately one generation, well within the lifetime of a majority of the European and North American populations and close to the mean age of global population, we can see the changes that have occurred. (Mean age in Western Europe is about 40 years of age.) Thirty years ago the majority of current industry and public sector senior leaders at national level, had already left school. Thirty years ago the world wide web did not exist. How many times in the last week have you used the internet to facilitate your learning, your social life and your work or commercial well-being? The answer to that question for all leaders of the top 20 countries in the world, the G20, when they were at university is a resounding 'none'. In fact it is unlikely that any would have recognised the word 'internet' when they were first at university. As well as the world wide web, there were no PCs – or at least anything we would recognise today as a PC. As well as this now taken-for-granted form of communication, there were no mobile phones or, of course, PDAs, iPods, laptops, smart phones or email. Communications have been revolutionised in recent decades and greater change is yet to impact the fundamentals of our working and social lives.

Politically, the world has changed equally as dramatically. Thirty years ago, highly authoritarian Communist governments ruled Eastern Europe, Russia and its 'empire', and many other countries. The threat of world war between the Western powers and the Communist bloc was very real. China was isolated and economically backward, India remained in a perilous economic state and the European Union had only just begun to expand. Globalisation, as we know it today, was in an embryonic state and the WTO did not exist. There was no global 'war on terror'; most terror organisations were nationalist groups 'fighting' within one country.

Environmentally, there was concern about the destruction of the rain forests and the potential exhaustion of natural resources. However, concern about the existence or impact of global warming was in its infancy; in fact the fear of a new ice age was frequently discussed. Genetic engineering was a fringe activity, HIV/AIDS was unknown and world population was around 2.3 billion lower than today, i.e. about two-thirds its current size.

Looking back at these points we can see just how much and how quickly the world has changed. The question then becomes: what of looking forward 30 years?

Perhaps the most significant factor regarding these dramatic changes is that most were not predicted. Had someone 30 years ago outlined the nature of the fundamental advances or changes in communication technologies or of global politics that have actually occurred, they would have been considered (at best) a dreamer. The history books are littered with examples of poor forecasting or predictions. We need only go back to late 2007 to note that the bulk of governments, economists and commentators around the world completely failed to predict the extremely devastating and deep economic crisis which the world plunged into just months later. On a lighter note, many commentators have got it wrong regarding the

---

Minicase 9.6   The pace of change

Over the ten years to 2010 world population has grown by about 750 million. That growth figure alone represents more than double the total population of the world at the time of the Romans or ancient Greeks (when it was about 300 million). It was not until about 1750 that world population actually reached a total of 750 million. So, in just ten years we have added to world population what previously had taken many millennia to produce and support. In many ways this might be considered a great achievement of the modern world but it has its negative consequences. About 80 per cent of that increase is accounted for by growth in the developing world, where living standards are far lower than in the developed world. In the same time period the concentration of greenhouse gases has increased. Chlorine concentrations acting with other chemicals in the atmosphere have opened a hole in the ozone layer above the Antarctic, a hole which is now three times the size of the USA. Deforestation of tropical forests (never, realistically, to be reversed) proceeds at about 2 percent a year. Over half of all mangrove forests have been lost. Fish stocks have collapsed in many of our oceans, in some cases to irretrievable levels. Oil consumption and that of most finite mineral resources have increased by about 50 percent in the decade. Known reserves have fallen. More oil (and many other minerals) has been consumed in the lifetime of today's baby boomers (about 60-year-olds) than in the history of the world up to the time of their birth. A lot more!

Questions

1 To what extent are these trends predictable and how might they continue?
2 Could currently unknown factors radically alter future trends?

---

likely popularity of new technologies. Lord Kelvin, an eminent scientist of his day, said, in 1895 that 'heavier-than-air flying machines are impossible' and 'there is nothing new to be discovered in physics …'. A journalist wrote in 1939 in the USA that 'TV will never be a serious competitor for radio because people must sit and keep their eyes glued on a screen …'. *Minicase 9.6* demonstrates some of the changes to key social and ecological global concerns over a ten-year period by way of illustration.

It *is* remarkably difficult to hypothesise or predict discontinuous change. For example, it *might* be considered reasonable to assume that there will be an increase in the number of so-called 'failed states'. Some countries around the world are struggling with democracy and often violent extremist groups challenge for power. But what would a discontinuous global political change actually look like? A world of total peace and harmony perhaps, or one which saw a major nuclear-armed, Islamic mega-state challenge the existing global order? Perhaps it might be China assuming political and economic dominance in all aspects of global activity. Are these scenarios fanciful? Perhaps. Nevertheless, it is interesting to consider what one influential organisation predicts when looking at the global economy. Goldman Sachs have a view that the continuing growth in developing economies will result in a very different global distribution of wealth (and power and influence) by the middle of this century. As was seen in *Figure 9.5*, their idea of what the world will be like in 2050 shows it to be a very different place, with the US economy, currently the world's largest being overtaken by China – and with India not that far behind.

There are some trends which are already in place and which are to a large extent predictable. One such change is the aging of population in developed economies. How governments, organisations, groups and each of us as individuals cope with those changes, however, remains uncertain. For example, the global demographic situation is shifting with a rapidly ageing population in most of Europe, and to an extent in much of the developed and developing world, as life expectancy increases and birth rates contract. Will we see increasing retirement ages, major skill and talent shortages, ever-increasing taxation to pay for extra pension payments and healthcare provision? The answer is quite likely to be yes. Again socially, are we experiencing the early decades of the increasing dominance of women in society? Women achieve better than men in education, are released in many societies from many of the 'burdens' society previously placed upon them and, by all accounts, are increasingly ambitious. Women conduct around 70 percent of online banking in the USA, while two-thirds of wealth is owned by over-60-year-olds; the majority of this age group are women. By 2050 women may control around 60 percent of the total wealth in the UK. Will the top boardrooms and parliaments be female-dominated in 30 years times as they are male dominated today? And, then there is technology. What will technological changes in the next 30 years mean for industry, commerce and the public sector? Can we realistically predict that?

9.9 Conclusion

Our approach has been to focus on many of the environmental (PESTLE C) factors outlined in this text and on the increasing dynamism and uncertainty in the global business environment. In doing this we have commented upon some of the major changes that surround both the concept and impact of globalisation. We have also explored the implications of all this for organisations, groups, individuals and governments. In this final chapter we have concentrated on examining currently developing trends that we expect to continue to have a significant impact.

We have attempted to identify issues that may be important for organisations in the future, but have made few predictions, other than commenting on the unpredictable nature of many of the changes that have occurred and will continue to occur. We have used much factual data throughout this chapter – and the rest of the book. However, in a rapidly changing environment, there is a tendency for such data to become obsolete very quickly. This will, undoubtedly, mean that when you read this book there will be some information which no longer holds true. This will make it necessary for you to undertake your own research to update the figures as the world around you changes.

For this reason we recognise that the most lasting impact of the book will be your understanding of the processes and models used to examine the business environment. We have placed strong emphasis on ways of evaluating and understanding the business environment. For example, we have stressed the importance of examining problems from different perspectives. This includes a consideration of the individual, the group and the organisation at various different geo-political scales from local to global. The reason for this is simple: it seems to us that an analysis of the international business environment cannot confine itself to examining environmental factors in any one of these ways, as each influences all the others.

Summary of main points	This chapter has focused upon the nature of change in the business environment and organisational, individual, group and government responses to environmental dynamism. The main points are:

- The international business environment is increasingly complex, dynamic, uncertain (turbulent) and even chaotic for many organisations, individuals, groups and governments.
- Major economic, political, technological and social changes have transformed the business environment in the last decade, necessitating organisational change and increased flexibility.

- There may be a trend towards high-profile 'shock events' and non-linear chaotic patterns in many areas of the natural world (to some extent such patterns are also observable in the business world) which suggests that organisations might do well to make contingency plans.

- The nature of the international business environment calls into question the validity of organisational approaches to long-term planning and suggests the need for processes which build in flexibility and adaptability.

- There has been a rapid increase in previously considered 'non-standard' temporal and contractual patterns of work such as part-time work, teleworking, contracting-out, self-employment and temporary work as a means of enabling organisations to adapt to change.

- People of different generations have very different expectations and behaviours; culture is changing.

- Turbulent environments demand government attention.

- The future role of government is likely to remain a fiercely debated issue for some time.

- Global problems, such as climate change, demand global solutions.

Discussion questions

1 What are the implications of increased turbulence and chaos in the business environment for the ways in which organisations plan for the future?

2 Discuss the opposing ideological positions concerning the role of government in encouraging national competitiveness and technological development.

3 Assess the implications for individual workers of the increased use of flexible working practices by organisations.

4 Contrast your parents' work–life experiences with those of your grandparents. How do you expect your work–life experiences will differ from those of your parents?

5 Outline the ways in which the increasingly interconnected 'global' environment represents both a threat and an opportunity for business.

Further reading/sources of information

BBC (http://news.bbc.co.uk/) The BBC website provides up-to-date information on business topics, economics, politics, technology and much more from around the world.

European Union (EU) http://ec.europa.eu/index_en.htm Home page of the EC with access to the Directorate General for Competition of the EU.

Friends of the Earth (www.foe.co.uk) The website of one of the main green pressure groups, frequently updated with current issues. You may also want to look at **www.greenbiz.com/** which looks at the business end of the debate. **Innovation www.innovation.gov.uk/rd scoreboard** UK government site giving details on R&D.

Legal information can be found at **www.statutelaw.gov.uk/,** the UK statute law database which enables you to view UK laws and trace how they have changed over time. You can also consult **www.law.cornell.edu/world/** and **www.jus.uio.no/lm/index.html,** two excellent sources of material on international law and trade law by country.

OECD, *The* **www.oecd.org/** The OECD website covers the main industrialised countries. It provides a wide range of economic statistics and forecasts on these economies. It is good for most aspects of country data. Follow links to science and technology for information on effects on economic development.

Daniels, J.D., Radebaugh L.H. and Sullivan, D.P (2009) *International Business – Environments and Operations,* 12th edn. Upper Saddle River, NJ: Prentice Hall. This American textbook contains much useful information on both the international business environment and businesses' operations.

Dicken, P. (2007) *Global Shift; Mapping the Changing Contours of the Global Economy,* 5th edn. London: Sage A useful survey of how the global economy has changed in the last 30 years.

Johnson, G., Scholes, K. and Whittington R. (2008) *Exploring Corporate Strategy,* 8th edn. Harlow: FT Prentice Hall.

Sloman, J. and Wride, A. (2009) *Economics,* 7th edn. Harlow: Prentice Hall. A good introduction to economics. Wide range of short cases but a book that covers a lot more than just the internal macro economy.

Stiglitz, J. (2002) *Globalization and its Discontents.* London: Allen Lane. This book, written by a former chief economist at the World Bank, gives a devastating critique of the effects of many of the Bretton Woods institutions' policies in both economic and political terms.

Todaro, M.P. and Smith, S.C. (2009) *Economic Development,* 10th edn. Harlow: Addison-Wesley. A long-established book surveying global issues with an emphasis on a developing world perspective. Some sections are rather heavy on economic theory for non-economists, but there is still much of value and interest to be found.

Vignali, C. (2001) McDonald's: 'Think Global, Act Local' – the Marketing Mix, *British Food Journal,* 103 (2), 97–111.

This article focuses on the marketing mix of McDonald's and highlights how the company combines internationalisation and globalisation elements according to various fast-food markets. It illustrates the effect of McDonald's on the global environment and how it adapts to local communities.

Newspapers

Newspapers are a good source of information on many topics. Three of the more important UK papers may found on the following sites:

Financial Times	**www.ft.com**
The Guardian	**www.guardian.co.uk**
The Telegraph	**www.telegraph.co.uk**

References

Dollar, D. (2004) Policy Research Working Paper WP3333 Globalization, Poverty, and Inequality Since 1980, World Bank, available from **http://econ.worldbank.org/external/ default/main?pagePK=64165259&thesitePK=469382&piPK=64165421&menuPK=6416 6093&entityID=000112742_20040928096739**

Gleick, J. (1987) *Chaos: Making a New Science,* New York: Viking Penguin.

Johnson, G., Scholes, K. and Whittington, R. (2008) *Exploring Corporate Strategy.* 8th edn. Harlow: Prentice Hall.

Levitt, T. (1983) The Globalization of Markets. *Harvard Business Review,* May–June, 92–102.

Miles, R.E. (1980) *Macro Organisational Behaviour.* Sutt Foresman & Co.

Mintzberg, H. (2000) *The Rise and Fall of Strategic Planning.* Harlow: FT Prentice Hall.

Ohmae, K. (1989) Managing in a Borderless World. *Harvard Business Review*, 67(3), 152–161.

Pawley, M. (1974) *The Private Future.* London: Pan.

Stacey, R.D. (2007) *Strategic Management and Organisational Dynamics*, 5th edn. Harlow: FT Prentice Hall.

Toffler, A. (1985) *The Adaptive Corporation.* London: Pan.

Voda, J.J. (2006) Technological Change and Industry Structure: A Case Study of the Petroleum Industry. *Economics* of *Innovation and New Technology*, 15(3), 271–288.

Yip, G.S. (2003) *Total Global Strategy II: Updated for the Internet and Service Era*, 2nd edn. Upper Saddle River, NJ: Prentice Hall, NJ.

Index